EMBROIDERY
ENCYCLOPEDIA

XXXXX

Stitches and Techniques for Every Embroiderer

Other Schiffer Books on Related Subjects:
Whitework Embroidery: Designs and Accessories with a Modern Twist, Seiko Nakano, ISBN 978-0-7643-6423-5
Juno's Nature Embroidery Notebook: Stitching Plants, Animals, and Stories, Juno, ISBN 978-0-7643-6422-8
Embroidery Garden: Artful Designs Inspired by Nature, Yanase Rei, ISBN 978-0-7643-6424-2

Originally published as *Encyclopédie de la broderie à l'aguille*, by Éditions Eyrolles, Paris, ©2022
Translated from the French

Library of Congress Control Number: 2024932649

Cover design by Brenda McCallum
Type set in Heading Pro/TT Commons*

ISBN: 978-0-7643-6849-3
Printed in China

Published by Schiffer Publishing, Ltd.
4880 Lower Valley Road
Atglen, PA 19310
Phone: (610) 593-1777; Fax: (610) 593-2002
Email: Info@schifferbooks.com
Web: www.schifferbooks.com

MARTINE BIESSY

EMBROIDERY ENCYCLOPEDIA

XXXXX

Stitches and Techniques for Every Embroiderer

Foreword

For many people, embroidery conjures up images of antique, sumptuous, colorful, or all-white linens, or a simple decorative element. But embroidery is much more than that. Its history has social, cultural, economic, and religious aspects that speak volumes about the history of mankind. Embroidery is also a genuine means of expression, just like writing, music, or the graphic and plastic arts, and its many techniques are still practiced in France and all over the world today.

In my opinion, it's a real privilege to know how to embroider. Embroidery enables us to make every object, garment, and decorative element in our daily lives unique, to tell our own story.

As with any apprenticeship, it's important to learn the basics, to get to grips with the classics, and then to break free, explore, and experiment. Striking a balance between tradition and modernity then becomes a pleasure. But without help, it's often difficult to get started. We don't know where to start, or what materials and embroidery threads to buy. I learned these first steps from my maternal grandmother, then perfected them during numerous courses at the world's best embroidery schools.

This intergenerational and familial transmission is a treasure that I wish to perpetuate, since the know-how of embroiderers (previously handed down orally from generation to generation) virtually disappeared in the last century. Having taught both face-to-face and online courses, I felt it was important to put this heritage down in writing. For me, it's a real achievement!

In this book, I've gathered together the most traditional needlework techniques, commonly used in France, and brought them up to date on garments and accessories. Of course, there are others, but it would have taken me another 200 years and 2,000 pages to complete a full overview.

I hope this book will help you get started and perfect your embroidery skills.

Enjoy your embroidery!

—Martine Biessy

CONTENTS

2 | Library of Basic Stitches 45

3 | Color Embroidery 139

4 | White Embroidery 219

5 | Projects 273

Appendixes 407

A Brief History of French Embroidery

Textile embroidery has existed since the dawn of humankind. The oldest embroidery stitch found in Denmark dates back to the Bronze Age: the buttonhole stitch. However, it is impossible to know the origin of every single embroidery stitch. They have appeared over the centuries and have continued to evolve, giving rise to a considerable number of variations and combinations. The use of thread (initially animal hair and sinew) and needle dates back to prehistoric times: the eye needle appeared around 15,000 BCE.

During antiquity, embroidery developed around the Mediterranean via Egypt and the Roman Empire, playing a major role in commercial and cultural exchanges. Embroidery techniques spread throughout the world with the help of invasions, crusades, and wars.

In medieval times, under the influence of the Christian Church, embroidery was a sacred art, illustrating faith and magnifying God.

During the Renaissance, embroidery became a veritable needle painting. The Italians were masters of this art, and their work was imitated throughout Europe. The most famous artists provided embroiderers with models.

A draftsman at the court of Louis XIV, Charles-Germain de Saint-Aubin defined the role of drawing as "the basis and foundation of embroidery, which determines the forms and the beautiful distribution; it gives harmony, regulates proportions, adds a new merit to the work."[1] He published a technical treatise in 1770 titled *L'Art du brodeur*.[2] To emphasize the design, embroidery was created in "ronde bosse" relief, reminiscent of sculpture. Over the years, embroidery techniques were perfected: gold, pastels, couchures, pearls, chenille, and all kinds of supplies were used to embellish embroideries. Sacred art, sober at first, became ostentatious, sacrificing the spirit of piety and adoration to the richness of embroidery.

From the Middle Ages onward, secular embroidery was a sign of luxury. The court of kings was the most important client for embroiderers.

Between the 13th and 15th centuries, in the age of chivalry, coats of arms appeared. Coats of arms with brightly embroidered motifs were forbidden to commoners.

Art embroidery—previously the preserve of clerics, craftsmen, and professionals—evolved over the centuries into an art form for pleasure. In the mid-16th century, embroidery became a leisure activity. In 1587, Dominique de Sera published *Le Livre des lingeries*, the first book of embroidery patterns. Later, royal horticulturists and embroiderers collaborated, providing court ladies with drawings and engravings of plants as models for works executed in silk and gold. For example, in 1608, Jean Robin (gardener) and Pierre Valet (royal embroiderer) published *Le Jardin du Roy*, dedicated to Queen Marie de Médicis and containing images of plants for embroidery.

---

1 *Autour du fil, l'encyclopédie des arts textiles*, volume 3, Fait Main/Collection Bonniers, 1988.

2 Printed by Louis-François Delatour.

In 1884, Thérèse de Dillmont's *Encyclopédie des ouvrages de dames* became an embroiderer's bible. It compiles all the author's knowledge of needlework. Immediately translated, it was sold in seventeen countries. At the same time, Thérèse de Dillmont founded her own embroidery school in close collaboration with DMC near Mulhouse.

The early 20th century saw the triumph of *Journal des Dames* magazine. Embroiderers embellished both their homes and their outfits. But in those days, embroidery wasn't just an embellishment, it was also a necessity: a small row of picot buttonhole stitches was added to the cuff to prevent wear, or a small embroidery was made to prevent tears at the bottom of a slit.

Later, the great couturiers—such as Sonia Delaunay, Elsa Schiaparelli, André Courrèges, Paco Rabanne, Christian Lacroix, Coco Chanel—made use of prestigious Parisian embroidery workshops like those of Lesage and Vermont, with a recognition that resonates internationally. This is still the case today.

For several decades now, embroidery has been back in vogue with the general public, whatever the generation. It adorns garments (both haute couture and ready-to-wear), everyday objects, and top-of-the-range household linen and can be used to restore old works. It has also made a foray into contemporary art, with artists such as Ghada Amer and Maurizio Anzeri. For the general public, it's a creative hobby that's back in the spotlight, on a par with knitting and crochet.

Introduction

A Few General Points about Embroidery

Embroidery can be divided into two main families:

- **Color embroidery**, which groups together works made with colored or gold thread, pearls, and sequins
- **White embroidery**, which in the past was made with white thread on white fabric. Today, white embroidery techniques are also executed with colored threads and fabrics.

Two working techniques coexist in color and white embroidery:

- **Surface embroidery:** A design is transferred to the embroidery backing. The embroidery stitches then hide the design.
- **Counted-stitch embroidery** is performed on regular textile fabrics using geometric stitches. Stitches are embroidered by counting a precise number of warp and weft threads on the ground fabric. The drawings used to create the motifs are diagrams.

What You Need to Know

Many of the traditional embroidery stitches worked with these two techniques can be produced using both tracing and counted stitches.

These two techniques encompass two types of embroidery:

- **Linear embroidery**, which uses certain traditional embroidery stitches (such as backstitch and stem stitch) to create contours, borders
- **Filler embroidery** covers larger or smaller surfaces, often delineated by outlines. Filling is made up of tightly packed stitches such as laidwork or in the form of a grid.

What You Need to Know

Some linear embroidery stitches are also used as fillers, by joining embroidered lines together.

Finally, embroidery can be done in two ways:

- **in "rocking"** (one movement): The needle is threaded and pulled out in a single movement. The embroiderer's hand remains permanently on top of the work. It's a fast technique, best suited to certain embroidery stitches, such as front, back, stem, and buttonhole.
- **in "stab"** (two movements): The first movement is to prick the needle, and the second to pull it. The hand moves back and forth between the top and bottom of the work. This technique is more precise than the previous one, but half as fast.

Who Is This Book For?

With its detailed step-by-step explanations and diagrams, this book is just as much for beginners making their first embroidery stitches as for experienced embroiderers wishing to consolidate their knowledge or discover new techniques. It's also a real teaching manual for embroidery students.

The embroidery models at the end of the book enable you to apply your knowledge, according to your level.

The Structure of the Book

This manual for learning and perfecting modern needlepoint and hand embroidery is divided into five main sections.

What You Need to Know

In parts 2 to 4, each chapter ends with a visual library of most of the embroidery stitches explained in the previous pages. You'll be able to compare them with the results of your own work and choose the right stitches for your project.

- **PART 1: MATERIALS AND TECHNIQUES** (pages 17–43)
This first part presents the equipment and supplies needed for embroidery, as well as the basics common to all techniques.

- **PART 2: THE BASIC POINTS LIBRARY** (pages 45–137)
This section is divided into several chapters, each focusing on a particular stitch and its variations. Once you've mastered these basic stitches, you'll be able to create any type of embroidery, color or white.

- **PART 3: COLORED EMBROIDERY** (pages 139–217)
Color embroidery consists of adding a flat or raised design to a support, usually textile, the basic element of which is the stitch, embroidered with thread and ribbons (silk, wool, cotton, or metal). Other elements (pearls, sequins, feathers, mother-of-pearl, etc.) can be added later. These supplies remain on the surface of the fabric to embellish it.

- **PART 4: WHITEWORK EMBROIDERY** (pages 219–271)
Whitework embroidery is a refined and very broad category, encompassing techniques originally executed on white canvas (often linen) with white linen or cotton thread. It's difficult to date the appearance of whitework embroidery, but in the 15th through 17th centuries, it was in vogue mainly in European countries that cultivated linen and transformed it into fabrics of incomparable quality. During this period, the church played a major role in the spread of these techniques. Priestly vestments and worship linen, often white and adorned with embroidery and lace, were made in convents all over Europe. These techniques were used in decoration and clothing, especially lingerie. They were revived in the 19th century. It wasn't until 1950 that colored yarns and fabrics were introduced. Today, "white" refers to all linens, whatever their color.

In France, plumetis (or "French embroidery" abroad), jours, Richelieu and Renaissance embroidery, and boutis are the main whitework embroidery techniques.

White Embroidery in Europe

- **In Germany: embroideries from Schwalm and Dresden**
- **In Norway: Hardanger embroidery**
- **In Denmark: Amager and Hedebo embroideries**
- **In England: English embroidery (Madeira embroidery), Ayrshire, Coggeshall, and Mountmellick**
- **In Switzerland, around the town of Appenzell: there's a technique similar to plumetis.**

- **PART 5: PROJECTS** (pages 273–405)
This final section features examples of real-life projects that illustrate each chapter in the previous sections.

"Frieze": a frieze punctuates most of the chapters in this book. It can be embroidered to any length; simply repeat the design several times.

"Discover" introduces you to the technique and lets you create a small piece of work.

"Going the extra mile" takes more time to achieve the model and often includes more delicate technical elements.

What You Need to Know

When the garment is embroidered on a commercial pattern, the exact pattern is indicated. Otherwise, it's a ready-to-wear garment or a homemade pattern. To achieve a similar effect, use the same type of fabric as that shown. Interlining is sometimes necessary; this is specified in the supplies.

All the full-size drawings in part 5 can be downloaded by scanning the QR code below or by entering the internet address. At the end of the book, you'll find a bibliography of my reference works, a list of my partners, and a list of good places to buy tools and supplies. Finally, an index of embroidery stitches in alphabetical order will help you find your way around the book. For example, if you're looking for chain stitch, go to the "chain" entry

editions-eyrolles.com/go/EncyclopedieBroderie

3685
N° 25 - 32 m
100% Хлопок · 纯棉 · 綿 100%
400
COTON 100 % COTTON
10 m - 10,9 y.
COTON 100 % COTTON
10 m - 10,9 y.
COTON 100 % COTTON
10 m - 10,9 y.
COLORFAST
COLORFAST
IN FRANCE
2118030
Antimite - Mothproof
ER A SOIE
OIE D'ALGER
DEPUIS 1820
5 m.
100%
E - SILK - SEIDE
SETA - SEDA
PARIS
ADE IN FRANCE
352

1

MATERIALS AND TECHNIQUES

EMBROIDERER'S EQUIPMENT

Embroidery requires very little equipment. If you're just starting out, an assortment of embroidery needles, a small 12cm hoop, scissors, and an erasable pen.
After that, it's important to choose the right materials and tools to progress. You'll find my list of good addresses on page 410 to find out where to buy.

Needles

Needles need to be adapted according to the technique chosen, the threads to be embroidered, and possibly, the ground fabric. Boutis needles, for example, are highly specific and specially manufactured by Bohin.

What You Need to Know

To help you find your way around, the packaging specifies the type of needle and its size, using a number: the higher the number, the finer the needle, and vice versa.

- **Long needles** for embroidering round threads such as perlé (cotton or silk) and Coton à Broder DMC, whatever the medium. They have a round eye and a pointed tip.
- **Milliners** or **mode needles** for embroidering knotted stitches (knot stitch and post stitch), whatever the medium. Very long and regular in diameter, they feature a round eye and pointed tip.
- **Chenille needles** with points for embroidering ribbons and chenille threads on all materials. These extra-large needles have a longer eye and a pointed tip than conventional embroidery needles.
- **Jersey needles** for embroidering round threads (such as perlé and Coton à Broder DMC), on linen or cotton backing. Long, with a ballpoint, they have a round eye and a rounded tip. Ideal for daytime work.
- **Tapestry needles** for embroidering several strands of embroidery floss, Retors cotton, and wool. They feature a rounded tip. Perfect for counted stitch on canvas, Aïda, linen, or cotton fabrics.
- **Needles for embroidering beads** on any surface. Thin and long, they guarantee passage through the bead hole.
- **Specific needles for boutis padding**. Thin and long, they guarantee passage through the vermicelli of the boutis (long lengths to be tamped on the surface).

Tips for Good Embroidery

Pay attention to the size of the eye: too small and the thread may not slide freely, causing premature wear; too large and the thread will constantly unthread.

Embroidery Needles

Chenille needles nos. 18 to 26 for embroidering ribbons and large supplies

Long needles nos. 1 to 12 for embroidery with round thread (like the Coton à Broder DMC) or with a single strand of embroidery floss

Tapestry needles without point and with rounded tip nos. 14 to 28 for embroidery on canvas and Aïda fabric and for cross-stitching on linen

Embroidery needles nos. 1 to 10 for multistrand embroidery embroidery floss

Needles nos. 3 to 5 for Sashiko embroidery

Boutis needles: long needle for padding small shapes, trapunto needles for long shapes and vermicelli

Milliners needles nos. 1 to 12 for embroidering knotted stitches (such as knot, seed, and post stitches)

Needle nos. 9 to 12 for appliqué Boutis needles: long needle for padding small shapes, trapunto needles for long shapes and vermicelli

Needle nos. 10 to 12 for sewing beads

Jersey needles with rounded tips nos. 5 to 9 for embroidering pulled threads and openwork grounds

Hoops and Slate Frames

A hoop (or slate frame) is most often indispensable in embroidery, to ensure even tension on the ground fabric and prevent it from deforming as you work.

However, it is sometimes possible to dispense with it when embroidering certain stitches (such as stem stitch or backstitch) and with certain techniques (such as daystitch). In this case, the index finger of the hand opposite the one holding the needle is used as a support. The work is placed astride the index finger, and the fabric is tensioned and advanced by sliding the thumb and middle finger. This type of embroidery, known as "worked in hand," is also used in sewing; for example, to hem fabrics by hand. Our grandmothers commonly embroidered this way.

Tip

If the fabric to be embroidered is too small to be stretched on a hoop or frame, machine-sew four strips of fabric around it. This will increase the size of the fabric so that it can be properly stretched.

Wooden hoops

First introduced in Europe around 1760, small circular wooden frames, more commonly known as "embroidery hoops," are the simplest to use. They consist of two interlocking rings. The outer ring is fitted with a screw to adjust the tension on the backing. The fabric is slid between the two and held in place by tightening the screw.

These wooden hoops are also available on a stand for placing on the floor, or with a screw system for hanging on a table, or fixed on a rod and base that locks under the thigh when seated. These three solutions free up both hands for easier work, especially when making knotted stitches. Alternatively, two small clamps can effectively secure the hoop, cantilevered over the edge of a table (*see opposite*).

Wooden hoops are available in several diameters. The most common diameters are 10, 12, and 15 cm, depending on the work to be done. If you're embroidering buttonholed stitches, for example, a 10cm diameter is preferable, since you'll need to hold both the hoop and the working thread with your thumb. It's also important to take into account the size of your hand: small diameter for small hands, and vice versa.

If you're embroidering ribbon, smooth purl, or other materials that can't withstand crushing, choose a hoop larger than the size of the design, or switch to an slate frame for more extensive work. Here's how to mount a hoop.

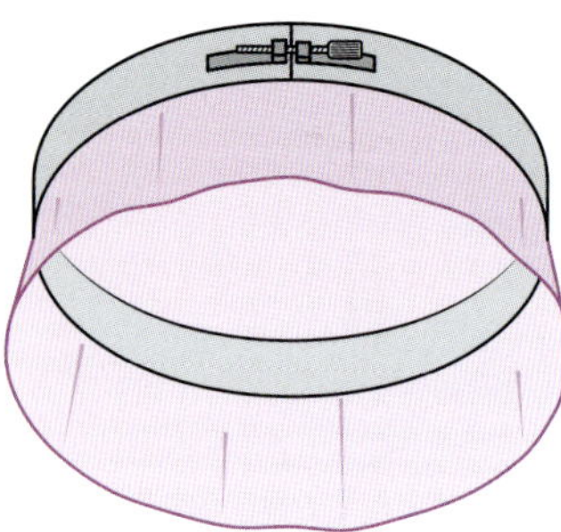

1 Separate the two wooden rings.

2 Place the inner ring on the worktable.

3 Place the embroidery fabric on top.

4 Fit the outer ring (with screw) onto the inner ring and screw to secure.

Tips for Good Embroidery

To avoid damaging the ground fabric and prevent it from slipping, the hoop rings should be wrapped with a cotton twill tape that will stay in place for years (see p. 22).

Method for wrapping an embroidery hoop

Supplies

- white cotton twill, 20 mm wide
  (see below for length)
- a needle with ecru sewing thread

To determine the length of twill required per ring, simply measure its circumference with a tape measure and multiply by four.

1 Wrap the twill tape once around the hoop ring. Make a few small stitches with the thread to secure the ribbon.

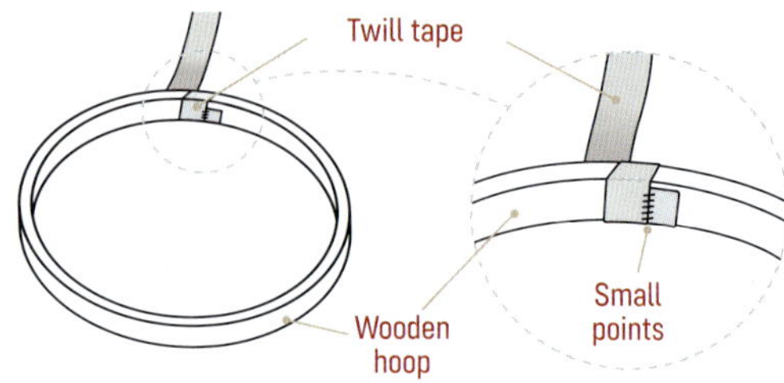

2 Continue winding the ribbon tightly around the hoop, overlapping each turn by 5 mm.

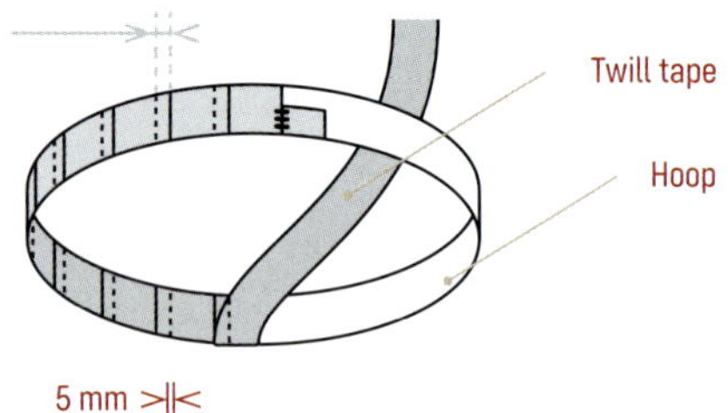

3 On the last lap, make a small tuck in the twill ribbon to prevent it from fraying, and sew a few small stitches: on the inside of the inner ring and on the outside of the outer ring.

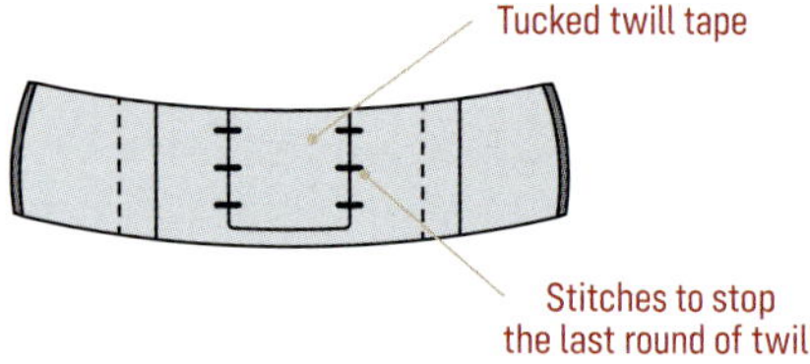

Rectangular slate frames

Rectangular slate frames date back to Greco-Roman antiquity. They enable the entire backing to be stretched perfectly, to prevent it from deforming during work. They consist of

- **two mortises,** the wooden pieces that make up the large top and bottom sides of the frame;
- **two laths**, wooden pieces forming the left and right sides of the frame;
- **four screws** to securely join mortises and battens at the four corners of the frame;
- **two lengths of twill tape**, twill tapes generally stapled to the mortises to sew the textile support to be embroidered in order to stretch it across the width; and
- **pull tabs**, twill tapes wound on slats and pinned to the ground fabric to stretch the ground fabric lengthwise.

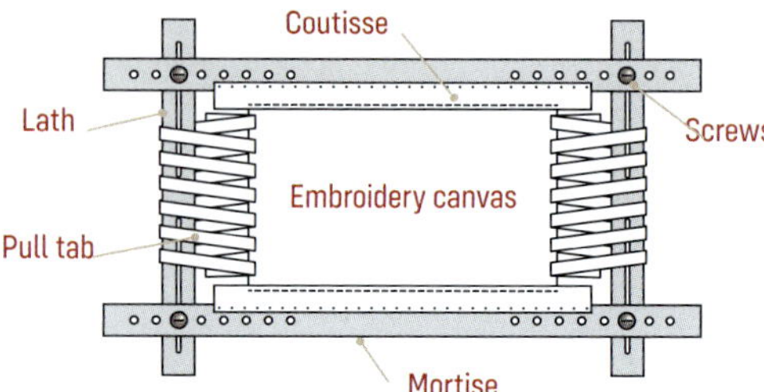

More cumbersome and more difficult to set up than a conventional embroidery hoop, these frames are most often used by professional embroiderers, although they remain accessible to amateurs who have the space. The frame must be laid flat; for example, on two trestles or between a table and trestle. Work is performed with one hand about the work and the other below.

How to Assemble a Slate Frame

Supplies

- white cotton twill: 4 to 6 m long and 30 mm wide
- extra-strong thread, 4 times the frame length of the frame
- pins
- a long needle

1 When the edges of the canvas are not straight, fray them by hand to restore straightness. In this way, you'll be able to mount your canvas perfectly plumb in the frame.

2 Disassemble the frame if mortises and battens are screwed together.

3 To center the fabric support on the mortise, start in the middle and pin the edge of the long side of the fabric to a seamstitch. Stitch with a sufficiently long double needle of extra-strong thread.

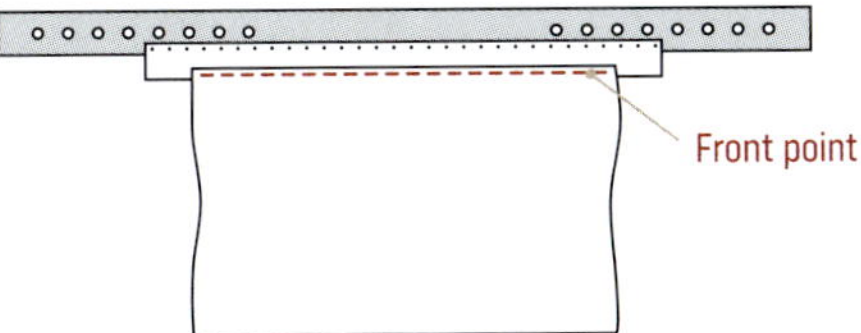

4 Do the same on the opposite mortise. Ensure that the textile support is centered as on the first mortise.

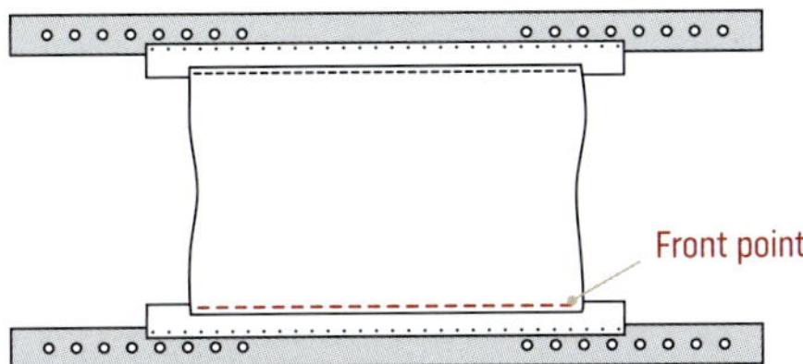

5 Loosely assemble the slats and mortises, using the screws. Tension the canvas, keeping the mortises as far apart as possible. Tighten screws securely.

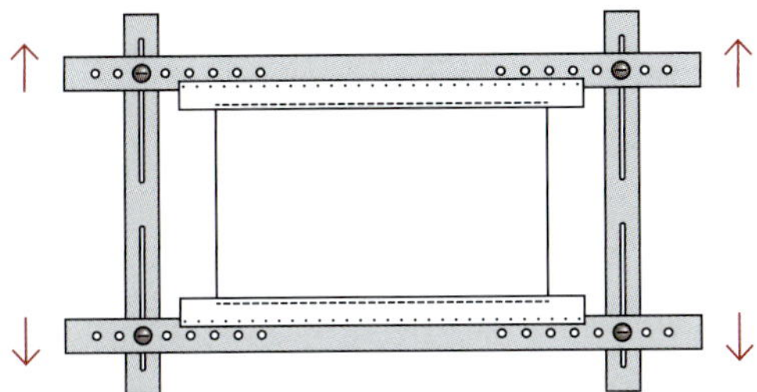

6 Pin the pull tabs on each side 2 cm from the edge of the canvas, wrapping them around the slats.

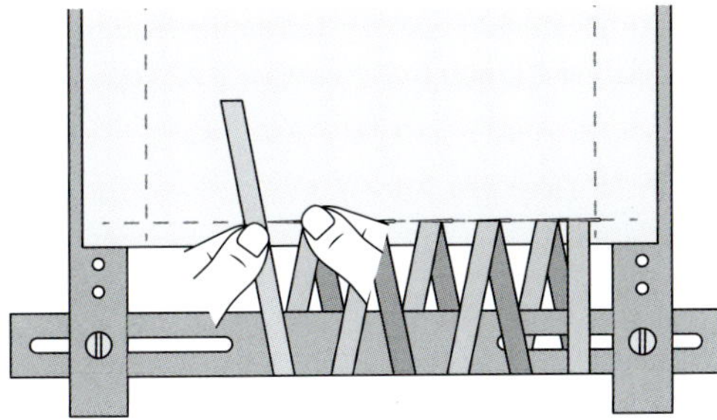

7 Place the frame on trestles set at a comfortable height for working.

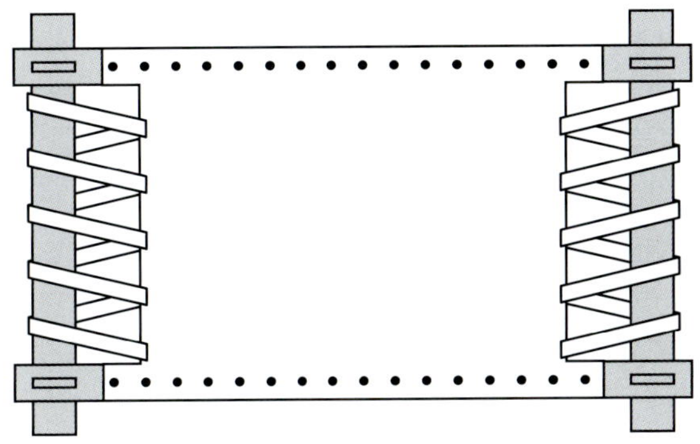

Rectangular or square plastic frames

There are also small plastic or wood-and-plastic frames, which are very practical and more accessible to amateur embroiderers, thanks to their ease of assembly. All you have to do is wedge the fabric support in place with clips that replace the stitching—instructions are supplied with purchase. They also take up less space.

Small Tools

In addition to the needles and the hoop or frame, other tools are required to produce high-quality embroidery.

- **Embroidery scissors**. These are indispensable. Fine, pointed, and small, they need to be perfectly sharp to cut embroidery threads and various supplies cleanly. Make sure you have two pairs: one for cutting threads and another for metal and plastic supplies (such as jaseron and smooth purl). Special scissors with rounded, pelican, or lens blades are also available to avoid cutting the fabric backing.
- **Cutting scissors** for canvas and interlining.
- **Transfer tools** to reproduce a motif. Pencil, felt-tip pen, chalk, transfer pen, disappearing-ink pen (the line remains visible for just a few hours), or with the heat of an iron or hairdryer (such as Pilot's Frixion), pounce . . . the choice is vast! You'll also need pins, tape, a ruler, a circle tracer, tracing paper and textile carbon, tissue paper, sheets of acetate, and the indispensable light table. Select your tool according to the transfer method (see page 33). Always carry out a trial run on the chosen textile.

Embroiderer's Tools

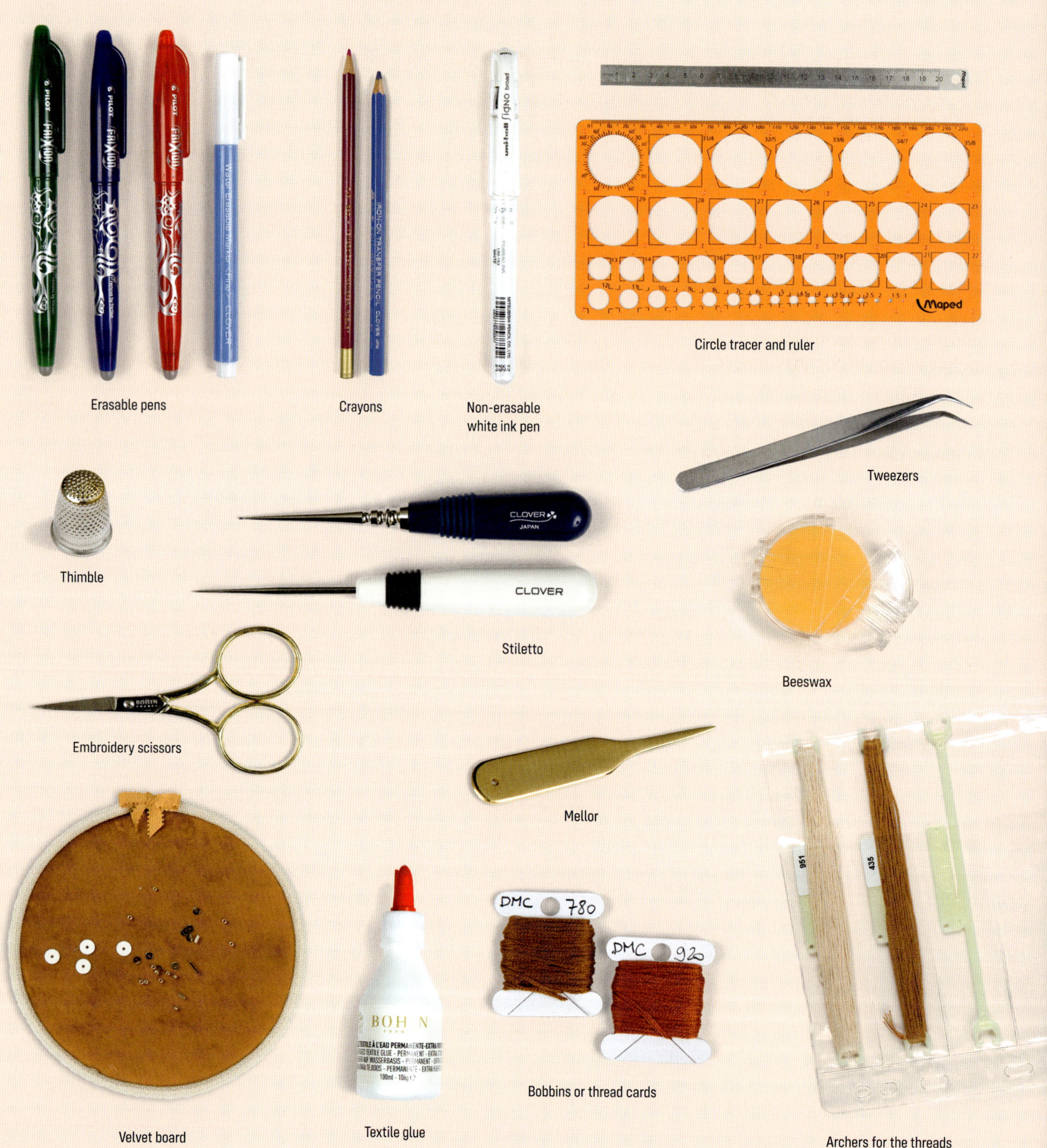

Erasable pens

Crayons

Non-erasable white ink pen

Circle tracer and ruler

Tweezers

Thimble

Stiletto

Beeswax

Embroidery scissors

Mellor

Velvet board

Textile glue

Bobbins or thread cards

Archers for the threads

• A **thimble**: The right size, neither too big nor too small. Made of metal or silicone, it can be worn on the middle finger.

Tip

If your die tends to slip, lightly moisten the tip of your finger, blow into the die, then thread it quickly.

• **Stilettos** for piercing fabrics without tearing them, to pass large supplies like cords through. They are pointed and come in different sizes.

• A **mellor** for handling metallic threads, purls, and ribbons and positioning them correctly when embroidering. A boutis needle (see page 19) can replace this hard-to-find tool.

• **Tweezers** for undoing embroidery and handling beads, sprinkles, and small supplies

• **Beeswax** to lightly coat the threads holding the metal supplies

• A **velvet board** to place the small supplies (pearls, sequins, etc.) to catch them easily with the needle, or to cut the smooth purl. It can be of any shape and is generally made by the embroiderer themselves. Its bottom is covered with a velvety fabric, and its high edges prevent the supplies from escaping.

• Tools for **finishing embroidery fixtures** (such as brooches): textile glue, double-sided iron-on glue such as Vliesofix from Vlieseline

• **Boxes** and **binders** to store yarns and various supplies. Wrap skein threads around cardboard boxes. DMC has also developed a storage system for archers, which you can slip into a plastic binder pocket. Don't forget to note the color references and brand name.

How to Make a Velvet Board

Supplies

• strong cardboard, 2 mm thick: 11 × 21 cm

• light-colored velvety fabric: 15 × 15 cm

• cotton fabric: 15 × 15 cm

• light wadding: 11 × 11 cm

• 12mm diameter cord (or 12mm high double piping): 35 cm long

• 1 to 2cm wide ribbon: 4 cm

• white acrylic glue

• clothespins, plastic clips, or clamps

• pins

• a compass

• a brush

Optional: sewing thread to match the cord

1 Cut two 10cm circles from cardboard, one 13cm circle from fabric, one 13cm circle from cotton, one 10cm circle from wadding.

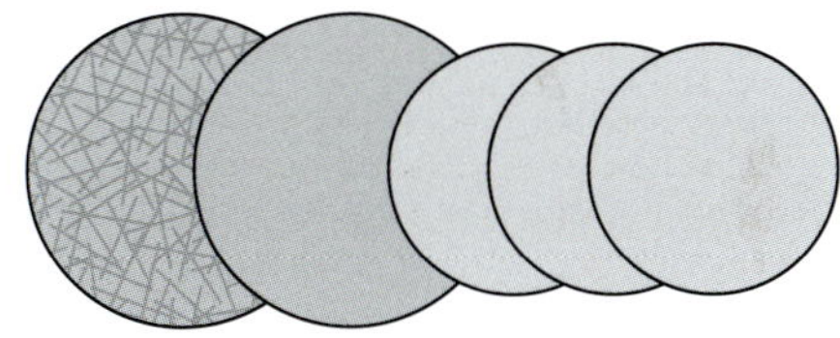

2 Place the wadding on a cardboard circle and the velvety fabric on top. Secure with pins on the edge of the cardboard.

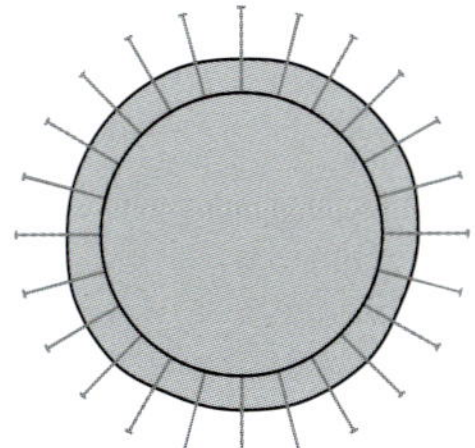

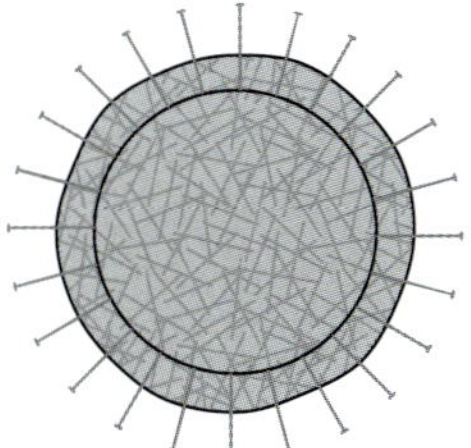

3 Trim margins and glue with white acrylic glue.

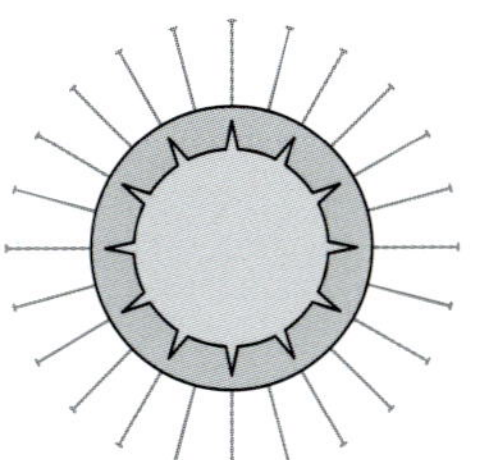

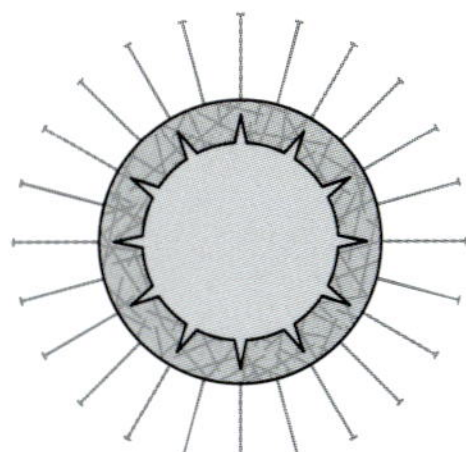

Embroidery Backing and Stabilizers

Fabrics for clothing

Linen canvas for embroidery

Batiste

• FABRICS •

Aïda

Silk gauze, 19 stitches/cm

Wool viscose and linen, 12 threads/cm

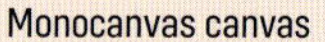

Monocanvas canvas

Penelope canvas

• INTERLINING •

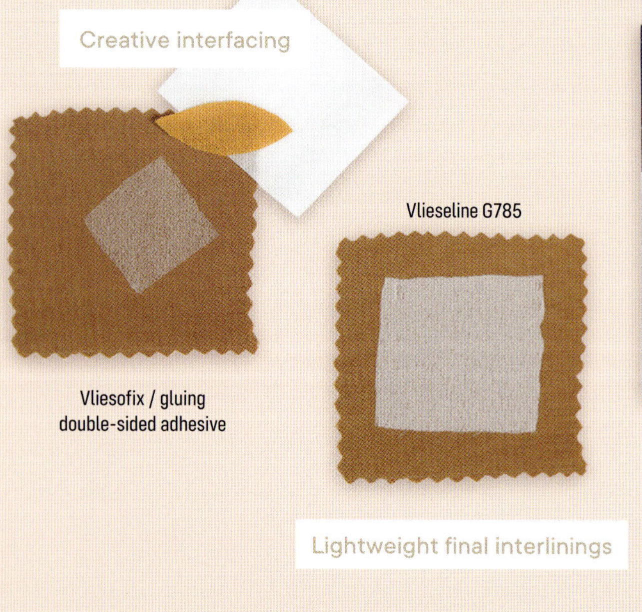

Creative interfacing

Vliesofix / gluing double-sided adhesive

Vlieseline G785

Lightweight final interlinings

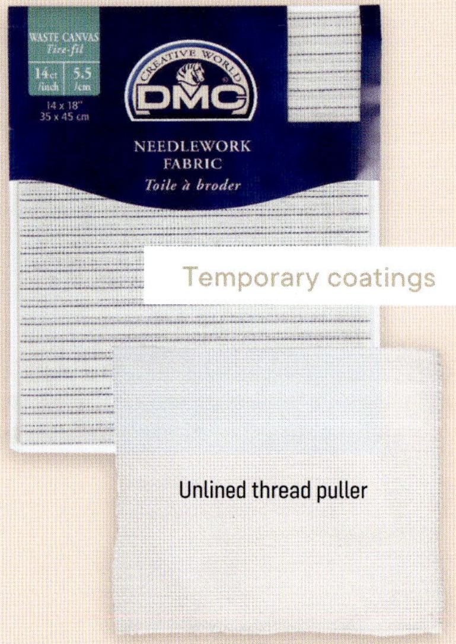

Temporary coatings

Unlined thread puller

Soluble stabilizer

Soluble canvas

4 Do the same with the second cardboard circle and absorbent cotton, without adding any wadding.

5 Glue the two circles together. Hold them together with pliers while they dry.

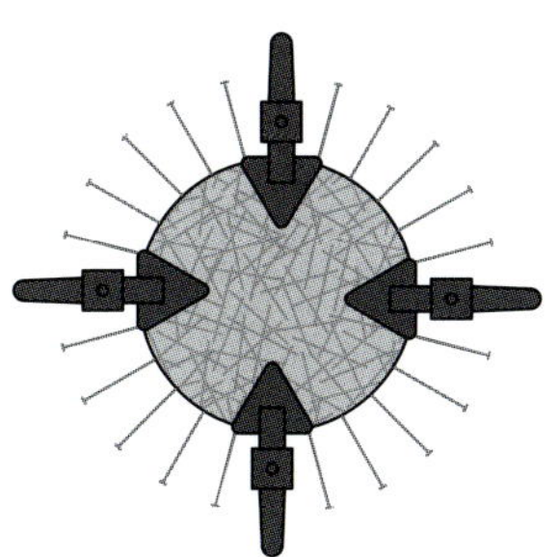

6 Glue or sew (or both) double piping or cord all around to create a trough on the velvety side.

7 Cover the junction with tape.

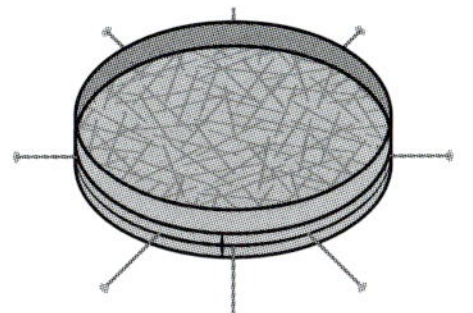

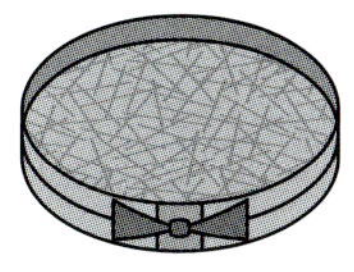

Tips for Good Embroidery

- Work in good lighting conditions. Equip your lamp with a "daylight" bulb for greater comfort. Special "small jobs" lamps are sometimes fitted with a magnifying glass built into the structure of the lamp.
- Close-up glasses dedicated to embroidery can help. Conventional spectacle lenses are often unsuitable for embroidery, since the distance between the eyes and the work to be embroidered is less than when reading. Talk to your ophthalmologist.

Supplies

"Supplies" refer to all embroidery materials and their backings.

Embroidery backings

On fabric, leather, cardboard, mesh, plastic . . . there are no limits to embroidery! Bear in mind that some materials lend themselves better than others, such as fabric, which beginners will prefer.

Fabrics

The most common medium for embroidery is the woven or knitted fabric of a garment, accessory, or household linen, whether home-sewn or ready to wear.

Woven fabrics are formed by an interlacing of threads (the "weave") arranged longitudinally (the warp threads) and horizontally (the weft threads).

Vocabulary

Selvedges are the edges of the fabric in the direction of the warp threads.
Straight-grain corresponds to the direction of the threads in the weave.
The **warp thread** is parallel to the fabric selvedge; the **weft line** is perpendicular.

The weave of a woven fabric can be divided into two categories.

- The **simple weave** has threads that cross over each other, top and bottom, like a basic weave, giving the fabric a smooth appearance. This type of fabric, like cotton or linen canvas, is the easiest to embroider; designs shift easily, and the needle passes easily through the fabric.

- The **compound weave** is made up of warp and weft crossings that can adopt different rhythms. These fabrics include twills, satins, piqués, velvets, sponges, etc. Embroidery is much more complicated, since their surface is not smooth and the design is difficult to transfer. Special interlining is recommended (see pages 26 and 28).

- **Knit fabrics** such as jersey and the wool of machine- or hand-knitted sweaters can also be embroidered. However, they require special interlining (see pages 26 and 28) to counter their elasticity.

Tips for Good Embroidery

To get started with trace embroidery, it's best to choose light-colored fabrics without elastane. This will make it easier to transfer the design and eliminate the need for interlining.

Embroidery Canvas

Aïda canvas, canvas, and waste canvas (which is a stabilizer; see pages 26 and 37) are specifically made for counted-stitch embroidery. Their weave is very regular and square (the number of threads on the warp and weft is identical), more or less tightly woven.

- **Aïda** fabric is for all counted-stitch embroidery, mainly cross-stitch. Invented in 1907, its threads are woven four by four, leaving small holes for easy embroidery. It is defined by a number of stitches/cm: most commonly, 5.5 cross-stitches/cm or 7 cross-stitches/cm.

- **Linen canvas** is for all counted-stitch embroideries. Its linen fibers are irregular and its weave regular. It is defined by its thread count/cm. The higher the thread count, the smaller and more difficult the crosses, and vice versa. For example, Zweigart offers Dublin (10 threads/cm); Belfast (12.6 threads/cm), the most common; Edinburgh (14 threads/cm); and Newcastle (16 threads/cm).

Each cross-stitch is generally made on two warp and weft threads: on Dublin, this gives 5 stitches/cm, on Belfast 6.3 stitches/cm, on Edinburgh 7 stitches/cm, and on Newcastle 8 stitches/cm.

- **Etamine** is for Hardanger and Hedebo embroidery, cross-stitch for beginners, and traditional embroidery. It's a 100% cotton or cotton/modal fabric, supple, smooth, and pleasant to work with. The thread count of monocanvas is regular and constant in both warp and weft. Like linen, it is generally embroidered on two warp and weft threads, but the threads are easier to count because they are more regular. Its weave is defined by a number of threads/cm. At Zweigart, for example, you'll find Lugana (10 threads/cm), Murano (12 threads/cm), and Floba superfine (14 threads/cm).

- **Needlepoint canvas**. This is a warp-and-weft fabric that is weighted and therefore rigid. It has a very regular weave, defined by a number of stitches per 10 cm. Canvas comes in two forms.

- The **monocanvas canvas** for diagonally embroidered stitches such as Saint-Cyr.

- The **double canvas** (or "Penelope" canvas) for straight stitches such as Gobelin or Hungarian.

- **Silk gauze** for miniature embroidery. This fabric is fairly rigid but light, openwork, and transparent. It is made of silk threads. With a regular weave, it is defined by a number of threads/cm. For example, Au Ver à Soie offers 16 and 19 threads/cm. It is embroidered with a single strand of embroidery floss. This fabric is not recommended for beginners.

Interlining

The Vlieseline brand offers a wide range of high-quality interlinings, easy to find in haberdasheries.

Tips for Good Embroidery

Before you begin, refer to the manufacturer's recommendations and test a sample of your ground fabric to assess the fall of the fabric and the adhesion of the interlining.

- **Iron-on stabilizers** for final reinforcement. When embroidering on garments, some very soft fabrics, such as viscose or silk, require definitive backing. In most cases, superfine woven G785 stabilizer is ideal. It is fixed with an iron.

- **Temporary embroidery stabilizers**. Sulky (for use, see page 36) is self-adhesive and water soluble. It sticks to the top of the work to help transfer a design onto dark fabrics. It is also useful for removing the elasticity of a fabric (such as knitwear) during embroidery.

- The **waste canvas** (for use, see page 37). This temporary stabilizer enables you to embroider textiles not originally intended for counted-stitch embroidery. This is the case with clothing fabrics that have tightly woven webs or are sometimes irregular or contain elastane. The waste canvas creates a grid, which is then removed. It is available in various weaves for embroidering; for example, 5.5 or 7 cross-stitches/cm. This simple technique is highly creative!

• **Soluble canvas** (for use, see page 37). Like the thread puller, this temporary stabilizer is water soluble. It can be used to embroider textiles that are not suitable for counted-stitch embroidery. DMC's precut sheets measure 20 × 22 cm for 5.5 cross-stitches/cm, making them ideal for embroidering small designs on T-shirts, for example.

Embroidery Threads

Cotton, silk, linen, wool, polyester . . . the choice of embroidery threads is vast. The most common manufacturers are DMC (for cotton and wool), Maison Sajou (for cotton, wool, and silk), Anchor (for cotton), and Au Ver à Soie (for silk and metallic threads). Above all, beware of cheap yarns whose quality is not always up to scratch. Some yarns can bleed onto the fabric after the first wash. So be careful when you buy, and put your trust in reputable brands.

The brand, product name, material, size, and color of the thread are generally indicated on the spools or skein rings. Each manufacturer has its own thread color references.

What You Need to Know

Switching from one brand to another, or even from one material to another, can be useful to clear your thread stocks or change the appearance of the embroidery (silk, for example, is much brighter and more luminous than cotton, but also more delicate). To help you, Au Ver à Soie retailer Atelier 196 (www.atelier196.com) converts references from cotton embroidery floss to silk embroidery floss.

Cotton or silk embroidery floss

Embroidery floss is a multistrand thread with a shiny satin finish. Very versatile and easy to embroider, it is the most commonly chosen thread for embroidery. It is available in a wide range of colors from all manufacturers.

• At DMC and Anchor, it consists of six separable cotton strands packed in skeins.

• At Maison Sajou it's called "Retors du Nord." Presented on a cardboard sleeve, it consists of four separable cotton strands.

• At Au Ver à Soie, Alger silk is made up of seven separable strands packaged in skeins.

All these embroidery flosss can be embroidered as is or by removing the number of strands required for the job.

Pearl cotton and pearl silk

Pearl cotton is a shiny twisted thread. Well-rounded, it can be used as is without separating the strands in all types of embroidery, giving them incomparable relief and texture.

At DMC, perlé is made of cotton. It is sold in several sizes, identified by numbers: the smallest thread is no. 8, the medium no. 5, and the largest no. 3. Au Ver à Soie's pearl silk, on the other hand, comes in just one size, made up of three inseparable strands.

Coton à Broder

DMC Coton à Broder is a round, long-fibered cotton thread with a silky appearance. It is made up of four inseparable strands and is available in different sizes: from the thickest, no. 16; to the medium, no. 25; to the finest, no. 30 and no. 35. This thread is mainly used for white embroidery (plumetis, Renaissance, and Richelieu embroideries, borders).

Tips for Good Embroidery

This thread can sometimes become untwisted during embroidery. If this happens, roll the needle between your fingers to restore the thread's shape. If, on the other hand, the twist increases, let the needle hang down: the thread will untwist by itself under the effect of gravity.

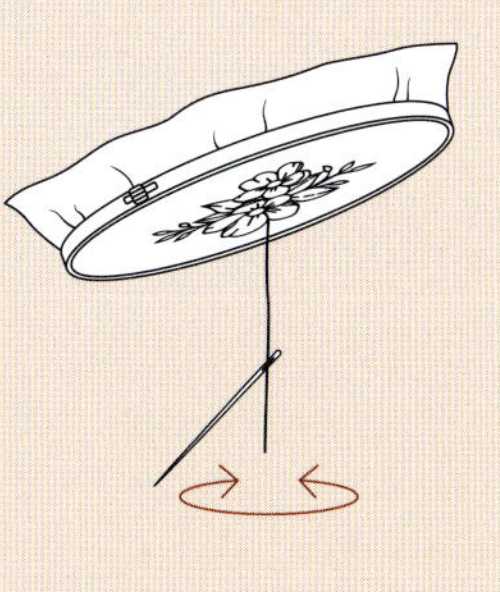

DMC Retors matte cotton

Retors matte DMC cotton is a combed yarn with a soft, supple matte appearance. Sold in a single size, it is made up of five inseparable strands. This yarn is traditionally used for canvas.

Embroidery Threads

• COTTON •

Embroidery floss

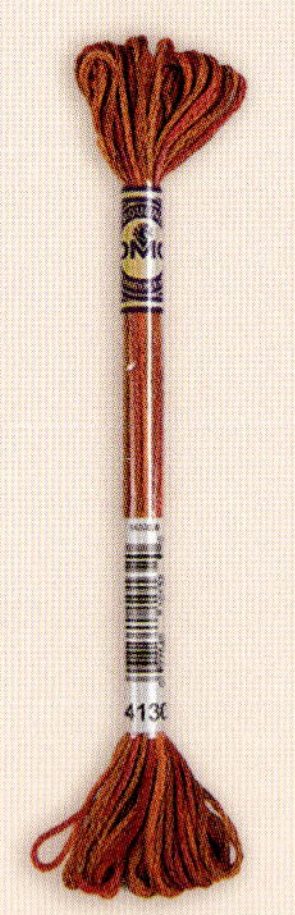
Variegated embroidery floss

Embroidery floss Anchor

Coton à Broder White DMC nos. 20, 25, 30 and 35 (packaging: 10 g)

Coton à Broder White DMC (10 m)

Coton à Broder DMC 25 colors (10 m)

Cotton Retors matte DMC

Retors du Nord Sajou

Cotton Pearl DMC

• BRISTLES •

Soie d'alger, Au Ver à Soie

Soie perlée, Au Ver à Soie

Chenille threads, Au Ver à Soie

• METALLIC •

Metallic Ets J. Toulemonde

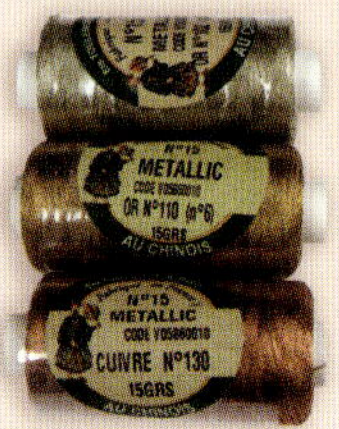
Metallic, Au Chinois Ets J. Toulemonde

Braided metallic 4, Au Ver à Soie

DMC Diamant

• WOOL•

Saint-Pierre wool Ets J. Toulemonde

Aubusson fine wool La Route de la Laine for Au Ver à Soie

Colbert DMC Wool

Wool

All knitting wools can be adapted for embroidery. Some are specially made for tapestry and traditional embroidery.

- Colbert DMC is a brightly colored 100% wool yarn. It is usually worked in half stitch on Penelope canvas.
- Ets J. Toulemonde Saint-Pierre wool is half wool and half polyamide. It consists of four separable strands. Initially intended for darning, it is also suitable for embroidery for a matte result.
- La Route de la Laine Aubusson fine wool is a 100% merino wool yarn. It is made up of four separable strands. Its high quality makes it ideal for tapestry and traditional embroidery.

Metallic threads

Metallic threads come in a wide variety of sizes, compositions, and colors. They are suitable for all types of embroidery, but some are easier to embroider than others. They can sometimes be too stiff or split.

At Au Ver à Soie, Metallic Tressé is a round, easy-to-embroider thread that can be worked without separating the strands. It is available in four sizes: in 1 strand and in 4, 8, or 16 twisted strands.

Attention

Items embroidered with metallic threads should be washed and ironed at low temperatures. Sometimes made of plastic, they can melt under heat.

Silk ribbon

Depending on the manufacturer, you'll find silk ribbons in widths of 2, 4, 7, 9, 10, 13, and 15 mm. Choose them according to the stitches used for ribbon embroidery.

Chenille thread

Chenille thread is a hairy thread that adds a lot of softness to embroidery.

Please note that not all chenille yarns can withstand abrasion as the needle passes through the textile backing. Rely on the manufacturer's recommendations or do a test before you start; use a stiletto to pre-punch.

Fantasy thread

Depending on what you find, these threads (hairy, curly, plastic, etc.) are ideal for embellishment and extremely creative embroidery.

Threads for beads, sequins, and special supplies

Au Chinois Ets J. Toulemonde glove thread is a cotton thread. It was once used for sewing and repairing gloves. Today, it is used for hand sewing. This thread is glazed, so it doesn't need to be dipped in wax to glide smoothly. Fine and very strong, it is available in some 30 colors.

Beads, sequins, and special supplies

For centuries, embroidery has been embellished by supplies other than thread. Glass, metal, plastic, and stone beads in all shapes, sizes, and colors; sequins; bowls; navettes; cabochons; sewing stones; rhinestones; mirrors . . . there's a vast choice of sparkling little supplies to enhance your designs.

In gold embroidery, purls and jaceron are small metallic or metal-plastic threads, wound like a spring (hollow for the former, tight for the latter). They are available in a variety of diameters and colors.

GOOD EMBROIDERY TECHNIQUES

Preparing the work is an important step in guaranteeing the success of the embroidery. It must not be neglected. Only then can the actual embroidery work begin.

A Few Tips before You Start

Getting inspired, choosing colors and threads . . . preparing a project is always very motivating! Here are a few tips to keep in mind before you get started, so that the pleasure of embroidery continues when you actually embroider.

• When starting out in embroidery, it's important not to put too many technical constraints on yourself. Choose a small motif, prefer a light-colored warp-and-weft fabric (cotton or linen), transfer the motif by transparency, and embroider with cotton embroidery floss.

• Preparing embroidery requires special care. The choice of design, embroidery stitches, and ground fabric depends on the use of the embroidered item. A garment (which will be worn and washed) requires embroidery that is much more resistant than a decorative item that will be hung on a wall. So a decorative embroidery design won't necessarily suit a garment.

• Feel free to adapt the templates in this book to your own work. To do so, photocopy, reduce or enlarge, cut out, and rearrange the motifs.

• To calculate the amount of thread required, make a sample of each embroidery element, measuring and noting the length of thread for each. Then multiply this length by the number of repetitions of each design. Alternatively, rely on your own experience to make the calculation!

• Whatever your project, it's best to do a trial run first. On a piece of fabric identical to the one you want to embroider (weave it if necessary), perform a few stitches with the chosen thread. This will ensure that the thread, needle, and backing are perfectly suited to your project.

Choosing the Right Amount of Fabric

The amount of fabric needed for embroidery should always be larger than the finished work. In this way, the fabric will be large enough to hold perfectly in the hoop and not slip. Don't forget to take into account any hems and seam allowances. For placed embroidery, the yardage also depends on the size of the design to be transferred.

For counted-stitch embroidery, which is characterized by the number of stitches represented on the diagram, it is necessary to calculate the surface area according to the number of stitches per centimeter on the chosen fabric (see page 28). For example, if your diagram has 55 stitches at its widest point and you embroider on 5.5 stitches/cm Aïda fabric, your finished embroidery will measure 10 cm. Make the same calculation for the height and plan your canvas surface accordingly.

What You Need to Know

The design can be adapted to the project, and therefore to the fabric, by reducing or increasing it slightly (by no more than 15%) on a photocopier.

Preparing the Textile Substrate

Before embroidering a fabric for a garment, accessory, household linen, etc., several steps are necessary to remove its primer and give it its final size (fabric, often new, can shrink on first washing). We therefore recommend scouring the fabric (i.e., soaking it in cold water for several hours) then washing and ironing it once dry.

Please note that, in some cases, no washing is required.

• Needlepoint canvas, Aïda canvas, congress cloth, or linen canvas for counted-stitch embroidery do not require any treatment; otherwise they may lose their rigidity.

• Similarly, with certain techniques (such as pulled-thread days), you should avoid washing the supports. The risk is that the threads will felt, which would then complicate the preparation work for pulling them.

• The boutis is washed once the embroidery has been completed, so that the holes caused by the padding in the fabric weft close up.

In all cases, don't forget to overcast the edges of the fabric, either by hand or on the sewing machine, so that they don't fray during embroidery.

Tips for Good Embroidery

• Would you like to sew a garment and then embroider it? Embroidery takes place before sewing. Roughly cut the fabric around the pattern, leaving a margin of 5 to 10 cm. Pay particular attention to the straight grain (generally, the design is positioned vertically on the garment) and the center of the piece to be embroidered. Then overcast, hem, or tape the fabric to prevent fraying. Finally, sew up the embroidered fabric according to the sewing pattern.

• For a hand-sewn garment, it's best to include a lining that hides the back of the embroidery.

Heat-Seal the Substrate

Some fabrics require fusing to stiffen them so that the embroidery does not weigh down the finished work. This is the case with very light fabrics (e.g., viscose, silk), or when the weft is so loose that the threads passing from one stitch to another on the back of the work would be visible ghosting on the right side (e.g., fine cotton batistes or light fabrics). In this case, a final light interlining is recommended (see page 26). Iron-on is applied to the reverse side of the fabric by using an iron, following the manufacturer's instructions.

When embroidering on knitted fabrics or fabrics with elastane, a temporary stabilizer, such as Sulky, will help you to embroider evenly. (For how to use it, see page 36.)

Transfer a Design for Line Embroidery

When it comes to traced embroidery, there are many ways of transferring the design. Bear in mind that if the design is not accurate, the embroidery will be even less so. This is an important step that needs to be carried out with care!

Note

Feel free to modify the composition of the designs to suit your projects! Remember that the borders in this book are to be transferred as many times as necessary to cover the surface to be embroidered.

Before you start

1 Use a ruler for the straight lines and a circle for circles.

2 Use the photocopier to enlarge or shrink the design to the correct size. If the pattern requires it, make a mirror copy.

3 Pin or tape the design in place to prevent it from moving, while respecting the straight line.

The different transfer methods

Choose the transfer method that's easiest to use, depending on the constraints of your textile. For example:

• For thin, relatively light-colored linen or cotton canvas, transfer the design by transparency (see opposite).

• For velvets, woolens, and dark fabrics of any composition and weave, use Sulky (see page 36).

For a lightweight, single-weave fabric and light color

Fix the drawing on a light table (or glass table lit from underneath by a flashlight) or window and transfer it transparently, using an erasable pen (air or heat) or mechanical pencil.

For medium to heavy single-weave fabrics to heavy weave in any color

Several techniques are available. Choose the one that suits you best.

Using carbon tissue paper

1 Select the color of the carbon sheet to be interleaved according to that of the substrate: dark for light fabric and vice versa.

2 Iron over the design lines with a round-tipped drypoint, a 2H hard-core pencil, a used ballpoint pen, or a patterned pinwheel.

Using heat transfer paper

Note that this technique is possible only if the fabric, such as cotton or linen, can withstand high temperatures.

1 Transfer the design to a sheet of thin paper, using a transfer pen.

2 Using an iron (very hot and without steam), transfer the design to the fabric.

> **What You Need to Know**
>
> **Some specialized embroidery magazines and haberdashery stores offer directly transferable designs. These are supplied already printed on transfer paper, which makes the job easier: all you have to do is iron them onto the embroidery backing.**

Prick and Pounce

This time-consuming and meticulous professional technique is not easy to implement in a hobby embroidery project. However, it is useful when the same design (and therefore the same tracing paper) has to be used several times for mass production. It can be used on all textile materials.

1 Draw the pattern to be transferred on tracing paper with a pencil. Turn the sheet over and pierce the line every millimeter with a fine needle (no. 10) or quilter. Turn it over again so that the line is facing you, and secure it to the fabric with tape or pins.

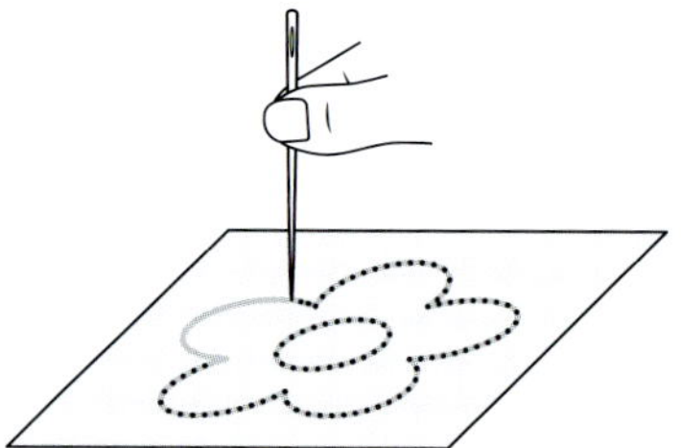

2 Take some light or dark pounce powder (choose according to fabric: dark for light fabrics, light for dark fabrics). Using the pouncing tool, spread it with circular movements on the tracing paper, so that it penetrates through the small holes. Gently remove the sheet.

3 Fix the powder by spraying with 70° alcohol, then with a hot iron without steam, remembering to interpose a sheet of tissue paper between the iron soleplate and the sanded pattern.

Using thread and tissue paper

1 Draw the pattern on tissue paper.

2 Pin the pattern to the ground fabric.

3 Using a strand of embroidery floss in a color matching the future embroidery, embroider small front stitches all along the design.

4 Gently tear away the tissue paper, retaining the running stitches as a design for the embroidery.

Using a template or stencil

For simple, repetitive designs, it's possible to make templates from transparencies or acetate sheets (available from hobby shops).

1 Offset the design on transparencies or acetate sheet.

2 Cut out the shapes with a thin cutter blade to create a stencil.

3 Position the stencil on the fabric to be embroidered and trace the shapes with a Frixion-type erasable pen.

Reading a Diagram for Counted-Stitch Embroidery

Counted-stitch embroidery patterns are represented by a diagram in which each stitch is represented by a square in a grid. Inside the square, a symbol or color (or both) indicates the stitch to be performed and the thread to be used. The diagram is accompanied by a legend giving this information.

This type of embroidery begins at the center of the design. Before starting work, it's essential to locate this point on the diagram (marked by arrows on the edge of the grid) and on the fabric (fold the fabric in four to find it).

How to Use Sulky

For precise lines and results, Sulky (see pages 26 and 28) is the modern solution when it's not possible to transfer the design directly onto the fabric. Use it on single-weave or compound-weave fabrics, with or without elastane, or on knitted fabrics of any color.

1 Cut a sheet of Sulky. It should be larger than the design, so that it can fit inside the embroidery hoop. Using a Frixion-type erasable pen, transfer the design to the fluffy side of the soluble stabilizer.

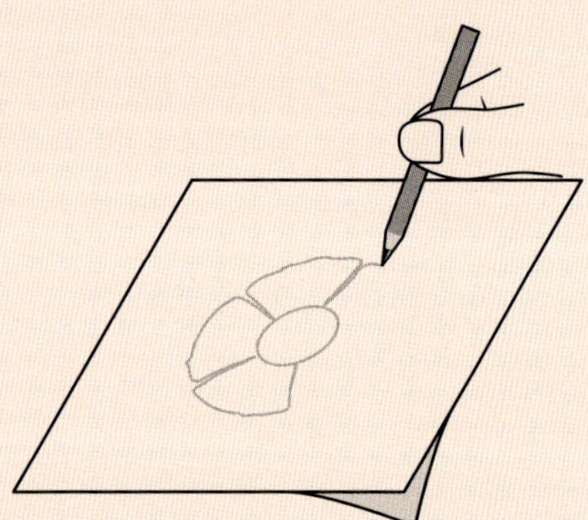

2 Remove the glossy paper and stick the Sulky to the right side of the backing, over the area to be embroidered. If necessary, use a needle and sewing thread to create a few large basting stitches around the design to hold the Sulky in place.

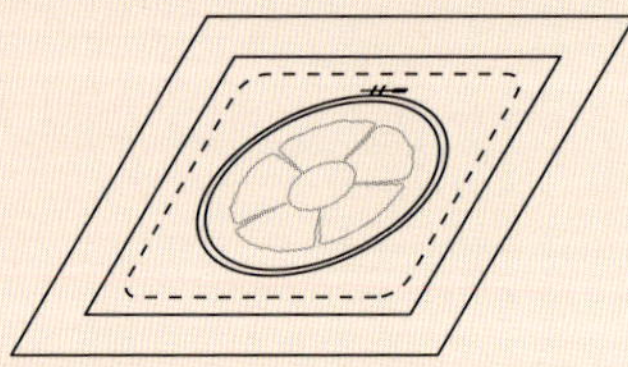

3 Once embroidery is complete, soak the work in cold water to dissolve the Sulky completely.

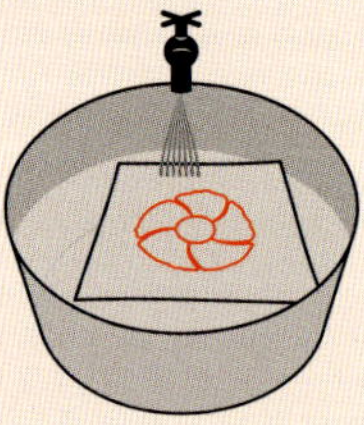

Some printers accept Sulky sheets in their paper tray and print the design directly onto them. In this case, check that the ink does not bleed onto the embroidered fabric during soaking. Try it out first.

Use a Waste Canvas or Water-Soluble Canvas

If you wish to embroider counted stitches and your fabric is not suitable, use a thread puller or water-soluble canvas (see pages 26 and 29).

The waste canvas

1 Cut a piece of waste canvas at least 5 cm larger than the surface to be embroidered.

2 Baste the waste canvas flat on the surface to be embroidered, respecting the straight thread. Make several basting lines if the work is large, spacing them 5 cm apart.

3 Embroider the whole with a hoop and a pointed embroidery needle. Be careful not to prick the needle into the threads of the waste canvas; you'll have trouble removing it later.

4 Once the embroidery is finished, soak it for an hour in lukewarm water.

5 Remove the threads from the waste canvas one by one, in both directions, starting with the shortest threads. Use small tweezers.

Water-soluble canvas

1 Cut a piece of water-soluble canvas. It should be larger than the surface to be embroidered: allow at least 5 cm more.

2 Lay the canvas flat on the surface to be embroidered, respecting the straight thread to hold it in place.

3 Once the embroidery is complete, soak the work in lukewarm water to dissolve the canvas completely.

Preparing Embroidery Work

Once the fabric has been correctly placed in the hoop or on a slate frame, it's time to embroider. This work begins with the preparation of the first needle, the length of thread required for embroidery, threaded through the eye of the needle.

For embroidery to remain intact over time, it must be strong. So, when you start embroidering, it's vital that the thread is firmly attached to the backing, so that it doesn't slip away. The reverse side of the work should be as clean as possible. To achieve this, start without tying a knot at the end of the needle.

Tips for Good Embroidery

You are free to follow the instructions given in the embroidery explanations or to personalize your creations. I advise you to prepare and color your future embroidery (using colored pencils, felt pens, or watercolors) on paper before starting. This way, you won't have to search for colors as you work.

Conditioning Large Cotton Skeins

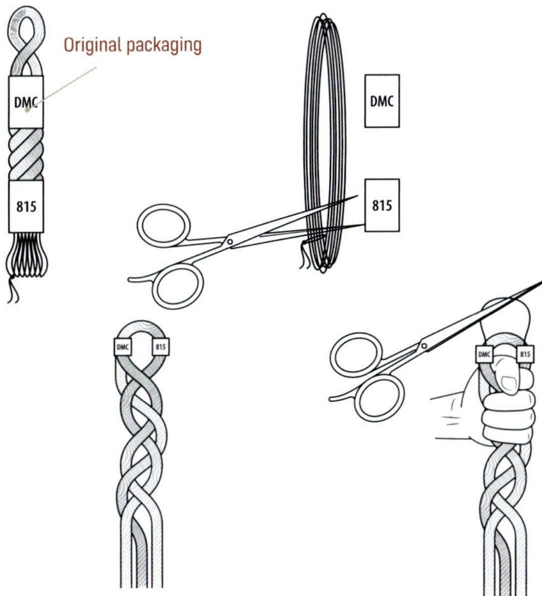

Some DMC threads, such as Coton à Broder and pearl cotton, are sold in very large skeins. Here's how to condition them to prevent tangling during use.

1 Remove the rings and untwist the skein completely. Cut all threads at once at the knot.

2 Pass the threads through the labels to keep the references. Divide the threads into thirds and braid them.

3 To grab a thread, put your thumb under the labels and hold the threads in your hand. With the tip of the scissors, extract a thread by lifting and pulling on it. The braid stays in place and doesn't tangle.

How to separate the strands

Some threads (such as embroidery floss) require the strands to be separated before threading the needle. The number of strands required is specified in the embroidery pattern legends.

> **Reminder**
>
> **Round threads (Retors, Coton à Broder DMC, etc.) are highly twisted and indivisible. The needle threads as is.**

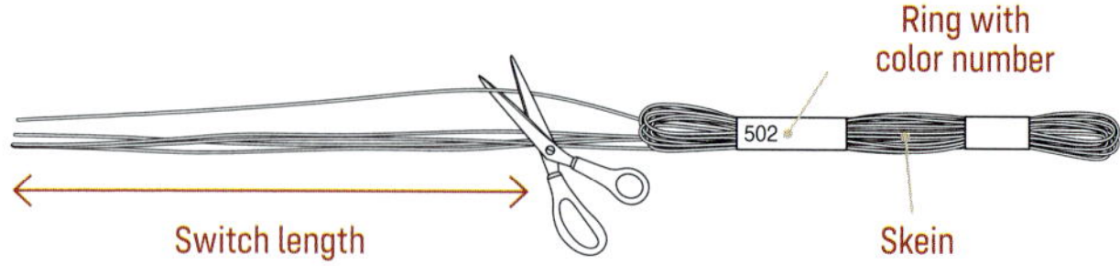

1 Take the skein and pull all the strands to the side of the ring marked with the color number.

2 Determine the length to be cut.

3 Lift a strand at this point with the tip of the scissors, cut, and gently pull the strand out.

4 Repeat the operation for each strand required.

This way, you can detach only what you need from the skein and avoid wastage.

Which switch length to choose

A single lead consists of a single thread or strand, a double lead of two threads or strands, and a multiple lead of more than two threads or strands. Follow the instructions supplied with your model.

To prevent thread damage or tangling, standard needles should measure a maximum of 45 cm. They may be longer with certain embroidery stitches (such as knotted stitches) or shorter with certain delicate threads (such as chenille and metallic threads).

Depending on the number of strands in the needle and the embroidery technique, the way to start work will differ.

Making an embroiderer's knot

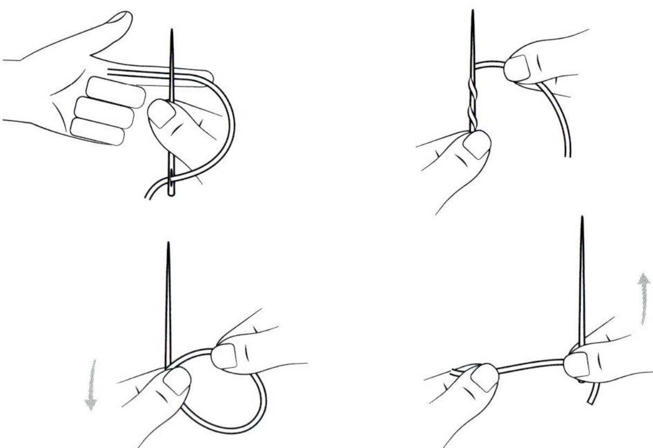

Here's how to tie a knot at the end of the needle.

1 Lay the thread along your left index finger and place the needle perpendicular to the thread.

2 Hold it between the thumb and forefinger of your left hand. With your right hand, wrap the thread twice around the needle.

3 Bring the turns down along the needle and clamp them between the thumb and forefinger of your left hand.

4 Without letting go of your left hand, gently pull the needle with your right hand. The knot forms between the thumb and forefinger of your left hand.

Anchoring Your Thread

There are different techniques for starting a needlework without tying a knot on the back of the work, because the back of the work must be as clean as possible.

Split strand

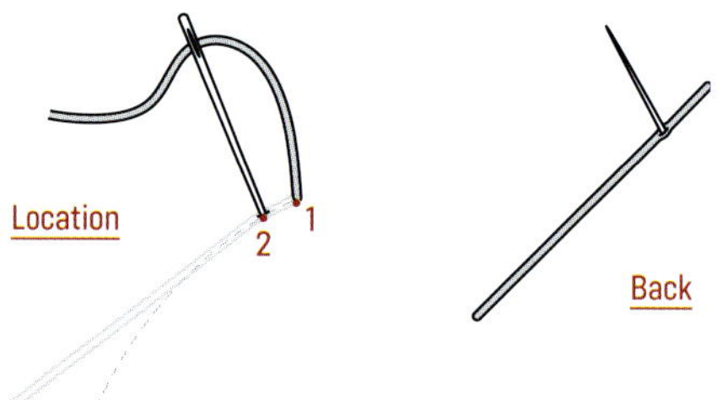

This split-strand start is required only for linear stitches.

1 Tie a temporary knot in the thread and stitch 2 cm outside the line. The thread should be positioned under the trace, 8 mm from starting point 1.

2 Take out the needle in 1 and stitch in 2, splitting the taut thread below the line.

3 Switch back to 1 and start the embroidery stitch.

4 After a few stitches of embroidery, cut the knot and the excess thread on the reverse side.

Lassoing

This is a starter for use with an even-numbered switch.

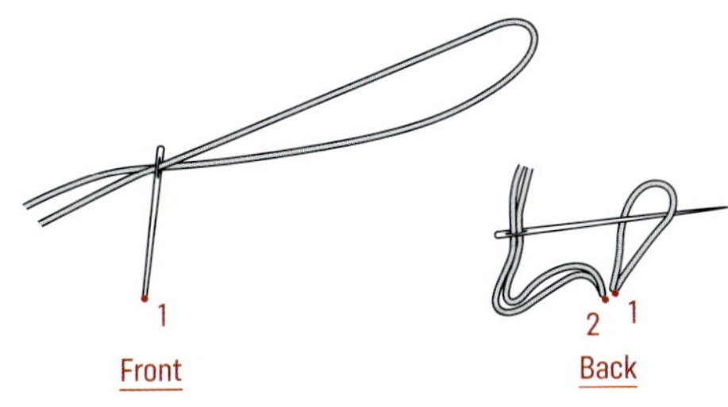

1 Prepare a 90cm length of thread or strand of floss (this is the double needle): cut one strand/thread for double embroidery, two strands/threads for embroidery with four strands/threads, and so on. The strands/threads are folded in half to obtain a final length of 45 cm.

2 Fold the strands/threads in half and pass the ends through the eye to thread the needle. A loop forms at the bottom of the needle.

3 On the wrong side, stitch in 1 and out in 2. Pass the needle through the loop before pulling the needle all the way through.

With a waste knot

This method requires you to rethread the needle along the way, which is not always easy. You'll need a 50cm needle.

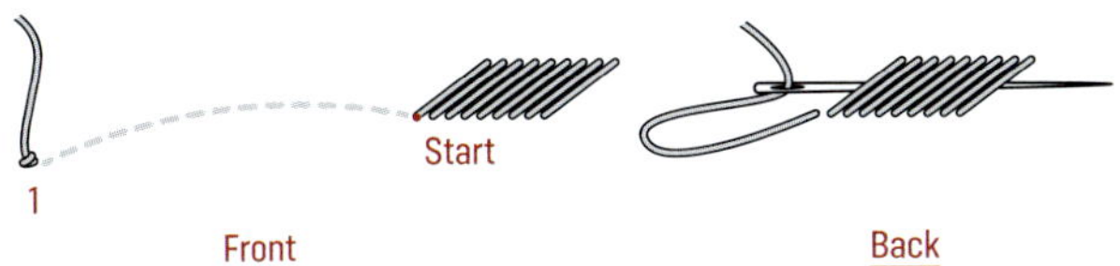

1 Tie a temporary knot at the bottom of the needle.

2 Stitch in 1 on the right side, 5 cm from the start, and leave the thread on hold while you do a few embroidery stitches.

3 Cut the thread flush below the knot to remove it.

4 Rethread the needle and block the thread by passing under a few embroidery stitches (on the reverse side).

5 Cut the excess thread flush on the reverse side.

At the starting point

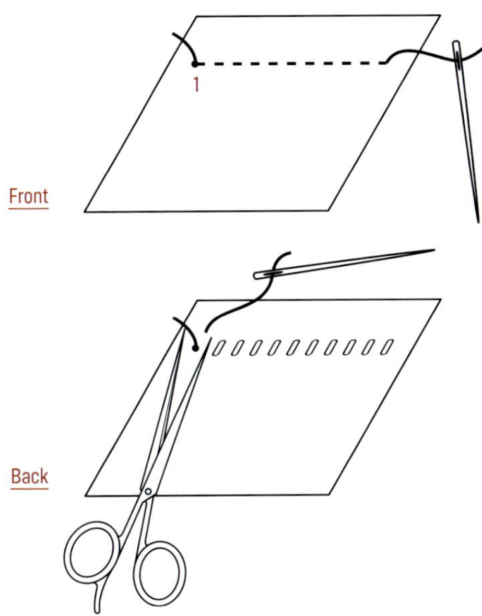

This technique is mainly used in tapestry, when the work is mounted on an embroidery frame.

1 Tie a knot in the thread.

2 Stitch in 1 on the right side and use a straight stitch (see page 59) to bring the needle out to the starting point. Position 1 so that the embroidered straight stitch is covered by the first embroidery stitches.

3 Embroider the final stitch by trapping the cast-off stitch.

4 Cut the knot when it becomes awkward: on the right side, pull it up to pass the scissor blades underneath, then cut and remove the knot.

Running stitch with a temporary knot

This technique can be used only if the embroidery covers the running stitch sufficiently, trapping it in place; for example, with a satin stitch or buttonhole stitch.

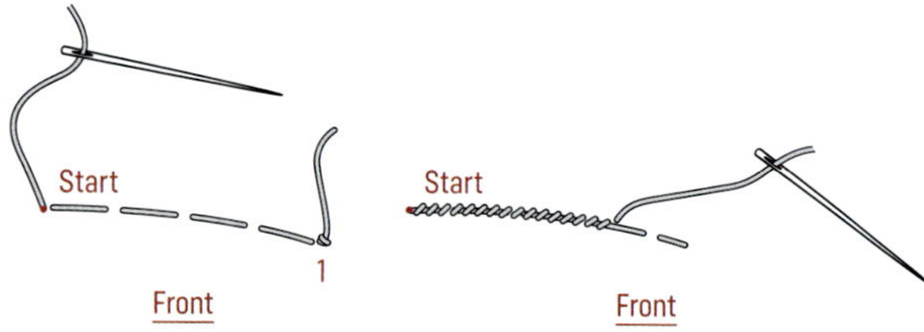

1 Tie a knot in the thread.

2 Stitch in 1 on the right side and stitch four front running stitches (see page 46) to bring the needle out to the starting point.

3 Embroider the final stitch by trapping the running stitch.

4 Cut the excess thread flush on the reverse side and remove the knot by simply pulling on it.

Boulogne point

This technique allows you to start laying thick supplies (cords, soutaches, etc.) which are then embroidered in appliqué with a couching stitch, for example

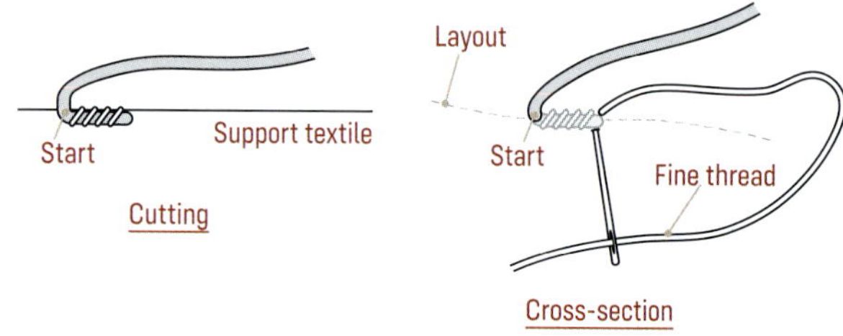

1 Using a stiletto, make a hole at the start of the embroidery to pass the supplies through.

2 Using a single needle of fine thread in the color of the ground fabric, or invisible thread, create a few couching stitches (see page 122) to block the supply under the outline—the embroidery will then conceal them.

3 Do the same to stop the supply.

4 Cut the supply about 1 cm after the end of the embroidery. Make a hole with a stiletto at the end of the line to pass the supply through. Fold it under the embroidered part and secure it with a few stitches (as in step 2).

With three small stitches

This technique is useful when you're embroidering on a frame that's difficult to turn. All the work is done on the right side.

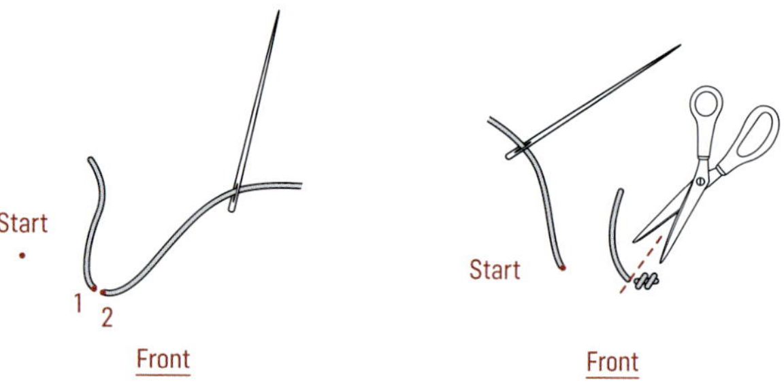

1 On the right side, close to the start, stitch in 1 and pull out in 2, leaving 2 cm of thread overhanging in 1. The stitch should be very small.

2 Straddle the first stitch with two others to bring the thread out to the starting point of the embroidery.

3 Cut the excess thread flush with the back.

4 Cover the small stitches with filler embroidery, best done in the same color.

With a thread slipped under the embroidery

When embroidery is already at an advanced stage (when you need to change needle), this method allows you to anchor the starting thread on the reverse side. A temporary knot (to be cut flush on the reverse side, after a few stitches) may be necessary before slipping the needle under the stitches, to avoid pulling too hard on the needle for the first few stitches.

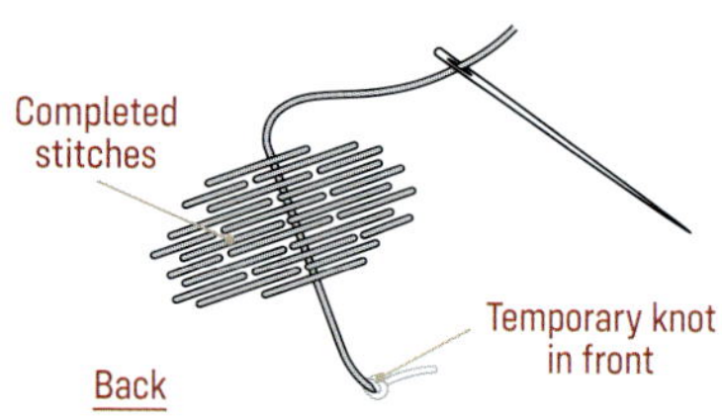

1 Tie a knot at the end of the needle.

2 Stitch the right sides together, 1 cm from the embroidery.

3 On the reverse side, go under the embroidery stitches already made.

4 Embroider a few stitches as shown in the pattern.

5 Cut the thread flush on the reverse side.

Tips for Good Embroidery

- If you're embroidering on a hoop, the fabric must be tightly stretched for even results and ease of use. During embroidery, it is often necessary to retension the fabric. To do this, without unscrewing, simply pull the fabric carefully, always in straight thread, to avoid distorting the work.

- With an embroidery hoop, stitches can be embroidered vertically or horizontally. To position yourself correctly, simply turn the hoop in your hand. On the other hand, it's impossible to turn your work on a slate frame set on trestles or on a hoop fixed to a table: the embroiderer must therefore adapt and learn to embroider all stitches regardless of the direction of the line.

- As you work, move the hoop over the work as you go along. It can be positioned astride the embroidery already made, but only if the embroidered materials allow it (as is the case with all threads). Please note that this is not possible with pearls, purls, jaceron, etc.

- When you embroider dark threads on a light canvas, they may appear ghosted and therefore be visible on the right side of the work. Make sure you have as few floating threads as possible between the embroidered parts and from one stitch to another. In this case, you need to stop the needles after each embroidered motif.

- Follow this basic rule: take out the needle in the nonembroidered part and then stitch in the embroidered part. Of course, as always with rules, there are exceptions: such is the case with the long and short stitch. Don't forget that the embroidery must cover the design lines.

- In the course of embroidery, when there are frequent color changes, it is sometimes necessary to leave a few needles waiting to be picked up later. In this case, they should be pulled out and left free on the right side to avoid creating unwanted tangles and knots on the reverse.

- To undo stitches that don't fit, remove them one by one from the right side, using the eye of the needle—this rounded part prevents the thread from being damaged. If the thread is still damaged, stop the needle (see page 42) and start again with a new thread. If the length or embroidered surface to be unraveled is too great, carefully cut the threads on the embroidery site before removing them.

How to Embroider

With the thread of the first needle now attached to the work, the next step is to embroider the entire work with precision.

Handling the needle

In embroidery, there are two ways to handle the needle:

- In a **single movement**. On a slightly slackened fabric on a hoop, the needle is inserted and withdrawn in a single movement. The embroiderer's hand remains permanently above the work. This fast technique is better suited to some embroidery stitches than others. For example, running, back, stem, and buttonhole stitches are best embroidered this way. On the other hand, it is less precise than the following. It can be embroidered "in hand" (see page 20) or on a hoop.

- **Back and forth** (i.e., in **two movements)**. On a canvas stretched tightly on a hoop or slate frame only, the first gesture pricks the needle and the second pulls it. The embroiderer's hand moves back and forth between the top and bottom of the work. This highly precise technique is, however, half as fast as the previous one.

Depending on the embroidery stitches you're doing, and whether you're right- or left-handed, you can work from right to left or left to right, and sometimes from top to bottom or bottom to top.

Adapting model instructions

If you've enlarged the design on the photocopier, you need to be careful about the length of the stitches to be embroidered. They will vary. In principle, they should not exceed 8 to 10 mm in length. If this is the case, you'll need to choose a more suitable stitch; for example, replacing the stem stitch with a long and short stitch.

Sparse embroidery

This expression is inherited from our grandmothers. Sparse embroidery means trying to use as few threads as possible on the back of the work, so as to keep embroidery costs to a minimum. Sparse embroidery is also more flexible and less "cardboardy" than conventional embroidery. To do this, take the shortest route from one stitch to the next.

This technique is frequently used for padding, particularly in plumetis embroidery.

Reserve embroidery

With this technique, it's not the motif (or text) itself that's embroidered, but its outlines and the background outside the outline. It can be used with all embroidery stitches, like Assisi embroidery.

Stopping a Lane

When there's not enough thread left on the needle, at the end of the embroidery or when changing color, the needle must be stopped. Different techniques are used for different stitches (linear or filling).

Tips for Good Embroidery

For a clean reverse side, stop the threads carefully at the end of the needle.

Under the linear points

It is possible to stop the needle under the embroidery:

- By overcasting. Wind the thread several times in the last embroidery stitches.

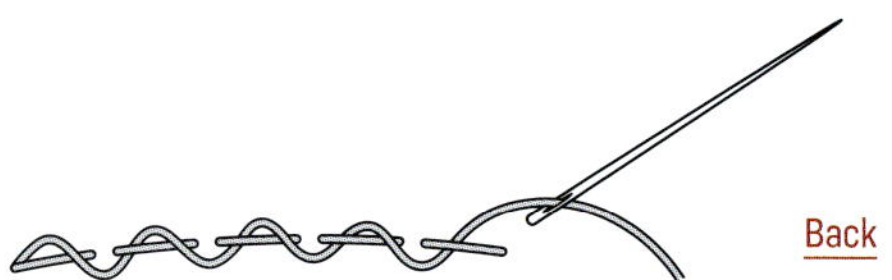

- With a thread backstitch or interlaced running stitch (see page 47). On the reverse side, pass the needle under the last embroidery stitches.

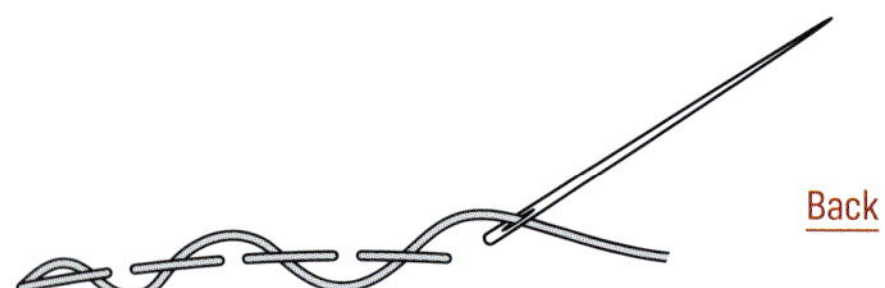

Under the filling points

It is possible to stop the switch by using these methods:

- By passing the needle, on the reverse side, under the nearest embroidery stitches under the filling stitches.

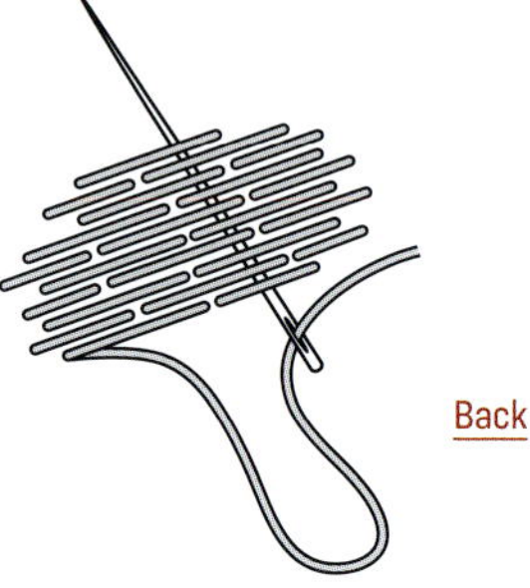

- By using three small stitches (when the frame is difficult to turn) on the right side. Using a thread of the same color as the filling embroidery, make the three small stitches straddling each other, hidden in the embroidery. Reach underneath the frame and, without turning it over, carefully cut the thread flush with the backing.

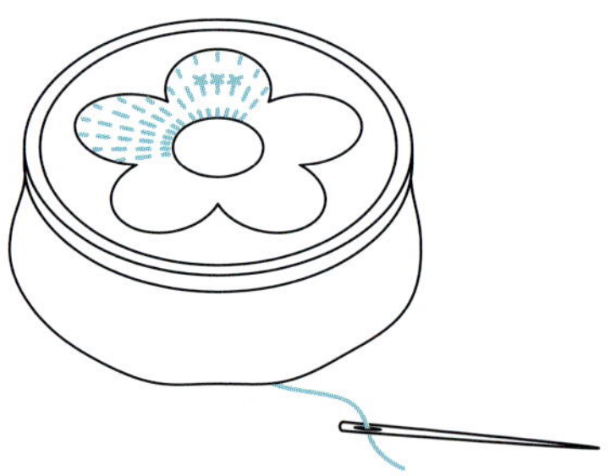

- With a straight stitch: this technique is mainly used in needlepoint and canvas embroidery, when the work is mounted on a hoop.

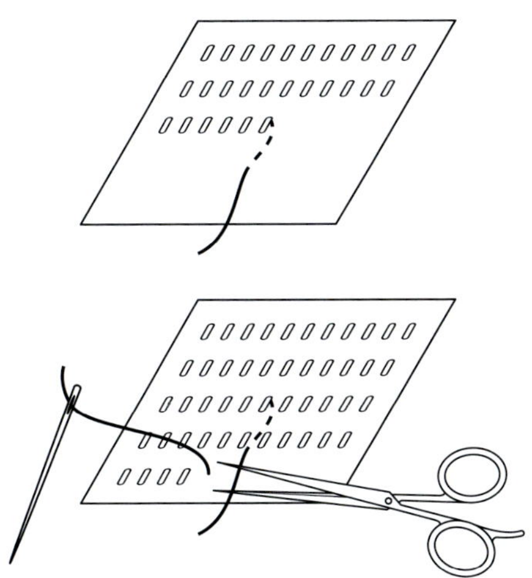

1 Pull out the needle from wrong side to right side, 2–3 cm from the last stitch. Unthread the needle and leave the thread on standby.

2 Continue embroidering. When you reach the height of the waiting thread, cut its end. The thread is now blocked by the embroidery.

Ironing and Maintenance

Once the embroidery is finished, always iron it on the reverse side to avoid shining and damaging the threads. Then wash the work at the temperature recommended for the fabric, let it dry flat, then iron it again on the reverse side. Washing will "felt" the embroidery threads, consolidating the work.

Attention

With certain techniques (gold, ribbon, or embossed embroidery), this final ironing step should be avoided, since the pressure exerted by the iron may damage the fabric. In these cases, we recommend gently spraying the reverse side with a little steam, without pressing with the iron, before removing the work from the frame or embroidery hoop.

2

LIBRARY OF BASIC STITCHES

RUNNING STITCH AND ITS VARIATIONS

Running stitch is probably one of the oldest embroidery stitches. It's also the simplest to make. It's embroidered all over the world, whether for quilting, boutis, patchwork quilting, kantha embroidery (in India), blackwork (in England), or sashiko (in Japan).

In Italy, in the Assisi region, the double running stitch (a variation of running stitch) is associated with cross-stitch: this is Assisi embroidery (see page 90), often featuring stylized animal motifs embroidered in symmetry. In Germany, this same stitch, known as "Holbein stitch," draws geometric figures.

The running stitch is characterized by its linearity and regularity—its stitches are of the same length on the right and wrong sides of the work. It is also used in sewing to build up or gather work, as well as to form gathers.

Unless otherwise specified, running stitch and its variations are embroidered from right to left, in a line, on a line drawing or in counted stitches.

Embroidered sashiko kimono, Japan, mid-19th century

Running Stitch

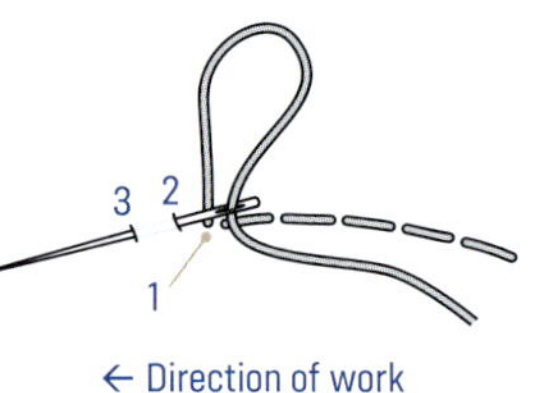

Take out the needle in 1, stitch in 2, and take out in 3.

For left-handed people

Embroider from left to right.

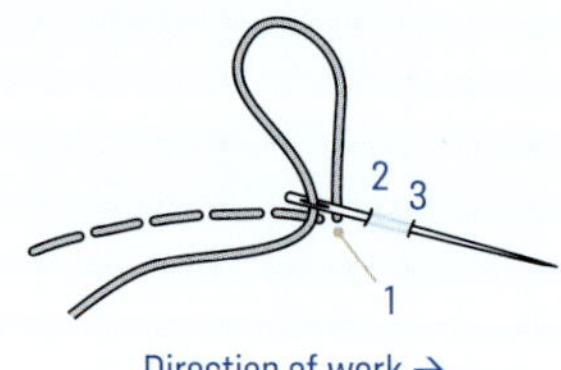

Whipped Running Stitch or Cast-On Stitch

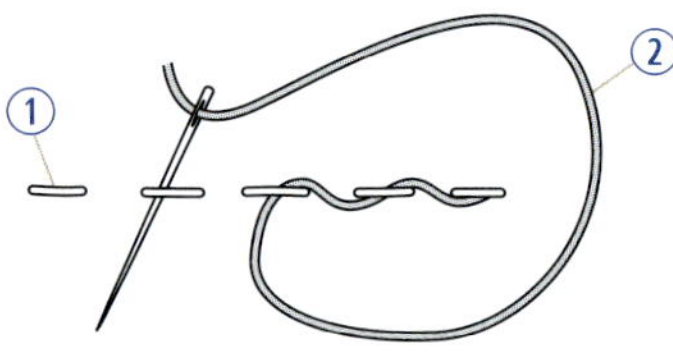

1 Embroider a line in front stitch.

2 Using the same thread or a thread of a different color, start at the beginning of the line and embroider, passing the needle under each stitch, from top to bottom, without piercing the fabric.

Line Stitch or Holbein Stitch or Double Running Stitch

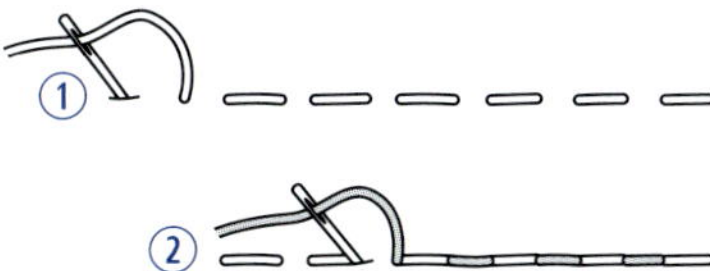

The double running stitch is reversible: the finish is identical on the front and back of the project.

1 Embroider a line in running stitch.

2 Using the same thread or a thread of a different color, start at the beginning of the line and stitch a new line in running stitch, inserting the stitches between those of the first line. Stitch and pull the needle through the same holes as the first line.

Threaded-Through Running Stitch or Interlaced Running Stitch

Threaded backstitches or interlaced running stitches create elegant borders. For more fantasy, change the color of the threads used to embroider the different lines.

Warning

When re-embroidering a threaded backstitch, work preferably with a round-tipped needle to pass under the running stitch lines. It should not go through the fabric.

On one line

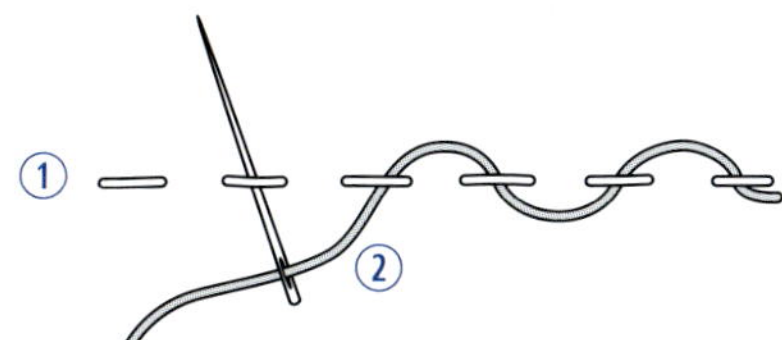

1 Embroider a line in running stitch.

2 Using the same thread or a thread of a different color, start at the beginning of the line. Pass the needle under the stitches of the first line, alternately from bottom to top and then from top to bottom.

Whipped running stitch on two staggered lines

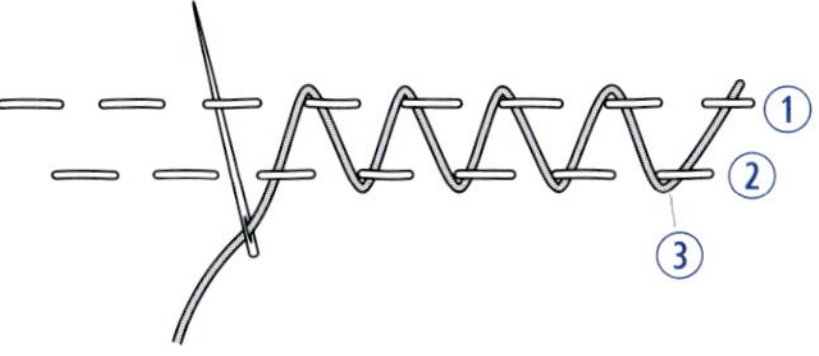

1 and 2 Embroider two even, parallel lines in staggered running stitch.

3 Using the same or a different color thread, start at the beginning of the lines. Pass the needle under the first stitch of the first line and under the first stitch of the second line from top to bottom, then under the second stitch of the first line from bottom to top.

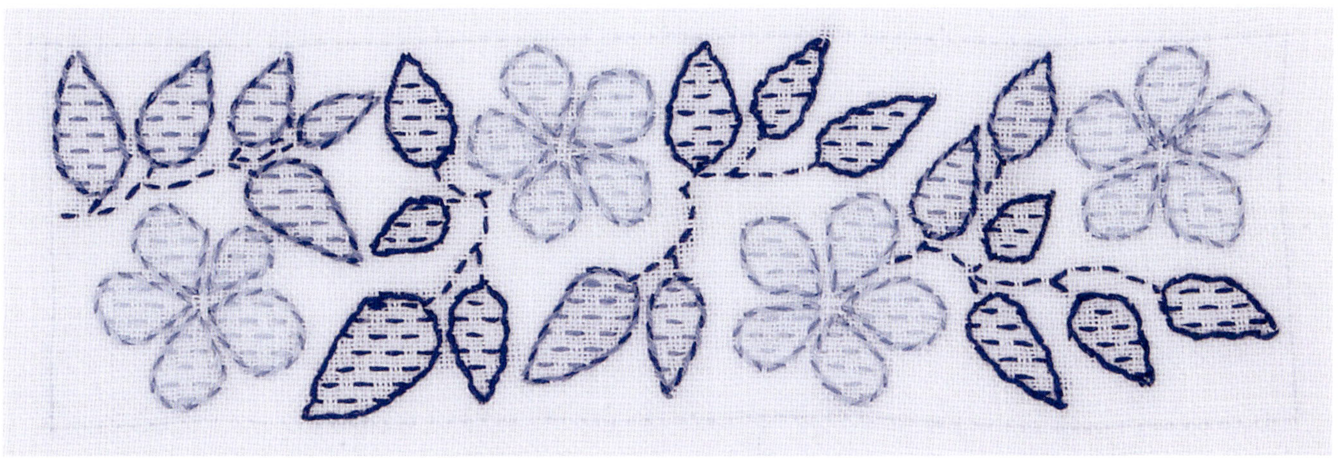

Interlaced running stitch on two parallel lines

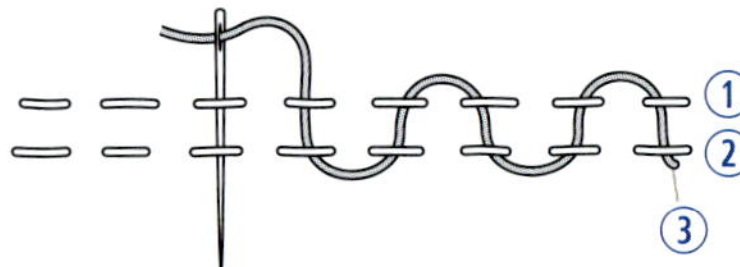

1 and 2 Embroider two even lines parallel to the running stitch. The stitches must be opposite each other.

3 Using the same thread or a thread of a different color, start at the beginning of the lines. Pass the needle under the first stitches of both lines from bottom to top, then under the second stitches from top to bottom.

Double interlaced running stitch on two parallel lines

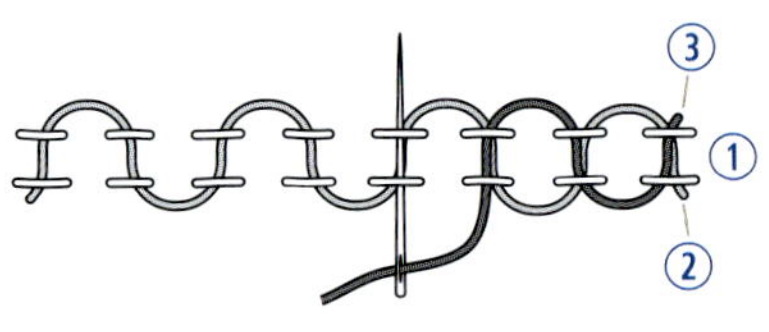

← Direction of work

The double interlaced running stitch is always embroidered in opposition to the previous line.

1 Embroider two even lines parallel to the running stitch. The stitches should be opposite each other.

2 Using the same thread or a thread of a different color, start at the beginning of the lines. Pass the needle under the first stitches of both lines from bottom to top, then under the second stitches from top to bottom.

3 Using the same thread or a thread of a different color, start at the beginning of the lines. Pass the needle under the first stitches of both lines from top to bottom, then under the second stitches from bottom to top.

Visual Library of Embroidery Stitches

BACKSTITCH AND ITS VARIATIONS

The backstitch is easy to achieve and is widely used in all types of embroidery. As far back as the Renaissance, it was used on silk or openwork embroideries to underline and surround embroidered grounds.

Today, the backstitch is embroidered onT-shirts in the form of naive motifs, or on decorative works displayed in embroidery hoops. Use it to embellish tattoos, coloring books, or children's designs. The backstitch is also used in sewing to securely join fabrics without a sewing machine.

Unless otherwise specified, the backstitch and its variations are embroidered from right to left, in a line, on a line drawing or in counted stitches.

Open Backstitch

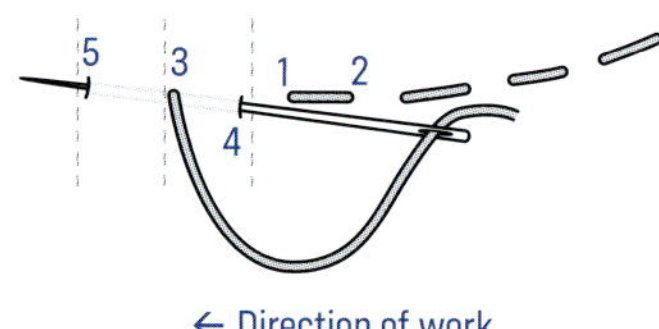

← Direction of work

On the right side of the work, the backstitch resembles the running stitch and, on the wrong side, a stem stitch (see page 55).

Take the needle out in 1, stitch in 2, take out in 3, stitch in 4, take out in 5.

For left-handed people

Embroider from left to right.

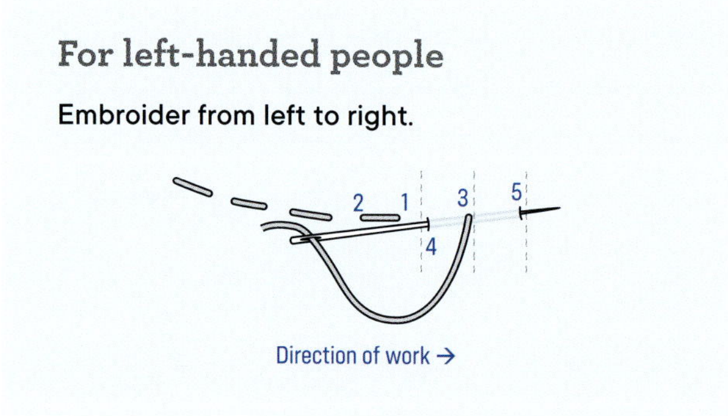

Direction of work →

Closed Backstitch

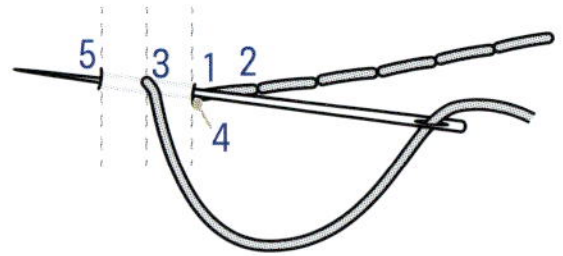

This stitch is more widely used than the open or dashed backstitch. It's done in the same way, but the needle is stitched into the hole of the previous stitch, so there's no space between each stitch. It thus resembles sewing machine stitching. This stitch can be used for filling.

Take the needle out in 1, stitch in 2, take out in 3, stitch in 4, take out in 5.

What You Need to Know

For convenience, in embroidery, the closed backstitch is often called "the backstitch."

Whipped Backstitch

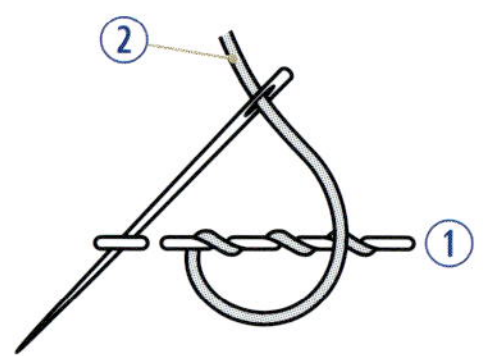

1 Embroider a line in backstitch.

2 Using the same thread or a thread of a different color, start at the beginning of the line and embroider, passing the needle under each stitch, from top to bottom, without piercing the fabric.

Double Lines of Whipped Backstitch

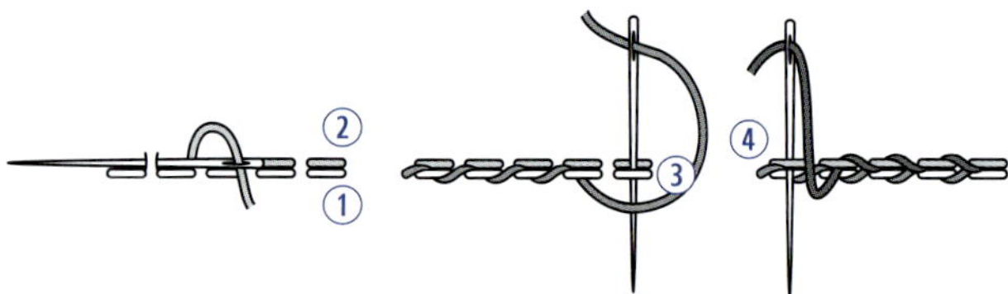

1 and 2 Embroider two even, parallel lines in the backstitch.

3 and 4 Whip around a first line and then a second, reversing the direction of thread winding to create a chevron pattern.

Threaded or Interlaced Backstitch

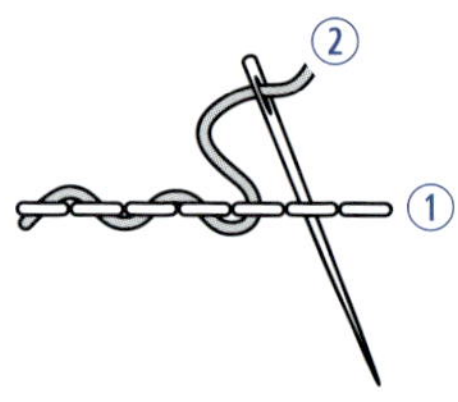

1 Embroider a line in backstitch.

2 Using the same thread or a thread of a different color, start at the beginning of the line and embroider, passing the needle under each stitch, alternately from bottom to top, then from top to bottom, without piercing the fabric.

Double-Interlaced or Double-Threaded Backstitch

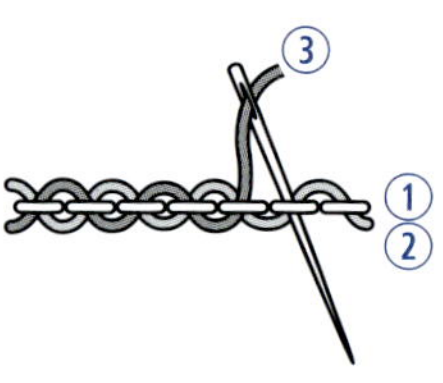

1 Embroider a line in backstitch or stitch.

2 Using the same thread or a thread of a different color, start at the beginning of the line and embroider, passing the needle under each stitch, alternately from bottom to top, then from top to bottom, without piercing the fabric.

3 Using the same thread or a thread of a different color, start at the beginning of the line and embroider, passing the needle under each stitch, alternately from top to bottom, then from bottom to top, in opposition to the previous passage, without piercing the fabric.

Pekinese Stitch

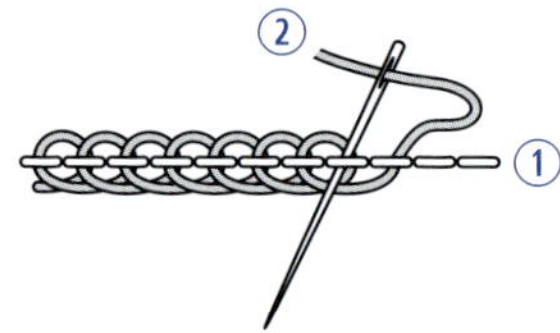

1 Embroider a line at the stitching point.

2 Using the same thread or a thread of a different color, start at the beginning of the line and embroider, passing the needle from bottom to top under the second stitch, then from top to bottom under the first stitch, then from bottom to top under the third stitch, then from top to bottom under the second stitch, without piercing the fabric.

Backstitch for Filling

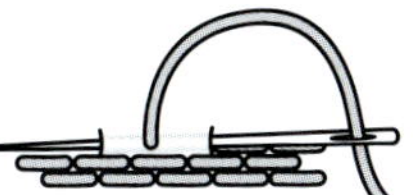

This stitch is ideal for embroidering text. Stitch several rows together, staggered.

Linen case embroidered with wool, England, 1669

Visual Library of Embroidery Stitches

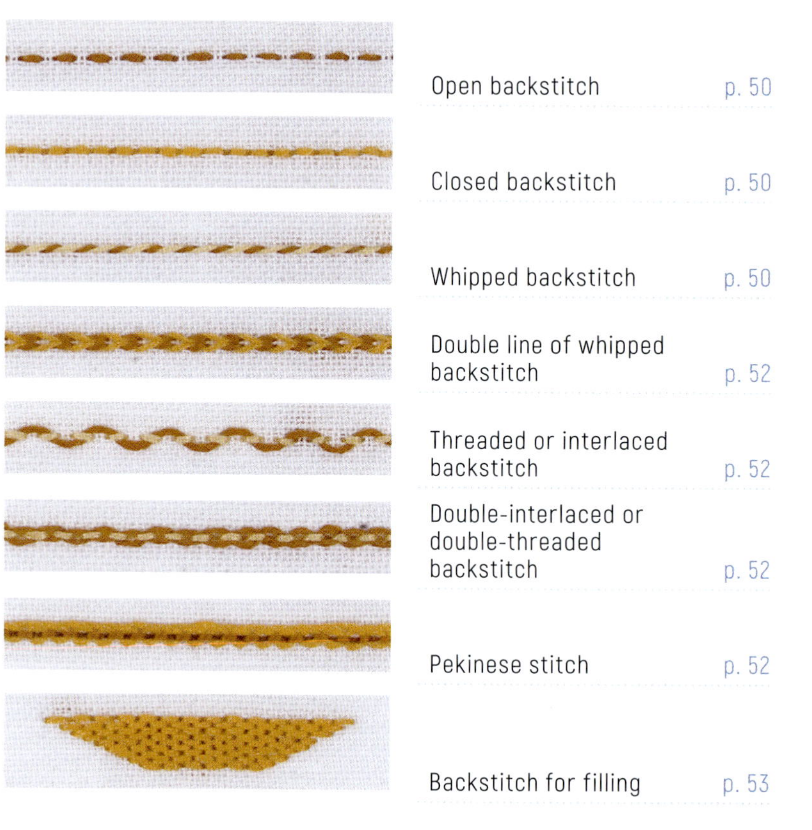

STEM STITCH AND ITS VARIATIONS

Stem stitch has been used throughout the history of embroidery. From the beginning of the 17th century, it was widely used in Europe and America for redwork embroidery on white and ecru canvas, using red-dyed embroidery threads—very resistant to washing—with the pigments of madder, a plant grown in Turkey. This technique then spread to Alsace, where it was used as a popular art form to depict naive motifs.

This linear stitch has the appearance of a cord. It's perfect for embroidering straight lines and curves, and for following the contours of shapes.

Unless otherwise specified, stem stitch and its variations are embroidered from left to right (or top to bottom). The working thread should always be positioned downward, held by the thumb of the left hand.

Stem Stitch

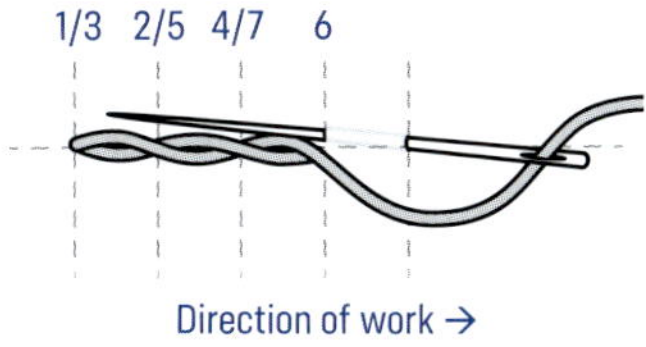

Each line at the stem point begins with a half-point between 1 and 2.

Take the needle out at 1, pick up at 2, and take out at 3. Pick up at 4 and take out at 5, in the hole of the previous stitch (2 and 5 are mixed up). Stitch in 6 and out in 7, in the hole of the previous stitch (4 and 7 are mixed up).

For left-handed people

Embroider in a line, from left to right The working thread should always be positioned downward, held by the thumb of the right hand.

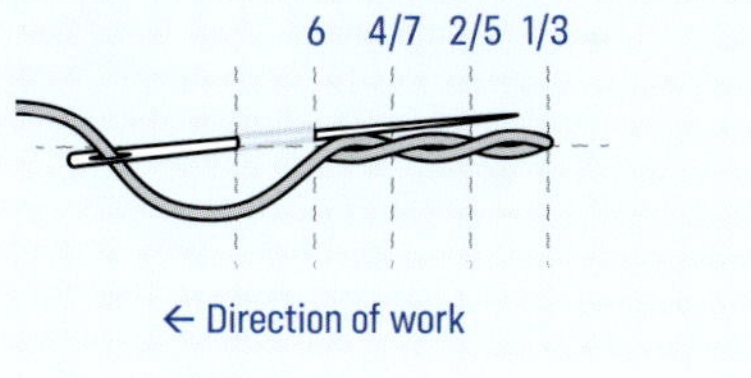

How to embroider an angle in stem stitch

To embroider a line in stem stitch. finish with a half stitch, which you stitch in 1. Pass the needle under the last stitch on the back of the work to block the thread. Return to 1, turn, and start in the other direction with a half stitch.

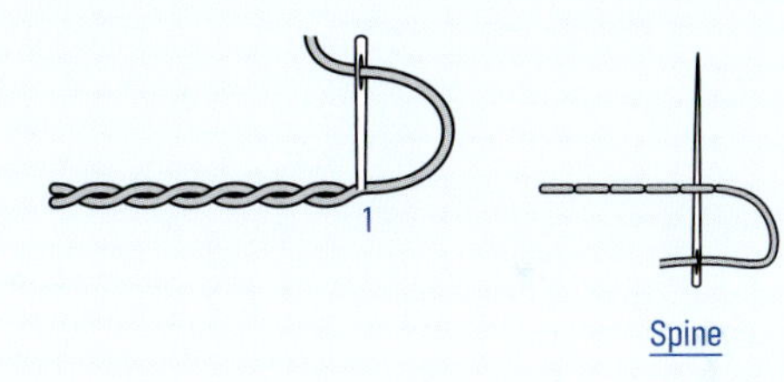

Curved Stem Stitch

Embroider a line at the stem stitch, gradually decreasing the stitch length in tight curves to maintain a clean line.

Diagonal Stem Stitch or Thick Stem Stitch

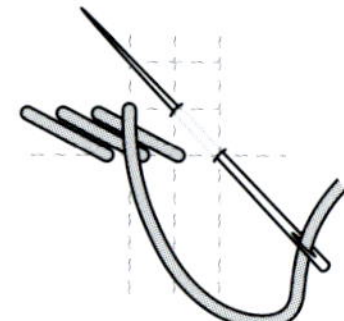

Embroider a line in stem stitch by pricking the needle at an angle, slightly above the point where the previous stitch exits. The stem stitch thickens.

Encroaching Stem Stitch

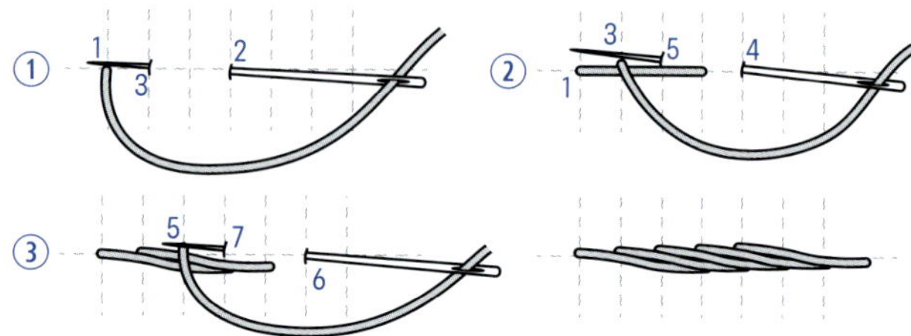

This variation of stem stitch is thicker and resembles a twisted cord.

1 Take out the needle in 1, stitch in 2, and take out in 3 (at the first third of the stitch).

2 Stitch in 4 and out in 5 (the second third of the first stitch).

3 Stitch in 6 and out in 7 (at the end of the first stitch).

Reverse Stem Stitch

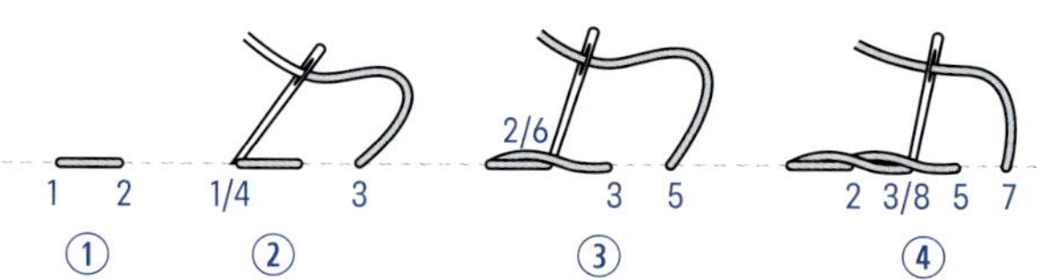

On the right side, the reverse stem stitch renders the same as the classic stem stitch. The reverse side, however, is denser.

1 Take out the needle in 1 and stitch in 2.

2 Take out 3 and prick 4 (4 and 1 are confused).

3 Take out 5 and prick 6 (6 and 2 are confused).

4 Go out on 7 and prick on 8 (8 and 3 are confused).

Thwarted Stem Stitch

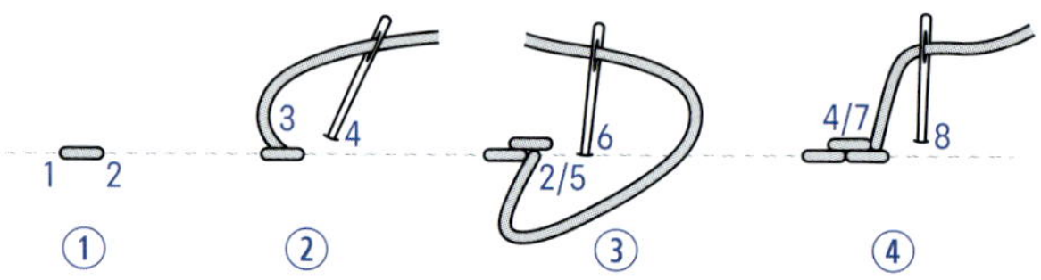

This stitch is embroidered on two very close parallel lines.

1 Take out the needle in 1 and stitch in 2.

2 Take out in 3 and prick in 4.

3 Take out in 5 and insert in 6 (5 and 2 are confused).

4 Go out on 7 and prick on 8 (7 and 4 are the same).

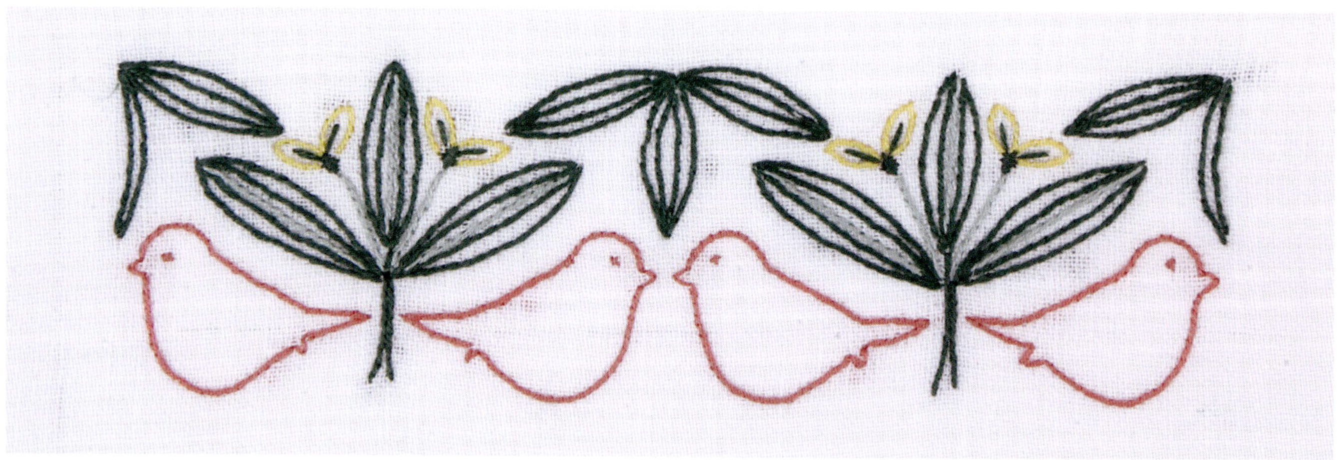

Knotted Stem Stitch

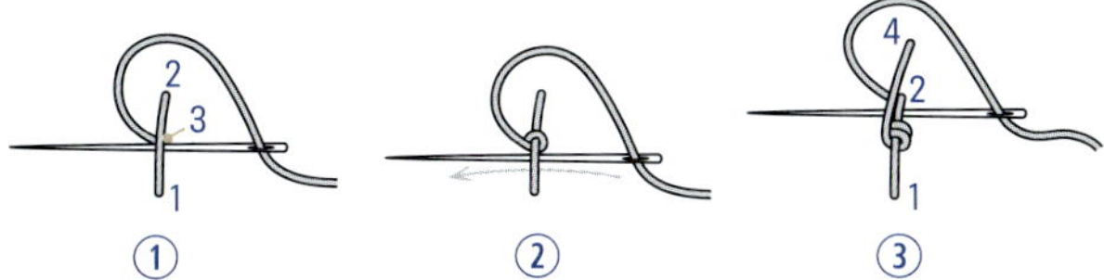

Knotted stem stitch is embroidered from bottom to top.

1 Take out the needle in 1, stitch in 2, and take out in 3.

2 Pass the needle twice under the stitch from right to left.

3 Stitch in 4 and out in 2 (at the end of the previous stitch). Pass the needle twice under the two stitches.

Whipped Stem Stitch

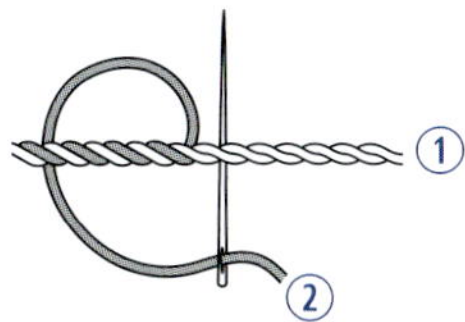

1 Embroider a line of stem stitch.

2 With a contrasting color thread, start at the beginning of the line and pass the needle under each stitch, without piercing the fabric. The thread will then wrap around the stem stitch.

Split Stem Stitch with Two Strands

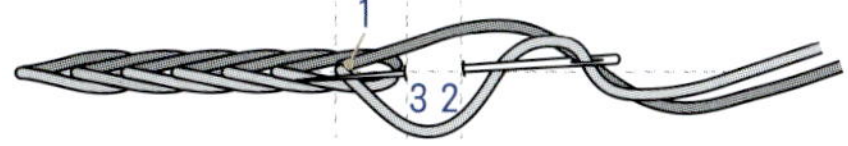

Split stem stitch is embroidered with two different colored threads in the eye of the needle. Always use the same color of thread at the top and bottom.

Take out needle 1 and stitch in 2. Take out needle 3, between the two needle threads.

Stem Stitch Filling

With this stitch, filling an embroidery surface is quick and easy. Work in tight rows.

1 Embroider a first line in stem stitch.

2 Turn the hoop 180° and embroider a second line.

3 Turn the hoop 180° and embroider a third line.

Split Stitch

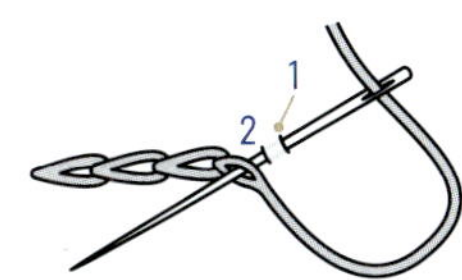

In the Middle Ages, the faces, feet, and hands of religious figures were embroidered in split stitch, using tapestry or Medici wool. Today, it's embroidered with a round thread (pearl cotton or Coton à Broder DMC) so you can stitch in the thread. The result resembles a chain stitch.

Insert the needle in 1 and pull out in 2 in the middle of the thread to split it with the needle tip. Use relatively short stitches.

Visual Library of Embroidery Stitches

STRAIGHT STITCH AND ITS VARIATIONS

Straight stitch is a simple embroidery stitch. It can be used alone (in a line, for example, to form braids), in seeding (small stitches embroidered in all directions, without a precise design), or as a filling. It can also be embroidered as a counted stitch on regular-weave fabrics. More complex embroidery stitches can be created by combining several straight stitches.

For even, straight stitches, draw parallel lines or use the fabric's weft or a waste canvas (see page 37).

Straight Stitch

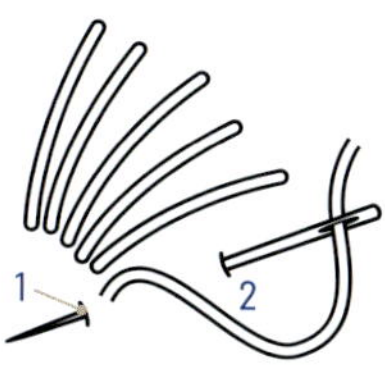

Straight stitch can be embroidered in any direction. Vary the stitch length according to the desired effect. Take the needle out in 1 and stitch in 2.

Star Stitch

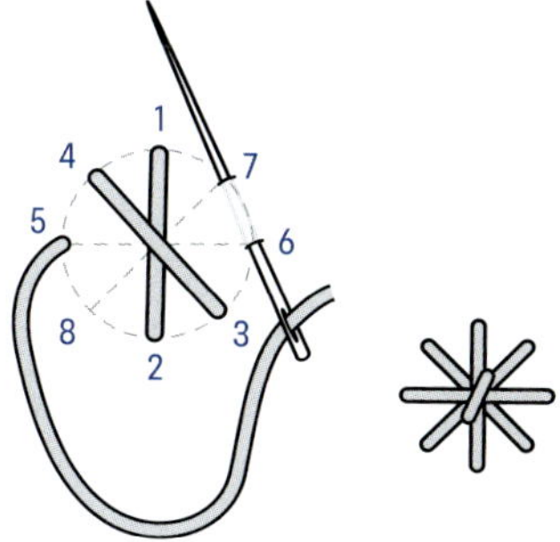

This stitch is used to embroider stars with an even number of branches. If the stars are large, embroider a small straight stitch in the center of each one to hold them together.

Use a circle marker to draw a circle. Mark every 45° on the circumference. Take out needle 1 and stitch in 2 (diametrically opposite). Take out needle 3 and stitch to 4. Continue in this way to 7 and 8.

Rhodes (Round or Square) Stitch or Tight Star Stitch

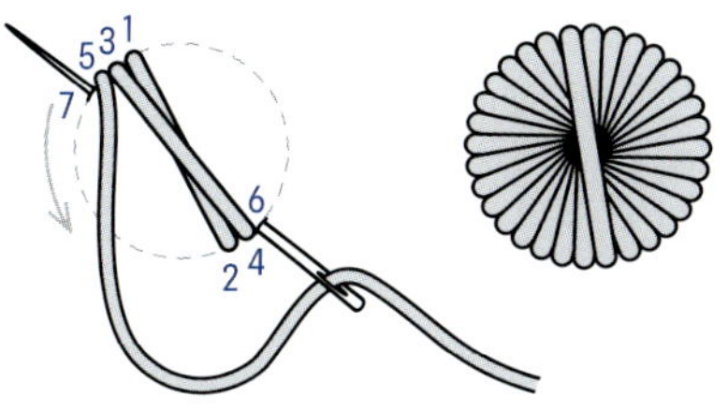

1 Using a circle template, draw a circle. Take out the needle at 1 and stitch at 2 (diametrically opposite 1).

2 Continue on half the circle to cover the entire surface. The stitches overlap, passing through the center of the design and creating a relief.

Eyelet Stitch

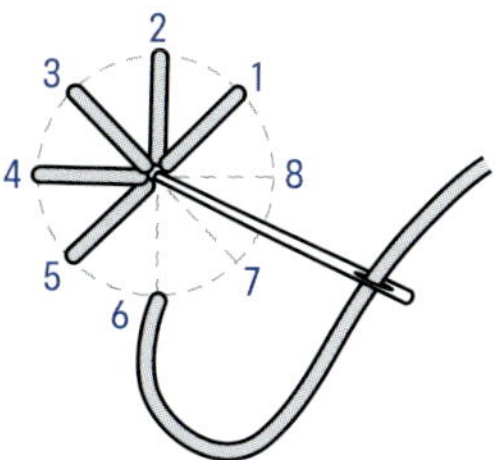

Using a circle template, draw a circle. Mark every 45° around the circumference and in the center. Take out needle 1 and stitch in the center. Take out needle 2 and stitch in the center.

Fern Stitch

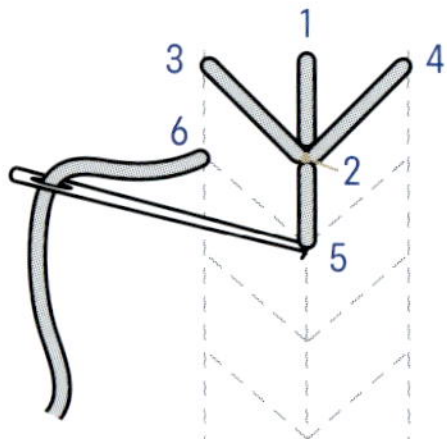

Fern stitch is used to embroider foliage. It is embroidered on three lines, from top to bottom.

Take out needle 1 and stitch in 2. Take out needle 3 and stitch in 2. Take out needle 4 and stitch in 2. Take out needle 5 and stitch in 2. Take out needle 6 and stitch in 5, and so on.

Seeding

Embroider small stitches thrown in all directions.

Double Seeding

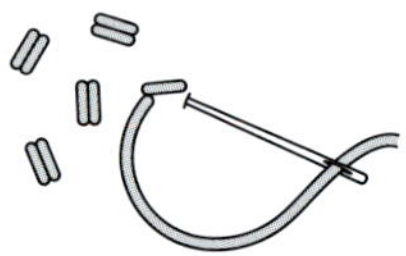

Embroider two small stitches thrown together in all directions.

Knit Stitch or Knitting Stitch

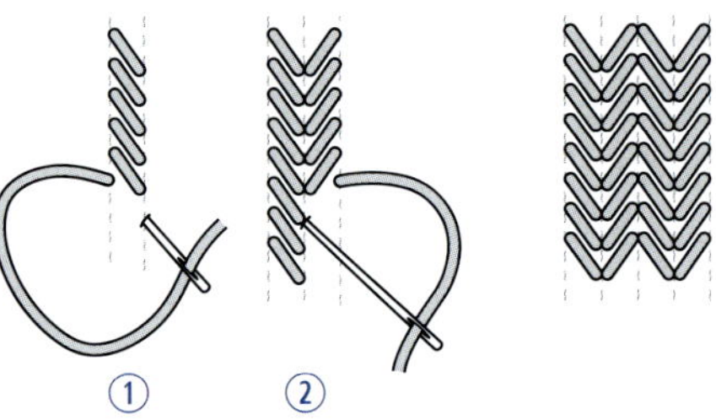

The knit or knitting stitch is embroidered between parallel lines. It can be used as a filling.

1 Embroider between two parallel lines with diagonal straight stitches.

2 Draw a third parallel line on the right and embroider opposing rows of knitting stitch to form a chevron.

Tips for Good Embroidery

You can embroider other knitting stitches adjoining the previous ones to form wide embroidered bands. In this case, work on a regular weave fabric such as those suitable for counted stitches, or with a waste canvas (see page 37).

Sheaf Stitch

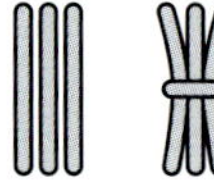

1 Embroider in three parallel throws, slightly spaced apart.

2 Connect the points at the center with a small perpendicular straight stitch.

Fan Stitch

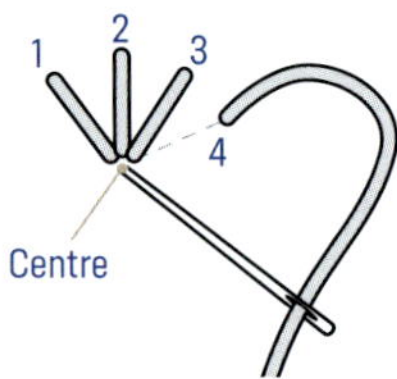

Fan stitch is embroidered by exiting at the top and stitching through the center.

1 Draw a circular arc, its center, and evenly spaced markers around the circumference.

2 Take out the needle in 1 and stitch in the center.

3 Take the needle out in 2 and prick in the center.

Eyelet Wheel

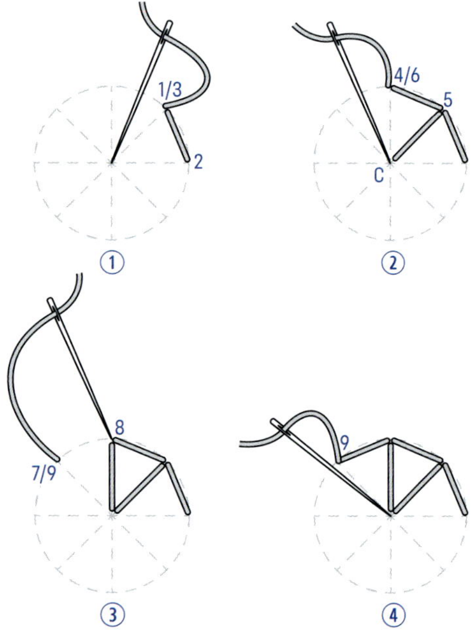

The eyelet wheel is embroidered in the same hole, without the thread overlapping.

Using a circle tracer, draw a circle, its center, and marks every 45° on its circumference.

1 Take out the needle at 1, stitch at 2, and take out at 3 (1 and 3 are mixed up). Stitch in center C.

2 Exit at 4, stitch at 5, and exit at 6 (4 and 6 are the same). Stitch in center C.

3 Exit at 7, stitch at 8, and exit at 9. Stitch in center C.

Tips for Good Embroidery

Widen the central hole with a stiletto before starting work.

Forget-Me-Not Stitch

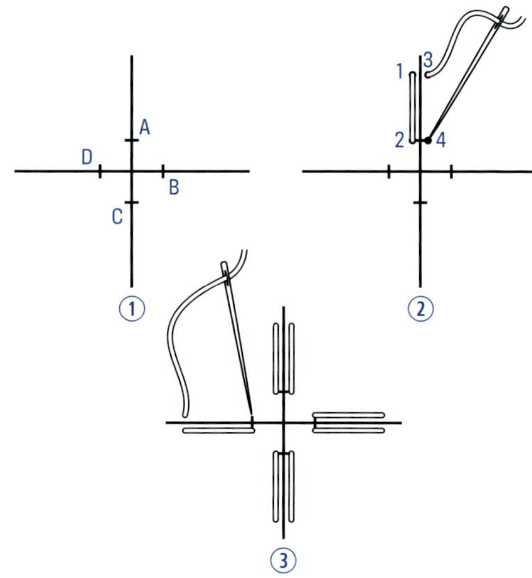

Forget-me-not stitch is used to embroider four-petal flowers.

1 Draw a cross and mark four points (A, B, C, and D) on each branch, 2 mm from the center.

2 Take the needle out in 1, stitch in 2 right next to A, take out in 3, then stitch in 4 on the other side of A.

3 Repeat step 2 for the rest of the cross.

The straight stitch and its variations

Embroider a flower (for example, a daisy).

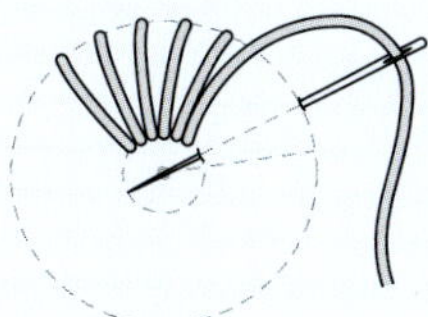

Using a circle template, draw two concentric circles. Embroider the stitches, systematically pointing them toward the center of the circles.

Embroidering a trim or band

In different widths and used like ribbons, trims are used to decorate the edges of a garment, curtain, or tablecloth, for example.

Forget-me-not trim or band

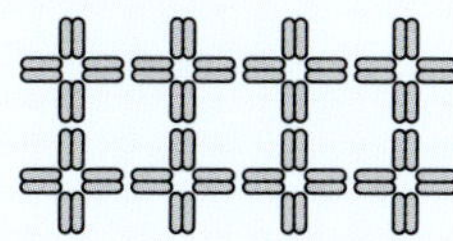

Embroider forget-me-not stitches on a grid, one against the other.

Straight stitch for a stem

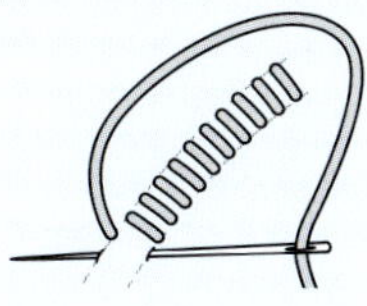

Draw two parallel lines and stitch evenly spaced throws between them.

Norwegian stitch braid

Norwegian stitch is a variation of forget-me-not stitch.

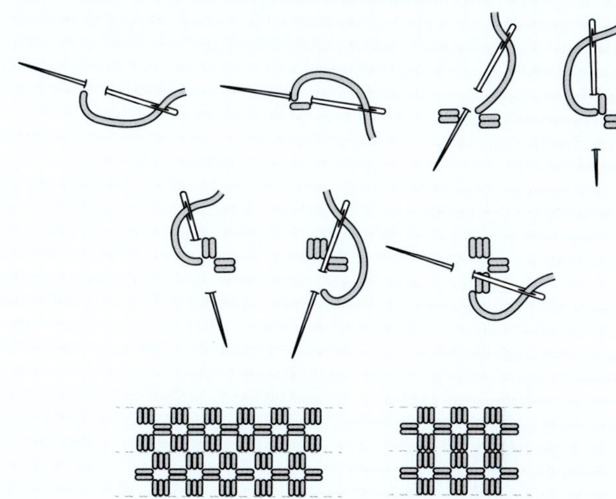

On a grid, embroider in forget-me-not stitch, making the following changes.

- Embroider three vertical throws instead of two.
- Use each of the horizontal points to form petals common to two flowers.

Alternating or staggered straight stitch

Draw as many parallel lines as necessary to delineate the heights of the stitches to be embroidered. Embroider a succession of straight stitches of varying heights, inspired by the designs shown here. All variations are possible, so give free rein to your creativity!

Square eyelet fill

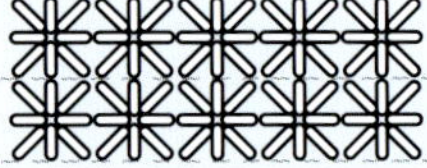

On a grid, embroider eyelet stitches against each other.

Diamond-shaped band or trim

On a grid, embroider stitches thrown to form a succession of lozenges.

Two-sided insertion stitch band

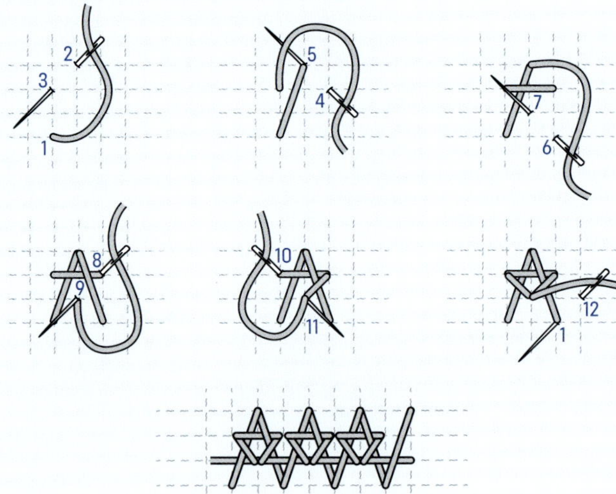

On a grid, stitch from left to right. Each stitch is made on six squares of the grid (three in height and two in width).

1 Take out the needle in 1, stitch in 2, and take out in 3.

2 Stitch in 4 and out in 5 (5 and 2 are confused).

3 Stitch in 6 and out in 7.

4 Pierce in 8 (8 and 4 are the same) and exit in 9 (9 and 7 are the same).

5 Pierce in 10 (10 and 3 are mixed up) and take out in 11 (11, 9, and 7 are mixed up).

6 Stitch at 12 and exit at 13, which becomes the starting point for the next stitch.

Visual Library of Embroidery Stitches

DARNING STITCH AND ITS VARIATIONS

Darning stitch (or mending stitch) has always been used to mend damaged textiles, especially when clothes and household linen were scarce and expensive. Mending, darning, patching, mending, remaillage, reweaving . . . the vocabulary for all garment repair techniques!

With the advent of cheap industrial clothing in the 1950s, these repair techniques disappeared. Today, however, mending damaged garments is making a comeback for more sustainable consumption or for purely artistic purposes.

In contemporary embroidery, the darning stitch has been hijacked and is now used as a filling or in pulled-thread embroideries such as Hedebo. Pleasant and quick to create, it offers a host of possibilities. Textiles embroidered with darning stitch remain supple, since very few threads pass through the back of the embroidered fabric.

What supplies do you need for mending?

For invisible mending, use the same type and size of thread as the fabric to be repaired. For artistic mending, on the other hand, anything goes!
An embroidery hoop is essential for working.

Embroidery Darning Stitch

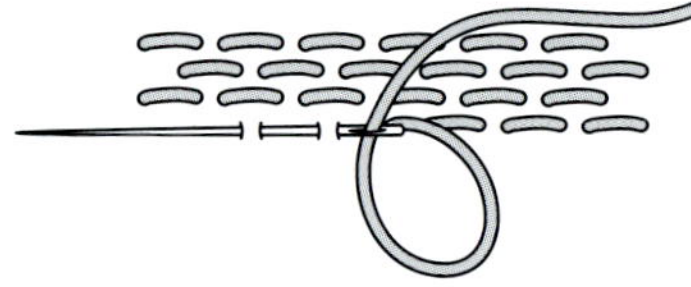

The darning stitch is embroidered on slightly spaced lines on the right side of the work.

Line by line, embroider the stitches in aligned or offset, depending on the desired effect.

What You Need to Know

The stitch length visible on the right side will be much greater than on the wrong side (e.g., 6 mm on the right side and 2 mm on the wrong side).

Invisible Mending

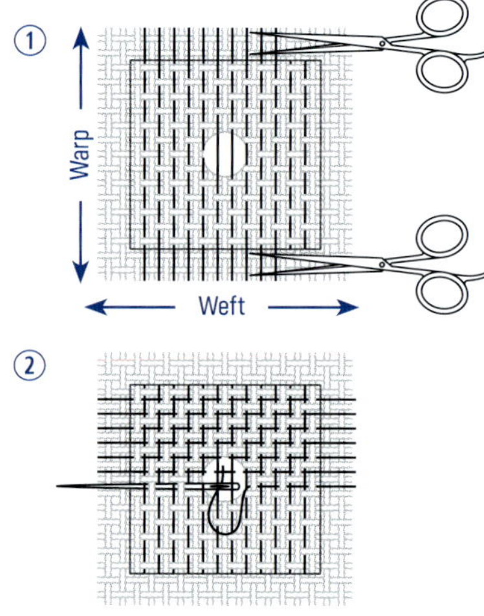

Invisible mending is done on the reverse side of the work.

1 Using a felt-tip pen or erasable pencil, mark out the area to be darned in the straight grain, adding 1 to 2 cm around the hole. Respecting the number of threads used in the warp and weft of the fabric, add needle-weave threads in the direction of the weft onto the surface to be darned. Cut off the ends of each thread.

2 Carry out the same work in the direction of the warp.

Tips for Good Embroidery

For completely invisible darning, use threads taken from the fabric to be repaired. Take them from a hidden part of the garment, such as a hem or the bottom of a pocket. Alternatively, embroider a very similar thread.

Rework samples

Mending or Surface Darning Stitch

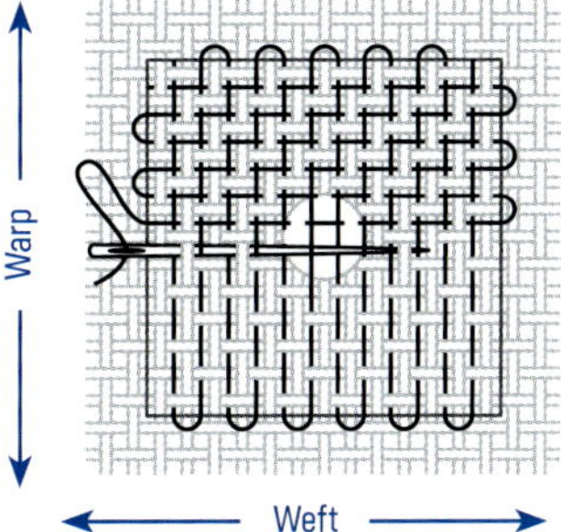

Canvas stitch is worked on the reverse side of the work. Using a felt-tip pen or erasable pencil, mark out the area to be darned in the straight line, adding 1 to 2 cm around the hole.

Embroider the warp back and forth with lines in running stitch on the surface; pass over the hole. Leave a small loop at each change of direction, so that the warp is elastic enough to let the weft threads through. Then embroider the weft in the same way, weaving the threads over the hole.

Visual Library of Embroidery Stitches

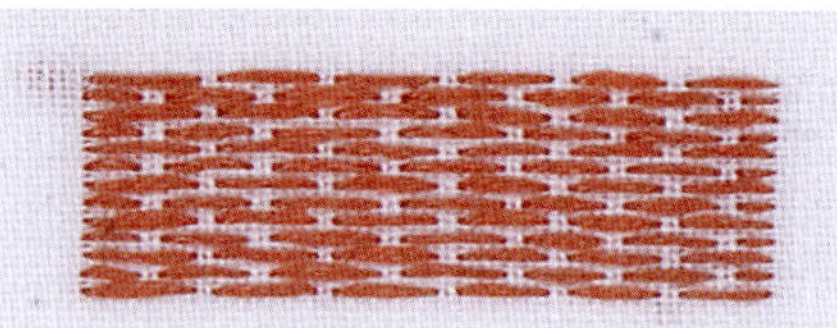

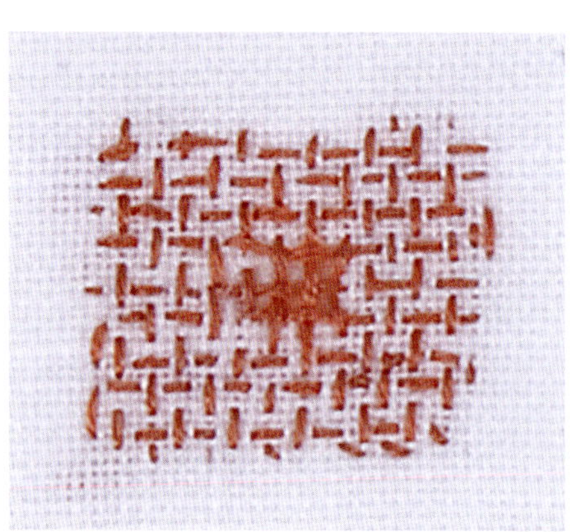

Dior

BUTTONHOLE STITCH AND ITS VARIATIONS

Blanket stitch or buttonhole stitch is one of the oldest embroidery stitches. Its history dates back to the Bronze Age. Excavations in Denmark have uncovered embroidery dating back 3,000 and 6,000 years, and, in Switzerland, dating back 4,000 years. In those days, plant fibers were used as thread to make useful objects such as fishing nets.

It is the basis of tulle stitch, which is used in needle lace, Richelieu and Renaissance embroidery (see page 258). Grébiche or closed buttonhole stitch (see page 71) is also a variation, characterized by the formation of triangles.

The buttonhole stitch is made up of simple loops. It can be used to create a decorative border on the edge of a fabric.

Unless otherwise specified, buttonhole stitch and its variations are embroidered from left to right (or top to bottom).

Buttonhole Stitch

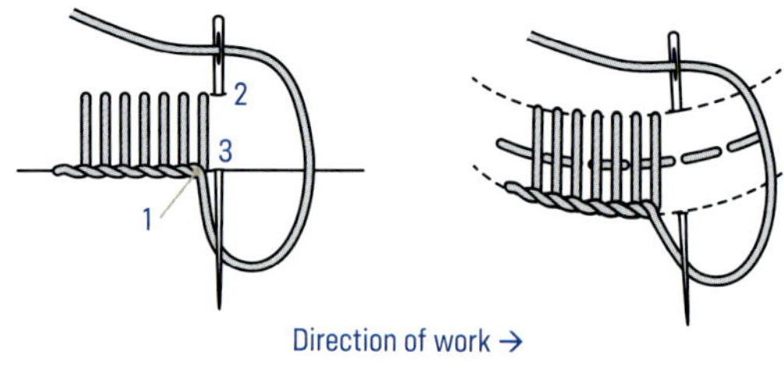

The buttonhole stitch has a cord-like border: the scalloped line. These stitches are made directly on the fabric and can be embroidered tightly or more widely apart.

Pull the needle out in 1 on the line to be scalloped. In a single movement, stitch in 2 and pull out in 3, passing the thread under the needle. Finish the row by straddling the thread under the last stitch.

To border a fabric, embroider the buttonhole stitch (stitches must be tight) around the entire piece, then trim the edge of the fabric.

For left-handed people

Embroider from right to left.

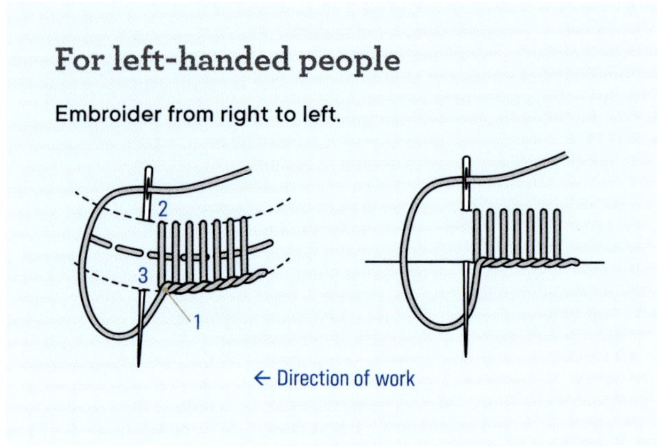

Up and Down Buttonhole Stitch

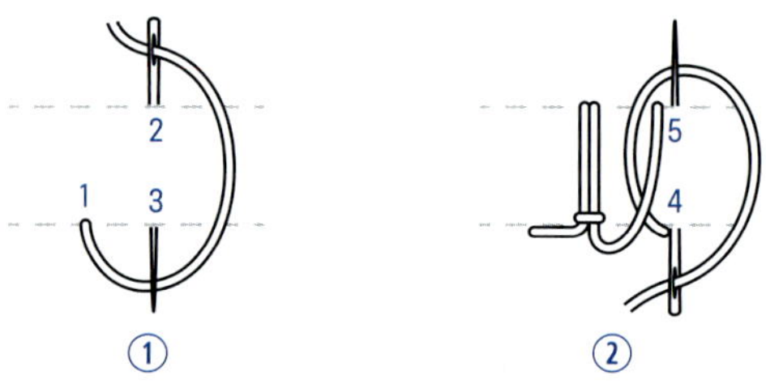

Up and down buttonhole stitch is embroidered on two parallel lines.

1 Pull the needle out in 1. In a single movement, stitch in 2 and pull out in 3, passing the thread down under the needle.

2 In a single movement, stitch in 4 and out in 5, passing the thread under the needle (4 and 3 are side by side; 2 and 5 are side by side). Continue in the same way, spacing the stitches.

Grébiche Stitch or Closed Buttonhole Stitch

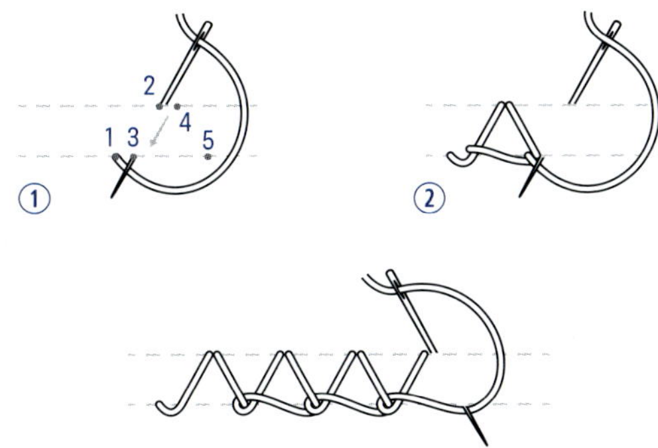

Grébiche stitch is embroidered on two horizontal lines. It forms a triangle.

1 Bring the needle out in 1 on the line to be buttonholed. In one movement, stitch at the top in 2, over the apex of the triangle, and exit in 3 next to 1, passing the thread under the needle. In a single movement, stitch in 4 at the top, right next to 2, and exit in 5, passing the thread under the needle.

2 Continue in the same manner to form triangles.

Knotted Grébiche Stitch

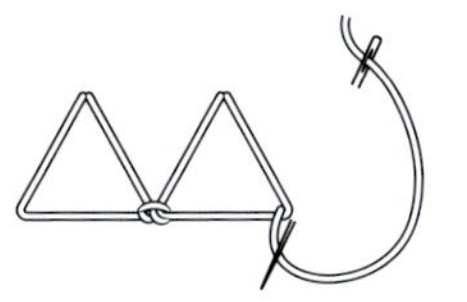

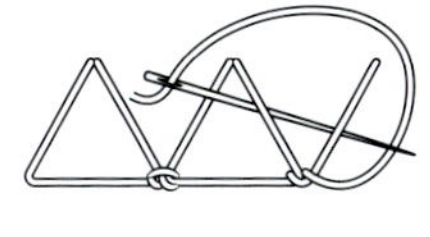

Knotted grébiche stitch is embroidered like grébiche stitch to form triangles.

As you embroider the first side of the next triangle, pass the needle under the second side of the previous triangle and under the first side of the current triangle. Pass the thread up and down under the needle to make a knot.

Crossed Buttonhole Stitch

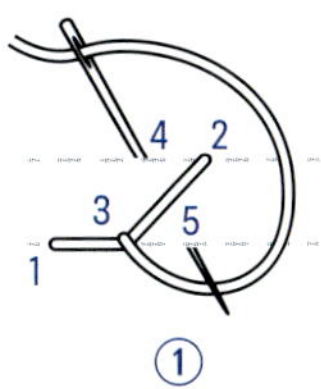

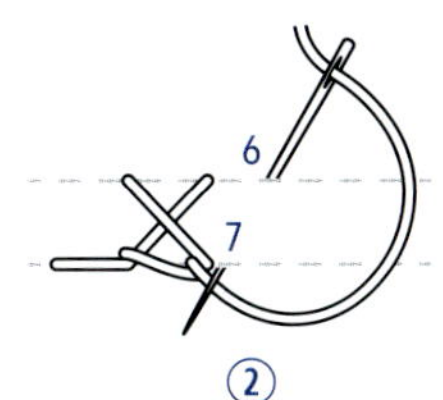

1 Pull the needle out in 1. In one movement, stitch in 2 and pull out in 3, passing the thread under the needle. In one movement, stitch in 4 and pull out in 5 to form a cross with the cross with the previous stitch.

2 Continue in the same way: 7 becomes point 3, and so on.

Whipped Buttonhole Stitch

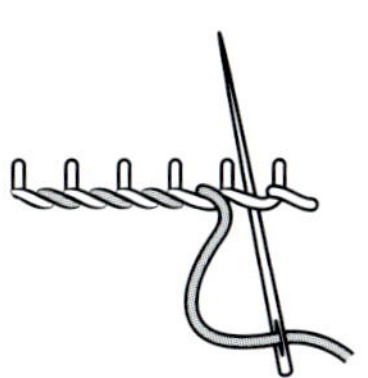

Embroider one row in buttonhole stitch. Preferably using a different color of thread, start at the beginning of the row and embroider, passing the needle under each stitch from bottom to top, without piercing the fabric.

Buttonhole Variation

Embroider one row in buttonhole stitch. If the stitches are wide apart, use a backstitch on the ends. If the stitches are tight, use a stem stitch.

Dovetail Buttonhole Stitch or Double Buttonhole Stitch

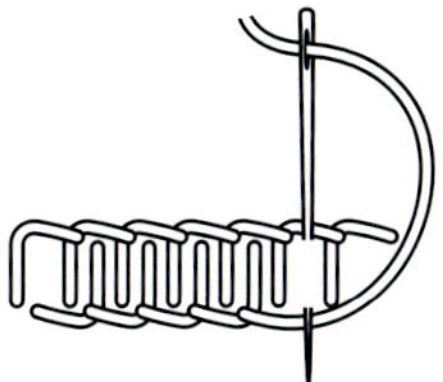

Embroider a first row in buttonhole stitch. Embroider a second row in mirror fashion, using head-to-tail stitches. The needle should penetrate and emerge at every stitch interval of the previous row.

Buttonhole Stitch Fill

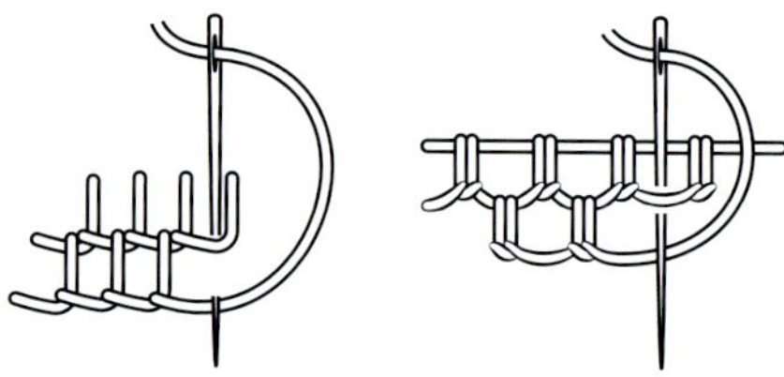

When embroidered regularly, buttonhole stitch rows form grids. They can be executed one above the other, in staggered rows or in pairs (or both).

Diagonal Buttonhole Stitch

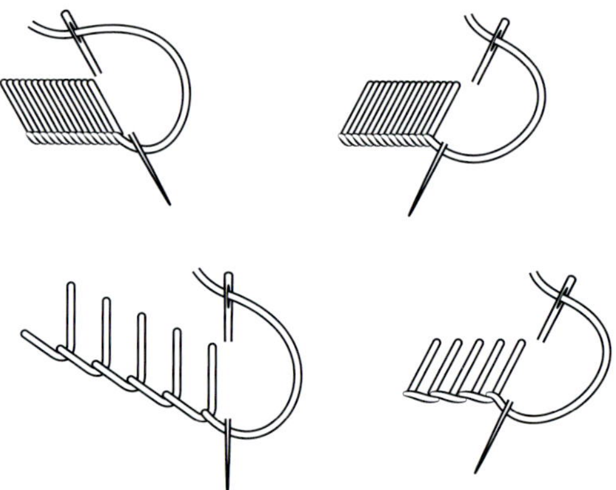

Buttonhole stitches are also embroidered on the diagonal, either close together or spaced apart. The needle is inserted at an angle rather than perpendicular to the stitched line.

Bullion Picot Stitch

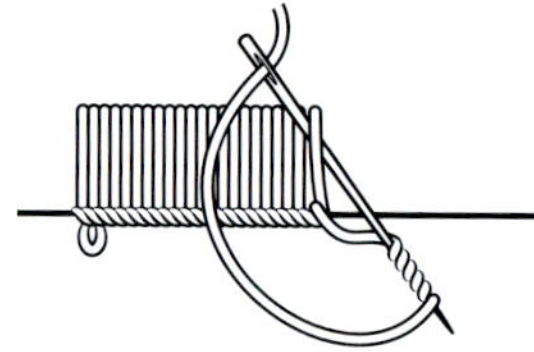

Bullion picot stitch is embroidered starting with a row of tight buttonhole stitch. A picot in bullion knot stitch is then added at regular intervals.

Embroider in buttonhole stitch up to the picot. Stitch the needle under the vertical stitch of the last buttonhole stitch.

Holding the needle down, wrap the thread six to eight times around the needle and pull gently. Be sure to hold the thread around the needle between thumb and forefinger to form a knot (picot). Secure the picot by working the following buttonhole stitch flush with the previous one.

Knotted Buttonhole Stitch

There are two variations for this point.

Variation 1

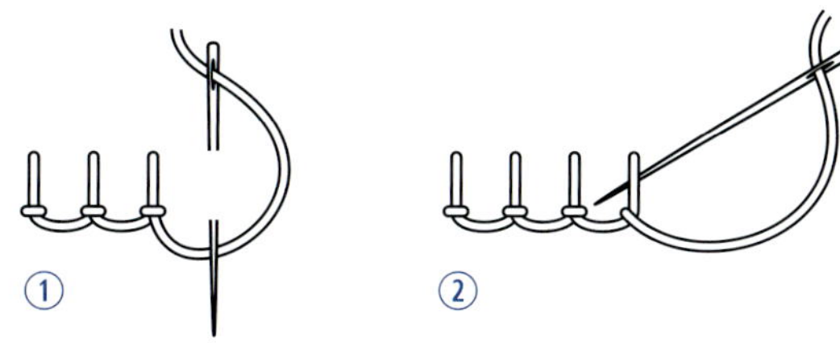

1 Embroider a classic buttonhole stitch.

2 Pass the needle from right to left through the stitch in 1, without piercing the fabric, to form a loop.

Variation 2

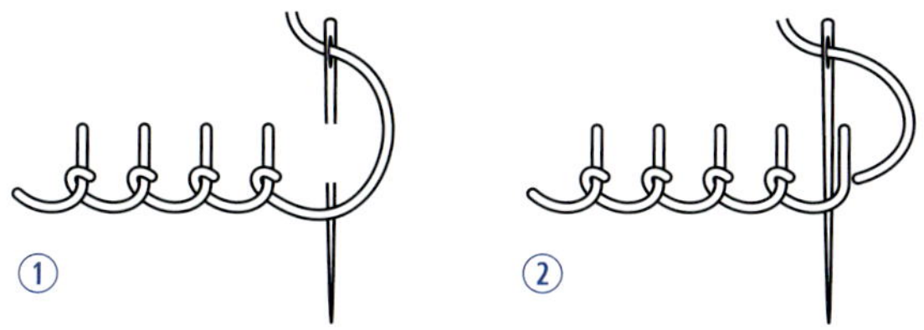

1 Stitch and pull out the needle as if embroidering a buttonhole stitch, but without passing the thread under the needle.

2 Pass the needle up and down under the thread of the stitch made in 1, without piercing the fabric.

Buttonhole Wheel Stitch

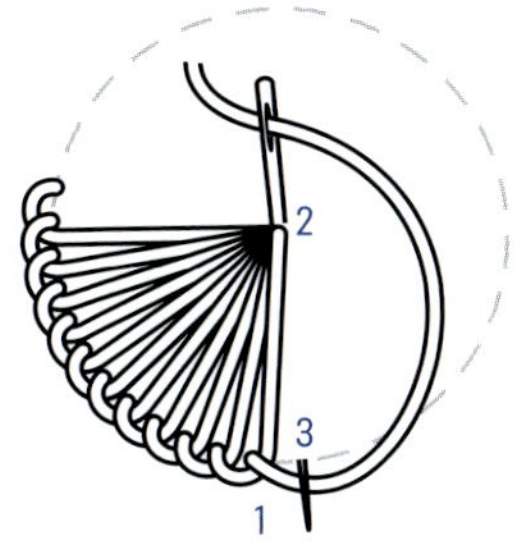

The buttonhole wheel stitch is embroidered with more or less spaced stitches, depending on the desired effect.

Using a circle template, draw a circle. Bring the needle out to the circumference of the circle, which will be the scalloped part. Pull out to 1 and, in a single movement, stitch to 2 (in the center), then pull out to 3, passing the thread under the needle. Always place the needle in the center, in the same hole.

Spoked Eyelet or Inside Buttonhole Wheel Stitch

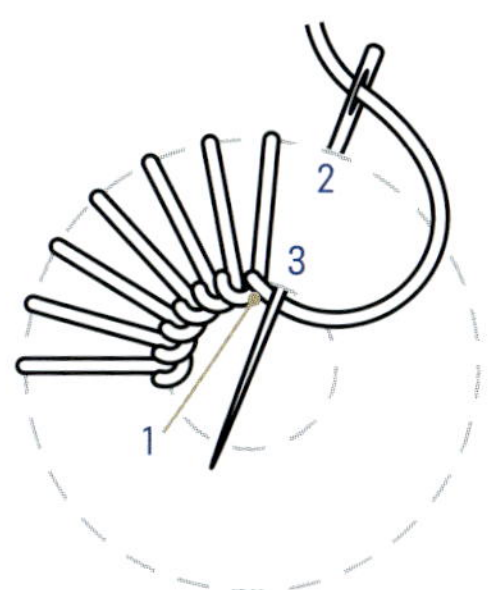

Using a circle template, draw two circles; the inner circle will be the scalloped one. Take out the needle on the inner circle. Pull out to 1 and, in a single movement, stitch to 2, then pull out to 3, passing the thread under the needle.

Tailor's Buttonhole Stitch

Tailor's buttonhole stitch is embroidered on two parallel lines. In contrast to classic buttonhole stitch, the needle is threaded on the side of the scalloped line.

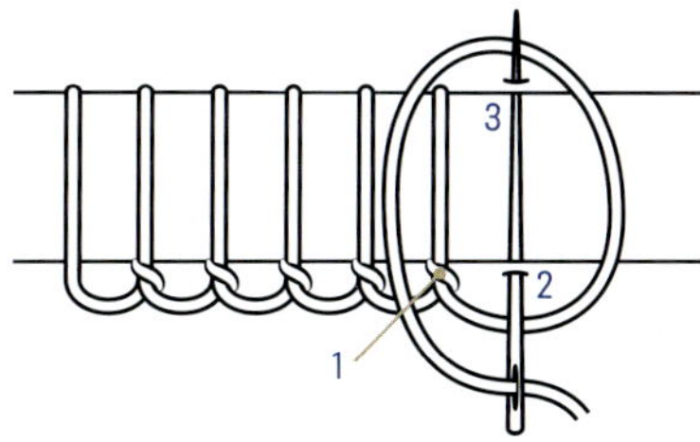

Pull the needle out in 1. In a single movement, stitch in 2 and pull out in 3. Pass the thread under the needle and gently pull the loop downward.

Buttonhole stitch and its applications

Embroidering a buttonhole bar

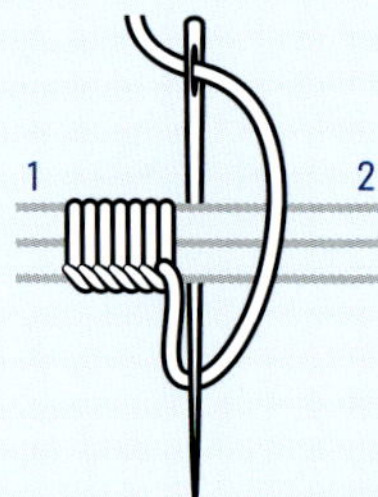

1 Draw a line between 1 and 2 the length of the bar. Take out the needle at 1 and stitch at 2. Embroider this straight stitch once or twice (see page 59) to create the frame of the bar.

2 Take out needle 1, then embroider in tight buttonhole stitch the whole length (up to 2), passing the needle under the bar frame, without piercing the fabric.

Embroidering a bar for a buttonhole in tailor's buttonhole stitch

This bar, which is the part opposite the button, completes the garment's edge-to-edge fastening system. The distance between points 1 and 2 must be equivalent to the diameter of the button, plus 1 or 2 mm.

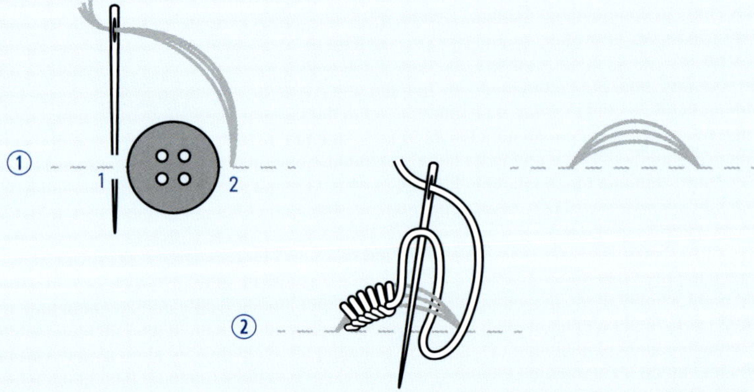

1 Make three or four passes with the straight stitch (see page 59) between 1 and 2 to create the bar frame. Use the button to define the length.

2 Embroider the thread bar in tailor's buttonhole stitch.

Embroidering a scalloped border on padding

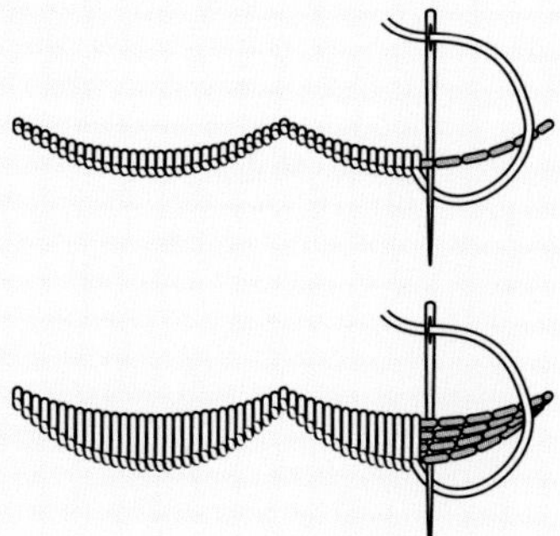

To achieve relief, start by filling the work with one or more lines in running stitch (see page 46) along the entire length to be embroidered. Then work a tight buttonhole stitch straddling the running stitches. The more lines you embroider in running stitch, the thicker your padding will be—a trial run may sometimes be necessary.

Caution: if the fabric is to be cut to the edge of the scalloped line, the embroidery must first be fully completed.

Embroidering leaves

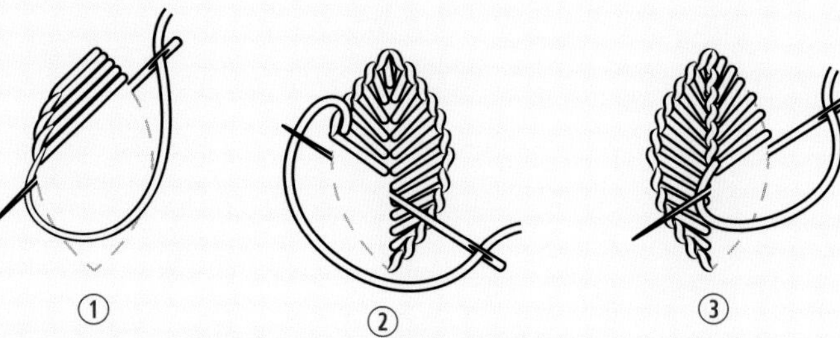

With the buttonhole stitch, leaves can be embroidered with the scallop positioned on the outside of the leaf or on the center vein (or both).

1 If the sheet width is less than 8 mm, a single row at the buttonhole stitch is sufficient.

2 If the width of the leaf is greater than 8 mm, draw a central vein on it. Then embroider, placing the buttonhole-stitched line around the edge of the leaf, starting at its base. Embroider up and down: stitch on the diagonal at the center vein and pull the needle out around the edge.

3 If the buttonhole-stitched line is around the edge of a leaf half and then on the center vein, start the embroidery at the base of the leaf. embroider a leaf half as before and, once at the top, reverse the direction of the needle to embroider the buttonhole stitched line on the center vein.

Visual Library of Embroidery Stitches

CHAIN STITCH AND ITS VARIATIONS

Chain stitch first appeared between the 10th and 5th centuries BCE. It is still embroidered today all over the world: from Peru to Turkestan, Mongolia, China, Greece, India, and North Africa.

This linear stitch is easy to embroider. It can be used to follow winding lines, emphasize an outline, mask an edge, create a braid, and even be embroidered as a filler.

Unless otherwise specified, chain stitch and its variations are embroidered from right to left, on one line.

Chain Stitch

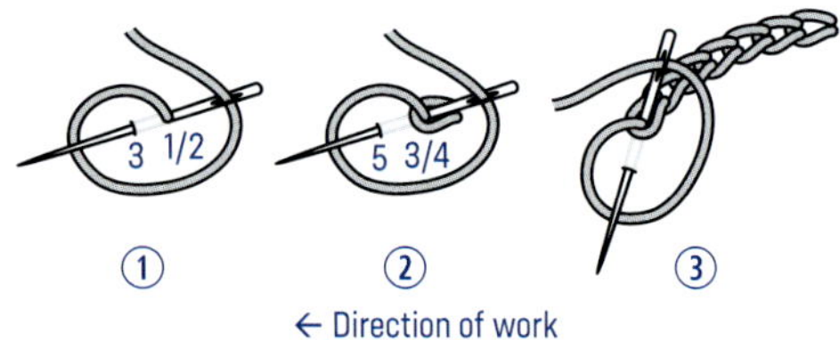

1 Pull the needle out in 1. In one movement, stitch in 2 (1 and 2 are the same) and pull out partially in 3 (1 and 2 are merged). Pass the thread under the needle to form a loop and pull the needle out completely, in a movement parallel to the fabric.

2 In a single movement, stitch in 4 (3 and 4 are the same) and pull out partially in 5. Pass the thread under the needle to form a loop and pull the needle all the way out.

3 Saddle-stitch the last loop to secure it.

For left-handed people

Embroider from left to right.

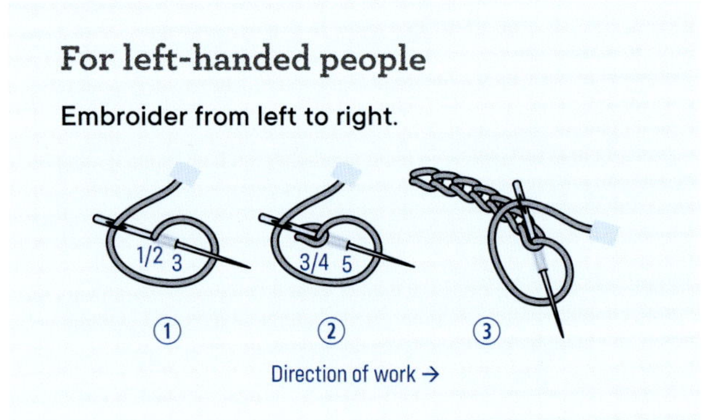

Whipped Chain Stitch or Molded Chain Stitch

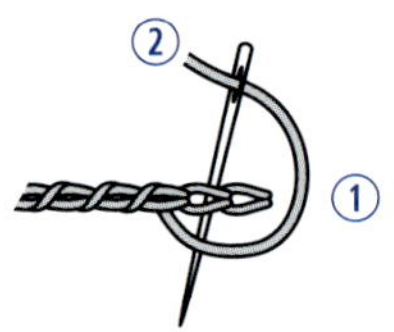

1 Embroider a line in chain stitch.

2 Whip by passing the needle under each stitch from top to bottom without piercing the fabric.

Chain Stitch Whipped on Both Sides

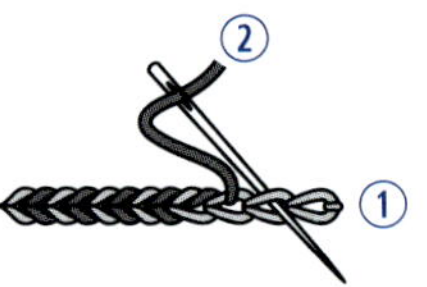

1 Embroider a line in chain stitch.

2 Using a thread of contrasting color, whip by each stitch on each side without piercing the fabric.

Twisted Chain Stitch

1 Pull the needle out in 1, stitch in 2, and partially pull out in 3. Thread over and under the needle. Pull the needle all the way out.

2 Stitch in 4, outside the chain, and pull out partially in 5. Pull the needle out completely.

Zigzag Chain Stitch

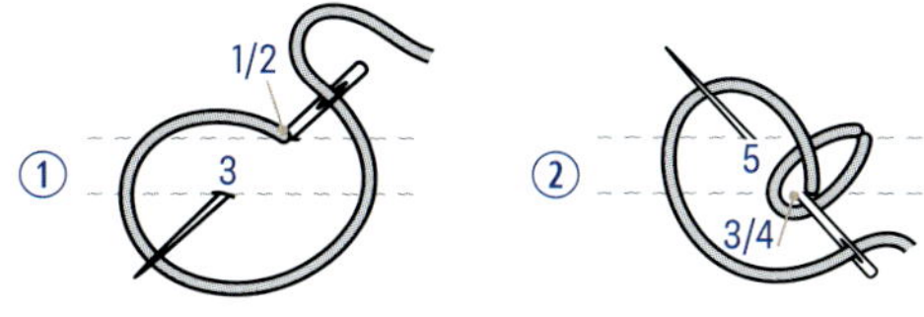

Zigzag chain stitch is embroidered on two parallel lines.

Embroider like a classic chain stitch, pricking the needle to obtain an open zigzag angle (slightly over 90°) at each stitch.

Feathered Chain Stitch

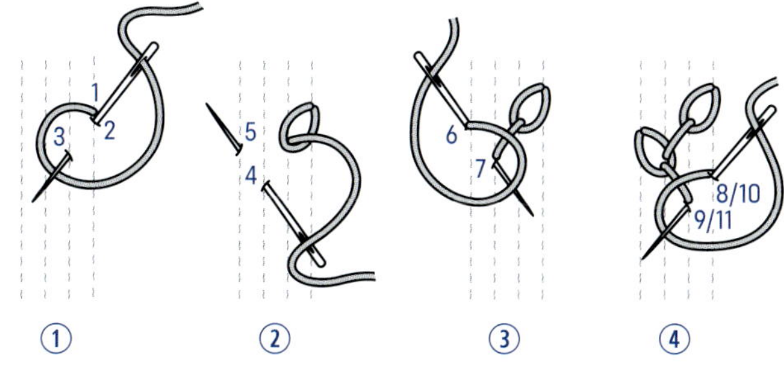

The feathered chain stitch is embroidered on four parallel lines, from top to bottom.

Embroider a line in chain stitch, intersecting it with running stitches to form the spine.

Quilted Chain Stitch

Quilted chain stitch is embroidered on a chain stitch line.

With a contrasting thread, embroider in backstitch on each stitch intersection.

Quilted Chain Stitch on the Sides

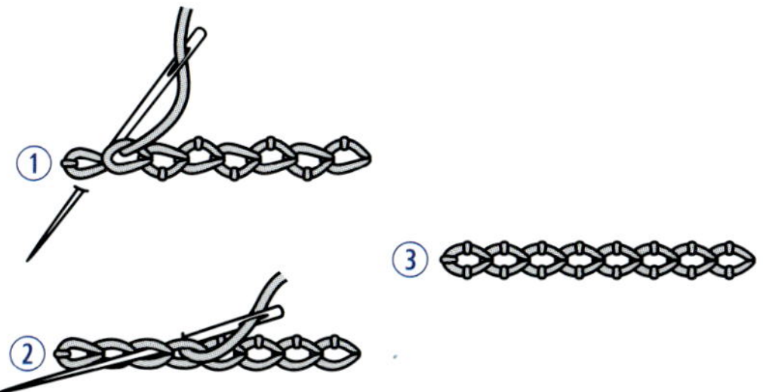

The chain stitch stitched on the sides is embroidered on a chain stitch line.

Embroider a backstitch straddling the sides of the stitches: zigzag (in 1), unilateral (in 2), and bilateral (in 3).

Two-Tone or Chequered Chain Stitch

Chequered chain stitch is embroidered with two different colored threads in the eye of the needle.

Embroider a line in chain stitch, passing a single thread under the needle. Alternate the thread for each stitch.

Tips for Good Embroidery

When you take out the needle, pull the threads apart so that the one not used for embroidery is the same length as the other, in order to achieve the following stitch.

Picot Chain Stitch or Crested Chain Stitch

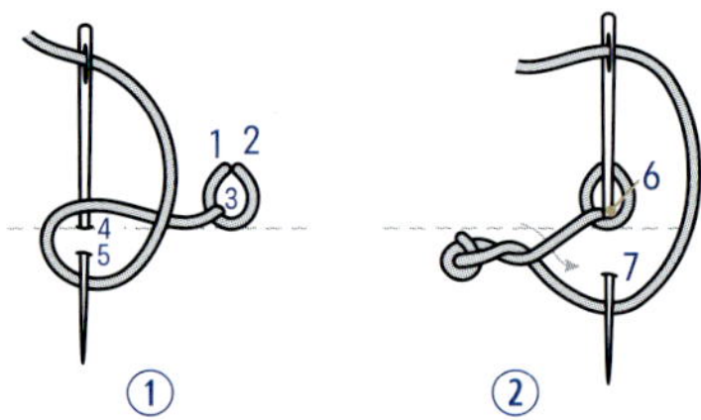

The picot chain stitch is embroidered on two parallel lines, from top to bottom.

1 Take out the needle on the right-hand line and stitch in classic chain stitch (1, 2, and 3). Embroider a stitch (4 and 5) on the left-hand line, stitching at the same height as the bottom of the stitch. Pass the thread over and then under the needle and pull.

2 Pass the needle under the thread in the middle. Stitch through the loop of the previous stitch in 6, exit in 7, and pass the thread under the needle.

Open or Square Chain Stitch or Ladder Stitch

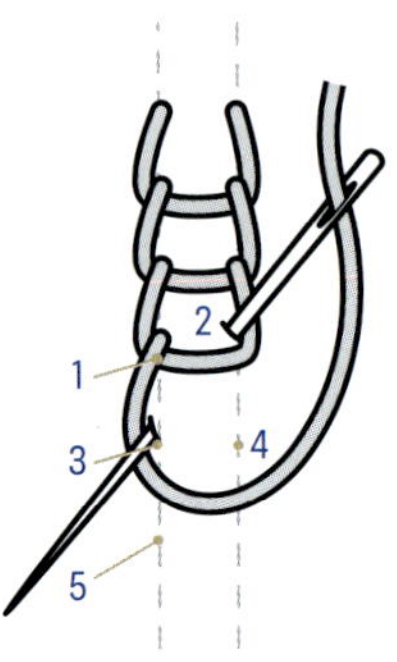

The open chain stitch is embroidered on two parallel lines, from top to bottom.

Take out the needle in 1. In one movement, stitch in 2 and partially take out in 3, needle at an angle. Pass the thread under the needle to form a loop. Pull the needle out completely. In one movement, stitch in 4, and pull out in 5. Pass the thread under the needle to form a loop. Pull the needle through.

Double Chain Stitch or Staggered Chain Stitch

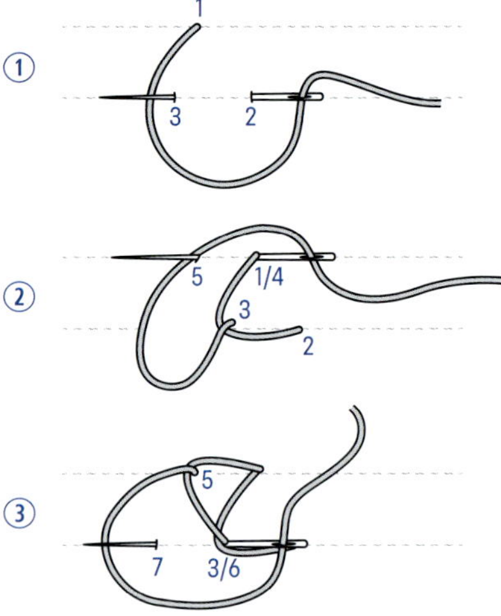

Double chain stitch is embroidered on two parallel lines, stitching alternately on the top and bottom lines.

1 Exit in 1, on the top line. In a single movement, stitch in 2 and partially exit in 3, on the bottom line. Pass the thread under the needle tip.

2 On the top line, in a single movement, stitch in 4 (4 and 1 are the same) and pull out partially in 5. Pass the thread under the needle tip.

3 On the bottom line, in a single movement, stitch in 6 (6 and 3 are the same) and pull out partially in 7. Pass the thread under the needle tip.

Chain Stitch Filling

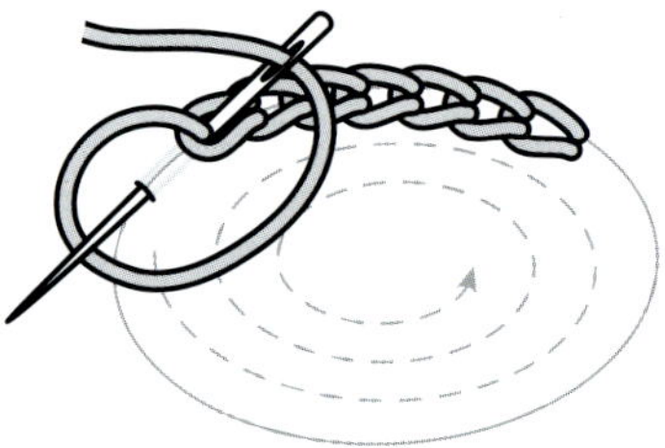

Embroider several lines of chain stitch against each other to fill the shape to be embroidered. Always start at the outside of the shape.

Heavy Chain Stitch

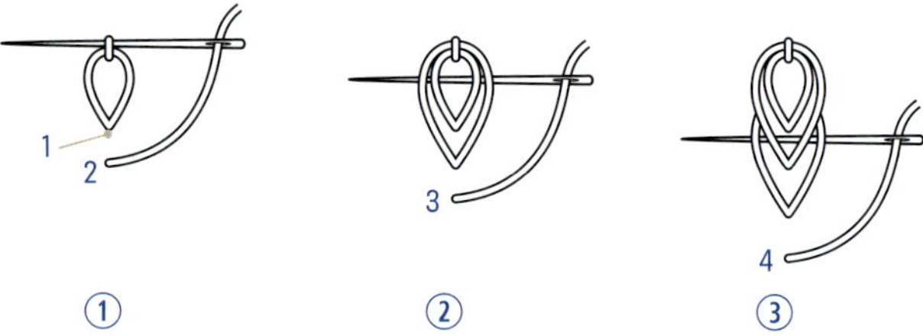

Tight chain stitch is embroidered from top to bottom.

Heavy chain stitch is embroidered from top to bottom.

1 Embroider two small stitches one on top of the other. Take the needle out in 1, pass under the stitches, and stitch in 1. Take the needle out in 2, pass under the stitches, and stitch in 2.

2 Exit in 3, pass under the penultimate loop (the first one made), and stitch in 3.

3 Pull out in 4, pass under the penultimate loop (the second one made), and stitch in 4.

Rope Stitch

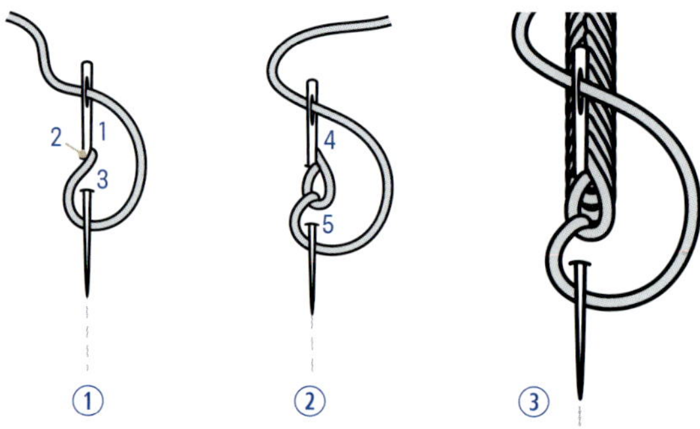

Rope stitch is embroidered from top to bottom.

1 Take out the needle at 1, stitch at 2, and partially take out at 3 (2 is to the left of 1). Thread over and under the needle.

2 Stitch in 4 on the left and slightly lower than 1, then out in 5. Pass the thread under the needle from left to right.

3 Stitch in the penultimate stitch and exit by passing the thread under the needle.

Cable Chain Stitch or Cable Stitch

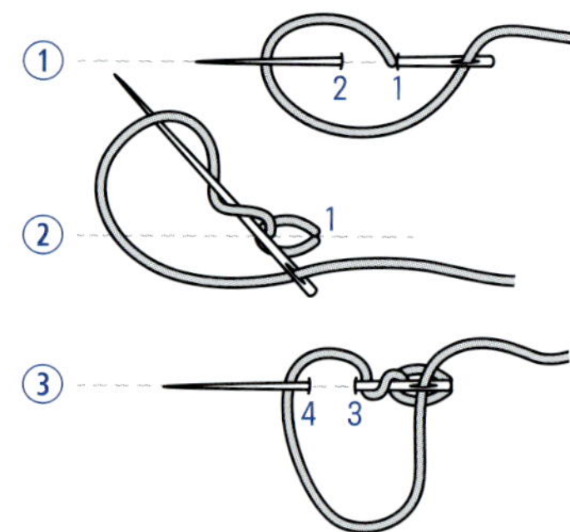

1 Embroider the first stitch of the chain stitch between 1 and 2.

2 Wrap the thread around the needle, passing it over the top then under and over again.

3 Hold this loop while stitching in 3 and out in 4 in a single movement. Pass the thread under the needle and place the loop correctly.

Etruscan Stitch

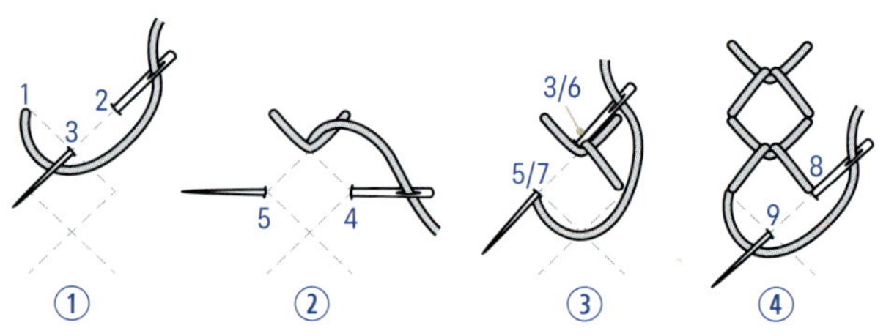

Etruscan stitch forms lines of checks. It is embroidered on a regular weft like those designed for counted stitches (see page 86).

Tips for Good Embroidery

If the fabric you've chosen doesn't have a regular weave, carefully trace the squares with a felt-tip pen or erasable pen.

1 Pull the needle out in 1. In a single movement, stitch in 2 and partially pull out in 3. Pass the thread under the needle and pull the needle all the way out.

2 Pierce the needle in 4 and out in 5.

3 Pierce the needle at 6 (3 and 6 are the same) and take out in 7 (7 and 5 are the same).

4 In a single movement, stitch in 8 and pull out partially in 9. Pass the thread under the needle and pull the needle all the way out.

Raised Chain Band

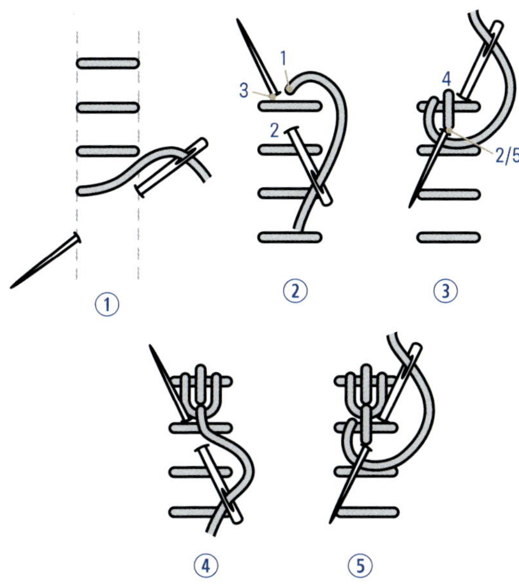

Raised chain band is embroidered on two parallel lines, from top to bottom.

1 Embroider regular horizontal stitches in straight stitch over the entire height to be embroidered.

2 Take out the needle at 1, stitch at 2, and take out at 3 (to the left of 1).

3 In a single movement, stitch in 4 and pull out partially in 5 (2 and 5 are the same hole). Pass the thread under the needle and pull the needle all the way out.

4 and 5 Continue in this way, straddling each rung of the ladder.

Detached Chain Stitch

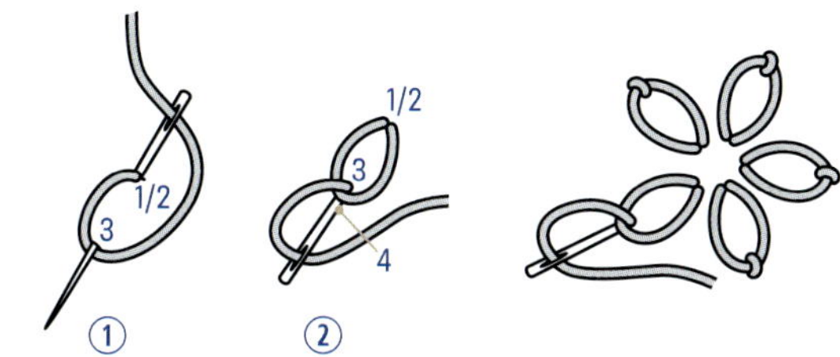

1 Pull the needle out in 1. In one movement, stitch in 2 (1 and 2 are merged) and pull out partially in 3. Pass the thread under the needle and pull out the needle completely.

2 Stitch in 4, straddling the loop, to secure it.

Visual Library of Embroidery Stitches

CROSS-STITCH AND NEEDLEPOINT

Embroidered in abundance all over the world, cross-stitch uses small crosses to draw patterns. By the second half of the 16th century it spread to northern Europe, where it became very popular. It can be found on handwoven fabrics—notably costumes, headdresses, and household linen—especially household linen—especially in northern Germany and the Alps, where it is embroidered in linen, cotton, or wool.

In Hungary, throughout the Balkans, and in the countries of the Levant, Ottoman influence led to the development of this technique in the late medieval period.

Throughout history, this stitch has been embroidered both in popular compositions and in prestigious creations such as sacred embroidery. More recently, this technique reached its apogee from the 1970s to the first few years of the 2000s.

From the Middle Ages onward, this stitch was also called "mark stitch," since it was used to mark (cipher) body and household linen. All girls from good families had to learn how to embroider it. Samplers then appeared. These were exercises carried out on fabric, on which girls cross-stitched letters of the alphabet, numbers, religious symbols and designs, and even mottos. Samplers flourished throughout the 19th century and up to the Second World War, not least because embroidery was taught in elementary school. Indeed, as early as 1882, when Jules Ferry made school compulsory, embroidery lessons became part of the curriculum for young girls. This teaching greatly contributed to the development of samplers and cross-stitch. Sewing and embroidery lessons were officially removed from the school curriculum in 1972.

Cross-stitch is made up of two intersecting stitches forming a cross. It is most often embroidered on textile supports with a regular weave—the symmetrical crossing of weft and warp ensures perfect work—but also on tracings or canvas-type supports called waste canvas (see pages 37 and 86). It's used for counted-stitch work that requires following a diagram.

Sampler, France, 1870

Supplies and Materials

Cross-stitching requires a specific ground fabric. It is therefore essential to choose your embroidery fabric or temporary stabilizer with care.

What You Need to Know

Hundreds of cross-stitch embroidery diagrams are available free of charge on www.dmc.com.

Canvas and backing materials

Cross-stitch is embroidered on regular-weave warp-and-weft fabrics, such as congress cloth, monocanvas, or Aïda canvas. They are available in cut pieces, by the meter, and in braids of various widths.

In haberdashery stores, you can also easily find ready-to-embroider baby accessories, household linen or decorative items with a band of fabric, cheesecloth, or Aïda.

Ready-to-embroider cuddly toy

Tips for Good Embroidery

Be careful not to wash these fabrics before starting to embroider, so that they don't lose their primer, a precious aid for regular embroidery. Cut them to size beforehand in straight thread and overlock the edges to prevent fraying.

Aïda canvas

This woven canvas is ideal for FRIEZEs to cross-stitch: its weave forms very regular squares with small holes for easy embroidery of a cross in each one. It is available in several weave thicknesses for embroidery of 5.5 or 7 stitches/cm, for example, and in different colors.

Congress cloth and even-weave linen cloths

On these even-weave fabrics, embroidery work is more difficult, since it is necessary to count the weft threads. However, the weave remains loose enough to locate and count the threads for cross-stitch embroidery.

Counted fabrics are defined by a number of threads/cm, depending on the thickness of the weave. The most common are 10, 12, 14, and 16 threads/cm (10 being the thickest and 16 the thinnest), which gives 5, 6, 7, and 8 stitches/cm if embroidered on two threads. They also come in a wide range of colors. Here, cross-stitch embroidery can be performed over one, two (most common), or three threads.

Waste canvas

A waste canvas is a temporary canvas with the same characteristics as cross-stitch canvas. It is available in various weave thicknesses for embroidering 5.5 or 7 stitches/ cm, for example. It can be used to cross-stitch all kinds of textiles (including knits). To find out how to use a waste canvas, go to page 37.

Soluble canvas

Water-soluble canvas is a temporary stabilizer that can replace the waste canvas for smaller embroideries. The DMC brand offers 20 × 22cm sheets for 5.5 stitches/cm embroidery.

1 Lay the soluble canvas flat, aligning the straight edge of the embroidery backing with the canvas grid.

2 Once the embroidery is finished, soak it for 10 minutes in 40° water to dissolve the canvas.

Threads

Cotton or silk embroidery floss are the most common materials for cross-stitch embroidery (see pages 29 and 30).

Needles

For canvas and Aïda fabrics, use embroidery needles with round tips. To embroider with two strands of embroidery floss, choose between sizes 26 and 22.

For embroidery on waste canvas, use size 26 chenille needles.

Embroidery hoop

Use a 12 or 15cm diameter hoop.

Cross-Stitch

Cross-stitch is made up of two half stitches embroidered in a cross. It is embroidered in the same way for right- and left-handers, starting from the center of the motif and working outward.

To learn how to follow a diagram and how to start embroidering, see page 36.

Sampler, Netherlands, 1745

Warning

To ensure uniformity, all crosses must be embroidered in the same way: half stitches must always be oriented and superimposed in the same order.

Embroidery on Aïda canvas

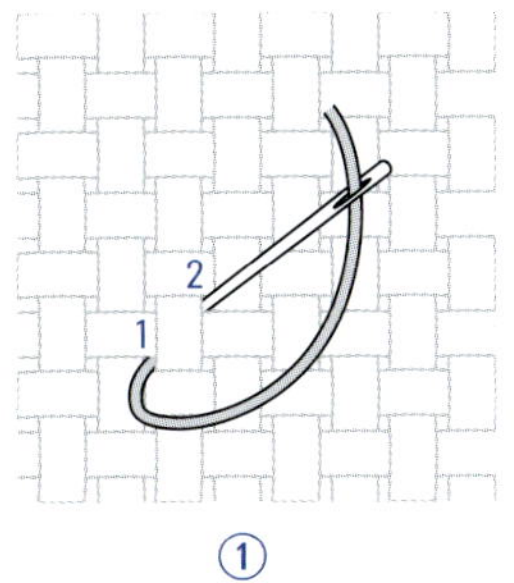

①

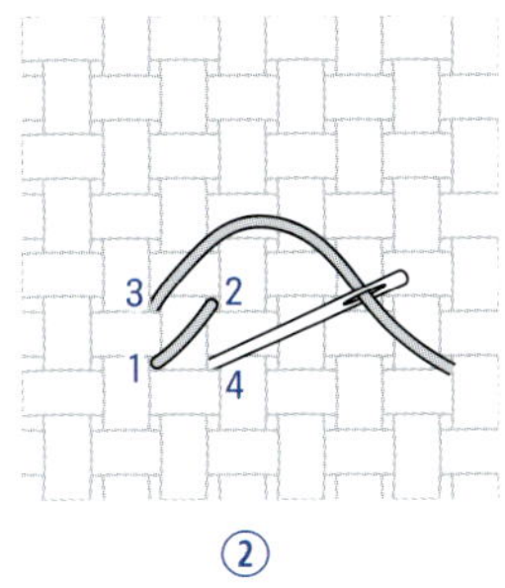

②

1 Take out the needle in 1 and stitch in 2.

2 Take out in 3 and prick in 4.

Embroidery on an even-weave canvas

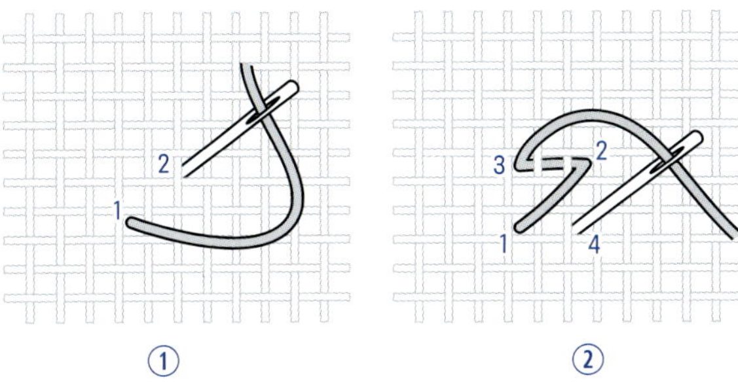

Unless otherwise specified in the diagonal legend, skip two weft threads to make a stitch.

1 Take out the needle in 1 and stitch in 2.

2 Take out in 3 and prick in 4.

Horizontal embroidery

Traditional cross-stitch or sampler cross-stitch

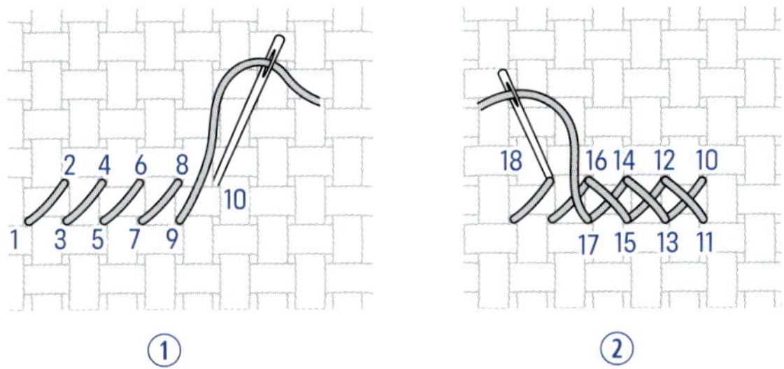

This technique is used to embroider long horizontal lengths.

1 Embroider a whole first row of half cross-stitches: take out needle 1 and stitch 2, take out needle 3 and stitch 4, and so on.

2 Embroider the second row back: take out 11 and stitch in 12, take out 13 and stitch in 14, and so on.

Individual or simple cross-stitch

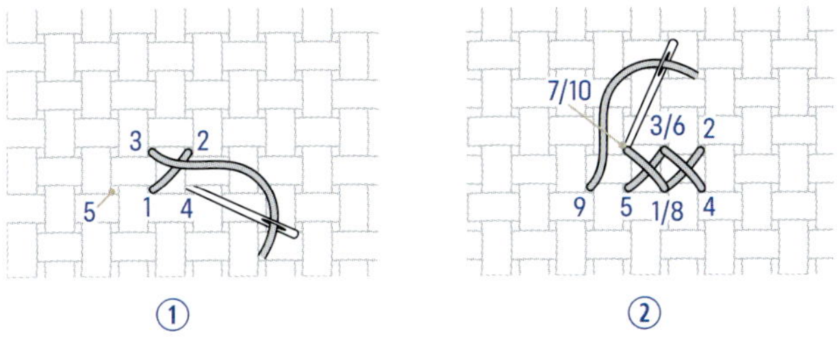

This technique is useful when there are only a few stitches to be made in a row.

1 Embroider the first cross: take out needle 1 and stitch 2, then then take out needle 3 and stitch 4.

2 Embroider the second cross: exit at 5 and stitch at 6, exit at 7 and stitch at 8 (1 and 8 are the same), and so on.

Vertical embroidery

Traditional cross-stitch—vertical

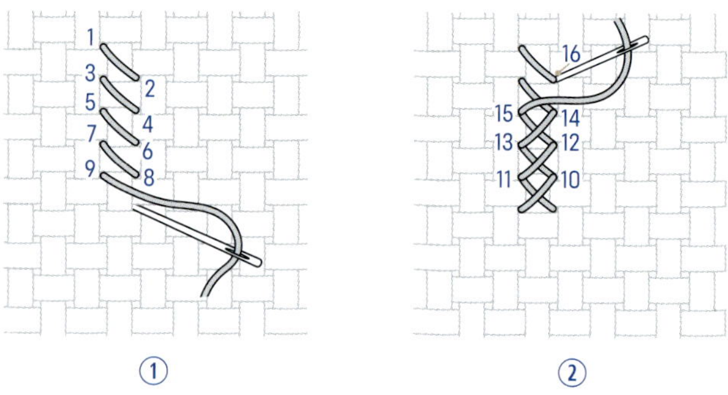

This technique is used to embroider long vertical lengths.

1 Embroider a first full row of half cross-stitches: take out needle 1 and stitch 2, take out 3 and stitch in 4, and so on.

2 Embroider the second row back: take out 11 and stitch in 12, take out 13 and stitch in 14, and so on.

Individual or simple cross stitch

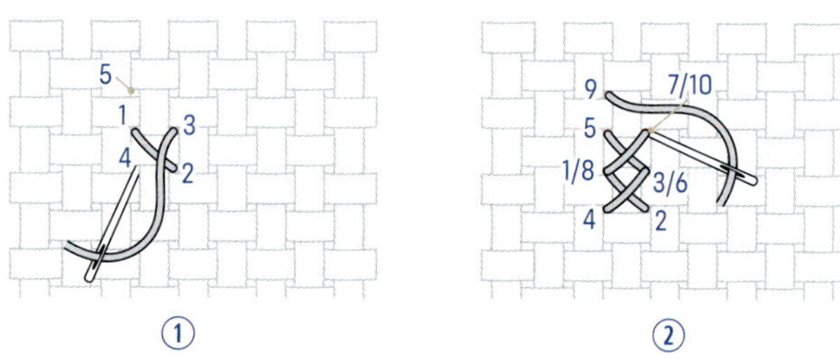

This technique is useful when there are only a few stitches to be made in a row.

1 Embroider the first cross: take out needle 1 and stitch 2, take out needle 3 and stitch 4.

2 Embroider the second cross: exit at 5 and stitch at 6, exit at 7 and stitch at 8 (1 and 8 are the same), and so on.

Diagonal embroidery

Moving upward

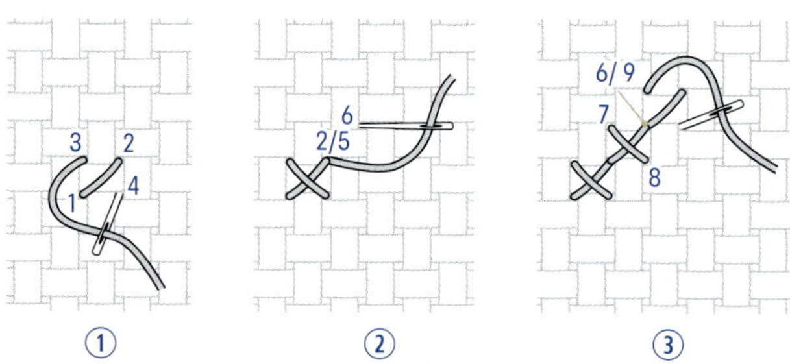

1 Embroider the first cross: take out needle 1 and stitch 2, then take out needle 3 and stitch 4.

2 Work diagonally upward to the right: exit at 5 (2 and 5 are merged) and stitch at 6.

3 Still on the diagonal, ascending to the right, exit at 7 and stitch at 8 to embroider the second cross.

Descending

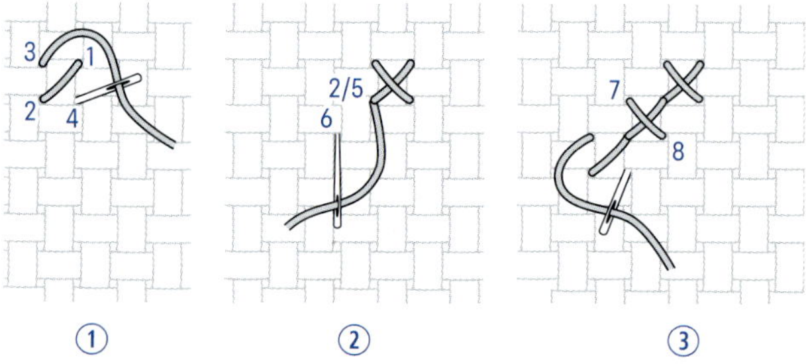

1 Embroider the first cross: take out needle 1 and stitch in in 2, then take out in 3 and stitch in 4.

2 Work diagonally down to the left: exit at 5 (2 and 5 are the same) and prick at 6.

3 Still on the diagonal, moving down to the left, exit at 7 and stitch at 8 to embroider the second cross.

Half cross tent stitch

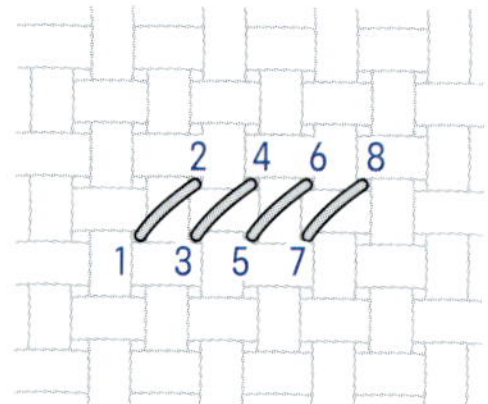

Embroider only the first row of the cross-stitch. Take out the needle in 1 and stitch in 2, take out in 3 and stitch in 4.

Two-Sided Cross-Stitch

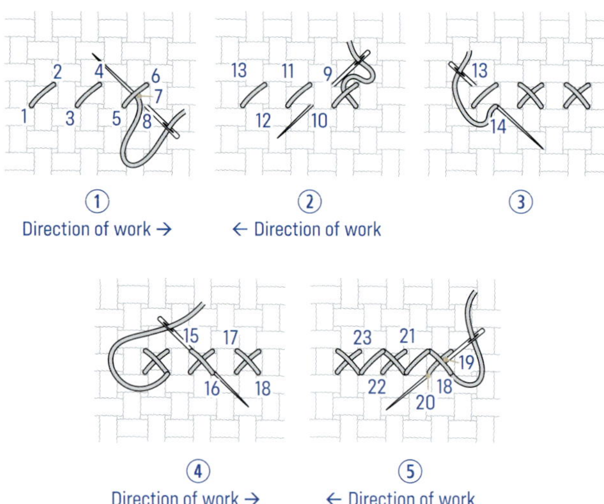

Two-sided cross-stitch is used when the embroidery is visible on both sides.

To embroider a row, proceed as follows.

1 Embroider every other half stitch until the end of the row. Take out the needle in 7 in the middle of the last half stitch embroidered, stitch in 8, and take out again in 7.

2 Stitch in 9 to embroider the remaining quarter stitch. Finish the crosses from step 1: exit at 10 and stitch at 11, then exit at 12 and stitch at 13.

3 When the last cross is embroidered, exit at 14, bottom right of the last cross.

4 Return to the right, embroidering a half stitch between each previously embroidered cross. Stitch in 15 and out in 16, then stitch in 17 and out in 18 (bottom right of last cross).

5 Stitch at 19 (center of last cross) and exit at 20 (bottom left of last cross). Finish the first row of crosses: stitch at 21 and exit at 22, stitch at 23, and so on.

Assisi Embroidery

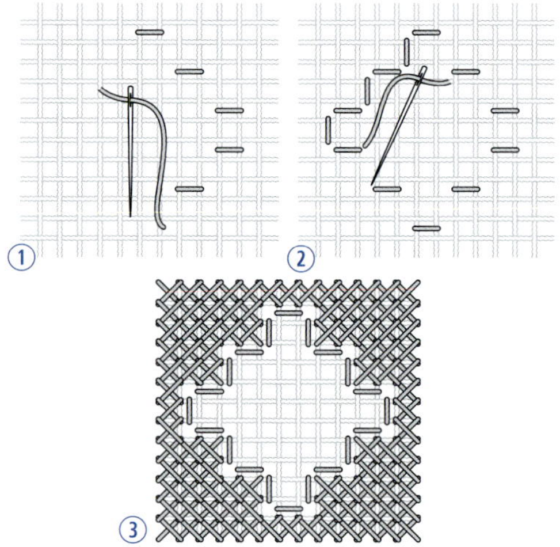

This resist technique first appeared in Assisi, Italy, in the 16th century. It allows motifs to appear in spaces not embroidered in cross-stitch. From the end of the 19th century onward, Assisi embroidery, which is generally symmetrical, became very popular. Traditionally, the colors used are black and brown for the outlines, and red and blue for the grounds. The motifs are hooped in line stitch with very fine thread.

1 and 2 Embroider all contours in double running stitch.

3 Embroider grounds in cross-stitch.

What You Need to Know

It is possible to start by embroidering the grounds, but the pattern is then much more difficult to locate.

Assisi embroidery

Rice Stitch

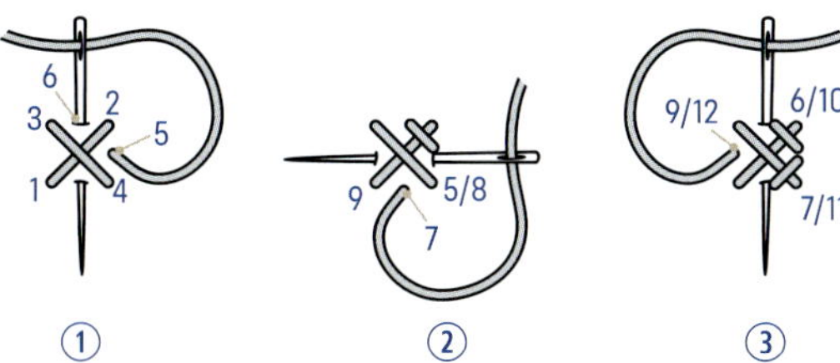

Rice stitch consists of a cross-stitch embroidered with four diagonal stitches. It is possible to change thread size or color (or both) between cross-stitch and diagonal stitch. In this case, first embroider all the cross-stitches with the thread of your choice, then change thread and embroider all the diagonal stitches.

1 Embroider a cross: take out needle 1 and stitch 2, then take out needle 3 and stitch 4.

2 and 3 Embroider the stitches on the diagonal: exit at 5 and stitch at 6, exit at 7 and stitch at 8, exit at 9 and stitch at 10, then exit at 11 and stitch at 12 (5 and 8, 6 and 10, 7 and 11, and 9 and 12 are the same holes).

Bee Stitch

Bee stitch is embroidered on a one-sided triangle.

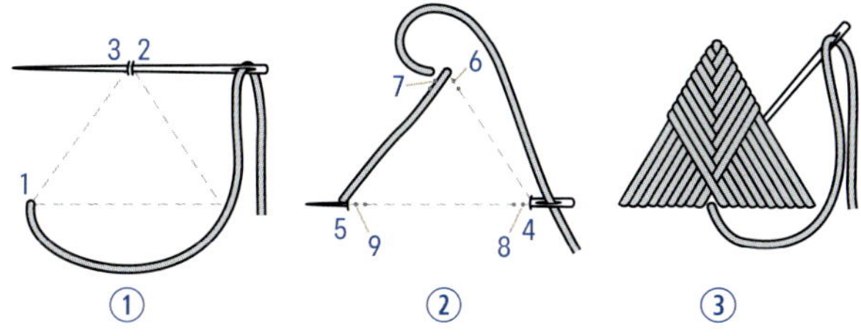

Work "rocking the needle" (i.e., in a single movement).

1 Take out the needle in 1, stitch in 2, and take out in 3 at the top of the triangle, using a tiny stitch.

2 and 3 Stitch at 4 and exit at 5 (5 is to the right of 1, on the base of the triangle). Stitch at 6 and exit at 7, stitching the needle horizontally (just below 2 and 3). Stitch to 8 and exit at 9 (8 is to the left of 4 and 9 is to the right of 5, on the base of the triangle).

Fishbone Stitch

Fishbone stitch can be embroidered on parallel lines or on petals and leaves.

Raised fishbone stitch or overlapping herringbone stitch

On a leaf or petal

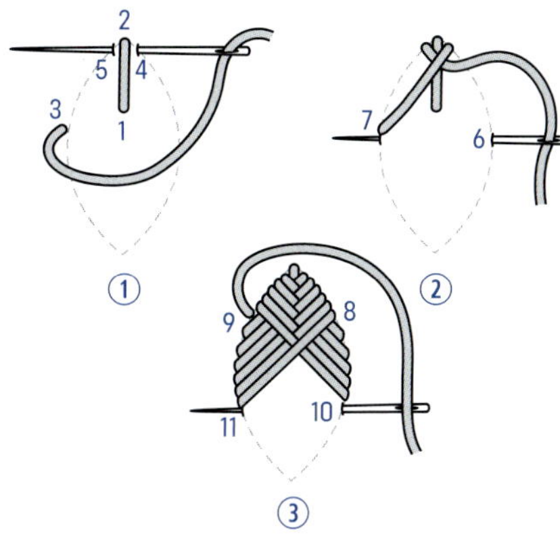

Work "rocking the needle" (i.e., in a single movement, embroidering stitches against each other).

1 Take out the needle in 1 and stitch in 2 to form the point of the design. Embroider alternately from the top and the bottom to cross the thread and fill the motif completely: pull out in 3, stitch in 4, and pull out in 5.

2 and 3 Stitch in 6, take out in 7 and stitch in 8.

Along parallel lines

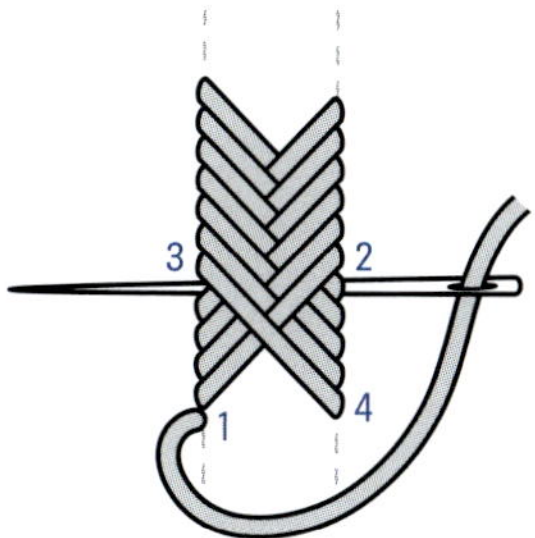

Work "rocking the needle" (i.e., in a single movement, embroidering stitches one against the other).

Embroider alternately in top and bottom stitches to cross the thread and fill the motif completely: take out the needle in 1 and stitch in 2, then take out in 3 and stitch in 4.

Open Fishbone Stitch

On a leaf or petal

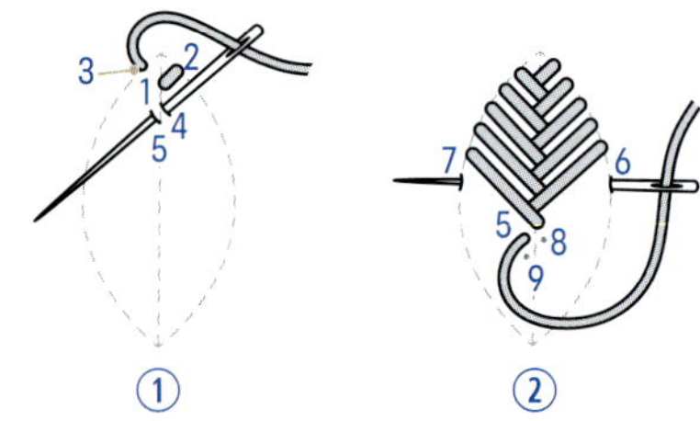

Work "rocking the needle" (i.e., in a single movement, moving downward along the pattern). Leave small spaces between stitches.

1 Take the needle out in 1, stitch in 2, and take out in 3, stitching the needle horizontally. Stitch in 4 to the right of the vein and exit in 5 to the left to create a small diagonal stitch.

2 Stitch at 6 and exit at 7, stitching the needle horizontally. Stitch in 8 to the right of the rib and exit in 9 to the left to create a small diagonal stitch.

Along parallel lines

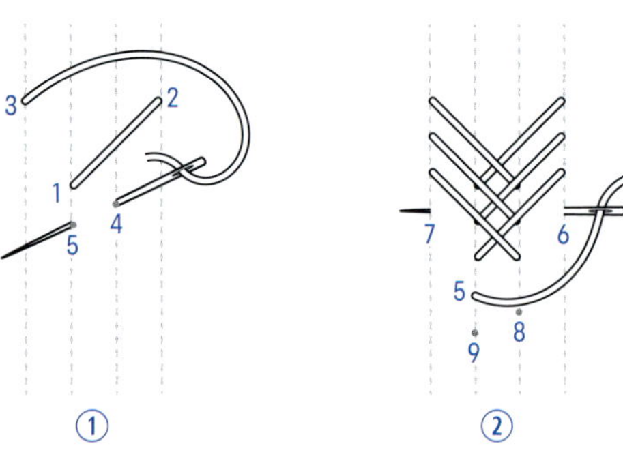

Work "rocking the needle" (i.e., in a single movement, moving downward along the pattern). Leave small spaces between stitches.

1 Draw two parallel lines and then two more inside the pattern. Bring the needle out in 1, stitch in 2, and bring out in 3, stitching the needle horizontally. Stitch at 4 on the right-hand line and exit at 5 on the left-hand line to create a small diagonal stitch.

2 Stitch at 6 and exit at 7, stitching the needle horizontally. Stitch in 8 on the right-hand line and exit in 9 on the left-hand line to create a small diagonal stitch.

Fishbone Stitch in a Line

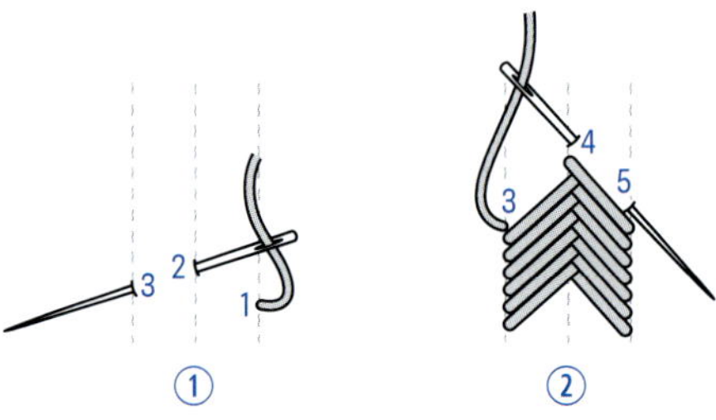

Start by drawing two parallel lines and a third in the middle.

1 Take the needle out in 1 on the right-hand line, stitch in 2 to the left of the middle line, and take out in 3 on the left-hand line.

2 Stitch in 4 on the right of the middle line and exit in 5 on the right. Continue, alternating.

Fishbone Stitch on a Motif

Fishbone stitch can be embroidered on two parallel lines or depict petals, leaves, and stars.

Tips for Good Embroidery

It is important to maintain a deep V shape when performing the stitches.

On a leaf or petal

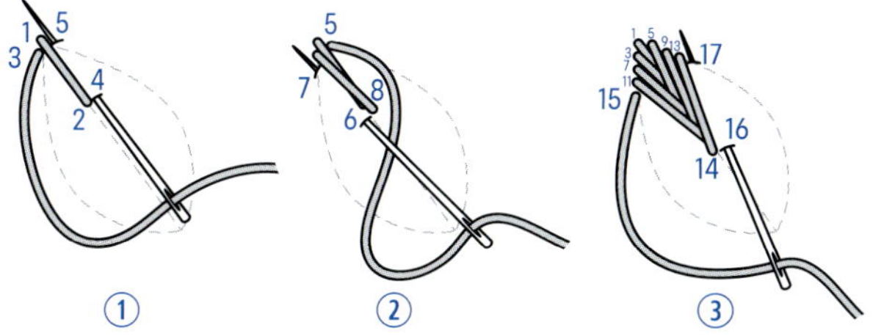

Start by drawing a central vein on the leaf or petal.

1 Embroider the first stitch on the center vein: pull the needle out in 1 and stitch in 2. Exit in 3 to the left of the outer edge of the sheet and stitch in 4 to the right of the center vein and 2. Exit in 5 to the right of the sheet.

2 and 3 Stitch in 6 to the left of the center vein and exit in 7. Continue alternating the stitches.

On a star

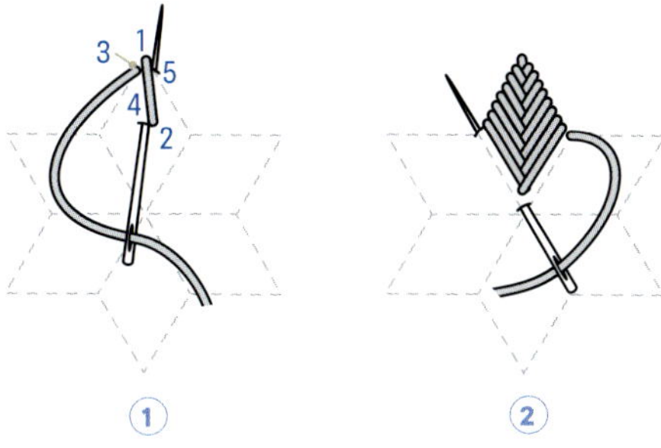

Start by drawing a five- or six-pointed star. In each point, draw a straight line between the apex and the center of the star, representing the central vein.

1 Embroider the first stitch on the center vein: take out needle 1 and stitch 2. Exit in 3 to the left of the outer trace of the star and stitch in 4 to the right of the center vein and 2. Exit in 5 to the right of 1 on the star and stitch in 6 to the left of the center vein.

2 Continue, alternating to finish each point of the star.

Tips for Good Embroidery

Embroider one point at a time.

Leaf Stitch

Leaf stitch is embroidered on three parallel lines, from bottom to top and from outside to inside. This stitch is also used to embroider leaves and petals.

Three parallel lines

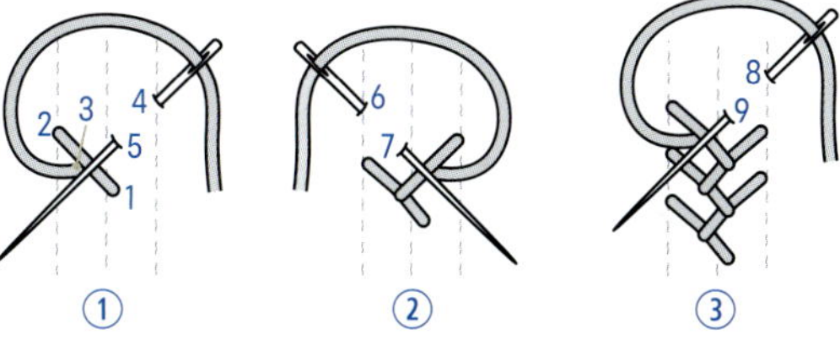

Start by drawing three parallel lines.

1 Take out needle 1 to the right of the middle line. Stitch in 2 on the left-hand line and exit in 3 (between the middle and left-hand lines). Stitch in 4 on the right-hand line and exit in 5 (between the middle and right-hand lines).

2 Stitch in 6 on the left-hand line and exit in 7 (to the left of the middle line).

3 Stitch in 8 on the right-hand line and exit in 9 (to the right of the middle line).

On a leaf or petal

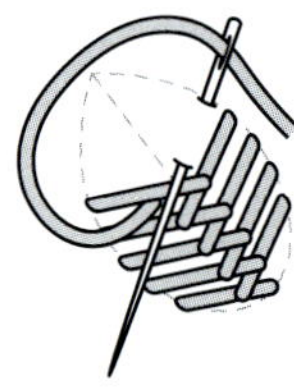

Do the same on a leaf or petal motif. Note that the last two stitches at the top of the leaf will be small and almost vertical.

Visual Library of Embroidery Stitches

HERRINGBONE STITCH AND ITS VARIATIONS

Since the Middle Ages, herringbone stitch has been used extensively, particularly for ombre or white embroidery and smocking. In sewing, it can be used for appliqués and hems. Variations of this stitch exist around the world.

Herringbone stitch and its variations can be embroidered on a free-line pattern or on counted-stitch fabric. It is worked "rocking the needle" (i.e., in a single movement).

Herringbone Stitch or Cross-Stitch

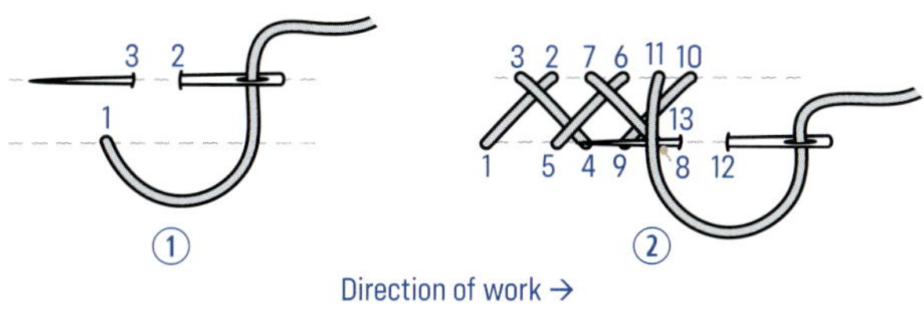

Herringbone stitch is embroidered on two parallel lines, from left to right and alternately on the top and bottom lines.

1 Take out the needle in 1, stitch in 2, and take out in 3 on the top line.

2 Stitch in 4 and out in 5 on the bottom line.

For left-handed users

Embroider from right to left.

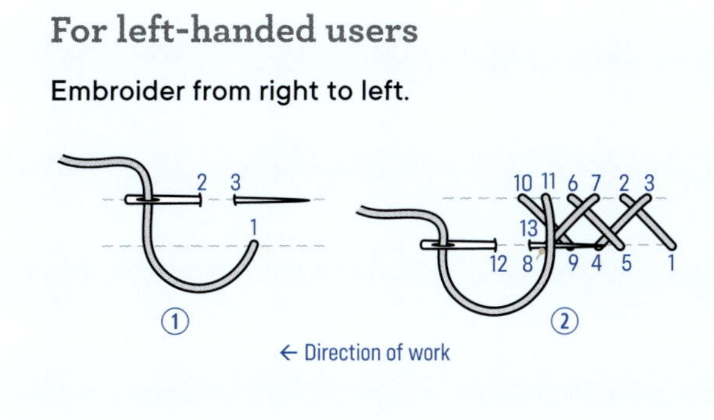

How to embroider a leaf in looped overlapping herringbone stitch

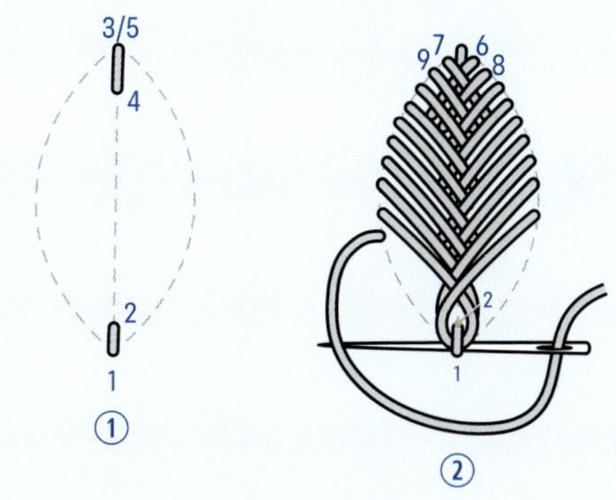

1 Embroider two straight stitches one on top of the other at 1 and 2 for a solid base. Embroider a straight stitch between 3 and 4 to form the tip of the leaf and exit at 5, very slightly to the left of 3.

2 Pass the needle under the vertical stitch at the base of the leaf and stitch in 6. Exit in 7, pass the needle under the vertical stitch at the base of the leaf, and stitch in 8.

Overlocking Herringbone Stitch

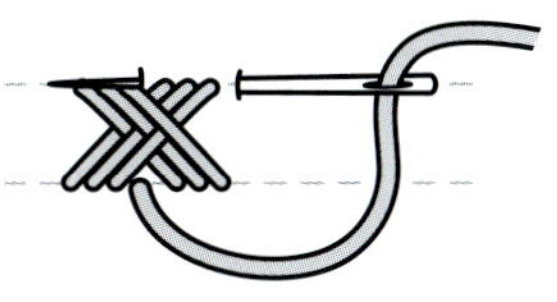

The overlapping herringbone stitch is embroidered by tightening the stitches: each stitch must touch the previous one.

Double Herringbone Stitch

The double bootie stitch can be performed in two ways.

Variation 1

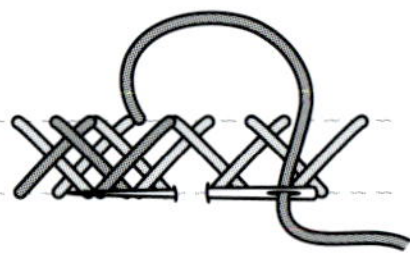

Work in two steps, using two different colored threads. With the first color, embroider a row in herringbone stitch; then with the other color, insert a second row into the first.

Variation 2

Work in the same way as for the first variation, but instead of pulling the needle out between two stitches, stitch and pull it out between the tops of the stitches in the previous row.

Braided Stitches

Braided stitches are embroidered all over the world. They combine cross-stitch (see page 87) and herringbone stitch (see page 95).

They are embroidered between two parallel horizontal or vertical lines. Before starting embroidery, mark regular spaces to indicate the width of the stitches, or work on counted-stitch fabric for greater ease.

Slavic variation

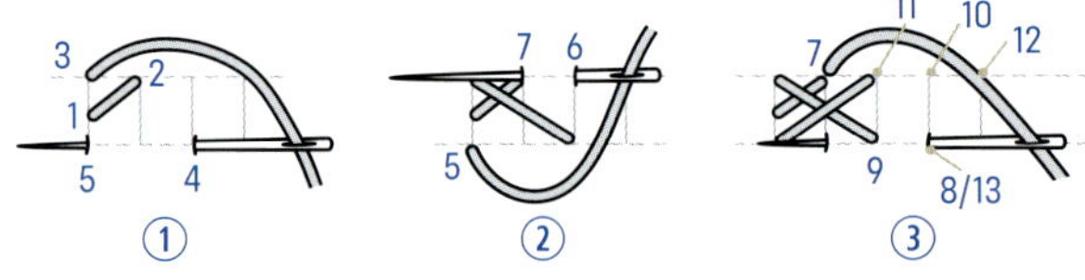

This variation is embroidered horizontally, from left to right.

1 Take out the needle in 1, halfway between the two horizontal lines, stitch in 2, and take out in 3 on the top line. Stitch in 4 and take out in 5 on the bottom line.

2 Stitch at 6 and exit at 7 on the top line (2 and 7 are merged).

3 Stitch at 8 and exit at 9 (plumb with 7) on the bottom line. Stitch at 10 and exit at 11 on the top line (11 and 6 are the same). Stitch at 12 and exit at 14 (14 and 4 are the same and plumb with 11).

Long-armed cross-stitch variation

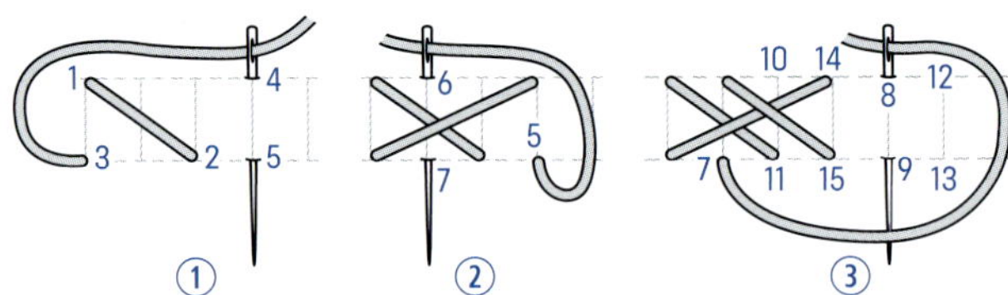

This variation is embroidered horizontally, from left to right. In contrast to the herringbone stitch, stitch the needle vertically in relation to the direction of work.

1 Take the needle out in 1, stitch in 2, and take out in 3 on the bottom line. Stitch in 4 and out in 5.

2 Stitch in 6 and out in 7.

3 Stitch in 8 and out in 9, stitch in 10 and out in 11, and so on.

Diagonal Slav variation

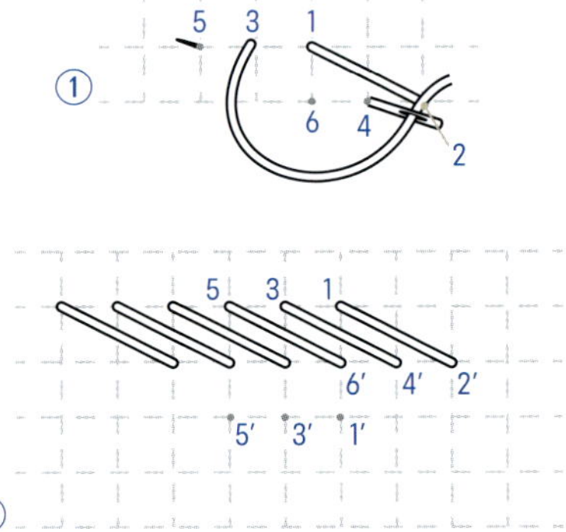

This variation is embroidered on three parallel horizontal lines.

1 Begin work by embroidering the bottom section (between the middle and bottom lines): take out the needle at 1 and stitch at 2, take out at 3 and stitch at 4, take out at 5 and stitch at 6, and so on.

2 Finish the bottom section and return to the beginning of the row. Then embroider the section (between the top and middle rows): exit at 1' and stitch at 2', exit at 3' and stitch at 4', exit at 5' and stitch at 6'.

Herringbone Stitch with Zigzag

Stitch one row in herringbone stitch, from left to right. Then stitch a zigzag straddling the herringbone stitch, from right to left.

Threaded Herringbone Stitch

The threaded herringbone stitch can be performed in two ways.

Variation 1

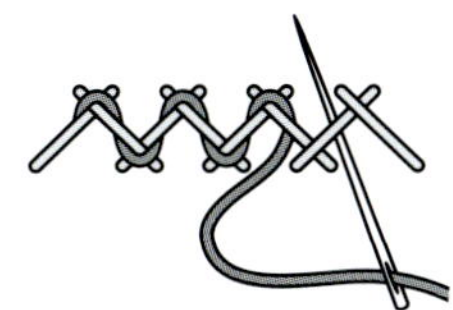

Embroider a row in herringbone stitch. Using the same thread or a thread in a contrasting color, take out the needle at the beginning of the row and stitch under each leg from top to bottom and from bottom to top, without piercing the fabric.

Variation 2

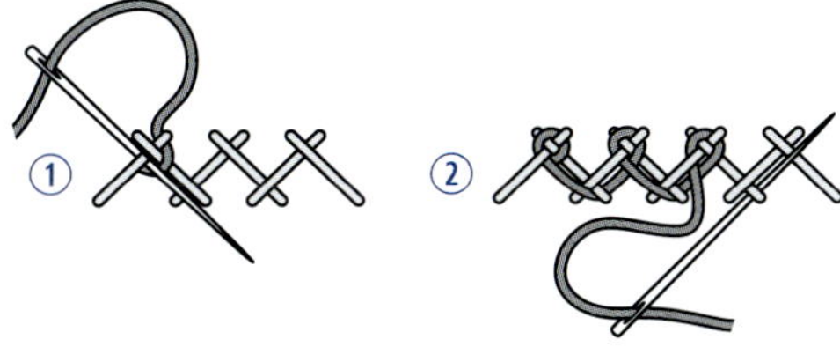

1 Embroider a row in herringbone stitch. Lace the top of the herringbone stitch as shown in the diagram, without piercing the fabric.

2 Pull the needle out from under the first stitch on the left. Turning counterclockwise, lace around the top intersection: pass over the first leg at bottom right, under the second, over the third, and under the fourth. Go down to the bottom intersection: pass over the first branch at bottom left and under the second. Go up to the next intersection at the top: pass over the first leg at bottom right, under the second, over the third, and under the fourth.

Tied Herringbone Stitch

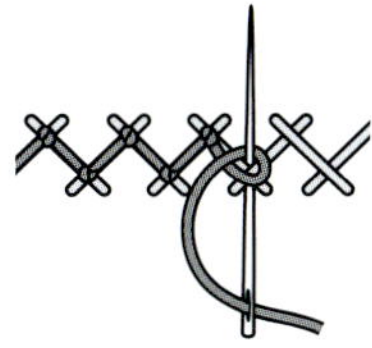

Embroider one row in herringbone stitch. Using a contrasting-colored thread, at the bottom of the herringbone stitch, pull the needle out from under the first stitch on the left and pass the thread from bottom to top under the crossing of the two legs. Make a loop by passing the thread over and then under the needle and pull to form a knot. On the top crossing, do the same, passing the needle from top to bottom.

Embroidered Herringbone Stitch

Stitch one row in herringbone stitch, then stitch a vertical backstitch over each intersection.

What You Need to Know

The holding stitches can also be horizontal *(left)* or cross-shaped (*right*).

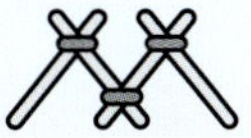

Chevron Stitch

The chevron stitch is embroidered on two horizontal lines.

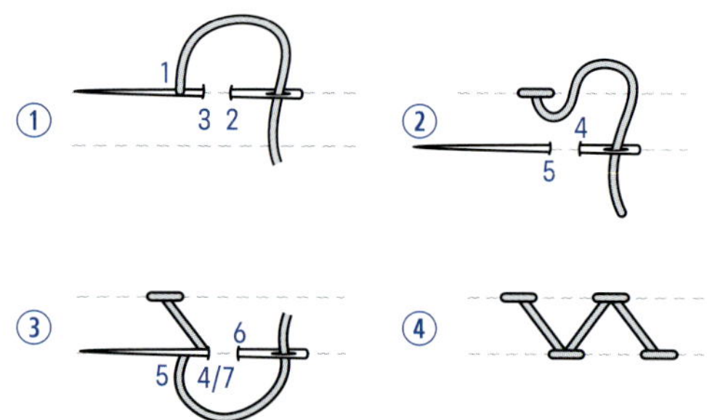

1 On the top line, take out the needle in 1, stitch in 2, and take out in 3, halfway between 1 and 2.

2 On the bottom line, stitch at point 4 and exit at point 5 to create an oblique stitch pointing to the right.

3 Stitch in 6 and out in 7 (7 and 4 are the same).

4 Continue alternately on the top and bottom lines.

Shadow Stitch or Double Backstitch

The shadow stitch is a tight, very regular herringbone stitch that appears on the reverse side of the ground fabric. On the right side, stitches are visible along the perimeter of the shape, as well as the ghosts of threads running along the back of the work.

This stitch should be embroidered on very fine, almost transparent fabrics (such as chiffon, organdie, or very fine batiste), so that the threads can be seen through to the right side. There are two ways to do this: on the wrong side or on the right side of the fabric. Choose the one that's easiest for you.

With face-to-face work

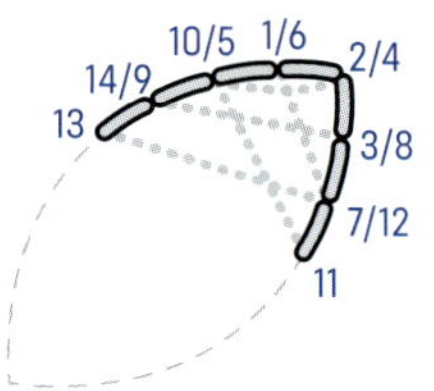

The stitches around the edge of the sheet must touch each other like a stitch.

Trace the design on the right side. Take the needle out at 1, stitch at 2, take out at 3, and stitch at 4 (4 and 2 are the same). Take out at 5 and stitch at 6 (6 and 1 are the same). Take out in 7 and stitch in 8 (8 and 3 are the same).

With face-to-face work

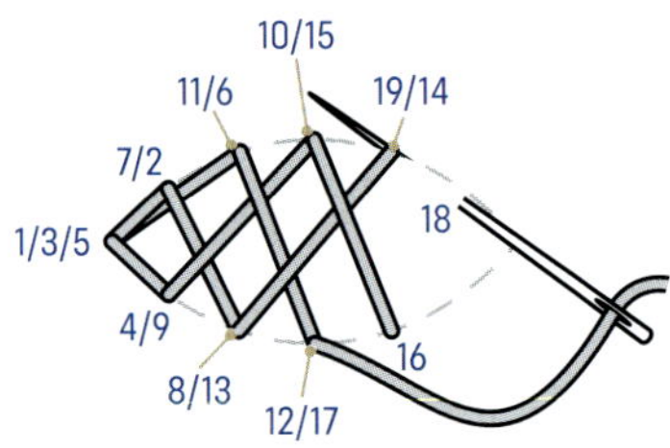

Trace the design on the reverse side. Insert needle 1, pull out 2, then insert 3 (1 and 3 are the same). Bring out 4 and pick up 5 (1, 3, and 5 are the same). Exit at 6 and pick at 7 (7 and 2 are the same). Go out at 8 and pick at 9 (9 and 4 are the same).

Visual Library of Embroidery Stitches

FEATHER STITCH AND ITS VARIATIONS

Feather stitch is similar to buttonhole and chain stitch. Highly decorative as a border or braid, it can also be used to embroider branches and leaves. Feather stitch and its variations are embroidered "en allant" (i.e., in a single movement).

Feather Stitch

Needlepoint can be embroidered in a variety of widths. Single, double, or triple, it's the width to be obtained that defines the number of lines to be drawn. Unless otherwise specified, the needle must be inserted and pulled out at an angle.

Single feather stitch

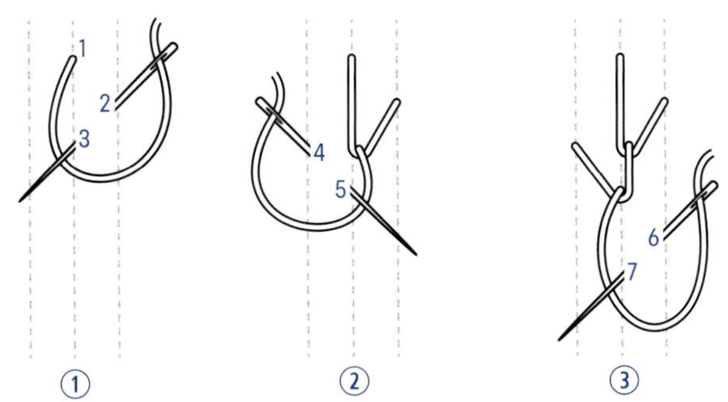

The simple feather stitch is embroidered on three parallel lines, from top to bottom.

On three lines:

1 Pull the needle out in 1 on the middle line. Stitch in 2 and pull out in 3. Pass the thread under the needle and pull out.

2 Stitch in 4 and out in 5. The needle should be stitched at the same height as the bottom of the previous stitch on the opposite side. Pass the thread under the needle and pull.

3 Stitch in 6, pull out in 7, and pass the thread under the needle and pull.

Feather stitch variation

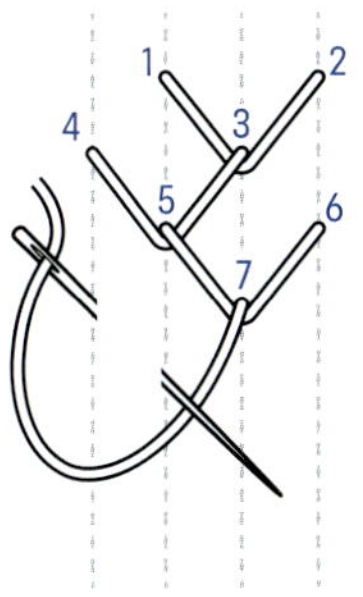

On four lines, the feather stitch will be wider and more tortuous.

1 Take out needle 1 on the second row from the left. Stitch in 2 and pull out in 3. Pass the thread under the needle and pull out.

2 Stitch in 4 and out in 5. The needle should be stitched at the same height as the bottom of the previous stitch on the opposite side. Pass the thread under the needle and pull.

3 Stitch in 6, pull out in 7, and pass the thread under the needle and pull.

Double feather stitch

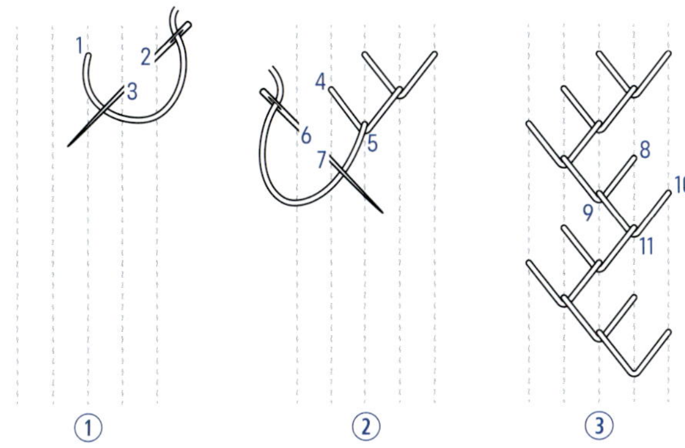

Double feather stitch is embroidered on five parallel lines, from top to bottom. The work is identical to single feather stitch, but with the addition of a stitch on either side of the middle line.

1 Pull the needle out in 1 on the middle line. Stitch in 2 and pull out in 3. Pass the thread under the needle and pull out.

2 Stitch in 4 and out in 5. Pass the thread under the needle and pull. Stitch in 6 and pull out in 7. Pass the thread under the needle and pull. Pick up in 8 and take out in 9. Pass the thread under the needle and pull. Pick up in 10 and take out in 11. Pass the thread under the needle and pull.

Triple feather stitch

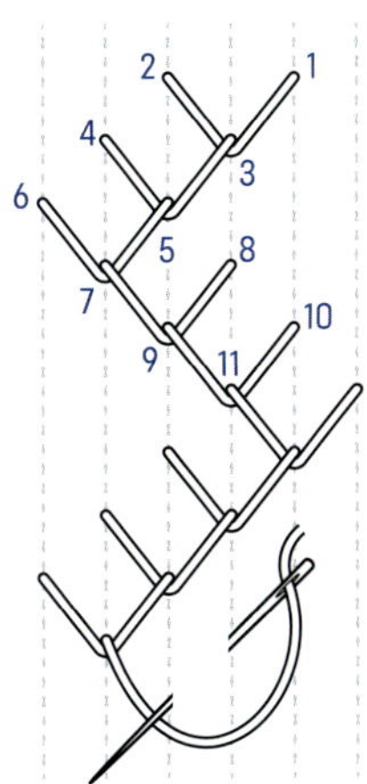

The triple feather stitch is embroidered on six parallel lines, from top to bottom.

1 Take out needle 1 on the fifth row from the left. Stitch in 2 and out in 3. Pass the thread under the needle and pull.

2 Stitch in 4 and out in 5. Pass the thread under the needle and pull.

3 Stitch in 6 and out in 7. Pass the thread under the needle and pull out.

4 Stitch in 8 and out in 9. Pass the thread under the needle and pull.

5 Stitch in 10 and out in 11. Pass the thread under the needle and pull.

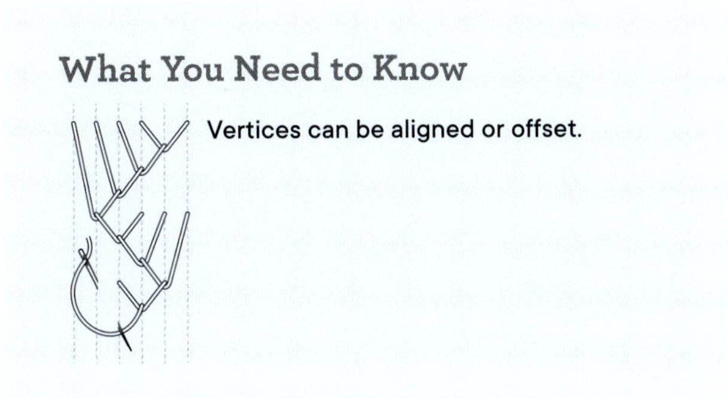

What You Need to Know

Vertices can be aligned or offset.

Unilateral feather stitch

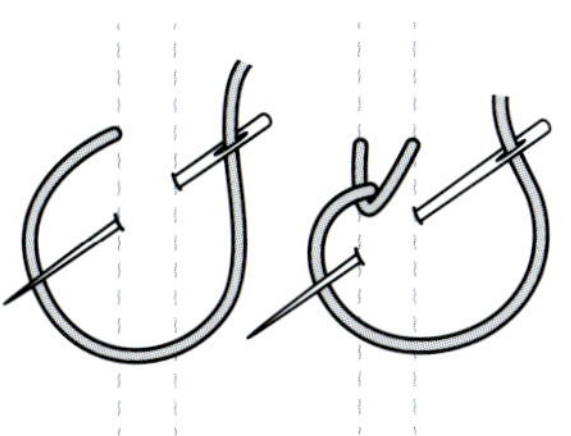

Unilateral feather stitch is embroidered on two parallel lines, from top to bottom. Embroider it in the same way as single feather stitch, always stitching in and out on the same side.

Closed feather stitch

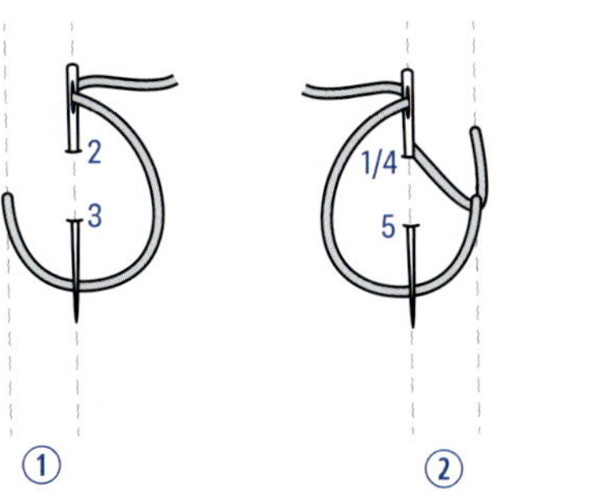

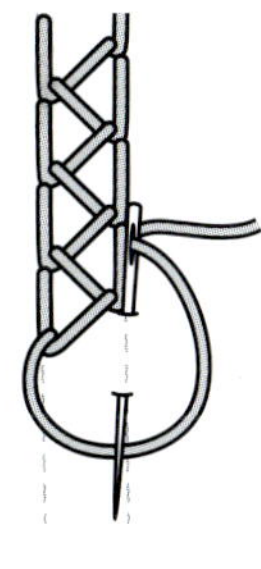

The closed feather stitch is embroidered on two parallel lines, from top to bottom.

Embroider it in the same way as the simple feather stitch, stitching just below the previous embroidered stitch. Be careful: the needle must be extended vertically.

1 Take out needle 1 on the left-hand line. Stitch in 2 and exit in 3, needle vertical, on the right-hand line. Pass the thread under the needle and pull.

2 Stitch in 4 and out in 5, needle vertical (1 and 4 are the same). Pass the thread under the needle and pull.

Variation of closed feather stitch

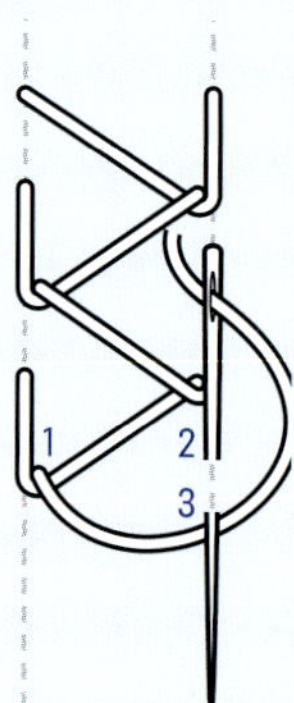

Take out needle 1 on the left-hand line. Stitch in 2 and exit in 3, needle vertical, on the right-hand line. Pass the thread under the needle and pull. Stitch in 4 and out in 5, needle vertical. Pass the thread under the needle and pull.

The result is very similar to a chevron stitch (see page 98).

Wheatear Stitch

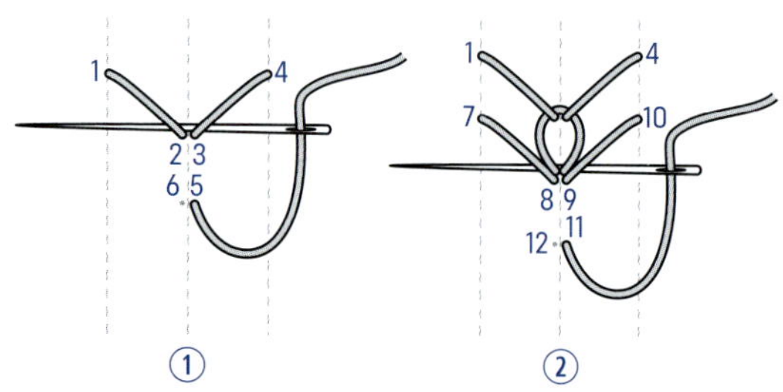

The wheatear stitch is embroidered on three parallel lines, from top to bottom.

1 Bring the needle out in 1 and stitch in 2 to the left of the centerline. Bring out in 3 to the right of the centerline and stitch in 4. Bring out in 5 to the right of the centerline, pass the needle under the first two slanted stitches, and stitch in 6, to the left of the centerline.

2 Make two new diagonal straight stitches on either side of the previously embroidered loop, repeating step 1 in its entirety. Exit in 11 and pass the needle under the two straight stitches and under the previous loop.

Cretan Stitch

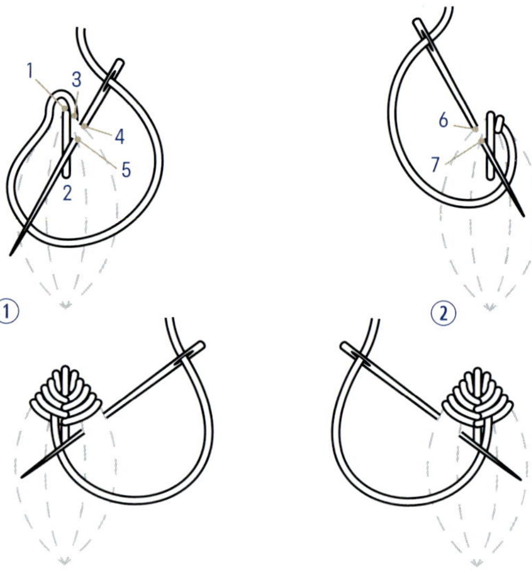

Cretan stitch is ideal for embroidering foliage. It is embroidered from top to bottom, alternating left and right and always pricking the needle at an angle, as with feather stitch (see page 101).

1 Trace two central veins. Embroider a vertical straight stitch between 1 and 2, about a third of the way up the leaf. Bring out the needle in 3 on the right-hand edge of the leaf, just next to 1. Stitch in 4 next to 3 and partially bring out in 5 on the right-hand vein. Pass the thread under the needle and pull.

2 Stitch in 6 on the left edge of the sheet and pull out partially in 7, on the left vein. Pass the thread under the needle and pull.

Fly Stitch

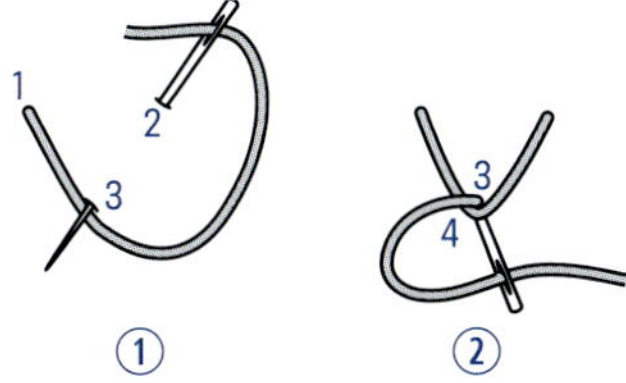

The feather stitch can be embroidered singly or in a line. It forms a V.

1 Pull the needle out at point 1, stitch at point 2, and partially pull out at point 3, with the needle at an angle. Pass the thread under the needle tip.

2 Stitch in 4, to lock the V-stitch at its base.

Visual Library of Embroidery Stitches

KNOTTED EMBROIDERY STITCHES

Knotted stitches are used to create decorative knots on the right side of the work. Preferably with a milliners needle, they can be embroidered singly, in fillers, or in rows.

French Knot

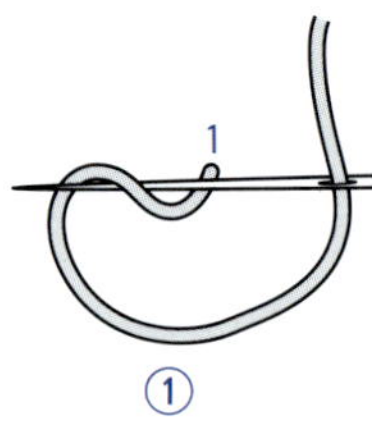

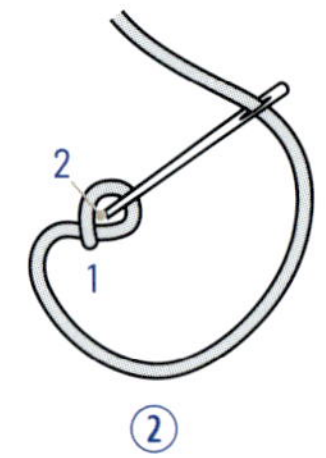

1 Take out needle 1. With your left hand, pull the thread toward you and place the needle perpendicular to the thread. Still with your left hand, wrap the thread around the needle.

2 Partially stitch the needle in 2, next to 1. Slide the knot to the fabric. Position the knot correctly and pull the entire needle through to the wrong side of the fabric.

Double-Turn French Knot

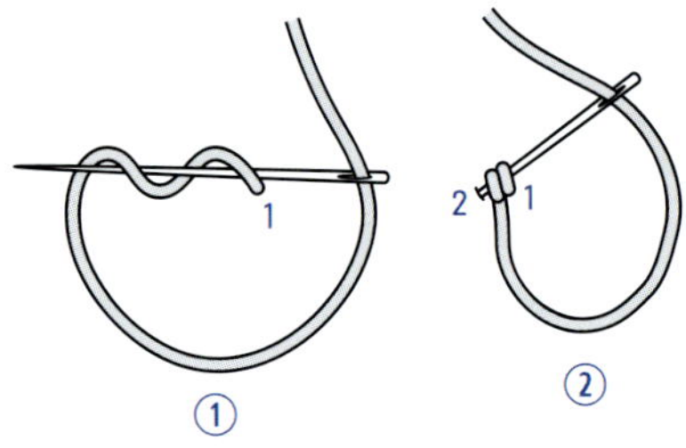

1 Take out needle 1. With your left hand, pull the thread toward you and place the needle perpendicular to the thread. Still with your left hand, wrap the thread twice around the needle.

2 Partially stitch the needle in 2, next to 1. Slide the knot to the fabric. Position the knot correctly and pull the entire needle through to the wrong side of the fabric.

Pistil Stitch

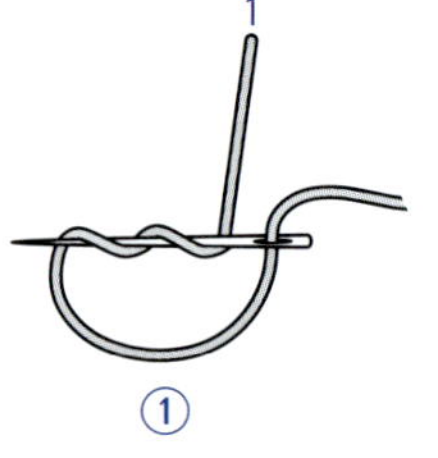

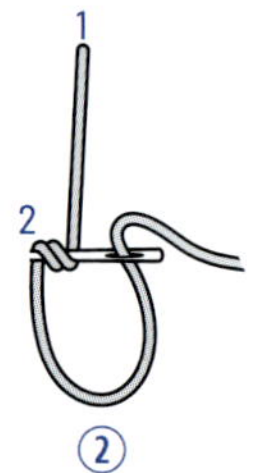

Embroider from right to left.

1 Take out needle 1. With your left hand, pull the thread toward you and place the needle perpendicular to the thread. Still with your left hand, wrap the thread twice around the needle.

2 Partially stitch the needle into the fabric in 2 (2 is more or less distant from 1, depending on the desired stem length). Slide the knot through to the fabric. Position the knot correctly and pull the entire needle through to the wrong side of the fabric.

French Knot Variation

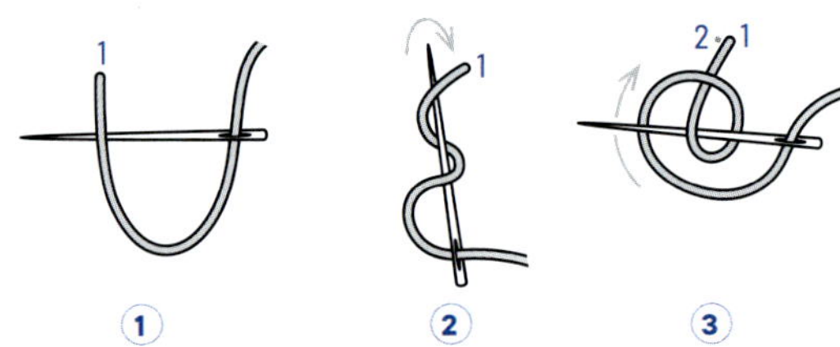

The French knot variation is rounder and more raised than the French knot. It is also less fragile on clothing.

1 Take out the needle in 1. With your left hand, pull the thread toward you and pass the needle perpendicularly under the thread.

2 Pointing toward the fabric with your right hand, turn the needle clockwise to wrap the thread around once.

3 Return the needle to its original position. With your left hand, place the thread in front of the needle, passing over it. Bring it back toward you, passing under the needle point with your left hand. Partially stitch the needle into the fabric in 2, to the left of 1. Slide the knot through to the fabric. Position the seed stitch correctly and pull the entire needle through to the wrong side of the fabric.

Colonial Knot Stitch

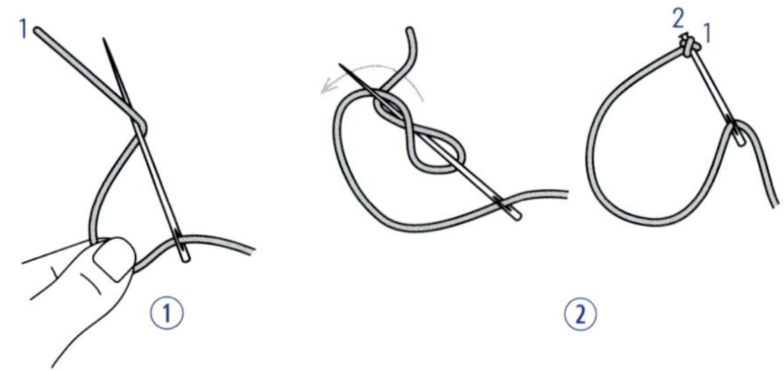

1 Take out needle 1. With your left hand, pull the thread toward you and pass the needle under the thread from the left. The needle tip is toward the fabric.

2 Pass the thread over the needle, from left to right, then under, from right to left. Partially stitch the needle into the fabric in 2, to the left of 1. Slide the knot through to the fabric. Position the colonial knot correctly and pull the entire needle through to the wrong side of the fabric.

Chinese Knot Stitch or Peking Knot

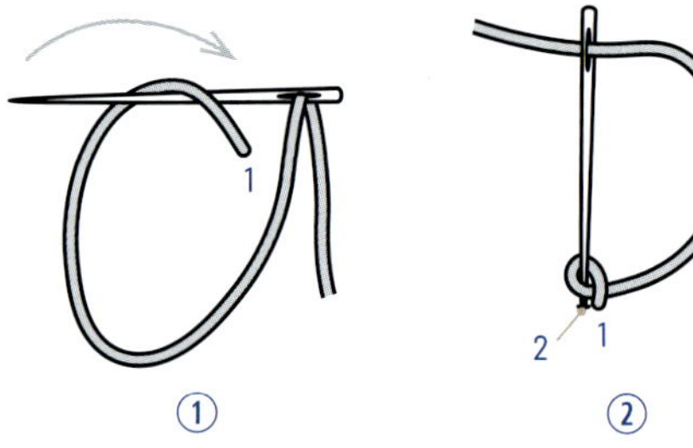

The Peking knot resembles the French knot but is flatter. Moreover, the knotting gesture is not the same.

1 Take out needle 1. With your left hand, stretch the thread to the left and pass the needle under the thread, from top to bottom. Still with your right hand, turn the needle clockwise, with the point toward the fabric.

2 Partially stitch the needle into the fabric in 2, to the right of 1. Slide the knot through to the fabric. Position the Peking knot correctly and pull the entire needle through to the wrong side of the fabric.

Single Pearl Stitch

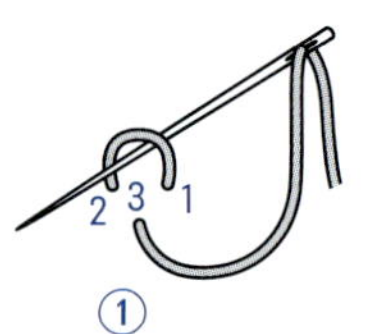

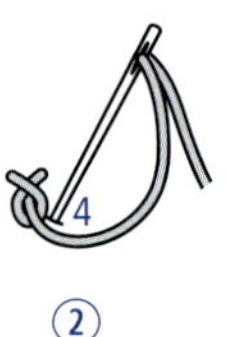

1 Take out the needle in 1 and stitch in 2, leaving a little length in the stitch. Pull out in 3 and pull the thread slightly to the right. Pass the needle up and down under the stitch formed. Rotate the needle clockwise to twist the loop, while pulling it downward.

2 Stitch in 4, to the right of the crossed loop.

Sorbello Stitch

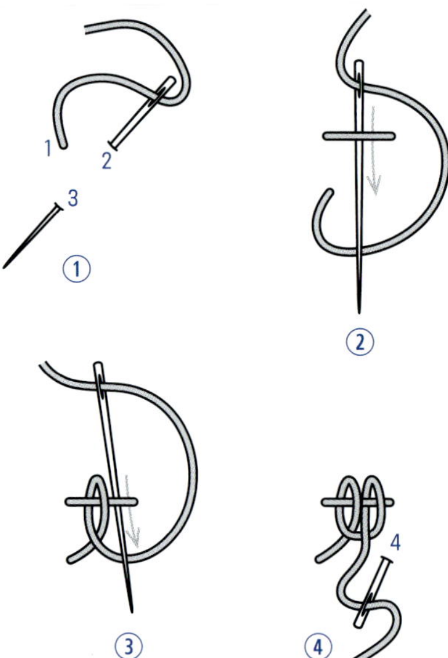

1 Take out the needle in 1, stitch in 2, and take out in 3.

2 Pass the needle up and down under the formed stitch.

3 Pass the needle up and down under the stitch a second time, this time with the thread under the needle tip.

4 Stitch in 4.

Knotted Cross-Stitch

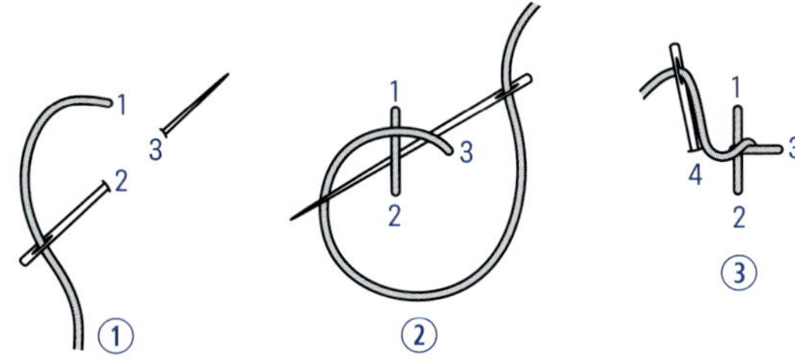

1 Take out the needle in 1, stitch in 2, and take out in 3.

2 Pass the needle from right to left under the formed stitch and slide its tip over the thread. Form the knot.

3 Stitch in 4 to make a cross.

Bullion Knot

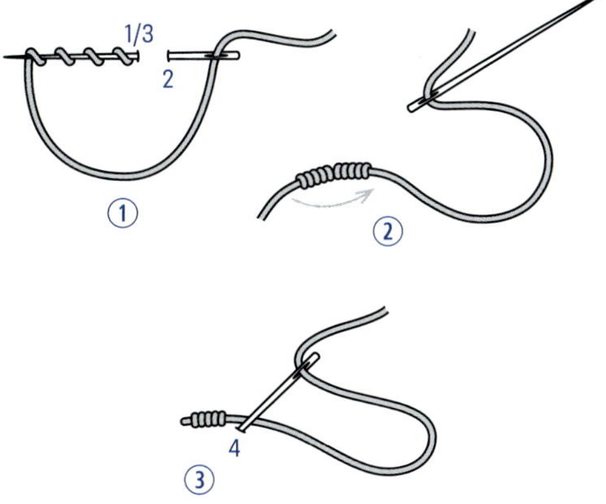

1 Extend the needle at 1, stitch at 2, and partially extend at 3 (1 and 3 are merged). The distance between 1 and 2 determines the stitch length. Wrap the thread around the needle until you reach the desired stitch length (i.e., the distance between 1 and 2).

2 Slide the loops along the needle to bring them closer to 1. Hold them between thumb and forefinger, then gently pull on the needle. Tilt the stitch to bring the output thread above 2.

3 Place the assembly correctly before inserting the needle in 4 (2 and 4 are the same).

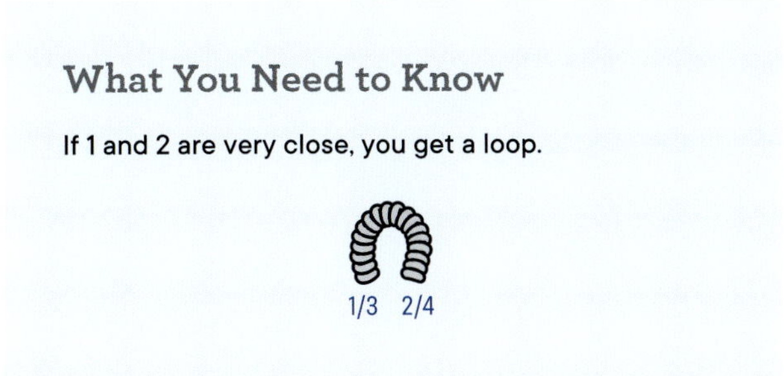

Cast-On Stitch

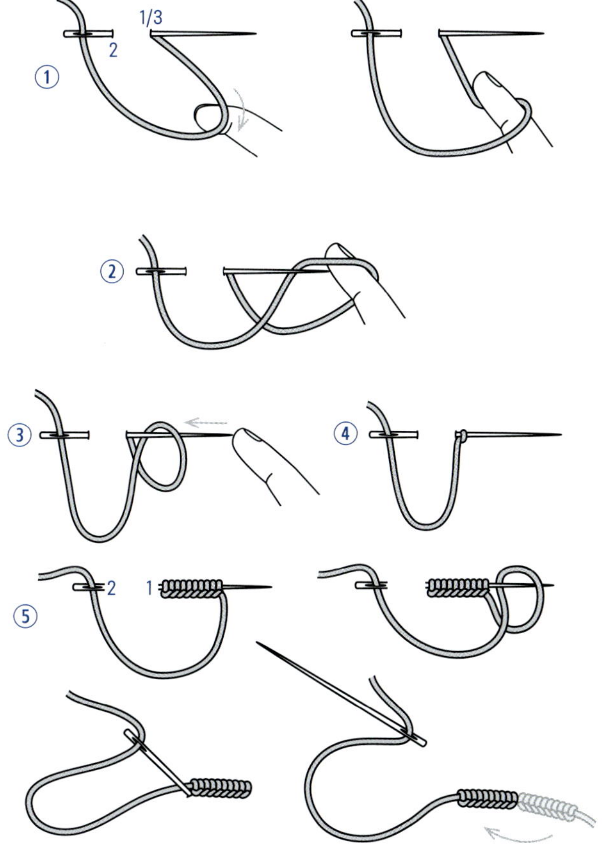

Carry out the same work as for the bullion knot, but instead of simply winding the thread onto the needle, cast on a series of buttonhole stitches.

1 Take out the needle in 1. Pass the thread around your left index finger.

2 Turn your left index finger to form a loop.

3 Place your index finger on the tip of the needle.

4 Slide the loop over the needle.

5 Make as many buttonhole stitches as necessary to cover the length between 1 and 2.

Drizzle Stitch

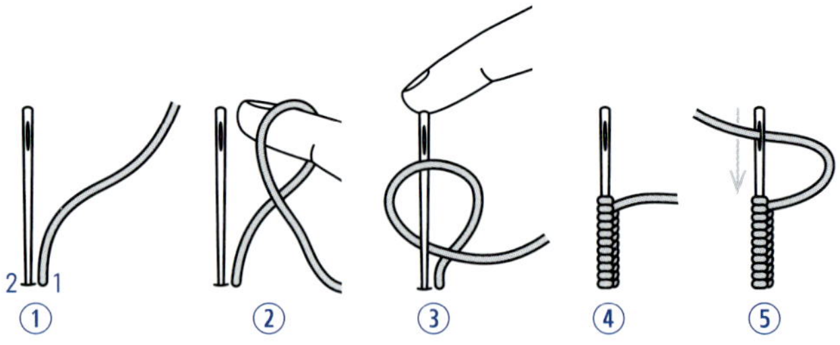

1 Take out needle 1 and unthread the needle.

2, 3, and 4 Partially prick the needle in 2. Wrap the thread around your finger and thread 10 to 12 scalloped loops onto the needle, as if knitting stitches.

5 Thread the needle and gently pull the needle through the back of the work.

Spanish Feather Stitch or Dutch Feather Stitch

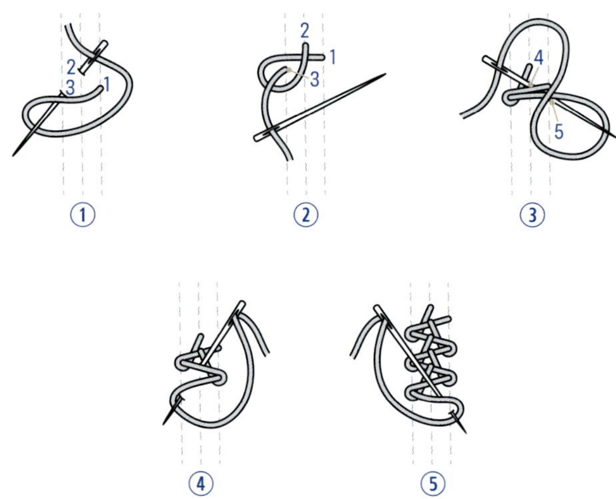

Spanish thorn stitch is embroidered on three parallel lines, from top to bottom.

1 and 2 Pull the needle out in 1, stitch in 2, and partially pull out in 3. Pass the thread over and then under the needle and pull. The thread forms a loop.

3 and 4 Stitch in 4 and partially out in 5 (4 is behind the thread crossing of the previous stitch and 5 on the third line). Pass the thread over and then under the needle and pull.

5 Continue, always stitching on the middle line, alternating each stitch on the right and left.

Coral Stitch

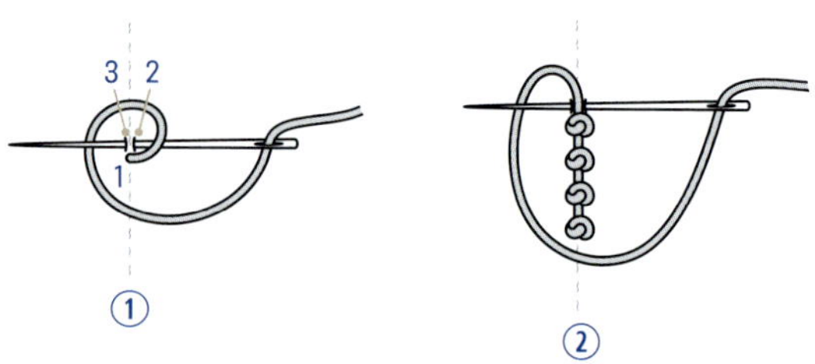

Coral stitch is embroidered on a line, from bottom to top.

1 Pull the needle out in 1, stitch in 2, and partially pull out in 3, on either side of the line. Pass the thread over and under the needle to form a loop. Pull the needle through to make the knot.

2 Repeat, spacing the stitches according to the desired effect.

Braided Coral Stitch

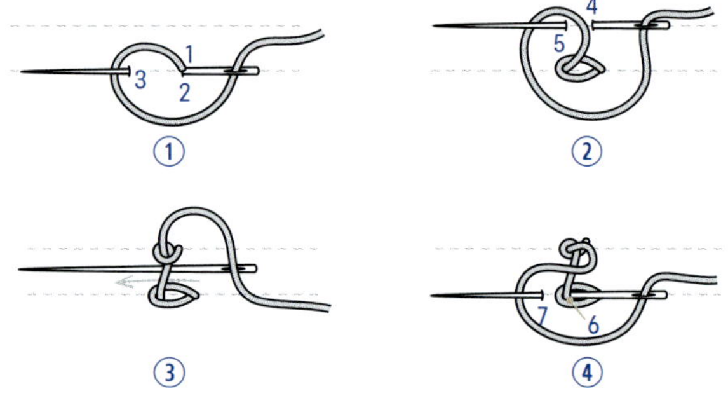

Braided coral stitch is embroidered on two parallel lines, from right to left, working alternately between the top and bottom lines. Don't forget to pass the needle under the thread on the way down.

1 On the bottom line, take out the needle at 1, stitch at 2 (1 and 2 are the same), and partially take out at 3. Pass the thread under the needle, from top to bottom, and pull out.

2 On the top line, stitch in 4 and out in 5. Pass the thread over and then under the needle and pull.

3 Pass the needle from right to left under the thread stretched between the two lines.

4 On the bottom line, stitch in 6 and out in 7 (6 and 3 are the same). Pass the thread under the needle from top to bottom and pull.

Weapon Stitch or Snail Stitch

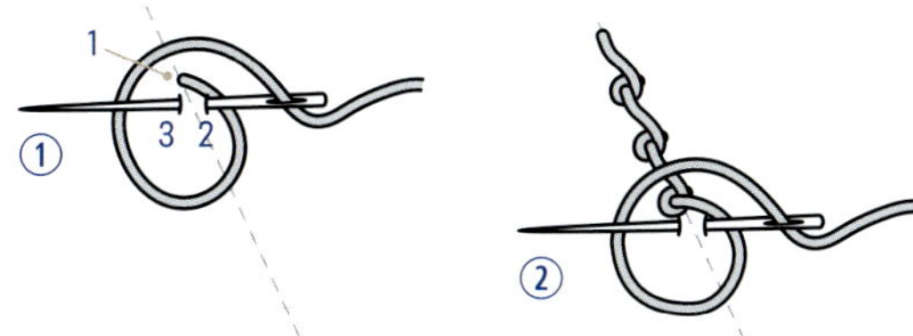

Weapon stitch is embroidered on a line, from top to bottom or from right to left. With wider stitches, a scale is formed.

1 Pull the needle out at 1, stitch at 2, and partially pull out at 3. Turning clockwise, pass the thread under the eye of the needle, then under its point.

2 Pull the thread through to form a loop.

Palestrina Stitch

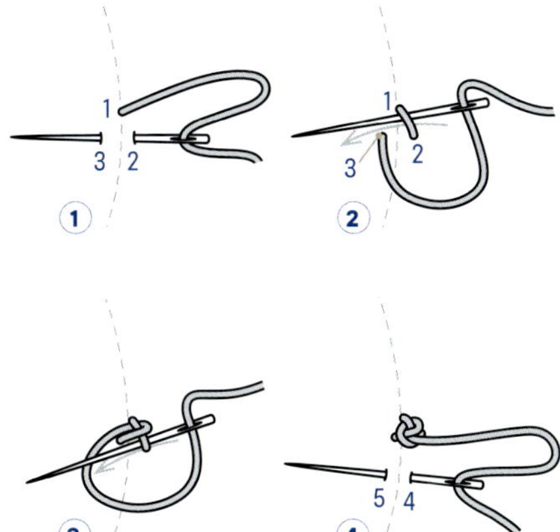

Palestrina stitch is embroidered on a line, from top to bottom.

1 Take out the needle in 1, stitch in 2, and take out in 3.

2 Pass the needle from right to left under the formed stitch.

3 Pass the needle again under this same point, but below the previous passage, sliding the thread under the needle tip. Pull gently to form a knot.

4 Stitch in 4 and out in 5.

Visual Library of Embroidery Stitches

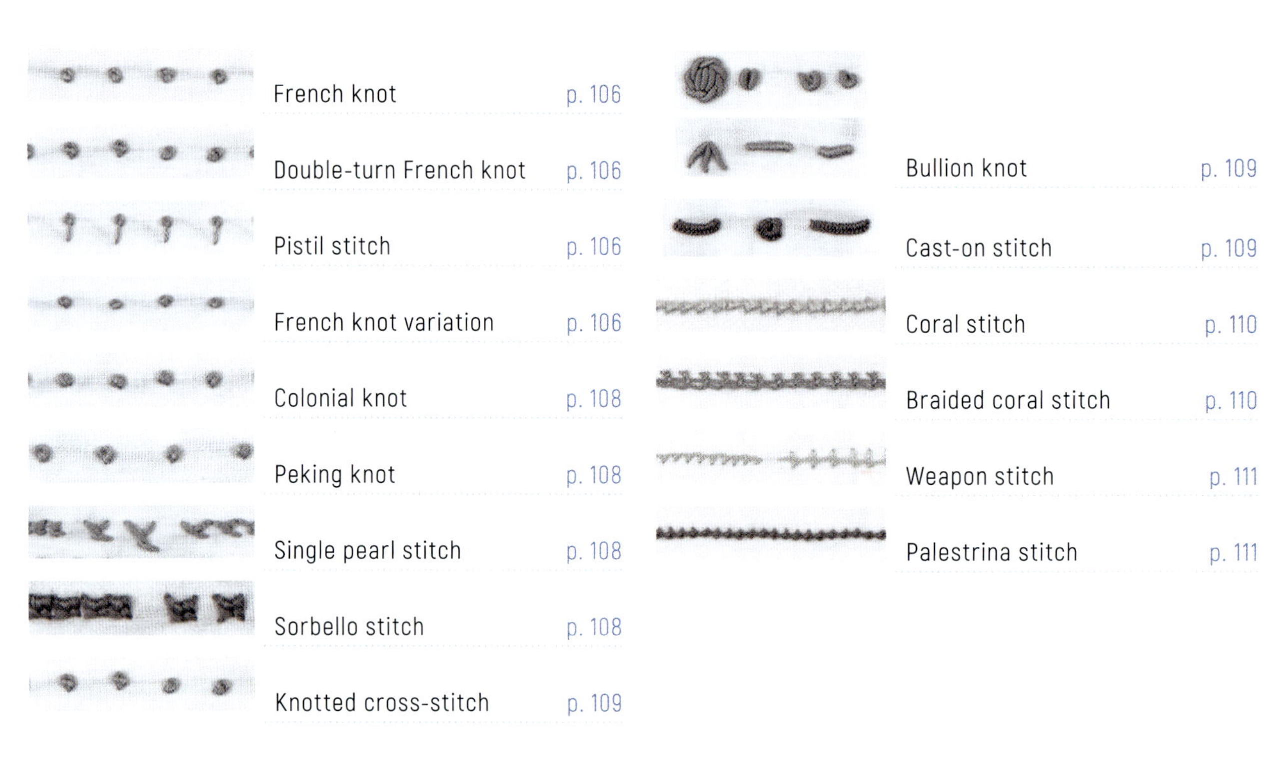

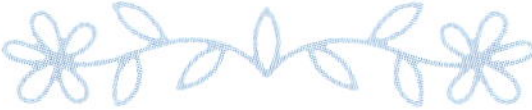

WOVEN STITCHES

Woven stitches seem to be as old as cloth weaving and fabric weaving, which dates back to at least 7,000 BCE. They have been known for centuries throughout the world: in Europe, Southeast Asia, and Latin America.

Embroidered on threads stretched over the right side of the work, most of these stitches are used for filling. Some are ideal for relief embroidery (see page 205), while others form braids or give the embroidered work a woven look.

Simple Woven Stitch

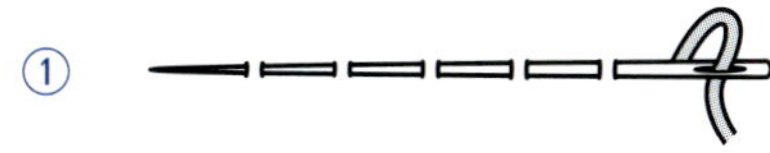

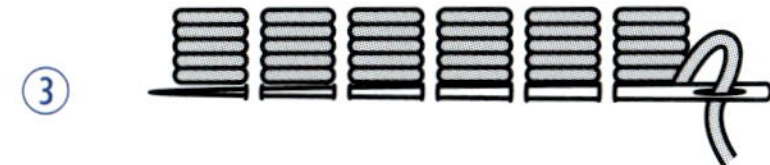

Simple darning fill stitch is made up of running stitches of variable length. It is usually embroidered in the straight thread of the ground fabric, on a fabric whose threads can be counted.

1 Embroider a line of running stitches, one fabric warp thread apart.

2 and 3 In order to conserve thread, turn the hoop 180° between each line to go back and forth.

Warning

Be careful not to overtighten the work to avoid puckering the fabric.

Simple darning fill stitch is embroidered following a design previously transferred to the ground fabric, or by creating your own motifs. To do this, count the warp threads left between each embroidered stitch and line.

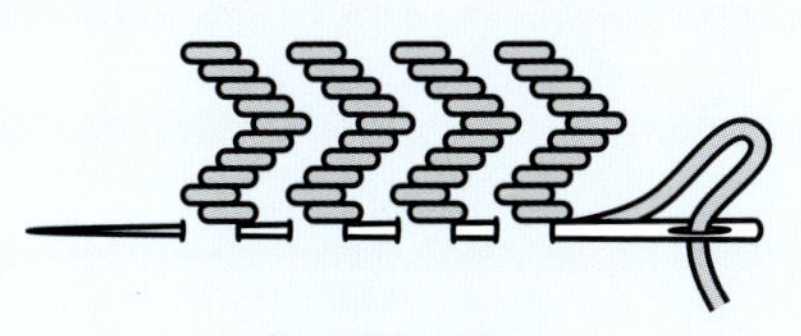

Geometric pattern

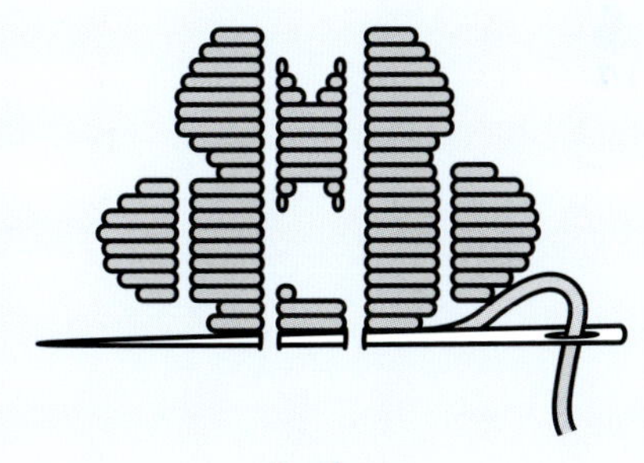

Freeform

Woven Wheel Stitch

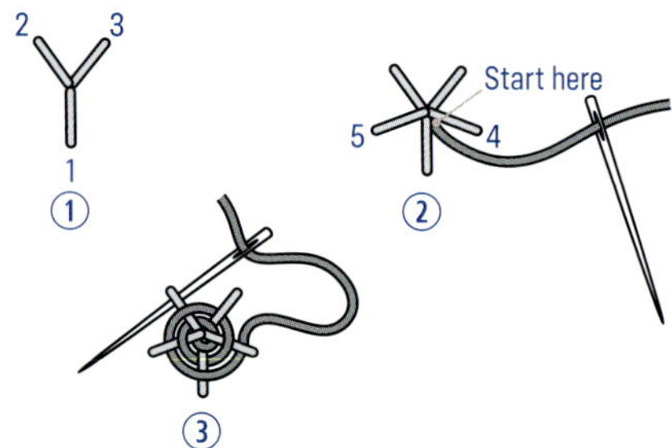

The wheel stitch is used to embroider roses. It is created by weaving a star with an odd number of branches (five or seven).

Tips for Good Embroidery

The star, which is the flower's skeleton, is embroidered first, so it's essential that the foundation star is solid.

1 Securely fasten the thread to the back of the project, using a lasso start, for example (see page 39). Form a Y with three straight stitches: exit at 1 and stitch in the center, exit at 2 and stitch in the center, then exit at 3 and stitch in the center.

2 Add a point on each side: take out at 4 and prick in the center, then take out at 5 and prick in the center. Take out between two points of the star, as close as possible to the center of the flower.

3 Pass the needle under one point, over the next, and so on, without piercing the fabric. When the wheel is full, pull the needle through to the wrong side.

Whipped Wheel Stitch

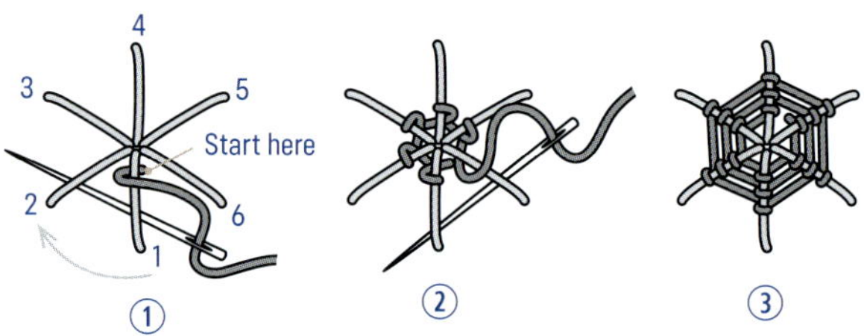

The whipped spider stitch is used to embroider flowers. The result is very pretty with threads in gradient colors, as with DMC Color Variations Embroidery Floss.

This stitch is made on a star with six to twelve branches. The number of branches increases with the diameter of the flower to be embroidered (e.g., six branches for a 6mm diameter rose, eight for a 10mm diameter rose).

Tips for Good Embroidery

The star, which is the skeleton of the flower, is embroidered first, so it's essential that the foundation star stitches are strong. Tighten the thread regularly to ensure clean work.

1 Securely fasten the thread to the back of the work, using a lasso start, for example (see page 39). Embroider the star in straight stitch, starting at the ends of the points and stitching through to the center. Pull out between two star legs, as close as possible to the center of the flower.

2 Pass once under leg 1, then a second time under leg 2, without piercing the fabric. Pass again under leg 2, also passing under leg 3, without piercing the fabric.

3 Each leg is thus whipped around. Spiral around the star, repeating these steps until the star is completely filled. Pass the needle over the wrong side of the work to finish.

Raised Stem Stitch Band

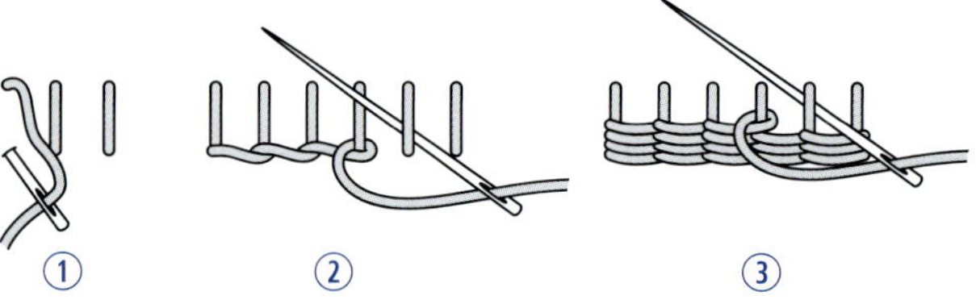

1 Embroider several parallel vertical straight stitches to form a ladder.

2 and 3 Embroider each line, always starting from the left: pass the needle from right to left under each bar.

Needle Weaving

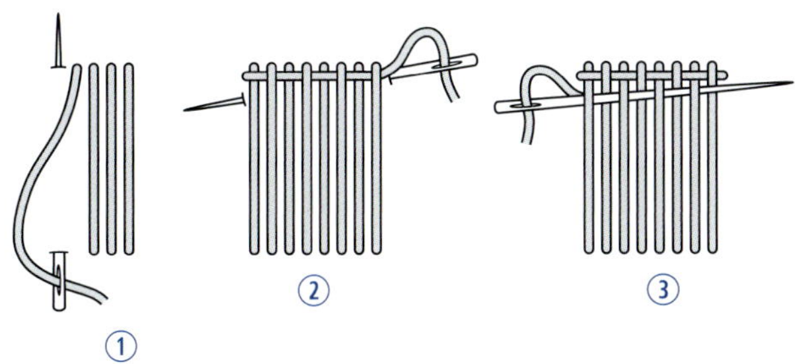

1 Form the embroidery warp by embroidering vertical straight stitches.

2 and 3 Weave the thread horizontally, alternating under and over the next thread. Embroider the next line, starting on the same side, but alternating above and below the previous line.

Two-Tone Raised Woven Band

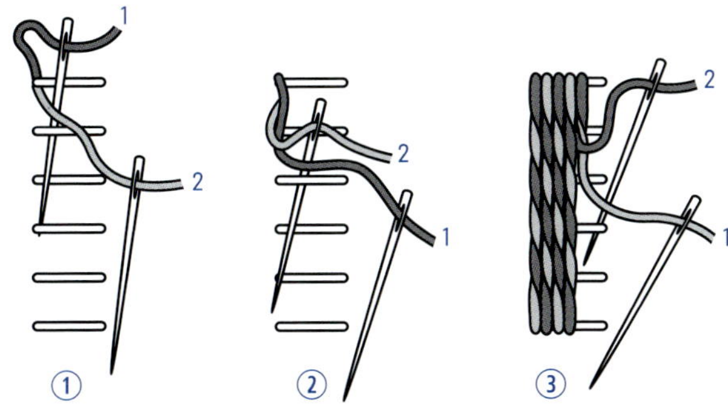

1 Embroider parallel straight stitches to form a ladder. Prepare two thread needles in contrasting colors. Bring out the top left of the ladder: needle 1 above the first rung and needle 2 below.

2 Weave the threads onto the rungs, passing needle 1 under the second rung and needle 2 under the third. Pass needle 1 under the fourth rung and needle 2 under the fifth, and so on to the bottom of the ladder.

3 Return to the top of the ladder for the next row. Make as many rows as necessary to fill the ladder.

Honeycomb Filling

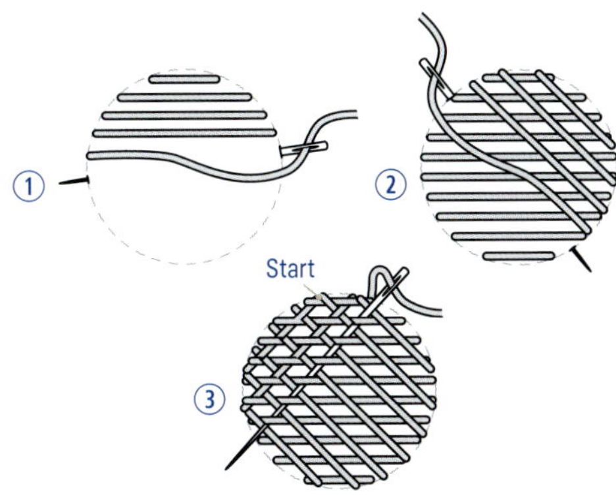

The honeycomb filling is used to cover a shape.

1 Embroider with parallel, evenly spaced horizontal straight stitches.

2 Starting at the top left, cover the horizontal dots with parallel, evenly spaced diagonal straight stitches.

3 Starting at the top right, weave in the second diagonal lines, passing the needle over the first diagonal stitches and under the horizontal stitches until the entire surface to be embroidered is covered.

Lattice Filling Stitch

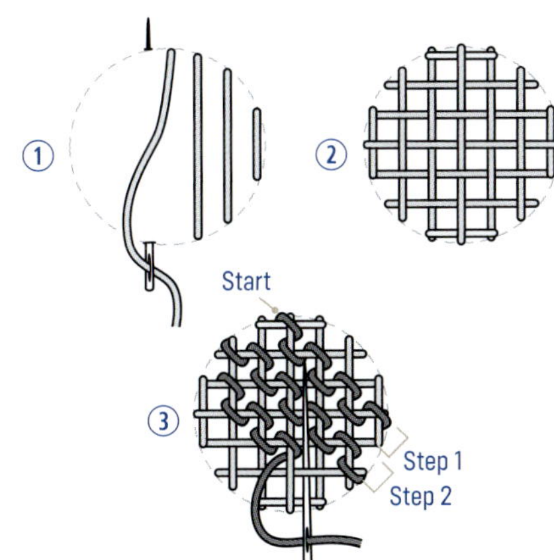

1 Embroider with parallel, evenly spaced vertical straight stitches.

2 Embroider a horizontal lattice on vertical straight stitches by weaving horizontal lines of straight stitches on vertical stitches.

3 With a contrasting color yarn, take the needle out at the top left and pass under the yarn from top to bottom and from right to left after the first intersection of row 1. Pass the needle from bottom to top and from right to left after the first intersection of row 2, and so on, always starting from the left.

Stitches Woven on a Stem Stitch Band

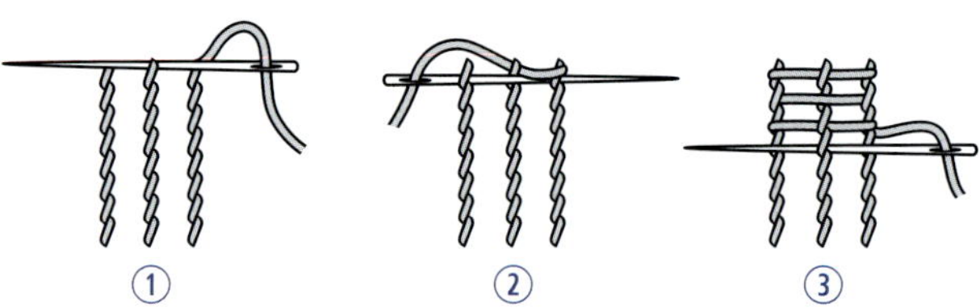

Stitches woven on a stem stitch band are embroidered in lines or curves and on an odd number of lines. The technique is exactly the same, whatever the number of lines embroidered.

1 Embroider three lines parallel to the stem stitch. Pass the needle from right to left, alternately over the right-edge stitch, under the middle stitch, and over the left-edge stitch.

2 For the bottom line, pass the needle from left to right alternately under the left-edge stitch, over the middle stitch, and under the right-edge stitch.

3 Continue, alternating the two previous steps.

Stitches Woven on a Chain Stitch

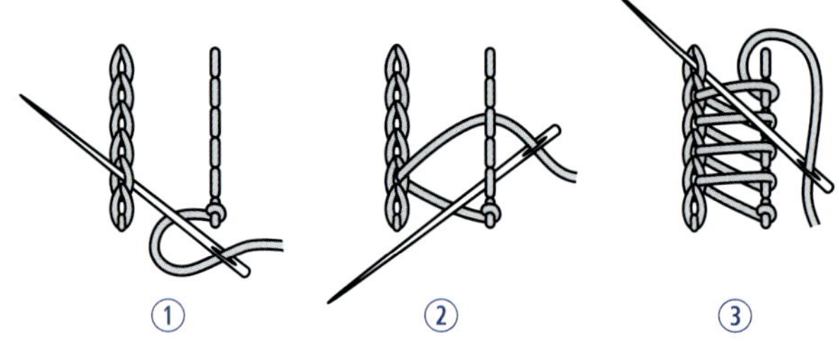

Stitches woven on a chain stitch are used to form braids. Trace the first stitches or work on counted-stitch canvases.

1 Embroider a line in chain stitch and a line in backstitch, perfectly parallel. Make sure the stitches are the same size and height. Exit at the base of the stitch. Pass under the first stitch and then under the second chain stitch.

2 Pass under the second stitch, then under the third chain stitch (right-hand chain thread).

Variations

Variation 1

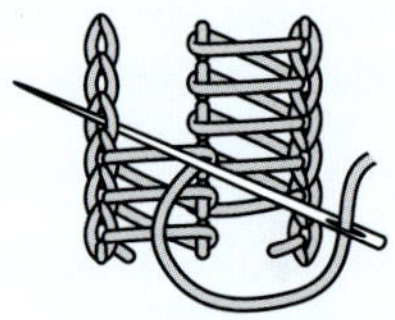

Embroider a second line in chain stitch to the right of the backstitch and then do the same weaving.

Variation 2

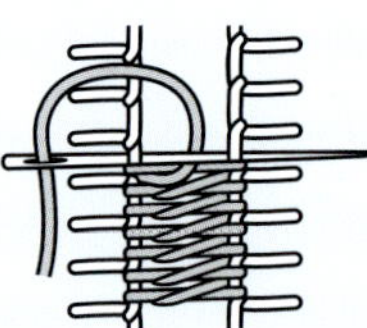

Embroider two parallel rows in buttonhole stitch, ensuring that the stitches face each other. Then perform the same weaving operation.

Variation 3

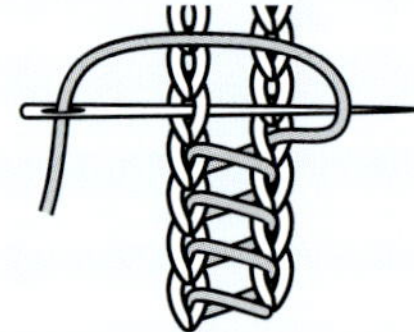

Embroider two parallel lines in chain stitch, making sure the stitches are facing each other. Then perform the same weaving operation.

Wheat Grain

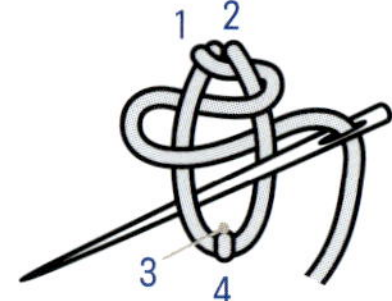

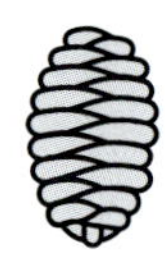

Highly embossed, the wheat grain is a small stitch well suited to embroidering insect bodies or congress cloth tips.

Embroider a large loop stitch: exit at 1, stitch at 2, exit at 3, and stitch at 4. Weave the loop stitch alternately under and over the left and right threads.

Interlaced Lattice

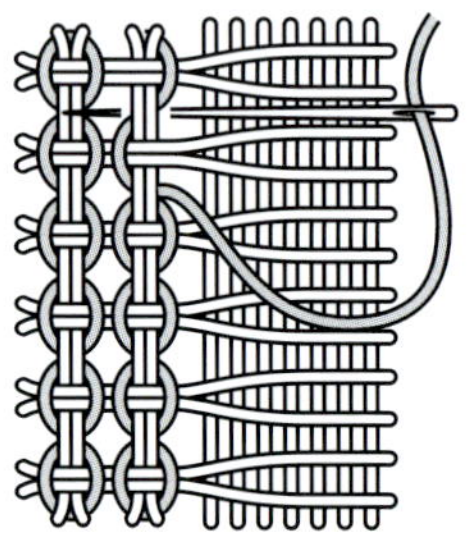

1 Embroider a regular lattice, using parallel, evenly spaced vertical throws. Then embroider evenly spaced horizontal throws at right angles to the vertical throws.

2 Using a different color yarn, interlace the first two vertical cast-off stitches of the network, from top to bottom: bring the needle out at the top between the first two vertical cast-off stitches. Pass the needle from left to right under the second vertical cast-on stitch.

3 Pass the needle over the first two horizontal cast-off stitches and from right to left under the vertical cast-off stitches.

4 Pass the needle over the next two horizontal throws under the vertical throws, then from left to right. Continue until you reach the bottom.

5 Carry out the same work from bottom to top, always on the first two vertical points of the trellis. Ensure that the new interlaced points are opposite those of the descending work.

6 Embroider the entire lattice in the same way.

Openwork Lattice

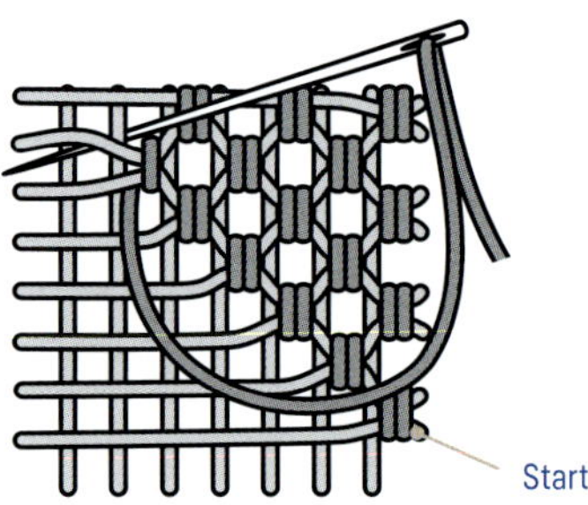

1 Embroider a regular lattice, using parallel, evenly spaced vertical throws. Then embroider evenly spaced horizontal throws at right angles to the vertical throws. Work diagonally from bottom to top and from right to left.

2 Using a thread of a different color, wrap the two horizontal threads together twice, stitching into the fabric. After the second stitch, pull out to the left, passing under the crossing. Turn half a turn at the end of each row.

Triple-Cane Lattice

①

②

1 Embroider a regular triple lattice: embroider groups of three parallel vertical throws side by side, evenly spaced. Embroider groups of three horizontal throws, parallel side by side and evenly spaced. Using a different color thread, pass the needle diagonally under the horizontal and over the vertical threads, without piercing the fabric.

2 Carry out the same work on the other diagonal, keeping the same thread or changing the color.

Two-Tone Algiers Braided Stitch

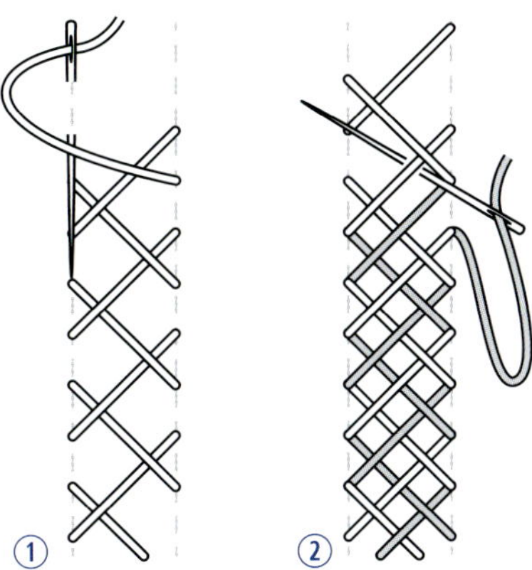

The two-tone Algiers braided stitch is embroidered on two parallel lines, from bottom to top.

1 Embroider a row in sock stitch.

2 Using a different color thread, embroider a second row of herringbone stitch by sliding the needle under the slanted stitch to the right of the first row.

Woven Roman Stitch

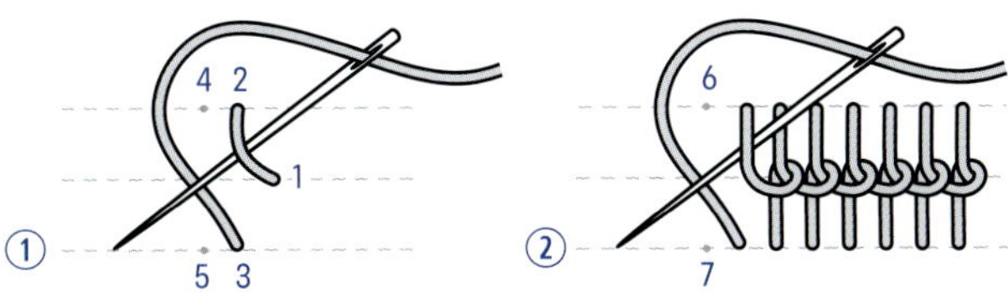

The woven Roman stitch is embroidered on three parallel lines, from right to left.

1 Take the needle out in 1, stitch in 2, and take out in 3. Pass the needle under the stitch from right to left, keeping the thread under the needle tip. Stitch in 4 and out in 5.

2 Pass the needle under the top of the previous stitch from right to left, keeping the thread under the needle tip. Stitch in 6 and out in 7.

Chalice Stitch

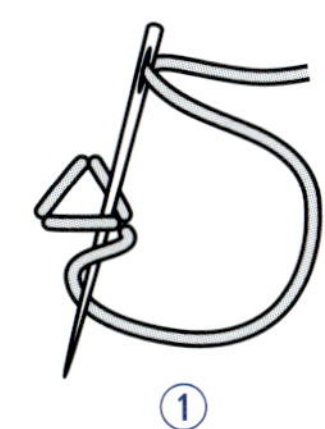

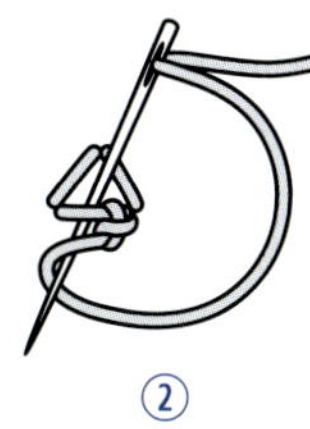

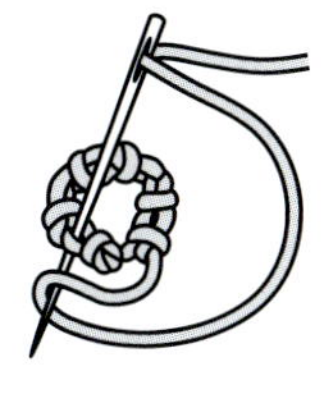

Chalice stitch is embroidered clockwise.

1 Form a triangle with three stitches. Pass the needle up and down under the triangle, and the thread over and under the needle in a counterclockwise direction.

2 Embroider all around the triangle, repeating this loop.

Simple Interlaced Stitch

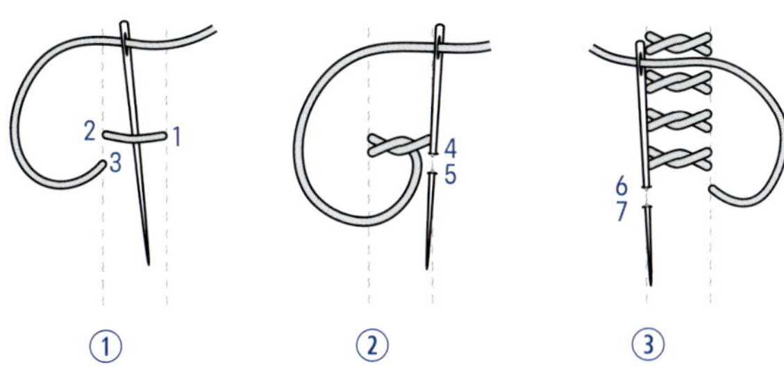

The simple interlaced stitch is embroidered on two parallel lines or by counting the threads, from top to bottom.

1 Take out the needle in 1 on the right line, stitch in 2 on the left line, and take out in 3, under 2.

2 Pass the needle under the stitch formed between 1 and 2.

3 Stitch in 4 and out in 5. Stitch in 6 and out in 7. Pass the needle under the previous stitch, from top to bottom, as you return to the right.

Breton Stitch

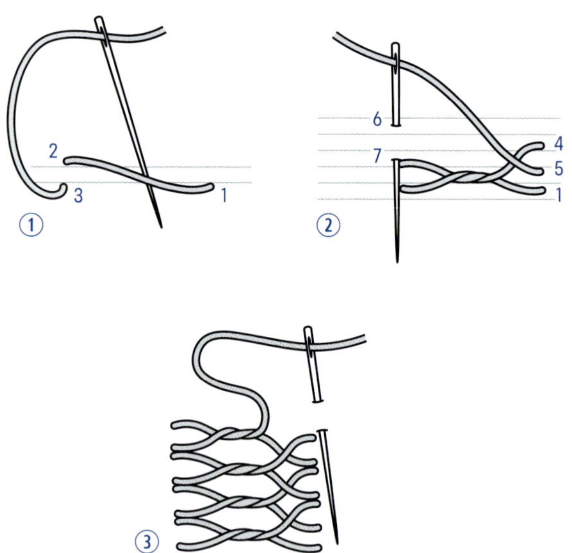

Breton stitch is embroidered on two parallel lines or by counting the threads from bottom to top. The needle must be inserted and withdrawn alternately on the right and left lines.

1 Take the needle out in 1, stitch in 2, and take out in 3. Pass the needle under the stitch formed between 1 and 2.

2 Stitch in 4 and out 5 on the right-hand line. Stitch in 6 and out in 7. Note that 1 and 3 are on the same horizontal line, and 5 is one thread above 1.

3 Always stitch two threads higher than the previous stitch to exit in the same hole and pass the needle under the previous stitch, from top to bottom, as you return to the right.

Visual Library of Embroidery Stitches

COUCHING STITCHES

Widely used in the Middle Ages, couching stitches were widely embroidered in Europe, notably in gold embroidery (see page 184), on ecclesiastical and ceremonial vestments and furnishings. Couching stitches are embroidered by filling.

Bayeux stitch belongs to this category of stitches. It is embroidered on the famous 11th-century Bayeux Tapestry, depicting the Norman Conquest of England in 1066. This perfectly preserved embroidery, measuring 70 meters by 50 centimeters, was mistakenly renamed "tapestry" in the 19th century.

Bayeux Tapestry

The famous Bayeux Tapestry (dating from the 11th century) is approximately 70 meters long and 50 centimeters wide.
Representing William the Conqueror's conquest of England in 1066, it is embroidered with wool yarns dyed with three plant dyes (madder, gaude, and woad), which are blended to produce around 10 different colors. Only four embroidery stitches are used: Bayeux stitch (see page 123), a couching stitch used for filling; stem stitch (see page 55) for outlines and text; chain stitch (see page 78); and split stitch (see page 54) to give more relief to certain motifs. In the 18th century, this embroidery was mistakenly renamed "tapestry."
It is on display at the Musée de la Tapisserie in Bayeux, Calvados (bayeuxmuseum.com).

Simple Couching Stitch

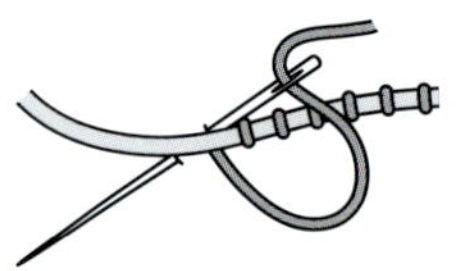

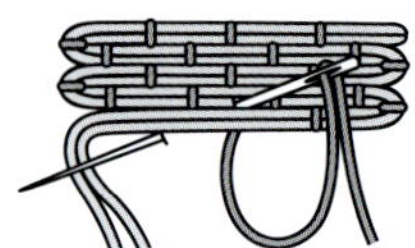

Couching stitch is embroidered with two different threads: one thick and one thinner. The thicker thread is held in place by small perpendicular stitches made with the finer thread.

It is also possible to embroider two coated threads at the same time.

Bukhara or Bokhara Couching Stitch

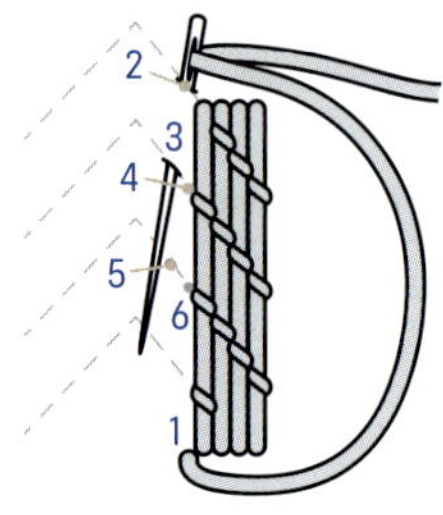

Bukhara couching stitch is embroidered on a motif from top to bottom. The thread is the same for both couched and holding stitches. Holding stitches can follow a previously traced design.

Embroider a straight stitch: take out the needle in 1 and stitch in 2 to cover the full height of the design. Take out needle 3 and stitch in 4 to embroider the couching stitch on the diagonal over the long straight stitch. Take out needle 5 and stitch in 6. Embroider in successive lines to cover the entire design.

Couching stitch, Greece, 18th century

Bayeux Stitch

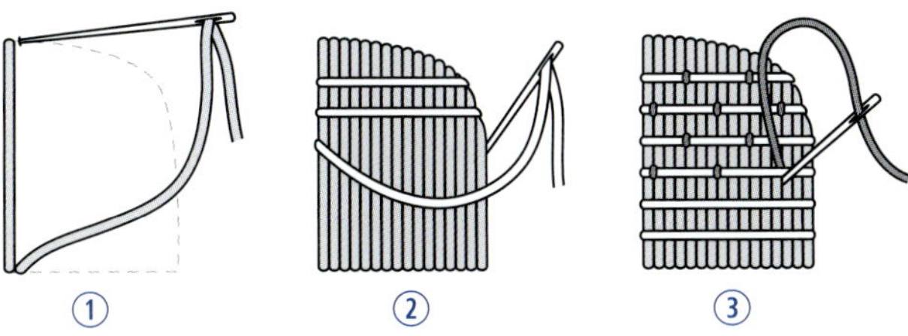

Bayeux stitch is embroidered on a motif with three different needles.

1 Fill in the traced pattern with tightly packed laidwork stitching.

2 Embroider perpendicular straight stitches across the width of the area, every 0.5 centimeter.

3 Embroider small, evenly spaced holding stitches on perpendicular lines.

Romanian Stitch

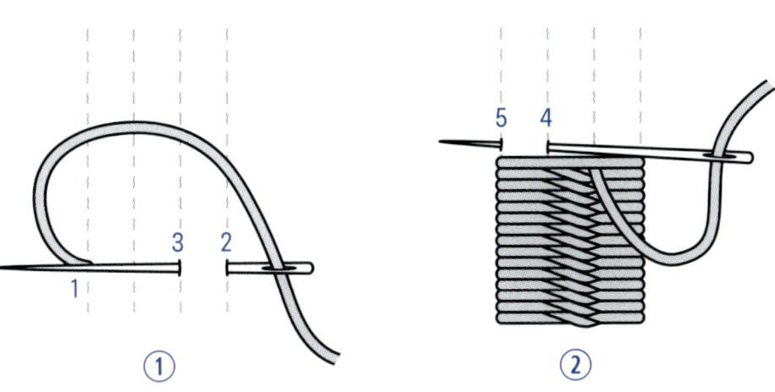

Romanian stitch is embroidered on parallel lines, from bottom to top. The thread is the same for the couching and holding threads.

1 Take the needle out in 1 and stitch in 2 to cover the entire motif. Remove in 3.

2 Stitch in 4 and out in 5 to form the holding stitch. If the pattern has a large surface area, there will be several rows of holding stitches.

Algerian Couching Stitch

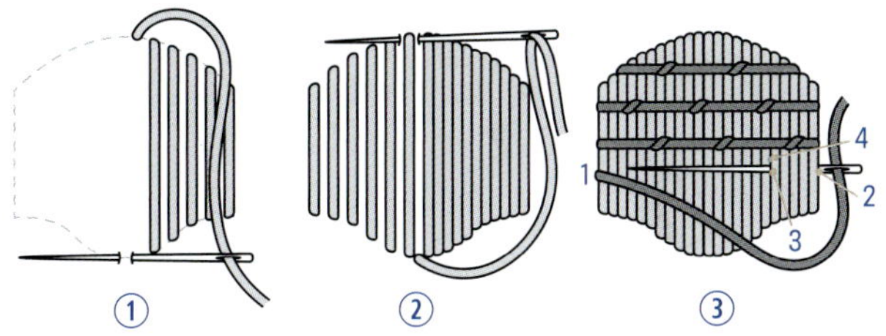

Algerian couching stitch embroidered on a pattern.

1 Fill in the traced pattern with evenly spaced vertical straight stitches.

2 Fill in the gaps by embroidering additional straight stitches to cover the surface.

3 With a new needle of a different color, layer the thread between 1 and 2. Take out the needle at 3 and stitch at 4 to embroider the holding stitch at a slight angle, straddling the couched thread.

Cross-Bar Filling Trellis

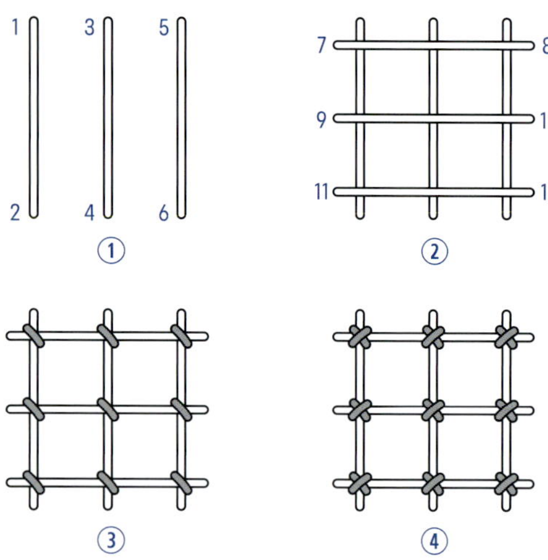

1 Embroider a regular trellis using parallel, evenly spaced vertical straight stitches.

2 Embroider evenly spaced horizontal straight stitches at right angles to the vertical straight stitches.

3 and 4 Embroider a cross-stitch on each intersection.

Trellis with Upright Cross Fill

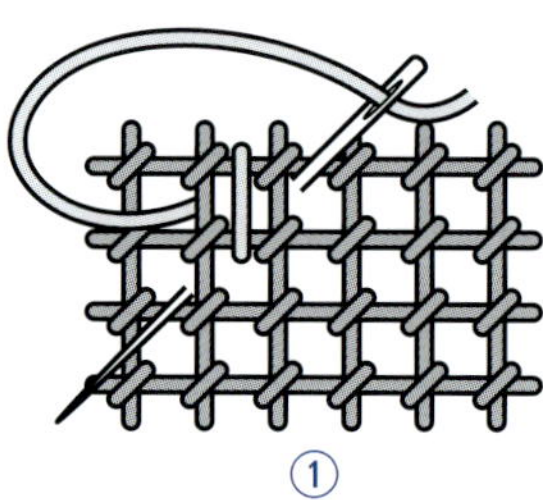
①

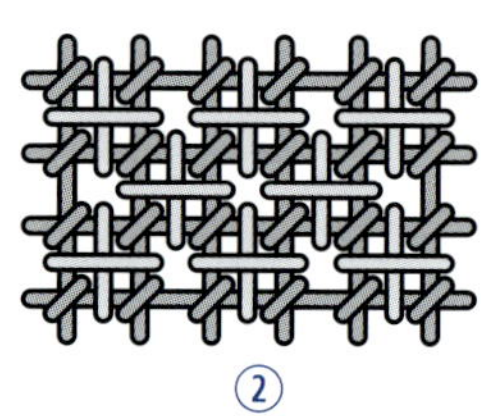
②

1 Embroider a regular trellis with evenly spaced vertical and parallel straight stitches. Embroider evenly spaced horizontal straight stitches at right angles to vertical throws.

2 On each intersection, embroider a diagonal half-cross stitch. In each square, embroider a large cross.

Trellis with Encroaching Cross-Stitch Fill

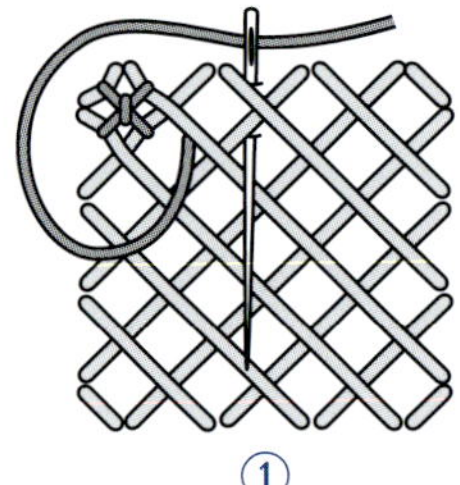
①

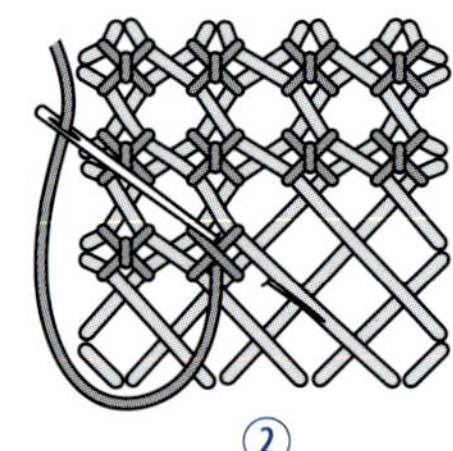
②

1 Embroider a regular trellis with evenly spaced vertical and parallel straight stitches. Embroider evenly spaced horizontal straight stitches at right angles to vertical straight stitches.

2 Straddling every other square on the trellis, embroider a large cross-stitch with a holding stitch over the center.

Trellis with Links

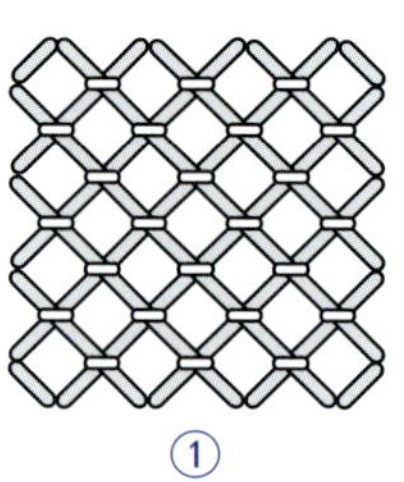
①

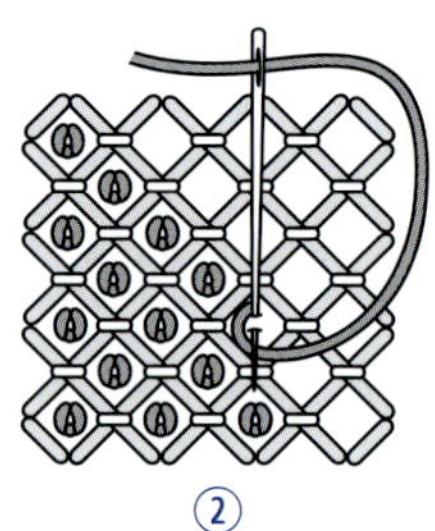
②

1 Embroider a regular trellis using evenly spaced vertical and parallel straight stitches. Embroider evenly spaced horizontal straight stitches perpendicular to the vertical throws. Embroider a small horizontal holding stitch on each intersection.

2 Embroider a detached chain stitch (see page 83) in each square.

Visual Library of Embroidery Stitches

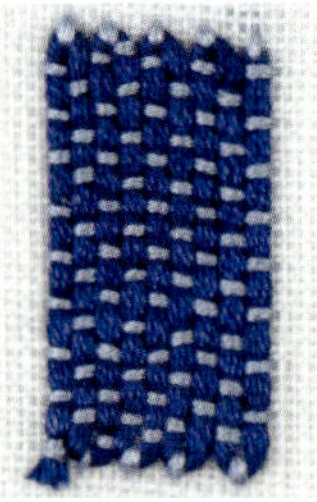

Couching stitch p. 122

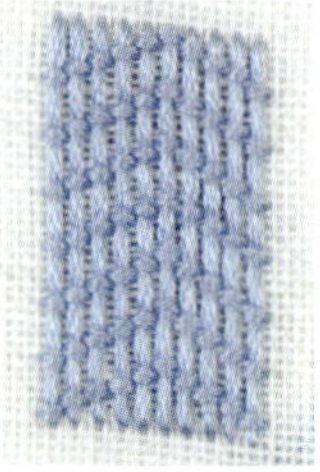

Bukhara couching stitch p. 122

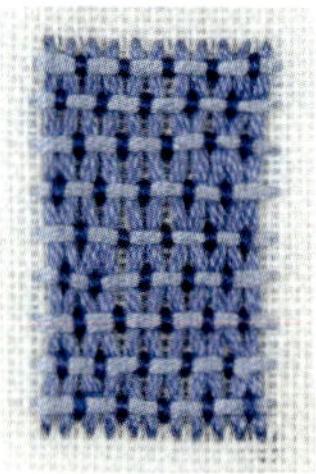

Bayeux stitch p. 123

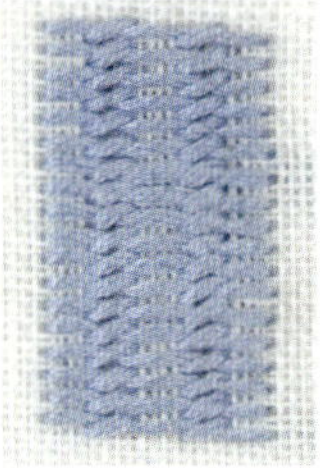

Romanian stitch p. 123

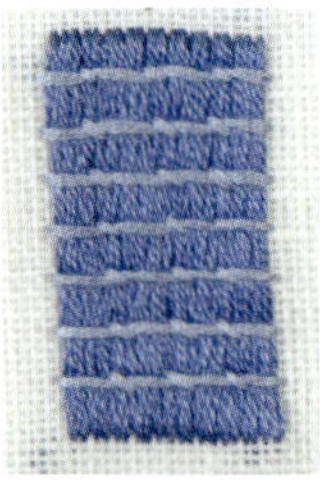

Algerian couching stitch p. 123

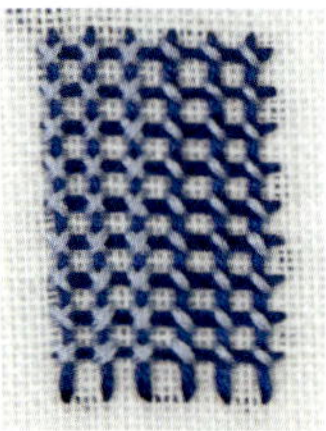

Cross-bar filling trellis p. 124

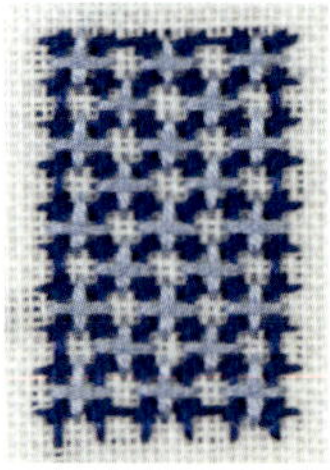

Trellis with upright cross fill p. 124

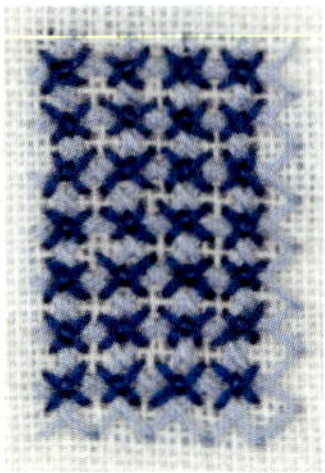

Trellis with encroaching cross stitch fill p. 124

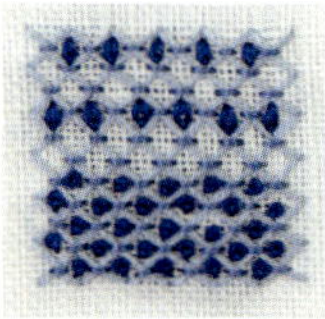

Trellis with links p. 124

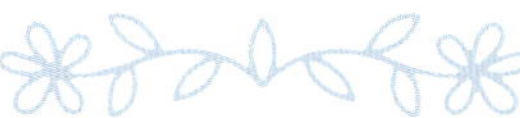

SATIN STITCHES

Satin stitches are used to fill patterns whose surface can be extended. These are the basic stitches of needlepoint.

These embroidery stitches have been around for a very long time. They were commonly embroidered in the Middle Ages, particularly in Asia—the origin of these techniques seems to come from China. In Europe, medieval liturgical embroidery is replete with gold threads worked in satin stitch and laidwork.

Depending on the period and the country, different threads were used. The Anglo-Saxons used wool for their Crewel embroidery, which was very popular in the 17th century. In Japan and China, silk thread is used, as it was in the floral bouquets embroidered in 19th-century Europe. The most delicate embroideries are embroidered with needles of very fine thread.

These stitches have many variations: the satin stitch, the laidwork, the long and short technique, the outlined satin stitch, and the long and short contoured edged.

Padded satin stitch is a succession of satin stitches embroidered side by side to completely cover a surface. It is also used in the plumetis technique (see page 220), where it is embroidered over padding.

Men's silk embroidered vest, 1780

Silk-embroidered man's vest depicting an opera scene, 1795

Satin Stitch

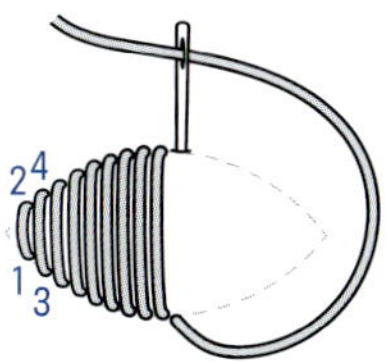

Satin stitch is used to cover narrow shapes up to 8 to 10 mm wide. For wider shapes, use long and short technique (silk shading) (see page 132). It is embroidered from left to right or right to left and from bottom to top. Stitch direction depends on design shape.

Embroider satin stitches evenly from one edge of the design to the other, one against the other, without gaps.

Diagonal Satin Stitch

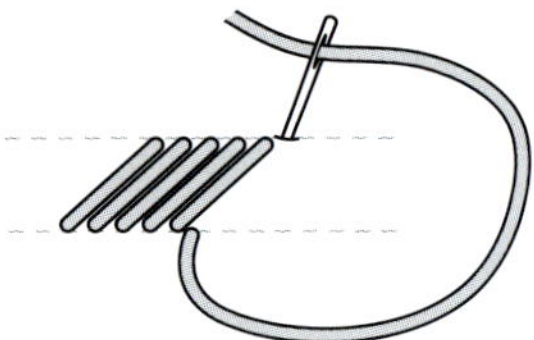

Stitches with a diagonal satin are embroidered at a very steep angle to the line.

Satin Stitch on a Curve

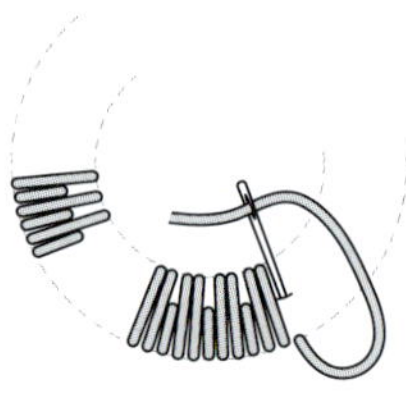

To fill in a curve correctly, insert small wedge satin stitches between the full-length satin stitches so that they do not overlap in the inner part of the drawing.

Embroidered silk sample, 1770

Tips for Good Embroidery

Before embroidering, draw evenly spaced lines. They illustrate the direction that the satin stitches should follow.

When the design is curved, for example, stitch from the outside of the motif inward.

For certain motifs, such as elongated leaves, it is a good idea to start embroidering the motif with a first stitch in the middle and then complete each half, starting from this first stitch.

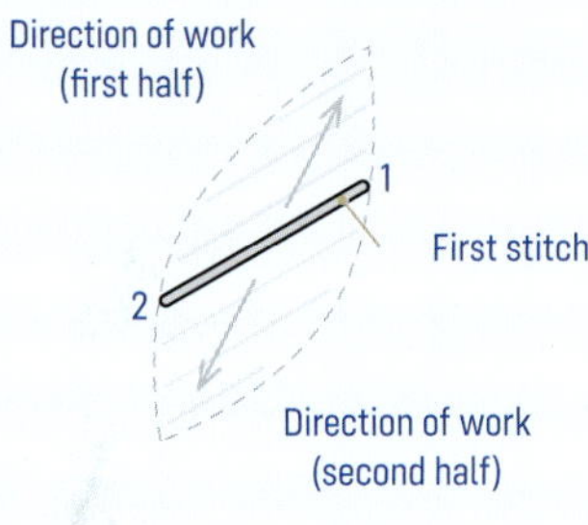

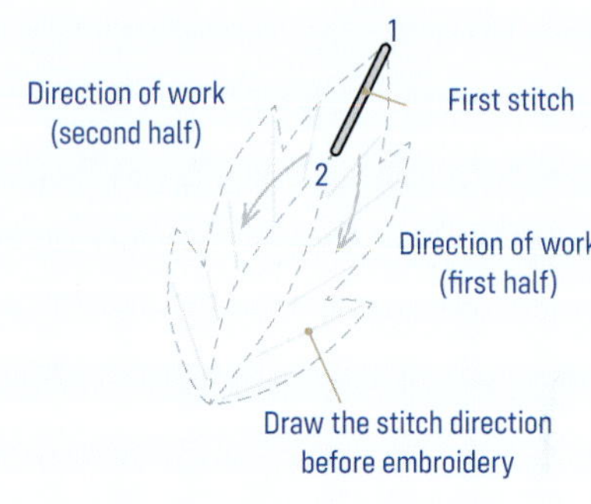

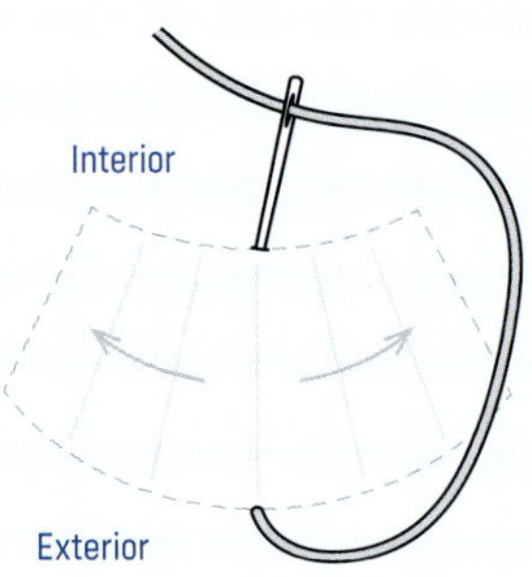

Laid Work

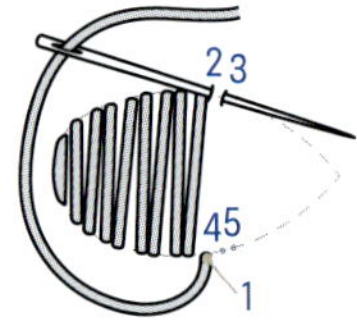

This technique saves a lot of thread, but the result is less smooth.

Take the needle out in 1, stitch in 2, and take out in 3 (right next to 2). Stitch in 4 and out in 5 (right next to 4).

Satin Stitch over Stem Stitch Outline

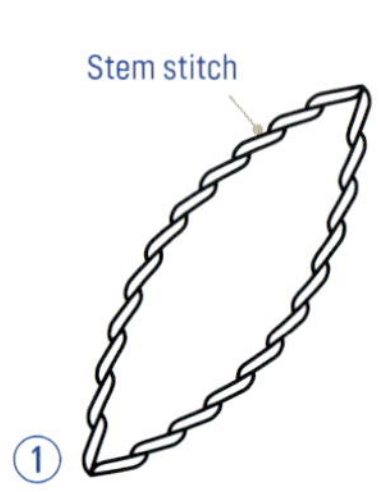

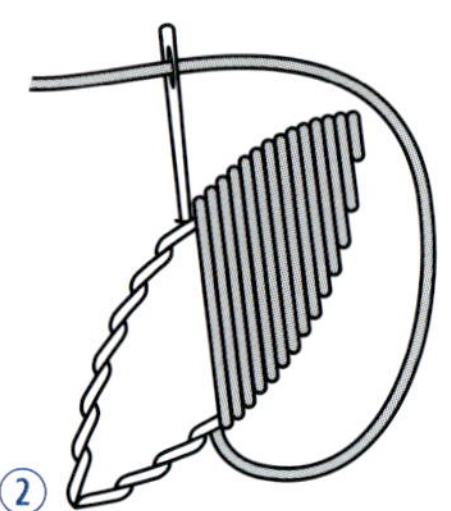

With satin stitch over a stem stitch outline, the embroidered surface has more relief.

1 Embroider the outline of the design in stem stitch.

2 Embroider the satin stitch over the stem stitch.

Long and Short Edge

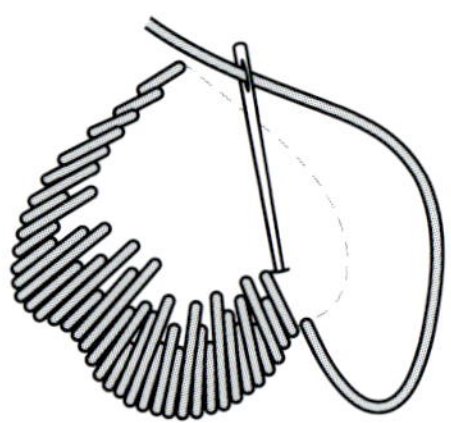

The long and short edge is used to embroider the outlines of a large motif, leaving the center open, free of embroidery. It is embroidered from bottom to top, with the needle extended on the outside of the design and stitched on the inside. For a natural look, use stitches of different lengths.

For very large designs, it is possible to embroider two or three rows of long and short edge and finish with a row that ends in the open space of the motif, leaving the center of the design without embroidery.

What You Need to Know

You can shade the long and short edge by changing the color and tone of the embroidery threads.

Embroidered silk sample, 1770

Visual Library of Embroidery Stitches

THE LONG AND SHORT STITCH

The long and short stitch is one of the main techniques of the satin stitch family, which are often combined in the same work. Its history is therefore linked to that of the satin stitch and the long and short edge (see page 127).

Long and short stitch is the most elaborate of these satin stitches. It is embroidered to depict fauna and flora, as well as landscapes that are "as real as nature": this is the "needle-painting" technique. This true art requires a long apprenticeship before it can be mastered.

As in painting, light and shade are very important. The embroiderers must therefore study the subject from a photograph or from nature to remain faithful to reality. In accordance with the rules of the art, they use a single strand of cotton or silk embroidery floss to embroider stitches nestled together so that the beginning and end of the rows of overlapping long and short are indistinguishable. The work is of remarkable finesse.

If you're modest about it, it's perfectly possible to discover this technique and enjoy making beautiful embroideries. For quick and easy embroidery, use two strands of embroidery floss.

Shaded satin rows (see page 136) is a variation of this stitch: the needle is tucked into the hole of the previous row and worked, splitting the threads of the previous row.

Embroidered skirt with yoke, 18th century

Long and Short Stitch

The long and short stitch is embroidered in monochrome or gradated colors.

There are several schools of embroidery for this stitch; here you'll find the two main ones. If you choose to embroider needles of different colors one by one, both techniques are ideal. On the other hand, method 2 (see page 135) is preferable if you wish to work several needles of different colors simultaneously to create the gradient.

What You Need to Know

It is possible to keep several working needles of different colors while you work to introduce them in turn within the same row of long and short stitch. Always leave these needles on standby at the top of the work, to avoid unwanted knots on the reverse side. In this way, you avoid having to stop and start a new needle again and again to change color.

A few recommendations before embroidering

Embroider from bottom to top if you're embroidering on a hoop, since the work can be turned to work in the same direction. On an embroidery frame placed on trestles, embroidery should be performed as shown in the drawing.

Whichever method you choose, always start embroidering from the outside of the design and work inward. Work from right to left or left to right; the important thing is not to change the direction during embroidery.

What You Need to Know

All the diagrams in this chapter are based on the left-hand side of the drawing. The work is identical with a right-hand start.

When the design features veins (leaves and petals, butterfly wings), start by embroidering them in stem stitch or encroaching stem stitch (see page 56), then continue with the long and short stitch.

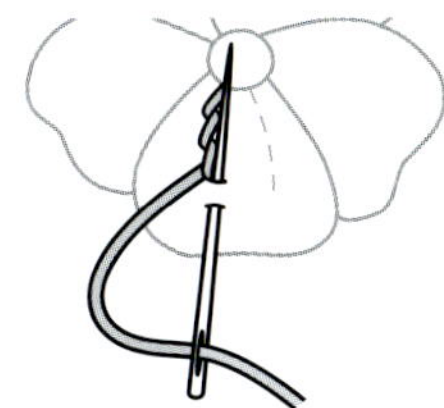

Anchoring your thread

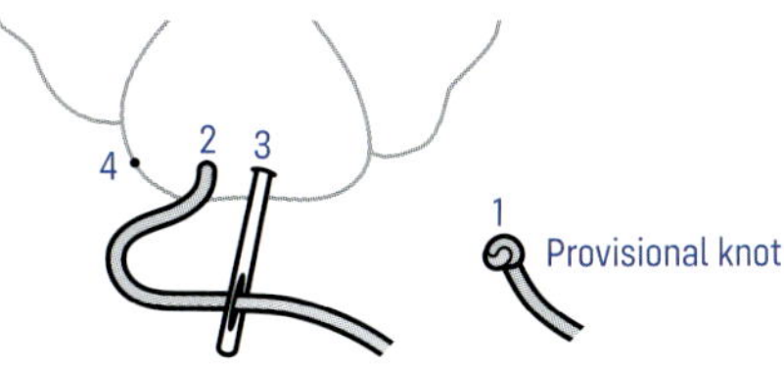

With the long and short stitch, the reverse side of the embroidery must be very careful. When it's done right, the reverse side is as beautiful as the front.

Make a temporary knot on the needle (see page 40). Stitch on the right side of the work and outside the area to be embroidered, so that the first stitches cover and block the starting thread. Embroider the entire design and cut the knot. Finally, pass the needle under the last stitches executed.

Tips for Good Embroidery

To make embroidery easier, use an erasable felt-tip pen to trace the direction of the stitches beforehand; for example, the direction of an animal's fur, a bird's feather, a flower petal, etc.

Embroidery with method 1

With this method, the needle is extended into the previous row and stitched into the unembroidered part. This makes it easier to respect the orientation of the stitches, for a coat or the veins of foliage, for example.

The first row

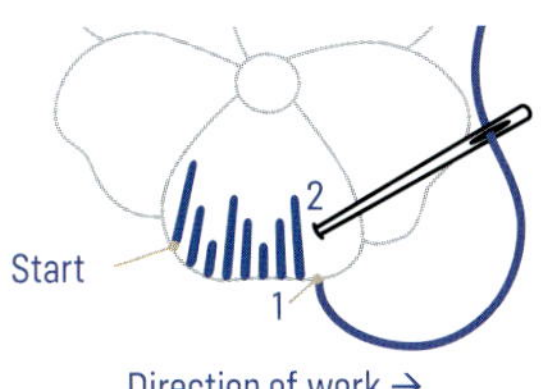

Embroider the first row in the same order.

1 Start with a large stitch. It can measure up to 8 mm.

2 Continue with a medium stitch. It can measure up to 7 mm.

3 Finish with a small stitch. It can measure up to 6 mm and should be larger than half the large stitch.

The stitches should touch but not overlap. Take the needle out in 1 on the outside of the petal and stitch in 2 on the inside of the petal.

The second row

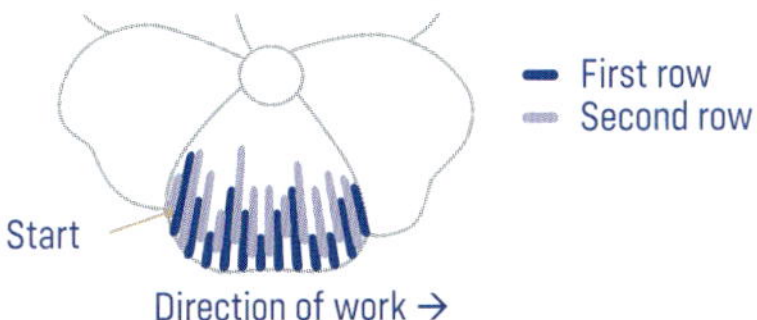

On the reverse side, pass the needle under the stitches to start again on the same side as the first row. Embroider the second row, taking the needle out between two stitches and inside the previous row, but at different levels. Stitch toward the inside of the design, following the directions. Continue in the same stitch order as the first row. The small stitch should come out on the outside of the previous row.

The following rows

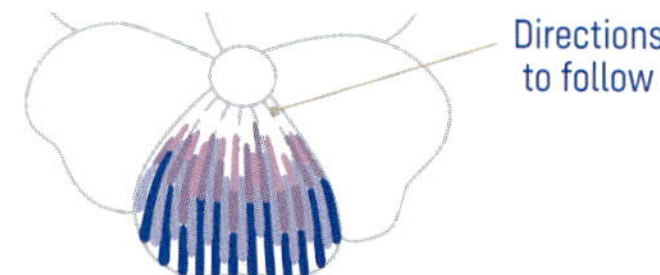

The following rows are done in the same way as the second row, keeping the stitch order. The start must always be on the same side: to do this, pass the needle on the back of the work under the last row completed.

Increases

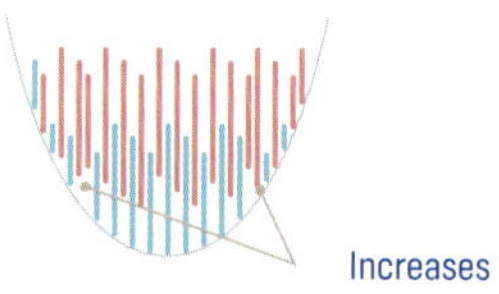

When a design widens, pull the needle out twice in the same space between two stitches of the previous row, as many times as necessary to cover the entire surface to be embroidered.

Reductions

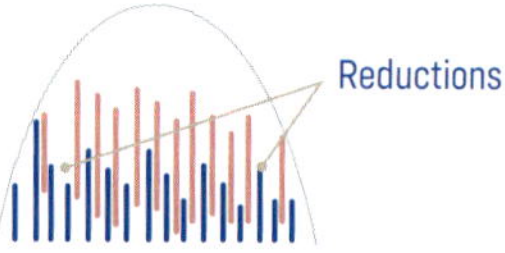

When a design shrinks, do not pull the needle out between all the stitches of the previous row, but only in those that are suitable for embroidering the stitches in the right direction and for covering the entire surface to be embroidered without packing the stitches.

Curves

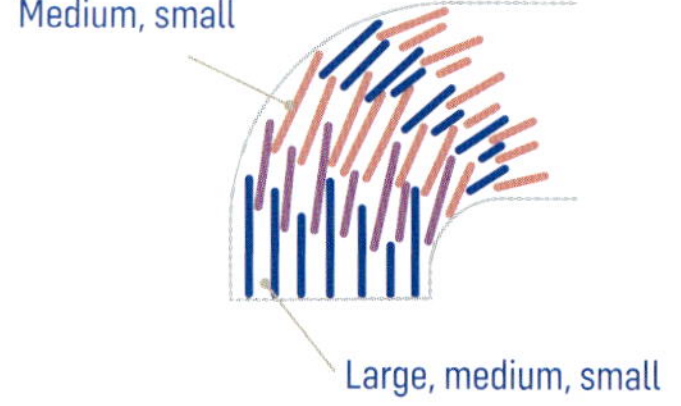

When the design has curves, embroider only small and medium stitches to avoid overlapping. If necessary, reduce stitch length too. As soon as the curve allows, resume embroidering the three stitch lengths.

Inserting a second color

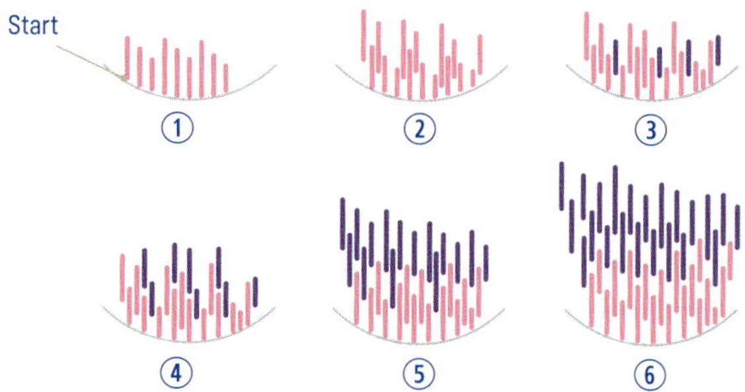

Changes of color or tone take place over several rows. The different threads must fit into each other without demarcation.

Gradient rows are created in two stages: first embroider a first color, leaving spaces for the second color. Then embroider the second color in the spaces left free. When a design widens, pull the needle out twice in the same space between two stitches of the previous row, as many times as necessary to cover the entire surface to be embroidered.

Row 1 (1) Embroider the three types of stitches with a first color (here, pink).

Row 2 (2) Embroider long and medium stitches in the same color (pink).

Row 2 (3) Embroider the stitches in a second color (here, purple).

Row 3 (4) Embroider the long stitches in the first color (pink).

Row 3 (5) Embroider medium and small stitches in the second color (purple).

Row 4 (6) Embroider all stitch types in the second color (purple).

Tips for Good Embroidery

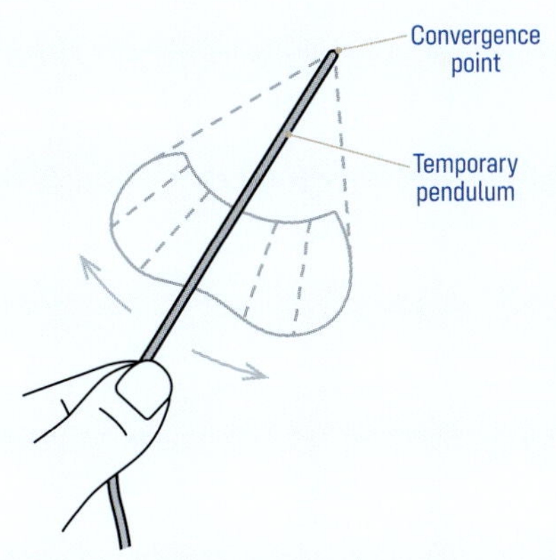

Depending on the design, it may be difficult to orient the points correctly. In such cases, a temporary pendulum, made with a loose thread exiting at the point of convergence, will be of great help. It will emerge from below to above. With a pendulum movement above the work, it determines the direction of the embroidery stitches.

Embroidery with method 2

With this second method, the needle is pulled out in the unembroidered part and stitched into the previous row. As a reminder, this is the preferred method if you're working several needles of different colors at the same time to create the gradient. The techniques for decreases, increases, embroidery in curves, and pendulum are identical here to the first method (see page 133).

First and subsequent rows

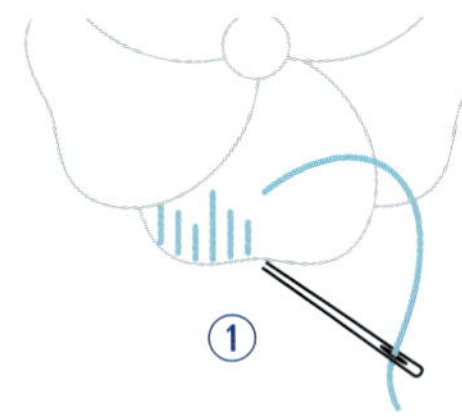

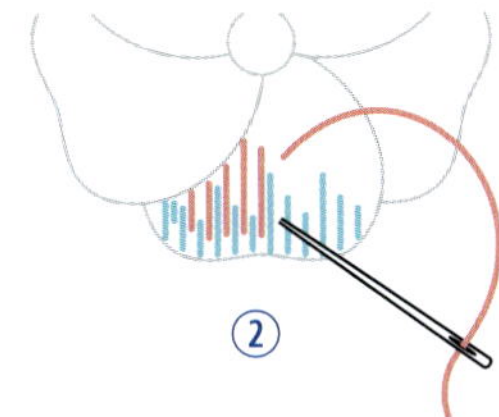

As with method 1, always follow the same stitch order (one large, one medium, and one small stitch) to achieve seamless embroidery.

1 The first row is embroidered in the same way as method 1 (see page 133).

2 To embroider the following rows, pull out the needle in the nonembroidered area and stitch in the embroidered area.

Embroidering with several needles at the same time

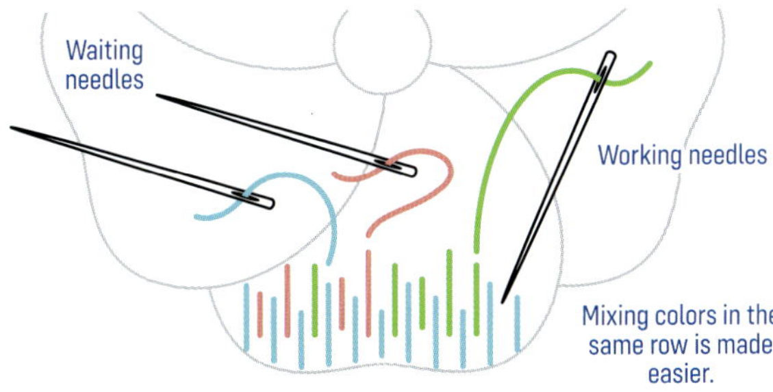

With this second method, it is easier to embroider with several needles at the same time in the same row, since they will be on standby (see page 41) in the unembroidered part.

1 Prepare all the color swatches used in the pattern, up to five or six simultaneously.

2 In the same row, embroider the stitches with the appropriate color.

3 To change color, pull out the last needle used in the unembroidered area. Take the new color and embroider the number of stitches required to follow the pattern colors.

4 To change color again, take out the last needle used in the nonembroidered area and take the appropriate needle, and so on.

Tips for Good Embroidery

Anticipate switch changes by leaving them on standby at the top of the structure (see page 41), where they will be needed.

Shaded Satin Rows

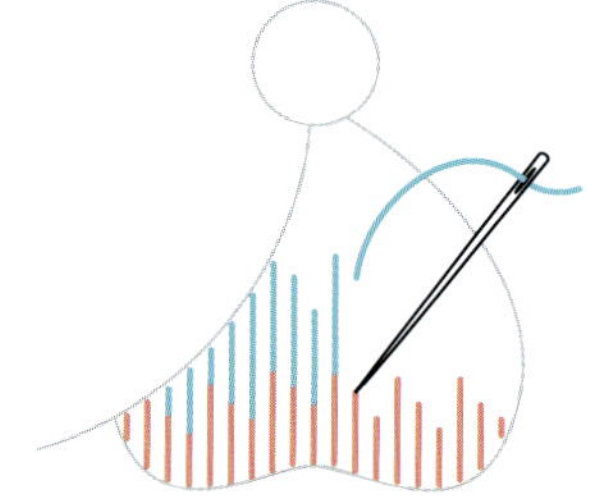

Stitch in the stitch hole of the previous row.

3

COLOR EMBROIDERY

INSERTION STITCHES

Insertion stitches (entre-deux brodé) are openwork embroidered-band decorative links between two pieces of fabric.

These embroideries have their origins in pulled-thread embroidery (see pages 228–240), used as early as the 15th century in Italy to decorate church linen. Since the 18th century, this technique has been used throughout Europe to embroider household linen.

The insertion stitches are often worked with buttonhole stitch and its variants (see pages 70–77).

Unless otherwise specified, insertion stitches are embroidered from left to right, and vice versa for left-handers, in straight or curved lines.

What You Need to Know

It is not necessary to embroider in the straight grain of the fabric, as is the case with pulled-thread days.

Before You Embroider

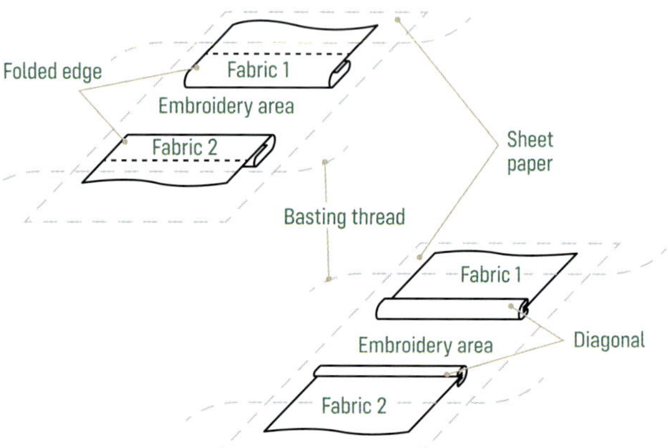

Turn the edges of the fabric to be embroidered under or lay a diagonal binding across the fabrics to be joined. Then carefully mount the whole on a conventional sheet of paper, placing the fabric edges in their final positions. This will ensure that the fabrics remain at the same distance from each other as you work. Once the embroidery is complete, tear off the paper to remove it.

Tips for Good Embroidery

For regular work, use a ruler and pencil to trace the location of future embroidery stitches on the paper.

Basic Insertion Stitches

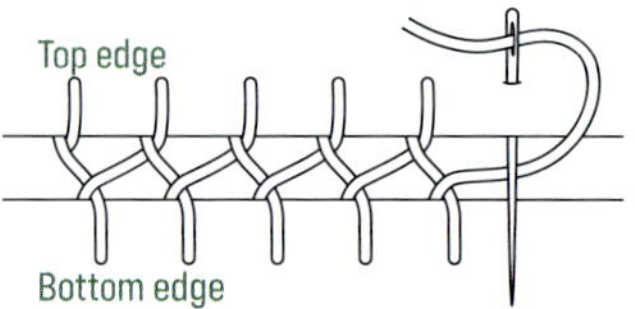

Embroider a single buttonhole stitch on each edge, alternating high and low edges and staggering the stitches. For each stitch, pass the thread under the tip of the needle, which should be tightened vertically.

Whipped Insertion Stitches

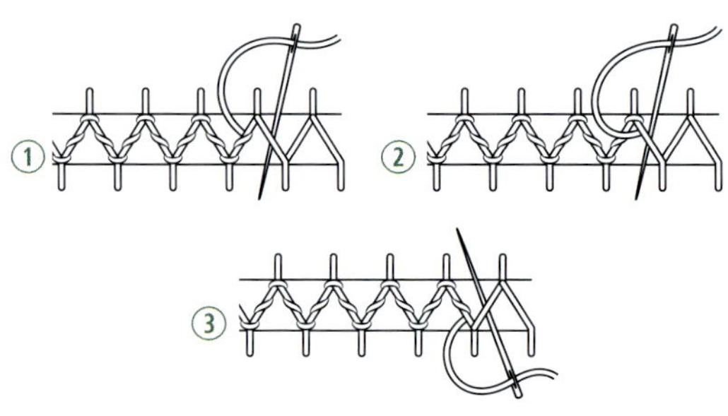

Embroider the insertion stitching with buttonhole stitch, then whip as follows.

1 Pass the needle up and down over the top crossing and under the thread of the next buttonhole stitch.

2 Pass the needle under the same thread a second time to wind it up.

3 Do the same work opposite, working from bottom to top with the needle.

Insertion Stitches with Buttonhole Groupings

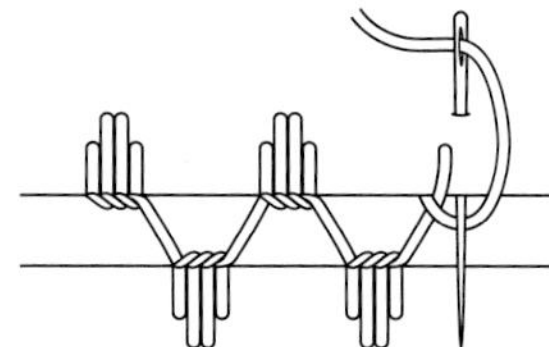

Embroider a series of buttonhole stitches, alternating each edge between groupings. Always work in the same way, either by embroidering buttonhole stitches of the same height or by varying their length (one short, two long, one short).

Laced Insertion Stitches

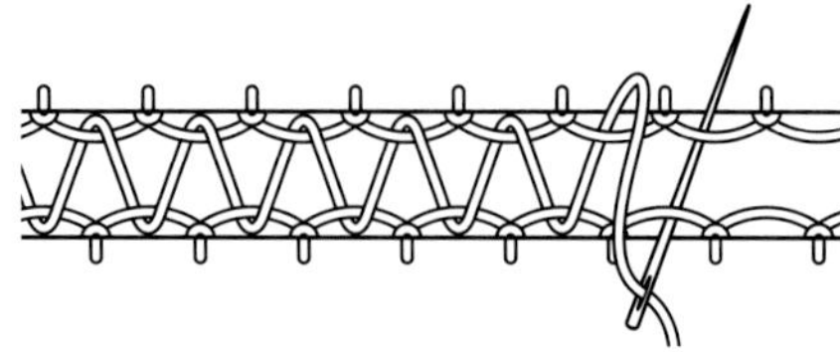

1 Embroider in tailor's buttonhole stitch on each edge, staggering the placement of the stitches on each edge.

2 Join the two edges by passing the needle under the arches of the tailor's buttonhole stitches, alternately between the top and bottom edges.

Woven Bars Insertion Stitches

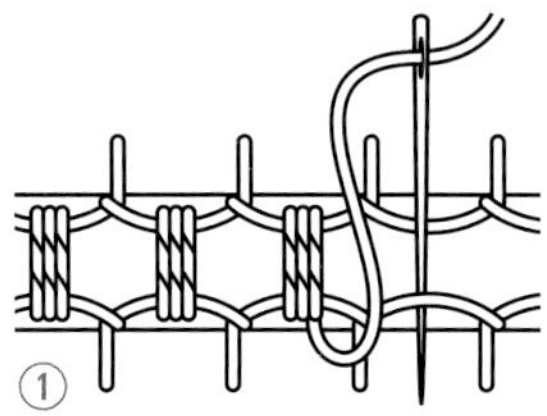

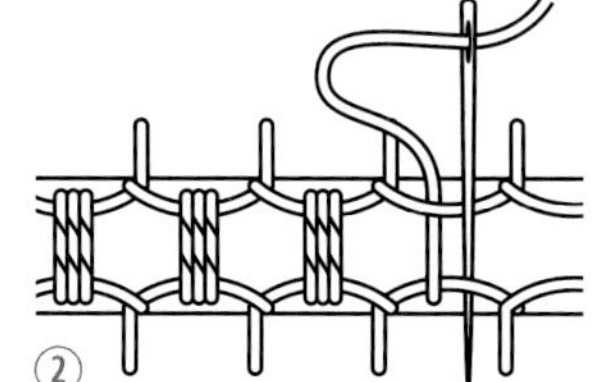

Embroider in buttonhole stitch on each edge, placing the stitches opposite each other.

1 Join the two edges by weaving three darning stitches between the loops on each edge.

2 Overcast the buttonhole loop to move on to the next loop.

Knotted Line Insertion Stitches

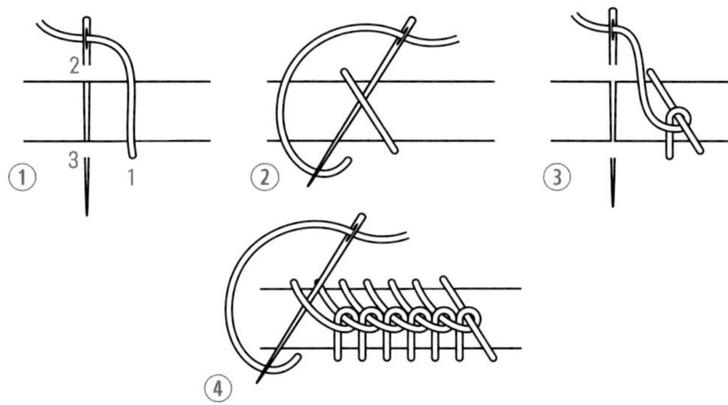

The middle knot is embroidered from right to left, and vice versa for left-handers.

1 Take out the needle in 1, stitch in 2, and take out in 3.

2 Pass the needle under the stitch and over the thread.

3 and 4 Tighten to form a knot.

Knotted Insertion Stitches

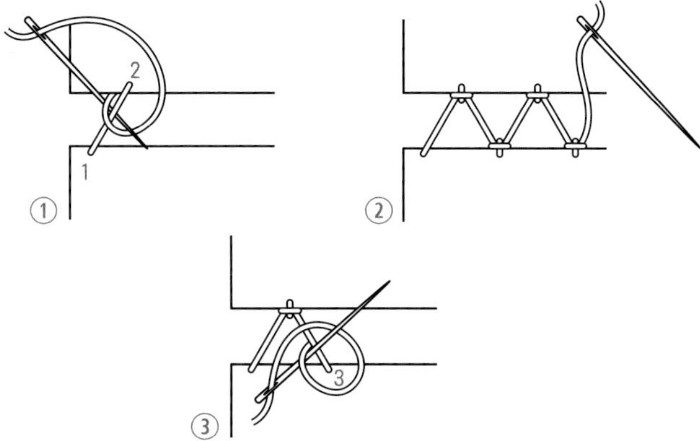

The knotted insertion stitch on each side is embroidered from left to right, and vice versa for left-handers.

1 Take out the needle in 1, stitch in 2, and take out to the left of 2. Pass the needle under the stitch, from left to right, and over the thread as if buttonholing. Pull to form a knot.

2 Stitch in 3 and repeat step 1 to form a new knot.

3 Continue alternating top and bottom edges.

Visual Library of Embroidery Stitches

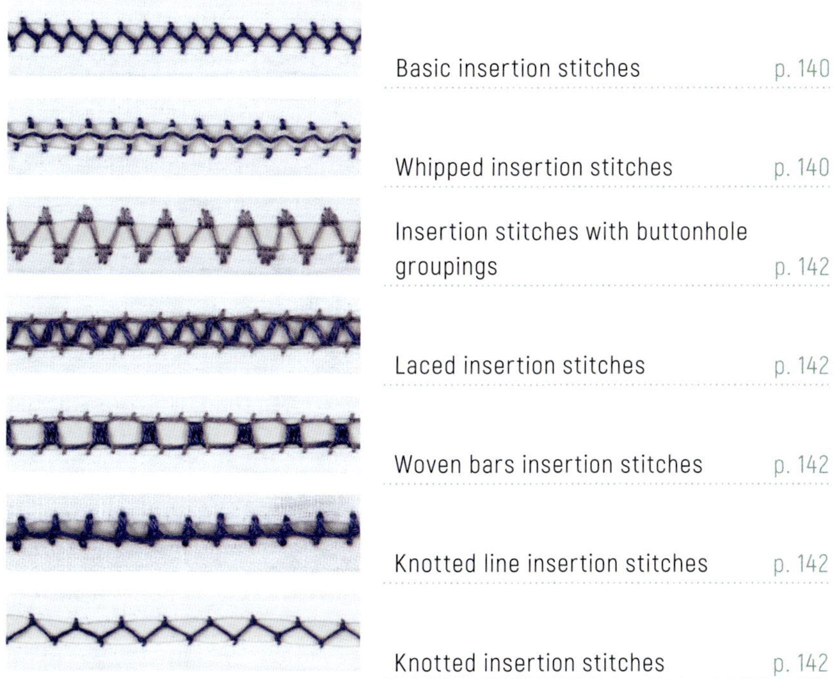

EMBROIDERING TEXT, LETTERS, AND NUMBERS

All over the world and for many centuries, embroidery of text and letters (embroider text) has been a decorative element adorning tapestries and church and household linen. Epigraphs, for example, have been found on church ornaments dating back to the Middle Ages.

In the 18th and 19th centuries, schoolgirls embroidered cross-stitched samplers (like a page of writing; see page 87) on pieces of fabric.

In the 19th century, embroiderers also embroidered household linen and lingerie in white, using plumetis stitch (see page 223). These embroideries, which followed very strict rules, were called "chiffrage": from handkerchiefs to tablecloths, the height of the letters could vary from 12 to 90 mm. Young girls' sheets and trousseaux were adorned with monograms embracing the initials of the bride and groom.

Alphabet, alphabet book, and text embroidery have always been popular in Europe and North America and remain so today.

To find numerous diagrams and drawings of antique alphabets, type "abécédaire broderie" or "monogramme" into a search engine; alternatively, type your message into a word processor to choose the font and letter size you prefer. Scan the QR code on page 14 to download all the alphabets in this book.

Backstitch

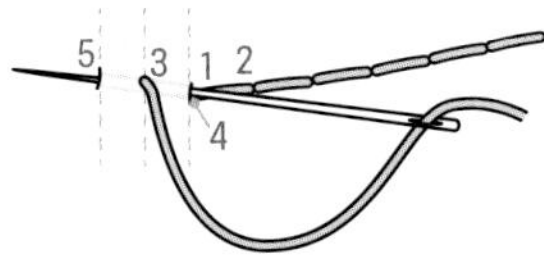

Easy to create, stitch-on stitch is used for embroidering fine-line fonts, and fill stitch for thick-line fonts. The amount of thread passing over the back of the work is important.

Whipped Backstitch

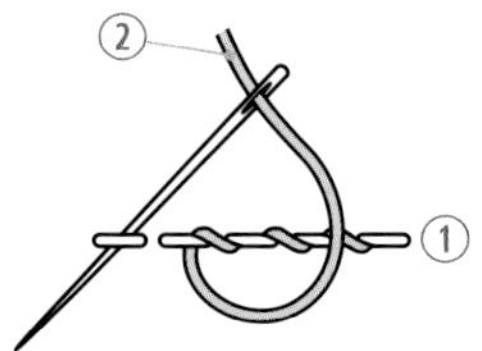

The whipped backstitch is ideal for embroidering fine, sinuous fonts.

Stem Stitch

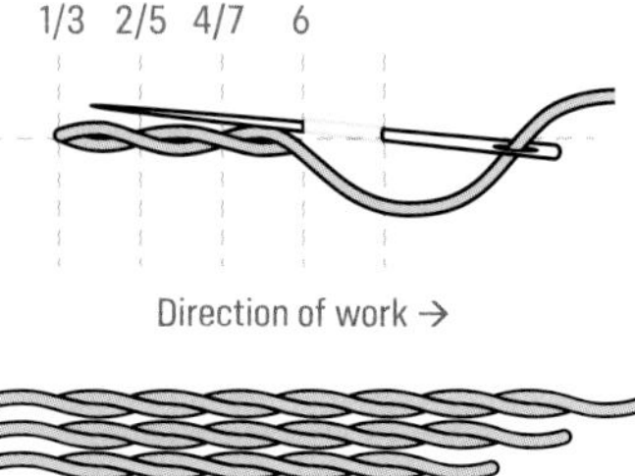

Any font can be embroidered with stem stitch. Note that curved letters are more difficult to embroider with this stitch, so you'll need to reduce the stitch length, as explained on page 55.

The amount of thread passing over the back of the work is less than with the backstitch.

Arthur

Backstitch filling

POURSUIS — Chain stitch

tes rêves — Stem stitch

Front point

décroche — Backstitch

LA LUNE — Basic satin stitch

Whipped backstitch — DES ETOILES

plein les yeux — Backstitch filling

Chain Stitch

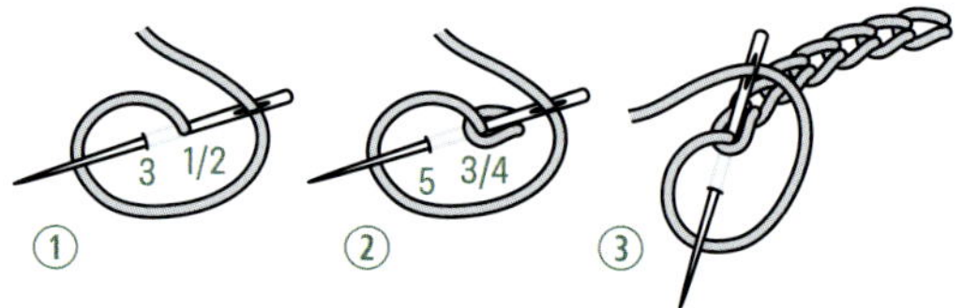

With or without filling, chain stitch is ideal for embroidering regular, fairly thick fonts.

Cross-Stitch

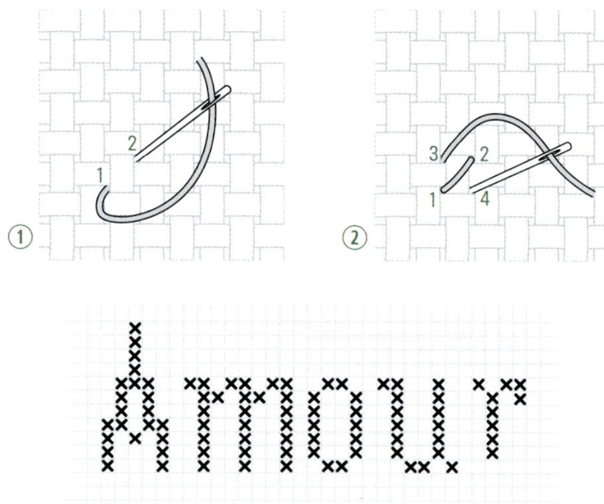

Widely used for embroidering primers and bookmarks, cross-stitch is perfectly suited for text.

Basic Satin Stitch

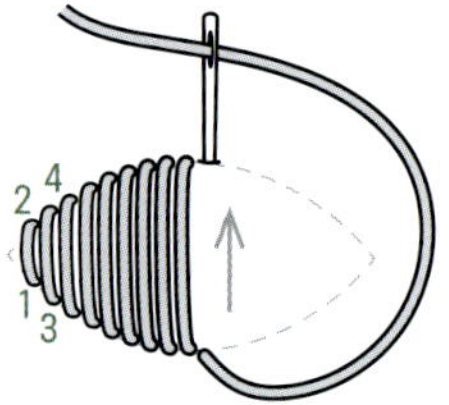

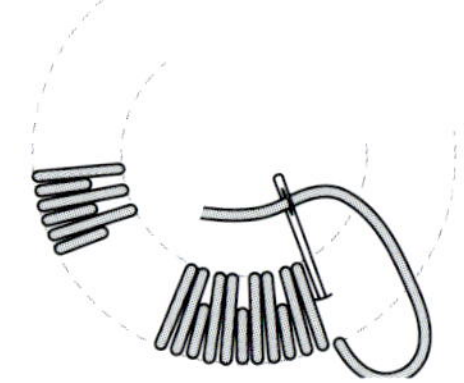

The satin stitch is ideal for embroidering very large fonts. Stitches must not exceed 8 mm in length.

Buttonhole Stitch

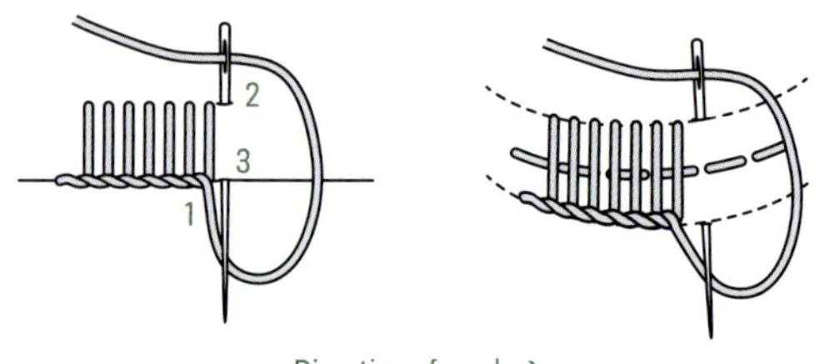

Direction of work →

A B C D E F G H I
J K L M N O P Q R
S T U V W X Y Z

The buttonhole stitch is suitable for embroidering wide fonts. For curves, it can be worked in the same way as the satin stitch.

SMOCKING

Smocking stitches are embroidered, elastic gathers. This technique was very much in vogue in 19th-century England. The term "smocks" was used to describe the traditional gathered shirts worn by men of modest means.

Made of cotton or linen, these loose-fitting, T-shaped shirts were soft, comfortable, and warm. Their back and front yokes and cuffs were tightened with small pleats held in place by embroidery stitches. These men's shirts gradually disappeared at the beginning of the 20th century.

It was at this time that this embroidery technique was taken up by the famous London store Liberty, which has since offered dresses for babies and girls every year. At the same time, in Europe in the 1930s, women fighting for the feminist cause replaced their corsets with much more comfortable smocked undergarments.

Today, smocking adorns blouses, dresses, lingerie, and feminine accessories. In children's fashion, girls and boys wear smocking for an elegant wardrobe.

Smocking is a two-stage process: first the fabric is pleated with gathers, then the pleats are embroidered.

Blouse with smocked cuffs, to be found in the creations on page 341

Supplies

Smock embroidery is performed with classic embroidery threads on apparel fabrics.

Fabrics

Smocking is done on woven fabrics (see page 27), ideally on lightweight fabrics. Choose cotton, linen, or fine woolens such as batiste, fil à fil, poplin, double gauze, Oxford, plumetis, or very light velvet. Piqué, twill, and pilou should be chosen in the lightest weights. Silk, on the other hand, is much more fluid and delicate and must be worked with great care.

> **Tips for Good Embroidery**
>
> **Choose fabrics weighing between 70 and 190 g/m^2.**

Before starting embroidery, it is necessary to scour the fabric. To do this, soak the fabric in water overnight, then wash it. Once the fabric has been ironed, gather it by hand or mechanically, using pleats threaded through the fabric.

Threads

You'll need thread to make the gathers and thread to embroider the smocks.

Gather threads should be strong, like polyester sewing-machine threads. They should be in a contrasting color to the fabric to be smocked, so that they can be easily identified. For embroidery, choose from the following threads:

- DMC embroidery flosses, easy to work with
- DMC pearl cotton no.8 (S)

- silks (such as Soie d'Alger from Au Ver à Soie) for a magnificent finish
- metallicized yarns to bring out the light (see page 30)

Equipment

Aside from needles and threads, which are easy to obtain, you'll need equipment to pleat the fabric. For this step, the choice of equipment and tools depends on the size of the project and the budget you wish to devote to it.

Embroidery needles

Work the smocks with a no. 7 embroidery needle with three strands of DMC mouliné or with two or three strands of Au Ver à Soie's Soie d'Alger.

Tools for making pleats

Pleating can be done mechanically or by hand.

Mechanically

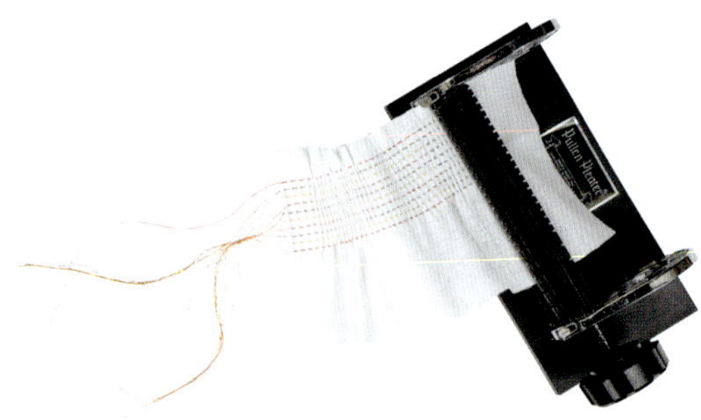

There's a very practical tool for mechanically pleating fabric: the pleating machine. Equipped with notched rollers fitted with needles, it allows you to precisely pleat the entire height of the work in just a few minutes, whatever the size of the project. The downside: this machine is expensive. You can find it at Stragier (see page 410).

Handmade

To pleat fabric by hand, it's necessary to draw a grid on the fabric to be embroidered beforehand, so you know where to prick the needle to obtain even pleats. To do this, choose the material of your choice.

- Thermo-transferable paper: easy to use, this can be bought at haberdashers. These are strips of parchment paper marked with small dots printed with a special ink. Once transferred to the fabric with an iron, these dots help you mark where to stitch pleats by hand.
- Water-soluble interfacing (such as Sulky; see page 36) to print marks for stitching folds.

- Water-soluble interfacing (such as soluble stabilizer; see page 36) to print marks for stitching folds.

If you don't want to draw the layout beforehand, there are other solutions available.

- DMC soluble canvas, originally designed for cross-stitch embroidery, is suitable for pleating small areas. Prick the gathering thread every fourth perforation hole.
- Use Zéphyr, voile de coton quadrille (5 × 5cm squares). This fabric can also be used on its own to make a smocked garment; note that it can be dyed after embroidery.

- Alternatively, opt for gingham or woven-dyed striped fabrics. Their geometric patterns will guide you through the pleats.

What You Need to Know

Woven-dyed fabric is when the threads used to weave the fabric are dyed before weaving. This technique produces fabrics of excellent quality. If the width of the stripes or checks—determined by the change in thread color during weaving—is a multiple of 5 mm, these can be used as markers for hand pleating without tracing.

Techniques

Smocks are made in two stages: pleating and embroidery.

The amount of fabric to be pleated should be about three times the width of the finished work. Allow a minimum margin of 3 cm all around the fabric. For example, for an embroidered cuff measuring 15 cm, allow 45 cm + 6 cm (3cm margins on each side), for a total width of 51 cm.

Pleating

Mechanically or by hand, this work prior to embroidery must be carried out with care.

Ideally, pleats are made on a 5 × 5mm grid, using gathers line by line.

Tips for Good Embroidery

Mechanical pleating can be more complicated with thick fabrics. Before you start, test samples to see if they are feasible and how they will look.

Preparing the switch

For gathering pleats, use sewing thread in your needle. The length of thread must be equivalent to that of the fabric to be pleated.

Choose five or six different colors that contrast with the color of the fabric to be pleated, so that the lines created are clearly visible during embroidery. The colors can be used alternately, whether working with a pleating machine or by hand.

Tips for Good Embroidery

It's better to have more gathering thread than you need, rather than too little. To be on the safe side, prepare one more needle at the top and three more at the bottom. For example, for a 5cm smocked piece, count 11 + 4 needles.

Preparing the gathering threads on the pleating machine

1 On the pleating machine, thread the number of needles indicated on the model to pleat the height to be embroidered in a single operation.

2 Turn the handwheel on the pleating machine to thread the gathers. Please refer to your machine's operating instructions.

Preparing gathering threads by hand

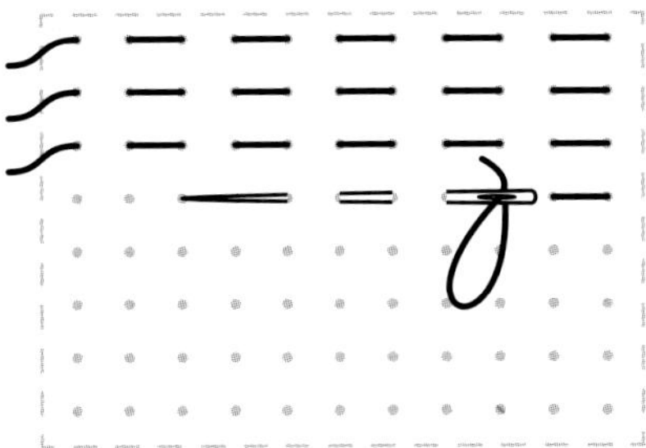

Prepare the layout of your work by hand, choosing the technique that suits you best.

→ With erasable pen and a ruler

Create a grid by using an erasable pen and a ruler.

→ With thermo-transferable paper

Transfer the markings for the folds, using an iron. Be careful: these little marks on the fabric don't always wash away.

1 Cut the transfer paper to the same size as the surface to be pleated.

2 Carefully pin the transfer side of the paper to the back of the fabric, where it will be pleated.

3 Press with an iron.

4 Remove and discard the paper.

→ With self-adhesive, water-soluble interlining

Download and print the grid (see QR code on page 14) directly on the Sulky interfacing, on an A4 or A3 sheet, depending on the printer. For larger formats, you'll need to trace or transfer the grid by hand. Then refer to the Sulky instructions for use (see page 36).

Before pleating, dip the interfacing in water to dissolve it. When the fabric is dry, form the pleats.

→ With Zephyr® fabric

1 Cut the Zephyr fabric to the same dimensions as the surface to be pleated, adding a 2cm margin all around.

2 Position the Zephyr fabric on the back of the smocking fabric, over the area to be pleated, and pin.

3 Thread the gathers in both thicknesses, using the squares as reference points for a regular result.

Zephyr fabric stays in place after embroidery is complete.

Pleating the fabric

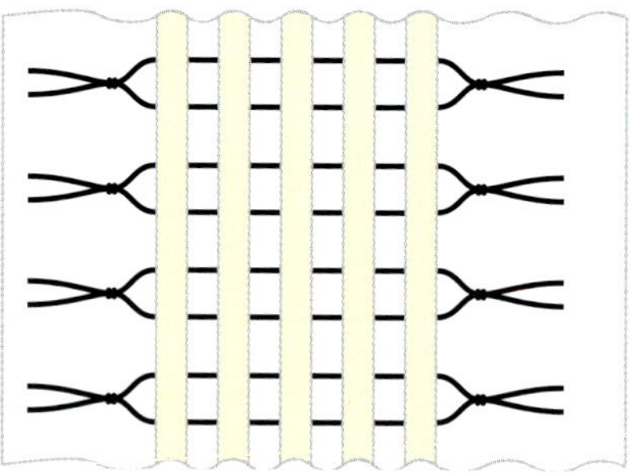

With a pleater or by hand, once the gathering threads have been passed through, pull on them to pleat the fabric to a width slightly less than that of the finished garment. Tie the gathers in pairs at the ends.

Embroidery

Gathering threads serve as a guide for smock embroidery.

Preparing the needle

The needle should be long enough to embroider a full row of smocks. Use a length of thread four times longer than the length to be embroidered.

Caution: if the needle is longer than 90–100 cm, it will be too difficult to pull the thread without tangling it. You'll need to stop the thread at the back of the work in the hollow of a fold, leaving it free, without tying a knot so as not to block the elasticity of the smocks. Then pull out precisely in the same fold, on the right side of the work, with a new needle.

Tips for Good Embroidery

Stop the threads with three small, discreet stitches, one on top of the other on the reverse side. Then conceal the end of the thread on the back of the embroidery. This operation should be carried out after final sizing, so as not to block the shaping of the work.

Embroidering a support row

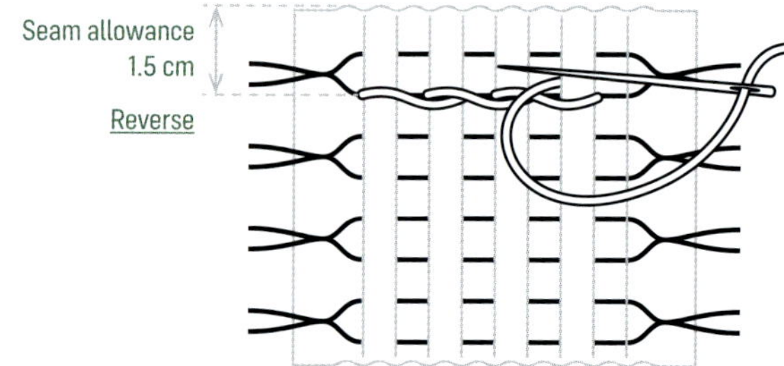

Support rows reinforce the work on the back of the work and are a precious aid during final sewing. They are embroidered in stem stitch.

Embroider a first support row on the first available line of gathering thread after the seam allowance. Then embroider one every ten rows of gathering thread.

Embroidering smocks

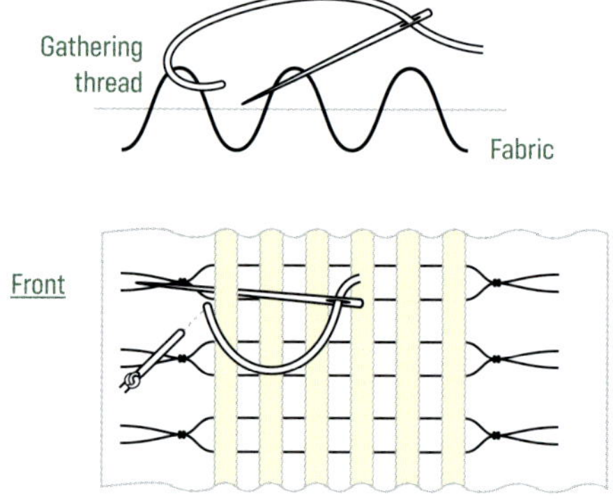

Smocks are embroidered on the right side of the work and follow the gathering threads horizontally and in zigzag, depending on the embroidery stitches used.

Stitch the needle over the gathering thread and catch the top of the pleat, without stitching into the gathering thread.

Tie a knot in the thread, take out the needle, and stitch in the first fold right next to the gathering threads. Embroider the first and following rows with the chosen embroidery stitch.

For left-handed people

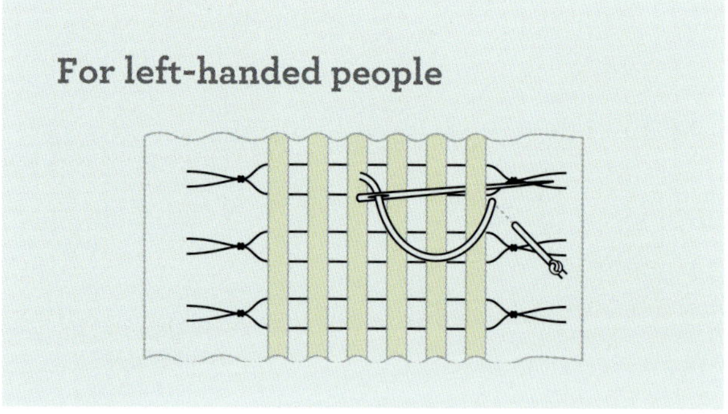

Finishing

Once embroidered, remove the gathering threads. Gently iron it on the wrong side, using steam or a damp pressing cloth, pulling the embroidery to enlarge it to fit the garment to be sewn.

If there are any threads left over from the needle changes, use stopper knots to lock them in place. All that remains is to sew the garment.

Embroidery Stitches

Smocking is worked without hoops. Unless otherwise specified, they are embroidered from left to right for right-handers and vice versa for left-handers.

What You Need to Know

Smocking can also be embellished with embroidery stitches: chain stitch, feather stitch, bow stitch, bullion knot for embroidering small roses, or loop stitch.

Note that it's not very complicated to make your own diagrams. The most important thing is to know how to make the embroidery stitches and how many folds they are embroidered on (see page 156).

Cable stitch or backstitch or braided stitch

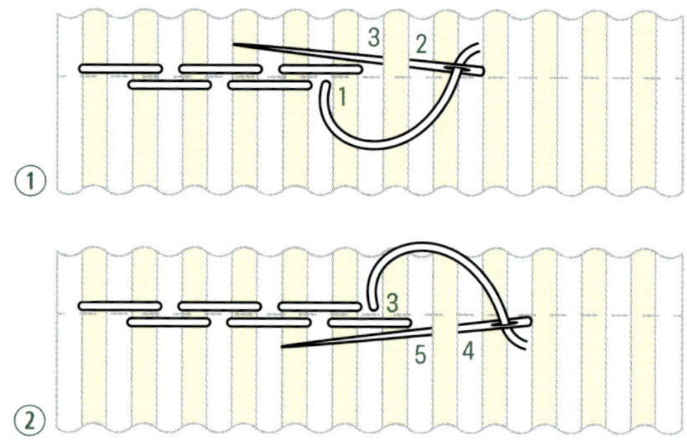

1 Take out the needle in 1, with the thread facing downward. Stitch in 2 in the next fold and pull out in 3.

2 Place the thread upward, stitch in 4 in the next fold, and pull out in 5. Work alternately with the thread upward and downward.

Cable-stitched flowerette

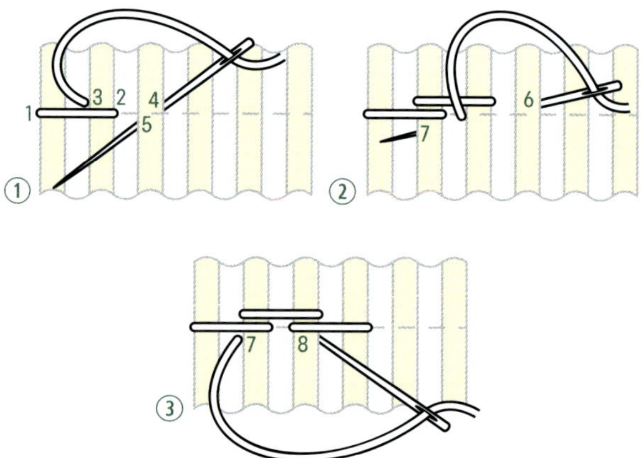

1 Take the needle out in 1, stitch in 2, and take out in 3 to embroider a cable stitch. Stitch in 4 and out in 5 to embroider a second stitch above the first.

2 Stitch in 6 and out in 7 to embroider a stitch following the first.

3 Stitch in 8. Finish the flower by tying a stopper knot at the back of the work, or move on to the next flower if it's close enough.

Parallel cable stitch

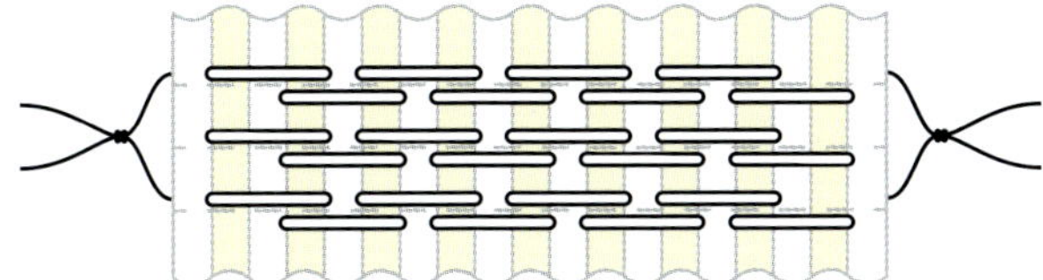

On gathering threads spaced 5 mm apart, embroider one row in cable stitch between each gathering thread. The top or bottom position of the cable stitches is identical for each embroidered row.

Opposite cable stitch

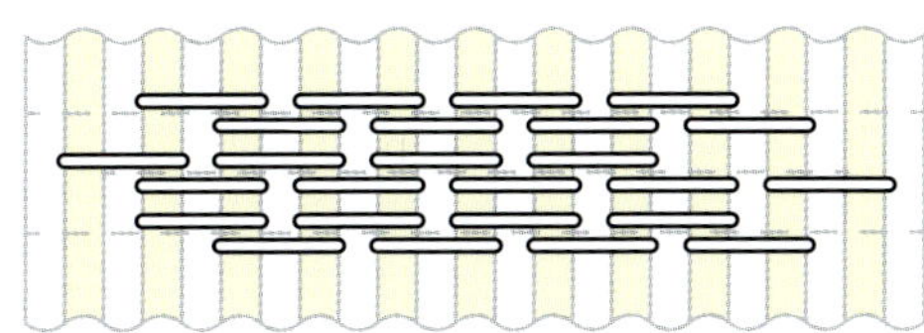

Cable stitches face each other from row to row to the other.

Embroider on the gathering threads, adding an extra row between each gathering thread. The rows of cable rows of cable stitch are therefore embroidered every 2.5 mm.

Picot cable stitch

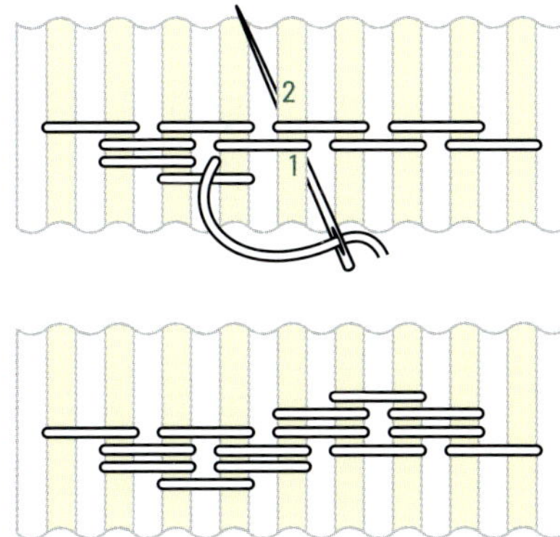

Embroider a first row in cable stitch. Under this row, embroider three cable stitches opposite the main row. Pass the needle under the main row: stitch in 1 and take out the needle in 2. Embroider three cable stitches above and opposite the next two stitches of the main row. Work alternately under and over the main row.

Diamond stitch or chevron stitch

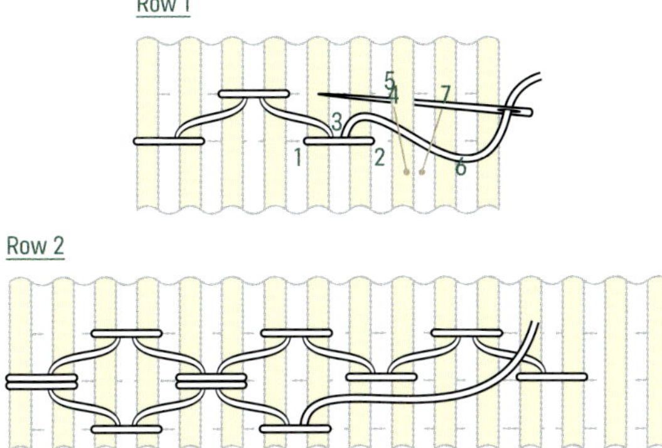

This stitch is a variant of the cable stitch, which is embroidered on two gathering threads.

Row 1 Take the needle out in 1, skip two pleats, stitch in 2, and take out in 3. Move up to one or two gathering threads higher, depending on the desired effect: stitch in 4, take out in 5, skip two gathering threads, stitch in 6, and take out in 7. Continue, embroidering alternately from one gathering line to the next.

Row 2 Embroider in the same way, facing each other.

Embroider the following rows, using these first two rows.

Surface honeycomb stitch

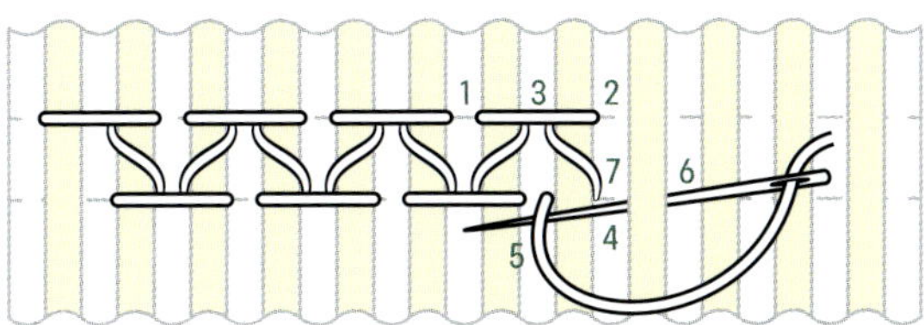

Honeycomb stitch is a variant of diamond stitch. Each fold is stitched alternately on top and bottom (unlike diamond stitch, where each fold is stitched on top or bottom). The embroidery is thus denser.

Take the needle out at 1, pick up at 2, and take out at 3 (3 is in the middle of the first and second folds). Move down to the next gathering thread: pick up at 4, take out at 5, pick up at 6, and take out at 7 (4 and 7 are in the middle of the second and third folds).

Elastic honeycomb stitch

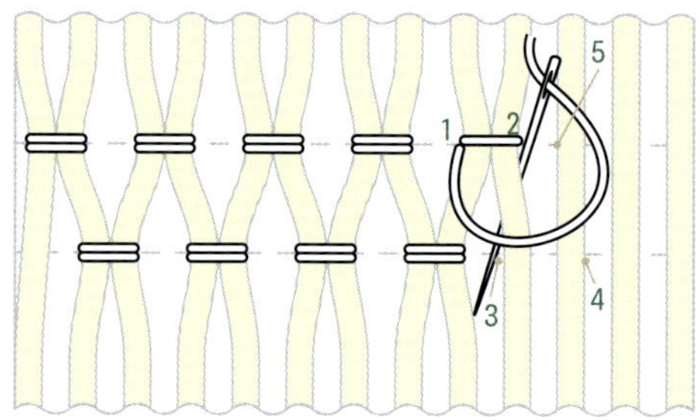

Embroider two folds together, alternating up and down. The stitches shift one fold each time.

Bring the needle out in 1 and stitch in 2, bring out in 1, stitch in 2, and bring out in 3, turning inside out, in the fold hollow (2 and 3 are in the same fold)—the needle should come out in 3 one or two gathering threads lower (as desired). Stitch in 4 and out in 3, then stitch in 4 and out in 5, turning inside out, in the fold hollow.

Wide honeycomb stitch

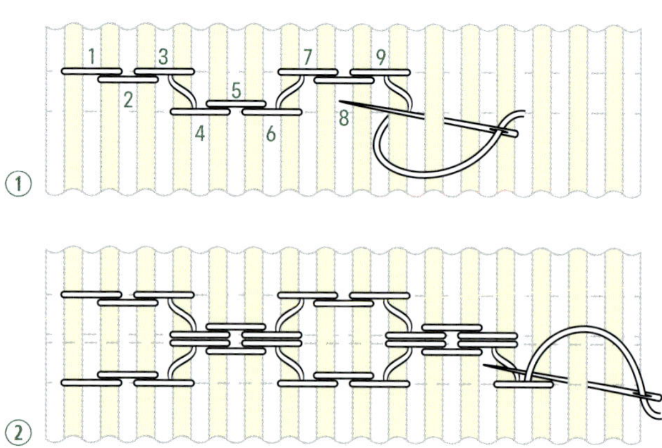

The wide honeycomb stitch is embroidered alternately up and down.

1 Embroider three cable stitches, in the order 1, 2, and 3. Go down one or two gathering threads (as desired) and embroider three cable stitches (4, 5, and 6). Go back up to the first stitches and stitch 7, 8, and 9.

2 Embroider the next row opposite the first row. The three cable stitches at the top of the second row are joined to the three cable stitches at the bottom of the first row.

Stem stitch

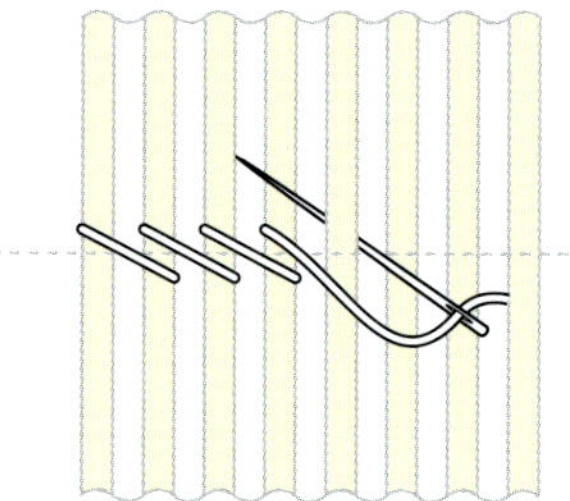

Embroider in stem stitch, working thread toward you as for classic stem stitch, and needle tilted upward.

Contour stitch

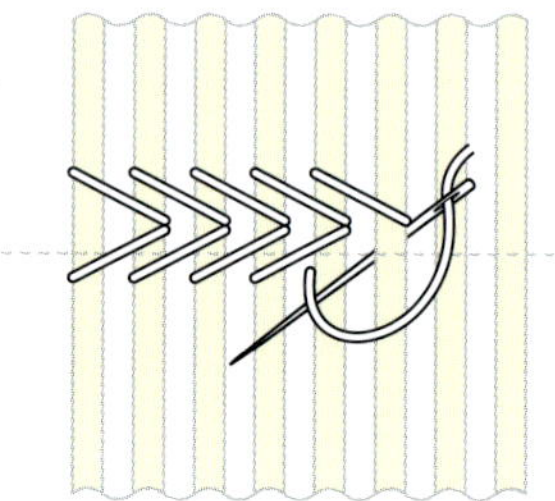

Contour stitch is a stem stitch embroidered by passing the needle under the working thread with the needle inclined downward.

Stem and contour stitches combined

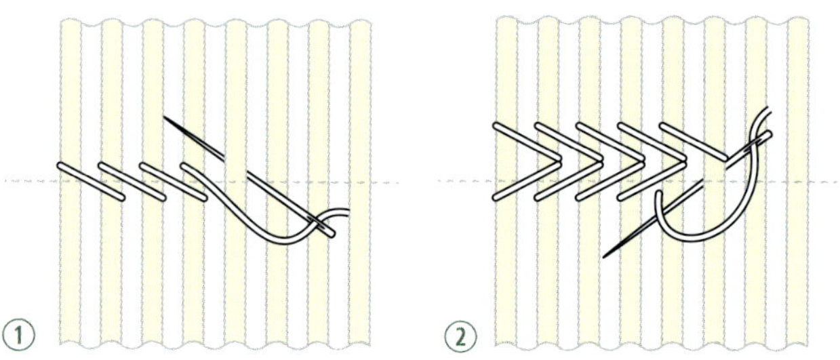

Combine the stem stitch and the contour stitch to form a chevron.

1 Embroider a first row in stem stitch.

2 Embroider the next row in contour stitch.

Wave and trellis stitches

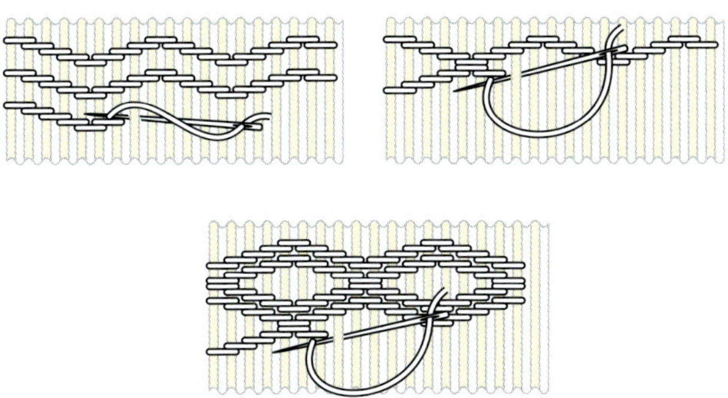

The zigzag stitch is embroidered by combining a stem stitch (working upward) and a contour stitch (working downward). Work upward and then downward to form zigzags.

Van Dyck stitch

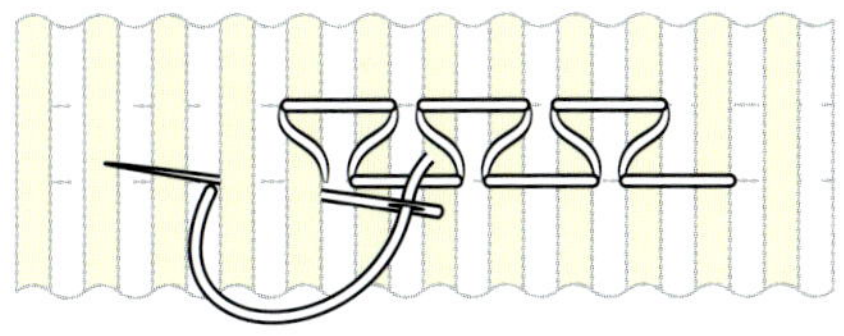

Van Dyck stitch is embroidered from right to left for right-handers, and vice versa for left-handers.

Pass the needle through two folds at the same time, then iron it in the same place. Work alternately up and down on two gathering threads.

Visual Library of Embroidery Stitches

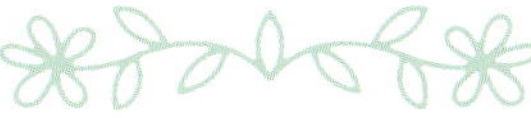

Reading symbols on a diagram

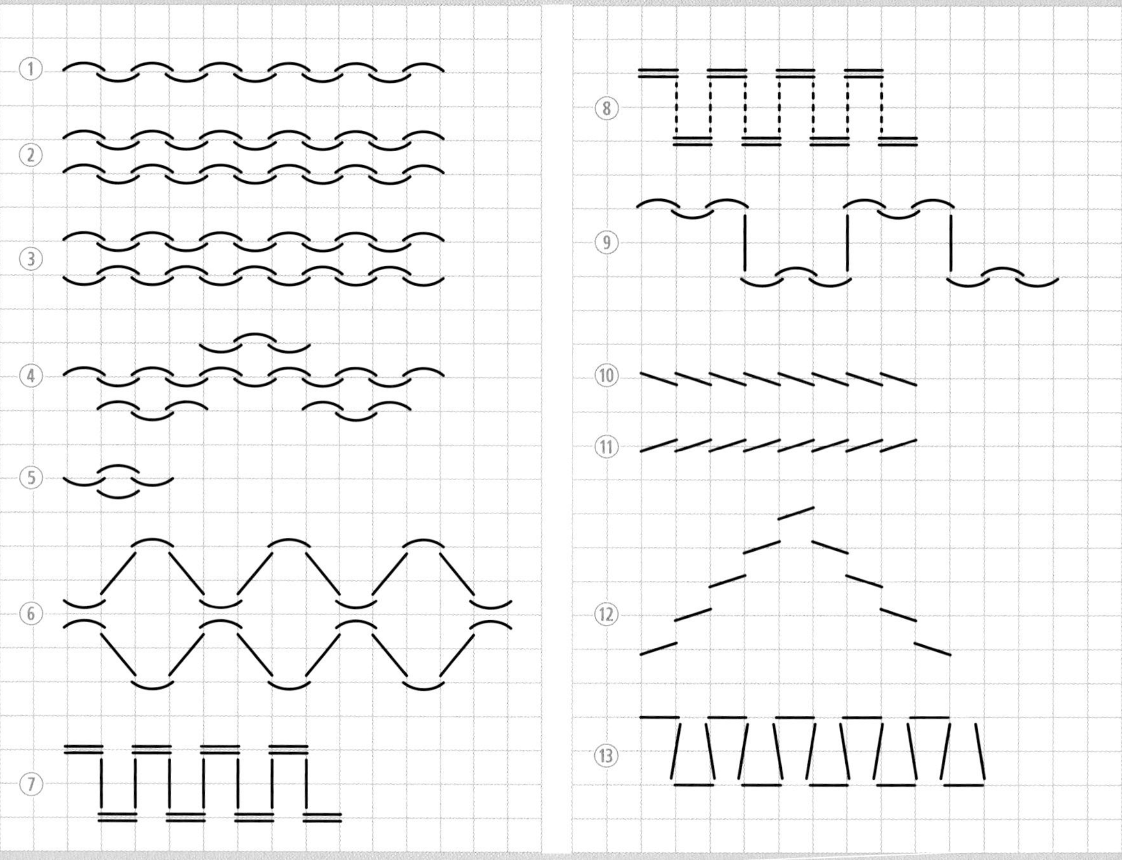

① Cable stitch
② Parallel cable stitch
③ Opposite cable stitch
④ Picot cable stitch
⑤ Cable-stitched flowerette
⑥ Diamond stitch
⑦ Honeycomb
⑧ Elastic honeycomb
⑨ Wide honeycomb
⑩ Stem stitch
⑪ Contour stitch
⑫ Wave stitch
⑬ Van Dyck stitch

On a grid, each vertical line represents the top of a pleat, each space between the lines the bottom of the pleat, and the horizontal lines the gathering threads.

NEEDLEPOINT AND WOOL EMBROIDERY

From the Middle Ages to the Renaissance, needlepoint embroidery (canvaswork or wool embroidery) enjoyed its heyday in Europe. Not only wool, but also silk, gold, and silver threads were delicately and imaginatively embroidered on painted hemp canvas.

For many centuries, basic stitches have been used to embroider with and on wool. Stem stitch and chain stitch remain the oldest in use. In England, for example, Crewel embroidery, also known as "Jacobean" embroidery, was popularized as early as the 17th and 18th centuries.

It is also possible to embroider a sweater knitted in stockinette stitch: the embroidery then reproduces a motif by superimposing itself on the knitted stockinette stitch.

Close-up of a cotton bedspread embroidered in England. The embroidery stitches are made in wool in pastel impiétant, flat purl, stem stitch, running stitch, and knot stitch.

Needlepoint on Canvas

Today, needlepoint is often used for furnishings, small decorative objects (such as boxes), and accessories. The embroidery completely covers the surface: designs and grounds are embroidered.

Traditionally, needlepoint is made with wool on a textile support called a "canvas," following a diagram or design painted directly onto the canvas with acrylic paint.

Supplies

The choice of supplies depends on the purpose of the embroidery and the stitch chosen.

Canvas

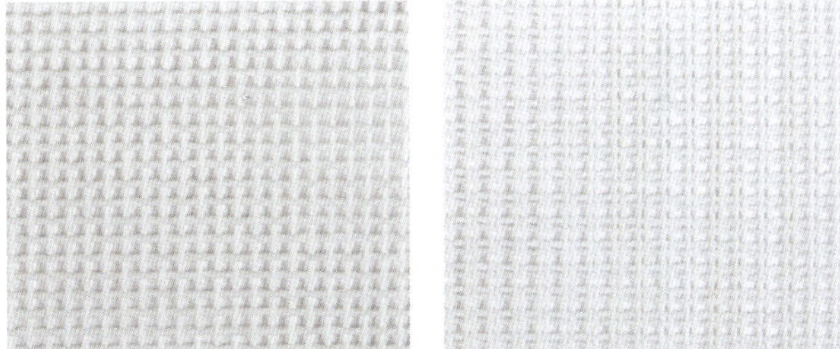

Left, monocanvas canvas; *right*, Penelope canvas

Canvas is a regular, resistant, and rigid textile support because it is highly primed with starch. There are two types:

- Monocanvas canvas, composed of simple warp and weft threads. It is suitable for all diagonal and diagonal stitches, such as the Saint-Cyr stitch.
- Double-thread canvas, or "Penelope" canvas, with doubled warp and weft threads. Suitable for straight stitches such as Gobelin or Aubusson.

White or beige in color, these canvases come in different sizes, defined by the number of holes per centimeter or decimeter. For example, at Tapisseries de la Bûcherie (see page 410):

- monocanvas 12 canvas with 10 2cm holes
- monocanvas 16 canvas with 13 holes over 2 cm
- monocanvas 20 canvas has 19 holes over 2 cm
- Penelope 18 canvas has eight 2cm holes
- Penelope 20 canvas has nine holes by 2 cm

The canvas must be tightly stretched on a rectangular or square embroidery frame. Round hoops are to be avoided, since they will break and deform the canvas, making it unusable.

Sewn to the stitching at the top and bottom, it is possible to wrap the canvas around the mortises if its height exceeds that of the frame. In this case, the mortises must be round to avoid damaging the canvas—you unroll one side and wrap the other around them as you work. On the other hand, the width of the frame must be greater than that of the canvas.

What You Need to Know

It isn't necessary to tension the canvas on these sides with pulls, since it is sufficiently rigid.

Needles

Embroidery is carried out with a tapestry needle with a round tip, to be adapted according to the size of the wool chosen. The no. 18 tapestry needle is versatile.

Threads

All wools are suitable for tapestry, but some are specific to this technique and to embroidery. Here are the main qualities and brands currently available, in a wide range of colors.

- La Route de la Laine Fine d'Aubusson wool, 100% merino wool yarn. It is made up of four separable strands.
- Ets J. Toulemonde Saint-Pierre wool, half wool and half polyamide yarn, also used for darning. It is made up of four separable strands.
- Colbert DMC wool, a brightly colored 100% wool yarn. It is usually worked in tent stitch on Penelope canvas.

With the first two types of wool (whose strands can separate), embroider with several strands of different colors to obtain mottled tones.

What You Need to Know

You'll find a wide range of needlepoint kits on the market featuring a painted canvas and Retors mat DMC cotton threads, which are less expensive than wool. Note, however, that the result will be less plush and less solid.

Aubusson Fine Wool
La Route de la Laine

Saint-Pierre wool
Ets J. Toulemonde

Laine Colbert DMC

Embroidery stitches

In needlepoint, both hands are used to embroider: the one above stitches the needle from right side to left side, while the one below grabs the needle, pulls it, and stitches from left side to right side. The smaller and tighter the stitches, the stronger the needlepoint.

Tips for Good Embroidery

Pull the needles straight up or down to avoid distorting the canvas and prematurely wearing out the wool.

A needlepoint or canvas pieces always begins at the top right, with a temporary knot and a covered straight stitch (see page 39). Stopping is also done with a covered straight stitch (see page 43).

The three basic stitches used in needlepoint are tent stitch, upright Gobelin, and oblique Gobelin. The first is preferred for so-called "seat" embroideries subject to heavy wear, such as the upholstery of armchairs, chairs, and stools. All other stitches are based on these three; there are hundreds of possible combinations.

The fancier stitches (such as Paris or Brighton stitch) are reserved for cushions, wall panels, and small objects.

Tent stitch or petit point (on very thin canvas) or gros point (on very thick canvas)

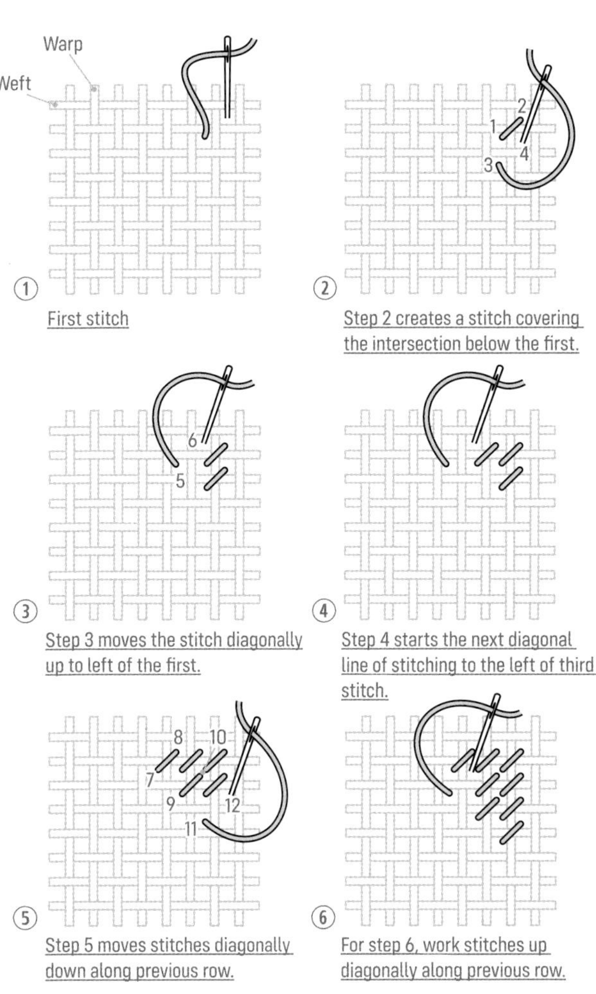

1. First stitch
2. Step 2 creates a stitch covering the intersection below the first.
3. Step 3 moves the stitch diagonally up to left of the first.
4. Step 4 starts the next diagonal line of stitching to the left of third stitch.
5. Step 5 moves stitches diagonally down along previous row.
6. For step 6, work stitches up diagonally along previous row.

Tent stitch is the most frequently used in needlepoint. It is embroidered in diagonal rows, on monocanvas, with four strands of Fine d'Aubusson wool.

Tips for Good Embroidery

It's very important to examine and locate the crossings in the weave of the canvas in order to start the embroidery at the right place on the weft: when the vertical warp threads pass over the horizontal weft threads, the direction of work is downward (this is called "going down the row on the warp"); when the weft threads pass over the warp threads, the direction of work is upward (this is called "going up the row on the weft").

Step 1 (1) The first stitch is embroidered on a crossing where the warp thread is above the weft thread: take out the needle in 1 and stitch in 2.

Step 2 (2 and 3) The stitches wrap the canvas intersection: take out the needle at 3 and stitch at 4, then take out at 5 and stitch at 6.

Step 3 (4 and 5) Bring the row down to start the next line of diagonal stitches: take out the needle at 7 and stitch at 8, take out at 9 and stitch at 10, take out at 11 and stitch at 12.

Step 4 (6) The stitches wrap the canvas intersection: take out the needle at 13 and stitch at 14, take out at 15 and stitch at 1, take out at 17 and stitch at 18, then take out at 19 and stitch at 20.

Upright or straight Gobelin stitch

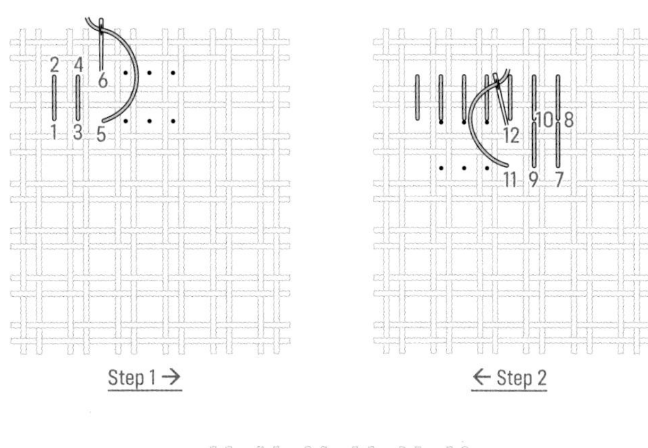

Step 1 → ← Step 2

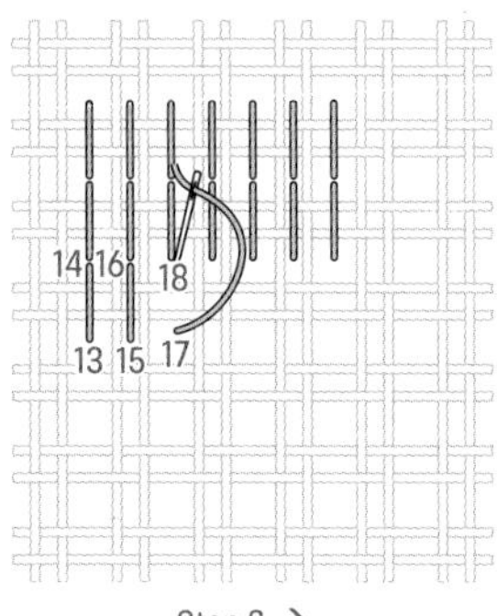

Step 3 →

Upright or straight Gobelin stitch is a straight stitch that is embroidered in horizontal rows (on several heights of weft thread) and back and forth, on Penelope canvas. Leave at least one warp thread and two weft threads between each stitch. It is used for wall panels.

Step 1 (1) Embroider from left to right: take out the needle in 1 and stitch in 2, take out in 3 and stitch in 4, then then take out in 5 and stitch in 6.

Step 2 (2) Embroider from right to left: take out the needle at 7 and stitch at 8, take out at 9 and stitch at 10, then then take out at 11 and stitch at 12.

Step 3 (3) Embroider from left to right: take out the needle at 13 and stitch at 14, take out at 15 and stitch at 16, then then take out at 17 and stitch at 18.

Oblique Gobelin stitch

Oblique Gobelin stitch, slightly slanted, is embroidered horizontally or vertically on Pénélope. It is used for wall panels.

→ Horizontal oblique Gobelin stitch

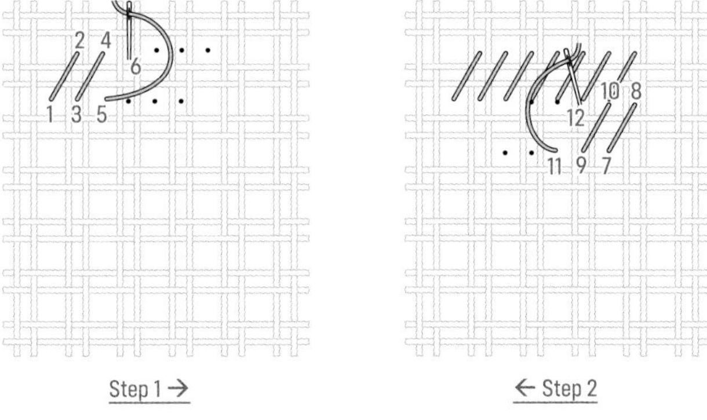

Step 1 → ← Step 2

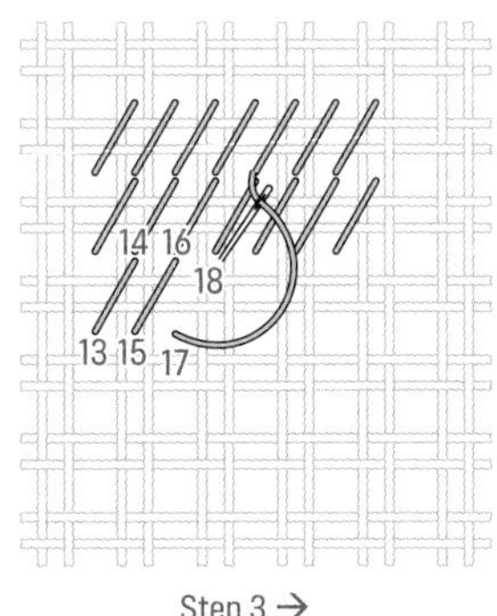

Step 3 →

Step 1 (1) Embroider from left to right: take out the needle in 1 and stitch in 2, take out in 3 and stitch in 4, take out in 5 and stitch in 6.

Step 2 (2) Embroider from right to left: take out the needle at 7 and stitch at 8, take out at 9 and stitch at 10, take out at 11 and stitch at 12.

Step 3 (3) Embroider from left to right: take out the needle at 13 and stitch at 14, take out at 15 and stitch at 16, take out at 17 and stitch at 18.

→ Vertical oblique Gobelin stitch

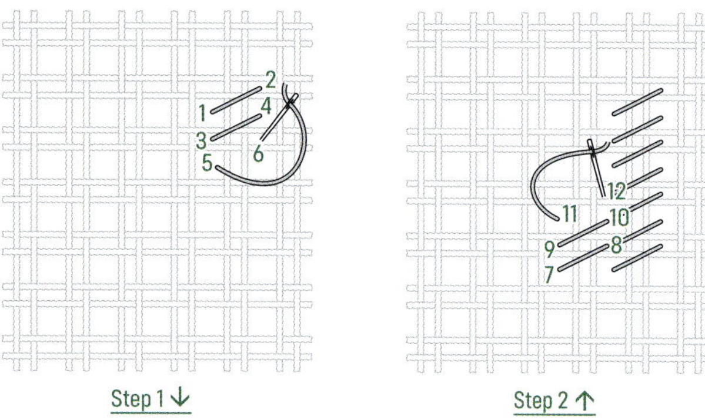

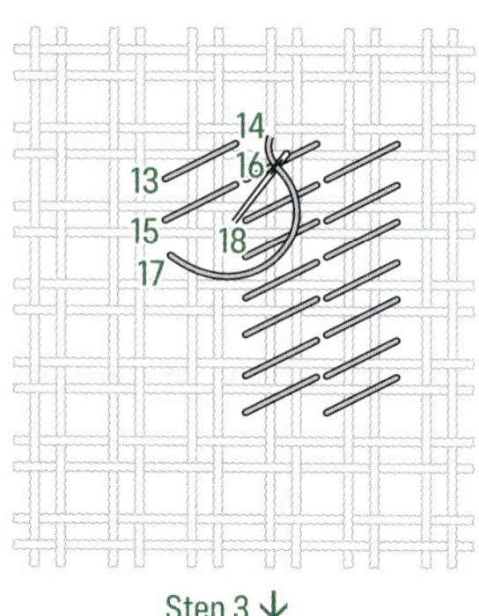

Step 1 (1) Embroider from top to bottom: take out the needle at 1 and stitch at 2, take out at 3 and stitch at 4, then take out at 5 and stitch at 6.

Step 2 (2) Embroider from bottom to top: take out the needle at 7 and stitch at 8, take out at 9 and stitch at 10, then take out at 11 and stitch at 12.

Step 3 (3) Embroider from top to bottom: take out the needle at 13 and stitch at 14, take out at 15 and stitch at 16, then take out at 17 and stitch at 18.

Bargello stitch

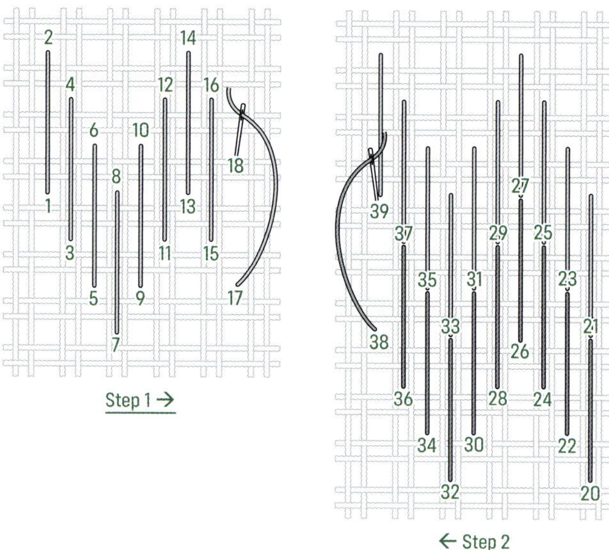

Bargello stitch is embroidered in vertical rows and back and forth, on Penelope canvas. It can be worked in several colors.

Start by embroidering a first row, defining the number of weft threads covered by a stitch, then maintain this space between each stitch.

Step 1 (1) Embroider from left to right: take out the needle in 1 and stitch in 2, take out in 3 and stitch in 4, then then take out in 5 and stitch in 6.

Step 2 (2) Embroider from right to left: take out the needle at 20 and stitch at 21, take out at 22 and stitch at 23, then take out at 24 and stitch at 25.

Cross-stitch

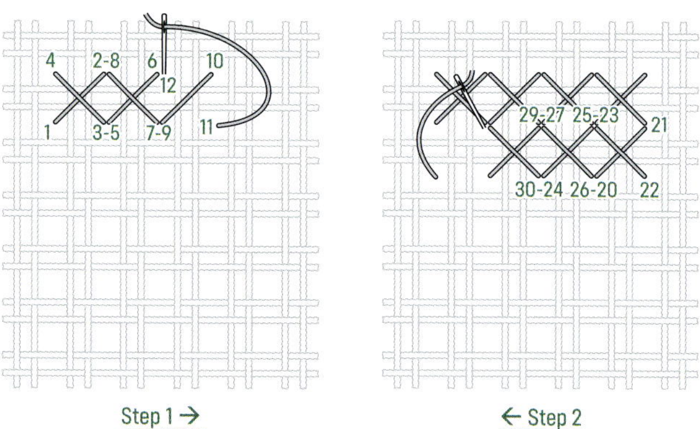

Cross-stitch is embroidered with full crosses (as shown in these diagrams) or with back-and-forth stitches (following classic cross-stitch techniques), on Penelope canvas.

Step 1 (1) Embroider from left to right: take out the needle at 1 and stitch at 2, then take out at 3 and stitch at 4 to embroider the first cross. Take out in 5 and stitch in 6, then then take out in 7 and stitch in 8 to embroider the second cross.

Step 2 (2) Embroider from right to left: take out the needle at 20 and stitch at 21, then take out at 22 and stitch at 23 to embroider the first cross. Exit at 24 and stitch at 25.

Half stitch or tent stitch or half-cross stitch

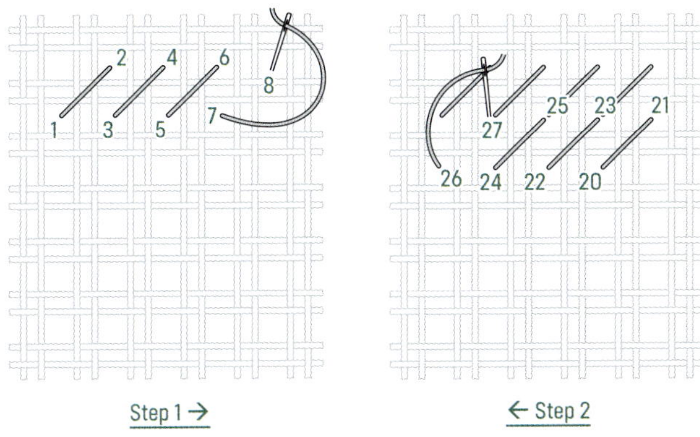

Half stitch is embroidered in rows and back and forth, on Penelope canvas.

Step 1 (1) Embroider from left to right: take out the needle in 1 and stitch in 2, take out in 3 and stitch in 4, then take out in 5 and stitch in 6.

Step 2 (2) Embroider from right to left: take out the needle at 20 and stitch at 21, take out at 22 and stitch at 23, then take out at 24 and stitch at 25.

Upright cross-stitch

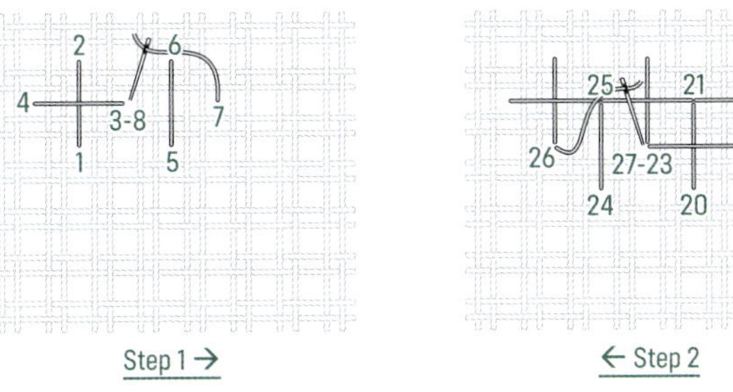

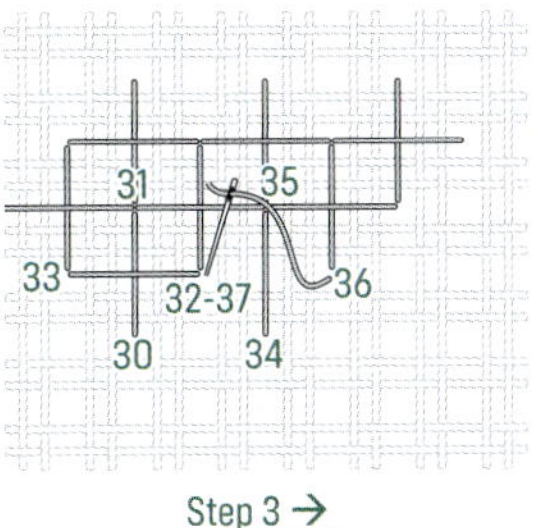

Upright cross-stitch is embroidered back and forth on Penelope canvas. Crosses must be straight.

Step 1 (1) Embroider from left to right: take out the needle at 1 and stitch at 2, then take out at 3 and stitch at 4 to embroider the first cross. Take out in 5 and stitch in 6, take out in 7 and stitch in 8 to embroider the second cross.

Step 2 (2) Embroider from right to left: take out the needle at 20 and stitch at 21, then take out at 22 and stitch at 23 to embroider the first cross. Take out at 24 and stitch at 25, then take out at 26 and stitch at 27 to embroider the next cross.

Step 3 (3) Embroider from left to right: take out the needle at 30 and stitch at 31, then take out at 32 and stitch at 33 to embroider the first cross. Exit at 34 and stitch at 35, then exit at 36 and stitch at 37 to embroider the next cross.

Parisian stitch

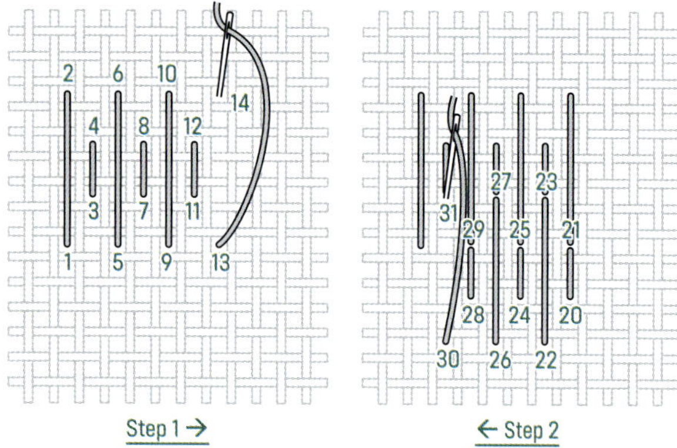

Parisian stitch is embroidered in vertical rows and back-and-forth, on a single-sided canvas.

Step 1 (1) Embroider from left to right: take out the needle in 1 and stitch in 2, take out in 3 and stitch in 4, then take out in 5 and stitch in 6.

Step 2 (2) Embroider from right to left: take out the needle in 20 and stitch in 21, take out in 22 and stitch in 23, then take out in 24 and stitch in 25.

Brighton stitch

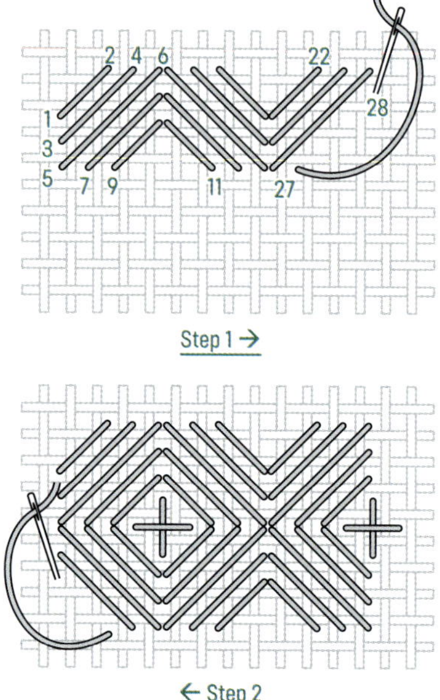

Brighton stitch is embroidered back and forth on monocanvas. The diamonds are worked in two stages: start with diagonal stitches, then make crosses in the spaces at the center of each diamond.

Step 1 (1) Embroider from left to right: take out the needle in 1 and stitch in 2, take out in 3 and stitch in 4, take out in 5 and stitch in 6.

Step 2 (2) Embroider from right to left: take out the needle at 20 and stitch at 21, take out at 22 and stitch at 23, then take out at 24 and stitch at 25.

Step 3 (3) Embroider the crosses in the center of each block.

Embroidering with Wool

All basic embroidery stitches can be performed with wool or on wool. However, the knit stitch is specific to embroidery on a jersey knit.

What You Need to Know

When embroidering traditional embroidery stitches on garments and sweaters, it is often necessary to use a temporary stabilizer such as Sulky (see page 36) to counter the elasticity of the knitted fabric during embroidery.

Knit stitch

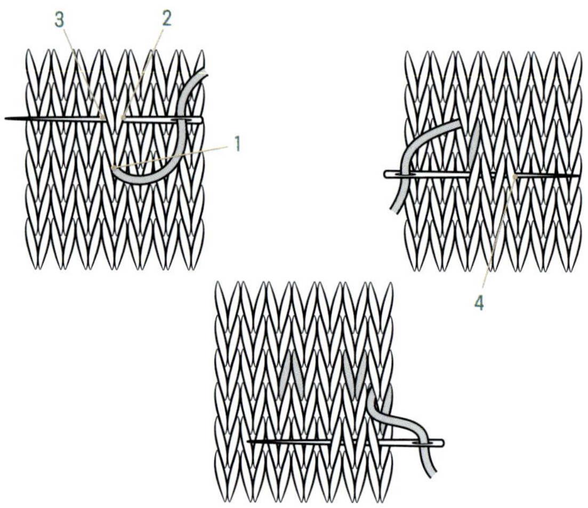

What You Need to Know

Diagrams for cross-stitch can also be used for surface embroidery.

Knit stitch is similar to jacquard. Like cross-stitch, it is embroidered using a diagram on which each stitch of the knitted fabric is represented by a cross. It is performed on the right side of a jersey knitted fabric, with the stitches clearly visible for ease of use. Each stitch is embroidered on top of a jersey stitch in the knitted fabric.

This stitch can be embroidered from left to right or right to left.

1 Take out the needle in the center of a stitch in 1, then pass under the two threads of the stitch above. Stitch in 2 and pull out in 3 to form the same loop as the jersey stitch below, then stitch back into the center in 1.

2 Go out in 4 and do the same as in step 1.

Visual Library of Embroidery Stitches

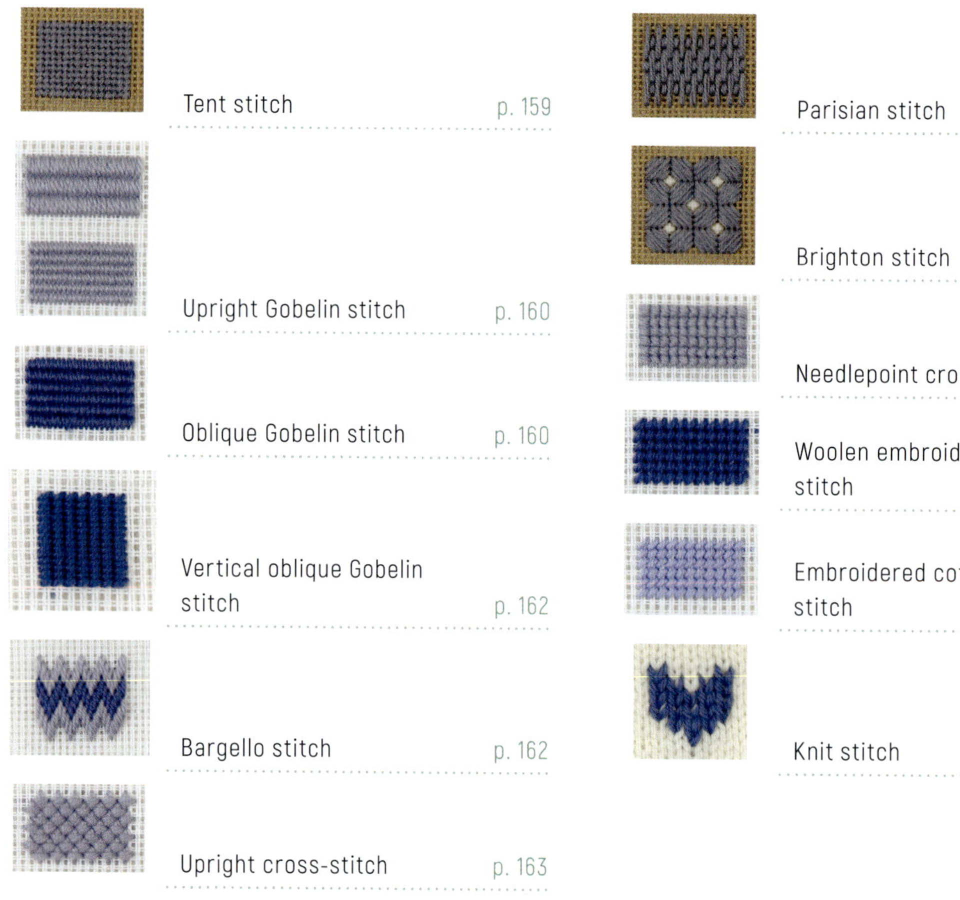

BEAD AND SEQUIN EMBROIDERY

For centuries, beads and spangles embroidery has been practiced the world over.

In Europe, this type of embroidery was very popular in the 18th and 19th centuries up until the First World War.

In Brittany, the regional term "perlage" (beading) had its heyday between the two world wars.

Sequin embroidery, a later arrival, enhanced princely and ecclesiastical garments with a touch of sparkle before the Napoleonic era.

Beads come in a variety of sizes and colors, and in a wide range of materials: mother-of-pearl, glass, crystal, amber, coral, horn, wood, stone, and plastic. Sequins, generally round, are made of plastic, metal, or glass.

Integral to this embroidery technique is the needlework of tubes, bowls, fancy sequins, sparkles, cabochons, mirrors, jewels, and rhinestones for sewing.

Pearl embroidery, Italy, 18th century

Bag embroidered with pearls, tubes, sequins, and jewels, shown in the projects on page 348

What You Need to Know

At the end of the 19th century, the Lunéville crochet hook revolutionized bead and sequin embroidery in Lunéville, Lorraine. The work was much faster, since the supplies were attached to the right side of the fabric, thanks to a chain stitch made on the reverse side of the work. This technique is still widely used in haute couture.

Glass bead embroidery, 1832

Supplies

In bead and sequin embroidery, there is an infinite variety of sizes and materials for each of the supplies. Suppliers have their own references, making it difficult to list them all here.

- Rock, crystal, and wooden beads have been around since the Stone Age, when men pierced shells, bones, and teeth to make necklaces. Later, the Egyptians made beads from a variety of materials, including wood, earth, coral, and horn. They even knew how to produce glass beads, whereas European glassblowers were unable to do so until the Middle Ages. Generally round or oval, but sometimes in more fanciful shapes, the beads were already pierced with a hole through which they could be threaded and fixed in place.

- Sew-on jewels, stones, and rhinestones: these are decorative elements with several holes or mounted on metal brackets that allow them to be stitched down and secured.

- Flat sequins and cupped sequins: flat sequins are generally round and flat (sometimes square or polygonal), with a diameter of less than a centimeter. They have a hole in the center for threading and fastening. Cupped sequins are curved and can be placed on either side, depending on the desired effect.

- Bugle beads are long beads.

- Paillettes are flat and come in a variety of shapes. The hole through which they are threaded and attached is off-center.

- Mirrors are round, 8 to 20 mm in diameter. They are often used in Indian embroidery.

Beads and sequins

Mirrors

Sew-on jewelry

• Threads, whether sewing threads (cotton and polyester or cotton only) or glove threads (fine, solid glazed cotton).

What You Need to Know

Glove thread was once used for sewing gloves. Today it is recommended for hand sewing and for attaching beads and sequins.

All these supplies are installed with a double needle: the thread is passed through the eye of the needle, and the ends are knotted together.

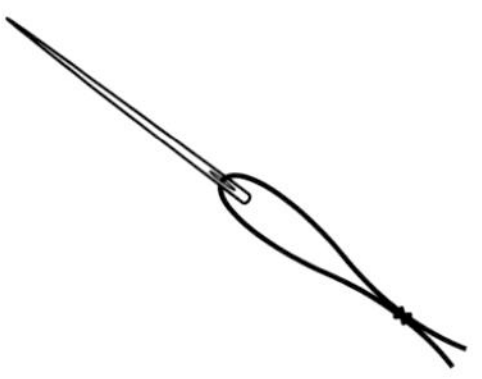

Equipment

Classic embroidery materials are required to embroider pearls and sequins:

• An embroidery frame or round hoop with a diameter greater than the embroidery surface

• Milliners and beading needles in various sizes, to be adapted to the size of the supplies

Don't forget a velvet board to make your work easier (see page 25). You can place your supplies in it to catch them with the needle before embroidering.

Techniques

Certain embroidery stitches (such as backstitch, running stitch, straight stitch, or cross-stitch) must be perfectly mastered in order to stitch with the supplies.

What You Need to Know

If you are left-handed, refer to the chapters on embroidery stitches to find out which way to work.

Setting a single bead

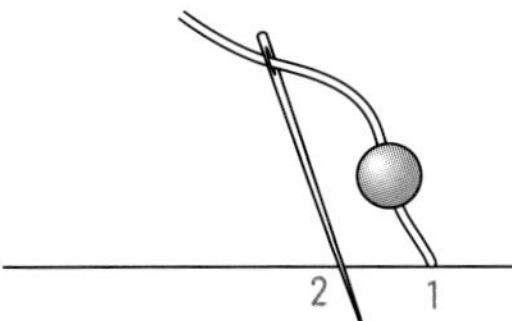

Take out the needle in 1, thread the bead onto the needle, and stitch in 2.

Stitching a single bugle bead

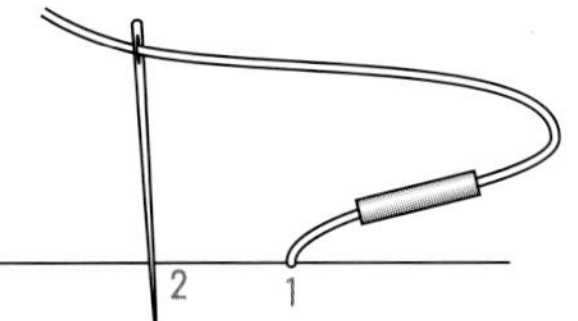

Remove the needle in 1, thread the tube over the needle, and prick in 2. Tube must lie flat.

Laying a seed pearl

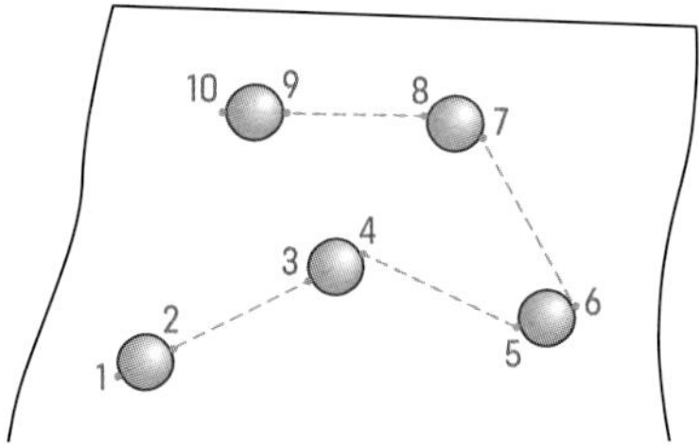

If the substrate is opaque, work with a single needle and lay the beads individually in backstitch or running stitch, moving from one to the other.

If the backing is transparent, start and stop the needle at each bead to avoid the thread running down the back of the work between each bead.

Several beads at once

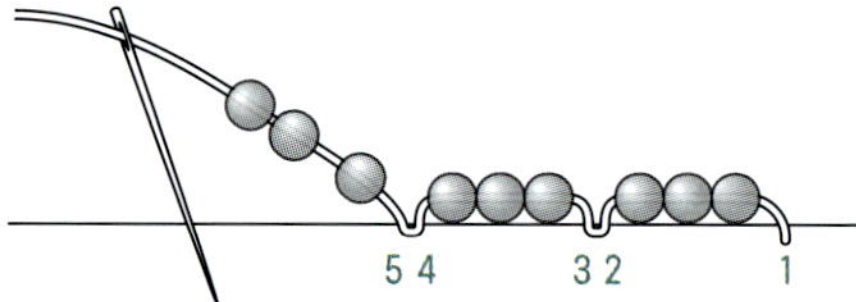

This work can be done with one, two, or three beads.

Take the needle out in 1, thread three beads onto the needle, and stitch in 2, just after the last bead. Take the needle out in 3, thread three beads onto the needle, and stitch in 4.

Tips for Good Embroidery

Make sure the beads lie flat and do not overlap when you place them.

Smoothed couched line of beads

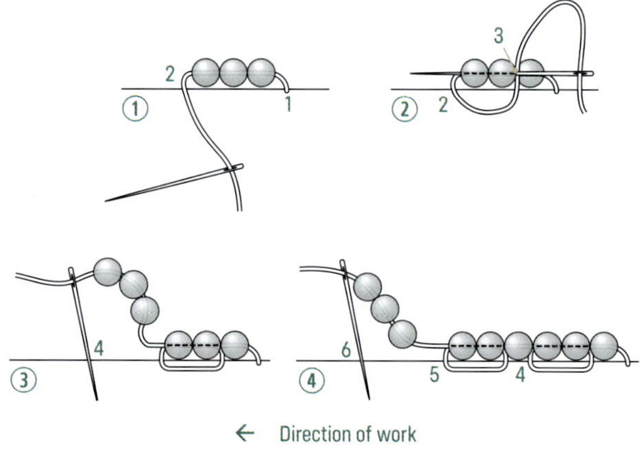

1 and 2 Take the needle out in 1, thread three beads on the needle, stitch in 2, take out in 3, and iron in the last two beads.

3 and 4 Thread three new beads onto the needle, prick in 4, pull out in 5, and iron in the last two beads.

Stem stitch beading

Create a stem stitch by stringing five or six beads at each point.

Laying beads in a satin stitch motion

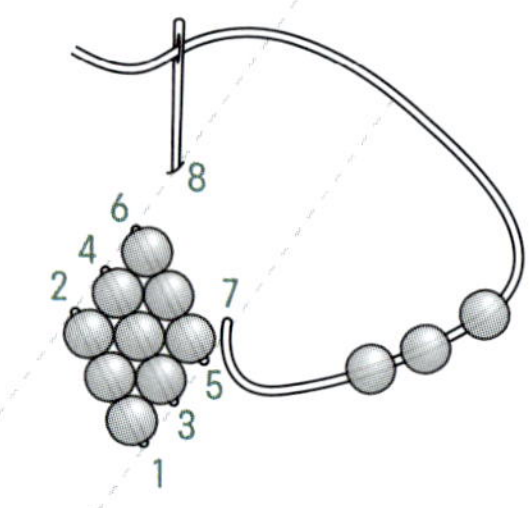

This technique is perfect for small surfaces. Embroider using the flat pastry technique, threading as many beads as necessary on the needle to cover the surface.

Laying beads with a straight stitch

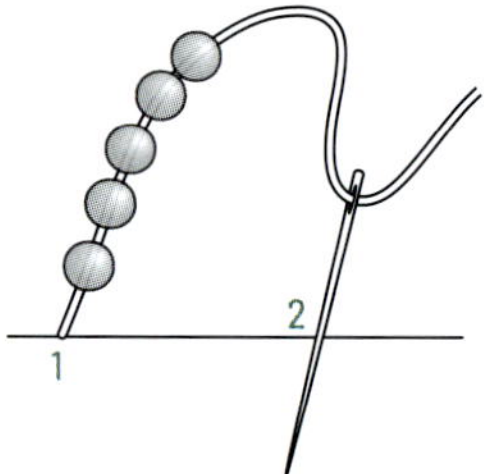

Embroider in straight stitch, threading as many beads as necessary to cover the length of the stitch.

Laying beads or tubes

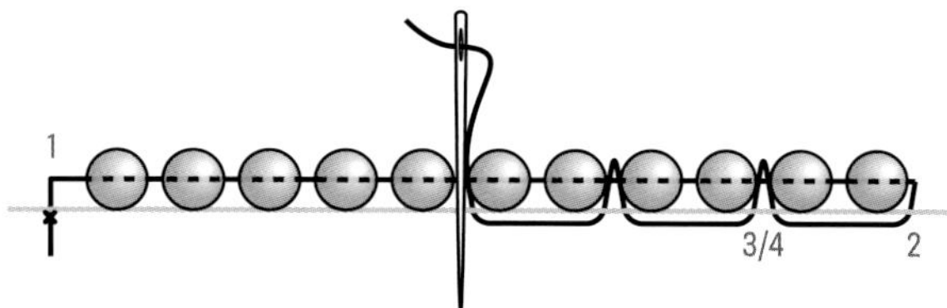

Take out the needle in 1, then thread as many beads as necessary onto the needle to cover the length to be embroidered. Pick up in 2, take out in 3, and pick up in 4 to make a couching stitch straddling the thread passing through the beads. Make a couching stitch every two beads.

Backstitch sequins

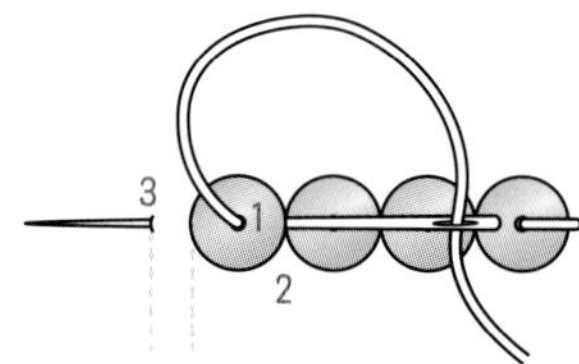

Spacing between sequin holes

Take out the needle in 1, thread a sequin onto the needle, and lay it flat on the work. Stitch in 2, just behind the sequin, and exit in 3 (one sequin radius away).

Line of flat or cupped sequins

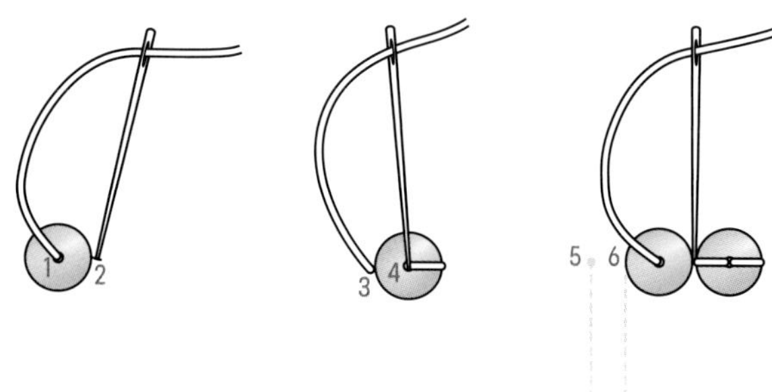

Sequin edge may or may not touch.

1 Take out the needle in 1 and thread a sequin onto the needle. Stitch in 2.

2 Take out 3 and back in at 4 (4 and 1 are the same hole).

3 Go out in 5 (one spangle radius away) and back in at 6 (6 and 3 are the same hole).

Line of overlapping flat or cupped sequins

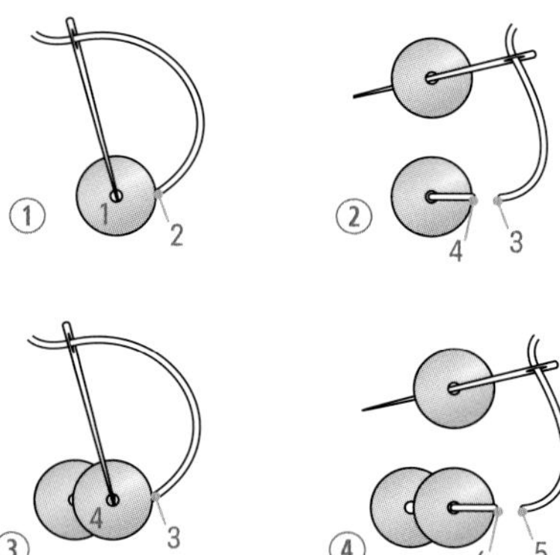

1 Take the needle out in 1, thread a sequin onto the needle, and stitch in 2 (one sequin radius away).

2 Go out in 3 (one sequin beam farther) and thread a sequin onto the needle.

3 and 4 Pick at 4 (4 and 1 are the same), exit at 5 (one sequin radius away), and pick at 6 (6 and 3 are the same).

Sequin filling

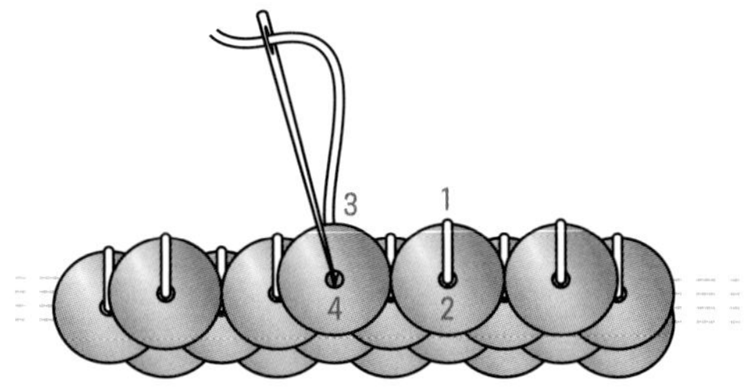

Work is carried out line by line.

Take out the needle in 1, thread a sequin with the needle, and stitch in 2. Pull out in 3, pick up a sequin with the needle, and stitch in 4.

Tips for Good Embroidery

To hide the working thread as much as possible, offset the lines by a value slightly smaller than the radius of the sequins.

Apply sequins (flat or cupped) with a pearl

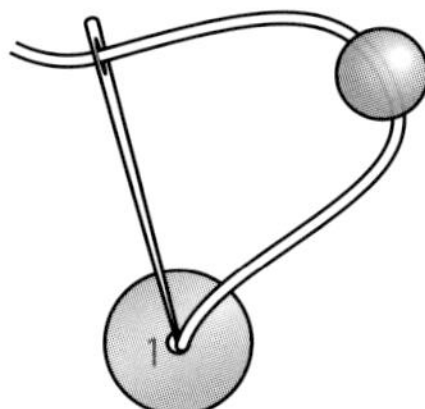

Take out the needle in 1, thread a sequin and a bead onto the needle, then thread again in 1.

Place cupped sequins with several beads

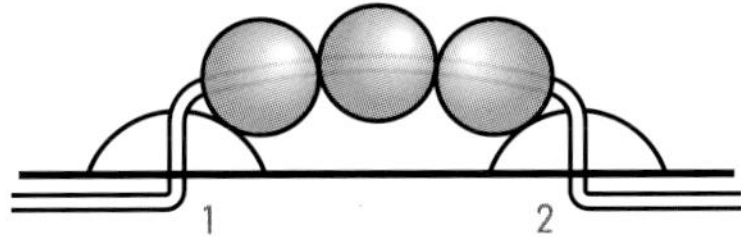

Take out the needle in 1 and thread a bowl, quilting it on the hollow side, and three or four beads. Thread a second bowl, stitching on the domed side, and stitch in 2.

Any combination is possible. Have fun with your supplies!

Attach jewels, bezels, and rhinestones (mounted on metal)

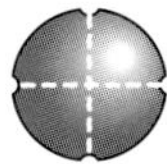

The metal support is available in a variety of shapes. Its base has four holes designed to sew these elements securely to the fabric. They form a cross-shaped passage, which enables the supply to be secured with two intersecting stitches. This technique is performed with a very fine milliners needle, able to pass through the cross.

Fasten each element with three or four cross-stitches through the holes provided.

Laying a stone

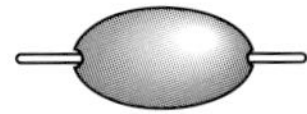

Embellishment stones have a flat back. One to four holes allow the needle to pass through.

Secure each element with three or four stitches passing through the holes provided.

Shisha or mirror embroidery

Mirrorwork (or shisha) originated in Asia. It's an ancient technique for warding off the devil with one's own reflection. Initially, mica flakes were embroidered.

Shisha stitching

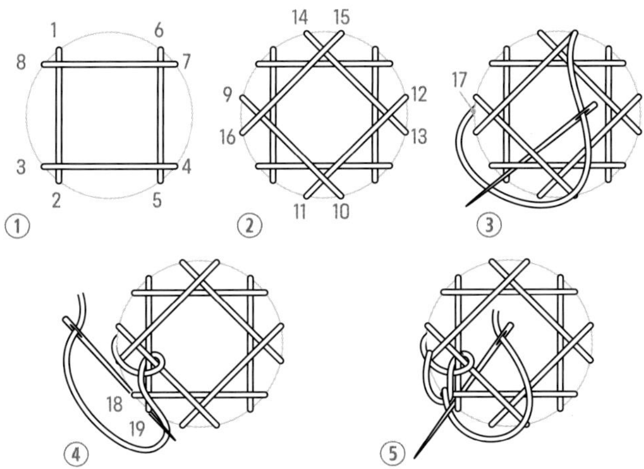

1 and 2 Place the mirror on the work and hold it in place with two perpendicular grids as shown in the diagrams, embroidering with straight stitches.

3 Take out needle 17 and pass it from the inside to the outside, perpendicular to the edge of the mirror, under the buttonhole stitches, on the thread.

4 Stitch in 18 and out in 19.

5 Repeat the same movements until you have completed the full circle of the mirror.

With chain and buttonhole stitches

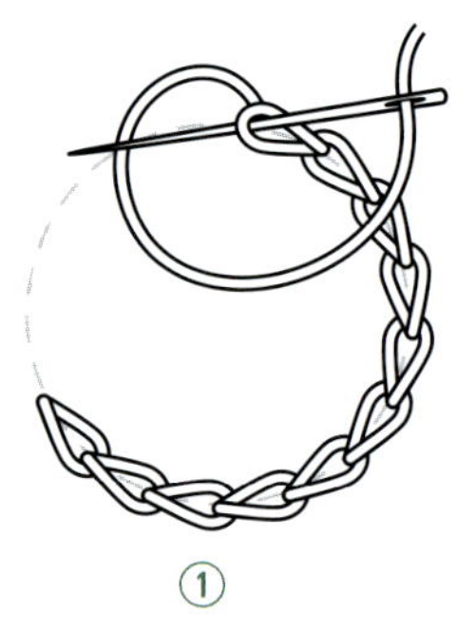
1

2

1 Use a circle template to trace the circumference of the mirror on the work. Remove the mirror and embroider a row in chain stitch on this line.

2 Replace the mirror inside the chain stitch and embroider a first row in buttonhole stitch, stitching through the chain. Embroider a second row in buttonhole stitch, stitching into the previous row.

Visual Library of Embroidery Stitches

RIBBON EMBROIDERY

More spectacular than it is difficult to achieve, ribbon embroidery, formerly known as "rococo embroidery" or "lace embroidery" in the early 18th century, is particularly creative. The volumes created by the specific stitches of this technique reproduce true-to-life flowers.

Presentation dress for the Saint James Court in London, made in the workshops of the Boué sisters' couture house, France, 1932–1934

Supplies

All ribbons, whatever their material, can be embroidered. The choice of textile substrates is equally vast.

Ribbons

Specific ribbons are available for this technique, usually in silk and in different widths (2, 4, 7, 13, and 15 mm). Monochrome ribbons, ribbons with varigated colors or hand-dyed ribbons—the wide range of shades offers great creativity.

Ribbons with picots on the sides are ideal for embroidering eyelets in gathered flower stitch.

Tips for Good Embroidery

Although most ribbons can be machine-washed on the "delicate" cycle, dry-cleaning is the best way to wash your embroidery. Ironing is not recommended, since it can permanently flatten the relief of the stitches. For this reason, this technique is preferable to embellish decorative works rather than garments.

Ground fabric

Silk ribbon can be embroidered on any type of fabric, provided its weight supports the entire embroidery.

It's possible to stabilize the fabric with a light iron-on stabilizer (such as Sulky) to support the embroidery. It's best to make a sample before starting embroidery.

Equipment

Here are the specific materials you will need to embroider with ribbons.

Needles

Ribbon embroidery is done with a chenille needle with a pointed tip. Choosing the right size is very important and depends on the width of the ribbon. Bring an assortment of needles (from 13 to 20):

- no. 20 needle for 2mm ribbons
- no. 18 needle for 4mm ribbons
- no. 16 needle for 7mm ribbons
- no. 13 needle for 10 to 15mm ribbons

Tips for Good Embroidery

To avoid damaging the fabric when using large chenille needles (such as no. 13), pre-punch the fabric with the stiletto.
If the ribbon gets damaged during embroidery, use a larger needle.

Also work with a mellor, an extra needle, or a boxwood manicure stick. They will help you manipulate the ribbon to give it volume and to position it as you wish during embroidery (especially when making straight and ribbon stitches).

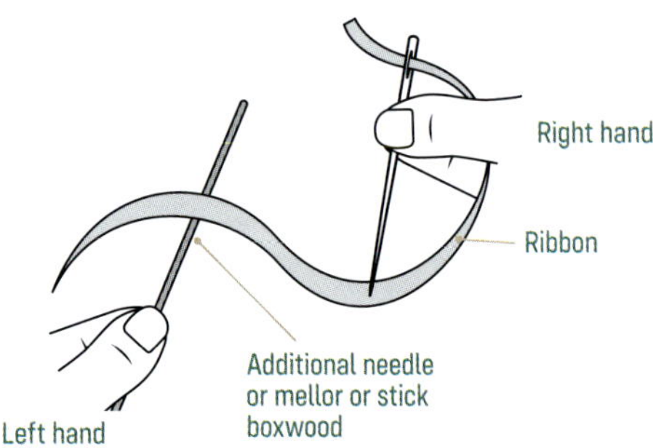

The hoop

The hoop must be larger than the design to be embroidered; otherwise the stitches produced will be damaged between the two circles.

For larger pieces, use an embroidery frame or, failing that, a q-snap frame (SuperFrame type; see page 21).

Techniques

Preparing a switch is different with ribbon.

Preparing a ribbon needle

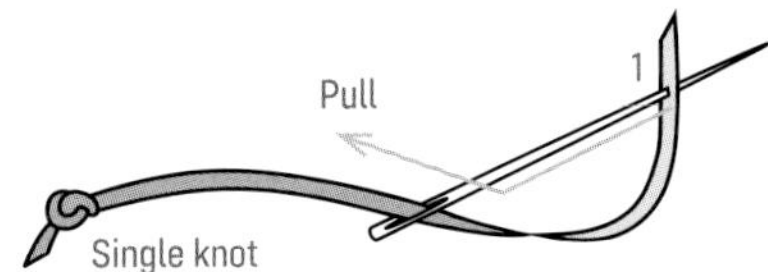

Since embroidery ribbons are fragile, they can be damaged when passing through the ground fabric. It is therefore essential to prepare needles that are shorter than normal, 30 to 40 cm maximum.

Cut the ends of the ribbon on the diagonal to prevent fraying, and iron it if it becomes creased. Pass the end of the ribbon through the eye of the needle. Using the tip of the needle, prick the same end at 1 cm (in 1). Pull on the other end to lock the ribbon in the eye.

Tying a knot at the end of the ribbon

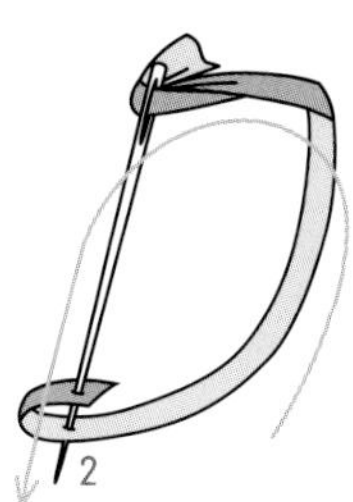

On 2- and 4mm ribbons, make a simple knot at the end of the needle.

On 7- and 13mm ribbons, make a loop knot: fold the end of the ribbon over itself (about 1 cm) and prick the needle (in 2; i.e., at 5 mm). Pull the ribbon all the way through.

Embroidery Stitches

Here's how to create the different stitches specific to ribbon embroidery.

Straight stitch

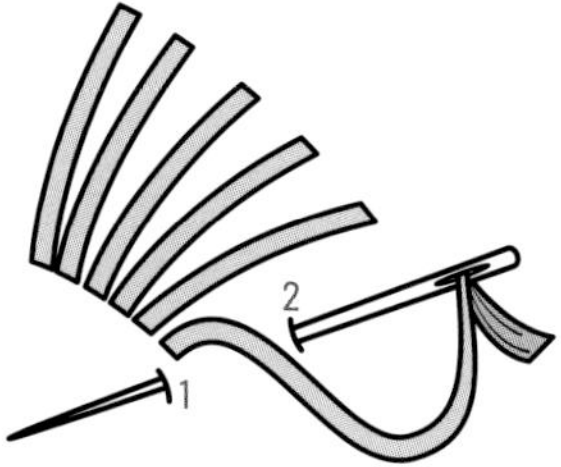

The ribbon can be embroidered in volume or flat with the help of a mellor.

Take the needle out in 1, stitch in 2, and gently pull the needle out.

Twisted straight stitch

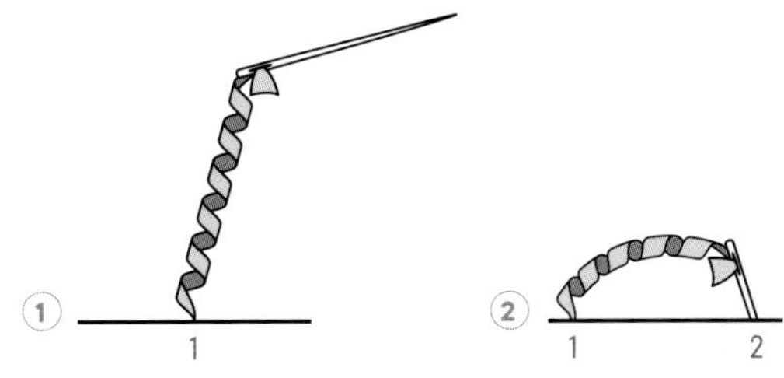

1 Take the needle out in 1 and twist the ribbon, turning the needle more or less depending on the desired effect.

2 Stitch in 2 while holding the twist above fabric.

Ribbon stitch

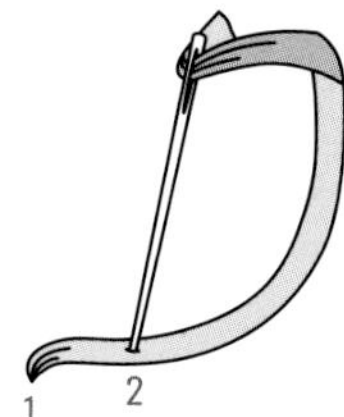

The ribbon can be embroidered in volume or flat with the help of a mellor. Stitching right or left across the width of the ribbon produces a different effect.

Take out the needle in 1, stitch in 2 in the ribbon, and gently pull out the needle.

Opposing ribbon stitch

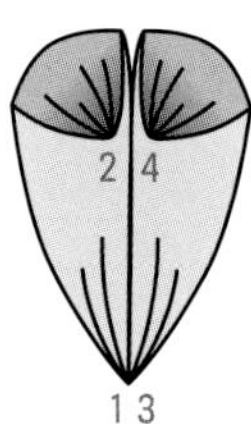

The opposing ribbon stitch is worked by embroidering two ribbon stitches against each other: the first stitched on the left and the second on the right.

Take out needle 1 and stitch in 2 on the edge of the ribbon. Take out 3 (next to 2) and stitch 4 on the edge of the ribbon, opposite 2.

Loop stitch

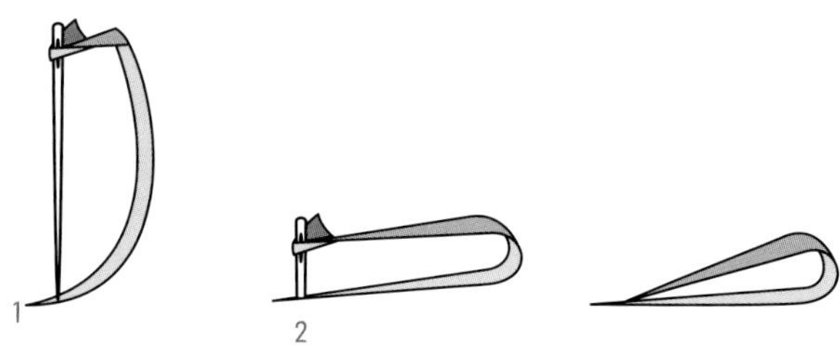

Take out the needle in 1, stitch in 2 on the base of the ribbon, and gently pull out the needle. The ribbon should be flat when you restitch in 2. Use a mellor to guide the ribbon into place.

Twisted rose stitch

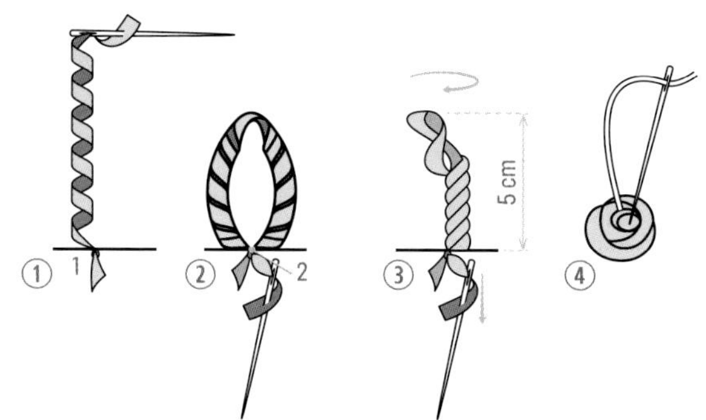

This rose is embroidered with a 7mm wide ribbon.

1 Prepare a needle of sewing thread to match the ribbon. Take out the needle in 1 and twist the ribbon by turning the needle between your fingers.

2 Insert the needle in 2, 2 mm from 1.

3 Gently pull the needle under the work to leave a 5cm loop at the top. Twist the loop with your fingers, holding it gently between thumb and forefinger, until a rose forms. At this point, you can control the size of the rose.

4 To hold the rose in place, make a few small stitches in the flower with the thread needle. To do this, stitch in the hollows formed by the ribbon to make them invisible.

Woven wheel stitch

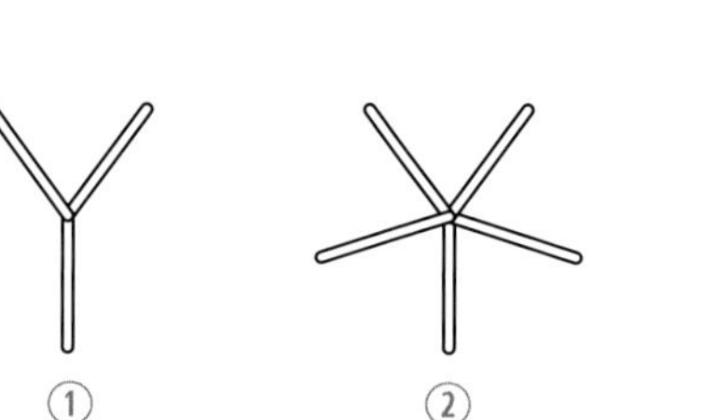

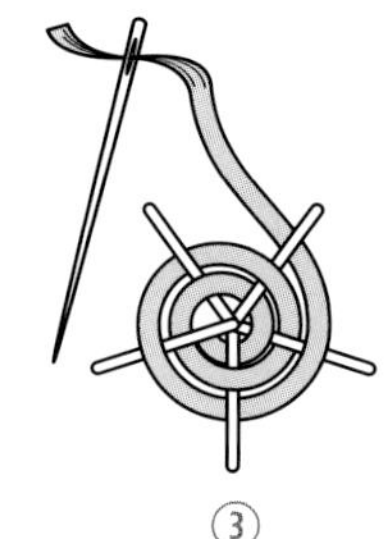

The woven wheel stitch is used to embroider a rose in two steps, with 4- or 7mm ribbons.

1 and 2 Using two strands of embroidery floss in the color of the ground fabric, embroider a Y, then add one or two points on each side, using straight stitches. This technique creates a regular star with five or seven points, depending on the diameter of the rose.

Tips for Good Embroidery

The start and end knots must be strong, since they form the skeleton of the flower that holds the ribbon in place.

3 With the ribbon needle, pull the needle out from the center of the flower and pass under and over a spoke. Work clockwise for right-handers, and counterclockwise for left-handers. Embroider gently to keep the ribbon loose; if necessary, lightly twist the ribbon. When the star is completely covered, pass the needle under the wrong side of the work, sliding the needle under the last turn. Stop the ribbon with a knot on the ribbon or a few stitches with a threaded needle.

Romeo et Juliette

Accordion rose stitch

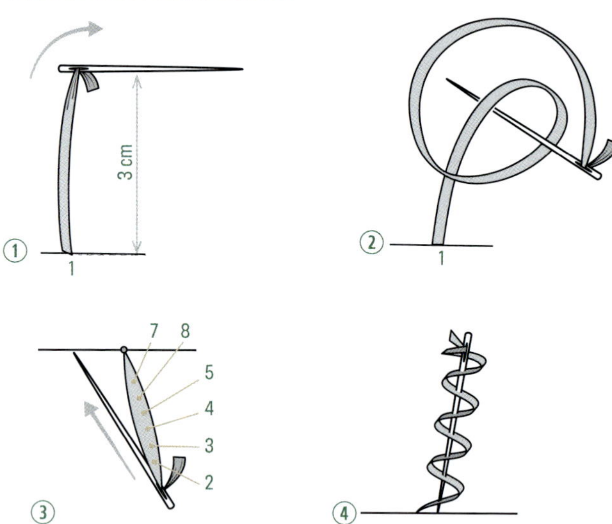

1 and 2 Take the needle out in 1. Hold the ribbon toward you with the opposite hand and wrap it once around the needle, leaving about 3 cm between the needle and the fabric. Position the needle and ribbon in the same direction, with the point of the needle toward the fabric.

3 Move the needle back to distribute three running stitches over the 3cm: stitch in 2 and out in 3, stitch in 4 and out in 5, and stitch in 6 and out in 7.

4 Stitch in 8, 2 mm from 1. Gently pull the needle under the work to form the rose.

Daisy

Ribbon is the ideal material for embroidering and creating true-to-life flowers.

Daisy with tied-down petals

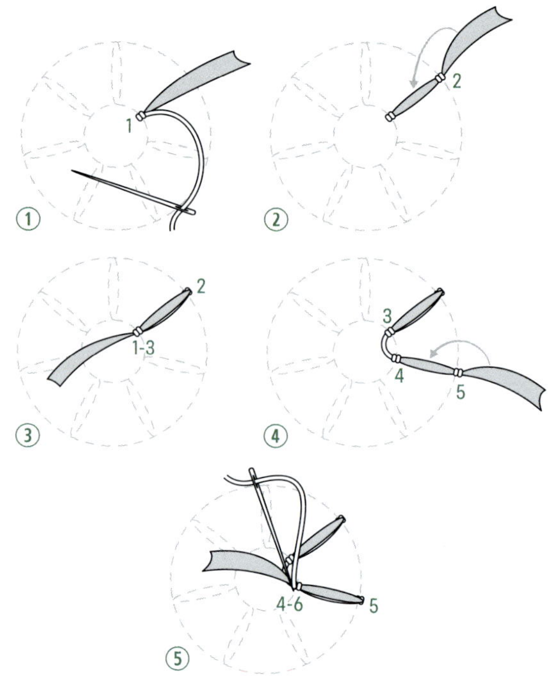

This flower is embroidered with a 7–, 13–, or 15mm wide ribbon and a matching needle of sewing thread.

Using a circle template, start by drawing two circles representing the outside diameter and the center of the flower:

- 20 mm and 5 mm for 7mm ribbon
- 30 mm and 10 mm for 13– or 15mm ribbon

Then draw six to eight lines to position the petals around the heart.

1 Take out the ribbon in 1 and embroider two couching stitches at the base of the first petal.

2 Place the ribbon flat on the petal design and make a couching stitch across the ribbon in 2 at the top.

3 Fold the ribbon back on itself and stitch over the ribbon in 3 (1 and 3 are the same).

4 Bring the ribbon to the base of the next petal. Couch over the ribbon in 4 and then in 5 at the top.

5 Fold the ribbon back on itself and make a couching stitch across at 6 (6 and 4 are the same).

Repeat these steps for each petal. After the last petal, use the large chenille needle and punch to pass the ribbon on the reverse side, just next to 1. Stop the ribbon with a few invisible stitches, using the sewing-thread needle, then anchor the thread.

What You Need to Know

You can finish by embroidering knotted stitches or pearls in the center of the flower.

Antique rose heart in folded ribbon

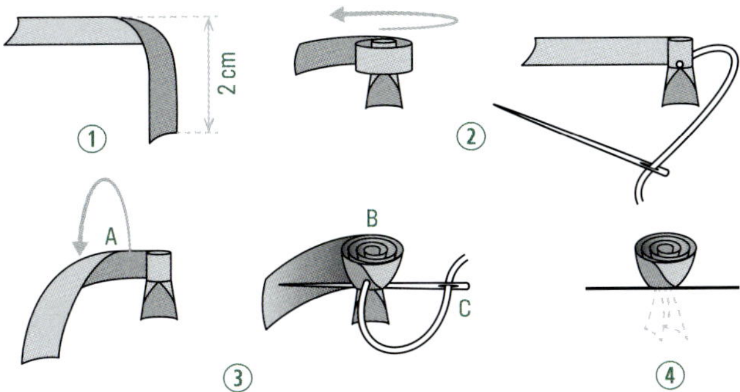

This flower is embroidered with a ribbon at least 7 mm wide and a matching needle of sewing thread. It can be embroidered alone or form the heart of a rose in wheel stitch.

1 Fold the end to form a right angle. Leave 2 cm of ribbon free.

2 To form the heart, wrap the ribbon around itself five or six times. Using the sewing-thread needle, make a few stitches at the base of the roll to secure the whole. Release and let the needle hang.

3 With your other hand, 1 cm from the rolled heart, fold the ribbon 90° toward you (A), then wrap it, with your working hand, around the heart. Shape the flower into a cone by aligning the top edge of the ribbon with the top of the heart as you wrap (B). Hold the top of the heart with your opposite hand and, using the sewing thread needle, make a few stitches at the base to hold it together (C). Repeat this step as many times as necessary to obtain the desired volume.

4 Finish by folding the unused ribbon 90° toward the base of the flower. Using the sewing-thread needle, turn around the base three times, then securely tie several knots.

Gathered ribbon flower

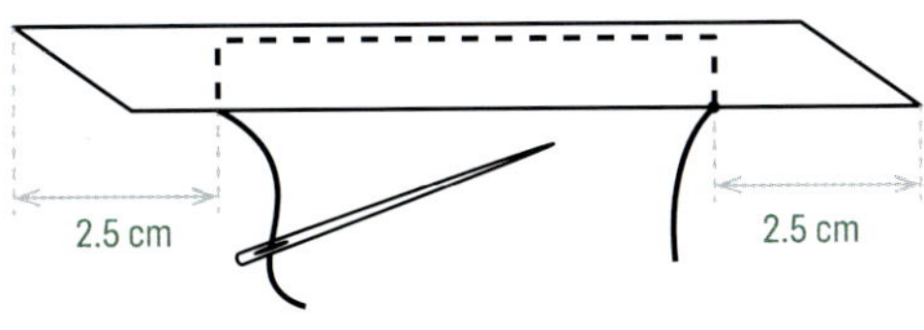

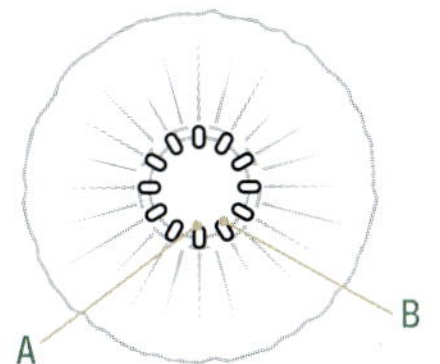

These flowers are embroidered with a ribbon at least 7 mm wide and a matching needle of sewing thread. The ribbon should be 15 to 25 cm long, with the ends cut on an angle. Using a circle template, trace a circle about 1 cm in diameter to represent the center of the flower.

1 Pass a gathering thread over the ribbon in small running stitches as shown in the diagram. Secure the thread on one side with a knot. Gently pull on the loose gathering thread.

2 Using a large chenille needle and, if necessary, a stiletto, thread the ends of the ribbon onto the reverse side of the work at A and B to conceal them. The beginning and end of the ribbon overlap. Divide the gathers around the circle to create a flower.

3 Secure the flower to the work with small stab stitches over the edge of the base of the petals, at the gathers.

4 Embroider the center of the flower with knotted stitches or pearls (optional).

Single rose with five gathered petals

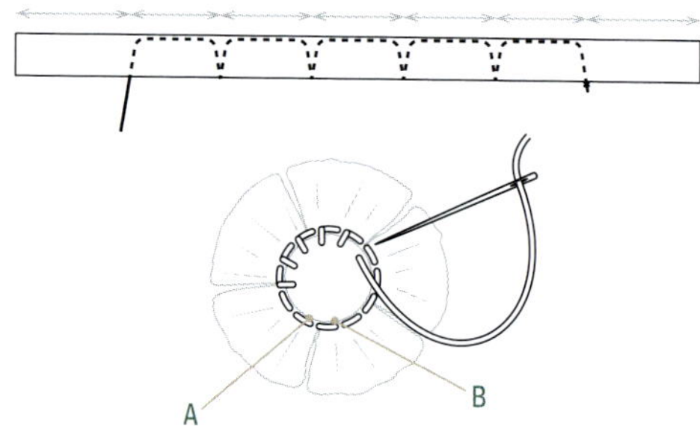

This flower is embroidered with a ribbon at least 7 mm wide and a matching needle of sewing thread. The ribbon should be 15 to 25 cm long, with the ends cut at an angle. Using a circle template, trace a circle about 1 cm in diameter to represent the center of the flower.

1 Pass a gathering thread over the ribbon in small running stitches as shown in the diagram. Secure the thread on one side with a knot. Gently pull on the loose gathering thread.

> **Attention**
>
> **The intervals between petals should be longer for wider ribbons (e.g., 4 cm for 15mm wide ribbons).**

2 Using a large chenille needle, and possibly a stiletto, thread the ends of the ribbon onto the reverse side of the work at A and B to conceal them. A and B should be as close as possible. Divide the gathers around the circle to create a flower.

3 Secure the flower to the work by stab stitching over the edge at the base of the petals at the gathers.

4 Embroider the center of the flower with French knots or pearls (optional).

Covering a Wooden Bead

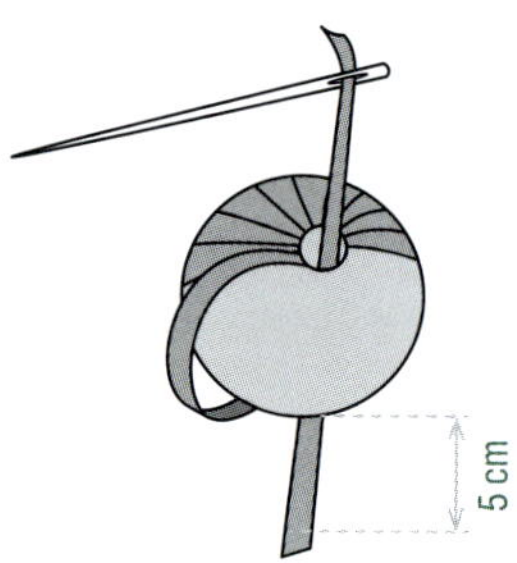

Equip yourself with a wooden bead with a large hole, a 4mm wide ribbon, a no. 24 chenille needle, and a matching needle of sewing thread.

Allow the ribbon to extend 5 cm beyond the base of the bead. To cover it, thread the ribbon through the hole, making sure it always lies flat. Secure the bead to the work by stitching both ends of the ribbon into the fabric. Pull the needle to the wrong side and stop with a few stitches of a sewing thread needle.

Visual Library of Embroidery Stitches

Straight stitch p. 177

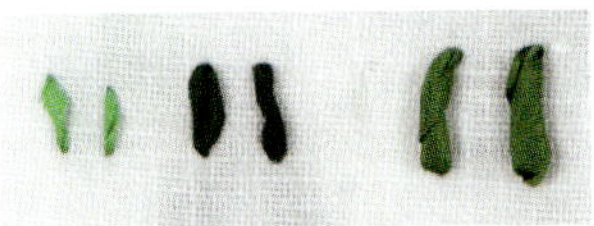

Twisted straight stitch p. 177

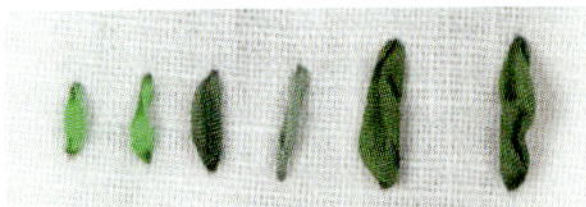

Ribbon stitch p. 177

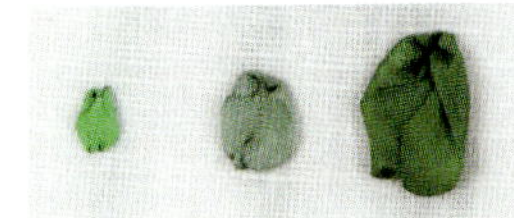

Opposing ribbon stitch p. 178

Loop stitch p. 178

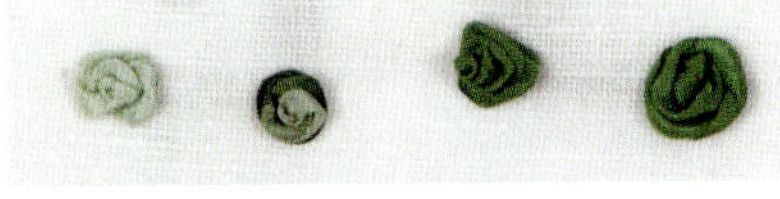

Twisted rose stitch p. 178

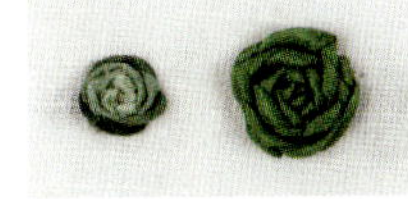

Woven wheel stitch p. 178

Accordion rose stitch p. 180

Daisy with tied-down petals p. 180

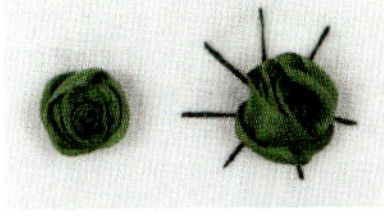

Antique rose heart with folded ribbon p. 181

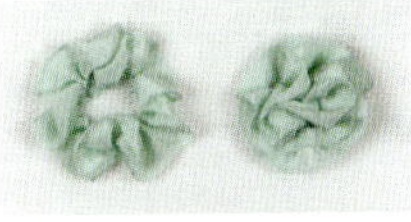

Gathered flower p. 181

Single rose with five gathered petals p. 182

Covering a wooden bead p. 182

GOLDWORK EMBROIDERY

Goldwork embroidery includes all embroideries made with metal or with metal or metallic materials, such as smooth purl, passing purl, and pearl purl, imitating metal (gold, silver, copper) in a variety of colors. These supplies can be found in the form of wires, passing threads, plates, twists, and braids.

It would appear that the first gold-embroidered garments appeared several centuries BCE. The book of Exodus, for example, mentions "garments embroidered with gold and purple."

Throughout the centuries, gold embroidery was considered a major art form in many countries of the world, from the Ottoman Empire (whose influence extended from the Mediterranean to the northern shores of the Black Sea, and from the Arabian Peninsula to the gates of Morocco) to Europe, where Christianity was developing.

In the Middle Ages, this technique adorned liturgical vestments. It was best mastered in England—this embroidery was known as Opus Anglicanum: it is generally considered that the work of the 13th and early 14th centuries reached the pinnacle of style and refinement in gold embroidery.

In France, gold embroidery developed with the arrival of the popes in Avignon in the early 14th century.

During the Renaissance, in the 18th century and throughout Europe, the great lords also appreciated richly embroidered costumes, with gold embroidery resplendent even on shoes, furnishings, horse harnesses, and standards.

Louis XIV, the Sun King, was particularly fond of the splendor of these embroideries. At the time, they were made in Parisian convents.

Napoleon I was the first to impose these embroideries on official costumes for major public services. Subsequently, on April 10, 1873, a ministerial decree specified the details of these embroideries (military insignia) on the kepis and epaulettes of soldiers, gendarmes, and customs officers.

Today, in France, these embroideries are still produced in the prestigious and highly specialized workshops of Rochefort. In haute couture, Paris is home to the workshops that master these techniques.

Supplies

Gold embroidery supplies are very specific, the most common being smooth purls and pearl purl.

What You Need to Know

In this chapter, all supplies are referred to as "gold," even if they are of a different color.

Embroidered peacock feather on a pouch, which can be found in the the creations on page 361

Attention

Goldwork embroidery must be dry-cleaned. In fact, some metallic supplies are fragile and cannot withstand water. Ironing should also be avoided to prevent damaging the relief.

Smooth purls and bullion

Bullion is a flexible, hollow thread wound into tight spirals of constant diameter. It can be smooth or bright check, and rough (matte) or smooth (shiny) finished. It is available in gold, silver, or copper, but also in a wide variety of colors. Bright check bullion is easier to install than smooth purl, thanks to its flexibility.

Mainly used for filling, the bright check must be cut to the desired length and threaded onto the needle, like a pearl, and set with a straight stitch.

Tips for Good Embroidery

In this book, the lengths to be cut for embroidery stitches are given as a guide. Experiment with your threads to adjust these lengths. The smaller the diameter of the thread, the more supple it is; in this case, you can reduce the lengths for stem stitch, loop stitch, and so on.

Pearl purl or jaceron

Pearl purls and jaceron are a fairly rigid metal. Made from very fine thread wound into spirals of constant diameter, it resembles a string of pearls. Each turn forms a spiral. Available in gold, silver, or copper, and in a wide variety of colors. Pearl purls and jaceron are mainly used to outline and delineate motifs. It is embroidered with a sharp needle, sewing thread of matching color, and a couching stitch.

Couching threads

The threads used for couching generally have a metal-wrapped fiber core. Japanese, imitation Japanese, rococo, passing, or twisted threads are used.

These threads are mainly used for filling. They are embroidered in a couching stitch, with a needle of matching or contrasting thread.

Threads for goldwork embroidery

Sewing thread is used to attach the metal threads and wires to the fabric. Sewing thread is used for greater strength; an alternative is glove thread (a fine, strong glazed cotton, see page 31).

If they are not originally waxed, they can be waxed by running them over natural beeswax to make them smoother and easier to work with. They are generally not visible once the work is finished.

Needle size depends on the size of the supplies to be stitched.

What You Need to Know

These threads are always used with a double needle, which is sturdier for laying the wires.

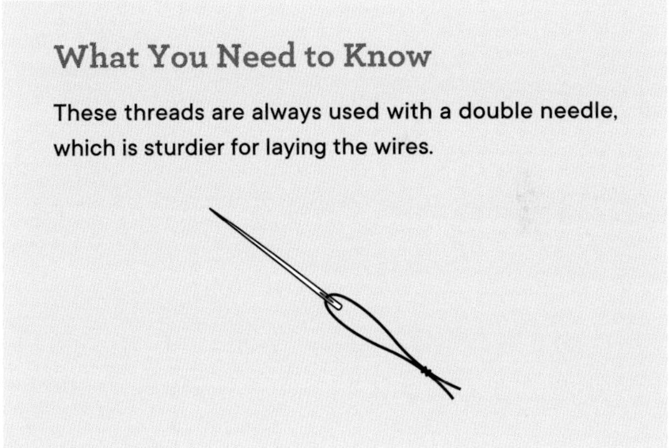

Metallic sewing threads

If the thread used to sew the supplies is visible once the work is finished, you can choose a metallic thread to match the supplies and blend in with the embroidery. Needle size depends on thread size.

Metallic embroidery thread

All the embroidery threads listed in the first part of the book are suitable. Needle depends on thread size.

Broad plate

Broad plate is a flattened strip of metal that looks like a ribbon.

Twists, braid, and soutache

These supplies are used to define a motif or for filling. They are generally laid with a couching stitch or backstitch, with a needle of thread in a contrasting or matching color.

- Twists and cords (also called "cordonnets") are obtained by twisting several threads together. They can be bought ready to use from haberdashers.
- The braid is a braid of cotton or silk threads, sometimes with a fiber core inside.
- Soutache is a braid made up of two strands of silk or cotton thread.

Padding

To add relief to the embroidery, some supplies, such as smooth purl, are placed over padding. The padding can be made of cardstock, vellum, soft cotton string, or felt in a color similar to that of the supplies.

Assorted beads and sequins

In gold embroidery, it's common to combine all kinds of sequins and pearls to bring out other textures and nuances.

Appliqués

Appliqués are integrated into gold embroidery to create flat areas that can be re-embroidered. Made from lamé fabrics, leather, etc., they can be used to cover both small and large surfaces.

Ground fabrics

Gold embroidery requires stable fabrics such as silk, percale, cotton batiste, or velvet. Since embroidered items are heavy, textile supports need to be stable and strong enough to support the weight of the embroidery.

Sometimes, for a better hold, it will be necessary to use another fabric for the ground fabric.

Equipment

Gold embroidery requires special equipment.

- Since the supplies are very fragile, gold embroidery is best worked taut on an embroidery frame. For small-scale work, it is possible to embroider on a wooden hoop with a maximum diameter of 15 cm; beyond that, the weight of the embroidery and the laying of the supplies would relax the work, and the embroidery would become difficult to achieve.

Tips for Good Embroidery

The size of the frame or hoop must be larger than the size of the embroidery to avoid damaging the metal wires and threads.

- Embroidery scissors for cutting metal supplies. Don't use your embroidery scissors if you don't want to damage the blades with metal.
- Long needles no. 7, 9, and 10 (for the finest work), to be chosen according to the fineness of the work
- An assortment of milliners needles for laying the smooth purl
- Beading needles
- Chenille needles for thick threads
- A stiletto to pass large supplies such as soutaches or cords on the reverse side of the work
- A velvet board for cutting supplies
- A mellor or large needle to support the metal wires while embroidering
- Tweezers to catch supplies

Supplies for goldwork embroidery

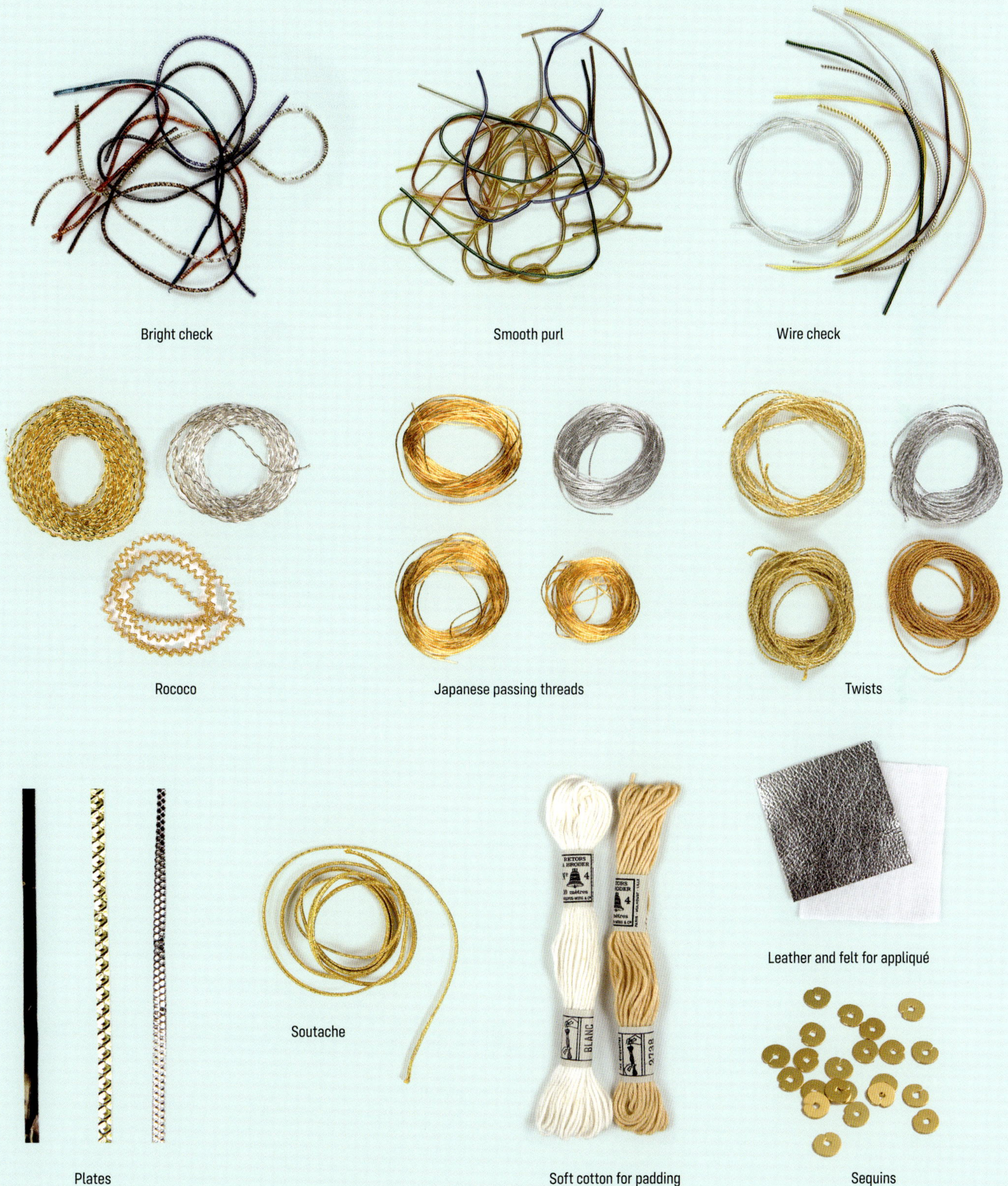

Bright check

Smooth purl

Wire check

Rococo

Japanese passing threads

Twists

Leather and felt for appliqué

Soutache

Plates

Soft cotton for padding

Sequins

Three Types of Goldwork Embroidery

- **Laid embroidery with passing,** a technique based on the satin stitch. It is possible only with metallic embroidery threads that can be threaded through the eye of the needle to penetrate the ground fabric. It's best done on cardboard padding to create volume. For easier cutting of the shape, cardboard can be replaced by wool felt.

Silk and metallic thread embroidery on silk satin, late 17th–early 18th century

What You Need to Know

Gold quilting requires a lot of raw materials, since there are as many threads to embroider on top as underneath.

- **Couching** to attach passing threads and twists, which are often thick and delicate. This technique enables large surfaces to be covered without too much added thickness: the passing threads then completely cover the motif to be embroidered. The threads are attached to the right side of the fabric by using small couching stitches and an embroidery or sewing thread.

Naked gold

Naked or nué gold is a variant of couching. A design painted on the textile support is covered with gold threads laid horizontally in pairs. These are then embroidered in couching stitch (see page 122) with colored silk threads to create flat tints, shadows, and highlights, rendering the design in minute detail.

Naked gold embroidery, Annunciation, 15th century

- **Relief goldwork embroidery** (or raised gold embroidery): this technique is characterized by its padding, which highlights the metal threads and wires (bullions and purl pearls). These embroideries include couched passing threads as well as pearls and sequins. They can also be embellished with braids, ribbons, twists, and cords sewn in invisible stitches.

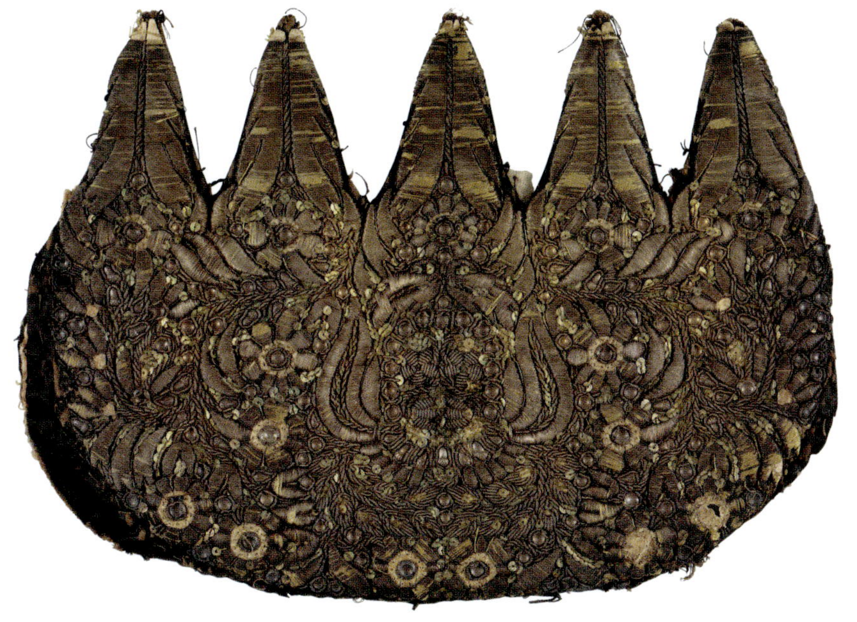

Padded relief goldwork embroidery, 19th century

Laid Embroidery

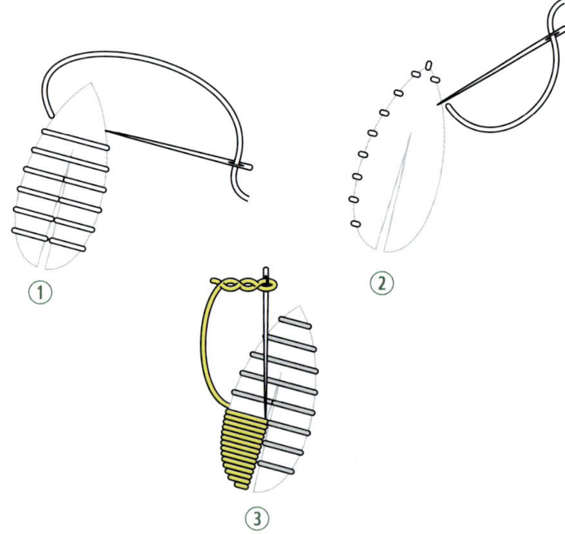

Laid embroidery is carried out using metallic embroidery thread and a filling made of cardboard (between 0.2 and 2 mm thick, depending on the desired effect) or good-quality wool felt, which represents the motif to be embroidered.

What You Need to Know

Embroidery is more precise with cardboard, but wool felt is easier to work with.

1 Make the padding by transferring the shape to be embroidered to the cardboard or felt; it should be about 5% smaller than the design, so that the outer lines of the design are clearly visible for the needle when embroidering. Cut all around and, using a double needle of sewing thread, secure the padding to the ground fabric on the area to be embroidered:

- On the cardboard, with long straight stitches stretching the width of the cardstock or cardboard cutout
- On the felt, with small stab stitches thrown around the perimeter of the felt cutout

2 Prepare a needle and use a chenille needle if the passing is thick. Pass it through the eye and twist it two or three times.

3 Embroider using the passing thread with satin stitch over the padding.

Couching Stitches

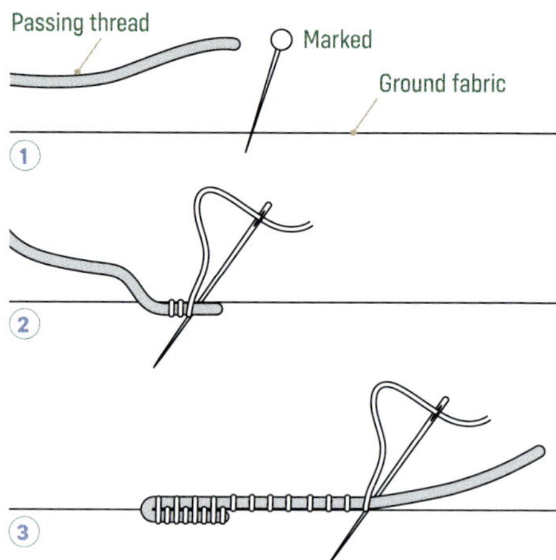

This work is carried out without padding, directly on the ground fabric. The threads chosen for the couching are attached with couching stitches, using a single or double needle.

Work with synthetic, silk, or metallic sewing thread, tone-on-tone or contrasting.

1 Using a stiletto, make an opening in the ground fabric for the couching thread.

2 To secure the couching thread at the start of the embroidery, sew the end of the thread to the back of the work, underneath the line to be stitched, using a sewing-thread needle.

3 Fold the couching thread over the design and start couching with small stitches perpendicular to the passing thread. This hides the first stitches from view with the embroidery.

What You Need to Know

To stop the couching thread at the end of the work, proceed in the same way: fold and sew the end of the thread to the back of the work under the embroidered couching.

Single-strand couching

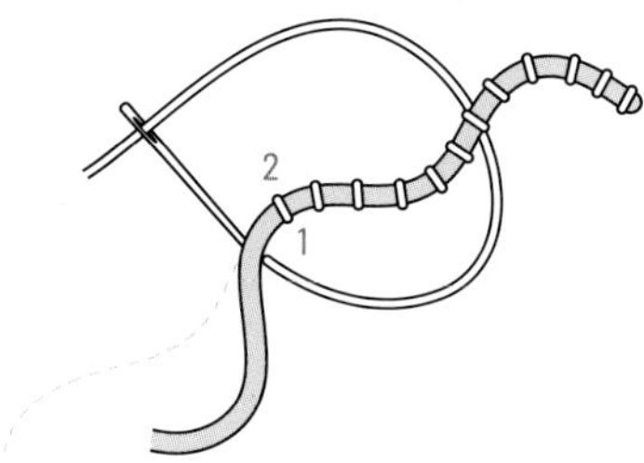

Sew the passing thread with a couching stitch, following the pattern.

Radial couching

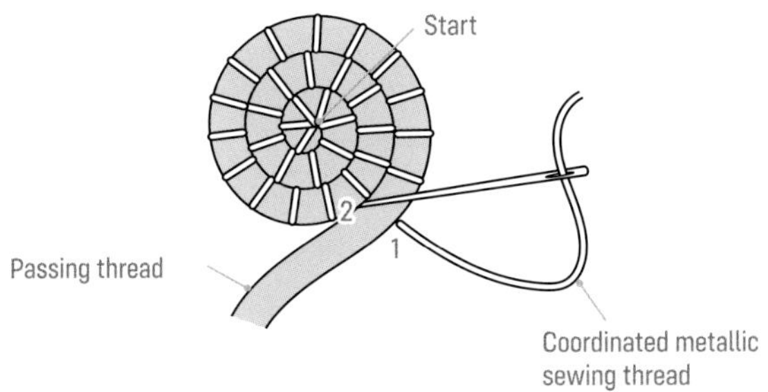

In a circle, work from the center outward, forming a spiral. Couching stitches should then be embroidered evenly with embroidery thread, staggering them from one turn to the next.

Rectangular couching

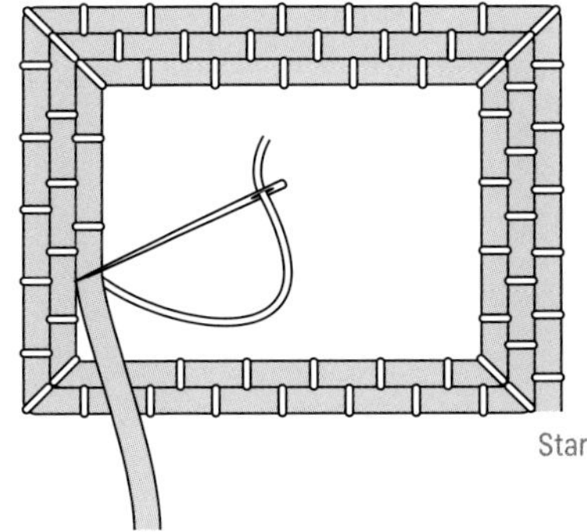

To embroider a rectangle or any other geometric shape, work from the outside in, using staggered couching stitches.

Turn the corner, securing the corners with a diagonal stitch until you reach the center of the rectangle.

Free-form couching

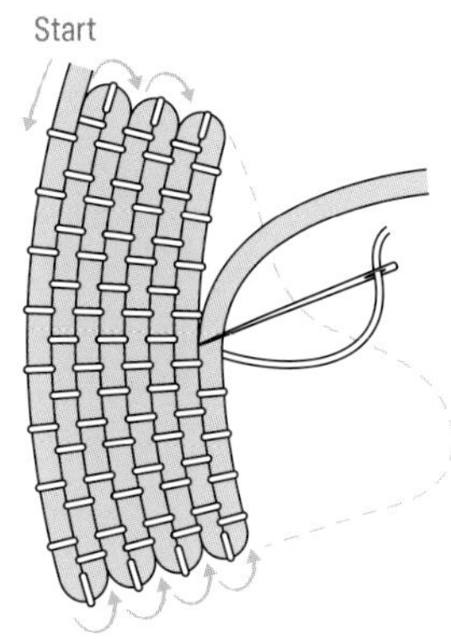

To embroider a free-form shape, start with the area where the lengths to be embroidered are longest, then work toward the shortest. Work back and forth.

Decorative couching stitches

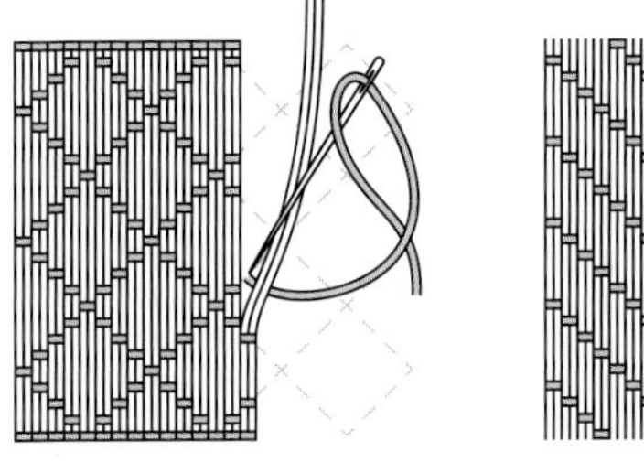

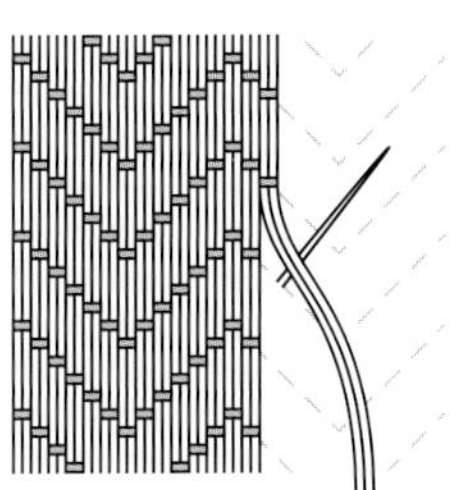

Decorative couching is embroidered with a thread that contrasts with the passing thread. As a decorative element, couching stitches follow a pattern, usually geometric, on the ground fabric, to form lozenges, zigzags, and so on.

Tips

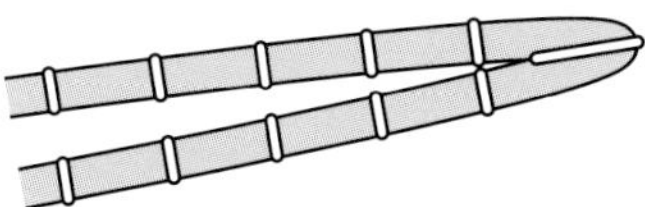

The sharpest points in a corner are obtained by placing a precise couching stitch in the fold.

Couching in pairs

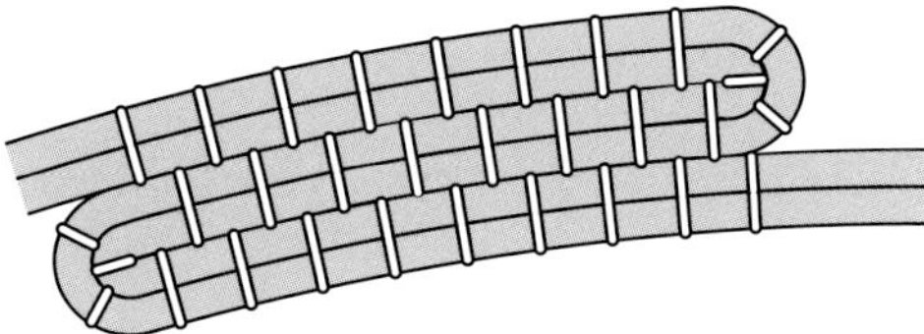

Two threads can also be used for couching. In straight lines, couching stitches cover both threads at the same time. On the other hand, for changes of direction, one stitch is embroidered on the inner thread in the fold, and two diagonal stitches on the outer thread.

> **Tips for Good Embroidery**
>
> **Make sure you have enough passing thread so that you don't stop and start in the middle of a design, which can be tricky. With sewing thread, on the other hand, you can easily stop one needle and start another; the stop stitches should then be hidden under the finished embroidery.**

Raised Gold Embroidery

Very creative relief embroidery is meticulous to make, but the techniques remain quite simple to implement.

Padding preparation

Padding adds relief to embroidery.

Felt padding

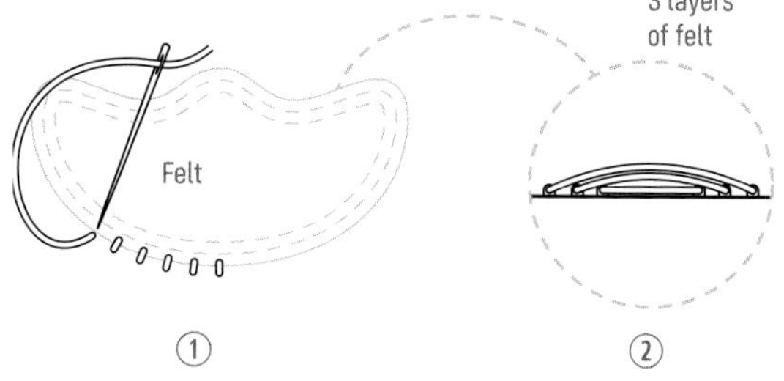

Very easy to use, felt is ideal for complicated shapes because it's easy to cut. To achieve the desired relief, several layers of felt may be required.

1 On the felt, transfer the shape to be embroidered three times: reduce its dimensions by a few millimeters so that the layers can be superimposed, as shown in the diagram. Cut these three shapes and, using a double needle of matching thread, begin by attaching the smallest one to the center of the design with small straight stitches all around, every 3 mm.

2 Overlap and secure all the felt layers in the same way, ending with the largest layer.

String padding with Retors matte DMC cotton

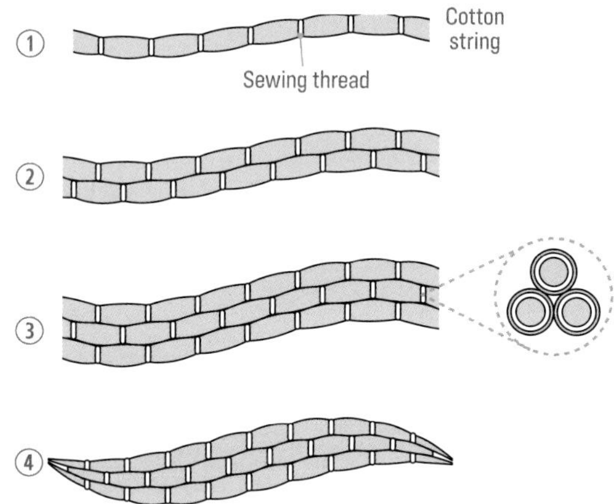

Retors matte DMC cotton is recommended for long, rather thin shapes, since its strands are easy to "sculpt." The surface of these fillings must be as smooth and uniform as possible for high-quality embroidery.

1 Cut and assemble four lengths of Retors matte DMC cotton. Hold the strands together with couching stitches on the area to be filled.

2 Go back and forth several times to cover the entire surface to be filled.

3 Several layers may be necessary to achieve the desired volume. Layer additional lengths of Retors matte DMC cotton.

4 The ends of these fillings can be tapered. These cotton strands are cut off cleanly, hidden in the layers in the middle of the padding, and firmly held in place by couching stitches.

Dior

Tips for Good Embroidery

Don't hesitate to multiply the couching points to obtain as uniform a surface as possible.

The cutwork technique

Bullion or smooth purl is sold by the gram, often cut into 50cm lengths. Each piece of bullion must be cut beforehand.

Preparation

The bullion, whether smooth or check, is prepared on top of the velvet board. Measure and cut all the pieces beforehand or as you go, depending on the work to be done on your motif.

Tips for Good Embroidery

If the cutwork pieces are to be the same size, use a ruler to draw a line with a Frixion pen on the velvet board of the desired length. This will serve as a template for cutting the bullion.
It's often easier to start in the middle of the pattern, especially if it's symmetrical or ends in a point (or both).

Embroidery stitches

Almost any embroidery stitch can be embroidered with bullion. Experiment and let your creativity flow!

What You Need to Know

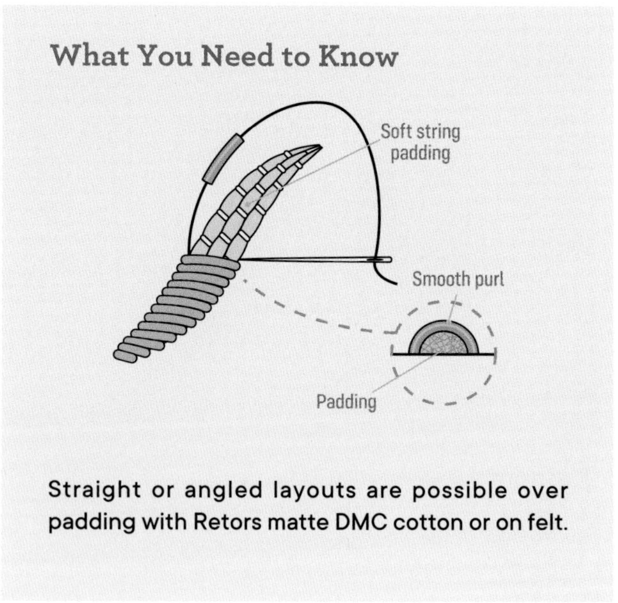

Straight or angled layouts are possible over padding with Retors matte DMC cotton or on felt.

→ Straight stitch

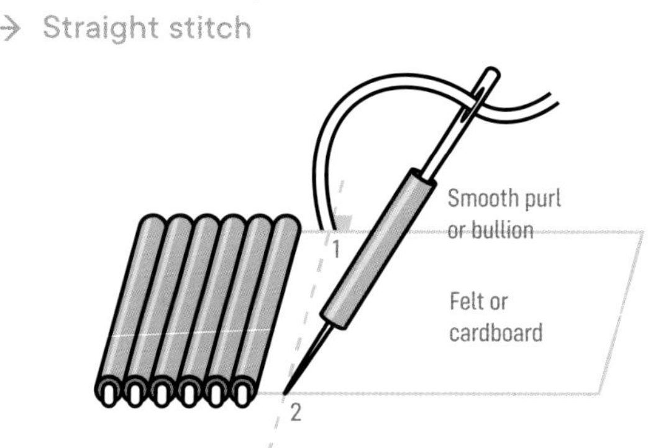

Prepare the padding and a double needle of sewing thread in the color of the smooth purl.

Anchor the thread with a small 1mm backstitch at the beginning of the work. Take out the needle in 1, thread the smooth purl cut to length onto the needle, and stitch on the other side of the motif in 2. The strands of purl, laid perpendicular to the padding, should lie against each other, not overlap. Apply strong tension to the thread to hold the purl in place. If necessary, apply a 1mm backstitch between the purls to secure the work.

For intersections, prepare a cross padding. The cutwork is then applied in straight stitch.

- **For the cross:** start with part 1, then embroider both sides of part 2.

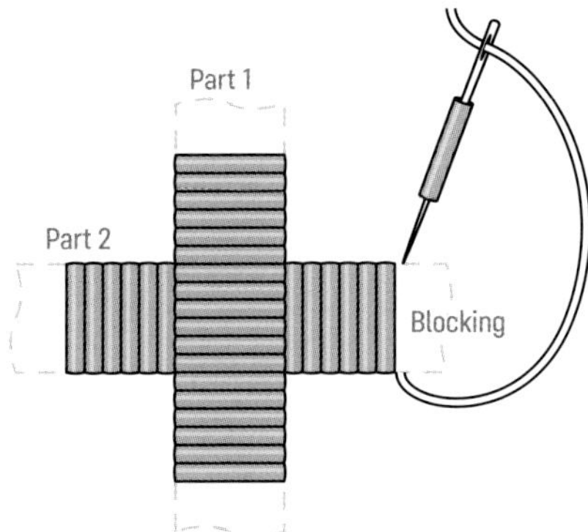

- **For the cross with cut intersection:** The lengths of the cutwork decrease in the center of the cross to form the diagonally cut intersection. Start at the center of the cross, with part 1, then embroider parts 2, 3, and 4.

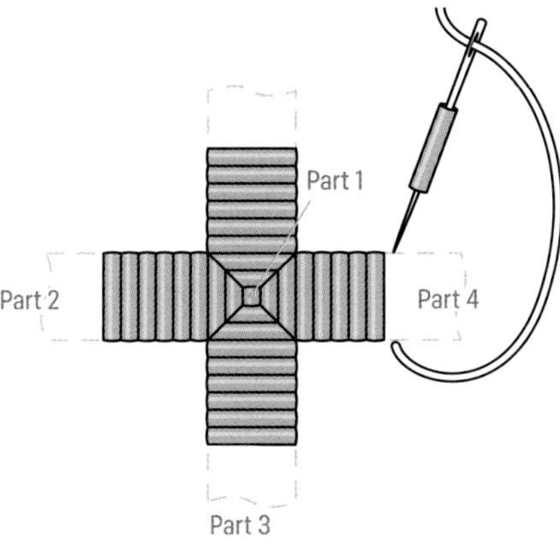

→ Cutwork on the diagonal

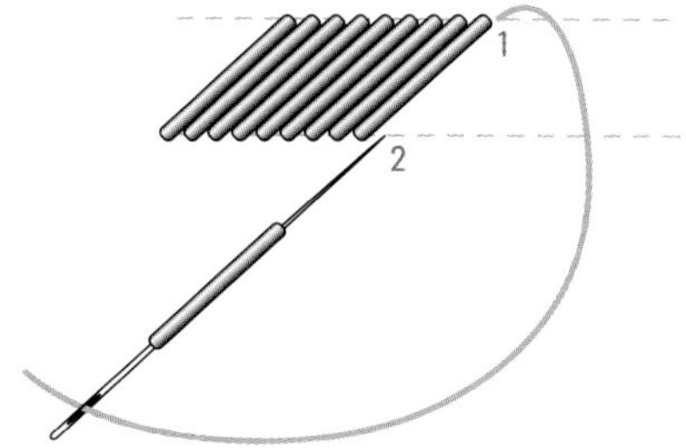

Prepare the padding and a double needle of sewing thread in the color of the bullion.

Anchor the thread with a small 1mm backstitch at the beginning of the work. Take out the needle in 1, thread the purl cut to length onto the needle, and stitch on the other side of the motif in 2. The strands of purl, laid at an angle on the padding, should lie against each other, not overlap.

Apply strong tension to the thread to hold the cutwork in place. If necessary, apply a 1mm backstitch between certain strands to secure the work.

- **For intersections:** Prepare a cross of padding. The cutwork is then applied in a diagonal stitch. Start with part 1, adjusting the lenghts to the shape of the intersection. Then embroider parts 2 and 3.

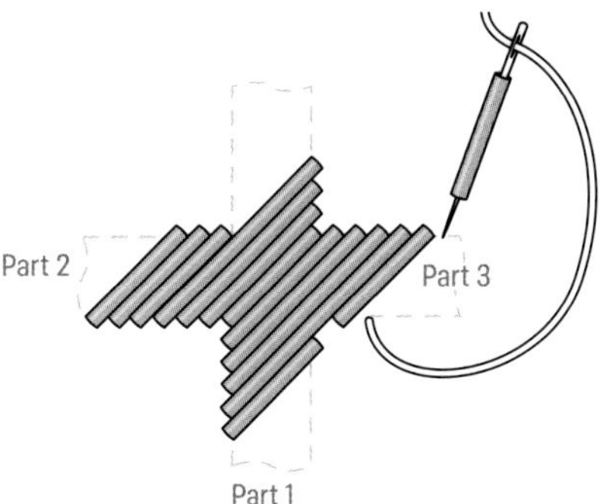

For corners, prepare a corner padding. The cutwork is then placed on the diagonal stitch.

- **For a right-angled corner:** Start by placing the cutwork in the corner. Then embroider the horizontal and vertical parts.

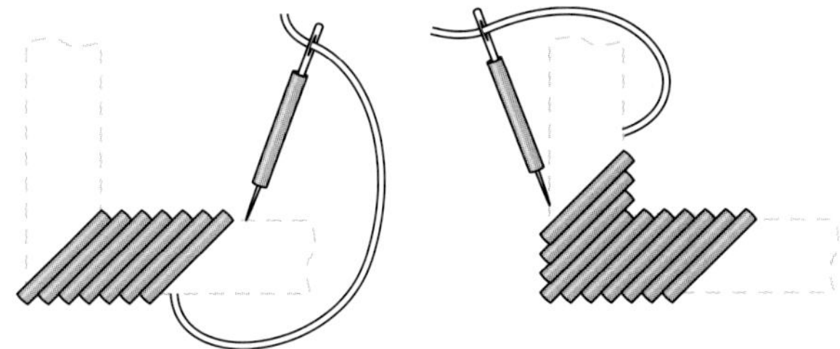

- **For an uncut right angle:** Start by placing the cutwork in the angle, following the diagram. Then embroider the horizontal part, followed by the vertical part. Finally, embroider the corner, carefully adjusting the length of the purl.

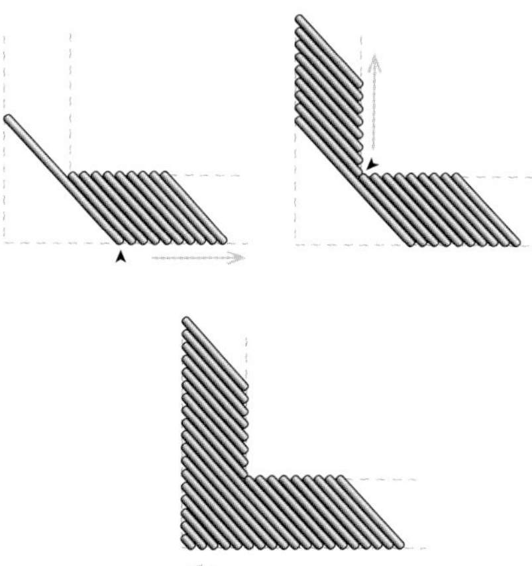

• **For a cut right angle:** Start by placing the cutwork in the angle. Then embroider the horizontal part, followed by the vertical part, starting inside the corner. Finally, embroider the corner, carefully adjusting the length of the purl.

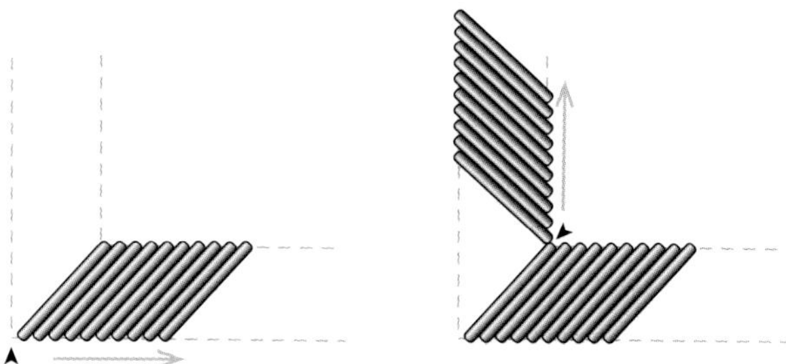

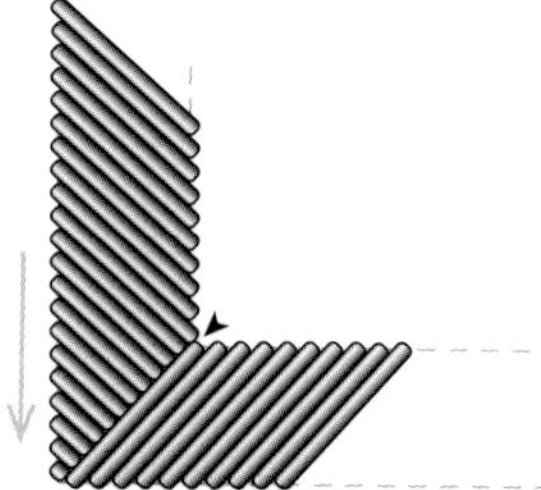

→ Cutwork around a circle

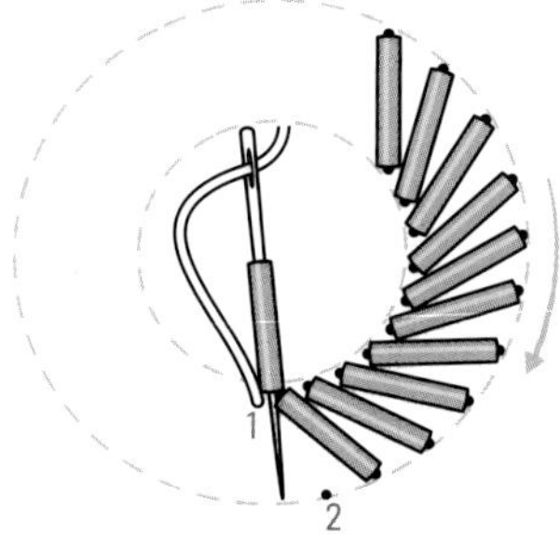

Take the needle out in 1 on the inside of the circle and stitch in 2 on the outside. Work counterclockwise.

→ Straight stitch

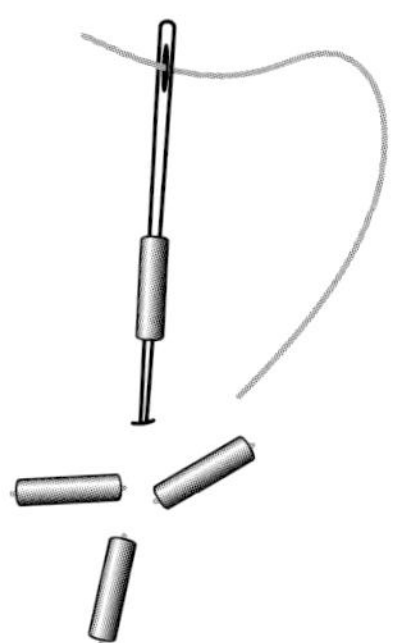

For straight stitches, cutwork pieces must not exceed 10 mm.

→ Chipping with purls

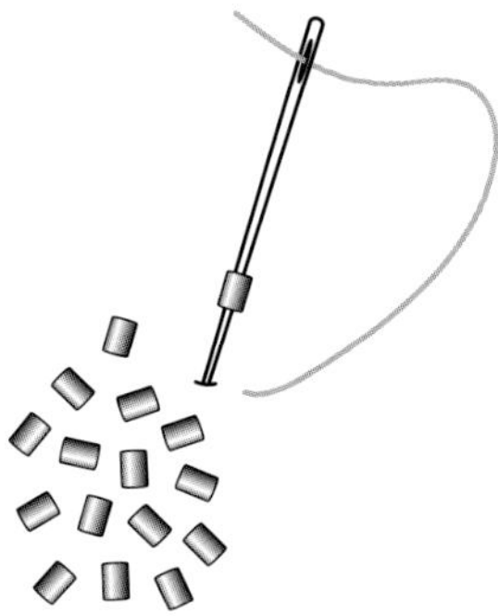

To create the chipping, the pieces of purl must not exceed 3 mm and are embroidered in all directions.

→ Backstitch line of bullion

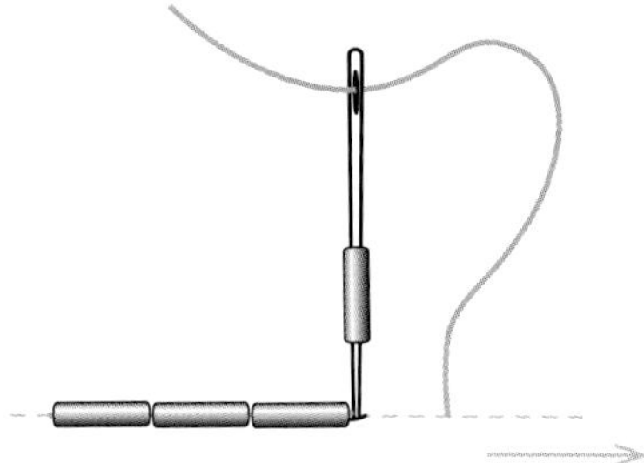

To create the stitch, the piece of purl must be slightly shorter than the stitch length.

→ Brick stitch

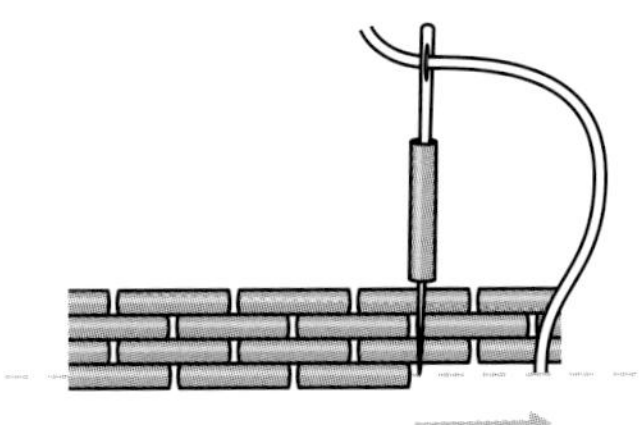

The pieces of purl must be the same length.

Embroider a first row at the stitch, then a second row in a staggered pattern.

→ S-ing

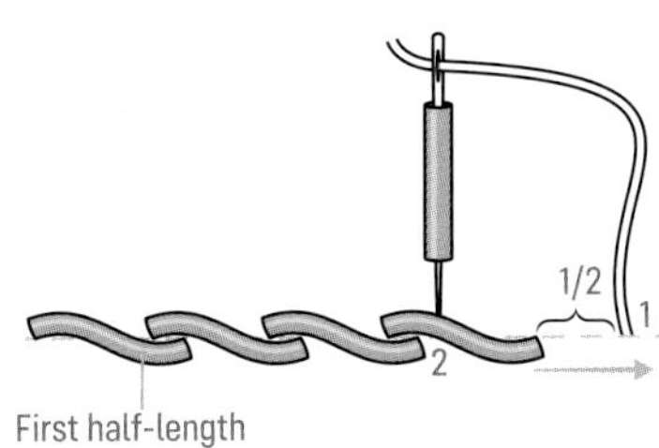

The pieces of purl must be cut very precisely (to 12 mm, for example) and to the same length.

Start the line by placing half a piece of purl (6 mm here). Take out the needle in 1, thread the 6mm piece purl onto the needle, and stitch in 2.

For each stitch, thread a 12mm purl on the needle. Take out the needle at 3 (6 mm from 2) and stitch at 4 (4 is above 1; as close as possible). Continue as follows: pull out at 5 and stitch at 6 (6 is above 2; as close as possible), pull out at 7, and stitch at 8.

→ Cable stitch

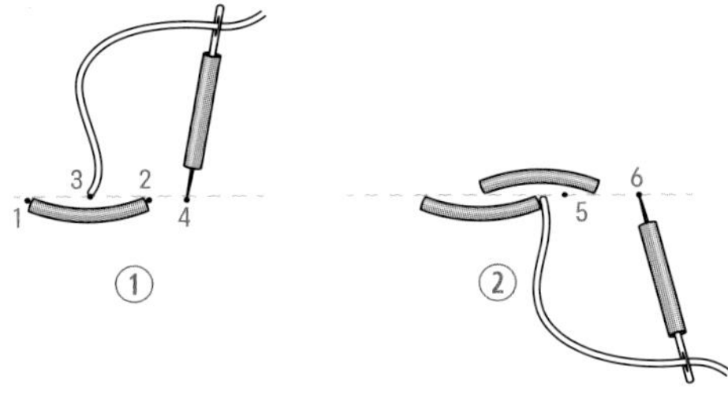

The pieces of purl should be slightly longer than the embroidery stitch, so that they form an arc when laid. For example, cut 6mm strands for 5mm stitches.

Place the purl, taking the needle out alternately above and below the line.

1 Take out the needle in 1, thread a piece of purl, and stitch in 2 (5 mm from 1, below the outline). Take out the needle in 3, in the middle and above the first stitch, thread a piece of purl, and stitch in 4 (there must be 5 mm between 3 and 4).

2 Go out in 5 (5 and 2 are the same hole), thread a piece of purl, and stitch in 6 (there must be 5 mm between 5 and 6).

→ Curl stitch

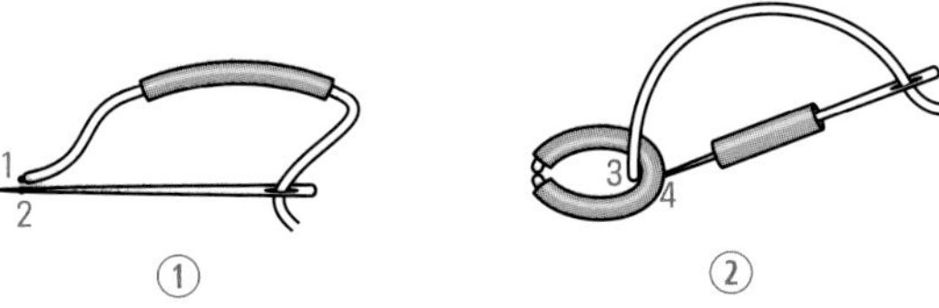

Cut 6- and 12mm pieces of purl.

1 Take out the needle in 1, thread a 12mm piece of purl onto the needle, and stitch in 2 (right next to 1) to form a loop.

2 Exit in 3, thread a 6mm piece of purl onto the needle, stitch in 4, and position it astride the end of the previously embroidered loop.

→ Purl French knot

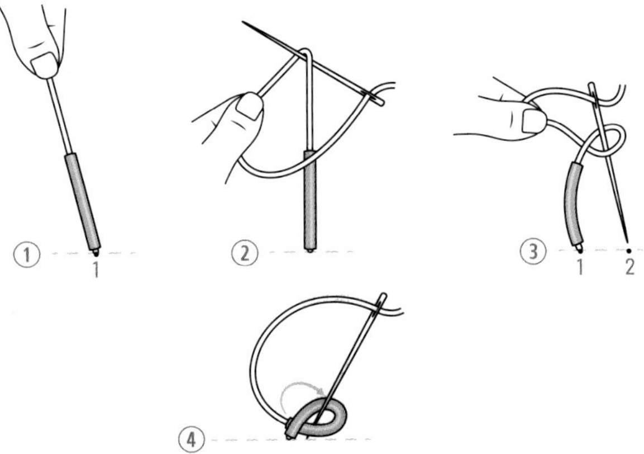

The pieces of purl must be long enough to knot. Test beforehand, since the length depends on the diameter of the purl.

1 Take out the needle in 1, thread a piece of purl onto the needle, and bring it down to the surface of the ground fabric.

2 Pass the working thread around the needle.

3 Make a loop as for a knot stitch with the thread on the needle. Stitch in 2 (1 or 2 mm from 1).

4 Using your fingers or the mellor, press the loop onto the fabric support and bring the second end of the purl to the center of the loop thus formed. Gently pull the needle under the work until the knot is secure.

→ Chain stitch

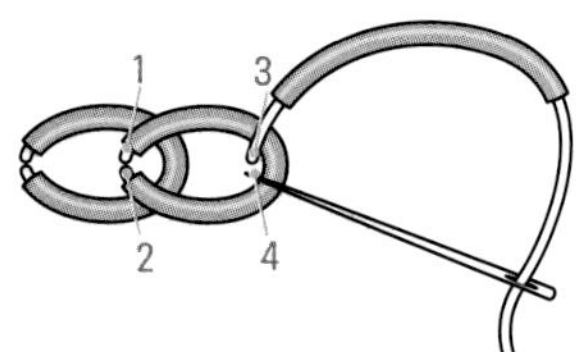

Cut 15mm pieces of purl.

1 Take out the needle in 1, thread a piece of purl onto the needle, and stitch in 2 (1 mm from 1) to form the first loop.

2 Exit in 3 (inside the first loop), thread a piece of purl onto the needle, and stitch in 4 (1 mm from 3), inside the first loop.

→ Fly stitch

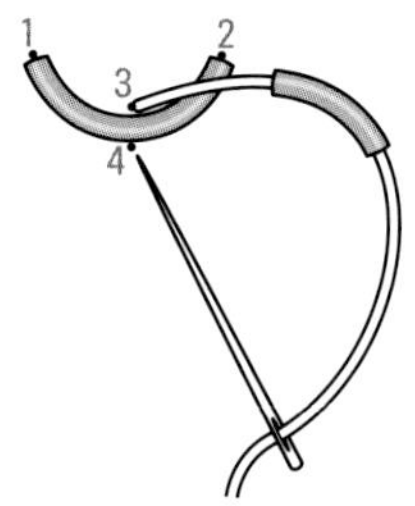

Cut 6- and 12mm pieces of purl.

1 Take out the needle in 1, thread a 12mm piece of purl onto the needle, and stitch in 2.

2 Exit in 3, thread a 6mm piece of purl onto the needle, stitch in 4, and position it astride the end of the previously embroidered loop.

→ Create a loop

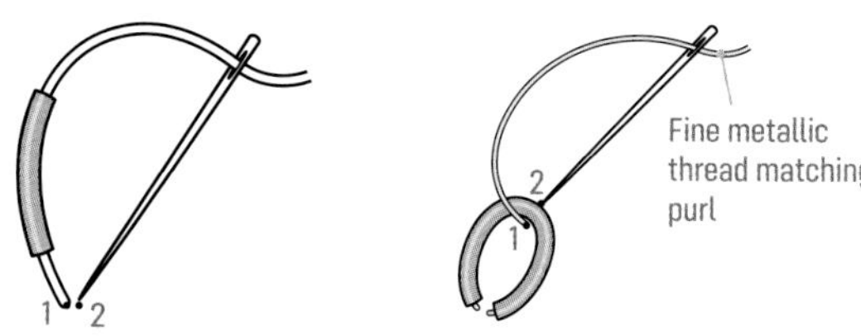

The loop is made like a detached chain stitch. It can be left free or held very delicately flat at the end by a small stitch made with a fine matching metallic thread.

Pearl purl or jaceron

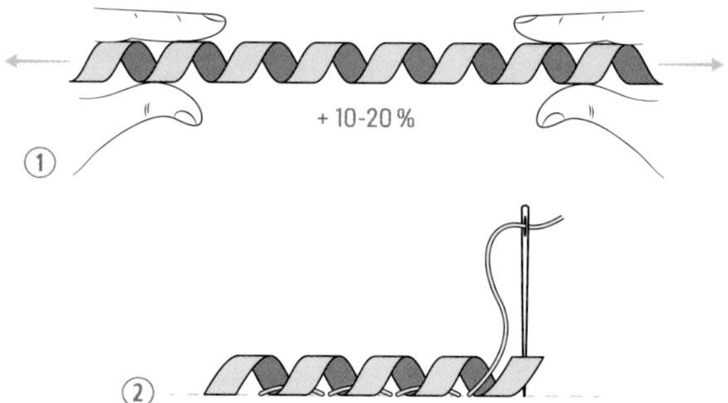

Sold by the meter, pearl purl or jaceron resembles a spring. It is attached to the work with couching stitches that sit between the coils.

1 Prepare the pearl purl. Gently stretch it lengthwise by 10%-20% to increase the space between the pearls. To do this, grasp it with both hands, between your fingers, and exert a gentle pull. Work on sections no longer than 3 cm to control the elongation of the pearl purl. Repeat the operation as many times as necessary to obtain the desired length.

2 Next, lay the pearl purl. Start by making a 1cm cut at the end to make a clean cut, removing the part you manipulated to stretch it. Lay it flat on the ground fabric, with its ends on top of the work. Hold it in place with couching stitches, inserted every 5 mm between the pearls. Increase the number of stitches at the ends of the pearl purl and in tight curves.

Tips for Good Embroidery

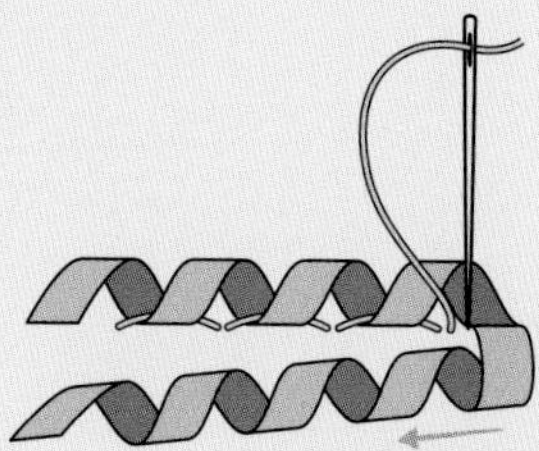

To fold the pearl purl at the points and corners of the motifs, use the needle: prick it partially, straight, at the fold, press the pearl purl on it to help it change direction, and place it in the right place. Secure with a couching stitch on the fold.

Sequins with purls

Sequins, spangles, and purls can be applied together.

Sequins with backstitch line of purls

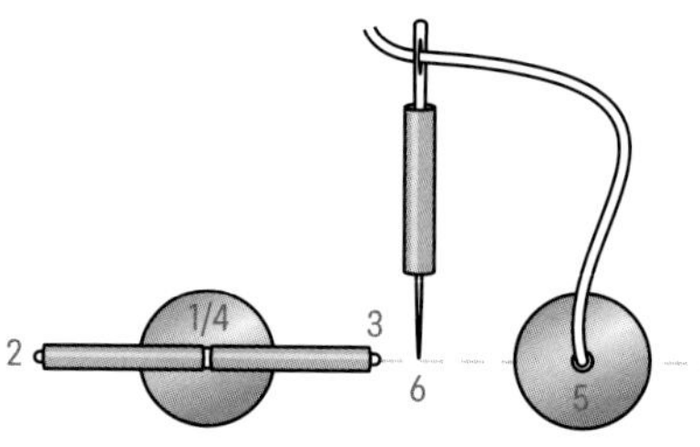

Cut pieces of purl slightly longer than the radius of the sequins. The sequins are placed on the backstitch.

Take the needle out in 1, thread a sequin onto the needle, then a piece of purl, and stitch in 2. Take the needle out in 3, thread a piece of purl onto the needle, and stitch in 4 through the sequin hole. Take the needle out in 5 and stitch in 6 (3 and 6 don't have to be the same).

Sequins with purl loops

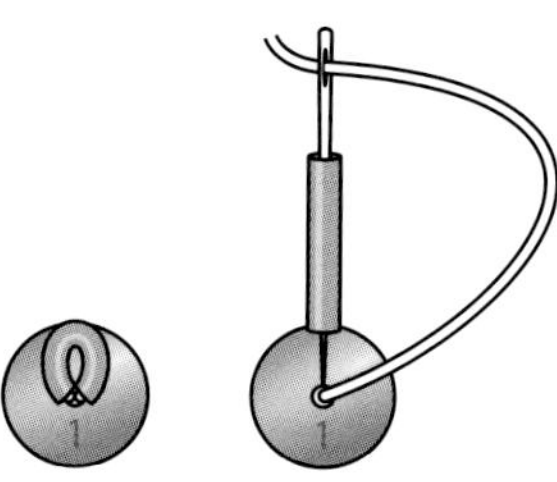

Cut 12mm pieces of purl.

Go out in 1, thread a sequin on the needle, then a piece of purl, and go back in 1.

Overlapping sequins with purls

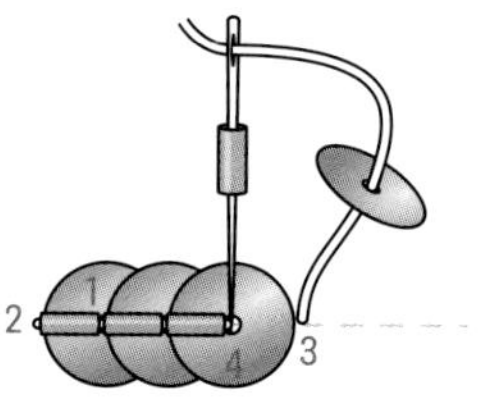

Cut pieces of purl slightly smaller than the radius of the sequins. The purls align with the holes of the sequins and stitch line.

Take out the needle in 1, thread a sequin onto the needle, then a piece of purl, and stitch in 2. Pull out needle 3, flush with the previous sequin. Thread a sequin onto the needle, then a piece of purl, and stitch in 4 through the hole in the previous sequin.

Line of overlapping sequins with s-ing

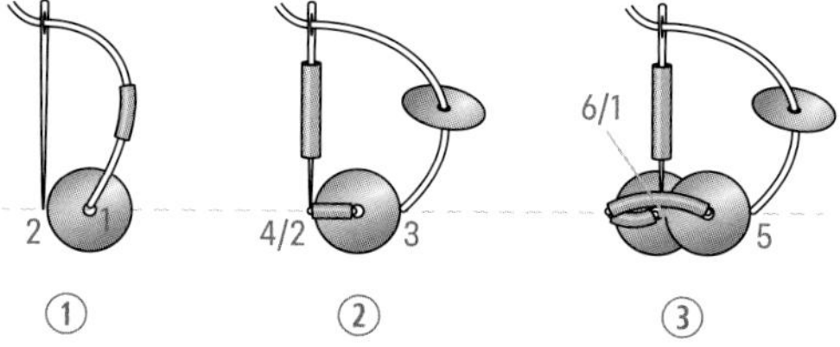

Cut a piece of purl the length of the sequin diameter and a small piece of purl the length of the radius. Place them on the stem point, from left to right.

1 Take out the needle in 1, thread a sequin onto the needle, then the small piece of purl, and stitch in 2.

2 Take out 3, flush with the first sequin. Thread a sequin onto the needle, then a piece of purl, and stitch in 4 (2 and 4 are the same).

3 Take out 5, flush with the previous sequin. Thread a sequin onto the needle, then a piece of purl, and stitch in 6 (1 and 6 are the same).

Laying pearls or stones with bullion

Pearls and bullion can be placed together.

Purl ring around a pearl

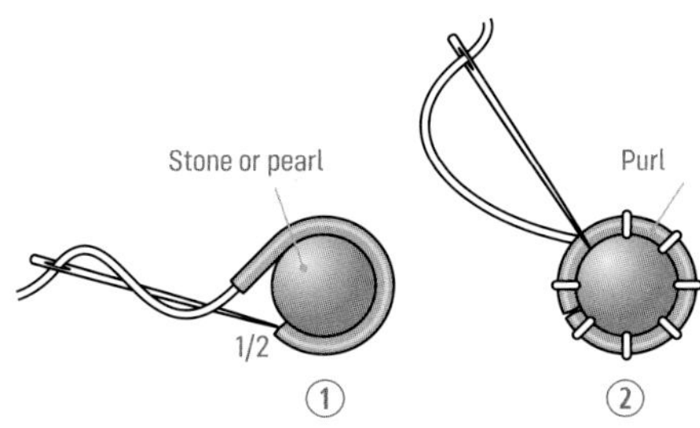

Calculate the circumference of the pearl or stone and cut a piece of purl of the same length.

1 Place the pearl or stone. Take out the needle in 1, thread the purl onto the needle and stitch in 2 (1 and 2 are the same).

2 Hold the purl in place around the stone or pearl, using small couching stitches made with very fine metal thread matching the purl.

Pearl embroidered with pieces of purl

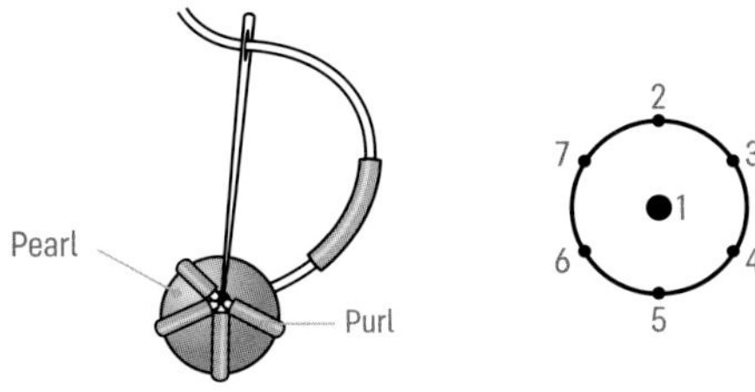

Calculate half the circumference of your pearl and cut five pieces of purls of the same length.

Take the needle out in 2, thread a piece of purl and the pearl onto the needle, and stitch in 1. Take out in 5, thread a piece of purl onto the needle, and stitch in 1 in the hole of the pearl. Exit in 3, thread a piece of purl onto the needle, and stitch in 1 in the bead hole.

Continue working opposite each other.

Broad plate

Couched broad plate

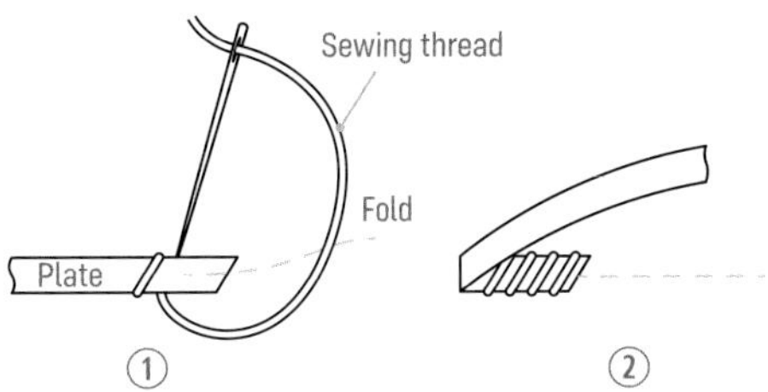

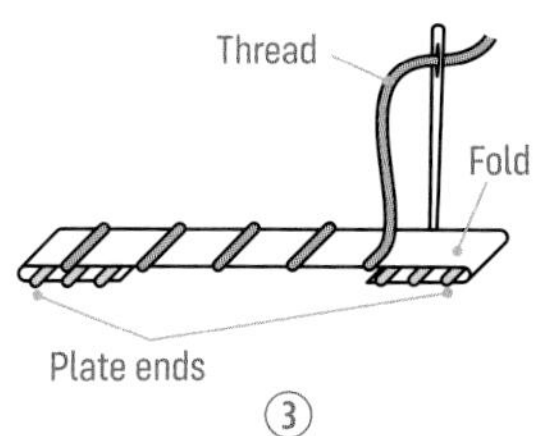

The ends of the plate should be bent over about 5 mm and secured with a few tacking stitches, using a double needle of thread matching the plate. Use a mellor to position and hold the plate during work.

1 Place the end of the plate on the line and stitch a few couching stitches across the plate.

2 Bend the plate to position it on the layout and create the couching stitches.

3 To finish the job, fold the plate back on itself to a length of about 5 mm and secure it with a few straight stitches, which should be slid between the two thicknesses of plate so that they are as invisible as possible.

Trellis of broad plate

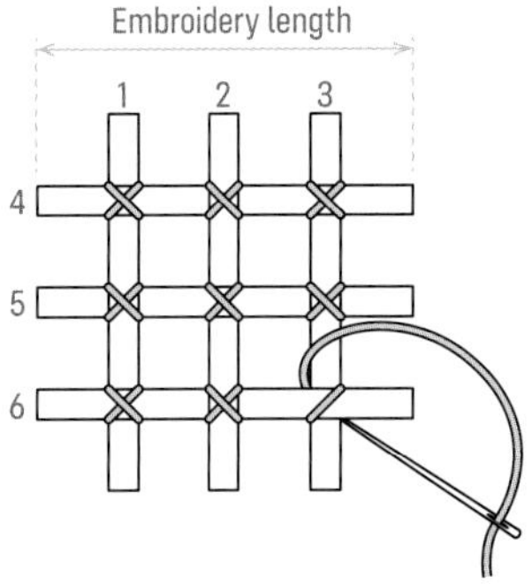

Draw a grid to your liking. Broad plate starts and stops are performed in the same way as for the line of broad plate (*see above*).

Cut as many plates as necessary to form the grid (six in this example). They should be slightly longer than the lengths to be embroidered and allow an extra 8 mm for the stop folds.

Lay the ends of the plate on the layout and make a few couching stitches to make the stop: all horizontal slats on their left-hand side and vertical slats from above.

Then gently weave the slats together. Embroider cross-stitches straddling the intersections of the slats. Tuck in and fasten the ends of the slats at the right and bottom.

Zigzagged broad plate

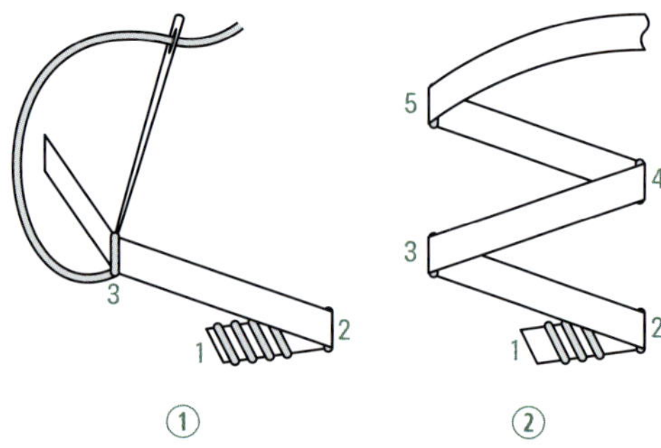

The broad plate is laid in a zigzag pattern, from bottom to top, between two pre-drawn lines. The plate bends alternately from side to side along these lines.

1 Secure the plate with anchoring stitches, as for the couched broad plate, at one end, next to the right-hand line in 1. Embroider two couching stitches one on top of the other in 2, on the right-hand line. Fold the plate up into a zigzag in 3, on the left-hand line. Embroider two couching stitches one on top of the other in 3.

2 Repeat as many times as necessary, ending with a folded stop, as for the couched broad plate.

Laying the twists, the braid, and soutache

It's not uncommon to find pretty trimmings (cords, soutaches, and twists) at haberdasheries and secondhand shops. Here's how to attach them.

Twisted thread and cord

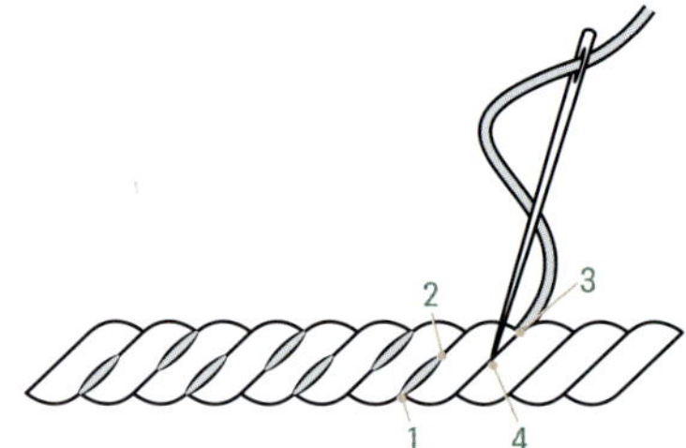

Embroider tiny backstitches in the same direction as the twists and cords to be laid. Bring the needle out in 1 on the outside of the twist and stitch in 2 in the hollow of a twist. Take out needle 3 and stitch in 4 in the hollow of a twist.

Embroider, alternating stitches on each side of the twisted thread or cord. This makes the holding stitches virtually invisible.

Ribbon

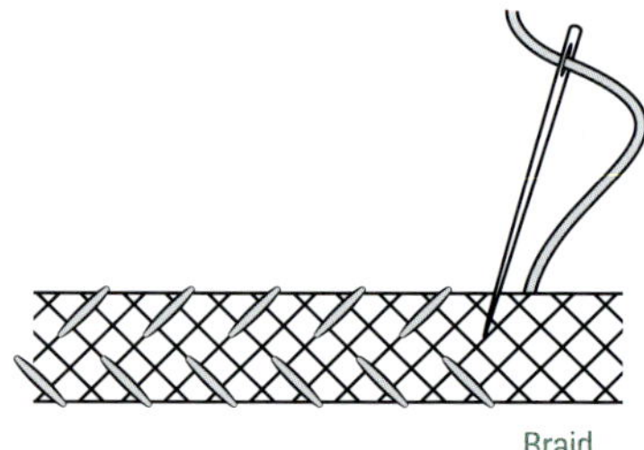

Take out the needle on the outside of the braid and stitch a tiny stab stitch in the direction of the braid, alternating stitches on each side of the braid. This makes the holding stitches virtually invisible.

Soutache

Embroider the soutache in the center rib with the backstitch.

Leather appliqué

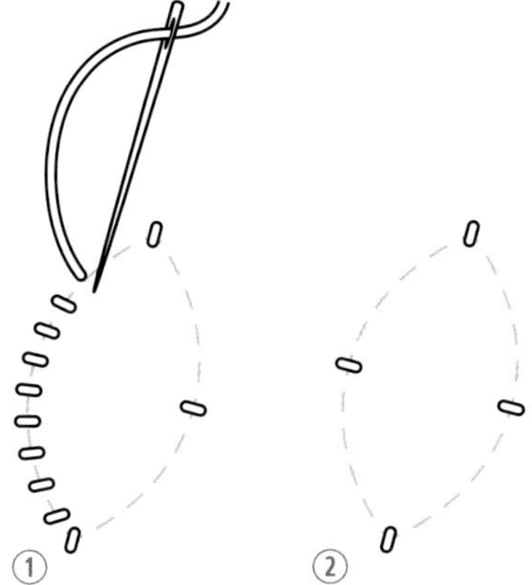

The leather is laid with small, evenly distributed stab stitches.

1 Trace and cut out the leather shape. If necessary, pad with felt to create relief. Hold the leather in place with a few stitches around the perimeter of the shape.

2 Embroider with equally spaced stitches between the holding stitches.

Visual Library of Embroidery Stitches

RELIEF EMBROIDERY

Traditional embroidery is itself already worked in relief. Threads and beads embroidered onto the ground fabric add dimension. Raisedwork embroidery is characterized by the padding underneath the embroidery and by the "slips" (elements embroidered separately on a fabric, which are then attached to the final ground fabric).

First produced in ancient Rome, this type of embroidery enjoyed a golden age in the 16th and 17th centuries, when it was used in textile furnishings and religious objects. The highly figurative designs depicted biblical scenes, flora and fauna, etc. Embroidery thicknesses could reach 15 mm.

Semi-precious stones, silk threads, mother-of-pearl, coral, wood, mica, feathers, pearls, etc. are also used for these embroideries.

Embroidery from the 17th century (England). The hangings are embroidered in needlelace. The hands are also embossed by wrapping embroidery thread around a wire.

Box depicting scenes from the story of Solomon and the Queen of Sheba de Saba (1670), embroidered in single Brussels stitch, double Brussels stitch, with pearls covered in Brussels stitch, sating stitch, and woven picots.

Supplies

- metal thread (brass, copper, etc.) from 0.2 to 0.5 mm (Le Beaufil or La Droguerie) for the reinforcement used to stiffen the uprights
- wadding for padding
- beads of different diameters
- textile glue to secure the edges of the slips

Techniques

For relief embroidery, you need to master the basic stitches as well as some specific techniques.

Felt padding

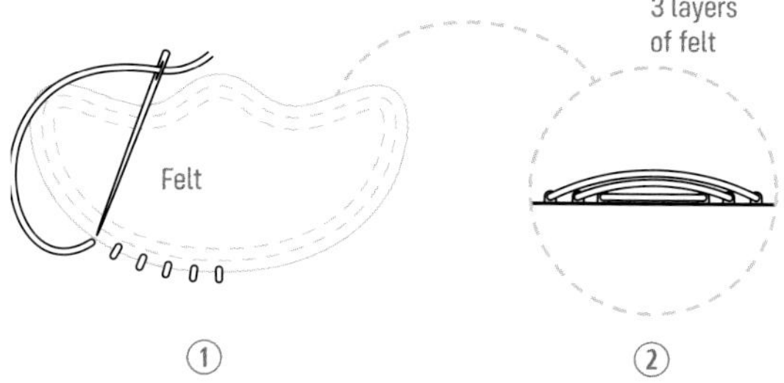

1 On the felt, transfer the shape to be embroidered three times: reduce its dimensions by a few millimeters so that the layers can be superimposed, as shown in the diagram. Cut these three shapes and, using a double needle of matching thread, begin by attaching the smallest one to the center of the design with small straight stitches all around, every 3 mm.

2 Overlap and secure all the layers of felt in the same way, ending with the largest.

Tips for Good Embroidery

Choose felt in the same color as the embroidery thread, so that it's completely invisible once the work has been embroidered. Work with matching sewing thread.

Woven picots

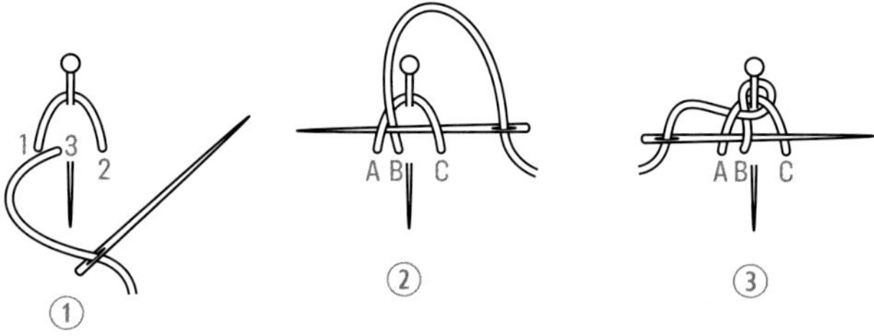

The woven picot is often used to represent petals. It is worked with a large straight pin, without piercing the fabric.

1 Place the straight pin to obtain the desired petal length. Take out the needle in 1, pass the thread behind the pin head, stitch in 2, and take out in 3 against the pin.

2 Pass behind the pinhead again from the left. These three taut threads form the warp (A, B, and C).

3 Pass the needle from right to left under C, over B, and under A, then from left to right over A, under C, and over A. Continue until the petal is completely filled, and finish by piercing the fabric to anchor the thread. Gently remove the pin.

Padded appliqué

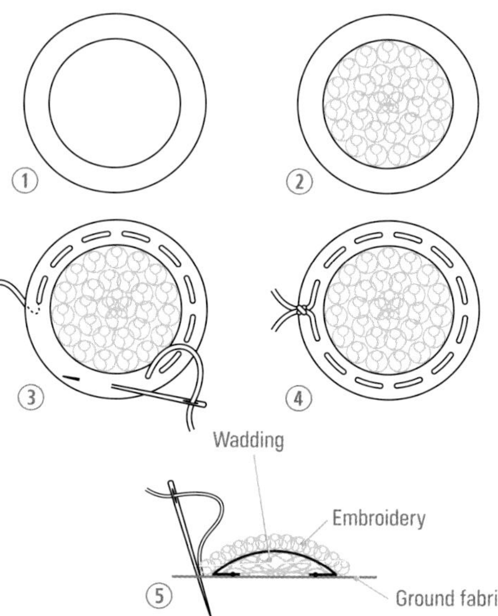

The padded appliqué is made on cotton batiste matching the embroidery. It is first embroidered on a small piece of fabric and then applied to the final work.

1 Using a circle template, draw a first circle the size of the embroidery and a second 10 mm larger.

2 Embroider French knots or beads in the inner circle.

3 Place a gathering thread on the remaining margin, in the middle of the space between the small and large circles.

4 Pull on the gathering thread. Thanks to the gathers thus created, the margin will fold itself onto the reverse side of the appliqué. If necessary, stuff the shape with wadding for extra volume.

5 Using a matching sewing thread, create an invisible stitch straddling the edge of the appliqué on the final work.

Wire frame

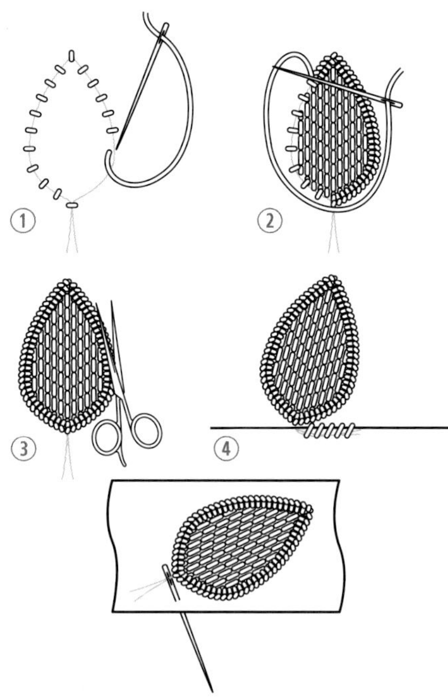

In addition to stiffening, a thread frame is used to attach lifted slips to the textile support. This technique is mainly used for foliage, petals, and insect wings. It is worked with very small-diameter thread and a small piece of cotton batiste to match the embroidery. Once embroidered, the raised motif must be attached to the final work.

1 Transfer the design to be embroidered onto the batiste—lift patterns are usually supplied with the design. Using thread matching the embroidery, embroider the thread with couching stitches around the shape to be lifted. Leave the ends of the thread overlapping by 3 cm; be careful not to let them overlap.

2 To embroider the inside of the design, follow the instructions on the pattern. You'll often need to use satin stitches or long and short technique. Then embroider, straddling the frame, a buttonhole stitch or tailor's buttonhole stitch.

3 Gently glue these buttonhole stitches on the reverse side and leave to dry overnight. Remove the embroidery from the hoop. While holding the raised side facing you (in this case, the front of the slip), carefully cut out the shape with small, precise scissors.

4 Using a large needle or stiletto, pass the ends of the thread through to the back of the work, fold them over, and secure them with small stitches (the thread must lie smoothly against the ground fabric).

Single Brussels stitch

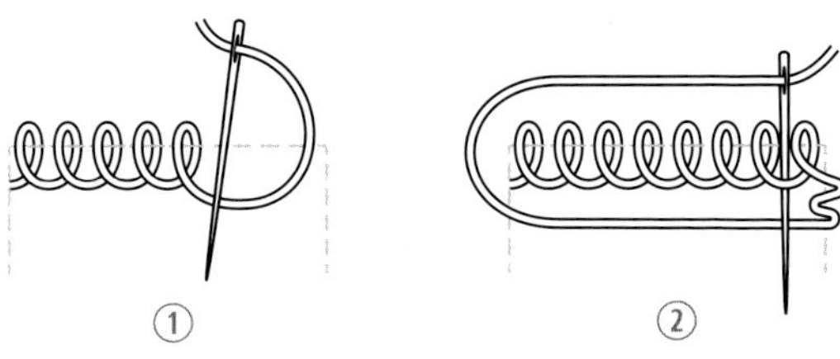

1 Embroider the perimeter of the shape with a 3mm backstitch. Starting from the left, embroider the first row with a detached buttonhole stitch and pass under each stitch, without stitching into the fabric.

2 At the end of the row, pass the needle right under the first vertical backstitch, then under the second, and start the second row. Embroider in detached buttonhole stitch from right to left, passing through each loop of the previous row. If necessary, increase or decrease the first and last loops of the rows, adding or removing detached buttonhole stitches.

Double Brussels stitch

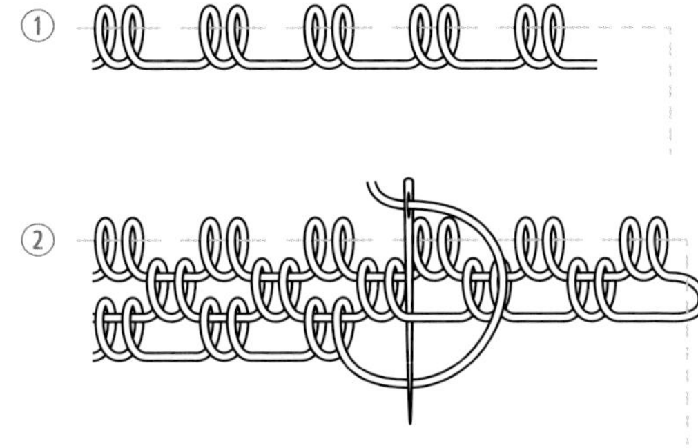

Double Brussels stitch is embroidered in the same way as single Brussels stitch, but with two tight detached buttonhole stitches in each loop. Two-by-two detached buttonhole stitches are staggered in relation to the previous row.

Corded Brussels stitch

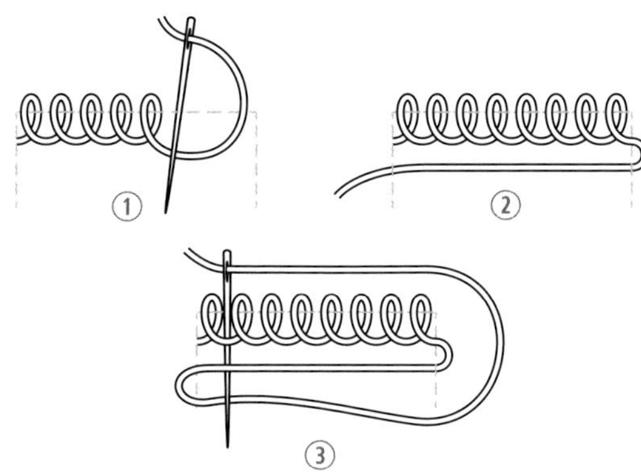

1 Embroider the perimeter of the shape with a 3mm backstitch. Starting from the left, embroider the first row with a detached buttonhole stitch and pass under each backstitch, without stitching into the fabric.

2 At the end of the row, pass the needle under the first vertical backstitch and then under the second. Tension the thread to pass under the second vertical stitch on the left. This taut thread becomes a filling thread or cord for the next row.

3 Embroider the second row in detached buttonhole stitch, from left to right, passing through each loop of the previous row and under the cord float. If necessary, increase or decrease the first and last row stitches, adding or removing detached buttonhole stitches.

Covering a bead

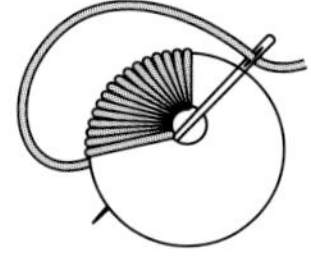

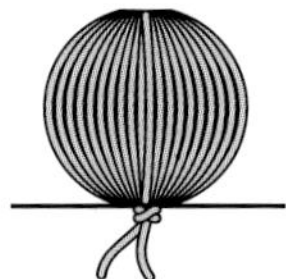

The work is carried out with the finest needle possible and on a bead with a large hole. Ideally, it should match the working thread. Whatever thread you choose.

Pass the needle through the bead, leaving 5 cm of thread protruding from the end of the needle. Wrap the thread around the bead until it is completely covered. The ends of the thread can help secure the bead to the ground fabric.

> **What You Need to Know**
>
> If you can't find a bead to match your thread, paint a rough wooden bead in the right color with acrylic paint. Allow to dry before you begin.

Covering a bead with needlelace

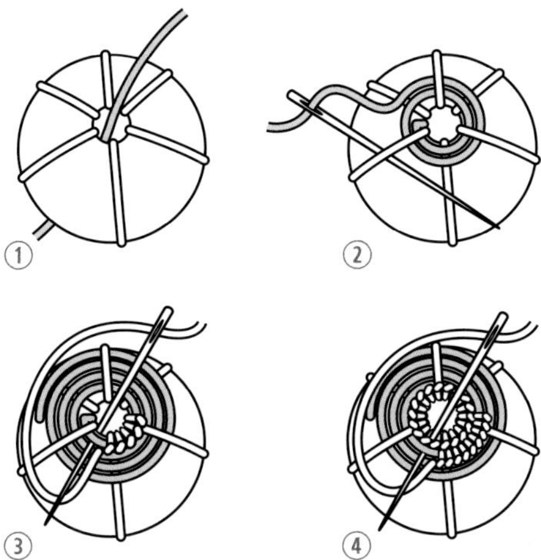

The work is carried out with the finest needle possible and on a bead with a large hole. Ideally, it should match the working thread. Whatever thread you choose.

1 Wrap the thread around the bead regularly (five, seven, or nine times, depending on the size of the bead).

2 On the top of the bead, pass the needle over and under each thread. Make three turns.

3 Make a first row in detached buttonhole stitch by passing the needle under the threads of the previous rounds.

4 Work the entire surface of the bead in detached buttonhole stitch. Add and reduce the number of detached buttonhole stitches to follow the contour of the bead.

Visual Library of Embroidery Stitches

APPLIQUÉS

Appliqués, or hand appliqués, are pieces of fabric sewn, or embroidered, on a textile background that serves as a support.

In China, Egypt, and Siberia, appliquéd embroidery dating back to 8,000 BCE was found in burial chambers. Embroiderers the world over then appropriated this art form, as they did in Europe as early as the Middle Ages.

Since the late 18th century, appliqué has been used on quilts and patchworks in North America. A famous little girl called Sunbonnet Sue, wearing a hat and carrying a bag or umbrella, is made in this way. Baltimore is the home of the finest embroidery.

Baltimore, USA: appliqué work with traditional motifs (wreath, bouquet, cornucopia, and bird), 1847

Mola is a reverse appliqué technique used by the Cuna people who live on the San Blas Islands off the coast of Panama.

In embroidery, there are two possible techniques for creating appliqués: tucked-edge or plain-edge. These two methods can be used alone or with any embroidery stitch.

Supplies

- appliqué or embroidery scissors for close trimming of appliquéd fabric edges

Pelican shears

- anti-fray textile glue to stabilize the edges of applied fabrics if they are very fragile
- Pellon or Sulky, a double-sided iron-on interlining for gluing full-edge decals
- needles for appliqué
- a Frixion pen for transferring patterns
- long needles adapted to the threads used
- glove thread, appliqué thread, or no. 50 sewing thread for sewing appliqués
- basting thread to baste work

Techniques

The appliqué technique involves sewing or gluing pieces of fabric onto a ground fabric to create a pattern. The edges of appliqués can be

- cut slightly larger than the motif—excess fabric is folded and hidden under the appliqué—or
- cut to size (i.e., the appliqué is cut to the exact size of the motif). Please note: the fabric must not fray.

Tucked-edge appliqué sewn with invisible stitches or turned-edge appliqué

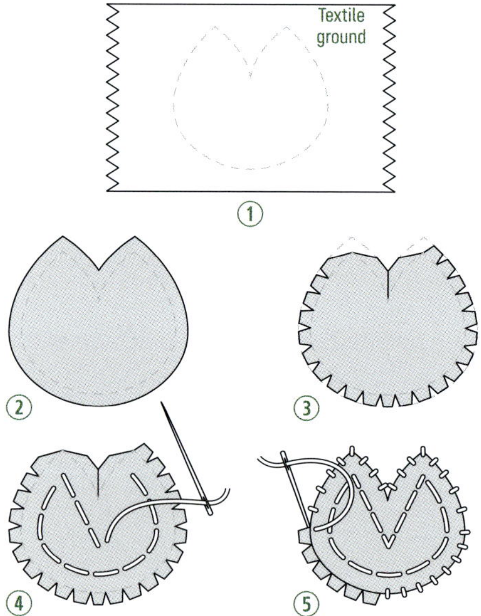

The geometrical shape of the patterns must be taken into account when working; for example, avoid excessively sharp angles, which are difficult to apply cleanly. If the curves are convex, they should be clipped beforehand; if concave, they should be notched.

1 Transfer the design to the right side of the ground fabric and the fabric to be applied.

2 On the right side of the fabric to be applied, mark a 5mm margin around the shape.

3 Depending on the corners, notch or clip all around the shape to a depth of 4 mm, within the margin. Be careful not to cut right up to the appliqué design: leave 1 mm to prevent fraying.

4 Baste the shape onto the ground fabric in large stitches, without coming too close to the edges, in order to bring in the seam allowances.

5 Using invisible stitches, secure the appliqué by folding the seam allowance as you go.

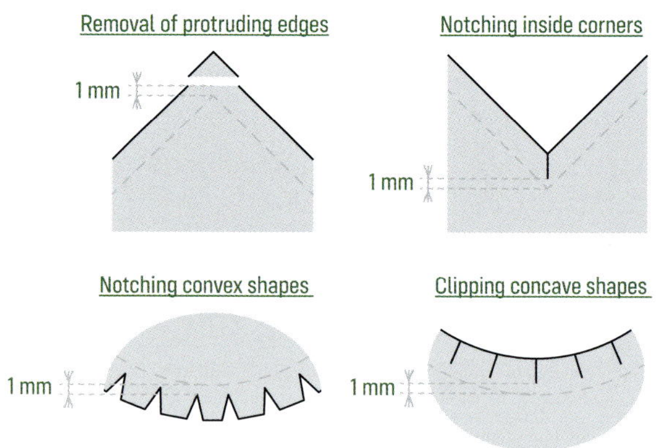

The appliqué with embroidered turned-in edges in hemstitch

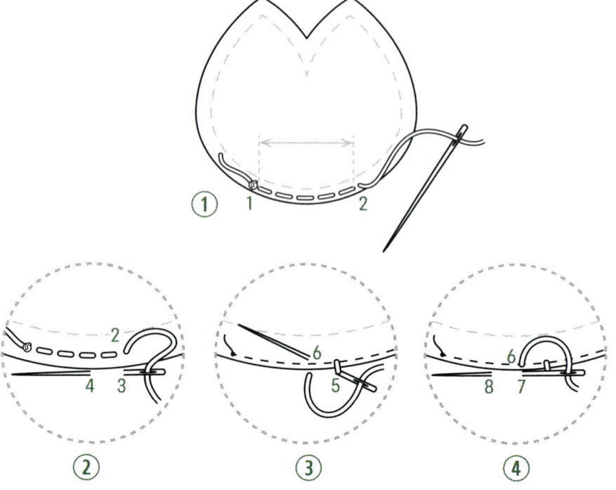

Hemstitch is one of the few embroidery stitches that doesn't have to be done with a hoop. It can be embroidered "in hand." It's up to you to choose the technique that suits you best!

This secure locking stitch is embroidered from right to left with a long needle and sewing thread (e.g., no. 50) or glove thread for 100–110 g/m^2 cotton fabric. Increase thread and needle size for heavier fabrics, and vice versa for lighter fabrics.

Start by preparing the appliqué as described in steps 1 to 4 above. Carefully tuck in the edges and baste.

1 Start and stop the needle in the thickness of this tuck: tie a knot on the needle, stitch in 1 on the top of the appliqué by sliding the needle into the fold of the tuck, and pull out the needle in 2 to 1 cm. The thread will then be cut flush under the small knot, after the first three stitches have been completed.

2 Stitch in 3 and out in 4 to create a 2mm stitch.

3 Stitch at 5 (5 and 3 are the same) and exit at 6 (in line with 4).

4 Continue in this way, stitching in 7, in the hole of the previous stitch, and exiting in 8.

For left-handed people

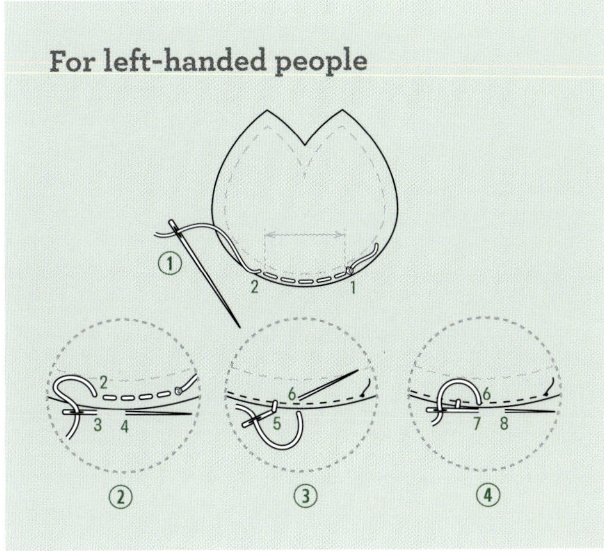

Clean-edge appliqué with fusible interfacing or stabilizer

1 Transfer the design onto the ground fabric.

2 Offset the design to be mirrored on the paper side of the stabilizer, then cut 2–3 cm around the design without biting into the details.

3 Apply the rough surface of stabilizer to the reverse side of the fabric to be applied, and iron for 5 seconds (medium to hot setting).

4 Cut out the motif precisely and remove the backing paper from the stabilizer.

5 Glue side down, place the pattern on the line of the ground fabric.

6 Cover with a cloth and press with an iron for 10 seconds (medium-hot).

To help you, please refer to the step-by-step instructions on page 357.

Reverse appliqué

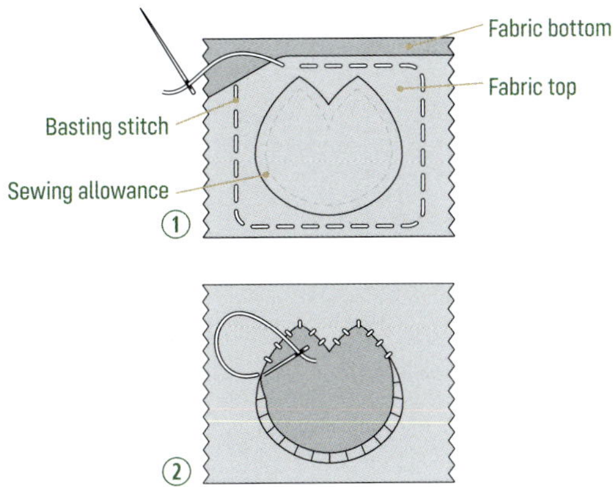

Reverse appliqué requires two identically sized pieces of fabric: one for the ground and one for the top (the motifs).

1 On the fabric above, trace the design and the 5mm seam allowances inside the shapes. Lay the two fabrics on top of each other and baste around the shape, without coming too close to the edges, so as to draw in the seam allowances. Trim the inside of the motif, then clip or notch.

2 Using invisible stitches, attach the appliqué following the final line, folding in the seam allowance as you go.

Embroidered appliqué

The embroidered appliqué is sewn in the classic way as described above: with tucked-in edges, with clean edges, or with raw edges. Embroidery stitches then straddle the edges of the appliqué to work the design.

Almost any embroidery stitch can be used to embroider an appliqué; here are the most common (see the explanations of each stitch in the Basic Stitch Libraries, pages 45 to 137):

- angled stem stitch (see page 56)

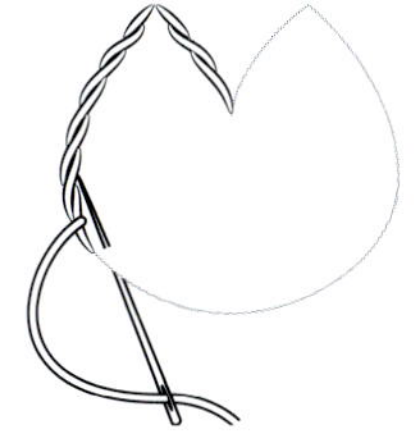

- couching stitch with a lying thread (see page 122)

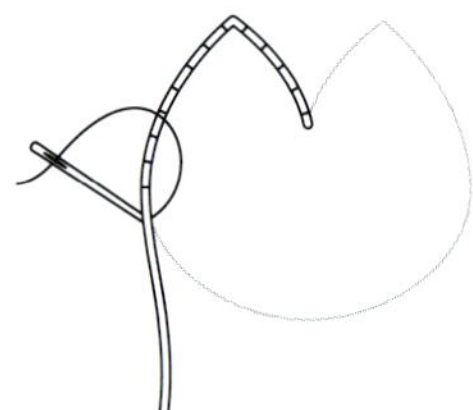

- twisted chain stitch (see page 79)

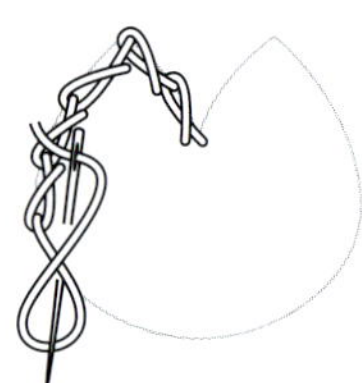

- herringbone stitch (see page 95)

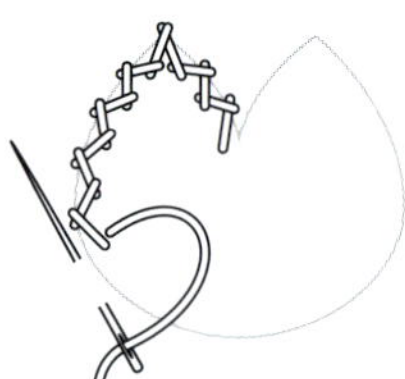

- buttonhole stitch (see page 70)

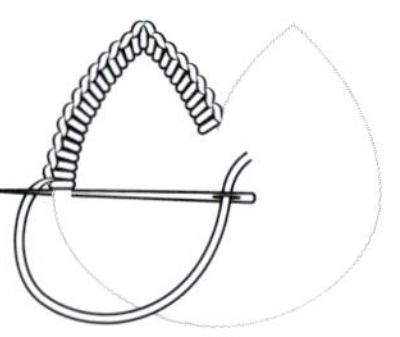

- the flat satin stitch (see page 127)

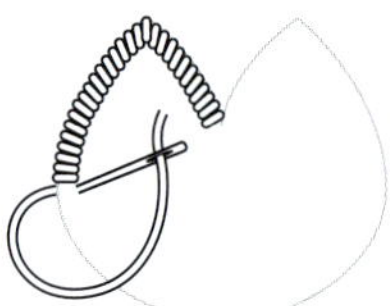

- coral stitch (see page 109)

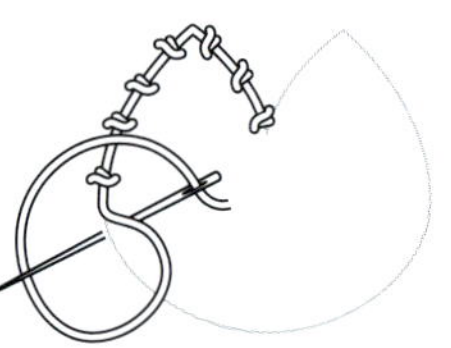

EMBELLISHMENT EMBROIDERY

Embellishment embroidery is very creative and a lot of fun. It involves combining all the embroidery techniques explained in this book to embellish a garment, accessory, or object, such as a pouch or wall hanging. No matter how regular the stitches, the embroidery must above all be original and pleasing to the eye.

All kinds of traditional and fancy threads (ribbons, chenille threads, raffia, lace, etc.) as well as pearls, sequins, and other supplies of all kinds are featured.

Small objects and mementos (such as cards or photos) can also be incorporated into the piece.

What You Need to Know

The core of a yarn is the central strand that supports the other strands making up a fancy yarn such as chenille.

Supplies

Needles should be chosen according to the threads being worked on.

Tips for Good Embroidery

Embellishment supplies and embroidery threads are often heavy. If necessary, when the ground fabric is too light to support the embroidery, use a backing (see page 28).

Chenille thread

There are two types of chenille thread.

- Those that pass through the ground fabric without deteriorating. At Au Ver à Soie, these are "satin" chenilles; their bristles are diagonal to the core thread.
- Those that get damaged when they cross the textile support. They are laid in couching. At Au Ver à Soie, these are "velvet" chenilles; their hairs are perpendicular to the core thread.

Not all suppliers specify whether chenille thread is suitable for passing through ground fabric. To find out, you'll need to do a test. Use a stiletto to pre-puncture the backing where the chenille thread is to pass through.

Embroidered raffia pouch, which can be found in the project on page 381

Embroidering raffia

Embroidery raffia comes in a variety of finishes (glossy, matte, satin, or iridescent) and widths. It can be embroidered like ribbon, using any traditional stitch.

Preparing a Satin Chenille Yarn Needle

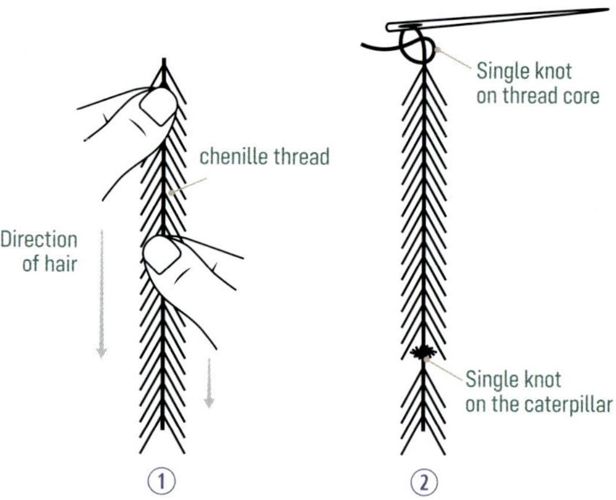

1 Cut 35 cm of chenille thread. Touch it to find the direction of the pile. On the top, remove 3 cm of the chenille thread, removing the chenille hairs with your fingernails, to find the central core thread.

2 Using a no. 16 chenille needle, pass the core thread through the eye of the needle and tie a simple knot.

Couching Stitch

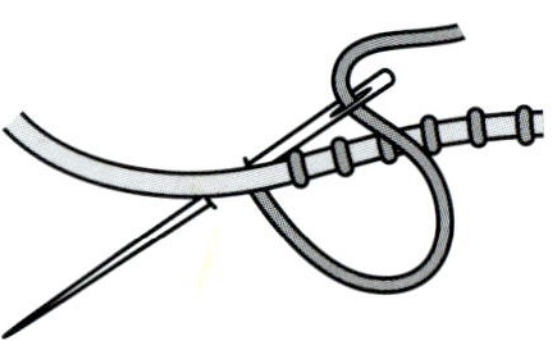

When certain fragile or rigid materials will not pass through the eye of the needle (such as silk chenille threads, braids, ribbons, etc.), they must be laid with couching.

What You Need to Know

The ends of the chenille threads and supplies are hidden under the embroidery or, if necessary, on the reverse side, thanks to a hole made beforehand using a stiletto.

4

WHITE EMBROIDERY

PLUMETIS

Widespread in the 19th century, plumetis is a white embroidery of French origin whose main stitch is the padded satin stitch.

In those days, well-born girls had to be able to embroider and plumetis their wedding trousseau. The higher their social standing, the more elaborate the embroidery and monogramming. In general, for a two-letter cipher, the first was the initial of the husband's surname, and the second the initial of the wife's maiden name.

What You Need to Know

Two expressions were used to designate the various forms of embroidery: chiffrage and marquage. The initial is said to be "chiffrée" when embroidered with padded satin stitch, and "marqué" when embroidered with cross-stitch. Beautiful body or household linen was ciphered, while everyday linen was marked.
The placement of initials and monograms varied according to whether they were padded satin or marked. Strict rules on this subject were taught to young girls.

From 1870 onward, specialized workers in the Vosges also offered complete trousseau production. Companies such as La Maison Malbranche in Paris (from 1860) took orders from wealthy customers and subcontracted the embroidery to these workers.

At the same time, plumetis was also used in Touraine embroidery for headdresses. Embroidered on muslin, its distinctive feature is the inlay of Valenciennes lace in the center of the floral motifs.

The most common motifs are flowers, leaves, garlands, polka dots, and letters that "chiffonize" linens and garments. Plumetis can be accompanied by openwork grounds (see pages 245 to 257), which are grids with or without drawn threads, particularly in the heart of flowers.

Supplies

- a tightly woven linen or cotton fabric, since this embroidery requires a dense weave
- Coton à Broder DMC no. 30 or 35 cotton for the padding, outlines, and embroidery
- glove thread (sewing thread ideal for working by hand) or no. 60 cotton sewing thread for openwork grounds
- a 12 or 15cm diameter hoop
- a no. 10 embroidery needle
- an erasable pen for transferring the pattern
- a circle template or compass for drawing neat circles on patterns

Techniques

Plumetis is worked in four stages: outling, filling, satin stitch, and grounds.

Design transfer

Start by transferring or sanding the design onto the fabric to be embroidered (see page 34).

Padding

Padding gives the embroidery more or less relief. It must be smooth but of variable thickness. It is carried out in the darning stitch, on the outline, and then on the inside of the shapes to be embroidered.

Plumetis-embroidered bodice with lace inlay and Paris-stitch laces

Fleur brodé au plumetis accompanied by rivière fantaisie border and Venice border. The center of the flower is embroidered with an openwork grid, and the inside of the leaves is filled with backstitch seeding (see page 226).

Touraine embroidery with plumetis and openwork grounds. Each petal is adorned with a lace inlay.

BR monogram embroidered in plumetis on an antique sheet

The recovery stitch

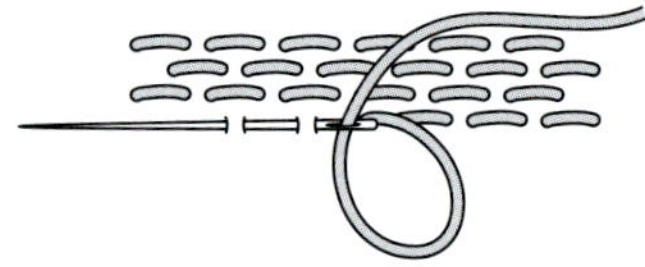

The darning stitch is embroidered on the right side of the work, on lines spaced very slightly apart. Line by line, stitch in staggered rows.

Stitched padded outline for contours and patterns

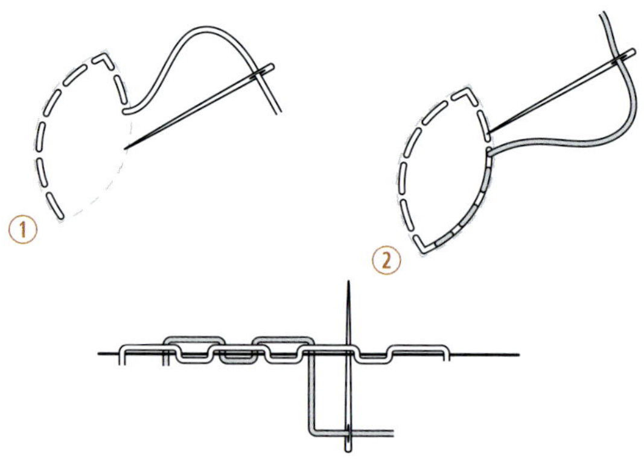

1 Embroider a first layer, using a row of darning stitch just inside the design.

2 When you return, stitch a second layer in running stitch, stitching through the first layer of stitches and the ground fabric, working in a staggered pattern.

Stitched padding inside motifs

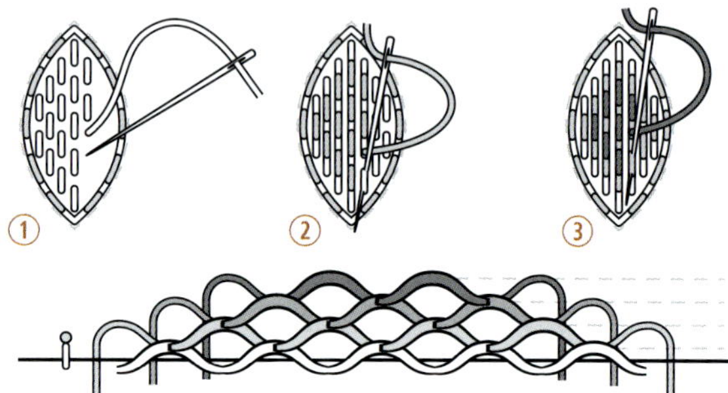

Padding is carried out in the same direction as the longest length of the motif. For example, on a leaf, padding should be parallel to the center vein.

1 Once the outline has been stitched and the direction of the future satin stitch embroidery has been determined, embroider the first layer of the padding in darning stitch. Stitch through onto the ground fabric.

> **What You Need to Know**
>
> **The stitched padding is always worked perpendicular to the direction of the future satin stitch and, generally, in the greatest length of the motifs.**

2 and 3 Embroider the second and subsequent layers by using straight and darning stitches that are stitched through the previous layer of stitches without going through the ground fabric—this way, the embroidery will not be too stiff.

By embroidering these layers, you create the desired relief only in the areas to be raised, to create a harmonious whole.

Whitework with flat satin stitch

Guide

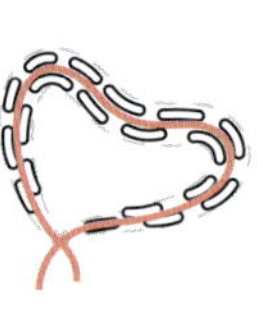

The guide is a thread laid between the padding and the satin stitch, enabling fine, precise embroidery. The thread used is Coton à Broder DMC cotton, a few centimeters longer than the shape to be embroidered.

This extra layer of thread, which is not attached to the padding, defines the edge of the design. Once the embroidery is complete, the ends of the guide thread are cut off flush.

Tips for Good Embroidery

If a guide thread continues past the padded motif to create a further padded line, the guide must be cut long enough to be laid in one piece over the entire motif.

If the design to be embroidered is divided into two parts, it is necessary to provide a second guide, which runs through the work so that it can then exit the second part of the design.

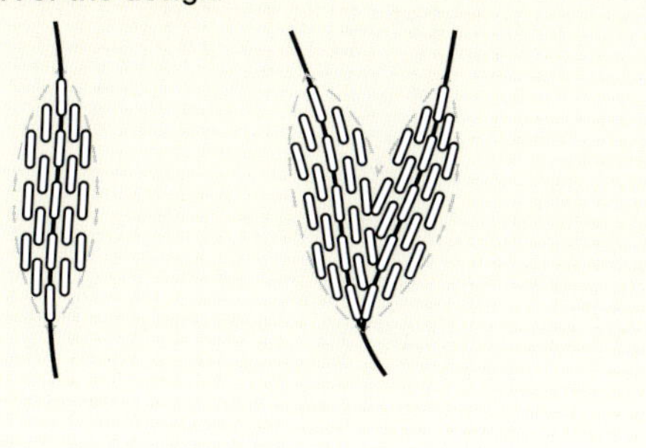

Padded satin stitch

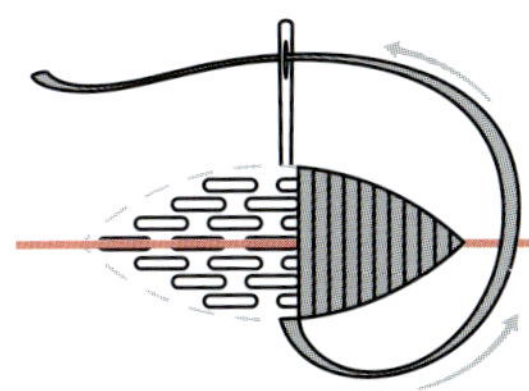

Satin stitches are embroidered perpendicular to the guide, which is laid in the same direction as the padding.

It's best to flip the direction of work, depending on whether you're right- or left-handed.

For left-handed people

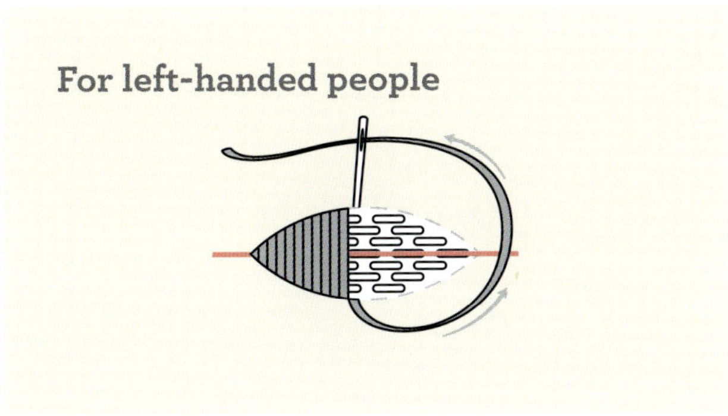

Single trailing

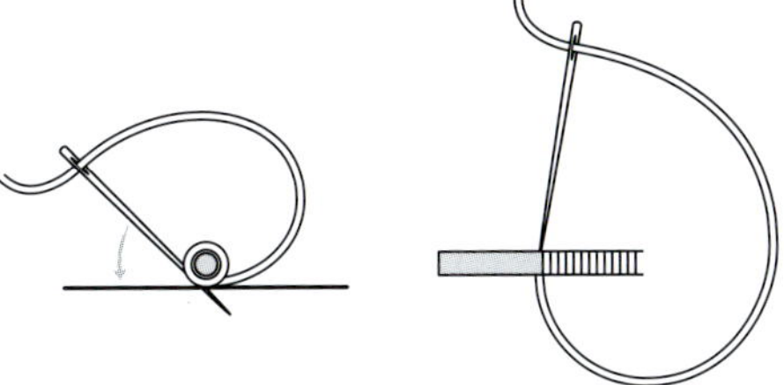

This linear technique has no variation in thickness. Embroider directly over the core thread with a tight satin stitch, tilting the needle to stitch under the guide on the design line.

Multiple cord trailing

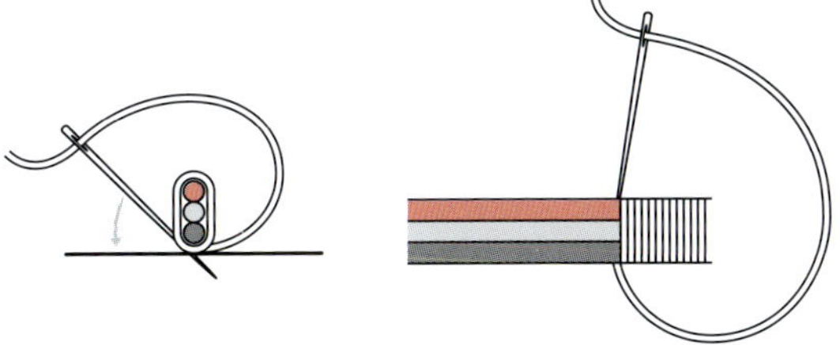

Embroider the trailing with multiple core threads, either stacked or gathered together. Place the core thread in place and embroider in the satin stitch perpendicular to it, angling the needle to stitch on the design line underneath the padding.

Complex motifs with satin stitch

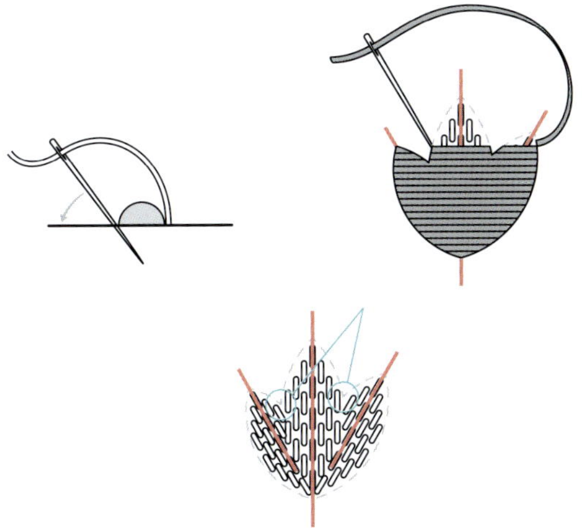

Lay the guide threads, stitch the outlines, and build up the inside of the motif with stitch padding. Place the core thread and embroider, using the satin stitch technique, placing the needle slightly at an angle to the design line.

At the end of the embroidery, cut the core threads flush with the first and last stitches.

What You Need to Know

When the motifs are pointed or complex, the area where the embroidery splits in two is called a "tip." The tips are embroidered in a second step, taking care to adjust and respect the direction of the stitches to achieve harmonious embroidery.

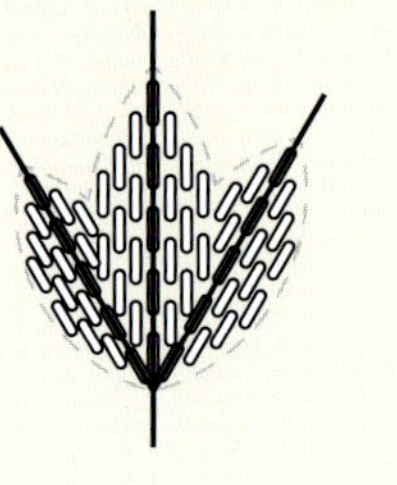

Padded tapered edges

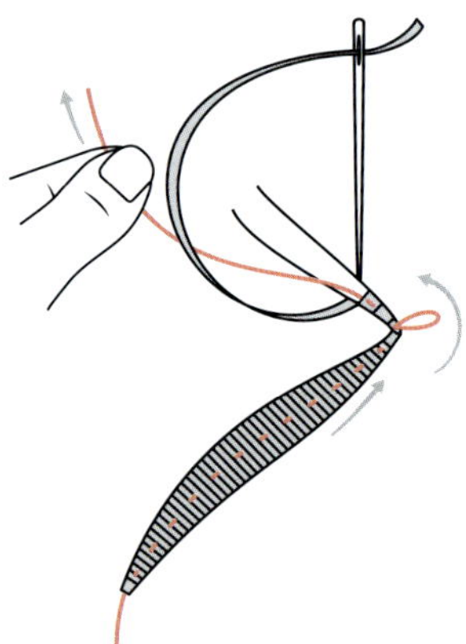

Design corners must be sharp. To achieve this, after padding the design, place the guide thread and satin-stitch the corner. Embroider three to four stitches past the corner, without stitching over the core thread and allowing the core thread to loop at the corner outside the satin stitch. Then gently pull the core thread under these last stitches to form the apex of the corner.

Polka dots with padded satin stitch

The embroidery steps are different depending on the diameter of the dots.

Polka dots 3 to 6 mm in diameter, with the direction of the final stitches vertical

1 Embroider a cross inside the motif.

2 Still within the design, embroider a layer of horizontal stitches.

3 Embroider the second and final layer of vertical stitches, stitching to the motif design line.

Polka dots 6 to 8 mm in diameter, with the final stitches horizontal

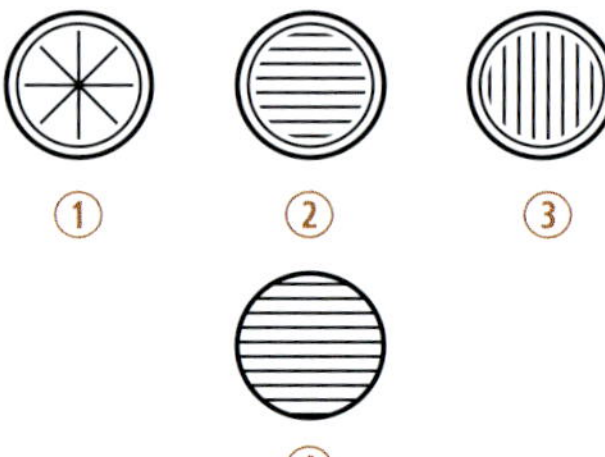

1 Embroider a line of split stitch inside the design, then two crosses, one on top of the other, offset at 45°.

2 Embroider a first layer of horizontal stitches inside the outline.

3 Still inside the stitched outline, embroider a second layer of vertical stitches.

4 Finally, stitch a third layer of satin stitches horizontal and stitching to the motif design line over the padded outline.

From 9 to 12mm diameter: Larger polka dots require more volume. Embroider in the same way as for the previous polka dots, adding a third layer of satin stitch padding on the inside. Finish the polka dot with the fourth layer, embroidering over the padding outline to the motif design line.

Richelieu embroidery and padded satin

Richelieu embroidery with satin dots (see page 224)

English embroidery with feathered dots

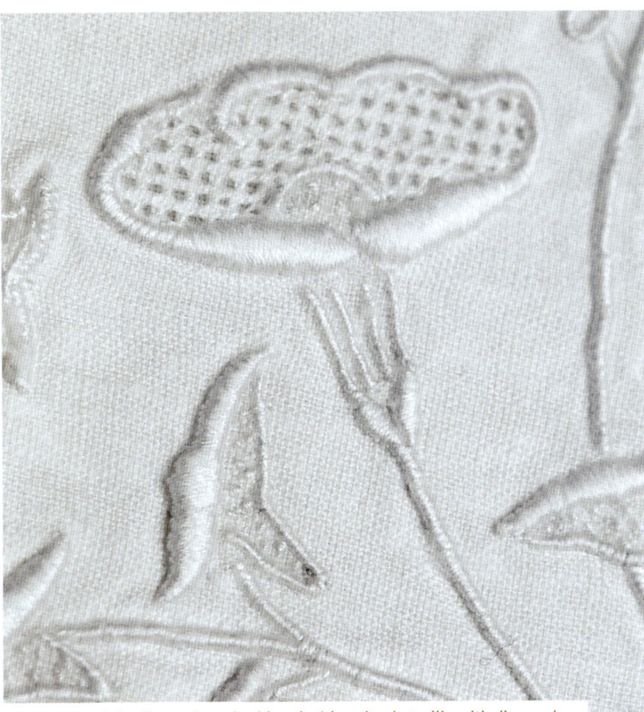

The center of the flower is embroidered with a simple trellis with diagonal holding stitch. The inside of the leaves is embroidered in backstitch seeding (see page 226).

What You Need to Know

In a sequence of polka dots, the final embroidery must have the same direction on all the dots, whether vertical or horizontal. It is therefore necessary to anticipate the work on the first level according to the size of the polka dots.

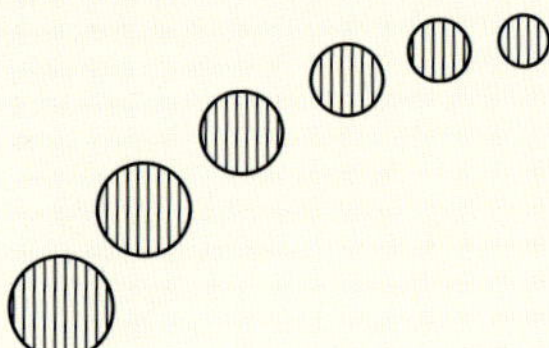

Filling techniques

Plumetis can be accompanied by filigree grounds (see pages 245–257) or seeding embroidery to fill the spaces inside the satin stitched and outlined motifs, particularly in the centers of flowers and sometimes leaves.

Filigree grounds are pulled thread patterns that can be embroidered with no. 60 cotton sewing thread or glove thread.

What You Need to Know

Pulled thread work and seeding stitches are applied after the motifs have been completed, using satin stitch, trailing, and outlining.

Backstitch seeding

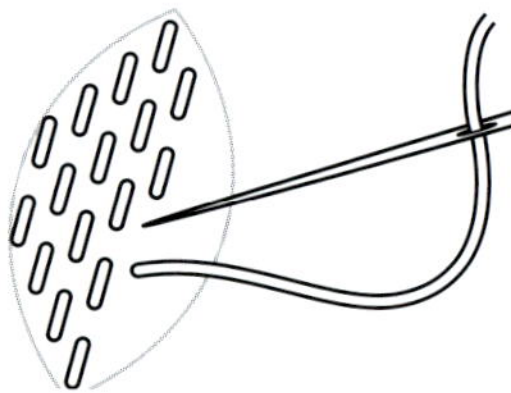

Backstitch staggered stitches measuring 1 to 1.5 mm, following the natural directions of the motif (e.g., veins for foliage). The space left between each stitch is equivalent to the length of the stitches visible on the top of the work. Close rows are spaced one-third of the stitch length apart.

Tips for Good Embroidery

Start embroidering the longest length to correctly orient the direction of embroidery.

BORDERS WITH DRAWN THREADS

Drawn threads embroidery is an embroidery technique that has been practiced all over the world for centuries, notably on Coptic textiles between the fifth and ninth centuries.

This technique, then known as "Punto Tirato," was developed in Italy in the 15th century. Threads are drawn out in only one direction and worked in continuous repeats over the remaining threads to create borders for sheets, tablecloths, handkerchiefs, and even pieces of lingerie.

Border from Venice

Drawn threadwork with decorative wheels

This technique is also known as "drawn thread" or "drawnwork."

The Italian Renaissance saw the emergence of designs with threads pulled in both directions, known as "Punto Tagliato." Threads are pulled through the warp and weft before the embroidery in hemstitching, trellis, and buttonhole.

Toward the beginning of the 20th century, in Europe and North America, days adorned blouses and undergarments. From the 1930s to the 1950s, the linear art deco style reinforced the presence of this embroidery in these countries.

Drawn-thread embroidered borders are made on fabric from which threads have first been removed in the warp or weft (or both): this is the "mark." Next comes the "openwork," needlework to create the final embroidery.

Days are usually embroidered on the reverse side.

Supplies

- Linen or cotton canvas, more or less fine, from which you can remove warp and weft threads. Test beforehand.
- Coton à Broder DMC no. 25, 30, or 35 cotton for openwork. Suitable for all types of canvas. Traditionally, it should be the same color as the fabric backing.
- No. 50 or 60 cotton sewing thread for the finest fabrics (such as batiste). It should be the same color as the fabric backing.

Tips for Good Embroidery

The thread used for drawnwork must be strong: make sure it is the same size as the threads of the linen to be embroidered.

- A 15cm diameter embroidery hoop. It's not compulsory, since borders can also be embroidered in hand. Choose the method that suits you best!
- Embroidery needles nos. 7, 9, and 10, to be chosen according to the thickness of the thread used, for openwork
- An assortment of embroidery and quilting needles to draw in threads when marking and to embroider any buttonhole stitches
- Embroidery scissors for pulling and cutting threads

Techniques

First, the fabric to be embroidered is marked by pulling out weft or warp threads (or both) one by one with a pair of embroidery scissors and an embroidery needle. It is then openworked by embroidery to create the patterns in the work.

Attention

The fabric should not be washed before working, since this would make it more difficult to make the mark—the fabric's weft threads may felt slightly in the wash.

Work preparation: Removing the threads

Marking—the space left free after the threads have been pulled—is an important and meticulous step. The number of threads to pull depends on the desired effect, defined by the weft of the fabric to be embroidered and the height of the embroidered borders. For example, if the fabric has 16 threads/cm and the band is to be 1.5 cm high, pull 16 × 1.5 = 24 threads.

Tips for Good Embroidery

To get started, follow a pattern. For the more experienced, don't forget that before you start, it's important to make samples to determine the number of threads to remove during preparation, as well as the thickness of the thread so that the work doesn't pucker. With experience, this will become easier.

Days running from one edge of the work to the other

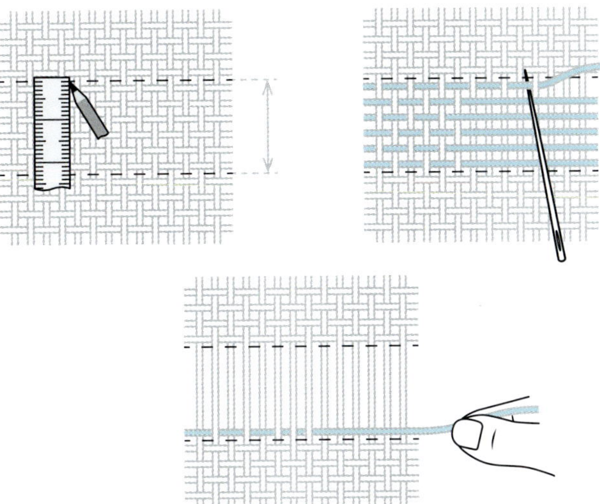

Work on the reverse side of the work. The use of an embroidery hoop helps achieve this.

1 Mark out the position of the strip to be marked with two pencil lines, counting the threads or measuring with a ruler.

2 Using an embroidery needle, clear about 2 cm of all the threads to be drawn out to one edge.

3 Remove the first thread along the entire length of the border; this is often the most difficult to extract from the weave. Continue marking, removing threads one by one in small sections.

Drawn threads removed from the center of the border

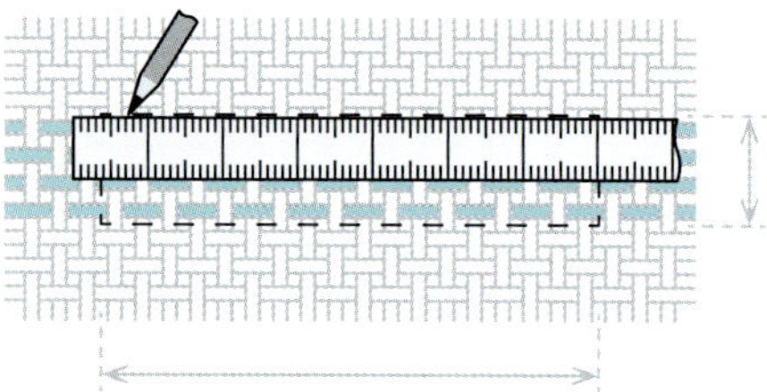

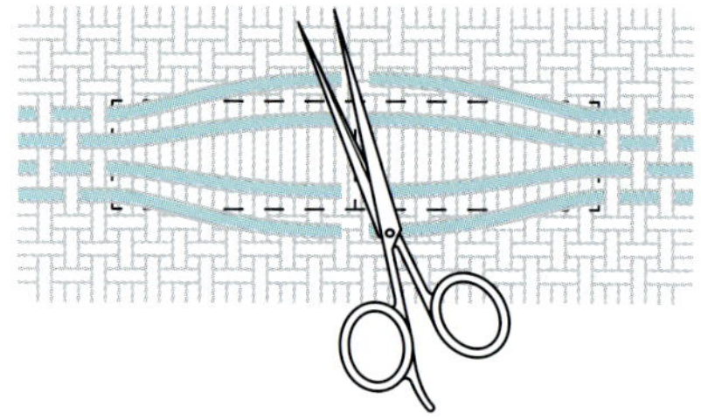

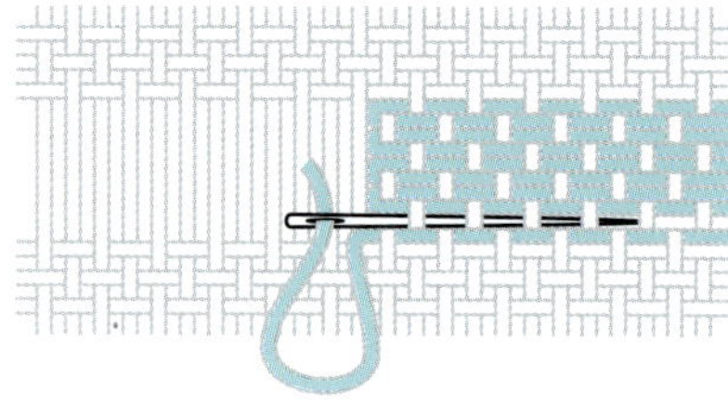

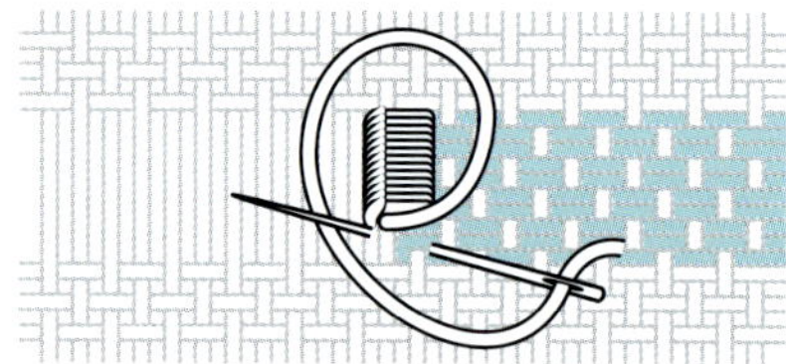

Work on the reverse side of the work. The use of an embroidery hoop helps achieve this.

1 Using a ruler, mark the length and width of the area to be marked with two pencil lines.

2 and 3 Cut a horizontal thread in the middle of the border and, using the eye of the needle, remove the threads to the border, taking care to keep a minimum length of 5 cm for the next step.

4 Thread each end of the previously removed threads onto an embroidery needle (choose an eye large enough for easy threading). Reweave for about 1 cm, taking care to respect the top and bottom of the weave. Do the same on the other end.

5 Buttonhole-stitch a tight bar over the edge at both ends.

Drawn threads at a corner

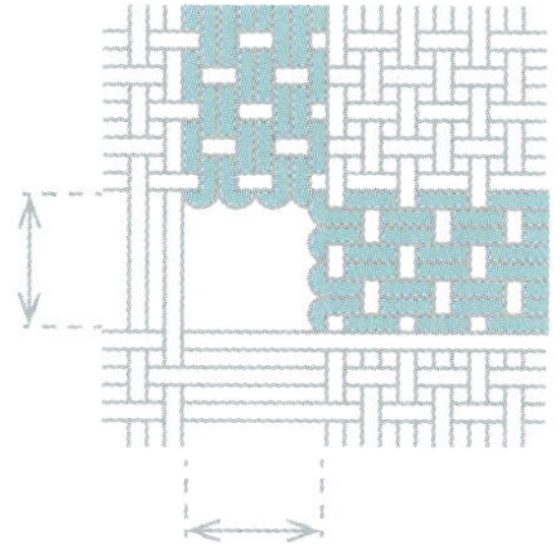

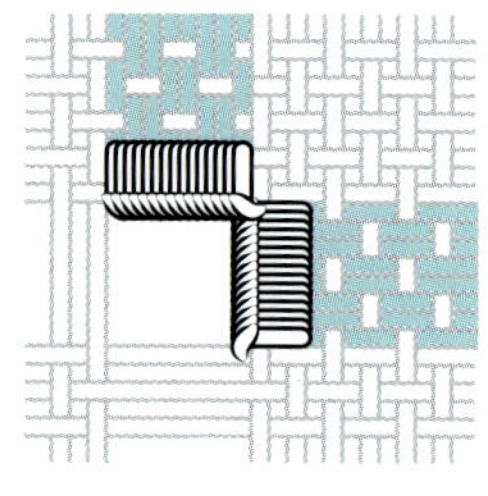

Work on the reverse side of the work. The use of an embroidery hoop helps achieve this.

Starting in the middle of the corner, remove the weft threads and reweave them back in above the corner. Once all weft threads are removed, remove the warp threads in the same manner, securing the end by reweaving them underneath on the corner edge. The corner thus worked will be completely empty.

Grouping the threads

Working-thread starts and stops must be invisibly integrated into the embroidery or canvas so as not to leave any knots in the work.

Working threads

When working on small surfaces, it's a good idea to have enough thread to cover the entire job. They should not exceed 60 cm, to prevent the thread from wearing out.

The start of the working thread

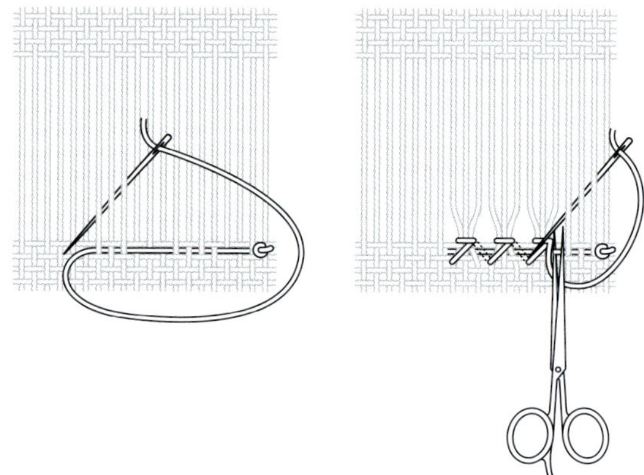

If embroidery has already been carried out on the work, slide the needle on the back of a few stitches to anchor the thread.

Alternatively, make a waste knot on the working thread and weave it on the wrong side at 2 cm, flush with the border and on the part that will be embroidered next. Embroider the first stitches including the working thread, then cut the small knot flush as soon as possible (when the start is well anchored). The working thread is thus anchored by the first stitches.

Stopping the needle

Finish by doubling the last stitch in the border and slide the needle, on the reverse side, under the stitches previously made.

Embroidery Stitches

Openwork embroidery is worked by counting the warp and weft threads of the fabric in the drawn border or the remaining threads in the band.

Unless otherwise indicated, days are embroidered on the reverse side.

Hemstitching

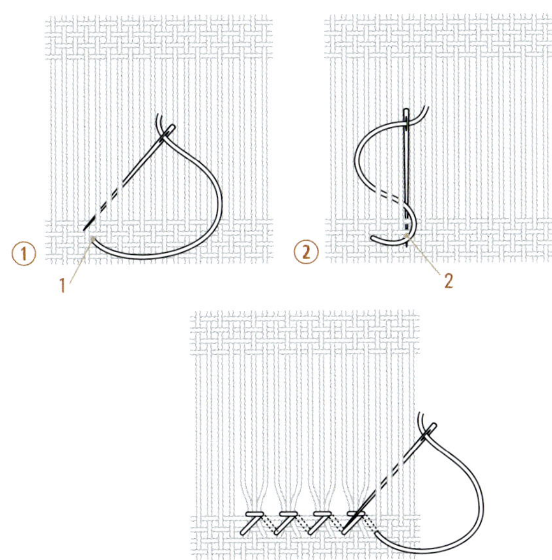

Hemstitching is worked from left to right. Stitches must be tight.

1 Pull the needle out in 1, taking two threads from the edge of the border. Slide the needle from right to left under three threads.

2 Pass the needle from behind, from top to bottom in the border, taking two threads, and exit in 2.

For left-handed people

Embroider from right to left. Work starts usually on the right.

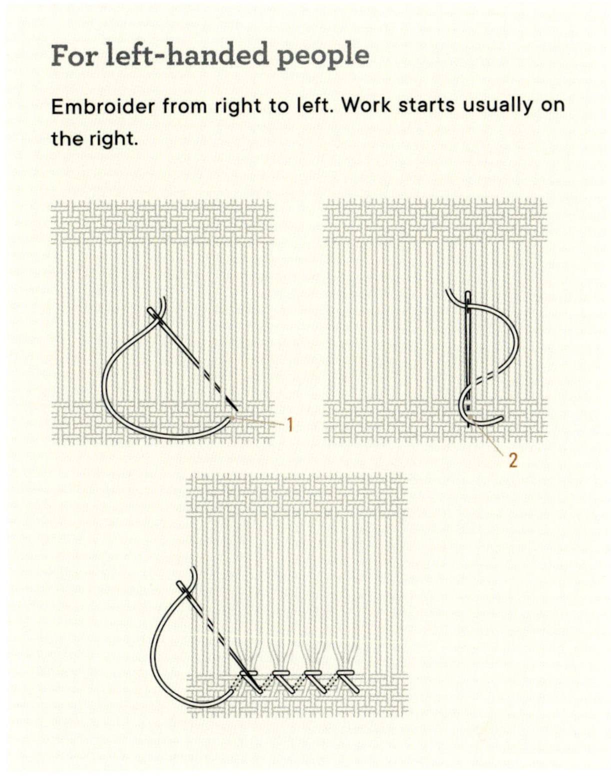

Ladder hemstitch

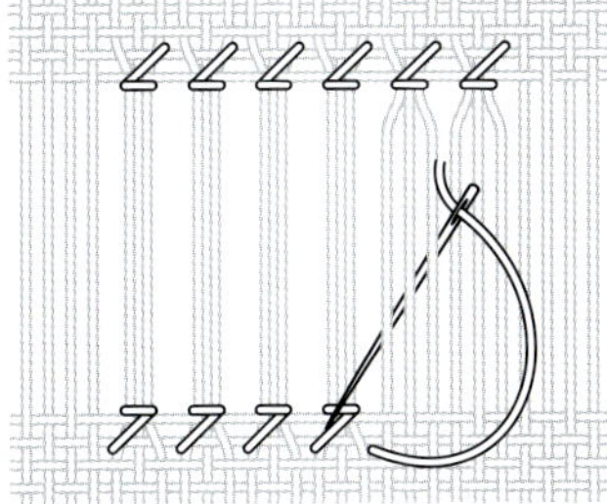

The ladder hemstitch is hemstitching worked on both edges of the border, from left to right.

1 Hemstitch one edge. Turn the work 180° to work the opposite edge.

2 Create a ladder hemstitch opposite the one created in step 1: bind the exact same threads to create a ladder.

What You Need to Know

All the threads grouped together are called "bundles."

Diagonal hemstitch or serpentine hemstitch

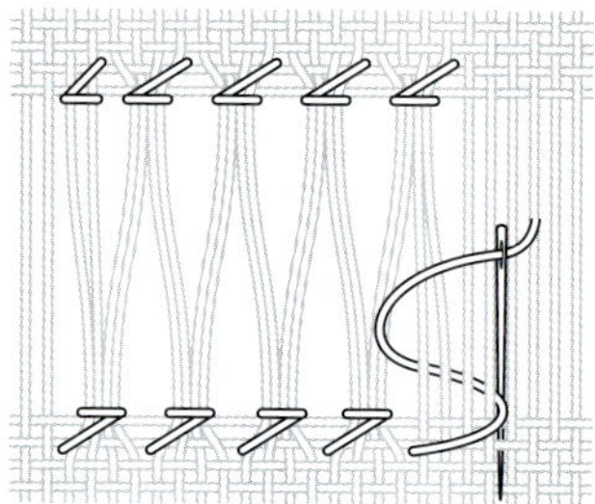

The split bundles form a V and are worked on an even number of threads (four or six threads), from left to right.

1 Make a simple hemstitch on one edge.

2 On the opposite side, hemstitch, staggering the placement across the first hemstitch side by taking half the threads from each bundle.

Interlaced border

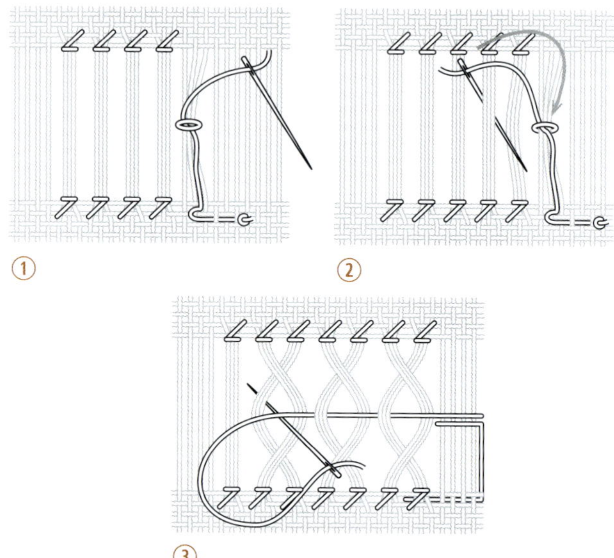

The ladder hemstitch is worked with two-thread bundles, from right to left; a working thread works through the middle of the border, twisting the bundles without puckering the textile backing.

1 Make a few anchor stitches and knot the working thread halfway up the first bundle so that it is firmly attached. Slide the needle tip, from left to right, under the second bundle and over the first.

2 In a rotating movement, tip the needle to the right, pointing downward, without catching the following bundles.

3 Work the bundles in pairs until you reach the end of the border: repeat steps 1 and 2.

Tips for Good Embroidery

Make sure you have enough length of working thread so that you don't have to change threads during work, since there's no place to anchor and start a new one.

Staggered interlaced border

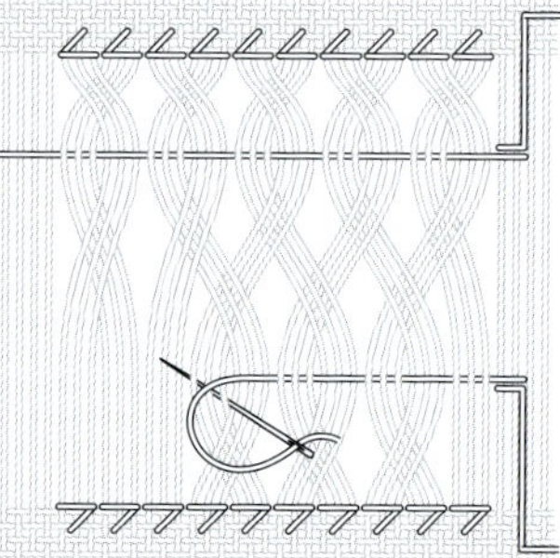

The staggered interlaced border is worked, from right to left, on a band wide enough to cross the threads without puckering the textile backing.

Step 1 Make a few anchor stitches and knot the working thread at a quarter of the border height to secure it. Cross the bundles in pairs. In a rotating motion, tip the needle to the right, pointing downward, without catching the following bundles.

Step 2 Make a few bartacks and knot the second embroidery thread at three-quarters of the mark, contrasting the bundles with those of the first row. Cross the bundles in pairs.

Knotted border

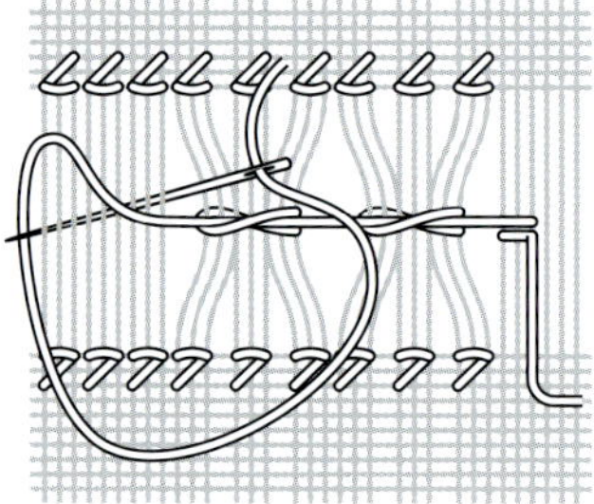

The knotted border is worked, from right to left, on a drawn band wide enough to knot the threads without puckering the ground fabric.

Make a few bartacks and knot the working thread halfway up the mark so that it is securely fastened.

Pass the needle from right to left under the bundles to be knotted, working thread down. Pass the working thread from bottom to top over the needle, then from top to bottom under the needle. Pull to tighten the knot.

Tips for Good Embroidery

The space between each node must be the same everywhere, to allow the beams to be distributed evenly. You'll need a bit of practice to achieve this.

Herringbone stitch border

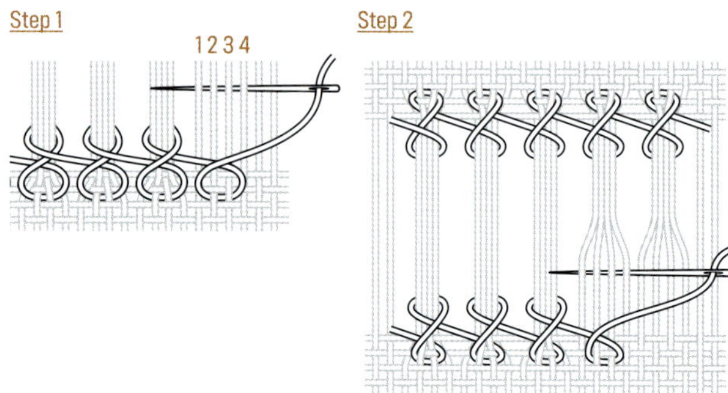

Herringbone stitch is worked from left to right, on the right side of the work.

Step 1 Stitch the needle, taking threads 2 and 3 from the edge of the border (under three horizontal threads).

Step 2 Pass the needle under threads 1 to 4 in the work opposite each other.

Zigzag border

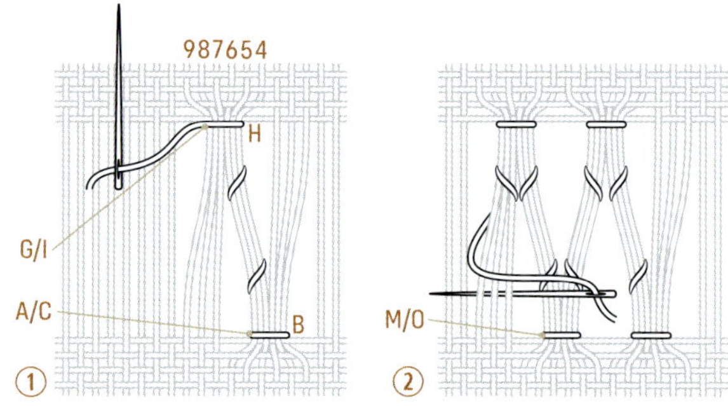

Zigzag border is worked from right to left, on the right side of the work, on three-thread bundles. It is embroidered alternately up and down.

1 Take out the needle at A, passing behind the first six threads at the bottom edge of the openwork. Stitch at B and exit at C. Overcast the working thread twice on threads 4 to 6 as you go up. Exit at G after thread 9. Stitch in H and exit in I to overlock together threads 4 to 9.

2 Overlock twice on threads 7, 8, and 9 on the way down. Exit at M after thread 12. Stitch in N and exit in O to overlock together threads 7 to 12.

Wrapped bars

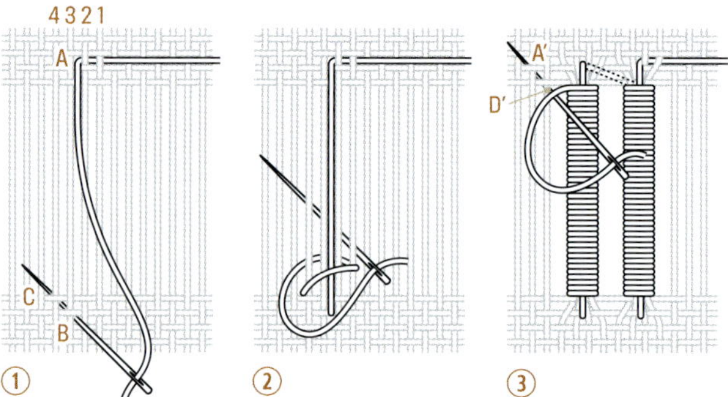

Wrapped bars are worked from right to left, on the right side of the work, on four threads. The working thread must be firmly attached to the top right-hand side of the openwork.

1 To start, pull the needle out at A, between the first two threads and two threads from the edge. Go down vertically, stitch in B, at the bottom, between threads 2 and 3, two threads from the edge of the border, and come out on the diagonal in C.

2 Gather the four threads together, wrap tightly around the threads, including the vertical working thread, as many times as necessary until you obtain an even, tightly wrapped bar.

3 Stitch in D and out in A to start the next wrapped bar.

Woven hemstitch

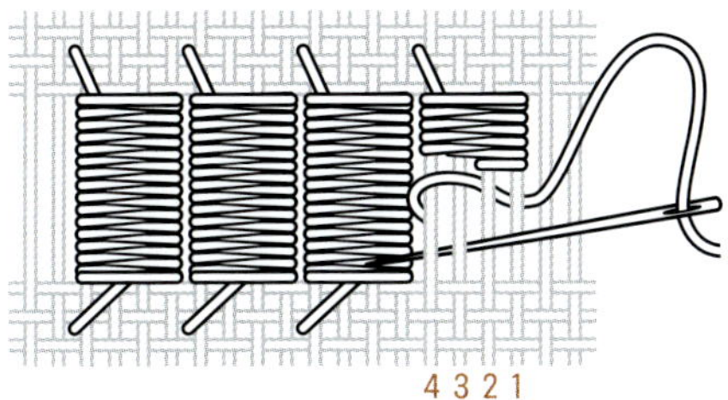

The woven bars are worked from left to right, on an even number of threads.

Embroider weaving around bars by pricking the needle in the middle of the bundle—between threads 2 and 3 when embroidering on four threads, and between threads 3 and 4 when embroidering on six threads. Alternately pull out to the right and left of the bundle (called a "bar" in this case) being embroidered. Embroider the first woven bar on the way down and stitch two threads away from the band edge before moving on to the next woven bar. Embroider the second woven bar upward.

Staggered woven hemstitch

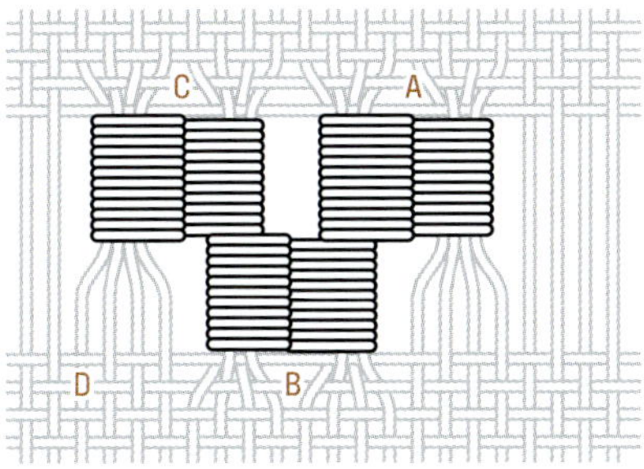

The staggered woven hemstitch is worked from right to left, on an even number of threads.

1 On the first eight threads, embroider weaving around bars to half height on section A. Work the second half with threads 5 to 12 on section B. Pass the needle around the bars on section B, working your way up.

2 Make the half-woven bar on threads 9 to 16 in section C. Pass the needle from top to bottom inside the stitches of section C, then make the half-woven bar of section D on threads 13 to 20. Pass the needle from bottom to top inside the stitches of section D and make the following half-woven bar.

Tips for Good Embroidery

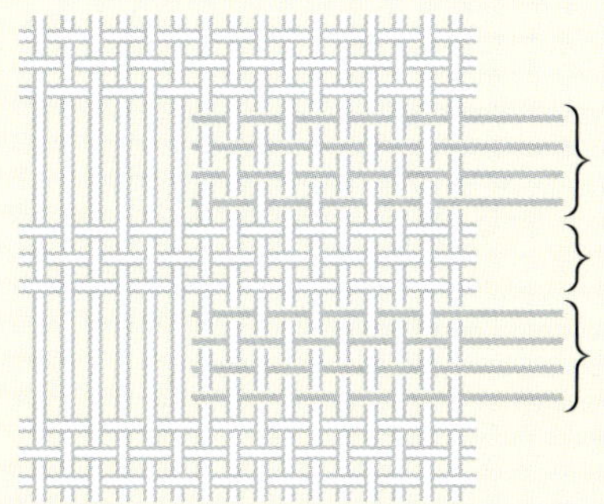

Some borders are worked on a double border (e.g., remove four threads, leave three threads, and remove four threads). Here again, it's best to test a sample to find the best combination for the fabric, stitch, and thread used.

Wave stitch on double border

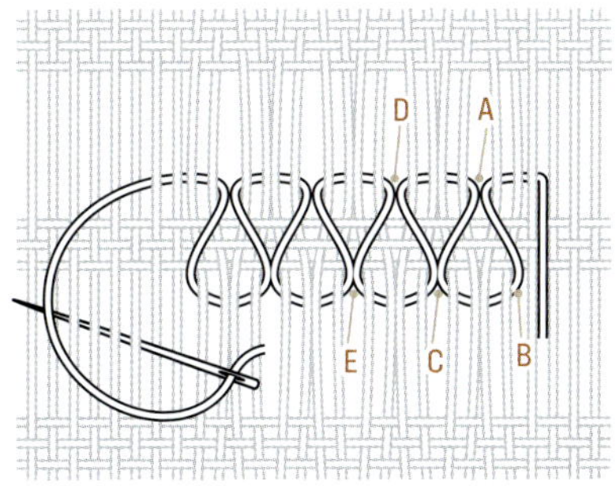

The wave stitch is worked from right to left, on the right side of the work, on a double border straddling the strip left intact in the center of this mark.

Remove the threads on both sides of the center band; for example: remove four threads, leave three threads, and remove four threads.

Pull the needle out at A between threads 2 and 3, above the band. Stitch at B and exit at C below the band after thread 4. Stitch in A and exit in D after thread 6. Stitch in C and exit in E.

Wave stitch variation

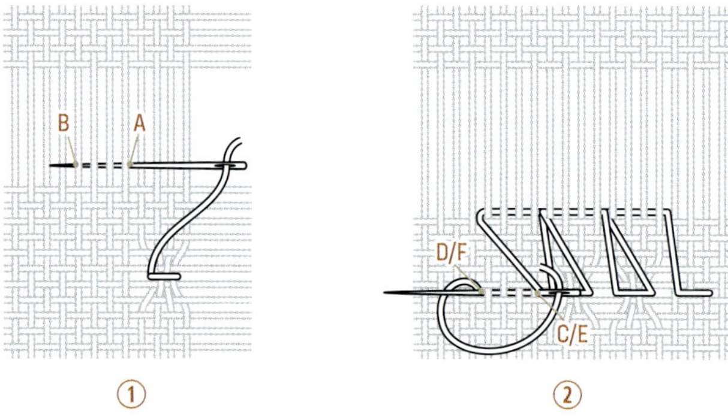

The wave stitch variation is worked from right to left, on the brand edge.

1 In the band, stitch at A and pull the needle out at B, passing the needle under four threads.

2 Six threads from the edge of the band, stitch in C and out in D. Stitch at E and exit at F (C and E are the same, as are D and F; A is vertically aligned with C and E, and B is vertically aligned with D and F).

Cable on a double border

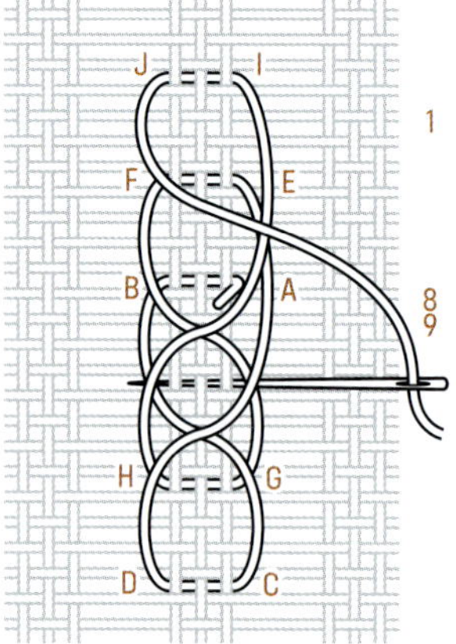

Cable stitch is worked from top to bottom on the right side, on groups of four threads.

Tips for Good Embroidery

The working thread must be firmly attached to the center band of the double border.

Remove threads to obtain a double border; for example: remove four threads, leave three threads, and remove four threads.

Stitch in A to the right of the band between threads 8 and 9 and take out the needle in B, to the left of the center band. Go down 12 threads: stitch at C and exit at D. Go up 16 threads: stitch at E and exit at F. Go down 12 threads: pick in G and exit in H. Go up 12 threads: pick at I and exit at J.

Italian hemstitching

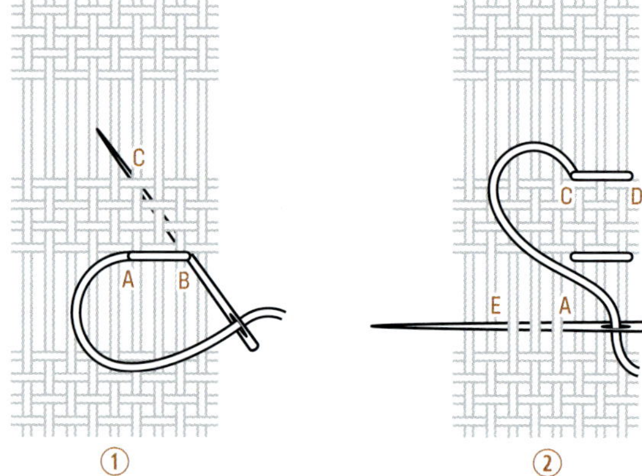

Italian hemstitching is worked from right to left, on the right side of the work. Remove threads to obtain a double border; for example: remove four threads, leave three threads, and remove four threads.

1 Take out the needle at A and make a loop around the first three threads. Stitch at B and exit at C—the working thread passes over the wrong side of the work.

2 Stitch at D and exit at C to make a loop at the top around the first three threads. Stitch at A and exit at E—the working thread passes over the right side of the work.

Four-sided stitch

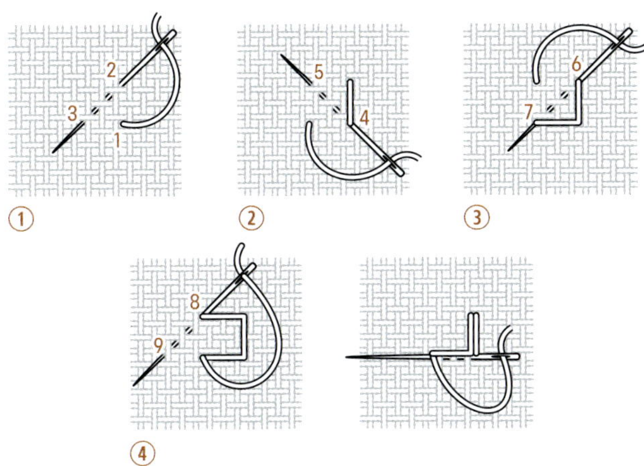

The four-sided stitch is worked on the right side, in order, on a line from left to right.

Make a square over the same number of warp and weft threads. Follow the stitch diagram above, pulling each stitch tightly and firmly.

What You Need to Know

The four-sided stitch can also be produced without pulling threads.

1 Take out the needle in 1, stitch in 2, and take out in 3, working over three threads between each stitch.

2 Stitch in 4 and out in 5, on the diagonal (1 and 4 are the same hole).

3 Pick at 6 and exit at 7 (2 and 6 are the same, as are 3 and 7, which is start 1 of the following square).

4 Stitch at 8 and exit at 9 (8 and 5 are the same, which is point 2 on the following square; 9 is point 3 on the following square).

Variation

To obtain more relief, you can double all the stitches: to do this, embroider a second stitch on the one you have just made.

Crossing hemstitch

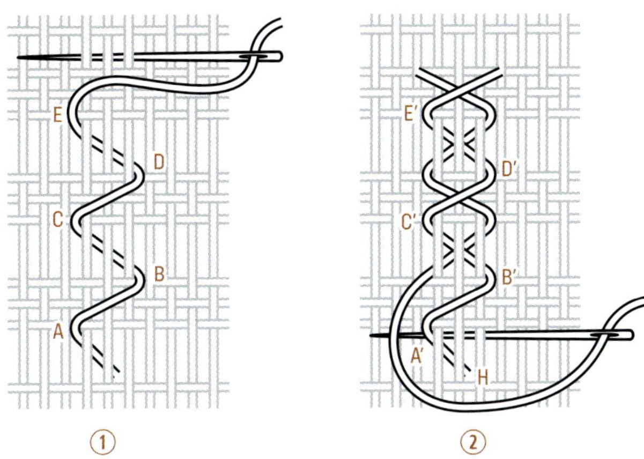

The crossing hemstitch is worked from top to bottom, then from bottom to top, on the right side.

Remove two threads, leave three threads, and remove two threads.

1 Going up: take out the needle at A, stitch at B, and take out at C.

2 Going down: in at D' and exit at E'. In at B' and exit at C'. In at H and exit at A'.

Square eyelet hemstitch

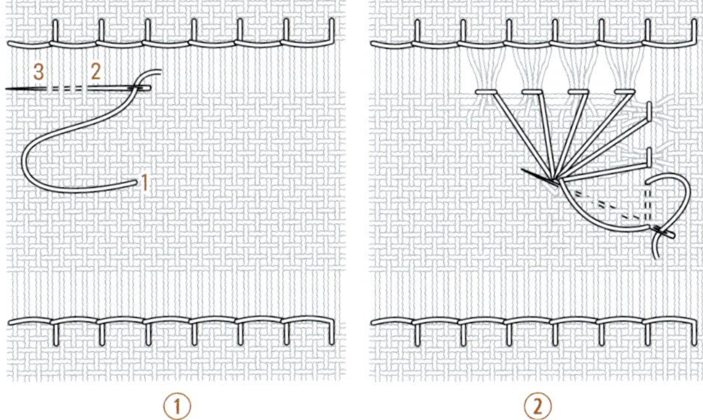

Square eyelet hemstitch is worked on the right side and on 16 threads: remove 4 threads, leave 16 threads, and remove threads. The idea is to group all the threads in a hemstitch by fours.

1 Take out the needle in 1 in the center, stitch in 2, and take out in 3.

2 Rejoin in 2 and exit in 1 to form the first loop. Continue working in a radial direction until the eyelet is complete.

Embroidering Corners

When the borders cross or form a corner, an empty zone is created. It can be embroidered using the working threads of the openwork or by adding others that form bars to create a "star" that will be the backbone of the work to follow.

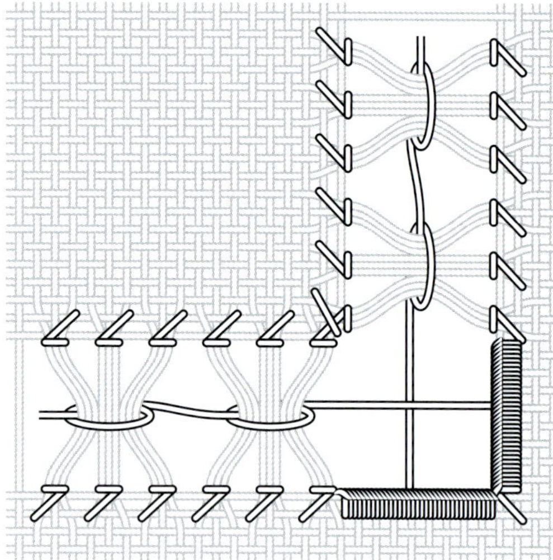

Wheel stitch or spider stitch

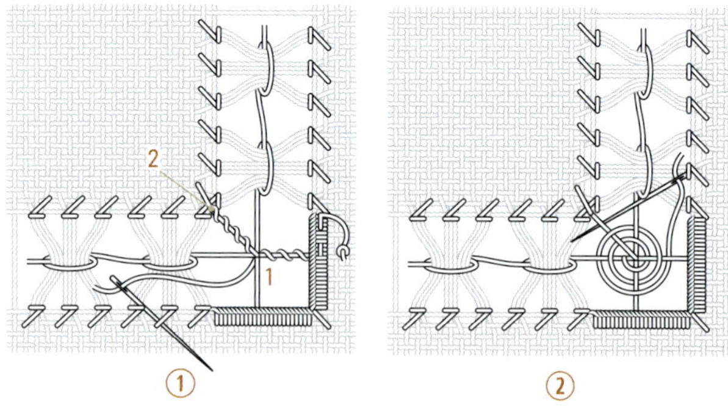

The wheel is a simple design for embroidering corners.

1 Create a five-pointed star structure by stitching a spoke with the working thread between 1 and 2: wrap the vertical thread around it to return to the center.

2 Embroider the wheel stitch, passing alternately over and under each spoke.

What You Need to Know

If the wheel has a diameter greater than 5 mm, it is possible to weave a larger number of odd-numbered spokes to support the weave (for example, nine spokes as shown in the diagram).

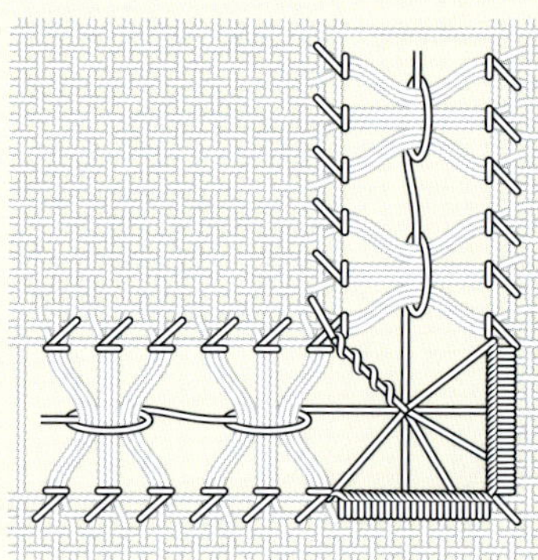

Whipped wheel stitch or whipped spider stitch

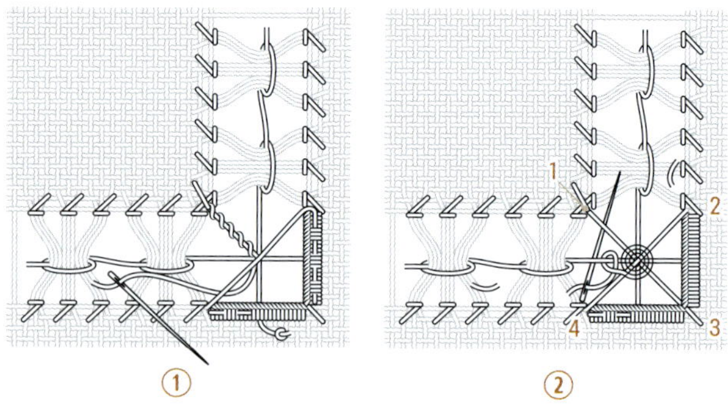

When the wheel diameter exceeds 5 mm, the whipped spider stitch will be stronger than a conventional wheel stitch.

1 Create a "star" structure by stitching straight stitches between 1, 2, 3, and 4.

2 Wrap the thread around the last spoke to return to the center. Embroider a whipped spider stitch.

Woven corner

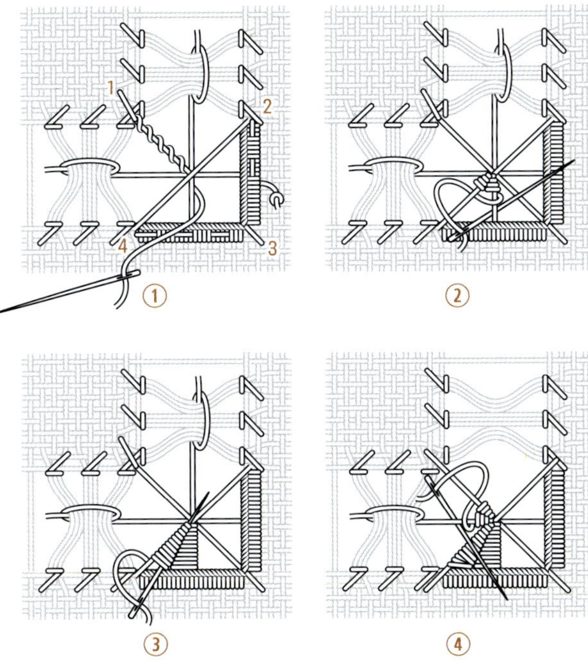

1 Create a "star" structure by creating straight stitches with the working thread between 1, 2, 3, and 4. Wrap the thread around the last spoke to return to the center.

2 Weave in and out around two spokes at a time.

3 Once the weaving is complete on the two spokes, move to the next pair of spokes and continue around the wheel of spokes.

Visual Library of Embroidery Stitches

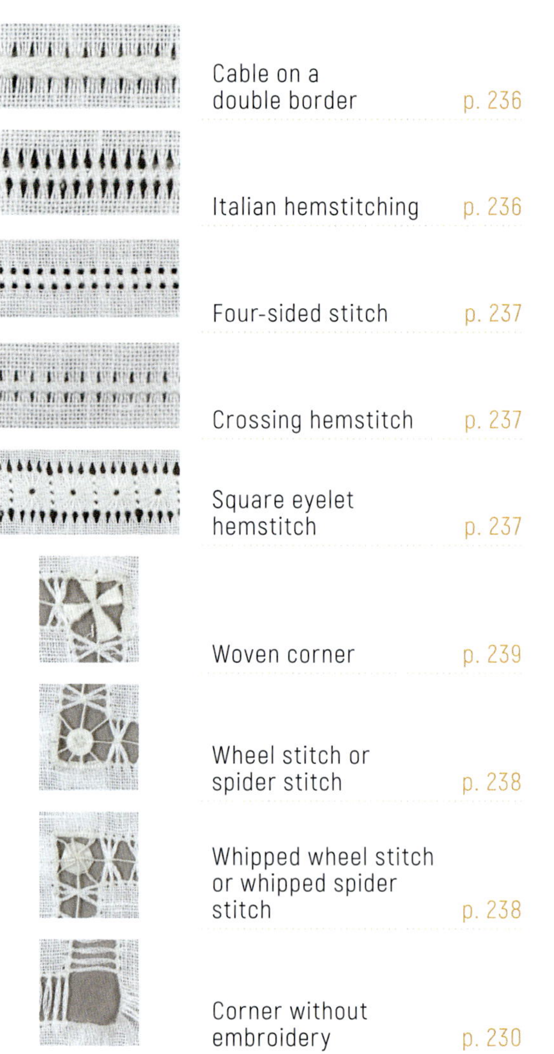

BORDERS AND LINES WITH PULLED THREADS

Tied threads embroidery can be embroidered without the need to respect the straight thread of the textile backing, since it is not necessary to prepare the work for embroidery.

It involves embroidering fine openwork following a pattern, being confined to a specific count for the pattern. Hemstitch is the best known for this technique.

What You Need to Know

Hemstitch is also used for perfect sewing finishes. This embroidery stitch is indispensable for seamstresses who like to finish the hems of their garments by hand.

Supplies

- Linen or cotton fabric of varying thickness, on which you can easily distinguish the warp and weft threads. These embroidery stitches are easier to make on fabrics with a loose weft. Test beforehand.
- Threads, to be chosen according to the desired effect. Use thinner threads for very fine canvas, thicker threads for relief. In order of thread size, from thinnest to thickest:
- no. 50 and 60 cotton sewing thread
- DMC 100% cotton Quilt Main Machine thread
- glove thread
- Coton à Broder DMC cotton no. 25, 30, or 35
- Retors DMC cotton
- a long no. 10 needle for trimming the finest fabrics
- an assortment of nos. 5 to 9 pointless needles for opening loosely woven fabrics

Techniques

Here are the three most commonly used stitches.

Three-sided stitch

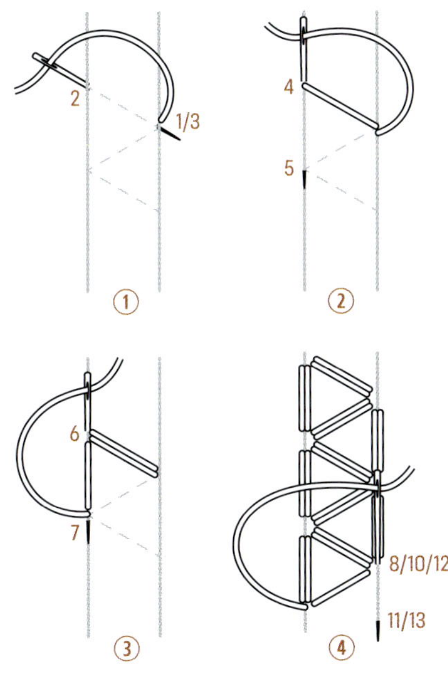

Three-sided stitch is worked from top to bottom on the right side. It forms small triangles that you can adjust to accommodate the shape of the embroidery motif. Each stitch is doubled and must be pulled tight. Draw two parallel lines.

1 Take the needle out in 1, stitch in 2, and take out in 3 (1 and 3 are the same hole).

2 Stitch in 4 and out in 5 (2 and 4 are the same).

3 Stitch in 6 and out in 7 (2, 4, and 6 are the same hole, as are 5 and 7).

4 In at 8 and exit at 9. In at 10, exit at 11, in at 12, and then exit at 13 (1, 3, 8, 10, and 12 are connected, just as 11 and 13 are connected and become start 1 of the following triangle).

What You Need to Know

The ground fabric may come out slightly embossed. You are free to iron or not.

Hemstitch

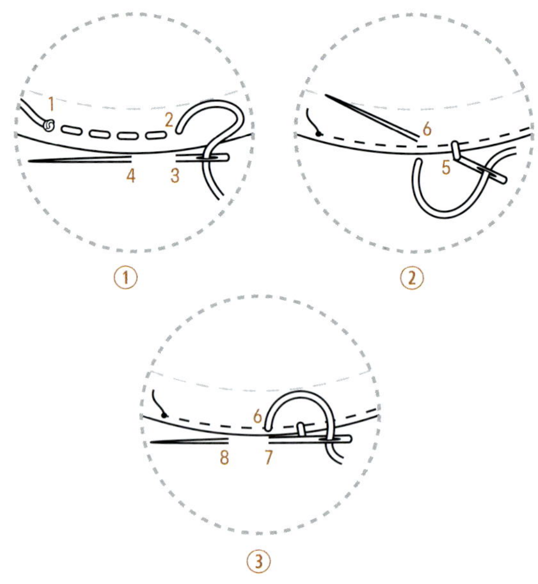

Hemstitch is embroidered in hand, from right to left. Choose one of the finest threads available. It's possible to make an extra stitch when pulling to make the small hole even more pronounced.

1 Embroider from left to right: take out the needle in 1 and stitch in 2, take out in 3 and stitch in 4, and take out in 5 and stitch in 6.

2 and 3 Embroider from right to left: take out the needle at 20 and stitch at 21, take out at 22 and stitch at 23, and take out at 24 and stitch at 25.

What You Need to Know

Hemstitch can also be used to attach lace, sew binding, hem, or appliqué (see page 212). It's best to build the work carefully before starting to embroider, for greater precision and ease of use.

Ladder stitch

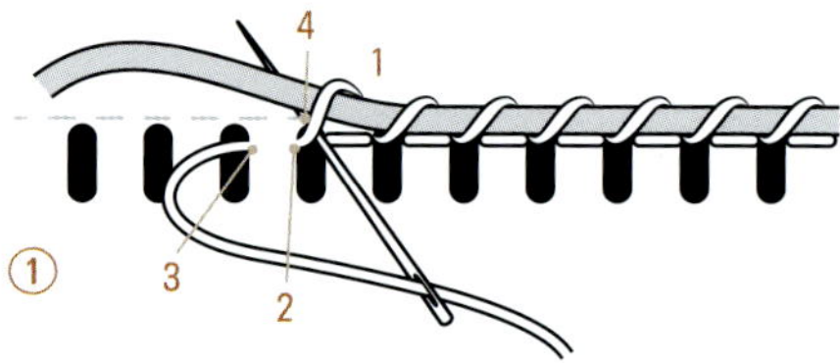

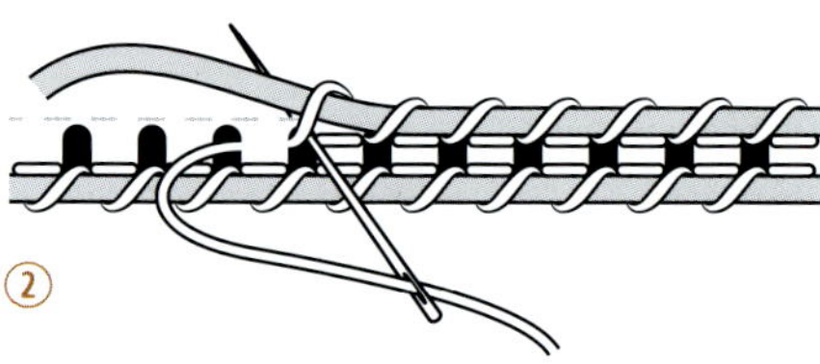

The ladder stitch with either single or double added relief is embroidered from right to left on the right side along a previously pulled line. Start by cutting a length of Retors DMC cotton greater than the total length of the embroidered line. Attach the cotton to the right-hand end of the line, using the couching stitch starting technique (see page 122), and leave it free.

1 Using a finer thread, depending on the fabric and the desired effect, embroider a hemstitch (*see above*) straddling the Retors cotton. Take the needle out in 1, stitch in 2, and take out in 3. Come back to stitch in the same hole as 2 and take out in 4 to position yourself for the next stitch. Tighten the stitches to form the pulled opening.

2 If you like, you can add another couched thread along the opposite side of the pulled-thread line. Draw a line parallel to the first line. Pick up the embroidery again, stitching through the holes formed during the first pass. At the end of the line, stop the Retors cotton in couching stitch on the reverse side of the embroidery.

Visual Library of Embroidery Stitches

OPENWORK GROUNDS WITH DRAWN THREADS AND PULLED THREADS

Openwork with drawn threads (fonds ajourés à fils coupés) entails openwork patterns in which certain warp and weft threads are removed in one or both directions, to embroider on the remaining threads. The number and direction of threads to be cut and pulled vary depending on the embroidery stitches to be produced.

Depending on the region or country, these openwork embroideries are formed with combinations of hemstitching, trellis, and buttonhole. In France, the jours d'Angles (from Angles-sur-l'Anglin) and the jours de Cilaos on Reunion Island are the most famous.

Openwork with pulled threads consists of surfaces where embroidery is performed without cutting or removing threads beforehand.

Embroidered doily in jours d'Angles by Stéphanie Michaud

Details of jours d'Angles embroidered by Stéphanie Michaud

Openwork grounds can be combined with drawn-thread embroidery, plumetis, Schwalm embroidery, Hardanger embroidery, Dresden embroidery, etc.

Supplies

- Linen or cotton canvas with a marked pattern (see page 28). To start with, Lugana canvas, with its sufficiently visible and loose weave, will help in counting the patterns.

What You Need to Know

For better visibility, the samples in this chapter were made with 10-count Lugana fabric and DMC Coton à Broder no. 16 cotton.

- Solid threads of the same size as the weft threads of the ground fabric
- For larger canvases, embroider with the DMC Coton à Broder in various numbers.
- For finer fabrics, embroider with no. 50 or 60 cotton sewing thread, DMC Quilt Main Machine thread, or glove thread.
- Hand-sewing thread in contrasting colors for thread tracing
- Embroidery needles nos. 5 to 10, to be chosen according to the thickness of the thread used
- Embroidery scissors for removing and cutting threads

Tips for Good Embroidery

To create an attractive relief on the work, use a thread thicker than the weft, as in the samples in this book.

A Few Tips Before You Start

Both these techniques require sufficiently long thread on your needles (60 cm maximum) to avoid having to change thread in the middle of rows.

Anchor stitches are stitched into the already embroidered edges, on the reverse side of the work. To carry threads from one row to the next, proceed in the same way.

Openwork fillings or openwork grounds are probably the most difficult to create in embroidery. It's delicate, technical work that takes practice. Start with simple patterns before exploring more-complex ones.

Before taking the plunge, it is essential to make a sample, using the same fabric and thread to ensure the final result.

Openwork Grounds With Drawn Thread Fillings

Openwork with drawn fillings is created in the center of a motif already embroidered around the edge, or the openwork itself delineates the motif. The resulting motifs have a different feel.

Whichever technique you choose, place the work upside down to remove and cut the weft or warp threads (or both) flush with the embroidery. Start removing and cutting the threads in the middle of the motif, then remove and leave the number of threads as indicated in the explanations provided.

As before, the type of filling pattern on the motif determines the number of threads to be cut and removed.

Openwork with drawn threads and embroidered outline

The insides of the motifs are filled with drawn-thread filling patterns, and the outlines reinforce the edges of the motifs. Prior embroidery around the openwork grounds guarantees the strength of the filling pattern. This is also the case for padded satin stitch: the satin stitch and the trailing stitch define the edges of the design, which can then be cut without risk of fraying. Schwalm and Hedebo embroideries are made using the same technique: darning, chain, coral, and buttonhole stitches are embroidered, alone or in combination, before the mark.

The number of threads to remove, cut, and leave depends on the desired effect, the type of embroidery, and the quality of the fabric backing.

The vocabulary used to describe this work varies from one technique and region to another. In general, the work done to pull the warp and weft threads together is called the "drawnwork." Openwork, or "rebrodé," is the embroidery work carried out with a working thread. Filigree ground is the finished result after the previous two stages.

What You Need to Know

- **Border system:** The drawn thread is made in one direction only, forming bands. Openwork is easy to execute in waffle stitch (see page 248).
- **Square lattice:** The threads are drawn in both directions, forming a grid of beams, squares, and blocks.
- **Schwalm embroidery square lattice:** Remove one thread and leave three.
- **The lattice in jours d'Angles:** For example, remove two threads and leave eight threads.
- **Even lattice**: Remove two threads and leave two threads.

Openwork grounds with drawn threads, without embroidery around the edges

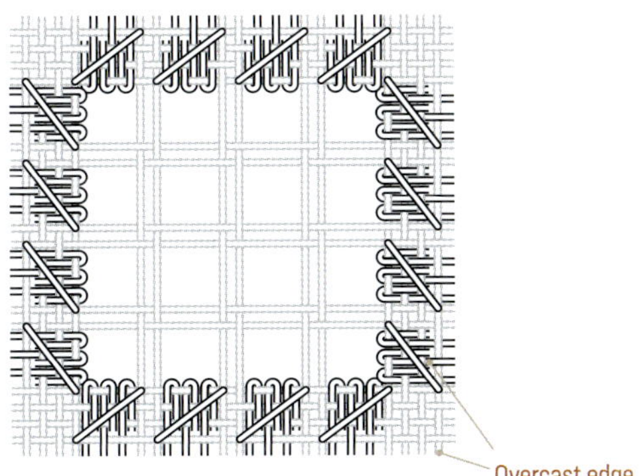

Reverse

Grounds are not always surrounded by embroidery. In this case, it's necessary to cut, remove, and reweave the threads around the edges, in the same way as for outlined openwork motifs.

1 Mark the design with a running stitch in contrast thread (thread tracing) on the pattern line: the thread tracing should pass over each thread to be pulled and under each thread to be left. In corners, create an additional backstitch. Remove the threads through the middle of the surface, cutting them off. Pull them up to the thread tracing, then fold them over, weaving them back into the edge of the fabric. When all threads have been removed and ends woven back in, remove the thread tracing by cutting it and pulling on it.

2 To secure the area to be worked, work in a whipstitch at an angle far enough away from the hoop not to interfere with the final embroidery. Remove this whipstitch by cutting and pulling it out once the embroidery is complete.

Embroidery stitches

Once you've secured the openwork area outline, you can move on to openwork.

Double wave stitch

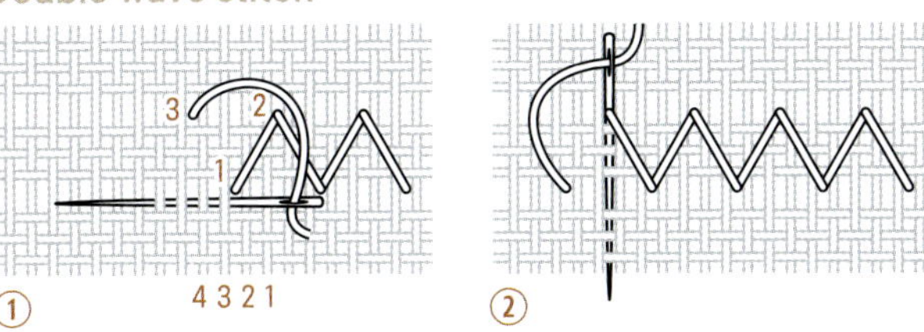

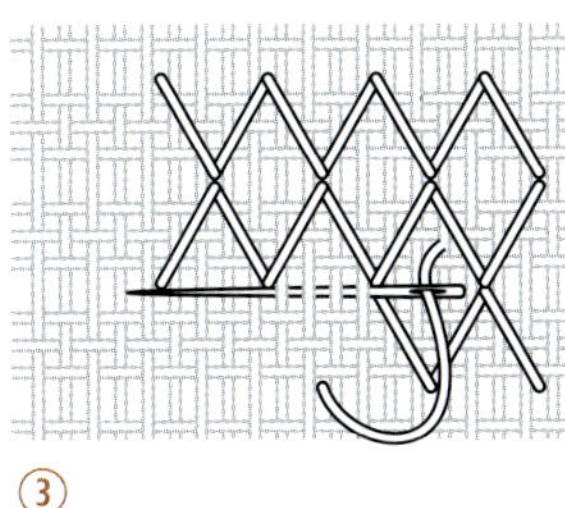

Double wave stitch is embroidered on the right side over four vertical threads. It is worked alternately up and down, from right to left, row by row, turning the hoop 180° between each row.

Start by removing threads for a band: remove one thread and leave three threads.

1 Take out the needle in 1, between thread 2 and thread 3. Stitch in 2, going back two threads, and take out four threads further on. Stitch in 4 (4 and 1 are the same) and pull out four threads further.

2 and 3 To make the next row, pull the needle out three threads below, opposite the apex of the previously embroidered triangle. Turn the hoop 180°. Repeat step 1.

Honeycomb stitch

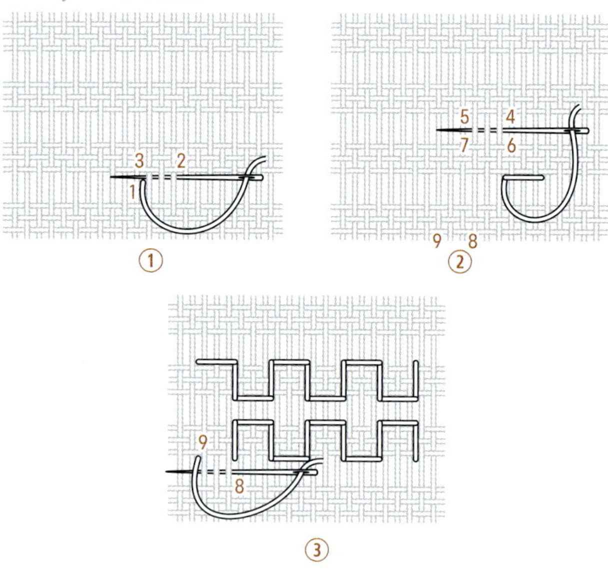

Honeycomb stitch is embroidered on the right side. It is worked alternately up and down, right to left, row by row, turning the hoop 180° between each row.

Thin the ground fabric weave of the area to be worked, removing some of the threads in one direction. Pull one thread and leave three threads.

1 Take the needle out in 1, stitch in 2, and then in 3 (3 and 1 are the same).

2 Climb vertically; pierce in 4 and exit in 5. Pierce in 6 (6 and 4 are the same) and exit in 7 (7 and 5 are the same). Go down vertically: pierce at 8 and exit at 9. Repeat this stitch pattern and go up vertically.

3 To make the next row, take out the needle on the next line, opposite the top of the previously embroidered stitch. Turn the hoop 180°. Repeat steps 1 and 2.

Greek cross filling stitch

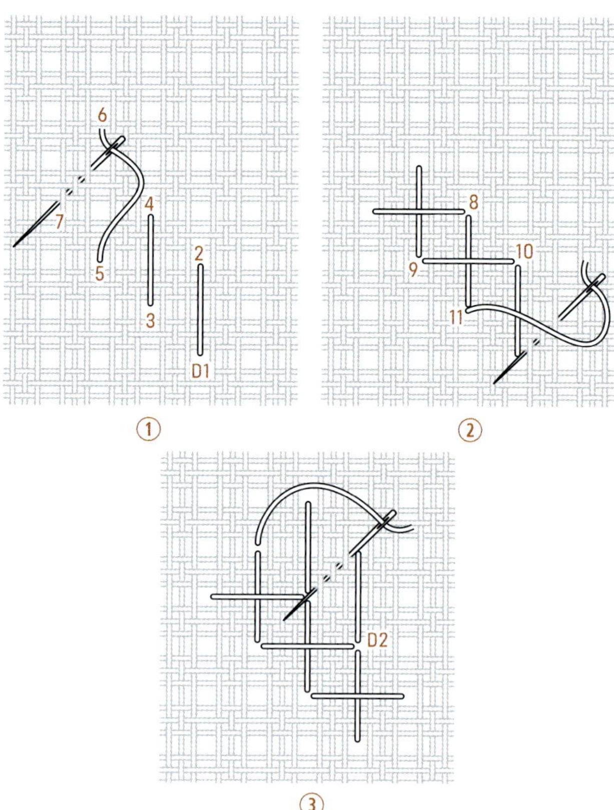

Greek cross filling stitch is embroidered on the right side, diagonally, in both directions.

Thin the ground fabric weave of the area to be worked, removing some of the threads in one direction. Remove a thread and leave three threads.

1 Take out the needle at D1, stitch at 2 (two blocks up), and take out at 3 (diagonally from 2, down). Stitch in 4 and out in 5. Stitch in 6 and out in 7.

2 Work your way back down. Stitch in 8 (two blocks to the right of 7) and exit in 9 (diagonally from 8, downward). Stitch at 10 and exit at 11.

3 Embroider the next diagonal in the same way, taking the needle out at D2.

Double four-sided stitch

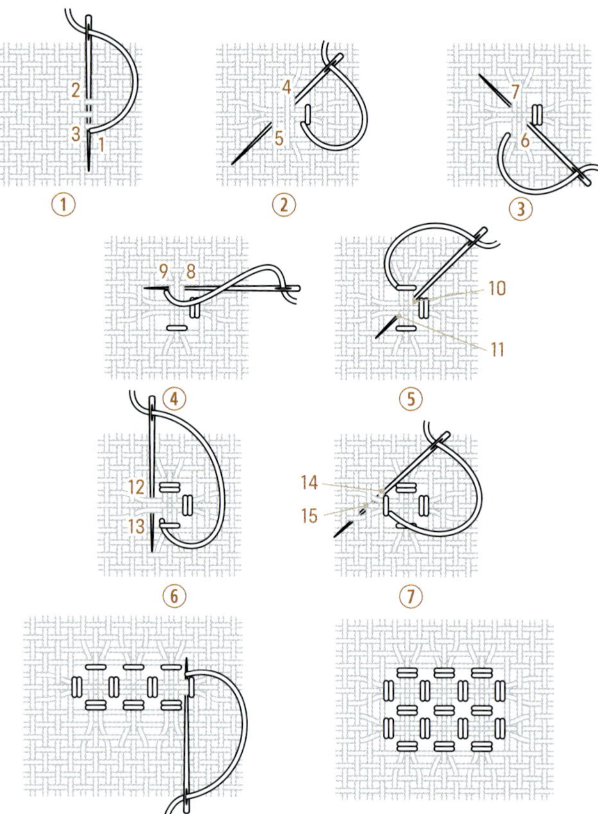

Double four-sided stitch is embroidered from right to left, row by row, turning the hoop 180° between each row, thinning the ground fabric weave by removing threads in both directions. Remove one thread and leave three.

Row 1 Leave three threads between each vertical and horizontal stitch.

1 Take the needle out in 1, stitch in 2, and take out in 3 (1 and 3 are the same hole).

2 Stitch in 4 and exit in 5, diagonally to the left (2 and 4 are the same hole).

3 Stitch in 6 and out in 7 (1, 3, and 6 are the same hole).

4 Stitch in 8 and out in 9 (2, 4, and 8 are the same).

5 Stitch in 10 and out in 11 (2, 4, 8, and 10 are the same hole, as are 5 and 11).

6 Pick at 12 and exit at 13 (7, 9, and 12 are the same hole, as are 5, 11, and 13).

7 Stitch at 14 and exit at 15, diagonally to the left (7, 9, 12, and 14 are the same hole).

Repeat only steps 2 to 7 for the rest of the squares. The first row is embroidered with two horizontal stitches at the top, two vertical stitches on the sides, and one horizontal stitch at the bottom.

Next rows Turn the hoop 180° and repeat the first row, but without carrying out step 4. All these rows are embroidered with a horizontal stitch at the top (which completes that of the previous row to obtain two stitches), a horizontal stitch at the bottom, and two vertical stitches on the sides.

Last row in step 3 Double the horizontal stitch at the bottom.

Keep in mind that all rows are made up of two vertical and horizontal stitches.

Satin stitch variations

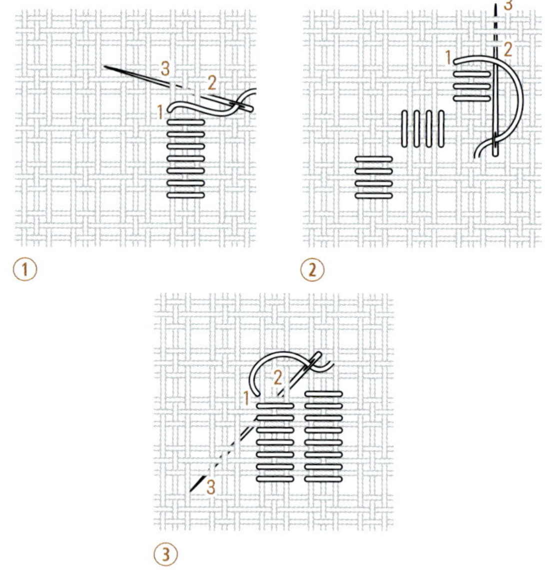

Satin stitch variations can be embroidered on the right side, as a bar, row of bars, or "staircase," to create motifs to suit your taste.

Start by thinning the ground fabric in both. Remove one and leave three threads.

In bars (1) This stitch is worked vertically, up and down. Take the needle out in 1, stitch in 2, and take out in 3 (between 2 and 3, the needle must be horizontal).

Step stitch (2) This stitch is worked diagonally up and down. Bring the needle out in 1, stitch in 2, and bring out in 3 (between 2 and 3, the needle must be vertical). Work three vertical stitches, then three horizontal stitches.

Row of bars (3) This stitch is worked up in vertical bars all the same height. Each time you move to the next bar, travel diagonally from top of current bar to bottom of next bar, then continue working up that bar.

Square eyelet

The square eyelet is a variation on the satin stitch. It is worked on the right side in the shape of a square, over four threads for each corner. This stitch is often combined with satin stitch and stepped-stitch patterns.

Start by thinning the ground fabric in both. Remove one and leave three threads.

1 Take out needle 1 in the center of the eyelet. Stitch in 2 and take out in 1. Stitch in 3 and take out in 1 (there's a weft thread between 2 and 3).

2 Continue like this in 4, 5, 6, 7, 8, and so on.

3 Finish by rotating around the center point in the same way until you return to 2 to form a complete rosette.

Waffle stitch on thinned ground

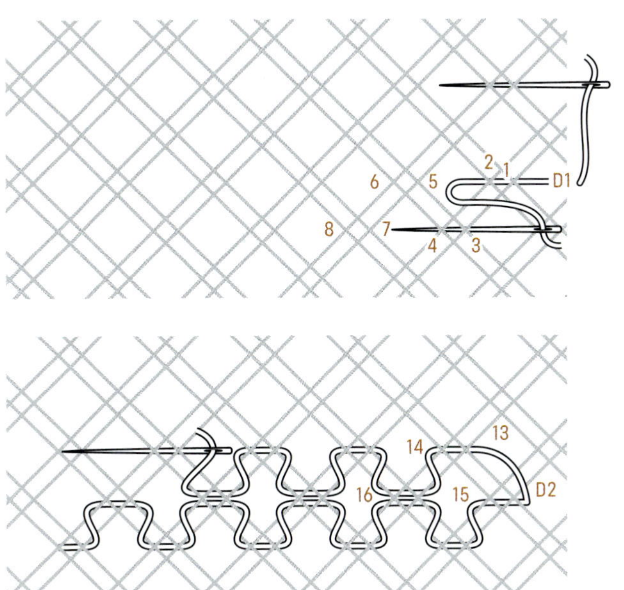

The basic stitch is embroidered before a more decorative stitch to consolidate the thinned ground fabric. This makes the whole work much more stable. It is embroidered on the reverse side from right to left and in the diagonal of the grid.

Start by thinning the ground fabric by removing the threads in both directions. Remove two threads and leave two threads.

Tips for Good Embroidery

Do not remove the work from the hoop between drawing the threads and stitching the openwork patterns. Unembroidered thinned ground fabric is very fragile.

1 Start in D1: stitch in 1 and remove needle in 2.

2 Stitch in 3 and out in 4. Stitch in 5 and out in 6. Stitch in 7 and out in 8.

3 Turn the hoop 180°. Start in D2 above previous row: stitch in 13 and exit in 14 (13 and 14 are diagonally opposite stitches 9 and 10). Stitch in 15 and out in 16 (8 and 15 are the same, as are 7 and 16).

Darning stitch

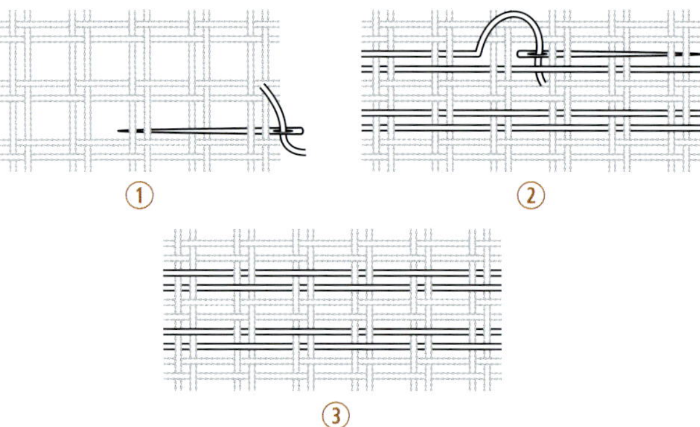

The darning stitch is used to create a variety of designs on a grid. It is embroidered on a light network reinforced with the basic stitch (*see above*).

Tips for Good Embroidery

On a piece of graph paper, draw the design you wish to embroider beforehand to make it easier to plan the drawnwork pattern.

Embroider the darning stitch back and forth, working the thread over and under the threads to "reweave" the fabric. The needle should work horizontally from right to left for right-handers, or vice versa for left-handers. Turn the hoop 180° each time. Make the same number of passes with the needle to fill the grid evenly.

1 Pass the needle over and under the weft of the thinned ground to be embroidered.

2 Turn the hoop 180°. Weave by passing the needle over/under, contrasting with the previous row.

3 For all subsequent rows, turn the hoop 180°. Weave by passing the needle over/under, contrasting with the previous row.

Continue in this way until all the spaces removed from the fabric have been filled.

Overcast mesh

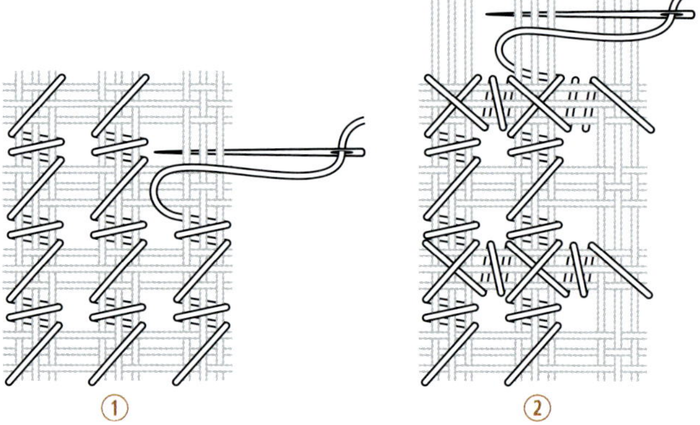

The overcast mesh is embroidered on the right side, vertically.

Start by thinning the ground fabric in both directions: remove two threads and leave three threads.

1 Embroider the grid vertically, overcasting twice in each square. At each thread crossing, pass the needle in front. At the top of the grid, make a small straight stitch in the border. Turn the hoop 180° and stitch the next vertical. Continue until you have embroidered all the verticals.

2 Turn the hoop 90° to work on the horizontals of 1—they are now oriented vertically. Complete the grid by embroidering the verticals in the same way as in 1 to form crosses.

Overcast filling or Russian overcast filling

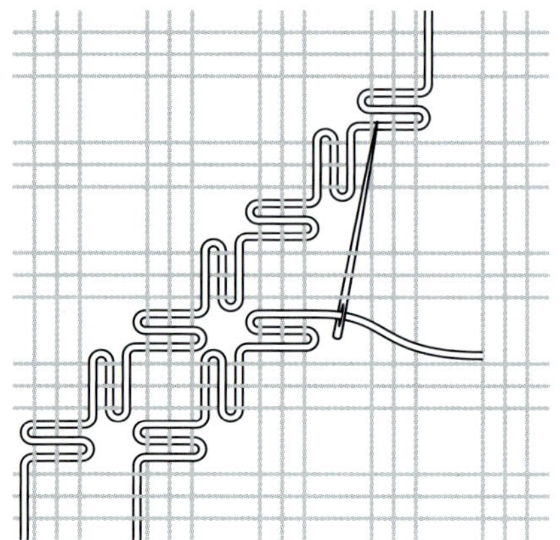

The overcast filling is embroidered on the wrong side, starting at the top left on the longest diagonal of the design. The rows to be embroidered run diagonally up and down the woven threads.

Start by thinning the ground fabric in both directions: remove two threads and leave three. Embroider by winding the working thread over the drawn area.

Descending rows Pass the needle twice under the vertical threads and once under the horizontal threads.

Ascending rows Pass the needle twice under the horizontal threads and once under the vertical threads.

Embroider the entire surface, alternating ascending and descending rows.

Lace stitch filling

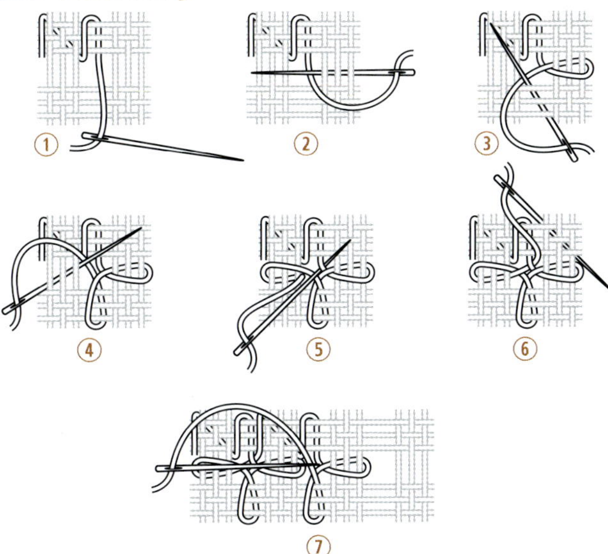

The lace stitch filling is embroidered on the right side.

Start by thinning the ground fabric in both directions: remove two threads and leave three threads.

Row 1 It is embroidered from left to right, turning the stitches forming the spirit stitch clockwise.

1 Embroider an overcast stitch on the upper beam.

2 Embroider a buttonhole stitch on the right bundle.

3 Embroider a buttonhole stitch on the lower beam.

4 Embroider a buttonhole stitch on the left bundle.

5 Pass the needle under the first diagonal stitch, between the upper and right beams.

6 Finish with an angled overcast stitch under the upper right block to move on to the next stitch.

7 Repeat steps 1 to 6 to embroider the next stitch. In step 4, slide the needle through the loop of the previous stitch.

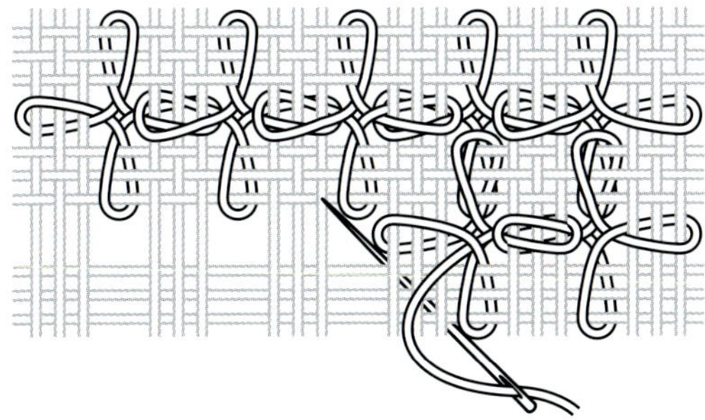

Row 2 It is embroidered from right to left by turning the stitches forming the lace stitch filling (steps 1 to 5) counterclockwise.

1 Embroider an overcast stitch on the upper beam, to the right of the stitch in the previous row.

2 Embroider a buttonhole stitch on the left bundle.

3 Embroider a buttonhole stitch on the lower beam.

4 Pass the needle under the first diagonal stitch, between the upper and left beams.

5 Finish with an angled overcast stitch under the upper left block to move on to the next stitch.

Repeat the work, alternating these two rows for the remaining rows.

Offset lace stitch filling

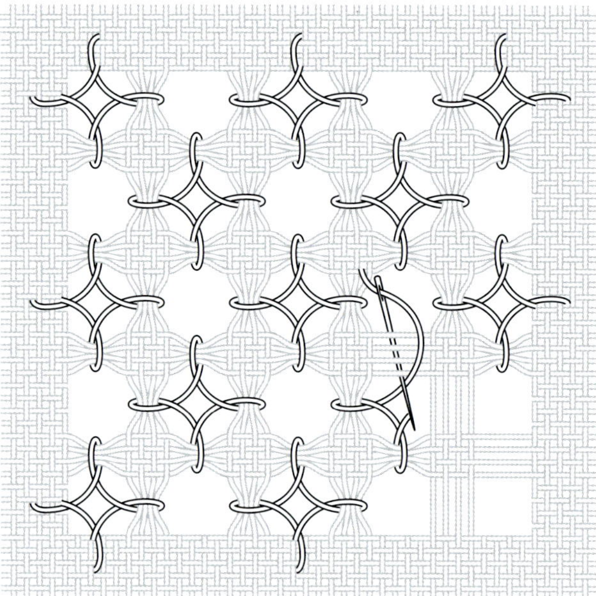

Offset lace stitch filling is embroidered on the right side.

Start by thinning the ground fabric in both directions: remove two threads and leave three threads.

The lace stitches are then embroidered in the classic way, but diagonally on every other row to create a checkerboard pattern: one embroidered and one nonembroidered opening. The working thread passes from one stitch to the other on the reverse side.

Diagonal drawn filling variation

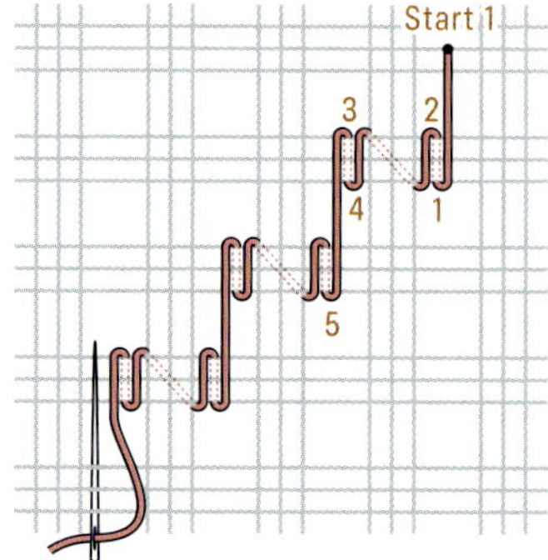

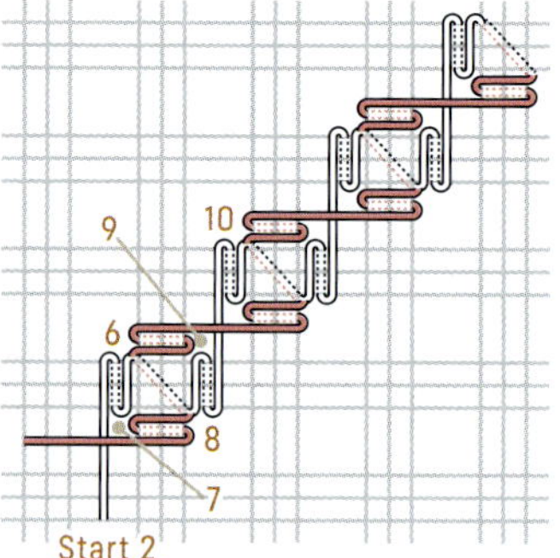

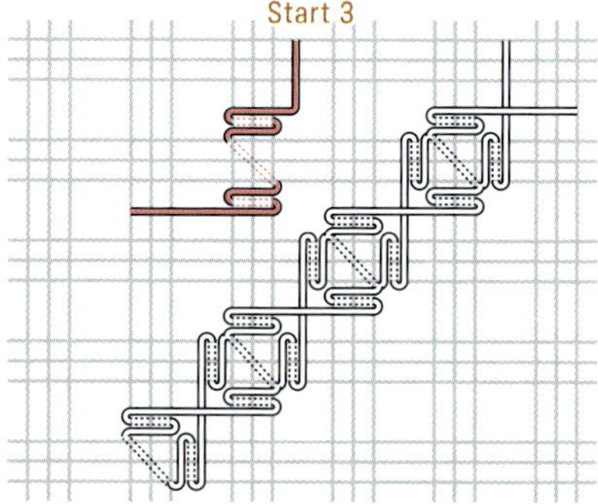

The diagonal drawn filling variation can be embroidered on either the wrong side or right side, starting at the top left on the longest diagonal of the design. Each row consists of a round trip: the forward (1) goes down and the return (2) goes up, overlapping on the same diagonal to form the cross.

Start by thinning the ground fabric in both directions: remove two threads and leave three threads.

Row 1 Descending, like a staircase.

Start 1 Stitch in 1 and remove the needle in 2. Stitch at 1 and lift out at 3 (to go to next block). Pierce in 4 and take out in 3. Pierce in 5.

Row 2 Ascending return, like a staircase.

Move up on the same diagonal as the descending row to form the cross.

Start 2 Pierce in at 6 and exit at 7. Pierce in at 6 and exit at 8 (to go to next block). Stitch at 8 and exit at 9.

Row 3 The new start 3 for the next row is two spaces farther away than start 1, to leave a diagonal without crosses between two rows.

Once the embroidery is complete, the crosses are positioned in staggered rows, filling every other square in both directions.

Openwork Grounds With Pulled Threads

Pulled-thread openwork grounds are often combined with other embroidery stitches such as shadow work, satin stitch, chain stitch, or buttonhole stitch.

Embroidered on the regular weft of a loosely woven linen or cotton fabric, the grounds are pulled with the working thread to form openings.

What You Need to Know

Most embroidery stitches on drawn thread grounds can also be done without removing or cutting threads from the ground fabric. However, this work is much more difficult to perform, as it is more difficult to find your way around without the threads being cut and pulled.

Straight stitch rows

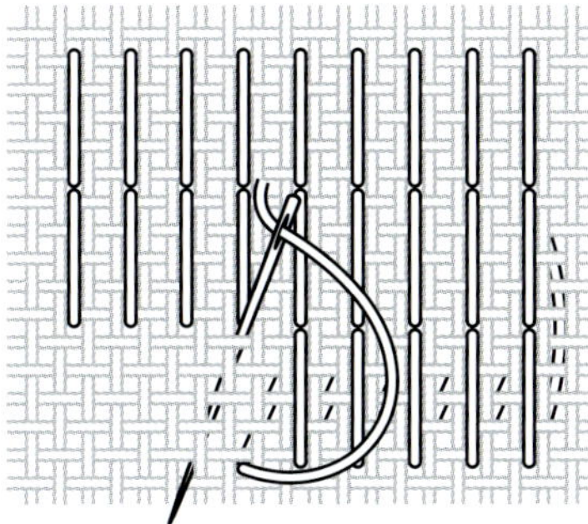

Embroider vertical bars by stitching a straight stitch over five horizontal threads, leaving two vertical threads between each stitch.

Ringed backstitch

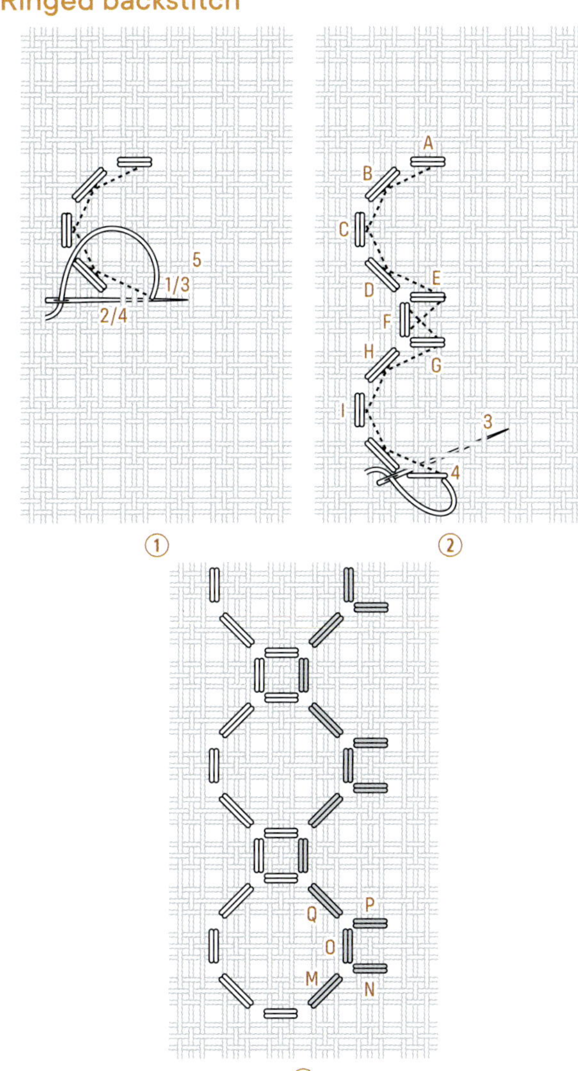

The embroidery forms octagons separated by small squares. Each stitch is doubled.

Work from top to bottom to create the first semicircle, then from bottom to top to close the pattern.

1 Embroider each stitch on three weft threads. Take out needle 1 and stitch 2. Double the stitch: take out at 3 and stitch at 4 (1 and 3 are the same, as are 2 and 4), then take out at 5. Stitches B and D are on the diagonal. Point C is vertical, and points A and E are horizontal.

2 Embroider F, G, H, and I the same way.

3 Embroider in the same way L, M, N, O, P, Q, etc., to close the octagons and prepare for the next row.

Diagonal backstitch filling

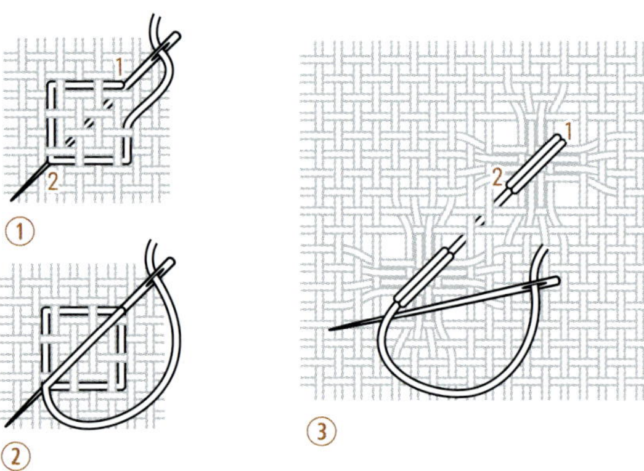

The diagonal backstitch is embroidered diagonally, from bottom to top.

1 Darning stitch a 4 × 4 thread square, starting at the bottom left. Pull the working thread through to tighten the fabric threads.

2 Stitch the needle twice in 1 and out in 2 to make two diagonal stitches.

3 To make the next stitch, pass under the diagonal work, leaving two horizontal and vertical weft threads.

Diagonal square stitch

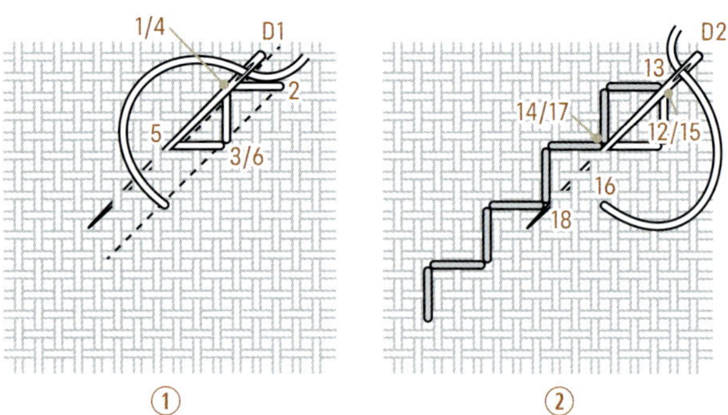

Diagonal square stitch is worked in two steps, in a staircase and from top to bottom. Each stitch is made on the same number of threads (generally three or four).

Embroider the first diagonal.

1 Start in D1: pull out needle 1 and stitch in 2. Take out in 3 and stitch in 4. Take out in 5 and stitch in 6 (1 and 4 are the same hole, as are 3 and 6).

2 Turn the hoop 180° and close the squares by embroidering a second diagonal, repeating the same work. D2 start: exit at 12 and stitch at 13. Exit at 14 and stitch at 15. Exit at 16 and stitch at 17. Exit at 18 (11 and 13 are the same hole, as are 12 and 15).

Square stitch

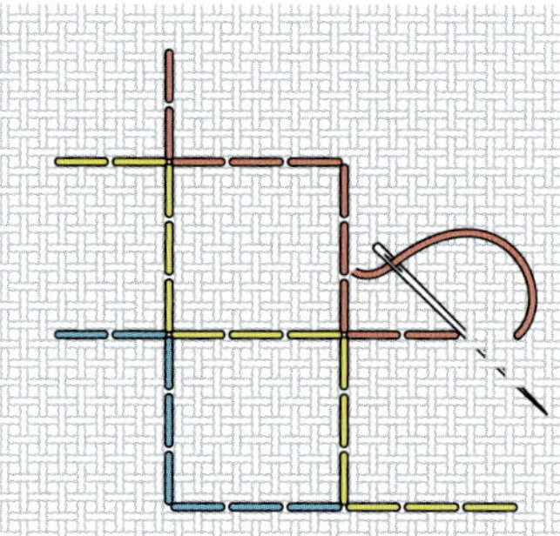

Over three fabric threads, staircase-embroider three vertical backstitches, then three horizontal backstitches. Pull on the working thread to create the openwork.

Row 1 (start 1) Stair-stitch the stitches three at a time.

Row 2 (start 2) Stair-stitch the stitches three at a time to close the squares.

Cable stitch

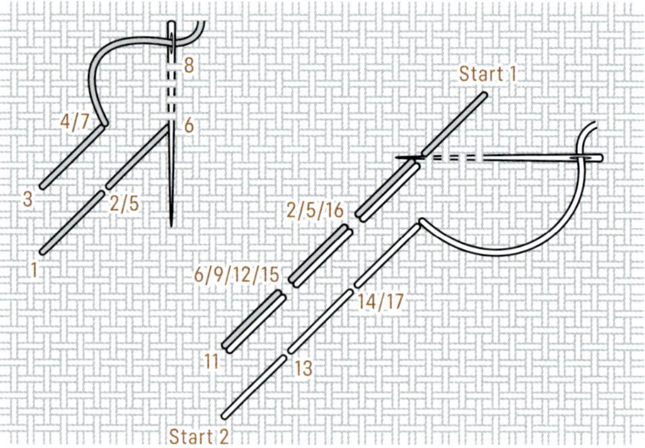

The shaded or raised ground is embroidered in backstitch, diagonally on three weft threads. Pull on the working thread to create the openwork.

1 (Start 1) Take out needle 1 and stitch 2. Pull out to 3 and stitch to 4. Pull out to 5 and stitch to 6. Pull out to 7 and stitch to 8 (2 and 5 are the same hole, as are 4 and 7).

2 (Start 2) Turn the hoop 180°. Exit at 11 and stitch at 12. Exit at 13 and stitch at 14. Bring out in 15 and stitch in 16, then bring out in 17 (2, 5, and 16 are the same hole, as are 6, 9, 12, and 15; the backstitches of the previous row are joined to those of this row).

Visual Library of Embroidery Stitches

RICHELIEU AND RENAISSANCE EMBROIDERY

Richelieu and Renaissance cutwork embroideries are white cut-stitch embroideries, as are English, Venetian, and Madeira embroideries.

They appeared during the European Renaissance period (late 14th to early 17th centuries) with the aim of imitating needle lace, such as the delicate Venetian stitch. Indeed, lace was much more expensive to produce than cutwork embroidery.

In these embroideries, the outlines of the motifs are outlined with embroidery stitch, cut out, and often crossed by buttonhole bars. The areas of the textile support left intact replace the dense parts of the lace.

Renaissance embroidery is characterized by motifs embroidered in buttonhole stitch (see page 70), which are then crossed by buttonhole bars. Finally, the ground fabric is delicately cut along the motifs.

Richelieu embroidery is more difficult to embroider, but also stronger. It is worked in a different order, and the embroidery stitch is not the same. The ground fabric is first cut, folded under to the reverse, then embroidered in overcast stitch (see page 260). As in Renaissance embroidery, the motifs are crossed by wrapped bars, often with a small picot in the center. Richelieu embroidery is sometimes done in buttonhole stitch, which can be confusing.

Supplies

- linen fabric with a very tight weft, such as linen percale or cotton bastiste
- DMC Coton à Broder no. 30 or 35
- a no. 10 embroidery needle
- HB mechanical pencil for tracing patterns

Attention

Don't transfer patterns with a dissolvable pen. An intermediate step requires ironing the work before cutting out the motifs, which would cause the design to disappear.

Richelieu Embroidery

Richelieu embroidery designs are overcast around the edges, and some edges are joined together by bars, also whipped and possibly bearing one or more picots. After embroidering the running stitch around the perimeter of the design and the flanges, the edges are cut, tucked in, and overcast.

What You Need to Know

Start by tracing the pattern with the HB pencil. If you wish, and to help you find your way around during the work, draw a cross on all the areas to be cut out.

Renaissance embroidery

Marking contours and wrapped bars

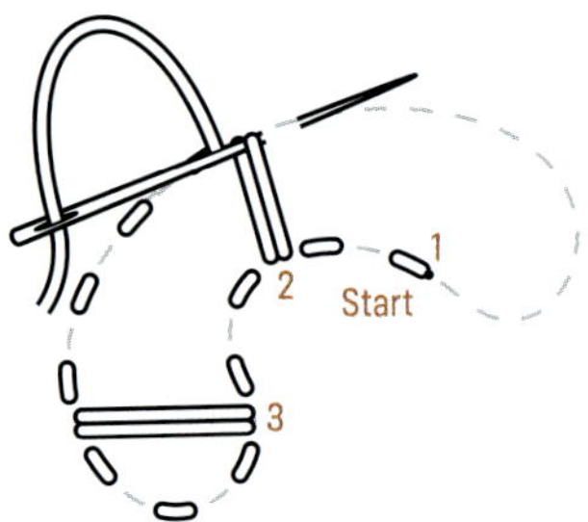

Round 1 Starting in stitch 1, stitch the outline of the design. In 2, stitch two threads back and forth to prepare the future bar. Resume running stitch on the outline between 2 and 3, then stitch two threads back and forth in 3 and wherever there are bars, then continue in running stitch.

Wrapped bars

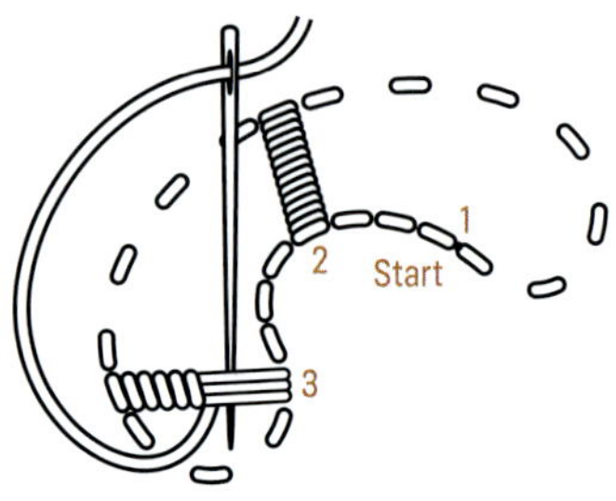

Tips for Good Embroidery

When you reach the top of a bar, pass the needle between the two threads of the future bar to secure the embroidery.

Round 2 When you reach stitch 1, stitch forward in the spaces of the previous row. In 2, thread the third support thread for the bar through to the other side and overlock, pulling the thread tight as you return to 2, without piercing the fabric. Thus embroider the perimeter in running stitch and overcast all the bars. Iron on reverse side.

Cutting, turning under, and overcasting

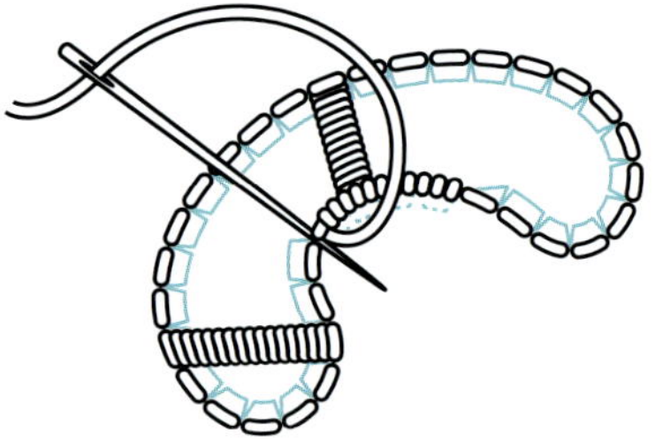

Cut the fabric 5–6 mm from the edge, inside the shape to be removed, taking care not to cut the edges. Sew the seam allowance into the curves and points. Turn the seam allowance under and embroider the outline in tight overcast stitch (*see below*) over the stitched outline. When the embroidery is complete, on the reverse side, trim the excess fabric that extends beyond the embroidery stitches.

Overcast stitch

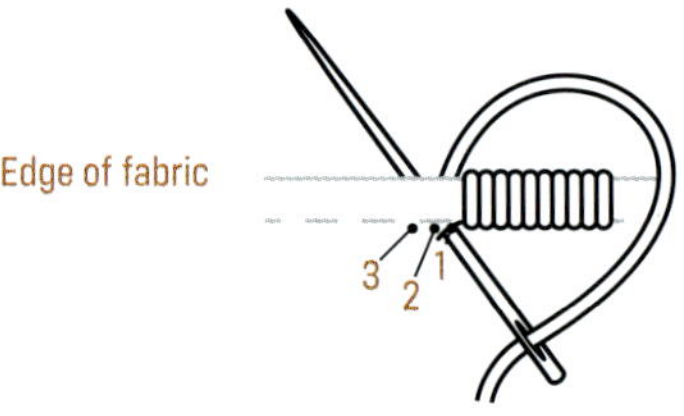

The stitches should be embroidered against each other. On the edge of the fabric, stitch in 1, pass under the fabric and return to stitch in 2, and so on. On the edges, wrap the thread around the previously stitched threads.

Bars with picots

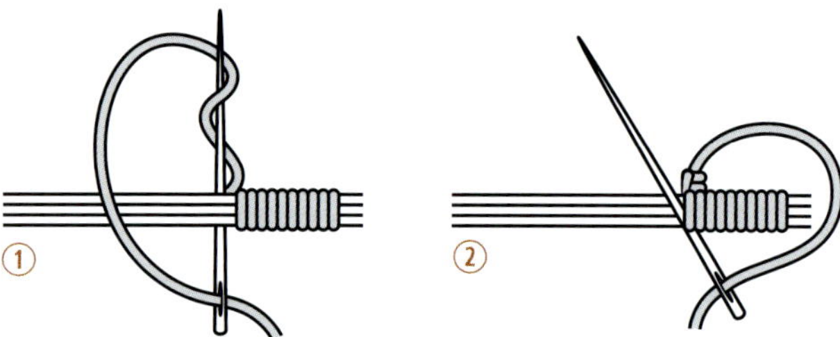

1 Pass the needle partially under the edge during embroidery. Wrap the working thread around the needle several times and pull it out.

2 Insert the needle back into the last loop of the overcast. Then overcast the entire bar.

Renaissance Embroidery

In Renaissance embroidery, the edges are embroidered in buttonhole stitch and joined together by buttonhole bars without picots.

After embroidering the running stitch and edges in buttonhole stitch, the edges are also embroidered in buttonhole stitch. Make sure all buttonholed edges are inside the design, which will then be removed. Once the embroidery is complete, carefully cut the fabric along the buttonhole stitch to remove it from inside the design.

> **What You Need to Know**
>
> **Start by tracing the pattern with the HB pencil. If you wish, and to help you find your way around during the work, draw a cross on all the areas to be removed.**

Marking bars and straight stitches

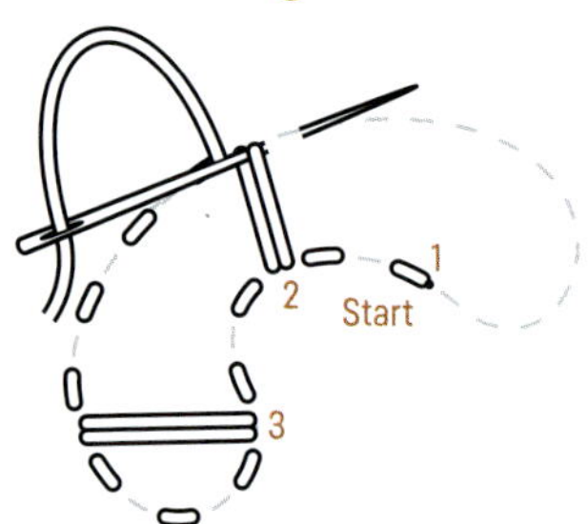

Round 1 Starting in stitch 1, stitch the outline of the design. In 2, stitch two threads back and forth to prepare the future bar. Resume running stitch on the outline between 2 and 3, then stitch two threads back and forth in 3 and wherever there are bars, then continue with the running stitch.

Buttonhole bars

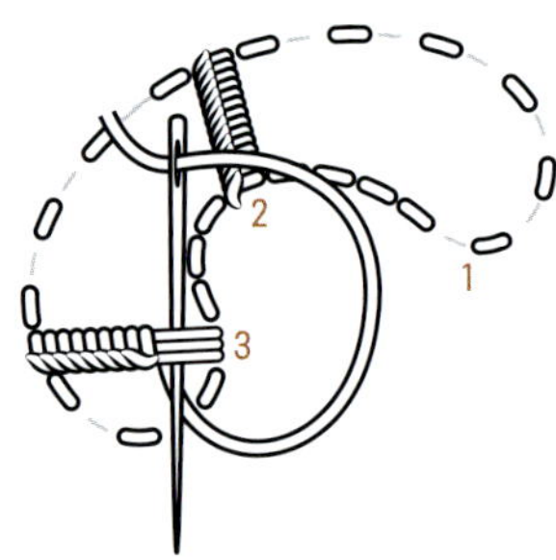

Round 2 When you reach stitch 1, embroider in running stitch in the spaces of the previous row. In 2, thread the third support thread for the bar through to the other side and embroider them in buttonhole stitch, returning in 2, without piercing the fabric. Embroider around the edges in running stitch and all bars in buttonhole stitch. Iron on reverse side.

Cutwork with buttonhole edge

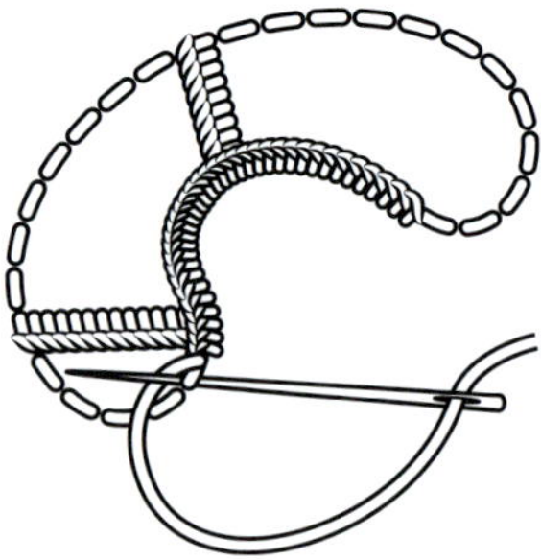

Embroider all edges in buttonhole stitch. Once the embroidery is complete, cut along the end flush with the stitches, passing under the bars and taking care not to cut the embroidery stitches.

Three-barred petal

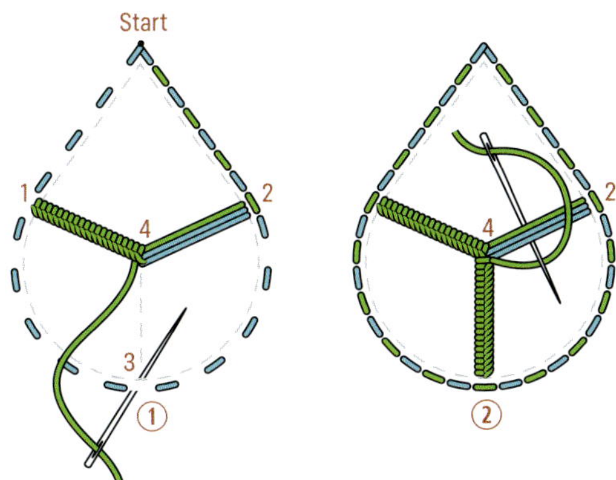

1 Embroider the first round in running stitch, stitching two threads between 1 and 2. Embroider the second round by making the third bar complete: embroider the half bar between 1 and 4 in buttonhole stitch. When you reach 4, cast on the three supporting threads between 4 and 3 and return to 4, embroidering in buttonhole stitch.

2 Finish the buttonhole stitches between 4 and 2. Then embroider the petal outline.

Eight-strap round flower

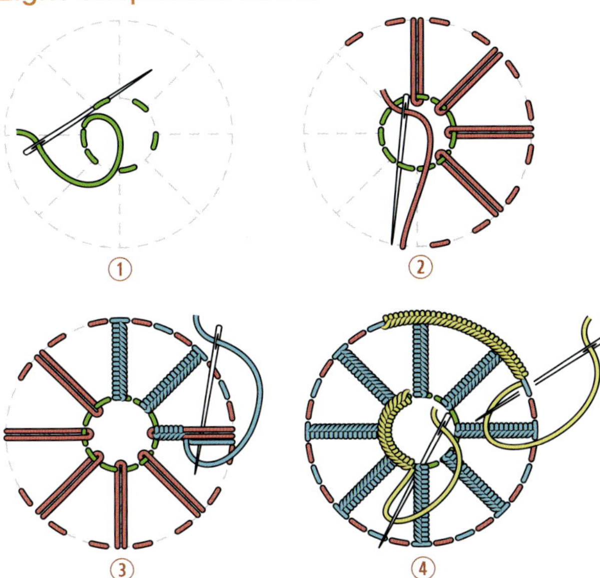

1 Embroider the center (inner circle) of the flower in running stitch in both directions.

2 On the outer circle of the flower, embroider the first round in running stitch, stitching two support threads for each bar between the outer and inner circles.

3 Embroider the second round, completing the bars with the third support thread and the buttonhole stitch.

4 Embroider the buttonhole stitch on the inner circle at the center of the flower, then on the outer circle.

What You Need to Know

The work is identical for a flower embroidered in Richelieu: instead of buttonhole stitch, embroider the flower in overcast stitch (see page 260).

BOUTIS

Boutis (or Provence embroidery) is a white embroidery.
In 2019, this technique was listed as an Intangible Cultural Heritage in France, under the names "boutis" and "Marseille embroidery."

It was in the 17th and 18th centuries that Provençal and Languedoc workshops saw the apogee of these techniques. Until the 19th century, boutis was still embroidered within the family circle, with young girls embroidering their wedding petticoats and trousseau.

"Petassons" and "bourrasons" were used to carry infants, while "vannes" (bedspreads) and pillows recounted the lives of these women. Symbols—such as a pair of birds for love, pomegranates, and a cornucopia for prosperity—initials, and flora and fauna described happy and unhappy events, love, births, mourning, wealth, and so on.

Boutis is most often embroidered in white, by stitching two layers of fabric together in running stitch (see page 46), following a design previously traced on the top of the work. Once the work is fully stitched, cotton strings are inserted between the two layers with a boutis needle to fill in the individual motifs, known as "embossed embroidery."

Real boutis can be recognized by the transparency of the quilting. Against the light, the light shines through the quilting, while the quilting remains opaque

What You Need to Know

Boutis should not be confused with quilting, piqué, or certain trapuntos (Italian embroideries resembling boutis), which are made up of three layers: the top fabric, the bottom fabric, and the filling (a wadding of silk, cotton, or wool). They are also made in running stitch. Quilting has been around for thousands of years, originating in China. Quilts (bedspreads) were often used to cover beds and were quilted on very large wooden quilting frames.
The term "boutis" has become overused. In fact, in the trade, any machine-stitched linen is mistakenly called "boutis."

Supplies

- a choice of white percale, batiste, or evenweave fabric, 10 to 20 cm larger than the work, for the top
- a cotton batiste fabric with a looser weave of the same dimensions for the underside
- a spool of DMC no. 50 white cotton sewing thread or quilting glove thread
- 10cm diameter embroidery hoop for quilting
- a 15 to 45cm diameter embroidery hoop for padding
- a boutis needle for padding
- no. 18 tapestry needle for padding
- a no. 10 embroidery needle for quilting.
- an erasable pen for transferring drawings
- a spool of special "Le Baufil" cotton no. 8 Ets J. Toulemonde for padding

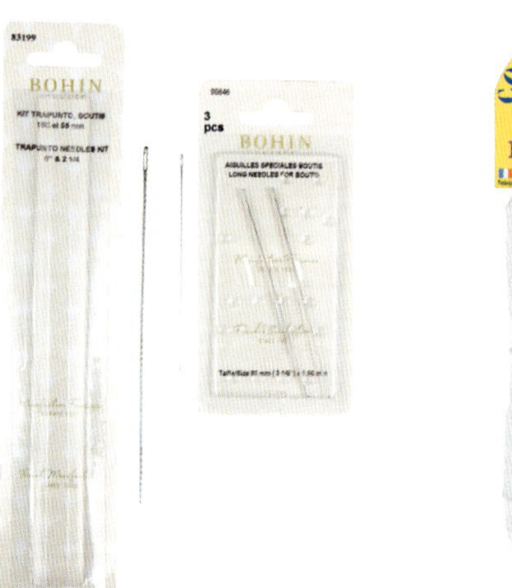

Knitting needles

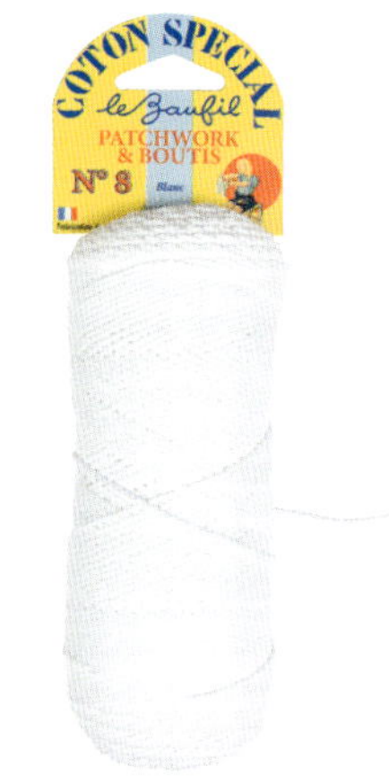

Coton spécial "Le Baufil" no. 8, Maison Sajou

Wedding petticoat

Baby blanket

Boutis against the light

Concentric waves

Padding gives relief to the boutis.

• double-sided tape or pins (or both) and basting thread to hold the work in place during the various stages

• a ruler and a circle template or compass to transfer the design

• *optional*: white bias binding, 1cm wide cotton twill tape, DMC Coton à Broder no. 16 or 25 cotton for finishing around the boutis

• a chopstick or toothpick to draw in the cotton strands when padding

Tips for Good Embroidery

To prevent shrinkage, do not wash or steam-iron fabric pieces before or during work.

Techniques

Once you have traced your pattern and joined the fabrics together, stitch and stuff the work.

Tracing

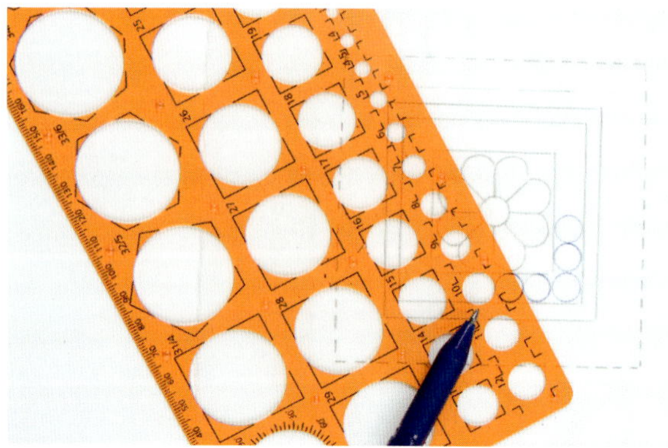

1 Find the center of the fabric to center the design. To do this, fold the fabric into quarters, respecting the straight edge, then mark the folds with an iron, without steam.

2 Using double-sided tape or pins (or both), position the top fabric over the pattern, then carefully transfer the design with an erasable pen.

3 Still using the erasable pen, draw straight lines with a ruler (the "channels"), measuring 4 mm wide.

4 Using the circle template, draw the circles.

Construction

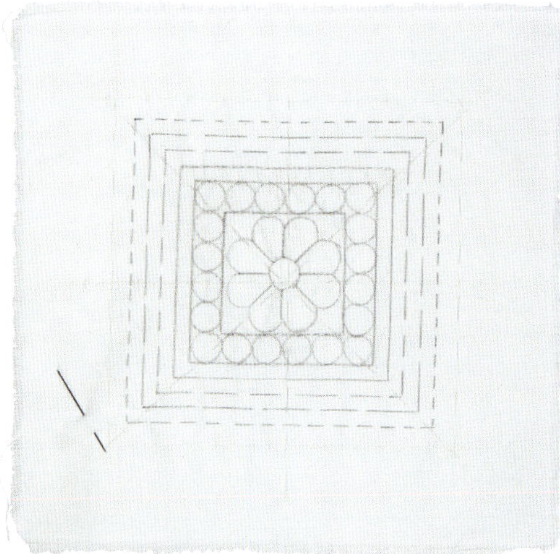

Using basting thread and a long needle, join the two layers of fabric together with large running stitches (see page 46), respecting the straight grain. The work must be secured with basting threads spaced every 15 cm.

Be sure to start at the center of the work and insert the needle between the lines of the design.

Stitch the pattern

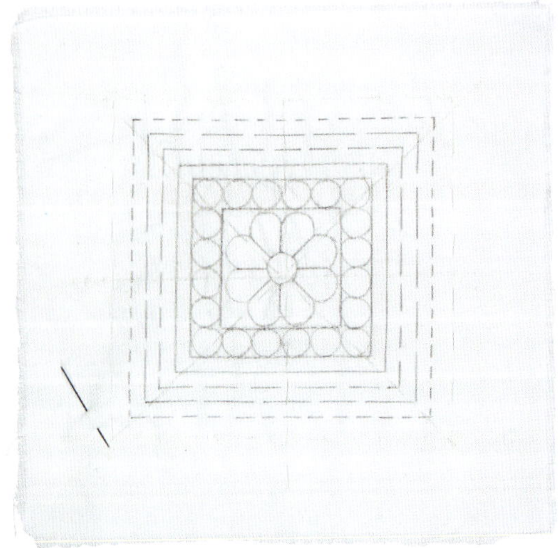

1 Refer to the diagrams on page 34.

2 Equip yourself with a 10cm diameter hoop, a #10 embroidery needle, and sewing thread.

3 To start a needlework, tie an overhand knot, leaving 2 cm of thread protruding from the end. Pass the needle 1 cm from the start, piercing between the two layers of fabric, and exit on the pattern line. Give a quick tug to pop the knot between the two layers and trim the excess thread. Make a small backstitch to secure the thread.

Tips for Good Embroidery

A backstitch is useful when starting or stopping a needle, when changing direction (like leaf tips) or pattern. To avoid systematically stopping the thread for each pattern, and if the next pattern is no more than 1 cm away from the previous one, slide the thread between the two layers of fabric to go to the next section, making a backstitch at the end of the first channel and at the beginning of the next.

4 Stitch the two layers of fabric together with running stitch according to the design—the stitches should be small (approx. five stitches/cm) and even. Start at the center of the fabric and gradually work outward from the design.

5 At the end of the stitched line, tie a knot on the working thread 2 or 3 mm from the last stitch, restitch the needle between the two layers of fabric, and give it a quick tug to pop the knot inside the work. Move on to padding when the design is fully stitched. Be careful not to let the quilting threads get in the way when padding.

6 Stitch the circles by stitching alternating semicircles one way and then completing the circles with alternating semicircles on the return.

Padding

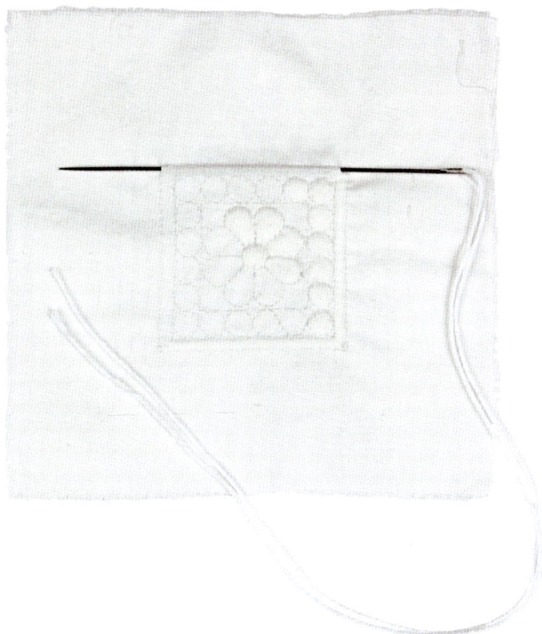

All padding is done on the reverse side, with the Le Baufil cotton passed twice through the needle's eye, and on the hoop with a minimum diameter of 15 cm.

1 Using the boutis needle and no. 18 needle threaded double without knots, fill in all the spaces, making several passes if necessary to obtain the desired volume.

What You Need to Know

These lengths of thread passed through the embroidery are also called "wicks."

2 Slide the needle between the two layers of fabric without breaking the fabric threads. Pull the needle until 1 mm of cotton is flush with the needle entry hole. Then cut the cotton thread 1 mm from the needle exit hole.

3 Using a toothpick or the tip of the needle, tuck the ends of the cotton string inside the shape to be stuffed. Repeat until the pattern is completely filled. It's up to the embroiderer to decide how much cotton to stuff into each shape; however, the work must remain supple for it to be comfortable and pretty.

4 Pass two strands of cotton through the padding channel (in a single pass of a double needle), using the boutis needle.

Finishing touches

There are several possible techniques for finishing the edges of a boutis.

Double-turned hem

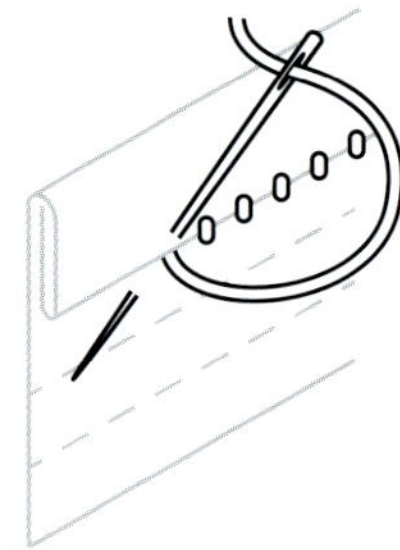

1 For a straight edge, cut the two layers of fabric together at 10 mm.

2 First fold 5 mm, then a second fold of 5 mm onto the reverse side of the work.

3 Use sewing thread to stitch the hem with invisible stitches in the hem fold groove.

4 Using the boutis needle, stuff the entire hem with a single strand of cotton.

Clean finished options

→ For a straight edge

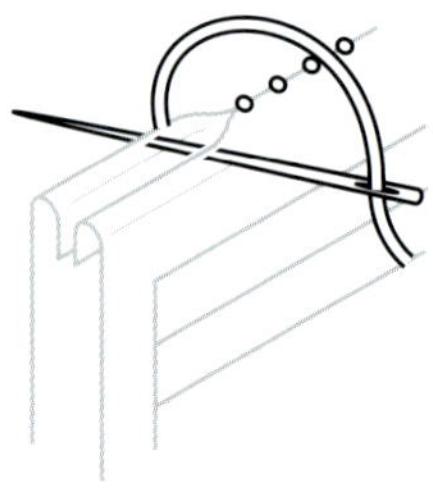

1 Pin the two layers of fabric together, 1 cm from the last raw edge.

2 Fold each layer inward by 5 mm, facing each other.

3 Sew with invisible stitches, using sewing thread.

4 Using the boutis needle, stuff the entire hem with a single strand of cotton.

→ Bound edge

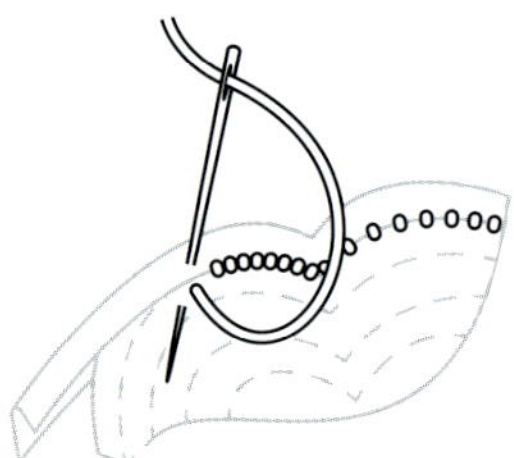

Using sewing thread, hemstitch over the edge of the binding all around the raw edge.

→ Buttonhole edging

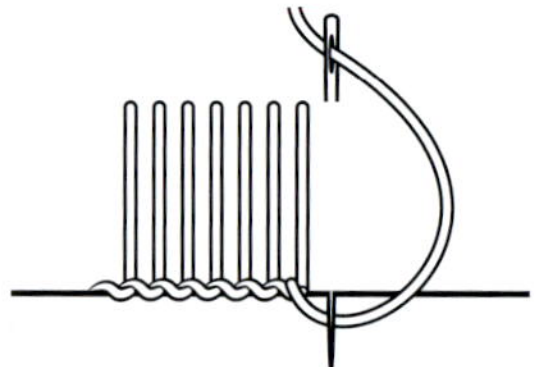

1 Before trimming the edges, embroider a tight buttonhole stitch all around the work, using DMC Coton à Broder no. 16 or 25, depending on the desired fineness.

2 Trim excess fabric very carefully all along the buttonhole stitched edge.

Cleaning

1 Iron the work on the right side to remove the erasable pen.

2 Wash with hot water and a gentle soap to shrink the fabric and secure the padding threads.

3 Wring it out in a towel and dry it flat.

What You Need to Know

Boutis generally have a shrinkage of 10–15%.

Tips for Good Embroidery

- To fill the padding channels in the large curves, remove the work from the hoop. Be careful not to cut the cotton strands permanently, since they may shrink when you put the work back on the hoop, making them too short. Place the work back onto the hoop to position the padding and cut to length.

- Tuck in the ends, using a toothpick. In narrow areas, pull the needle out before the end of the shape to be stuffed, to avoid overstuffing with too many cotton strands.

- For tightly curved or circular patterns, stuff in several steps. Stitch in 1, take out the needle in 2, stitch again in exactly the same hole as 2, and take out in 3, and so on until you come back and take out in 1. Once the padding has been threaded through the full length of channel, then even out the tension of the string padding and trim to length.

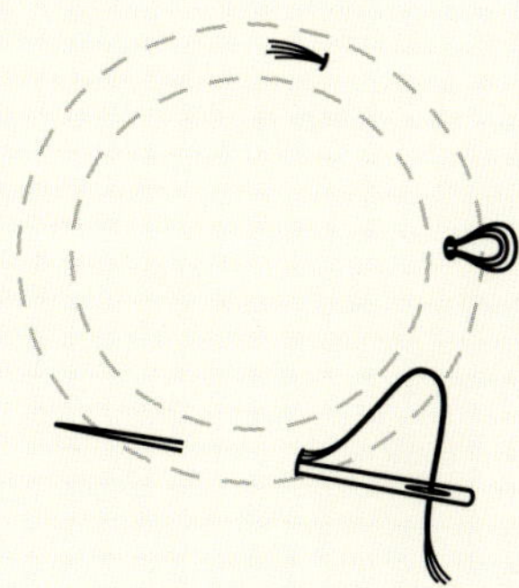

Template size 100%

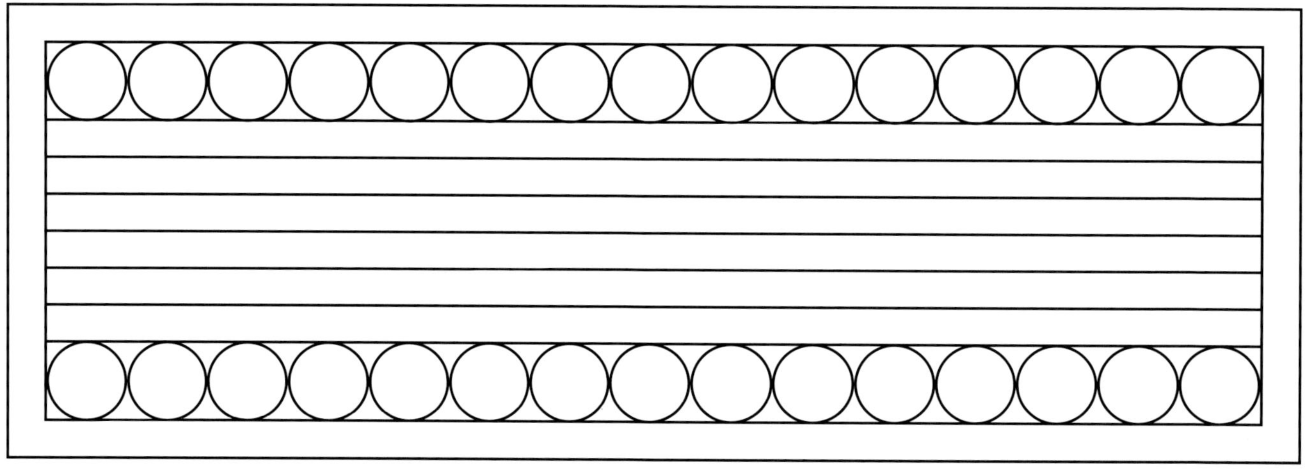

5

PROJECTS

FRIEZE

The photo of the design can be found on page 47.

Thread			
DMC Embroidery floss (stranded cotton)	312	334	3325

Transfer the pattern as many times as necessary on the chosen surface.

① Whipped running stitch with two strands color 334 and two strands color 3325 for whipping around the running stitch.

② Running stitch with two strands color 312.

③ Whipped running stitch with two strands color 334 or 312 and two strands color 312 for whipping around the running stitch. Running stitch with two strands color 312 or 334 in the sheet.

Template size 100%

DISCOVER

Shirt collars and cuffs

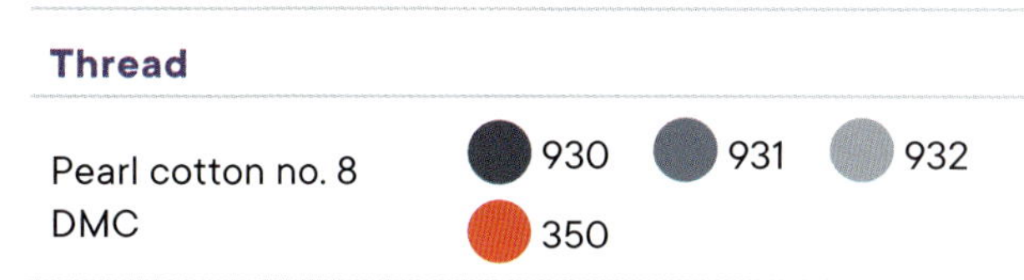

Thread

Pearl cotton no. 8 DMC	930 931 932 350

1 On the collar and cuffs, draw parallel lines 5 mm apart, starting from the outer edges.

2 Stitch before each line with the color of your choice.

3 To stop the needles, make a small knot on the working thread, 3 mm from the end of the line. Conceal it by sliding the needle through the layers of fabric forming the collar or cuffs, pull out to 3 cm, and cut the thread flush.

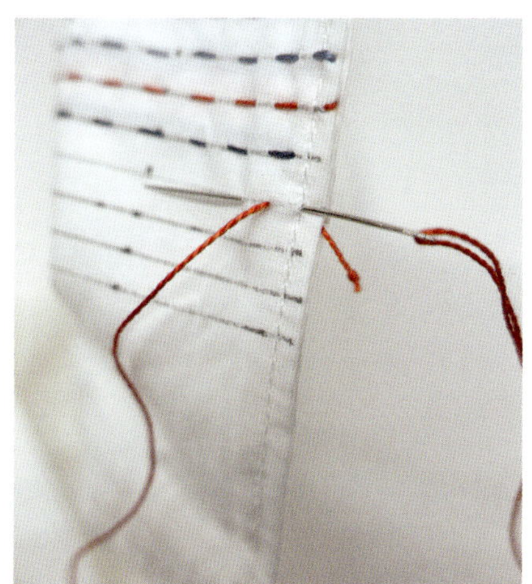

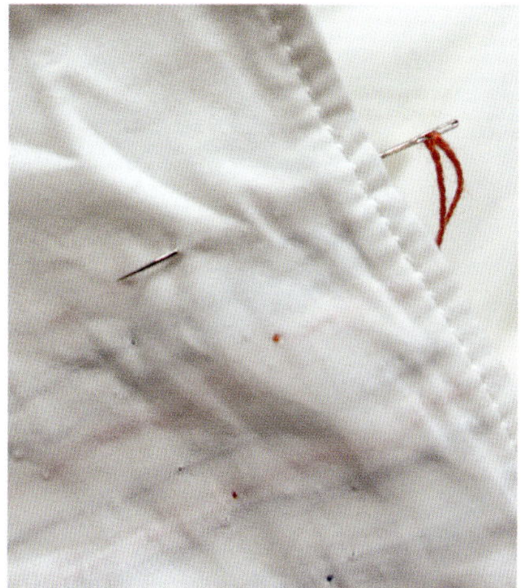

T-shirt

Thread	
DMC Embroidery floss (stranded cotton)	930, 932, 3824, 3340
Supplies	Sulky

① Whipped running stitch with two strands color 3824 and two strands color 3340 for whipping around the running stitch.

② Running stitch with two strands color 930.

③ Whipped running stitch with two strands color 930 and two strands color 932 for whipping around the running stitch.

Template size 100%

GOING THE EXTRA MILE

Thread	
DMC Embroidery floss (stranded cotton)	02, 3325, 3340, 3824
Fabric	Double gauze, denim blue (Stragier, ref. 0001 5655)
Supplies	Soluble stabilizer
Pattern	Sakura blouse by Ikatee

Transfer the central motif to the front yoke and the frieze on the sleeve edges. Place the frieze designs facing each other.

① Whipped running stitch with two strands color 3340 and two strands color 3824 for whipping around the running stitch.

② Running stitch with two strands color 3325.

③ Whipped running stitch with two strands color 3325 and two strands color 02 for whipping around the running stitch.

Tips for Good Embroidery

When whipping around a linear stitch,, prick the needle at the tip of each leaf and pull out just beside it to create a pretty point on the top of the leaves.

FRIEZE and DISCOVER

The photo of the design can be found on page 53.

Thread	
DMC Embroidery floss (stranded cotton)	● 939
Supplies	Soluble stabilizer

Stitch each animal with two strands color 939.

Template size 100%

GOING THE EXTRA MILE

Threads	
DMC Embroidery floss (stranded cotton)	780 783
Metallic braided 4 Au Ver à Soie	035
Supplies	Soluble stabilizer

① Backstitch color 783.

② Backstitch with three strands color 783 and three strands color 780 for whipping around the backstitch.

③ Backstitch with three strands color 783 and three strands color 780 for whipping around the backstitch.

④ Stab stitch the filling of the eyes with metallic braid color 035.

Template size 50%

STEM STITCH and Its Variations

Pages 55 to 58

FRIEZE

The photo of the design can be found on page 56.

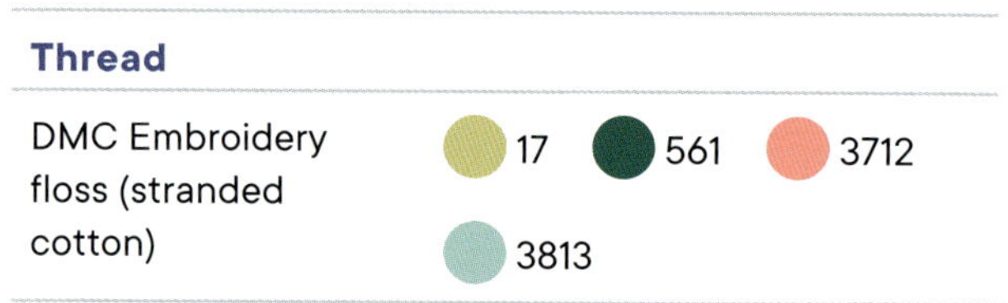

Thread	
DMC Embroidery floss (stranded cotton)	17, 561, 3712, 3813

Transfer the pattern as many times as necessary on the chosen surface.

① Stem stitch with two color strands 3712.

② Stem stitch with two color strands 561.

③ Stem stitch with two color strands 17.

④ Stem stitch with two color strands 3813.

⑤ Stem stitch and straight stitch with two strands color 561.

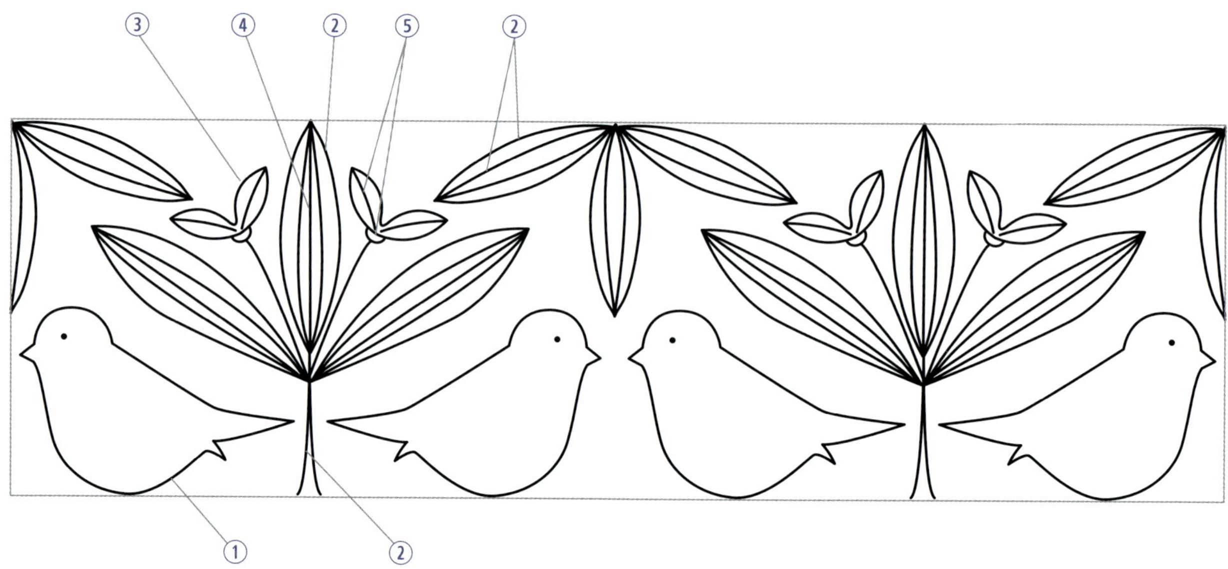

Template size 100%

DISCOVER

Thread	
DMC Embroidery floss (stranded cotton)	300, 561, 754, 780, 920, 3813, 3816, 3778

1. Stem stitch with three color strands 920.
2. Stem stitch with three color strands 300.
3. Stem stitch with three color strands 561.
4. Stem stitch with three color strands 3816.
5. Stem stitch with three color strands 3813.
6. Stem stitch filling with three strands color 780.
7. Three-strand color stab stitch 300.
8. Stem stitch with three color strands 3778.
9. Stem stitch with three color strands 754.

Template size 100%

GOING THE EXTRA MILE

Thread			
DMC Embroidery floss (stranded cotton)	04	06	224
	347	561	3712

① Stem stitch with two color strands 347.

② Three rows of stem stitch side by side, using two color strands 347, 3712, and 224.

③ Three rows of stem stitch side by side, using two color strands 347 and 06.

④ Three rows of stem stitch side by side, using two color strands 3712, 224, and 06.

⑤ Stem stitch with two color strands 04.

⑥ Stem stitch with two color strands 561.

Template size 100%

FRIEZE

The photo of the design can be found on page 60.

Thread	
DMC Embroidery floss (stranded cotton)	17, 726, 727, 3012

Transfer the motif as many times as necessary on the chosen backing and embroider, distributing the colors in the flower clusters as you wish.

① Rhodes stitch with two strands color 17, 726, or 727.

② Fern stitch with two strands color 3012.

③ Backstitch with two strands color 3012.

Template size 100%

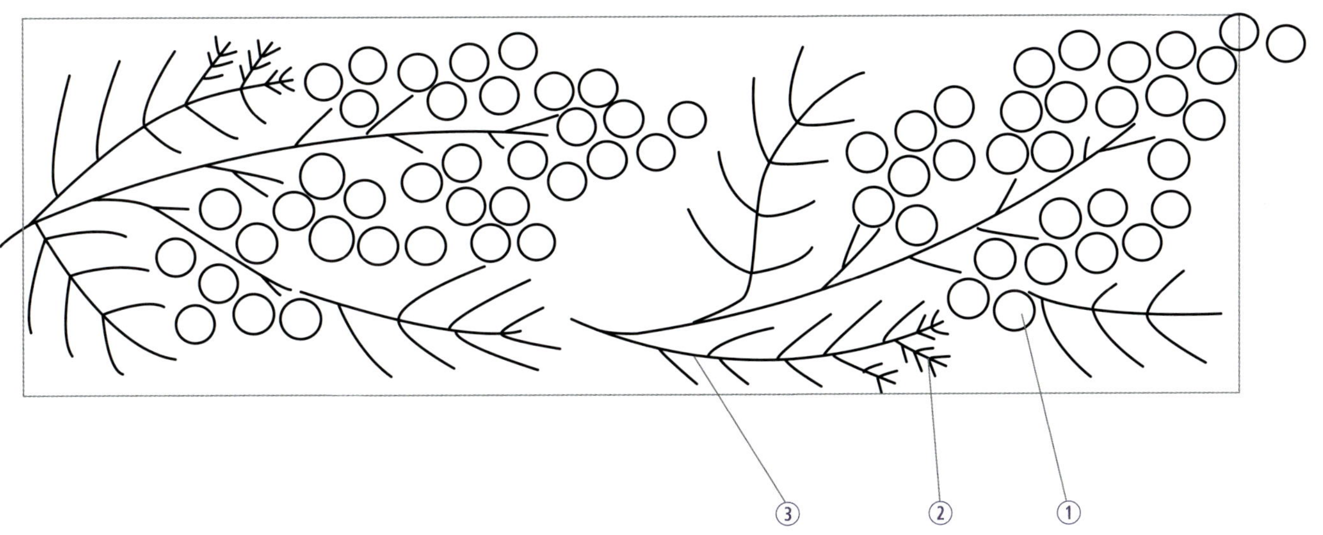

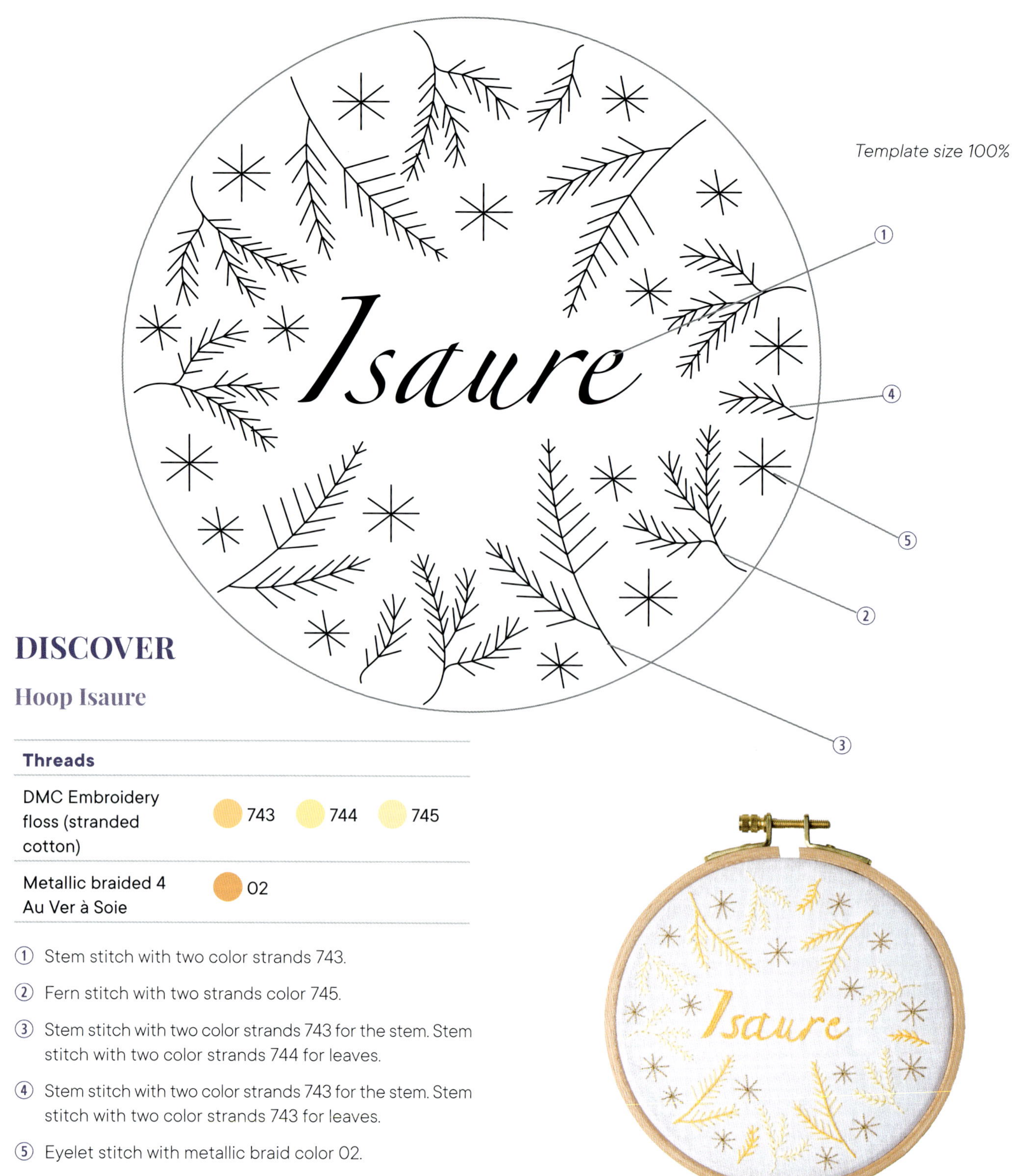

DISCOVER

Hoop Isaure

Threads	
DMC Embroidery floss (stranded cotton)	743 744 745
Metallic braided 4 Au Ver à Soie	02

1. Stem stitch with two color strands 743.
2. Fern stitch with two strands color 745.
3. Stem stitch with two color strands 743 for the stem. Stem stitch with two color strands 744 for leaves.
4. Stem stitch with two color strands 743 for the stem. Stem stitch with two color strands 743 for leaves.
5. Eyelet stitch with metallic braid color 02.

Violet flowers hoop

Thread			
DMC Embroidery floss (stranded cotton)	27	30	32
	34	208	676

① Fern stitch with two strands color 208.

② Stem stitch with two color strands 30 for the stem. Stem stitch with two color strands 30 for leaves.

③ Rhodes stitch with two strands color 676.

④ Stem stitch with two color strands 30.

⑤ Rhodes stitch with two color strands 32.

⑥ Stem stitch with two color strands 30 for the stem. Straight stitch with two color strands 32 for leaves.

⑦ Rhodes stitch with two color strands 676.

⑧ Straight stitch with two color strands 32.

⑨ Backstitch with two strands color 27 for stems. Straight stitch with two strands color 27 for leaves.

⑩ Sheaf stitch with two strands color 676.

⑪ Eyelet stitch with two strands color 34.

⑫ Stem stitch with two color strands 32.

⑬ Straight stitch with two color strands 32.

⑭ Straight stitch with two color strands 27.

Template size 50%

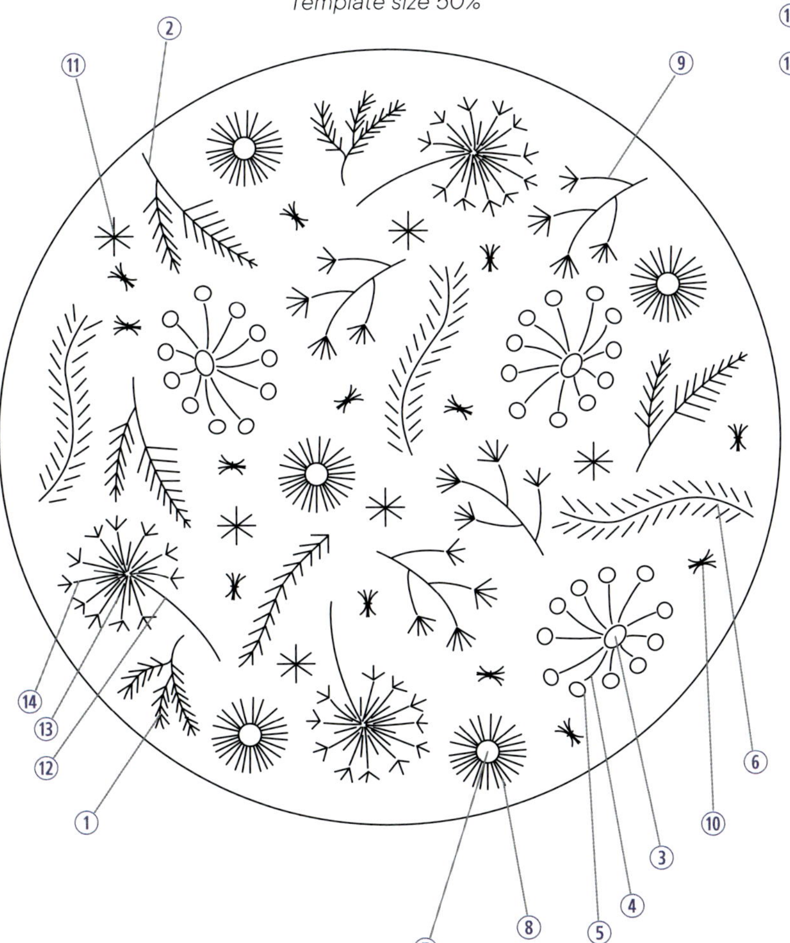

GOING THE EXTRA MILE

Thread	
DMC Embroidery floss (stranded cotton)	◯ White

① Fern stitch.

② Stem stitch for the stem and straight stitch for leaves.

③ Rhodes stitch.

④ Stem stitch.

⑤ Rhodes stitch.

⑥ Stem stitch for the stem and straight stitch for leaves.

⑦ Rhodes stitch.

⑧ Straight stitch.

⑨ Backstitch for stems and straight stitch for leaves.

⑩ Sheaf stitch.

⑪ Eyelet stitch.

⑫ Stem stitch.

⑬ Straight stitch.

⑭ Stem stitch for the stem and straight stitch for leaves.

Template size 50%

FRIEZE

The photo of the design can be found on page 72.

Thread	
DMC Embroidery floss (stranded cotton)	● 824 ○ 3865

Transfer the pattern as many times as necessary on the chosen surface.

① Stem stitch with two color strands 824.

② Buttonhole stitch with two strands color 824. Embroider the stitch on a diagonal, buttonhole to one side of the leaves.

③ Buttonhole stitch with two strands color 3865. Buttonhole along the base of the bells.

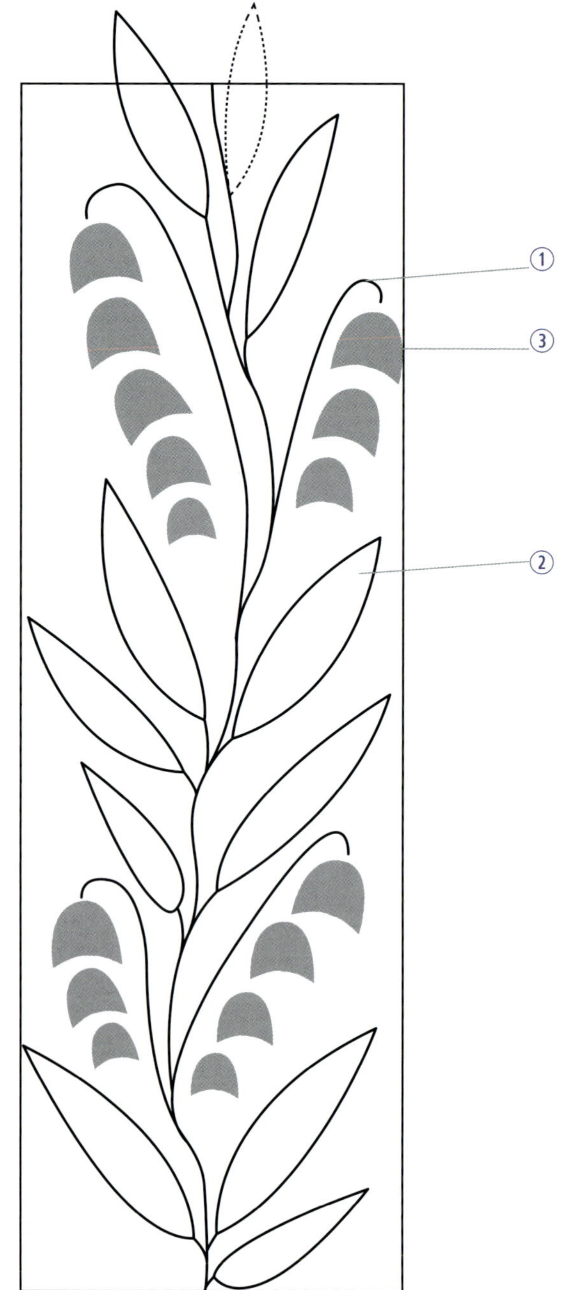

Template size 100%

DISCOVER

Threads	
DMC Embroidery floss (stranded cotton)	301 452 632 758 782
Metallic braided 4 Au Ver à Soie	002
Fabric	Pure organic cotton poplin, cream color (Stragier, ref. 0001 7389)

Find the alphabet on page 146, to download and print (see QR code on page 14).

① Buttonhole stitch with two strands color 782 and overlocked with metallic braid color 002.

② Buttonhole stitch with two strands color 758.

③ Buttonhole stitch with two strands color 301.

④ Buttonhole stitch with two strands color 452. Buttonhole the edge of the leaf.

⑤ Stem stitch with two color strands 452.

⑥ Buttonhole stitch with two strands color 632.

⑦ Buttonhole stitch with two strands color 758.

⑧ Buttonhole stitch with two strands color 452. Work the buttonhole toward the top of the leaf.

⑨ Flower buttonhole stitch with metallic thread color 002.

Template size 50%

GOING THE EXTRA MILE

Thread	
DMC Embroidery floss (stranded cotton)	01, 729, 780, 782, 783, 926, 927, 3768
Fabric	Sweatshirt knit extra, navy color (Stragier, ref. 0001 2527)
Supplies	Soluble stabilizer
Pattern	Irma Mum jacket by Ikatee

All leaves are embroidered with a side of buttonhole stitch worked toward the center vein and outer edge (see page 75).

① Buttonhole stitch with two color strands 780.

② Buttonhole stitch with two color strands 782.

③ Buttonhole stitch with two color strands 729.

④ Buttonhole eyelet or buttonhole wheel stitch with two strands color 783.

⑤ Stem stitch with two color strands 783.

⑥ Buttonhole wheel stitch with two strands color 783.

⑦ Stem stitch with two color strands 3768.

⑧ Buttonhole wheel stitch with two strands color 01.

⑨ Buttonhole stitch with two color strands 3768.

⑩ Buttonhole stitch with two color strands 926.

⑪ Buttonhole stitch with two color strands 927.

Template size 50%

RECOVERY STITCH and Its Variations

Pages 66 to 69

FRIEZE

The photo of the design can be found on page 67.

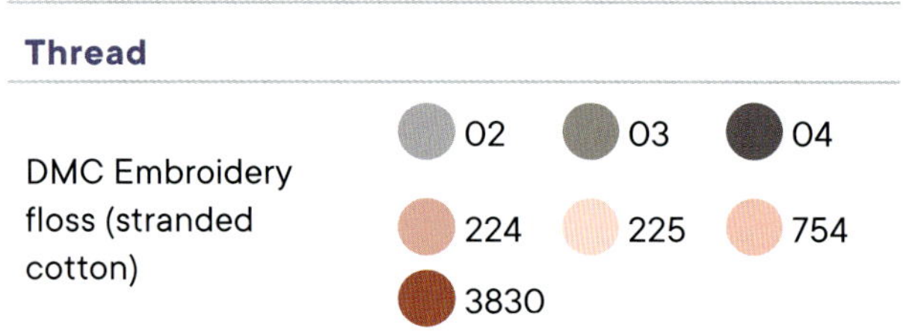

Thread	
DMC Embroidery floss (stranded cotton)	02, 03, 04, 224, 225, 754, 3830

Transfer the motif as many times as necessary on the chosen backing and embroider with two strands, using the color placement shown in the sample photo on page 67 as a guide.

① Mending or surface darning stitch for flowers.

② Mending or surface stitch for leaves.

③ Stem stitch for all bold petal and leaf edges, and for all stems

④ Seeding for the centers of flowers.

⑤ Straight stitch or satin stitch for the congress cloth above the rose buds.

Template size 100%

DISCOVER

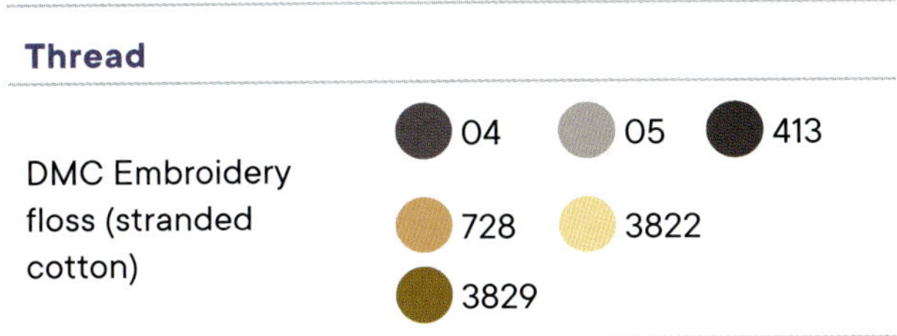

Thread	
DMC Embroidery floss (stranded cotton)	04, 05, 413, 728, 3822, 3829

- Darning stitch with two petal strands Stitches converge towards the center of the flower.
- Double strand mending or surface stitch for leaves. Stitches run parallel to the center vein.
- Stem stitch with two strands for all bold petal and leaf edges, as well as stems.
- Seeding with two strands for the center of the flower.
- For the stamens, stitch straight stitches with 2 strands above the rosebuds.

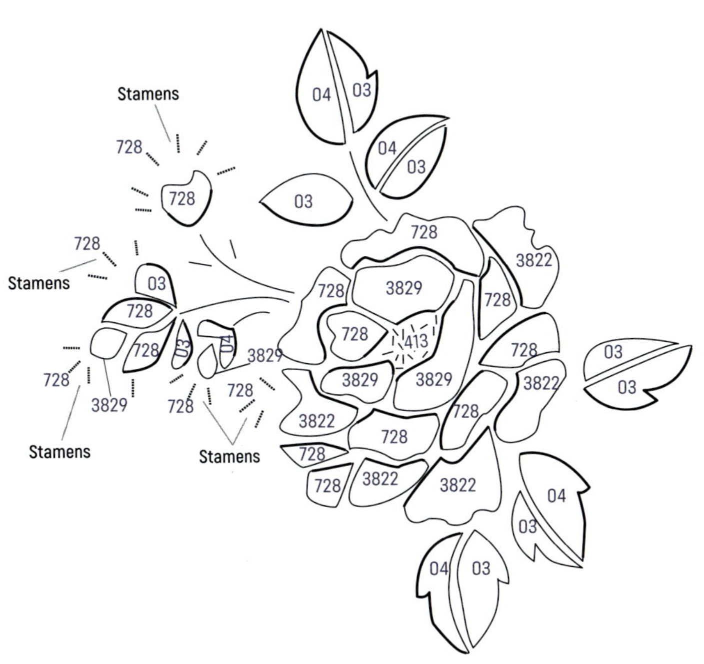

Template size 50%

GOING THE EXTRA MILE

Thread			
DMC Embroidery floss (stranded cotton)	02	03	04
	223	224	225
	355	754	758
	3770	3777	3778
	3830		

- Stem stitch with two strands for stems.
- Two-strand darning stitch for flowers. Stitches converge toward the center of the flower.
- Double-strand darning stitch for leaves. Stitches run parallel to the midrib.
- Stem stitch with two strands for all petal edges and leaf outlines.
- Seeding with two strands for the heart of the flowers.
- Straight stitch with two strands for the stamens above rosebuds and flowers.

Left side

Template size 50%

Right side
Template size 50%
3770
754
3770
754
355
355
754
3770
754
754
03
04
02
3770
3770
3830
03
3830
3778
3830
3830
3777
3777
3830
3778
3777
04
3777
3778
3830
3778
3778
3778
3778
3777
3777
3830
355
3777
3830
3830
3777
04
3777
3830
3778
03
04
03
03
03
355
355
355
3830
3830
3830
3830
03
03
02
04
03
03
03
03
03
02
03
04
03
03
03
03
3778
355
3830
3830
03
355
03
355
355
02
355

CHAIN STITCH and Its Variations

Pages 78 to 84

Tips for Good Embroidery

For each design, always start by embroidering the outline of the shapes before creating the filling.

FRIEZE

The photo of the design can be found on page 83.

Thread	
DMC Embroidery floss (stranded cotton)	02 823 3325
Supplies	Soluble stabilizer

Transfer the pattern as many times as necessary on the chosen surface.

① Three-strand chain stitch color 3325.

② Two small straight stitches one on top of the other with three color strands 823.

③ Three-strand chain stitch filling, color 02.

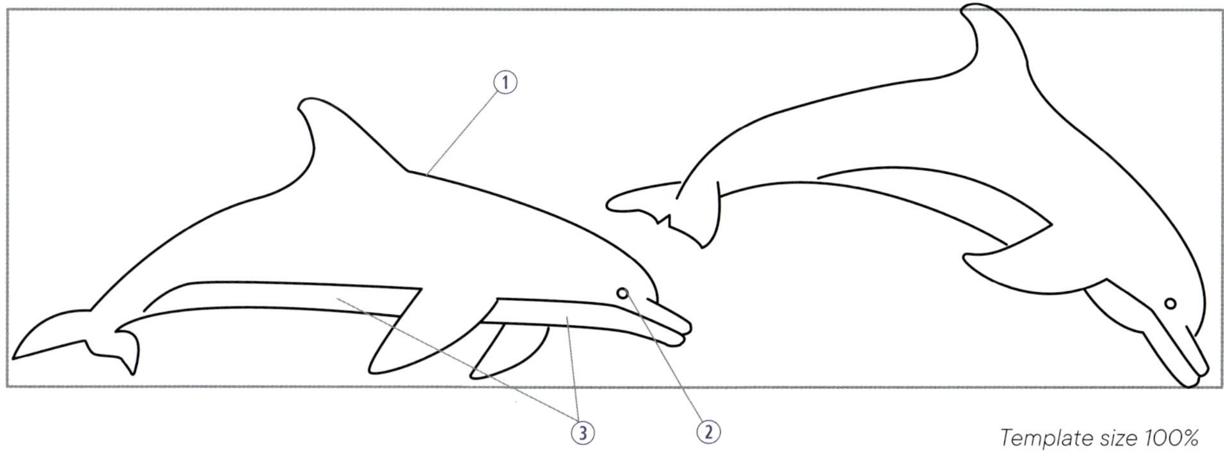

Template size 100%

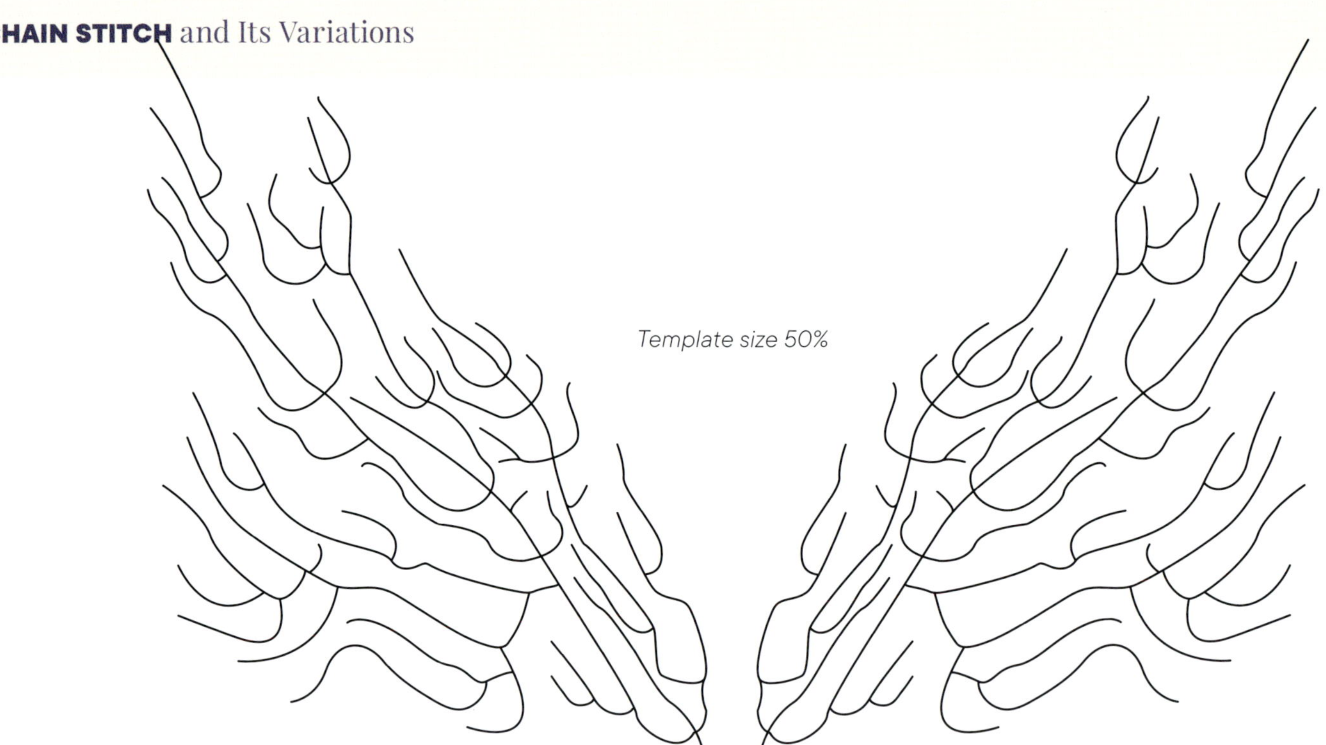

DISCOVER

Coral

Thread	
DMC Embroidery floss (stranded cotton)	350
Supplies	Soluble stabilizer

Embroider in twisted chain stitch with three strands color 350.

Seahorse

Thread	
DMC Embroidery floss (stranded cotton)	312  334

① Chain stitch with two strands color 334.

② Detached chain stitch with two strands color 312.

③ Detached chain stitch with two strands color 312.

④ Zigzag chain stitch with two strands color 312.

⑤ Backstitch with two strands color 312.

⑥ Backstitch with two strands color 312 for the outline. Two small straight stitches with two strands color 312 for the center of the eye.

Template size 100%

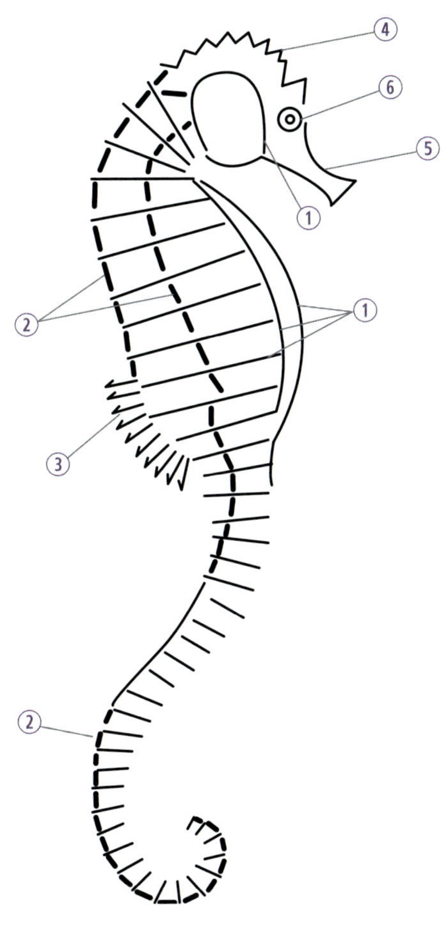

GOING THE EXTRA MILE

Thread	
DMC Embroidery floss (stranded cotton)	349, 350, 351, 817, 3777
Supplies	Soluble stabilizer

Chain stitch is for filling. Start by embroidering the outside of the shape, then fill in toward the inside.

Template size 100%

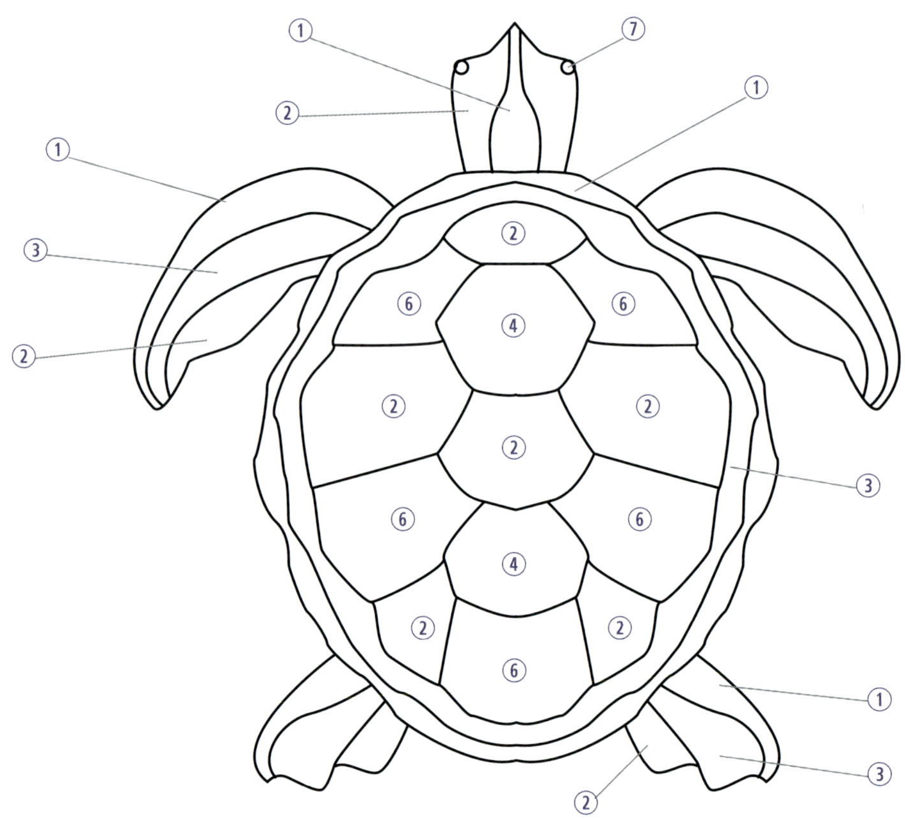

1. Chain stitch with two color strands 3777.
2. Chain stitch with two color strands 351.
3. Chain stitch with two color strands 817.
4. Chain stitch with two color strands 350.
5. Chain stitch with two color strands 351.
6. Chain stitch with two color strands 349.
7. Two straight stitches one on top of the other with two strands 3777.

CROSS-STITCH AND NEEDLEPOINT

Pages 85 to 94

FRIEZE

The photo of the design can be found on page 92.

Thread	
DMC Embroidery floss (stranded cotton)	03 04 782
Supplies	Toile Aïda 5.5 points or a ground fabric of your choice

Embroider as many times as necessary in cross-stitch with two strands of embroidery floss, following the color placement shown in the diagram.

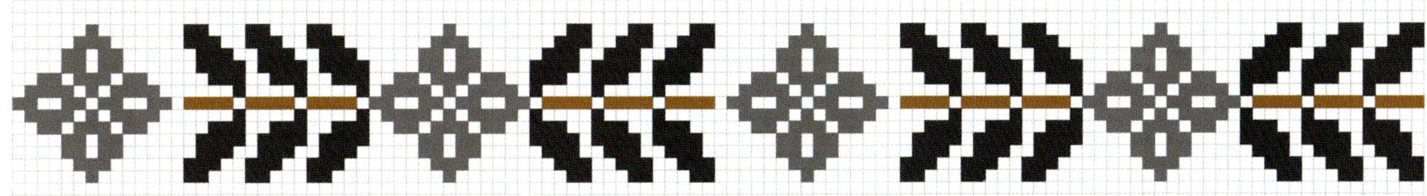

Template size 100%

DISCOVER

Thread	
DMC Embroidery floss (stranded cotton)	04 782 3799
Supplies	5.5 stitches/cm waste canvas Basting thread

1 Using basting thread, secure two squares of waste canvas 10 × 10cm squares on the collar. Align their edges perfectly with the collar.

2 Cross-stitch with two strands of embroidery floss, following the color placement in the diagram.

3 Soak embroidery in water and remove waste canvas.

Template size 100%

GOING THE EXTRA MILE

Thread	
DMC Embroidery floss (stranded cotton)	04 782 3799
Fabric	Lightweight cotton twill, color Anthracite (Stragier, ref. 0000 7028)
Supplies	5.5 stitches/cm waste canvas Basting thread
Pattern	Personal creation

1 Using basting thread, baste the waste canvas on the front of the garment.

2 Cross-stitch with two strands of embroidery floss, following the color placement in the diagram.

3 Soak embroidery in water and remove waste canvas.

Template size 100%

FRIEZE

The photo of the design can be found on page 98.

Thread	
DMC Embroidery floss (stranded cotton)	● 561
Fabric	Silk organza, Porcelain color (Stragier, ref. 0001 4284)

Transfer the pattern as many times as necessary onto a fabric suitable for shadow stitch (see page 95).

① Shadow stitch with two strands.

② Stem stitch with two strands.

Template size 100%

DISCOVER

Thread	
DMC Embroidery floss (stranded cotton)	502 561
Fabric	Striped cotton double gauze 10 mm, color Gris perle (Stragier, ref. 0001 5025)
Pattern	Personal creation

Along the entire length to be embroidered, draw a small line every centimeter with a dissolvable pen to mark stitch length.

① Herringbone stitch with six strands, color 561, on a height of three stripes (i.e., 1 cm).

② Three-strand laced running stitch color 501.

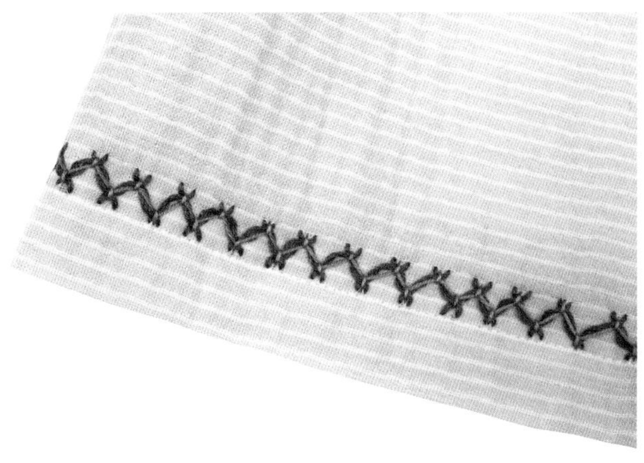

Tips for Good Embroidery

Stitch the running stitch with straight stitches perpendicular to the cross points of the herringbone stitch, then lace through those stitches.

GOING THE EXTRA MILE

Thread	
DMC Embroidery floss (stranded cotton)	502
Fabric	Striped cotton double gauze 10 mm, color Gris perle (Stragier, ref. 0001 5025)
Pattern	Louise Mum blouse by Ikatee

What You Need to Know

Each line of herringbone stitch is embroidered on the height of a gray stripe (i.e., 4 mm).

1 Along the entire length to be embroidered, draw a small line every centimeter with a dissolvable pen.

2 Embroider four vertical lines in herringbone stitch with color 502 in the center of the front yoke and on top of the sleeves.

3 Symmetrically reflect the foliage on either side of the front yoke.

4 Stitch the central veins with two lines of stem stitch and the leaves with herringbone stitch.

Template size 100%

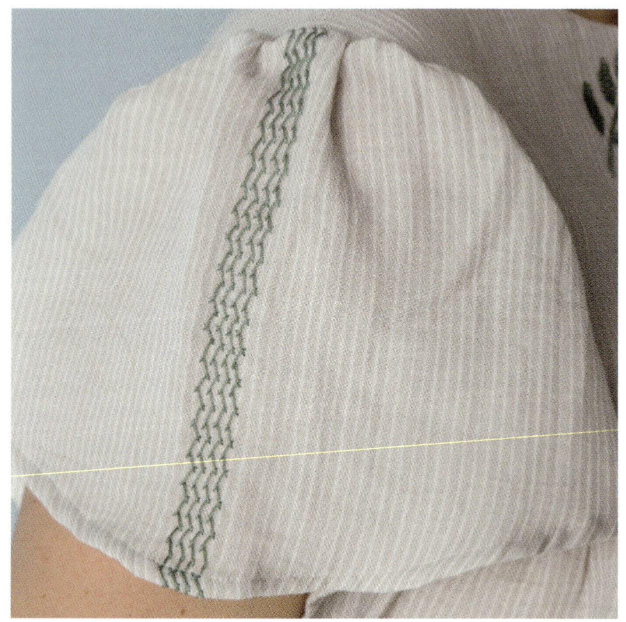

FEATHER STITCH and Its Variations

Pages 101 to 105

Thread	
DMC Embroidery floss (stranded cotton)	 30  783  823
Fabric	Pure organic cotton poplin, Crème color (Stragier, ref. 0001 7389)
Patterns	Personal creations

What You Need to Know

Supplies are identical for all products.

FRIEZE

Transfer the pattern as many times as necessary on the surface of your choice.

① Backstitch with two color strands 823.

② Cretan stitch with two color strands 823.

③ Cretan stitch with two color strands 30.

④ Rhodes stitch with two color strands 783.

⑤ Five straight stitches with two strands color 783.

⑥ Single straight stitch with two color strands 823.

Template size 100%

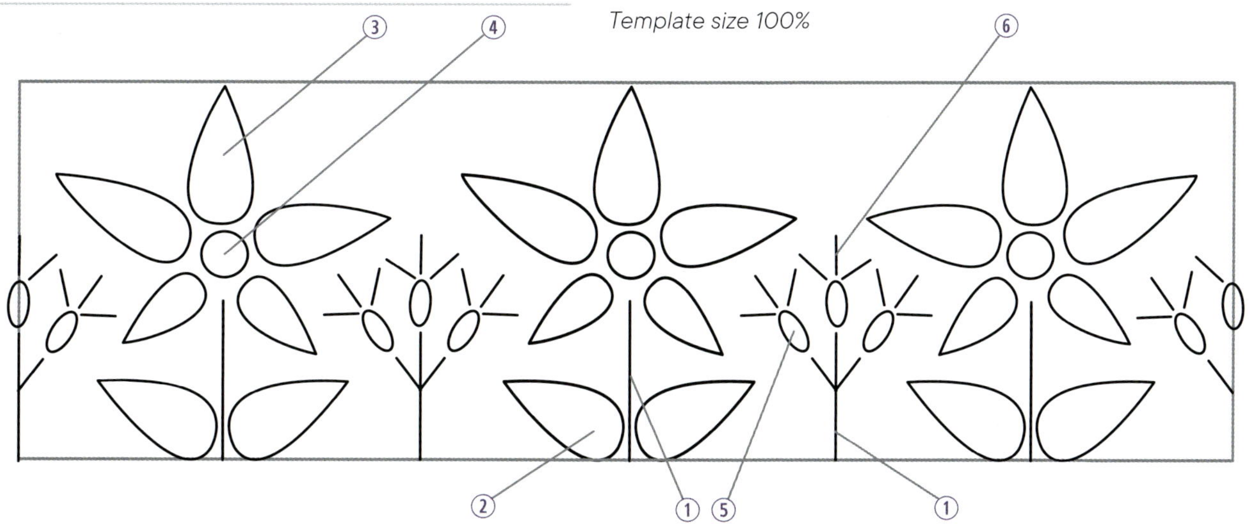

DISCOVER

① Backstitch with two strands color 823.

② Cretan stitch with two strands color 823.

③ Cretan stitch with two strands color 30.

④ Rhodes stitch with two color strands 783.

Template size 100%

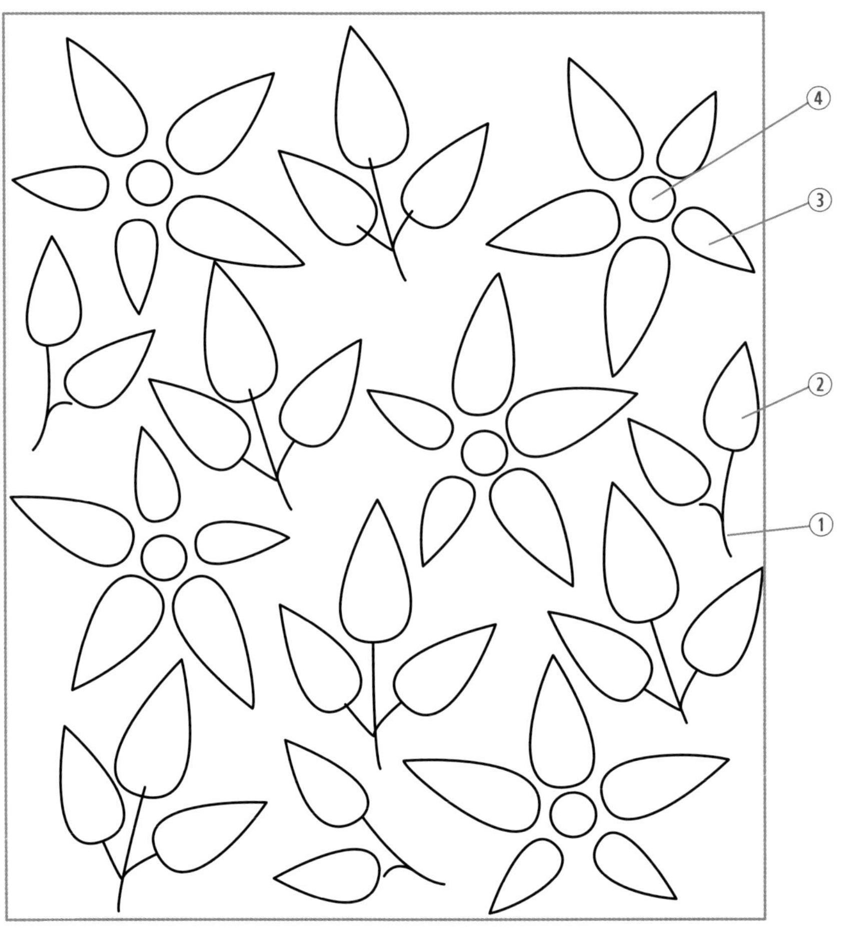

GOING THE EXTRA MILE

① Backstitch with two color strands 823.

② Cretan stitch with two strands color 823.

③ Cretan stitch with two strands color 30.

④ Rhodes stitch with two color strands 783.

⑤ Two-stranded feather stitch color 783.

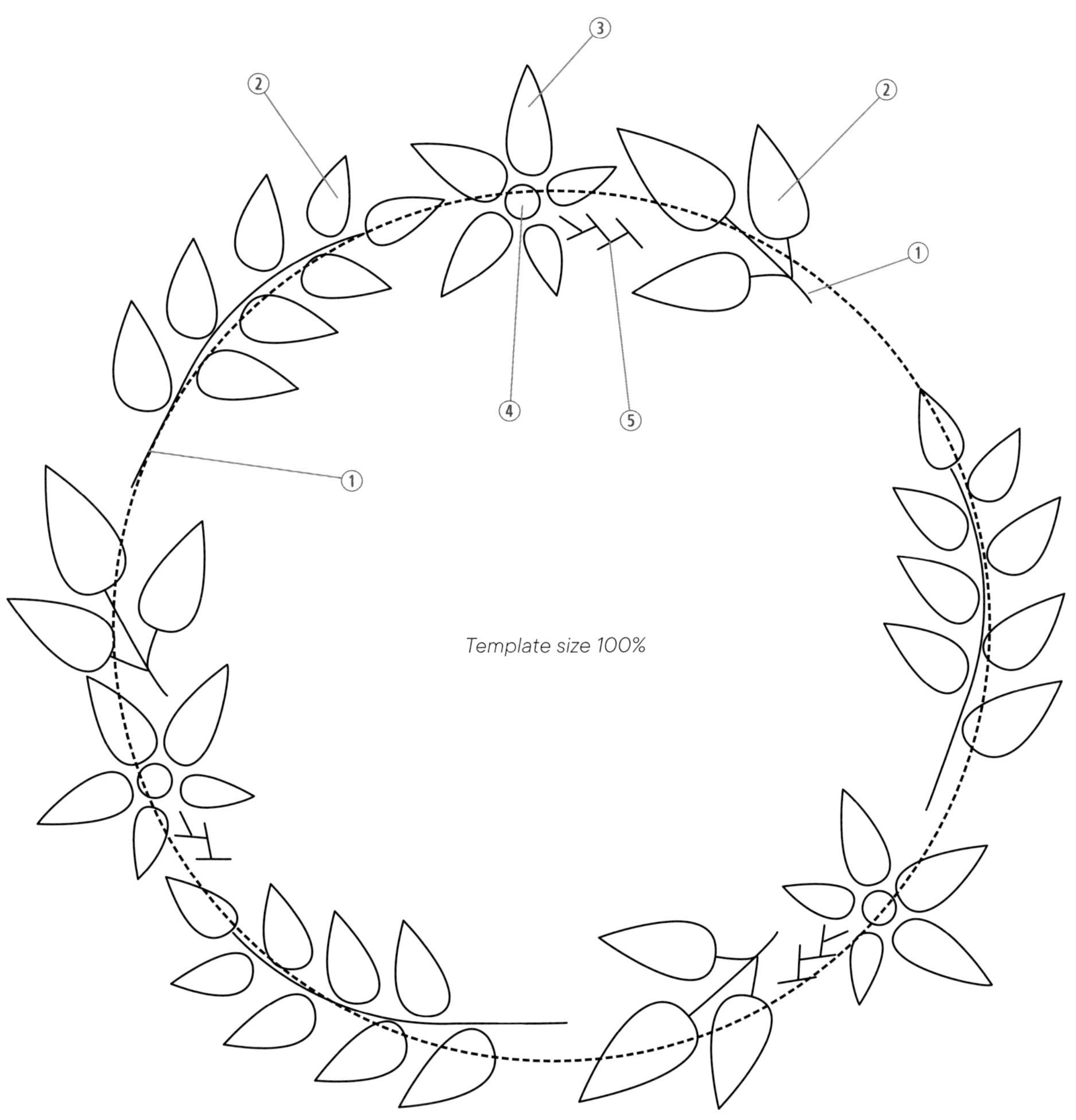

Template size 100%

FRIEZE

The photo of the design can be found on page 111.

Threads		
DMC Embroidery floss (stranded cotton)		03
DMC Color Variations embroidery floss		4180

Transfer the pattern as many times as necessary on the chosen surface.

① Coral stitch with two color strands 03.

② French knots with two color strands 4180.

③ Straight stitch with two color strands 03.

Tip

To embroider mimosa, replace Color Variations thread color 4180 with 4077 or 4075.

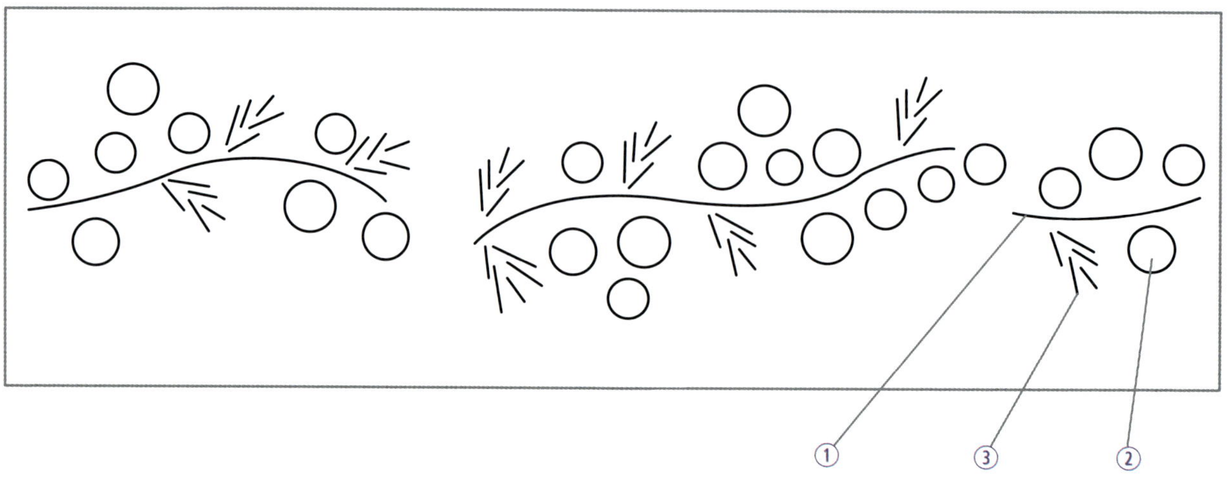

Template size 100%

DISCOVER

Thread	
DMC Embroidery floss (stranded cotton)	◯ 3865
Fabric	Pure cotton thread, color Pêche givrée (Stragier, ref. 0001 3711)
Pattern	Camelia dress by Ikatee

① Coral stitch with three strands of thread.

② French knots with three strands of thread.

③ Detached chain stitch with three strands of thread.

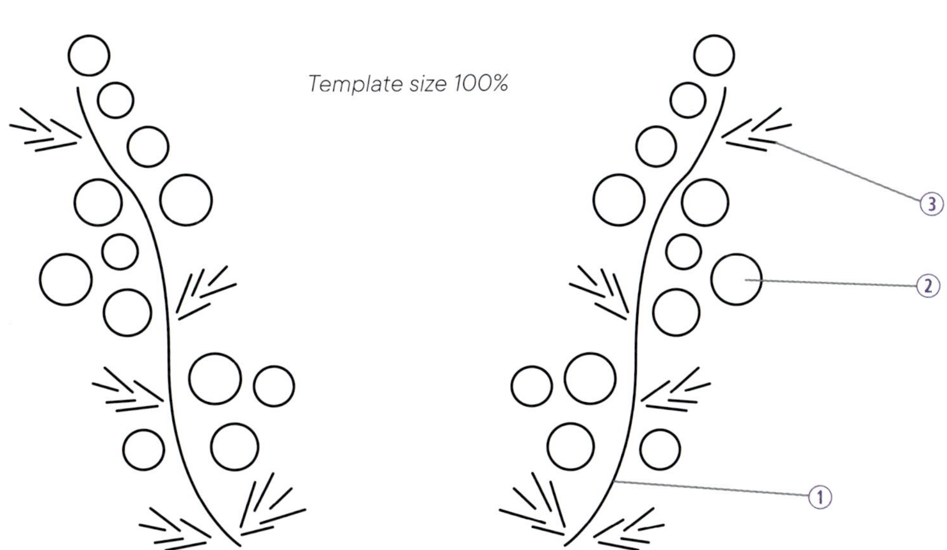

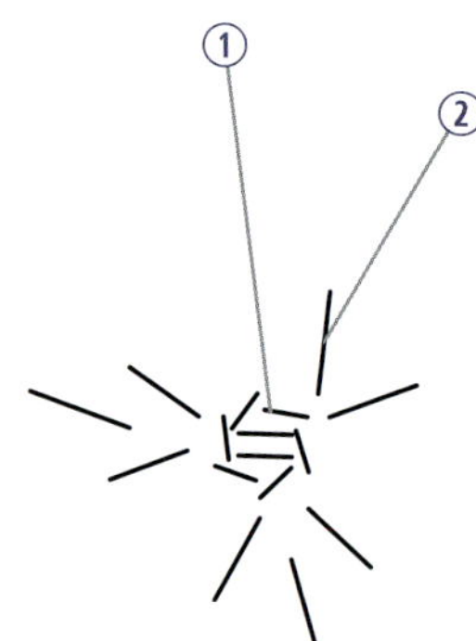

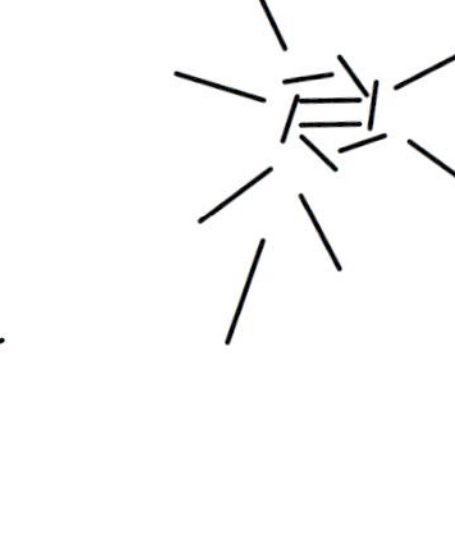

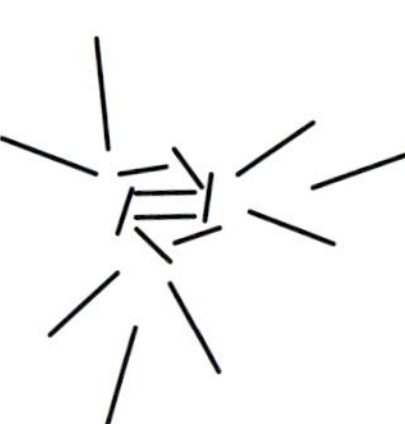

GOING THE EXTRA MILE

Threads	
DMC Embroidery floss (stranded cotton)	03 · 23 · 605
Metallic braid 4 Au Ver à Soie	002
Supplies	Soluble stabilizer

Tips for Good Embroidery

Take care to nest the first and last bullion knot together.

① Two side-by-side bullion knots with two color 605 strands at the center of the flower. Six bullion knots with two color 23 strands around the center.

② Detached chain stitch with two strands color 03 and a holding stitch on the end of the loops with metallic braid color 002.

WOVEN STITCHES

Pages 113 to 121

FRIEZE

The photo of the design can be found on page 120.

Threads	
DMC Embroidery floss (stranded cotton)	02 03 3771
DMC Color Variations embroidery floss	4120

Transfer the pattern as many times as necessary onto the chosen surface.

1. Stem stitch with two color strands 03.
2. Whipped wheel or spider stitch with two color strands 4120
3. Seven stitches thrown in herringbone with two strands of color 02.
4. French knots with two color strands 3771.

Template size 100%

DISCOVER

Threads	
DMC Embroidery floss (stranded cotton)	02 03 3689
Metallic braid 4 Au Ver à Soie (pour le bandeau seulement)	004
Fabric	Liberty Tana Lawn, color Capel-Petit Gris (Stragier, réf. 0363 3055K)
Supplies	Soluble stabilizer
Pattern of the headband	Personal creation

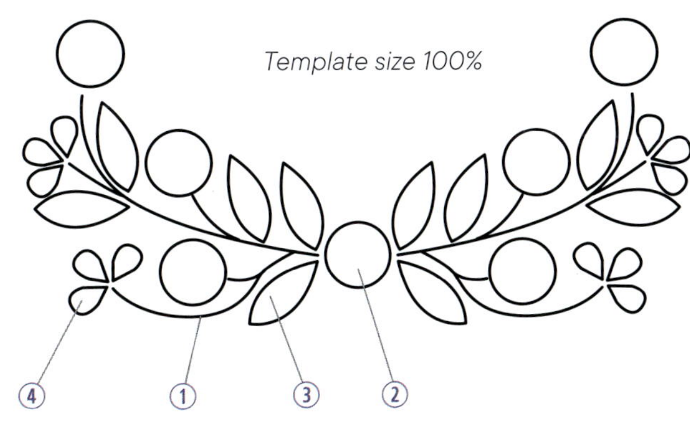

Template size 100%

Romper

① Backstitch with two color strands 03.

② Woven wheel stitch with two color strands 3689.

③ Diagonal satin stitch with two color strands 03.

④ Detached chain stitch with two color strands 02.

Headband

① Backstitch with metallic color thread 004.

② Woven wheel stitch with two color strands 3689.

③ Diagonal satin stitch with metallic color thread 004.

④ Detached chain stitch with two strands color 03. A holding stitch with metallic thread color 004 at the base of the loop.

GOING THE EXTRA MILE

Thread	
DMC Embroidery floss (stranded cotton)	***For the name Éloïse*** 824 3840 ***For the name Isaure*** 3328 3779 3830
Fabrics	Thin batting ***For the name Éloïse*** Lining and piping, UNE Mini Florie Ballet collection (Stragier, ref. 0001 8046) ***For the name Isaure*** Hespérides lining and piping, Mint-peach color (Stragier, ref. 0001 7510)
Supplies	Aïda cloth 7 stitches/cm, choice of colors Grid paper with small squares
Pattern	Personal creation

Tips for Good Embroidery

From the list of threads, choose two contrasting colors to form the cross.

1 Locate the front center of the future cover. The center of the cross is 8 cm from the top of the notebook. In width, it is centered on the front cover.

2 Transfer the drawing with a dissolvable pen.

3 Embroider the design with large, loose vertical straight stitches using six strands of embroidery floss.

Tips for Good Embroidery

Anchor threads on the back of the work (see page 42).

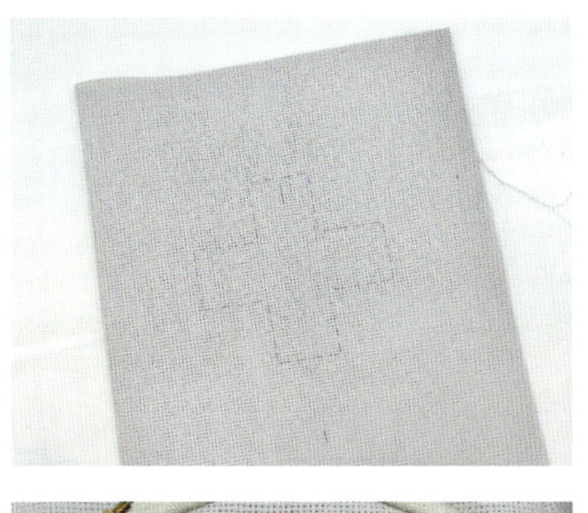

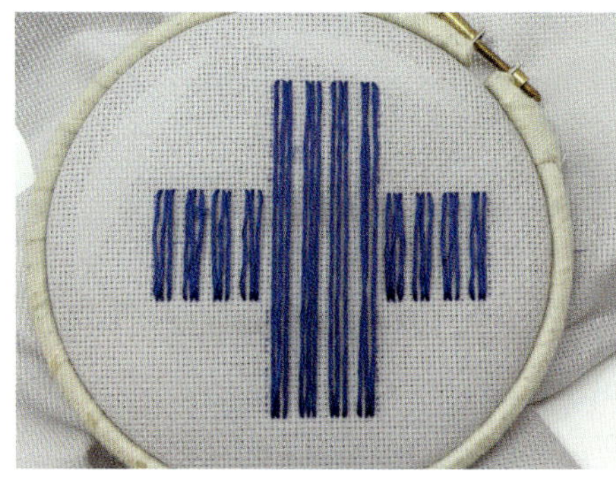

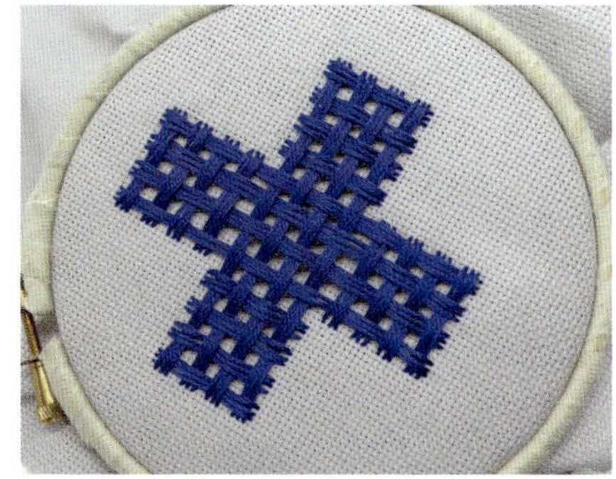

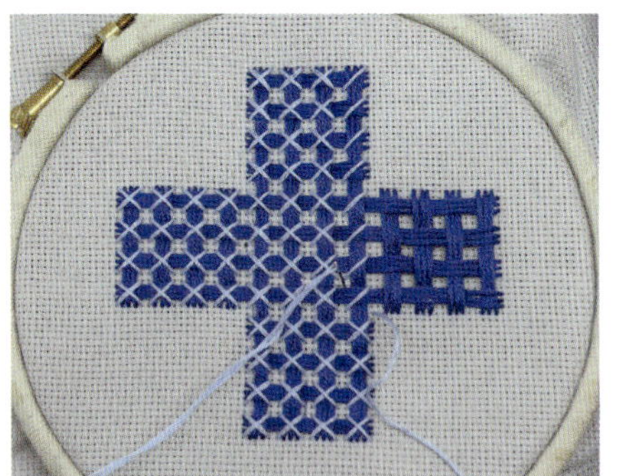

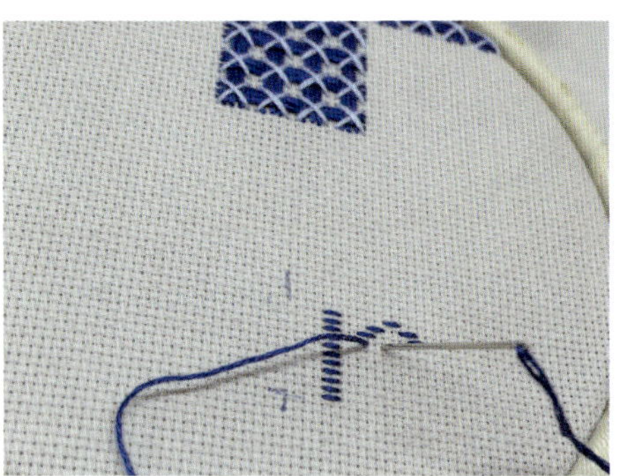

What You Need to Know

The squared sheet represents the diagram to follow: a 5 × 5mm square corresponds to a square (a point) on the Aïda cloth.

4 Weave the horizontal straight stitches, weaving through the vertical threads over/under in packs of three.

5 Embroider cross-stitches over each intersection with three strands of contrasting color.

6 On a sheet of squared paper, using the downloadable and printable alphabet book (see QR code on page 14), copy the letters of the first name. Locate the center of the letters to center them widthwise on the front of the cover. The base of the letters is 6 cm from the bottom of the cover.

7 Starting in the middle of the first name, stitch horizontal straight stitches with three strands in the color of your choice. Each straight stitch straddles two squares of Aïda cloth.

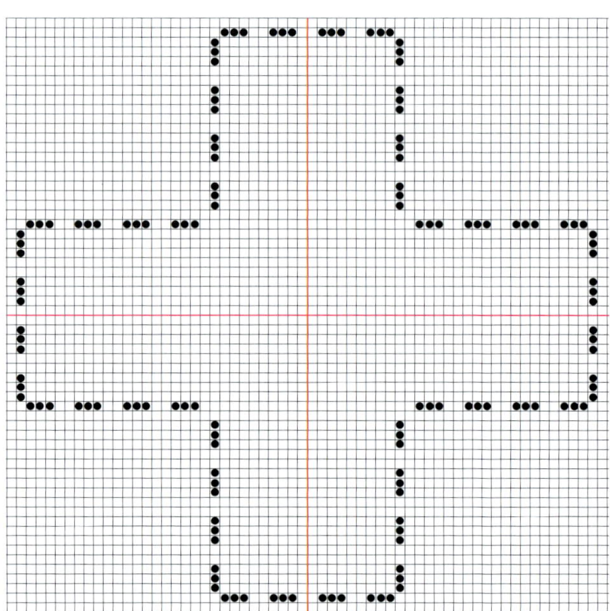

COUCHING STITCHES

Pages 122 to 126

DISCOVER

Thread	
DMC Embroidery floss (stranded cotton)	Écru 782
Fabric	Twill Tencel, cognac color (Stragier, ref. 0001 6999)
Pattern	Camelia dress by Ikatee

1 Draw a 5cm wide grid across the entire height, centered on the front center of the yoke. Space vertical and horizontal lines 1 cm apart.

2 Embroider single lattice with cross-stitches over each intersection. Start with long straight stitches to form the grid in both directions with six strands in ecru colors.

Tips for Good Embroidery

Work the straight stitches of the trellis back and forth to save thread on the back of the work.

3 Embroider a cross-stitch on each intersection with six ecru-colored strands.

4 In the center of each square, embroider a French knot with six strands in ecru.

5 Straddling the ecru, in the center of the sides of the squares, embroider a straight stitch with three strands of color 782.

Tips for embroidery

When working with couching stitches, use an embroidery hoop with a larger surface area than the embroidery. Plastic hoops with clips are ideal.

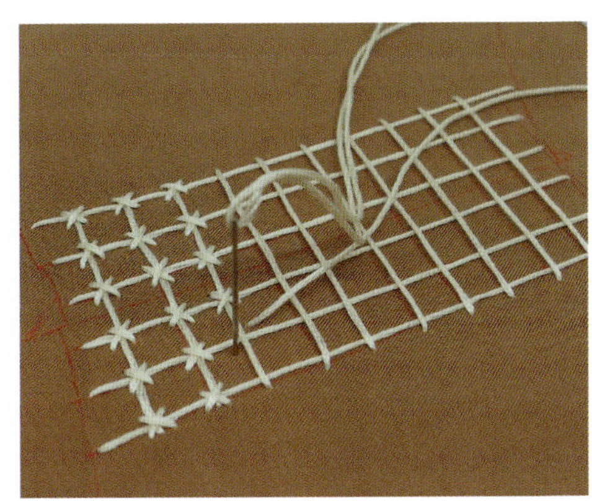

GOING THE EXTRA MILE

Thread	
DMC Embroidery floss (stranded cotton)	Écru 782 824
Fabric	Twill Tencel, color ink blue (Stragier, ref. 0001 6627)

1 Draw a lattice grid on the surface of the yoke. Space vertical and horizontal lines of 1 cm.

2 Next, embroider a lattice with holding stitches. Start with long straight stitches to form the lattice in both directions with six color strands 824.

Tips for Good Embroidery

Try to reduce the floats on the back of the work by working the trellis rows back and forth.

3 Stitch a diagonal holding stitch over each intersection with six ecru-colored strands. Work the diagonal stitches opposite each other on the second yoke.

4 Embroider a cross-stitch straddling every other square with six strands color 782. Stitch a smaller cross-stitch over the intersections of the straddling cross-stitches. Work in the same way on the second yoke, keeping the pattern symmetrical.

SATIN STITCHES

Pages 127 to 131

Tips for Good Embroidery

For each project, respect the direction of the stitches noted on the drawings.

FRIEZE

The photo of the design can be found on page 129.

Thread

DMC Embroidery floss (stranded cotton)	780	783

① Stem stitch with two color strands 783.

② Satin stitch with two color strands 783.

③ Satin stitch with two color strands 780.

Transfer the pattern as many times as necessary on the chosen surface.

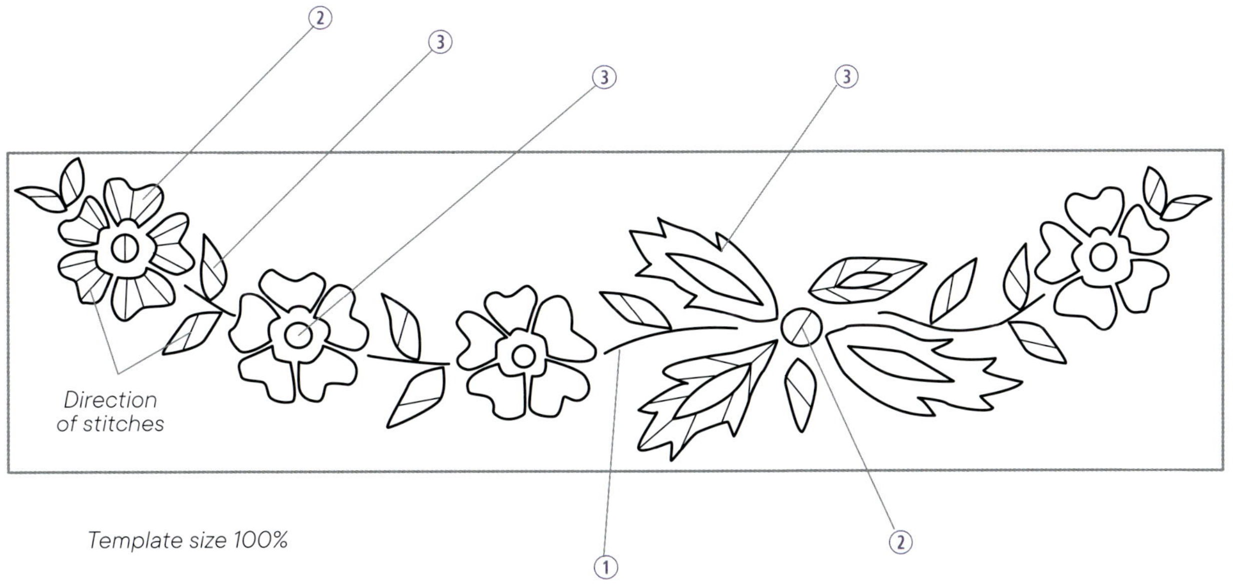

Template size 100%

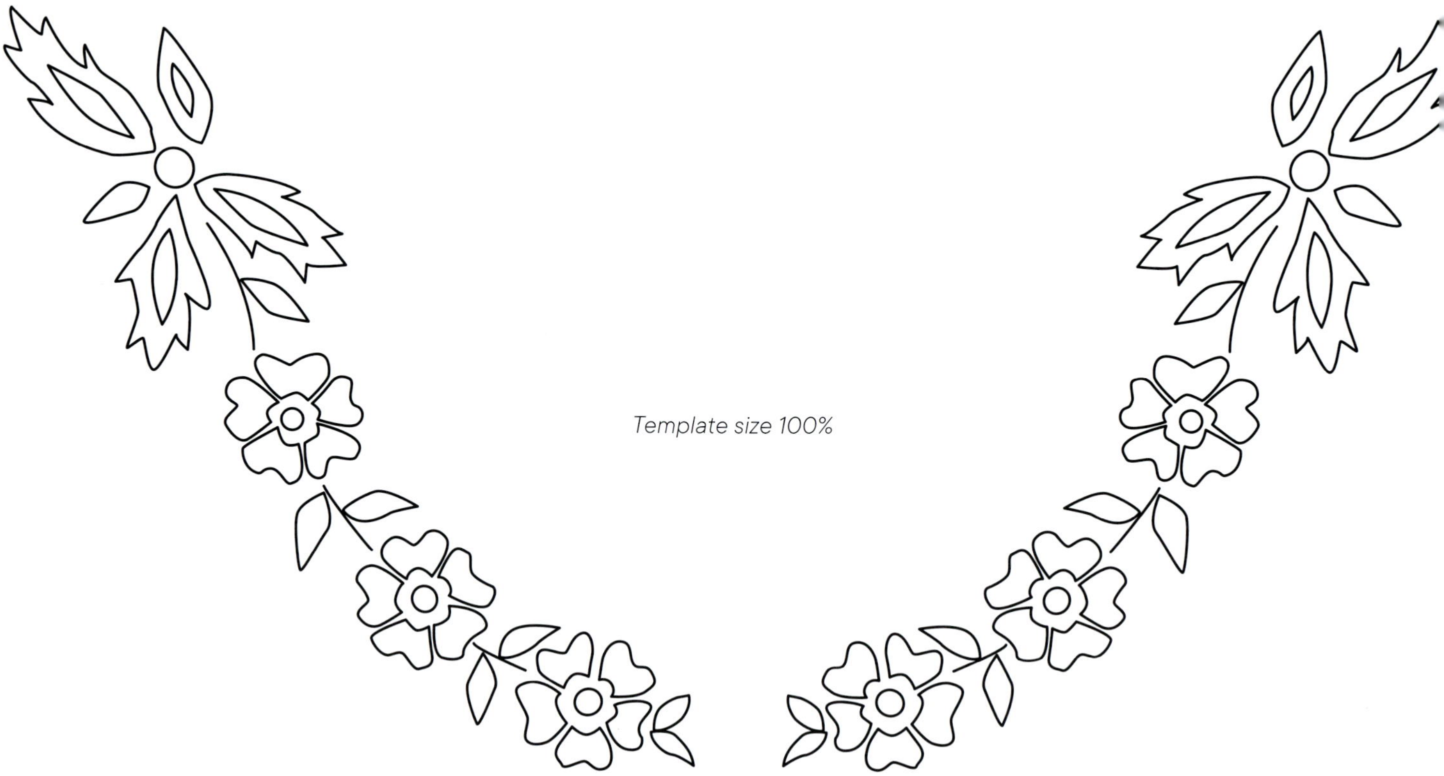

Template size 100%

DISCOVER

Thread	
Soie d'algers Au Ver à Soie	4636
Fabric	Cotton poplin, color White (Stragier, ref. 000 2390)
Pattern	Personal creation

① Stem stitch with two strands of thread.

② Satin stitch with two strands of thread.

③ Satin stitch with two strands of thread.

Signs of the Zodiac

Threads	
DMC Embroidery floss (stranded cotton)	312
Metallic braided 4 Au Ver à Soie	002

1. Stem stitch with two color strands 312.
2. Satin stitch with two color strands 312.
3. Stem stitch with metallic thread color 002.

Sweatshirt

Thread			
DMC Embroidery floss (stranded cotton)	301	452	632
	758	782	823
Supplies	Soluble stabilizer		

1. Satin stitch with two color strands 758.
2. Satin stitch with two color strands 301.
3. Satin stitch with two color strands 782.
4. Stem stitch with two color strands 632.
5. Stem stitch with two color strands 452.
6. Satin stitch with two color strands 823.

Template size 50%
1
2
3
1
6
Direction of stitches
2
3
3
4
5
Template size 100%

GOING THE EXTRA MILE

Thread	
DMC Embroidery floss (stranded cotton)	823 939
Fabric	Linen canvas, Caviar color (Stragier, ref. 0001 3755)
Pattern	Alex Mum blouse by Ikatee

① Satin stitch with two color strands 823.

② Satin stitch with two color strands 939.

③ Stem stitch with two color strands 823.

Tips for Good Embroidery

Embroidering with two very similar shades gives more relief to the design.

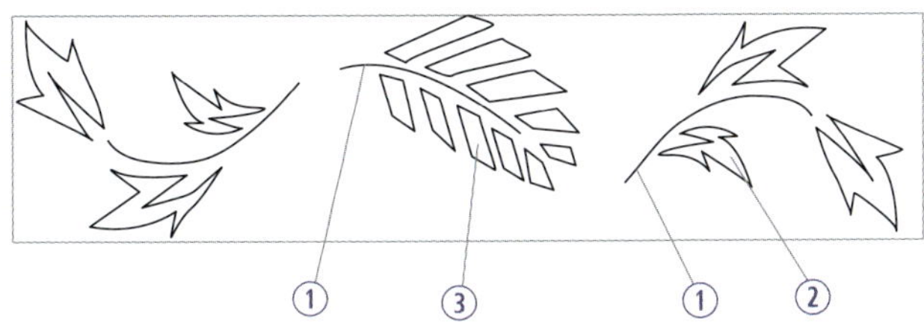

Template size 50%

Template size 50%

LONG AND SHORT STITCH

Pages 132 to 137

FRIEZE

The photo of the design can be found on page 136.

Thread

DMC Embroidery floss (stranded cotton)	17	355	561
	562	754	966
	3770	3778	3830

① Long and short stitch with a color strand 561, 562, and 966.

② Stem stitch with one strand color 561.

③ Shaded satin rows with a color strand 754, 3770, 3778, and 3830.

④ Rows of satin stitch with a color strand 355.

⑤ Three-strand French knots color 17.

Template sizes 100%

Embroidered notebook cover with two designs placed together

The notebook cover was embroidered by Ariane Andraud.

Thread

DMC Embroidery floss (stranded cotton)	10	11	12
	823	928	3813
	3816	3817	

① Long and short stitch blending colors 928, 3813, 3816, and 3817.

② Stem stitch with one strand color 3816.

③ Long and short stitch blending colors 10, 11, and 12.

④ Long and short stitch with color strand 823.

DISCOVER

Thread			
DMC Embroidery floss (stranded cotton)	17	355	562
	754	890	3778

Transfer the design on the ground fabric. Using another color, draw lines to guide the stitch direction for long and short stitch, which should converge toward the center of the flower.

① Three-strand color flat cord 17.

② Shaded satin rows with three color strands 355, 754, and 3778.

③ Diagonal satin stitch with three color strands 890.

④ Stem stitch with three color strands 890.

⑤ Stem stitch with three color strands 562.

⑥ Satin long and short stitch with three strands colors 890 and 562.

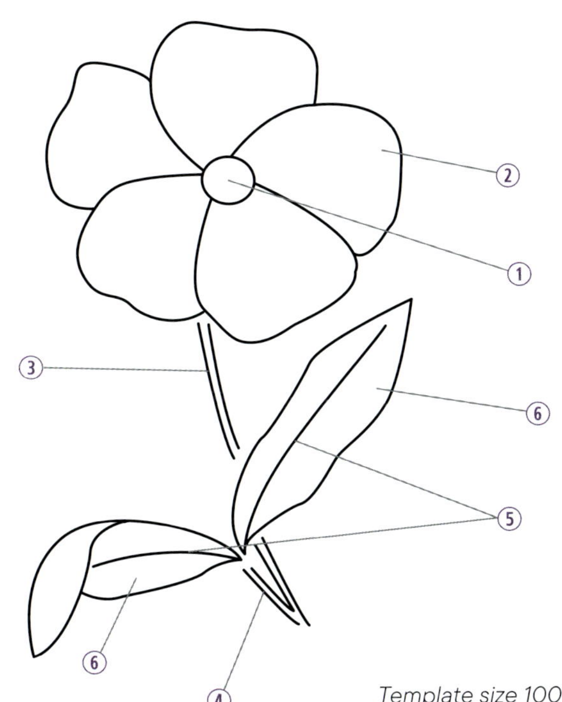

Template size 100%

LONG AND SHORT STITCH

GOING THE EXTRA MILE

Sweet peas

Thread	
DMC Embroidery floss (stranded cotton)	503, 676, 712, 738, 819, 961, 963, 991, 3716, 3813, 3831, 3832, 3865
Fabric	Soft Tencel jeans, Marine color (Stragier, ref. 0001 6735)
Pattern	Alex Mum dress by Ikatee

1 Embroider in long and short stitch.

- Leaves and sepals with two color strands 503, 991, and 3813.
- Flowers 1, 5, and 9 with two strands colors 819, 963, and 3865.
- Flowers 2, 7, and 12 with two strands colors 961, 3831, and 3832.
- Flowers 3, 8, and 11 with two strands colors 712, 676, and 738.
- Flowers 4, 6, and 10 with two strands colors 961, 963, and 3716.

2 Embroider stems and tendrils in stem stitch with two strands color 503.

Template size 50%

Peony

The peony was embroidered by Ariane Andraud.

Thread	
DMC Embroidery floss (stranded cotton)	01, 17, 23, 503, 601, 603, 605, 777, 924, 926, 927, 3813, 3816, 3817, 3350
Fabric	Linen Percale, colors Optique White (Stragier, ref. 0000 2666)
Pattern	Personal creation

- Petals 1 to 6 in long and short stitch blending colors 23, 601, 603, 605, 777, and 3350.
- Petal 4 turnover stitched in long and short blending colors 01, 23, and 605.
- Turnover of petal 5 in long and short stitch with colors 01 and 605.
- Petals 8 to 12 in long and short stitch with colors 601, 777, and 3350.
- Turnovers for petals 8–10 in long and short stitch with colors 01, 23, 601, 603, and 605.
- Turnovers for petals 11 and 12 in long and short stitch in colors 01, 23, and 605..
- Leaf 13 in long and short stitch blending colors 926, 927, 3813, 3816, and 3817.
- Leaf 14 in long and short stitch blending colors 503, 924, 926, 927, 3816, and 3817.
- Leaf 15 and 16 in long and short stitch with colors 503, 924, 926, 927, 3813, 3816, and 3817.
- Three-strand bullion knot for each congress cloth color 17.

Template size 50%

EMBROIDERED INSERTION STITCHES

Pages 140 to 143

What You Need to Know

The work is identical for right- and left-handed stitchers for whichever insertion stitch pattern is chosen.

DISCOVER

Thread	
Pearl cotton no. 8–S DMC	209 211
Fabric	Fil à fil, color Lilac clair (Stragier, ref. 0001 5194)
Supplies	A3 paper 80 g
Pattern	Personal creation

1 Hem the edges to be stitched: overlock the edge, turn under at 8 mm, and iron. Alternatively, make a very fine double-turned hem and then hem invisibly by hand.

2 Baste the two pieces to the sheet of paper, leaving a 5mm gap between the edges of the insertion stitching.

3 On the paper, using a pencil, mark every 5 mm. These will serve as a guide during embroidery.

4 Embroider a basic insertion stitch on alternating edges with color 211 and color 209 for basic insertion stitching.

5 Remove the paper and iron on the reverse side.

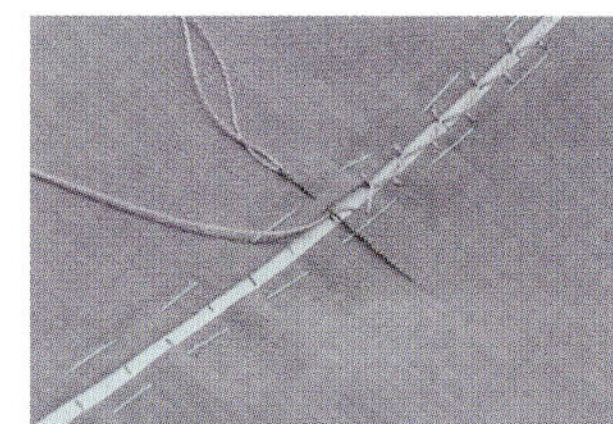

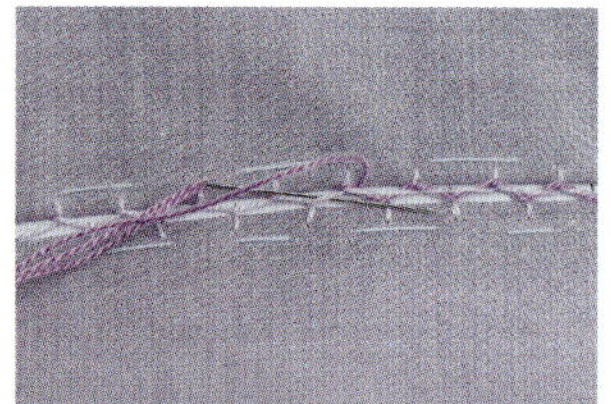

GOING THE EXTRA MILE

Thread	
Pearl cotton no. 8–S DMC	Écru
Fabric	Thread to thread, Cream (Stragier, ref. 0001 1765)
Supplies	Liberty Tana Long binding, color V (Stragier, ref. 0000 1663)
	Sheet of A3 paper 80 g
	Thread for basting
Patterns	Ida blouse by Ikatee
	Dakar Short by Ikatee

1 On the Ida pattern, remove 1 cm from the margin on the front panel 1b* and on the front panel 1*, at the seam joining these two pieces.

2 Cover the bib edge the diagonal binding and baste it on a sheet of paper.

3 Using a pencil, mark 5 mm from the edge all around the front. Pin the front to these marks, not forgetting to form the gathers, then pin the diagonal binding.

4 Temporarily remove the front from the paper sheet and stitch the binding by hand or sewing machine. Reposition the front, aligning the marks on the sheet, and baste.

Attention

Wheel 1c must not be cut or sewn.

5 On the paper, using a pencil, mark a mark every every 5 mm, to serve as a guide during embroidery.

6 With the pearl cotton, embroider a knotted insertion point, alternating each side.

7 Remove the paper and iron on the reverse side.

EMBROIDERING TEXT

Pages 144 to 146

DISCOVER

Thread	
DMC Embroidery floss (stranded cotton)	809
Fabrics	Cotton Percale, color White (Stragier, ref. 0000 2020): fabric A (12 × 70 cm: 2 times) Liberty Tana Lawn Queue for the Zoo, color G (Stragier, ref. 0363 4160 G): fabric B (48 × 28 cm: 3 times) Liberty Tana Lawn Pepper, color R (Stragier, ref. 0363 9010 R): fabric C (24 × 28 cm: 3 times)
Supplies	Silver lurex bias (Stragier, ref. 0001 0796): 3.5 m Gray and white sewing thread White microfiber fleece (Stragier, ref. 0001 8436): 70 × 100 cm
Pattern	Personal creation

Font : Snell roundhand

BE HAPPY MY BABY

Font : Andale Mono

Template size 50%

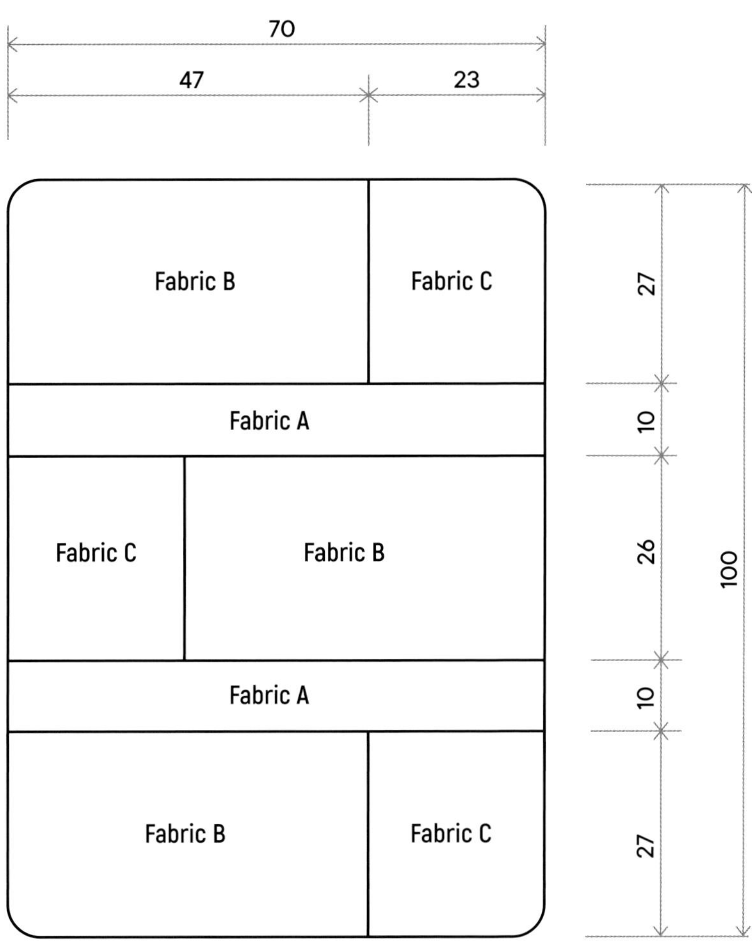

1. Transfer the chosen text on the white percale strips, ensuring that it is perfectly centered.
2. Embroider the text with two lines of chain stitch side by side using three strands of thread.
3. Sew the fabrics together like a patchwork quilt, following the pattern (finished dimensions: 100 × 70 cm).
4. 1 cm on each side, stitch white strips by hand or with a sewing machine.
5. Layer with the fleece and place the binding around the blanket.

What You Need to Know

The 1cm seam allowances are included in the pattern dimensions.

GOING THE EXTRA MILE

Thread	
DMC Embroidery floss (stranded cotton)	798
Fabric	Fine linen canvas, White (Stragier, ref. 0000 2589): 40 × 35 cm
Supplies	Strong cardboard: here, 28 × 20 cm for a 40 × 35 cm fabric Invisible white glue

Transfer the chosen text on the fabric, making sure it's perfectly centered and that horizontal lines are straight.

① Running stitch with three strands of thread.

② Backstitch (doubled in the wide parts of the of the letters) with two strands of thread.

③ Satin stitch with three strands of thread.

④ Chain stitch with two strands of thread.

⑤ Stem stitch (doubled in the wide parts of the letters) with two strands of thread.

⑥ Satin stitch with two strands of thread.

⑦ Satin stitch with two strands of thread.

⑧ Whipped backstitch with two strands of thread.

Template size 100%

Fonts used

Arthur — Cantoni basic

(1) (2)

(3)

(4) POURSUIS — Andale mono

(5) tes rêves — Cantoni basic

(1)

(6) décroche — Snell roundhand

(7) LA LUNE — Hobo std medium

(1)

(8) DES ETOILES — Andale mono

(2) plein les yeux — Snell roundhand

SMOCKING

Pages 147 to 156

The works in this chapter were produced by Karen Dobler Sauget, @liberty_smocks_addict

DISCOVER

Blouse

Thread	
Algiers silk Au Ver à Soie	3022
Fabric	Double cotton gauze, color Rose perle (Stragier, ref. 0001 4371)
Supplies	Pleating material (see page 148)
Pattern	See the table below

1 Cut the fabric, using the measurements in the table below.

What You Need to Know

For sizes 2 and 3, you'll need a single height of fabric for the front and back. For other sizes, you'll need two blouse heights: one fabric height for the back + one fabric height for the front.

		2 yrs	3 yrs	4 yrs	5 yrs	6 yrs	8 yrs	10 yrs	12 yrs
	Height (in cm)	86	98	104	110	116	128	140	152
	Chest circumference (in cm)	52	54	56	58	60	64	70	76
Fabric for the front	Width (in cm)	78	81	84	87	90	96	105	114
	Height (in cm)	32	33	34	35	37	40	43	47
	Length of front trim strip (in cm) × 5 cm	29	30	31	32	33	35	38	41
Fabric for the back	Width (in cm)	39	40.5	42	43.5	45	48	52.5	57
	Height (in cm)	34.5	35.5	36.5	37.5	39.5	42.5	45.5	49.5
	Elastic length (in cm) width: 12 mm	26	27	28	29	30	32	35	38
	Length of strap to tie (in cm) × 4 cm: cut 4	30	30	35	40	45	45	50	50
	Finished height excluding suspenders (in cm)	29	30	31	32	34	37	40	44

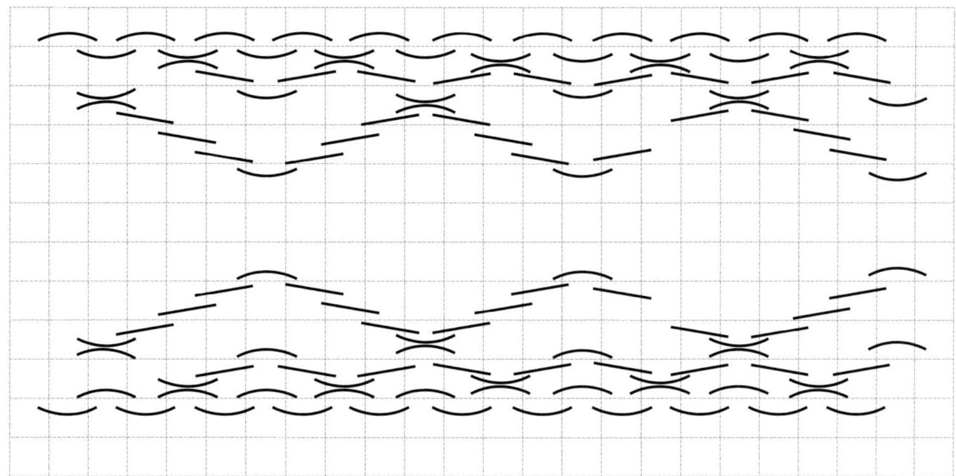

Smocking diagram

2 Smock the front.

> Starting 1 cm from the top of the front, pleat to a height of 6 cm, by hand or with a pleating machine, placing the gathering threads every 5 mm.

> Embroider with three strands of soie d'algers. Start with three rows of support row smocks on the reverse side. The first row should be 1 cm from the top edge, with subsequent rows 2.5 cm apart.

> On the right side, embroider 4 cm of smocking starting 1.5 cm from the top edge, following the diagram or your own design.

> Sew the facing: using the sewing machine, stitch right sides together 1 cm from the edge, stretching the work and distributing the smocks along the length of the facing. Stitch to the first support line on the back of the work.

What You Need to Know

At this stage, some of the gathering threads may break. Don't worry about this.

> Turn the facing edge under and hem, make a 1cm indentation, and hand-stitch on reverse side.

3 Make the back.

> At the top of the back, create the elastic tunnel: make an initial turnover at 1 cm, then turn again at 1.5 cm and stitch with the sewing machine. Pass the elastic through and secure it at each end with a few sewing machine stitches.

> Join the back and front with French seams on the sides.

> Hem the bottom: first turn at 1 cm, then 2 cm. Stitch or hand-sew the hem.

> Remove all gathering threads.

4 Make the four straps.

> Fold the straps like a bias and stitch them on the sewing machine or create an invisible seam by hand.

> Hand-tie each strap 6–7 cm from the sides of the dress.

Dress

Thread	
Soie d'algers Au Ver à Soie	3022
Fabric	Liberty Éloïse, color C (Stragier, ref. 0363 7015 C)
Supplies	Pleating material (see page 148)
Pattern	Personal creation

Repeat the steps for the blouse to make the dress. Please refer to the following size chart.

		2 yrs	3 yrs	4 yrs	5 yrs	6 yrs	8 yrs	10 yrs	12 yrs
	Height (in cm)	86	98	104	110	116	128	140	152
	Chest circumference (in cm)	52	54	56	58	60	64	70	76
Fabric for the front	Width (in cm)	78	81	84	87	90	96	105	114
	Height (in cm)	48	50	52	55	58	63	68	73
	Front trim strip length (in cm) × 5 cm	29	30	31	32	33	35	38	41
Fabric for the back	Width (in cm)	39	40.5	42	43.5	45	48	52.5	57
	Height (in cm)	50.5	52.5	54.5	57.5	60.5	65.5	70.5	75.5
	Elastic length (in cm) width: 12 mm	26	27	28	29	30	32	35	38
	Length of strap to be tied (in cm) × 4 cm: cut 4 off	30	30	35	40	45	45	50	50
	Finished height excluding straps (cm)	45	47	49	52	55	60	65	70

GOING THE EXTRA MILE

Thread	
Soie d'algers Au Ver à Soie	● 4636
Fabric	White (Stragier, ref. 0000 0148)
Supplies	Pleating material (see page 148) Tissue paper
Pattern	Personal creation

1 Modify the sleeve pattern according to the diagram below. For example, for an 18cm cuff, modify the sleeve to obtain 54 cm to pleat.

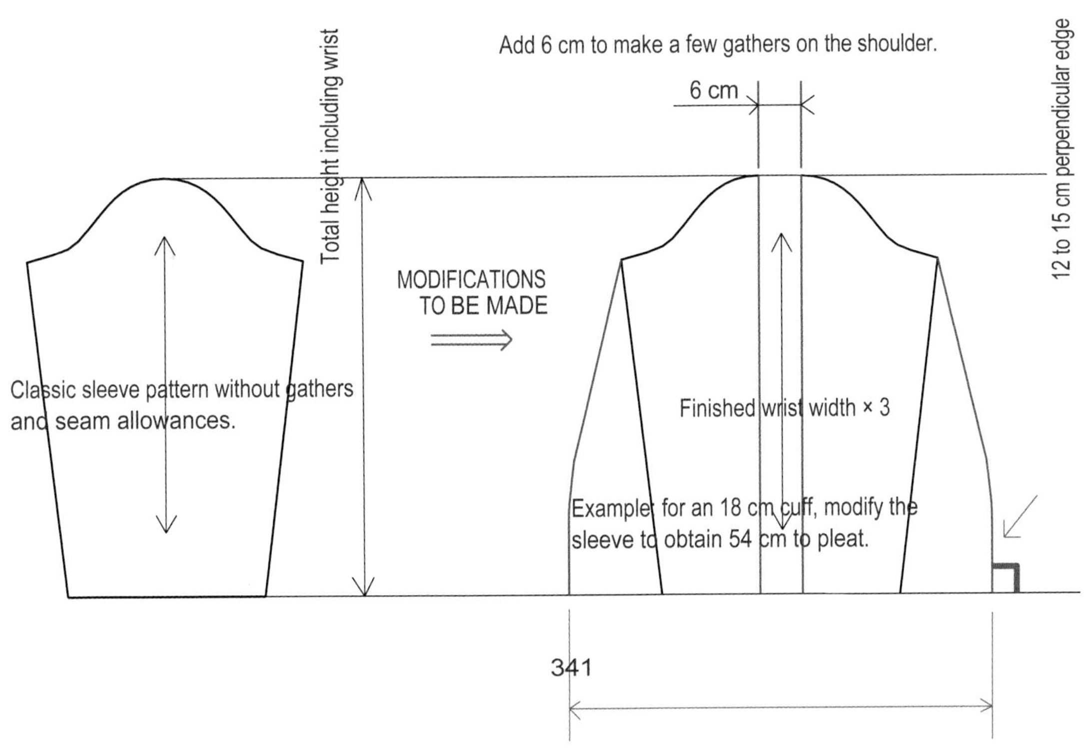

> **Attention**
>
> **Remove the seam allowances before making the pattern modifications and replace them before cutting the fabric.**

2 Once the fabric has been cut, hem the cuffs by hand by 0.5 cm.

3 Starting 4 cm from the edge of the wrist, pleat to a height of 3 cm, by hand or with a pleating machine, placing gathering threads every 5 mm.

4 Embroider with three strands of soie d'algers. Start with three rows of support row smocks on the wrong side. The first row should be 4 cm from the edge of the cuff on the first gathering thread, with subsequent rows 1.5 cm apart.

5 On the right side, embroider the smocks following the diagram below or your own design.

6 Sew the sleeve seam.

7 Remove the gathering threads.

8 Adjust the sleeve head to adapt it to fit the armhole.

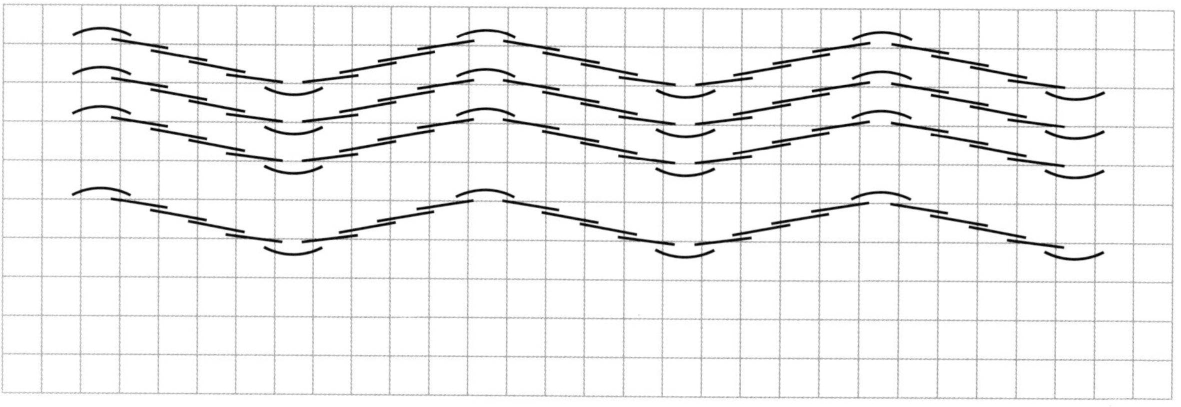

Smocking diagram

EMBROIDERING WOOL

Pages 157 to 166

FRIEZE

The photo of the design can be found on page 165.

Thread	
Saint-Pierre wool Ets J. Toulemonde	645 360 377
Supplies	Soluble stabilizer

Transfer the pattern as many times as necessary onto the soluble stabilizer and stick it onto the fabric.

① Rhodes stitch with four strands colors 360 or 377.

② Backstitch with two strands color 645.

③ Detached chain stitch with two strands color 645.

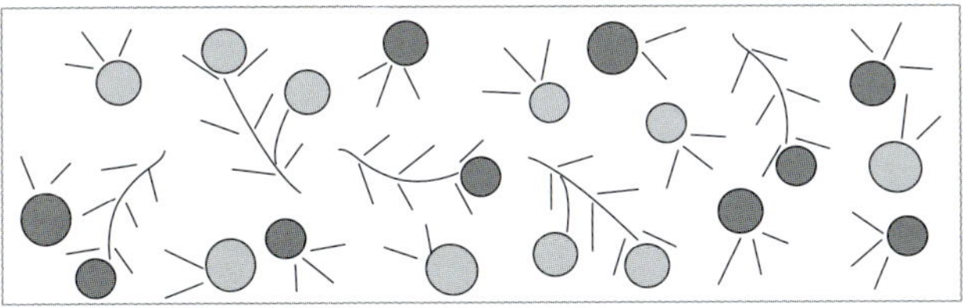

Template size 50%

DISCOVER

Collar

Thread	
Saint-Pierre wool Ets J. Toulemonde	565 118 422
Supplies	Soluble stabilizer

Modify the shape of the frieze to fit the neckline of the garment.

① Satin stitch with four strands color 422 or 565.

② Backstitch with two strands color 118.

③ Detached chain with two strands color 118.

GOING THE EXTRA MILE

Hat

Thread	
Laine Colbert DMC	7005, 7853, 7760, 7852, 7221
Supplies	Wool needle Grid paper

1 Knit the entire hat in jersey or buy one made from a coarse wool.

2 On graph paper, prepare the grid of the word you wish to embroider, using the letters to download and print (see QR code page 14).

3 On the right side of the jersey stitch, using the color of your choice, embroider letter after letter in knit stitch. Change color with each letter.

Cardigan

Thread	
Laine Colbert DMC	Écru
Supplies	Soluble stabilizer

① Two bullion knots for the center of each flower.

② Satin stitch for flowers and leaves.

Template size 100%

Scarf

Threads	
Laine Colbert DMC	7852, 7853, 7760, 7221, 7928, 7005
Wool Saint-Pierre Ets J. Toulemonde	360, 472
Fabrics	Double cotton gauze, Marine color (Stragier, ref. 0001 4380) Double cotton gauze, color Rose perle (Stragier, ref. 0001 4371) for lining
Supplies	Soluble stabilizer
Pattern	Personal creation

1 Transfer the pattern on the stabilizer.

2 Iron the double navy gauze to smooth it out.

3 Fix the stabilizer in a corner of the double marine gauze, 3 cm from the edges.

4 Embroidery

① Satin stitch with color 7005.

② French knots with four strands color 360.

③ Satin stitch for the leaf and stitching for the stem with color 7928.

④ Detached chain stitch with color 7760 for the petals and a straight stitch with four strands in color 472 for the central vein.

⑤ Sheaf stitch with color 7221.

⑥ Backstitch with four strands color 472 for stems and French knot with color 7852 for flowers.

⑦ Backstitch with four strands color 472 for stems and French knot with color 7221 for flowers.

5 Dissolve the stabilizer and let the work dry flat.

Template size 100%

Pages 167 to 174

FRIEZE

Thread	
Au Chinois glove thread	302
Beads and sequins	80 tubes Miyuki Bugles 6 mm, color Gold Silver
	71 Swarovski 4mm round beads, Topaz color
	11 Swarovski sew-on bezels 4 × 4 mm, Topaz color
	7 Swarovski sew-on bezels 6 × 6 mm, Topaz color
	Sequins Ø 5 mm, color Bronze satin
Fabric	Velours lisse miracle, color Marine (Stragier, ref. 0000 6608)
Supplies	Wooden or rectangular plastic embroidery frame
	Soluble stabilizer
Pattern	Cirri de République bag du Chiffon

Quantities are given for a 16cm long design.

1 Transfer the pattern as many times as necessary onto the stabilizer.

2 Stretch the fabric on the embroidery frame and stick the stabilizer to the fabric.

3 Place the beads and sequins.

① Single bugle beads to the backstitch.

② Overlapping sequins on the outer circle and then on the on the inner circle of flowers.

③ 6mm sew-on bezel crystals in the center of the flower.

④ Round beads in 9-by-9 couched lines and 4 and 4 for the ends.

⑤ 4mm beads at the end of each zigzag point.

4 Once the embroidery is finished, do not remove it from the frame, and gently dissolve the stabilizer under the shower. Leave the work to dry flat and taut, so that it remains perfectly flat.

Tip for good embroidery

Tuck the last sequin under the first to continue the overlapping pattern around the circle.

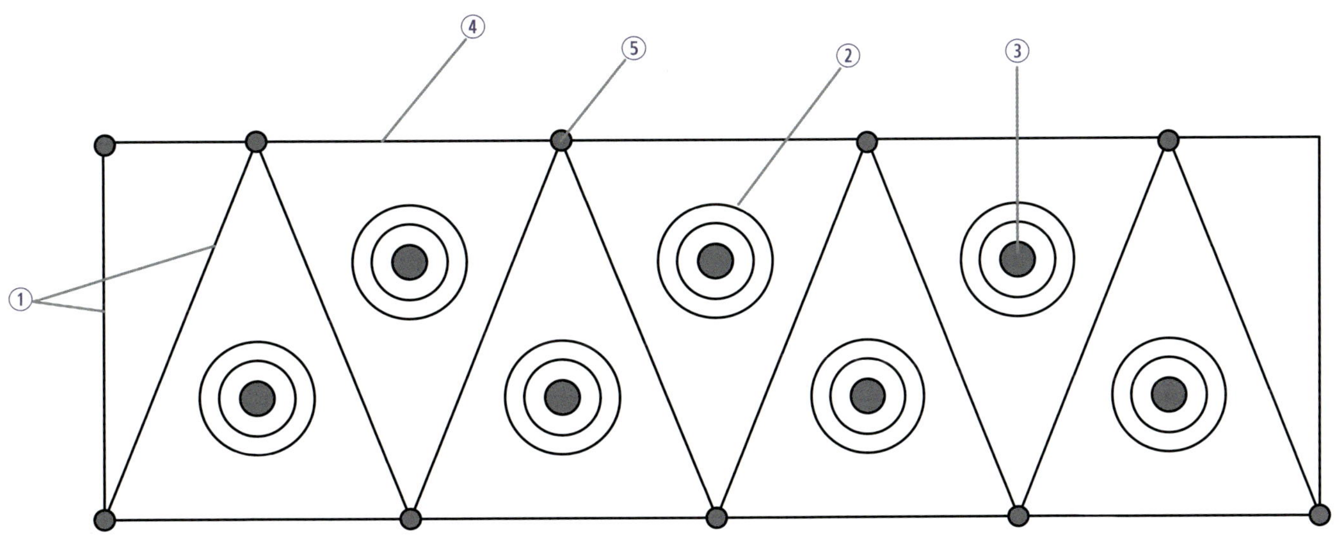

Template size 100 %

DISCOVER

Feather

Threads	
For the ocher version	
Metallic braided 4 Au Ver à Soie	002
DMC Embroidery floss (stranded cotton)	780 782 783
For the terracotta version	
Metallic braided 4 Au Ver à Soie	027
DMC Embroidery floss (stranded cotton)	918 920 921
Glove thread Au Chinois	302
Beads	*For the ocher version* 80 Miyuki Délicas 11/0 beads, Ochre DB1101 33 tubes Miyuki Bugles 3 mm, Gold color *For the terracotta version* 80 Miyuki Délicas 11/0 beads, pink DB1837 33 tubes Miyuki Bugles 3 mm, Gold color
Fabric	Silk organza, color Shale (Stragier, ref. 0000 2215) : 15 × 15 cm
Supplies	Textile glue Felt: 10 × 5 cm Sewing thread to match the embroidery Paintbrush Dissolvable black pen Brooch pin 38 mm long

1 Transfer the feather pattern on the organza.

2 Embroider and attach beads and sequins.

① Two rows in stem stitch with metallic thread.

② Lay 45 pearls along the topside of the central vein.

③ Place as many pearls as necessary on the veins.

④ Lay as many bugle beads as necessary on the veins.

⑤ Satin stitch with two strands of the darkest embroidery floss.

Tips for Good Embroidery

To cover the design perfectly, tuck the needle at an angle under the beads and bugles.

⑥ Satin stitch with two medium-sized strands of embroidery floss.

⑦ Satin with two strands of light embroidery floss.

3 Finish with a few French knots, using metallic thread on the satin-stitched areas.

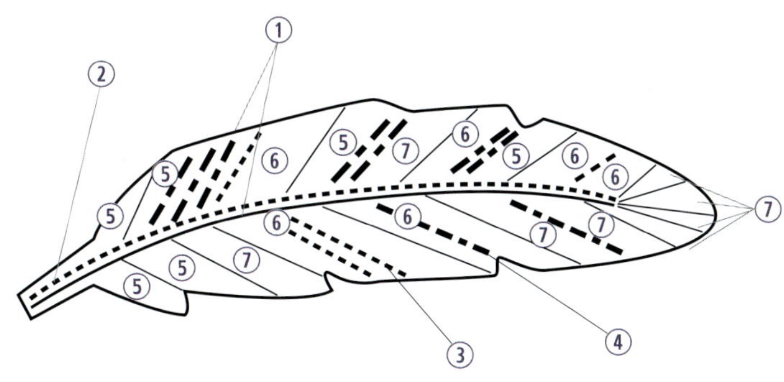

Template size 100%

Assembly for all the pins in this book

1 Using textile glue, carefully glue the back of the embroidery, covering the full size of brooch. Leave to dry overnight.

2 Cut the organza 8 mm from the outer edges of the embroidery. Clip or trim this seam allowance. Fold back all the way around and glue. Leave to dry.

What You Need to Know

When the width of the embroidery is small, it is necessary to trim the 8 mm to prevent the organza from protruding.

3 On the reverse side of the felt, use the embroidery to draw the shape for the back.

4 Cut two small slits to the length of the brooch pin. Open the pin and pass the ends through the slits. Hand-stitch between the felt and the pin back, in the holes.

5 Glue the felt to the back of the embroidery.

6 If necessary, trim the felt. Stitch buttonhole stitches or an overcast stitch with metallic thread (or a thread coordinated with the felt or embroidery).

Sweater

Embroidery by Guilaine Millour.

Thread	
Wool Saint-Pierre Ets J. Toulemonde, matching color creation	
Beads and sequins	*All sew-on stones are Swarowski.* 25 x 5mm bugle beads, Silver color 9 shuttle cabochons 18 × 9 mm, color Denim Blue 7 shuttle cabochons 12 × 6 mm, Silver Night color 7 drop cabochons 12 × 7 mm, Crystal color 4 drop cabochons 12 × 7 mm, color Denim Blue 9 sew-on rhinestones 4 mm, Crystal color 7 sew-on rhinestones 3 mm, Crystal color 5 sew-on rhinestones 6 mm, Crystal color 2 round stones 8 mm, Crystal color 1 round stone 12 mm, color Denim Blue
Supplies	Soluble stabilizer

Sew the elements one by one with Saint-Pierre wool a few stitches at a time, following the pattern of the beads.

Attention

Garments embroidered with Swarovski sew-on stones should be handwashed only to prevent breakage.

Template size 50%

1 Round stone 12 mm Denim Blue

2 8mm Crystal round stones

3 Drop cabochons 12 × 7mm Crystal

4 Drop cabochons 12 × 7mm Denim Blue

5 Shuttle cabochons 18 × 9mm Denim Blue

6 Shuttle cabochons 12 × 6mm Silver Night

7 Sew-on rhinestones 6 mm

8 Sew-on rhinestones 4 mm

9 Sew-on rhinestones 3 mm

10 / Silver tubes

GOING THE EXTRA MILE

Embroidery by Guilaine Millour

Threads	
Metallic braided 4 Au Ver à Soie (3 coils)	002
Au Chinois glove thread	302
Beads and sequins	66 Swarovski 4mm sew-on rhinestones, Topaz color 34 bicones in 5mm Swarovski crystal, Smoked Topaz color 31 6000 Swarovski drops 11 × 5.5 mm, Topaz color 33 Swarovski sew-on rhinestones, 5 mm, Topaz color 3mm cupped sequins from Beads & Co, color Doré Pail–011 Miyuki Délicas beads, color 11/0 DB 0042 (for setting drops) Miyuki Délicas beads, color 11/0 DB 0181 (to embroider with bowls)
Fabrics	Silk organza, navy blue (Stragier, ref. 0000 2222) Miracle smooth velvet, navy (Stragier, ref. 0000 6608)
Supplies	Textile glue Navy blue sewing thread Wooden embroidery frame large enough to embroider the entire collar (inner circumference: 45 cm, width: 17 cm) Paintbrush Pilot "Super Color permanent" White pen (caution: it does not erase) 2 small hooks and eyes
Pattern	Personal creation

Tips for Good Embroidery

It is imperative to create a sample in the final fabric first. The embroidery pattern must then be adapted and redesigned according to this canvas. The top edge of the embroidery design must match that of

1 Transfer the embroidery design on the organza. .

2 Embroider and attach beads and sequins.

① Embroider three rows together in stem stitch with metallic thread.

② Embroider five rows together in stem stitch with metallic thread.

③ Place three rhinestones on the middle band: thread together on the needle a 4mm rhinestone, a 5mm rhinestone in line with the A markings (secure with several stitches), and a 4mm rhinestone.

④ Place a bicone on the marks B and align the holes along the design line.

⑤ Place four needles of cupped sequins and beads color 0181 between two marks A: exit at C1, then thread one cupped sequin (catching it on the hollow side), three beads, and one cupped sequin (catching it on the curved side) onto the needle. Stitch at D1. Repeat on C2 and D2, C3 and D3, and C4 and D4.

⑥ Place a drop with color 0042 beads on marks A: exit at A, then thread three beads, a drop, and three beads together on the needle. Transfer to A. To secure the drop, thread the needle through all these elements a second time.

⑦ Place color 0181 cupped sequins and beads side by side: exit at E, then thread one cupped sequin (catching it on the hollow side), three beads, and one cupped sequin (catching it on the curved side) onto the needle. Stitch in F shape. Repeat to cover this area. Cupped sequins should be placed side by side, without overlapping.

4 Lightly glue the back of the work, extending past the sides of the collar. Leave to dry overnight.

5 Cut 1 cm around the collar, notch, and fold over to the wrong side, holding in place with large stitches, using the navy blue double thread.

6 Blindstitch the neckline by hand.

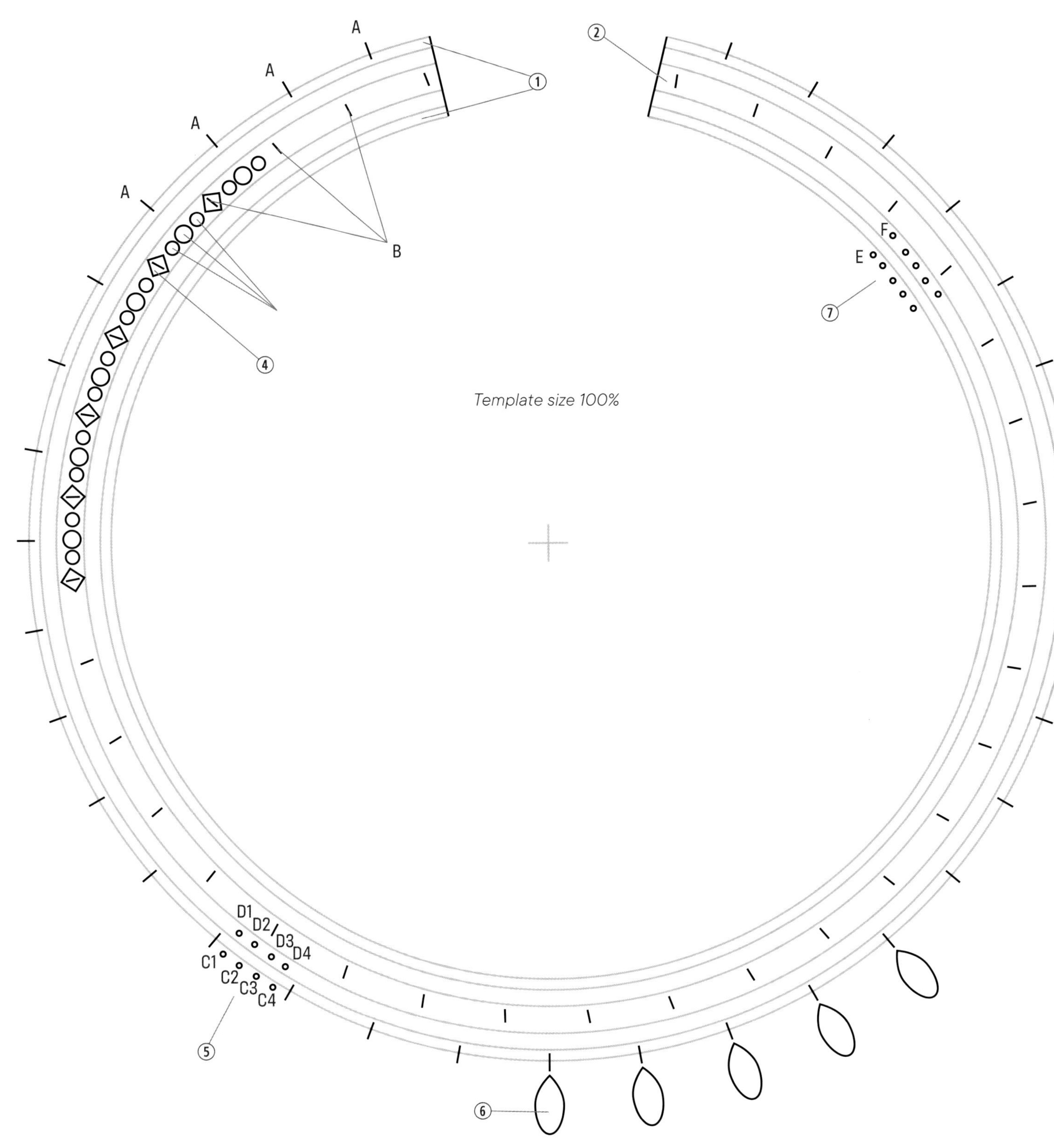

Template size 100%

RIBBON EMBROIDERY

Pages 175 to 183

FRIEZE

The photo of the design can be found on page 182.

Threads	
Soie d'alger Au Ver à Soie	2521
Metallic braid 4 Au Ver à Soie	002
Silk ribbons for embroidery	
Au Ver à Soie, width 4 mm	1840 920

Transfer the pattern as many times as necessary onto the chosen surface.

Tips for Good Embroidery

If the fabric is soft or delicate (such as silk), it is necessary to stabilize it on the back before embroidering (see page 175 for details).

① Straight stitch with ribbon color 920.

② Three-strand French knots, color 2521. Four to five knots per flower center with metallic thread.

③ Ribbon stitch with 1840 color ribbon. Straight stitch at the base of each leaf with metallic thread.

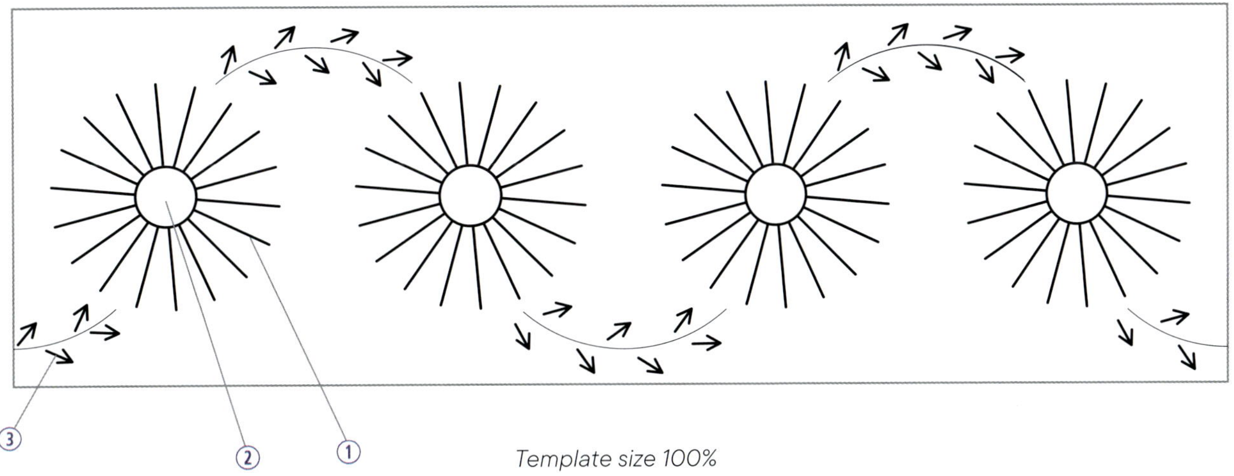

Template size 100%

DISCOVER

Threads		
DMC Embroidery floss (stranded cotton)	3770	
Metallic braid 4 Au Ver à Soie	002	
Silk ribbons for embroidery		
Au Ver à Soie, width 4 mm: 3 m	3596	
Au Ver à Soie, width 13 mm : 3 m	White	
Beads	Rocailles Toho 11/0, color Galvanized Starlight	
	Rocailles 11/0, color White	
Supplies	Ground fabric of your choice: 35 × 35 cm	
	Embroidery hoop larger than the embroidery area	

① French knots with three strands in color 3770 for the center. A few knot stitches with metallic thread in the heart of the flower.

② Straight stitch with three strands color 3770 for the seven branches of the wheel stitch. Wheel stitch with 7mm white ribbon.

③ Wheel stitch with 4mm pink ribbon. Place a golden pearl at the center of each small rose.

④ Stem stitch with metallic thread for stems.

⑤ Ribbon stitch with 7mm pink ribbon. Place a pearl at the base of the flower.

⑥ Straight stitch with 4mm pink ribbon.

⑦ Ribbon stitch with 7mm white ribbon. Straight stitch in each leaf with metallic thread.

⑧ Straight stitch with the 4mm pink ribbon. Place three white pearls at the center of each flower.

⑨ Apply gold beads with metallic thread scattered all over the ground.

⑩ Secure with a few stitches in the middle of the white ribbon, 13 mm for wedding rings.

⑪ Embroider the text of your choice.

Once the iron is hot, carefully iron around and under the embroidery, without flattening it, to remove pen marks. Mount the cushion flat on a cardboard hoop (here, 18 cm in diameter). Refer to the velvet board technique on page 25.

Template size 50%

GOING THE EXTRA MILE

Threads	
Metallic braid 4 Au Ver à Soie	002
Au Chinois glove thread	White
Silk ribbons for embroidery	
Au Ver à Soie, width 7 mm: 3 m	3596
Au Ver à Soie, width 13 mm: 1.5 m	White
Beads and sequins	Rocailles Toho 11/0; color is Galvanized Starlight Sequins 5 mm, colors Matte Gold
Supplies	Choice of fabric backing: 140 × 6 cm

1 Transfer the pattern as many times as necessary onto the chosen surface.

2 Embroidery.

① Make the gathered flowers: cut 25 cm of white ribbon and follow the instructions on page 181.

② Using a double needle of white thread, place the pearls and sequins in the center of the flower, stitching one pearl and one sequin with each stitch.

③ Embroider a ribbon stitch with 7mm white ribbon and a straight stitch in each leaf with metallic thread.

3 Scatter golden pearls with metallic thread.

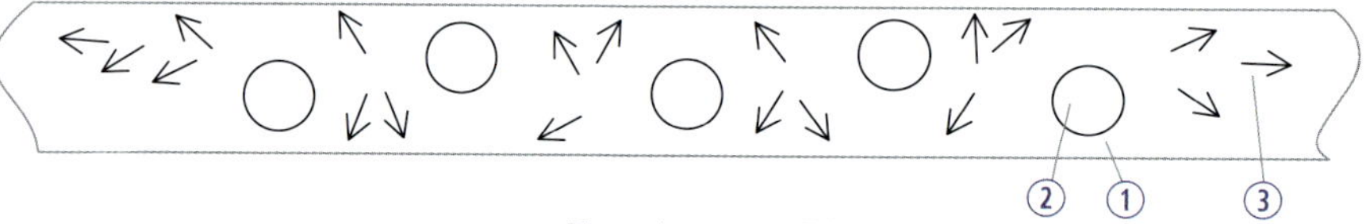

Template size 50%

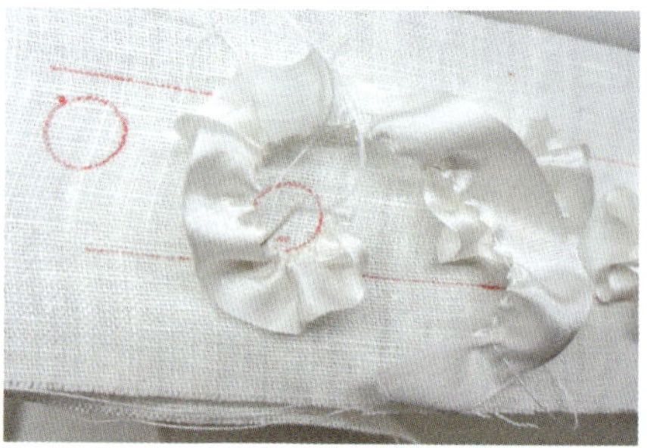

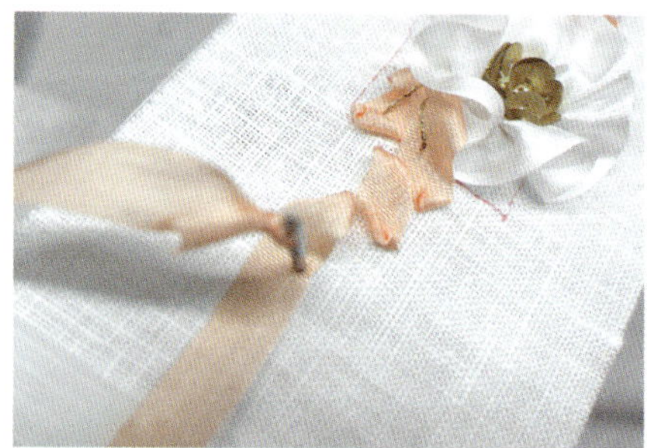

Tips for Good Embroidery

Take care not to flatten the ribbon fullness.

GOLDWORK EMBROIDERY

Pages 184 to 203

PATTERN

Thread	
Au Chinois glove thread	302 879
Metal embroidery wires	Neelam's bright check in Violet, Emerald, Copper Brown, and Green Jaseron by Neelam, Gold color
Fabric	Miracle smooth velvet, navy (Stragier, ref. 0000 6608)
Supplies	Japanese thread at Golden Hinde K2jap : 2 × 5 m Felt (for padding the center of the feather the purple chipping) Wooden or rectangular plastic embroidery frame Soluble stabilizer
Pattern	Cirri de République bag du Chiffon

Transfer the pattern to the soluble stabilizer and stick it to the velvet in the position of your choice.

① Embroider the pearl purl in couching stitch with the glove thread color 302 in double to outline the whole center of the feather.

② Lay the Japanese couching thread with glove thread color 876 in double: start at the base of the feather with the two Japanese threads, then embroider each thread back and forth for the left and right sides of the feather. Stop one thread at the base of the feather heart and work your way around with the remaining thread before stopping it when all is embroidered.

③ Place the felt in the center of the feather and stitch the purple bright check in a tight chipping with the color 302 glove thread.

④ Stitch the emerald bright check in a tight chipping with glove thread color 302.

⑤ Stitch the copper-brown bright check in a tight chipping pattern with glove thread color 302.

⑥ Stitch the green smooth purl in a tight sewing pattern with the color 302 glove thread.

Once the embroidery is finished, do not remove it from the frame. Gently dissolve the stabilizer under the shower and leave to dry flat and taut. This will keep the work perfectly flat.

Template size 50%

DISCOVER

Thread	
Au Chinois glove thread	302
Fabric (for the 2 projects)	Silk organza, color Shale (Stragier, ref. 0000 2215): 15 × 15 cm
Supplies (for the 2 projects)	Milliners needles Textile glue Felt matching the metal threads: 5 × 5 cm

The embroideries are made with double-needled glove thread.

1 Transfer the design on the silk organza stretched in the embroidery hoop.

2 Transfer and cut the padding from the felt, using the patterns. Secure with small stab stitches.

What You Need to Know

The felt padding pieces should be slightly smaller than the final shapes.

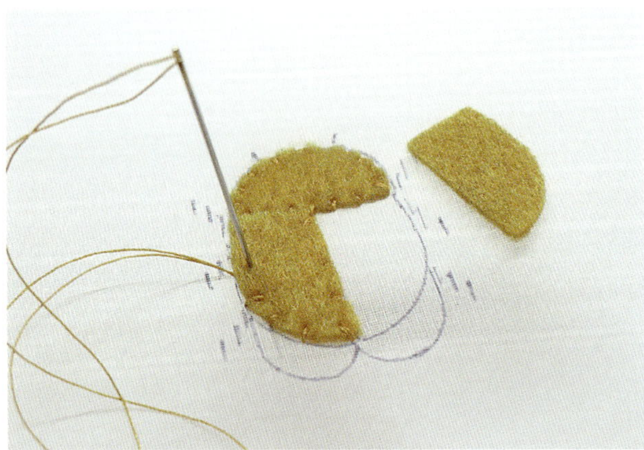

Small Beetle Brooch

Metal embroidery wires	Bright check from Neelam, Chocolate color Bright check from Neelam, in Copper Brown Jaceron by Neelam, Gold color
Beads	12 tubes Miyuki Bugles 3 mm, Gold BGL 1457 2 Matubo beads 8/0 3.15 mm, matte Gold color
Other Supplies	Bead needle Felt matching the embroidery Sewing thread to match the embroidery Brooch pin 28 mm long

1 Repeat steps 1 and 2 above.

2 Stitch the metal embroidery.

① Straight cutwork with brown bright check.

② Straight cutwork with chocolate bright check.

③ Secure a long piece of the chocolate bright check down the center.

④ Outline with the pearl purl.

⑤ Stitch the bugle beads as shown in the diagram, securing with a figure-8 stitch holding the two bugles side by side.

⑥ Two beads for the eyes, flush with the pearl purl.

3 Mount the beetle on a brooch pin (see page 351).

Templates for padding in felt

Start and finish of the pearl purl

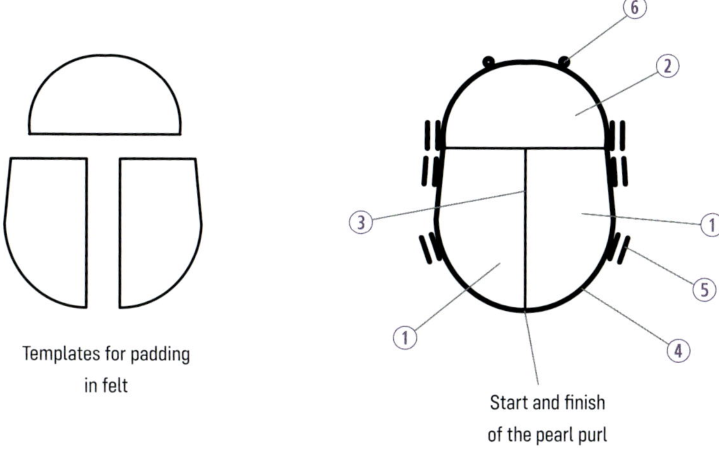

Template sizes 100%

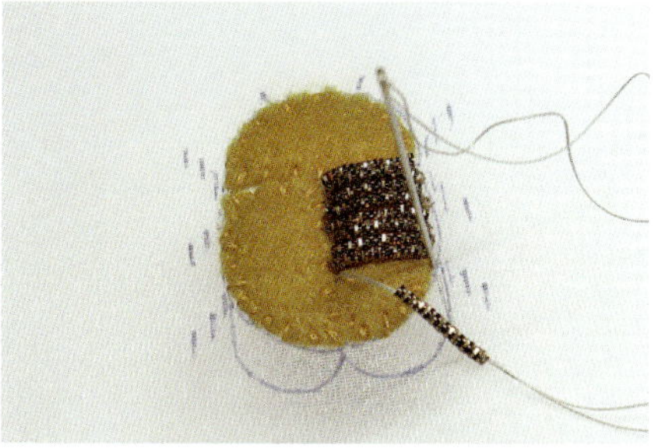

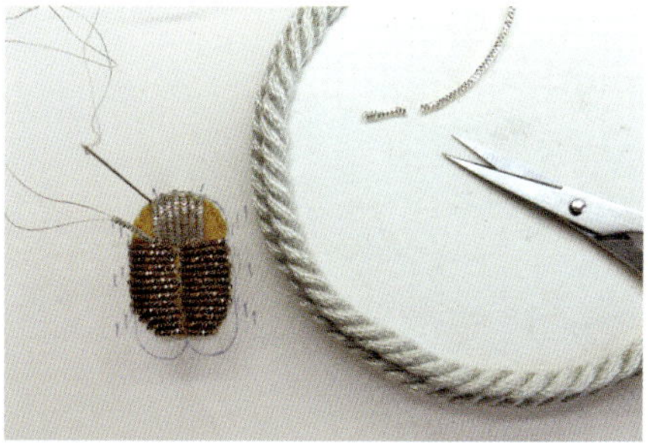

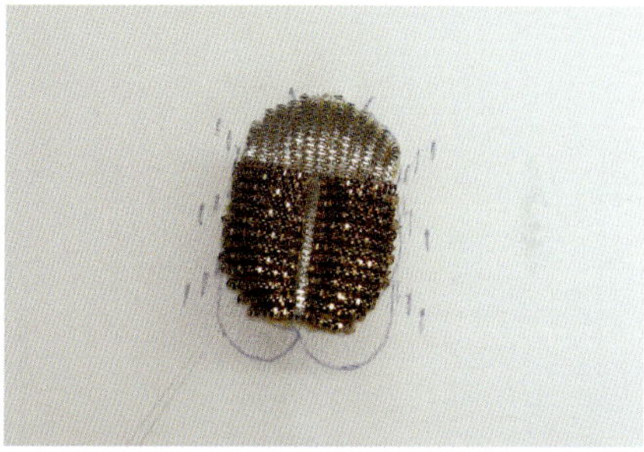

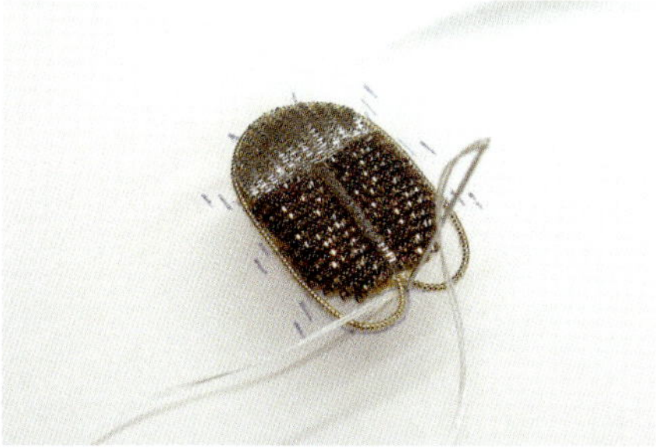

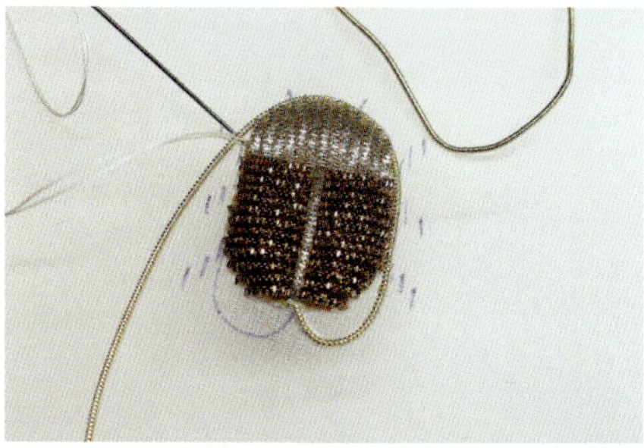

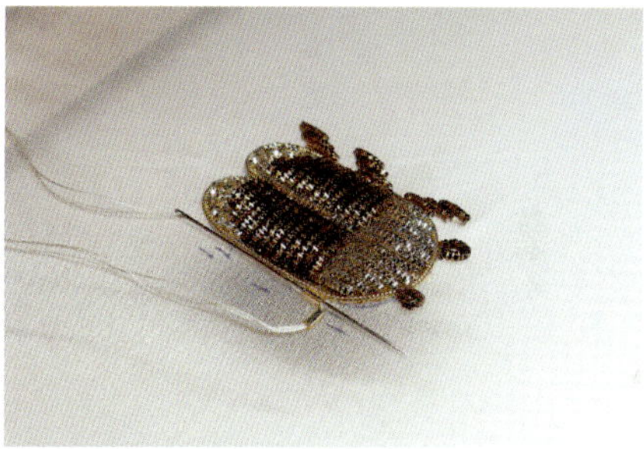

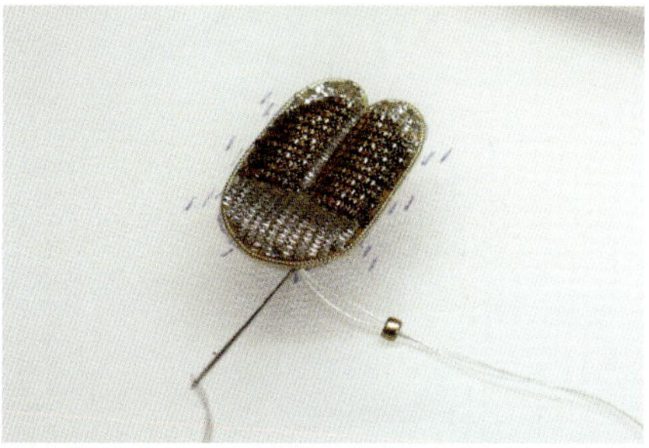

Tips for good embroidery

The textile support must not be pierced, since the beetle's legs will be free on either side of the spindle.

Scarab beetle on a hoop

Embroidery wires	Curly bright check from Neelam, Gold color
	Neelam's bright check, color Copper Brown
	Pearl purl by Neelam, Gold color

① Straight cutwork with brown bright check.

② Straight cutwork with gold bright check.

③ Long piece of gold bright check secured down center of wings.

④ Stitch pearl purl outline.

⑤ Tightly packed chipping with gold bright check.

⑥ One centimeter of brown bright check stitched as a standing loop.

⑦ Three times 5 mm of brown bright check for each leg secured with the backstitch.

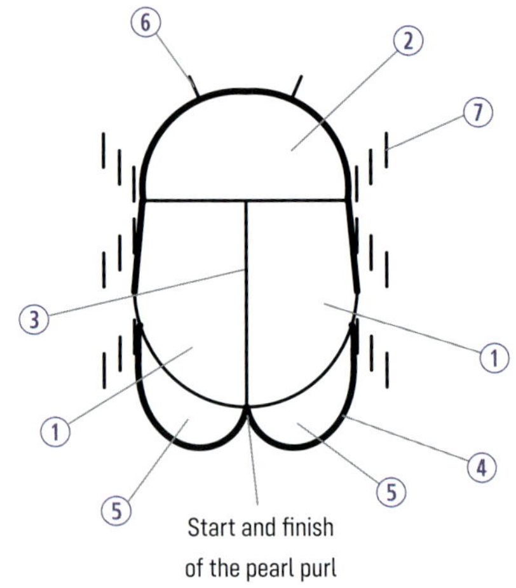

GOING THE EXTRA MILE

Thread	
Au Chinois glove thread	302
Embroidery wires	Smooth purl from Neelam, light copper brown color
	Bright check from Neelam, Gold color
	Neelam's bright check, Copper brown color
	Pearl purl by Neelam, Gold color
Beads	2 rocailles Matubo 8/0 3,15 mm, Galvanized Starlight color
Fabric	Silk organza, color Shale (Stragier, ref. 0000 2215) : 15 × 15 cm
Supplies	Textile glue
	Felt matching the embroidery
	Sewing thread to match the embroidery
	Dissolvable pen
	Brooch pin, length 32 mm

The entire embroidery is done with a double strand of glove thread.

1 Transfer the design on the silk organza stretched in the embroidery hoop.

2 Prepare and cut the felt padding, using the patterns, and attach them with small stab stitches.

3 Stitch the goldwork embroidery.

① Straight cutwork in light-brown smooth purl.

② Cutwork alternating light-brown smooth purl and bright check.

③ Stitch pearl purl outline.

④ Stitch pearl purl along design line.

⑤ Straight cutwork with gold bright check.

⑥ Tightly packed chipping with brown bright check.

⑦ Tightly packed chipping with gold bright check.

⑧ Two beads for the eyes.

4 Mount the embroidery in a brooch (see page 351).

Templates for stuffing in felt

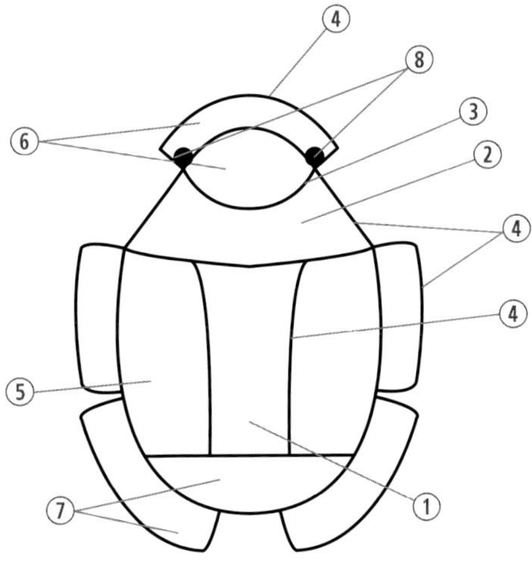

Template sizes 100%

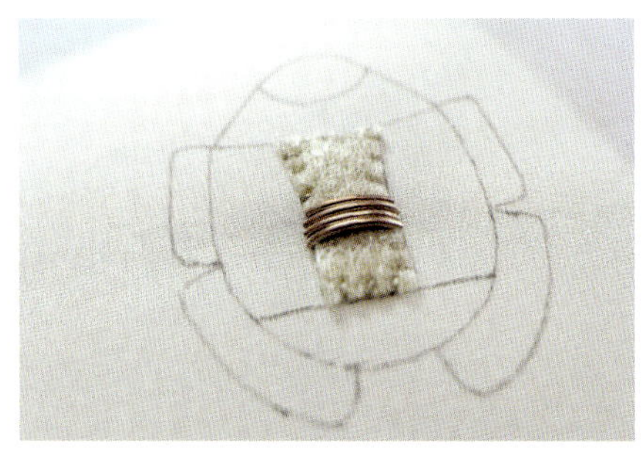

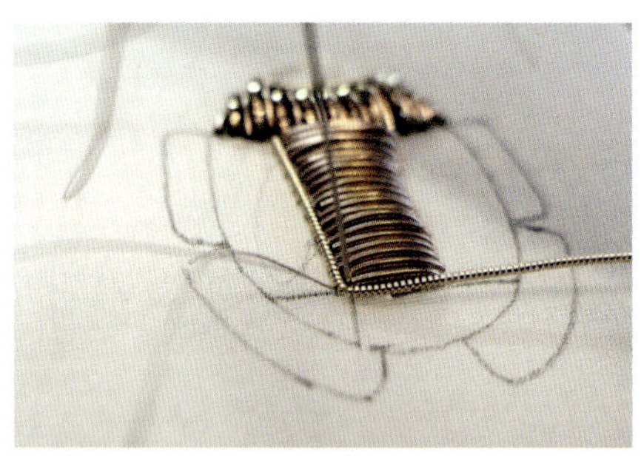

RELIEF EMBROIDERY

Pages 205 to 210

FRIEZE

Threads	
DMC Embroidery floss (stranded cotton)	02 03 3865
DMC Color Variations Embroidery floss	4075
Metallic braid 4 Au Ver à Soie	060
Beads	30 Toho 11/0 beads, Galvanized Starlight color 20 Toho 15/0 beads, Galvanized Starlight color 6 wooden beads Ø 7 mm with large hole
Fabric	Fine linen evenweave, Gold color (Stragier, ref: 0000 2585)
Supplies	Ecru cotton batiste : 15 × 15 cm Brass or copper thread Ø 0.3 mm

Transfer the pattern as many times as necessary on the chosen surface.

① Stem stitch with three color strands 03.

② Fishbone stitch with three color strands 03.

③ Woven picot stitch with three strands color 3865: embroider the first four in a cross, then four more in a cross staggered from the first ones.

④ Six French knots with six strands color 4075 in the center of the flower. Add beads 11/0.

⑤ Stitch an 11/0 bead in the center with two strands in color 4075, embroider six straight stitches, then place an 11/0 bead at each end.

⑥ Transfer the slip designs onto the cotton batiste. Embroider French knots with six strands in color 4075, then stitch a few 15/0 beads on the French knots.

⑦ Couch the wire along the design line, then embroider in buttonhole stitch over it. Then embroider the leaf in fishbone stitch.

⑧ Cut out the raised pieces, prepare them, and attach them in place with small invisible stitches, using the thread used for embroidery.

⑨ Cover the wooden beads with metallic thread and attach them to the work. Using a very fine beading needle, add a small 15/0 bead to each wooden bead.

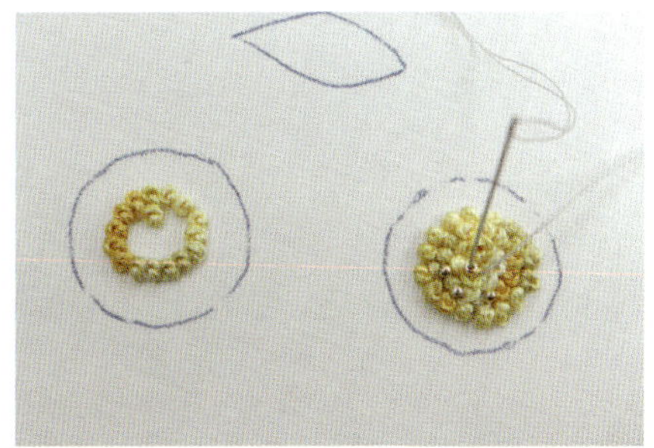

Template size 100%

Patterns for slips

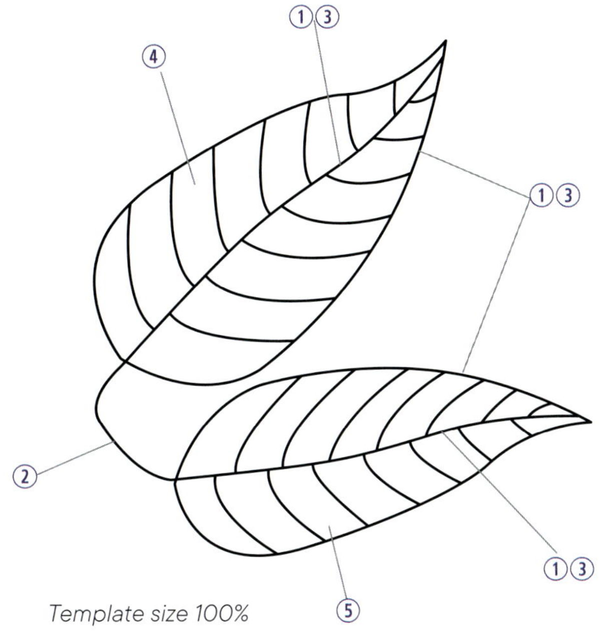

Template size 100%

DISCOVER

Threads	
DMC Embroidery floss (stranded cotton)	115, 895, 3346, 3345, 3347
Metallic braid 4 Au Ver à Soie	002
Supplies	Ecru or green cotton batiste or green: 15 × 15 cm Jewelry glue Textile white vinyl glue Spindle support length 32 mm Green permanent marker (for green batiste) Green felt: 10 × 10 cm Ø 0.5mm brass thread 2 wooden beads Ø 16 mm with large hole

1 Transfer the leaf pattern on the cotton batiste.

2 Embroider. All leaf embroidery is done with two strands of embroidery floss.

① Couch the wire down on the design line. Repeat for both leaves with color 895. Create the central veins with color 3346 for the large leaf and color 3347 for the small leaf.

② Whip two strands of color 3346 around the wire connecting the leaves, without piercing the fabric, so it is free from the surface.

③ Embroider the outside of the leaves in buttonhole stitch, using color 895. Cover the central veins of the large leaf with tightly packed couching stitches, using color 3346 and color 3347 for those of the small leaf.

④ For the large leaf, stem-stitch the side veins with color 3346, then use long and short stitch with colors 895 and 3345 (the light side against the center vein).

⑤ For the small leaf, stem-stitch the side veins with color 3347, then use long and short stitch with colors 895, 3345 and 3346 (the light side against the center vein).

⑥ On each leaf, embroider a few straight stitches, in the same direction as the long and short filling, with metallic thread.

3 Using fabric glue, glue the backs of the leaves, extending well beyond the outer edge. Allow to dry, then cut flush with the buttonhole stitch. If necessary, use a green permanent marker to cover the batiste cutout still visible.

4 Prepare the felt backs: on the reverse side of the felt. Using the embroidered leaves as a template, draw the shape onto the felt. Attach the brooch clasp (see page 351) to the back of the large leaf. Using textile glue, glue the felts to the backs of the embroidered leaves, taking care to glue right to the edges.

5 Cover the beads with six strands of color 115. Secure the ends of the strands with knots. Insert them into the bead hole and glue them in place.

6 Cut approximately 12 cm of brass thread. Without cutting the skein, glue six strands of color 3346 to one end of the brass thread, using jewelry glue. Allow to dry.

7 Start wrapping 1 cm of embroidery floss around the brass thread. Place a drop of jewelry glue on the remaining hole of a bead and insert the brass thread. Leave to dry.

8 Assemble the leaves of the cherry stems. Leave 3.5 cm of brass thread from the cherry and tie a loop around the middle of the leaves.

9 Cut the second cherry stem to 4 cm. Take the embroidery floss and continue winding it up the stem to the stem insertion. Completely cover the stem insertion with embroidery floss and hold it in place with a drop of fabric glue, as invisibly as possible. Wind the embroidery floss back down onto the second stem. At the end, glue the embroidery floss. Leave to dry. Put a drop of glue on the second cherry and proceed as for the first.

GOING THE EXTRA MILE

Threads	
Soie d'algers Au Ver à Soie	4236, 3825, 3823, 2536, 3846, 3842
Antique Metallic Thread Au Ver à Soie	901
Fabric	2 silk organza pieces, Shale color (Stragier, ref. 0000 2215): 30 × 30 cm
Supplies	Entomology box with minimum dimensions of 15 × 15 cm Fountain pen Permanent marker Ø 0.1 mm 2 Toho 15/0 beads, Galvanized Starlight color

The butterfly's wings are embroidered with a strand of Algiers silk.

1 Stretch the organza tightly over the hoop. Offset the design with a 0.1mm permanent marker.

2 Embroider. Start with a temporary knot on the outside of the embroidery and finish with two small cross-stitches in the future embroidery.

① Stem stitch with color 3846 for veins.

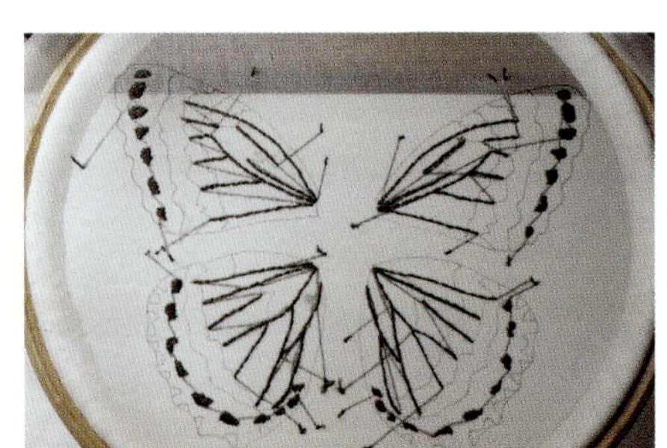

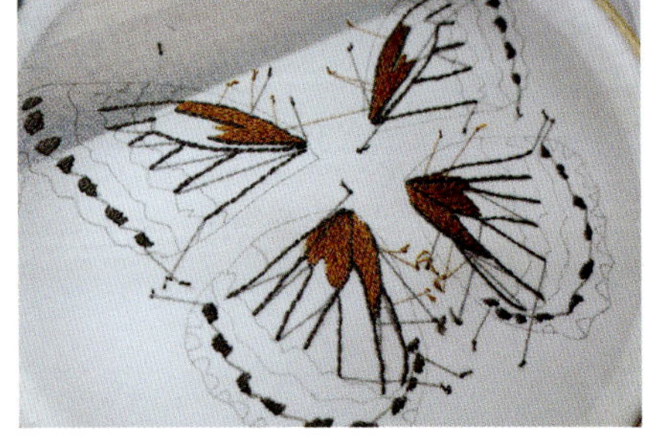

3 Then embroider each area of color in satin stitch or using long and short if the stitches are longer than 8 mm.

② Color 3846.

③ Color 4236.

④ Color 2536.

⑤ Color 3825.

⑥ Color 3846.

⑦ Color 2536.

⑧ Color 3842.

⑨ Color 3823.

⑩ A few straight stitches with metallic thread at the base of each wing.

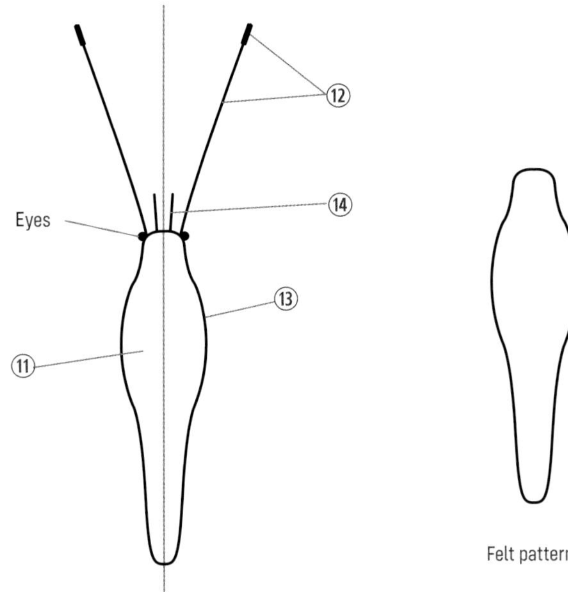

Template sizes 100%

4 Without dismantling the frame or hoop, gently glue the back of the embroidery, extending well past the outside of the wings. Allow to dry.

5 Cut flush with the embroidery as gently as possible.

6 Stretch the second piece of organza over the hoop or frame. Locate the center and the vertical straight thread. Using the permanent marker, transfer the body and antennae lines.

7 Cut out the body pattern from the paper and transfer it to the felt. Cut it out and position it vertically. Secure with a few stitches.

8 Embroider the butterfly's body.

⑪ Satin stitch with two color strands 4236 over the body, starting from the middle.

⑫ Stem stitch for antennas with metallic thread. Add two straight stitches at the ends of the antennas to thicken them slightly (anchor the thread with tiny backstitches on the back of the antenna).

⑬ Stem stitch with metallic thread for the outline of the body

⑭ Stitch a few straight stitches extending above head with metallic thread.

9 Place the eye beads.

10 Using metallic thread, attach the wings to the body, using a series of straight stitches that will pass through the organza.

Tips for Good Embroidery

Use a ruler to sew the wings symmetrically.

11 Cut the matboard to the inside dimensions of the box.

12 Center the butterfly on the matboard and pull it taut. Fold the organza over the back and glue it in place. Once dry, place in the box.

APPLIQUÉS

Pages 211 to 214

FRIEZE

The photo of the design can be found on page 214.

Thread	
DMC Embroidery floss (stranded cotton)	3777
Fabrics	Liberty Thorpe Burnt, color L (Stragier, ref. 0363 9005 L)
	Fabric of your choice (for textile backing)
Supplies	Two-sided fusible web

1 Transfer the pattern as many times as necessary onto the chosen surface: the stem with a pencil and the leaves with an dissolvable pen.

2 Transfer the leaves to be appliquéd to the paper side of the two-sided fusible web, then cut 2–3 cm around the design.

3 Apply the rough surface of the two-sided fusible web to the reverse side of the Liberty fabric. Fix the two-sided fusible web with an iron for 5 seconds (medium to hot setting).

4 Cut the prepared leaves flush, then remove the paper from the two-side fusible web.

5 Place the sheets face down on the ground fabric.

6 Cover with a press cloth and iron (medium to hot) slowly across the fabric, without slipping, for 10 seconds.

7 Embroider the leaf outlines using chain stitch with two strands of color 3777, flush with the edge.

8 Embroider the central stem with chain stitch with two strands of color 3777.

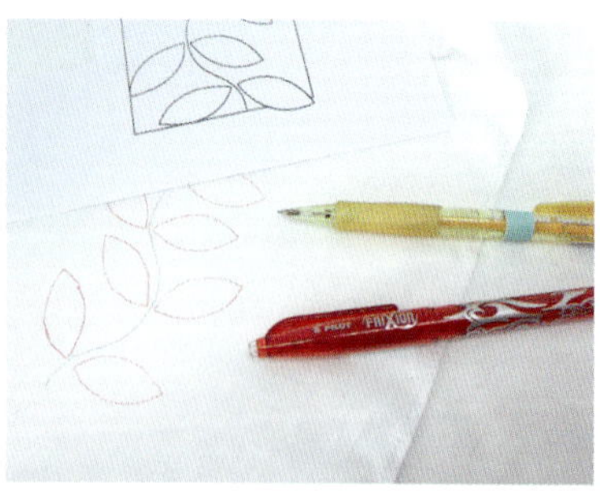

Template size 50%

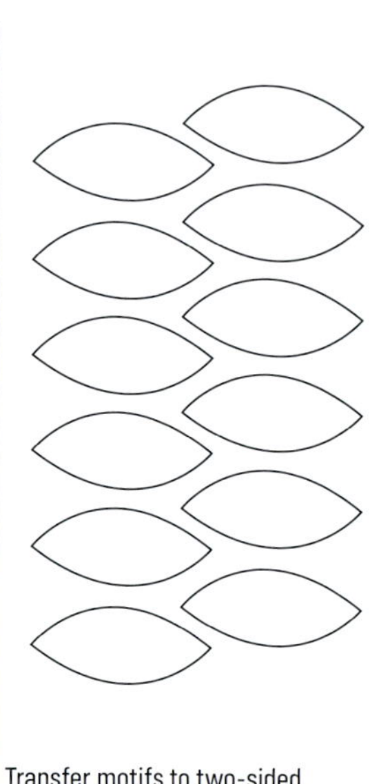

Transfer motifs to two-sided fusible web as many times as necessary.

DISCOVER

Thread	
DMC Embroidery floss (stranded cotton) to match fabrics	
Fabrics	Scraps of Liberty fabric
Supplies	Two-sided fusible web

1 Draw a horizontal line on the T-shirt and find the center by drawing a vertical line.

2 On the paper side of the two-sided fusible web, transfer the letters (download and print; see QR code on page 14), then cut 2–3 cm around each one.

What You Need to Know

Draw the mirror image of the letters on the back of the two-sided fusible web.

3 Apply the rough surface of the two-sided fusible web to the reverse side of the Liberty fabrics. Fix the two-sided fusible web with an iron for 5 seconds (medium to hot setting).

4 Cut the letters flush, then remove the paper from the two-sided fusible web.

5 Place the letters face down on the horizontal line, centering the word on the garment.

6 Cover with a press cloth and iron across the surface, without slipping, for 10 seconds (medium to hot).

7 Embroider the outlines of the letters in buttonhole stitch with two strands of embroidery floss over the edges of the letters.

Template size 100%

GOING THE EXTRA MILE

Thread	
DMC Embroidery floss (stranded cotton)	◯ White
Fabrics	Evenweave cotton, color Gris perle (Stragier, ref. 0000) Cotton thread, color White (Stragier, ref. 0000 0146)
Pattern	Louise Mum blouse by Ikatee

Appliqués are made on the yoke of the Louise blouse. The pattern on page 379 can be used to adapt the size of the appliqué to the project. The small gray appliqués are first sewn onto the white fabric, then applied to the fabric of the garment yoke.

1 Cut out the yoke pattern, removing the seam allowances.

2 Position the sides (points A and C) and the middle (point B) on the center of the circle—use three photocopies of the drawing. Trace the outline of the yoke.

Template size 50%

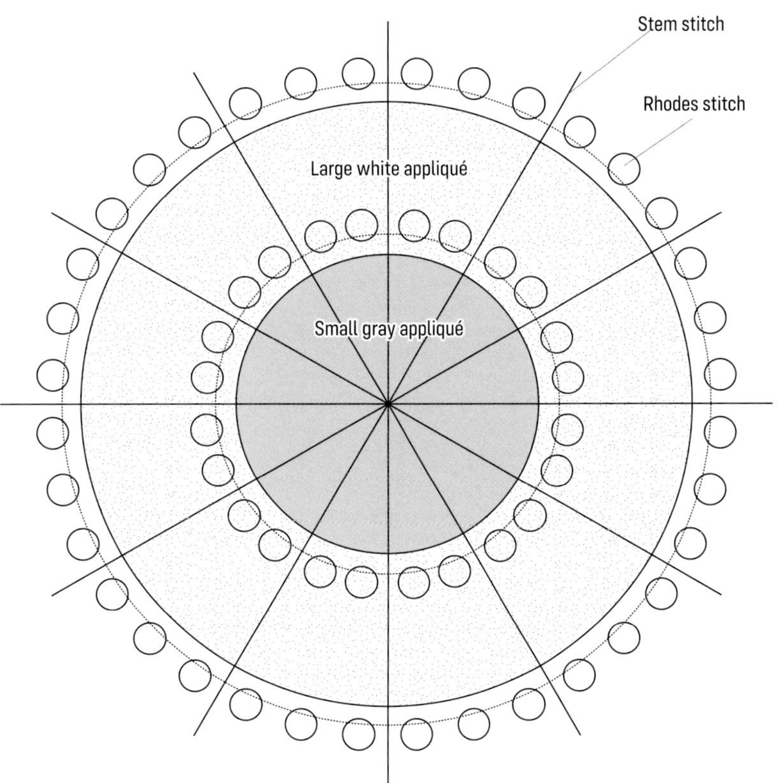

3 Photocopy each drawing of the appliqué sections from step 2 twice. Add the seam allowances for the small gray and large white panels: 1 cm for the machine seams and 0.5 cm for the appliqué edges. These are the six appliqué patterns.

4 Position the gray yoke patterns on the gray fabric along the straight grain. Cut.

5 Trace the seam lines of the fabric of the small appliqués to identify the seam allowance margins and carefully dip the seam allowances.

6 Baste the small appliqués on the white fabric, matching the straight grain.

7 Appliqué with an invisible hemstitch or slip stitch.

8 Cut the garment yoke from the gray fabric, adding the machine seam allowances.

9 Repeat steps 4 to 7 with the large white appliqués to be placed on the yoke of the garment.

10 Use a circle template to trace the spokes and polka dots.

11 Embroider the spokes in stem stitch with two strands of white.

12 Embroider the polka dots in Rhodes stitch with two strands of white.

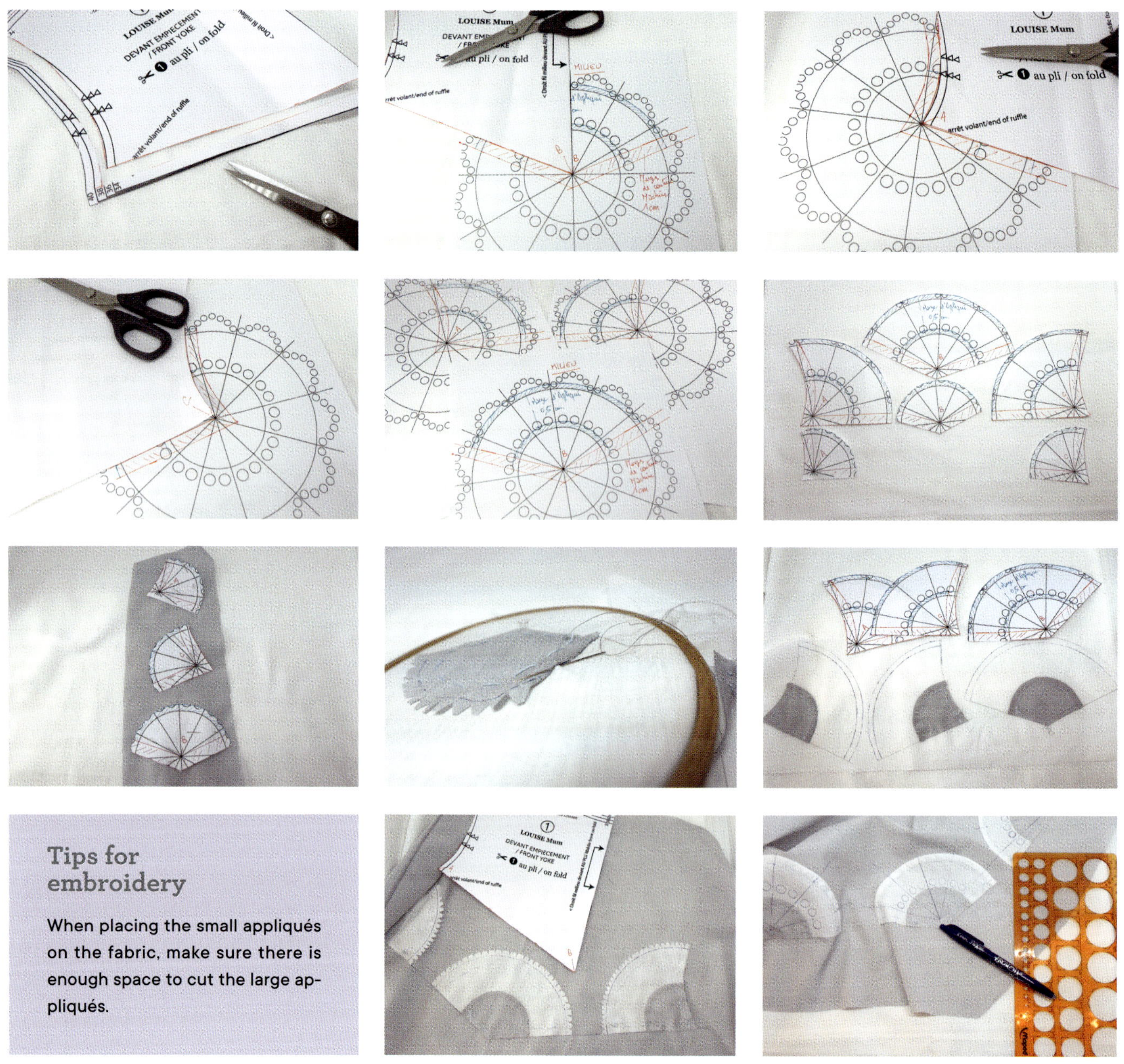

Tips for embroidery

When placing the small appliqués on the fabric, make sure there is enough space to cut the large appliqués.

EMBELLISHMENT EMBROIDERY

Pages 215 to 217

FRIEZE

Thread	Raffia to embroider blue and terracotta
Fabric	Raffia natural
Supplies	Beading needles
	Chenille needle no. 16
	Lining
	Sheet of acetate (to transfer the design)
	Beige sewing thread
	Q snap frame
	7 Khéops beads 6 mm, color Crystal Golden Rainbow

1 Back the raffia with interfacing, then prepare it in the Q snap frame.

2 Make a stencil in the acetate: transfer and cut out the motif. Transfer the motif as many times as necessary on the chosen surface.

3 Embroider raffia motifs with a straight stitch.

4 Place the beads at the base of each motif with the beige sewing thread.

Template size 100%

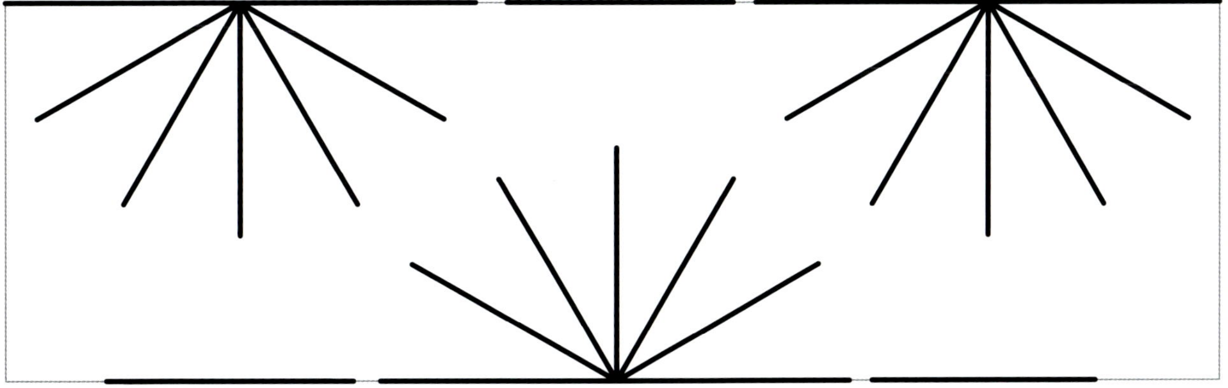

DISCOVER

Threads	
DMC Embroidery floss (stranded cotton)	3832
Au Chinois glove thread	535
Fabric	Liberty Tana Lawn Jannah, color A
Supplies	Chenille needle no. 16 Lining Bordeaux satin chenille thread 1 box of 3mm cupped sequins, color Doré 1 box of Toho 8/0 and 11/0 seed beads, color Galvanized Starlight 1 box of 3mm Miyuki Bugle Beads, color Galvanized Gold Metallic

All cupped sequins are laid with the convex side against the work and beads; bugle beads and cupped sequins with a double needle of color 535 thread.

① Straight stitch with chenille thread.

② Line of cupped sequins.

③ Place five cupped sequins in a circle, then embroider a French knot with chenille thread in the center.

④ Beads 11/0, scatter by attaching individually with a backstitch.

⑤ Beads 11/0 in a line with the backstitch

⑥ Beads 8/0 individually.

⑦ Diagonal satin stitch with three color 3832 strands.

⑧ Bugle beads stitched down individually.

PLUMETIS

Pages 220 to 227

DISCOVER

Thread	
Coton à Broder no. 30 DMC	◯ White
Fabric	Evenweave cotton, color Regata blue (Stagier, ref. 0001 5200)

1 Carefully trace the letter to be embroidered (download and print; see QR code on page 14). Transfer the dots, using a circle template.

2 To begin padding the letter, stitch with double running stitch around the full outline, down the thin lines, and on both sides of the thicker lines.

3 Using a darning stitch, stitch two layers of padding inside the thicker lines of the letter.

4 Embroider satin stitch all over the letter, not forgetting the guide.

>Take out the needle at the beginning of the letter.

>Position the guide and start embroidering in satin stitch.

>Embroider a satin stitch over the padding as you work down the letter.

>Continue stitching the satin stitch over the padding as the letter grows thick to thin to finish the letter.

5 Embroider the leaves.

6 Embroider dots less than 6 mm in diameter, without any padding or outline stitch.

7 Embroider dots larger than 6 mm in diameter, with satin stitch over a split-stitch outline.

Tips for Good Embroidery

For perfect embroidery, tuck the needle at an angle under the work, flush with the cord. For even greater finesse, use no. 35 thread instead of no. 30.

Template size 100%

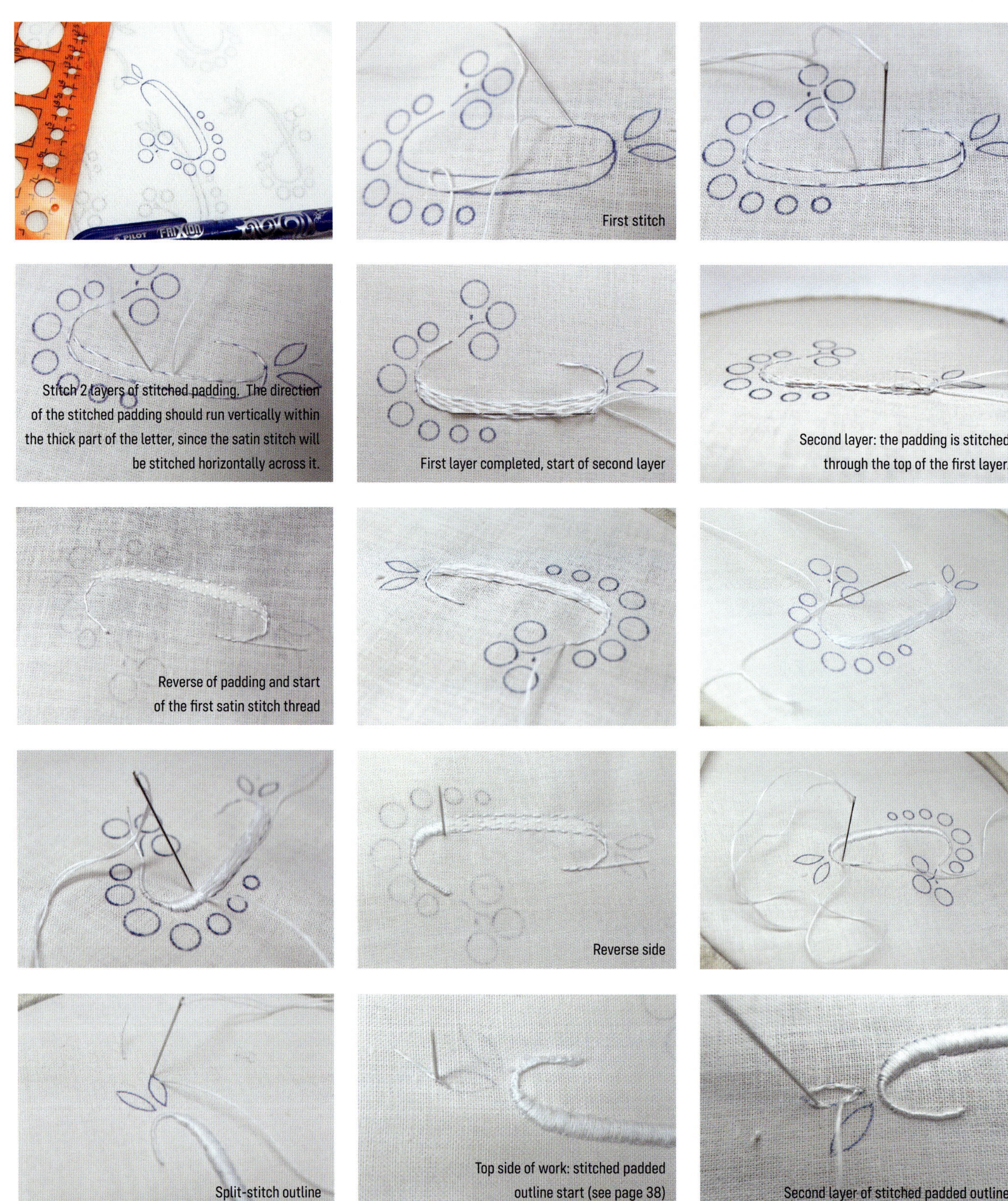
First stitch
Stitch 2 layers of stitched padding. The direction of the stitched padding should run vertically within the thick part of the letter, since the satin stitch will be stitched horizontally across it.
First layer completed, start of second layer
Second layer: the padding is stitched through the top of the first layer.
Reverse of padding and start of the first satin stitch thread
Reverse side
Split-stitch outline
Top side of work: stitched padded outline start (see page 38)
Second layer of stitched padded outline

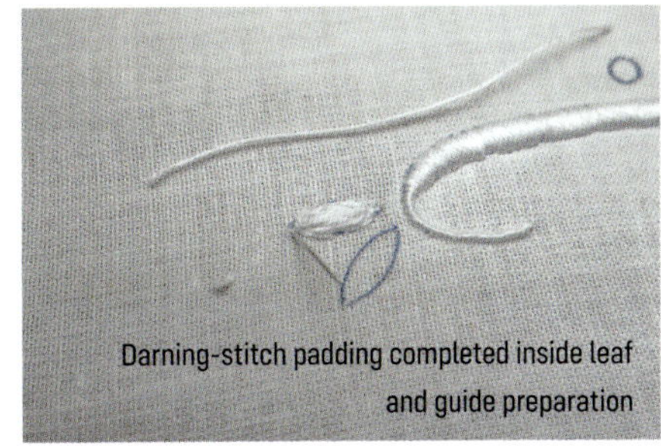
Darning-stitch padding completed inside leaf and guide preparation

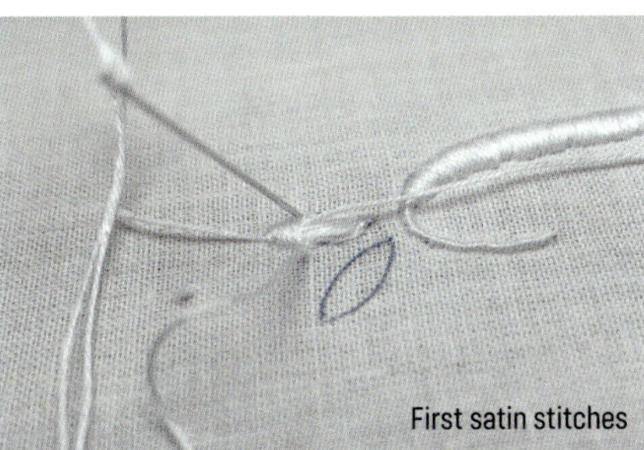
First satin stitches

Trim the ends of the guide once finished embroidering.

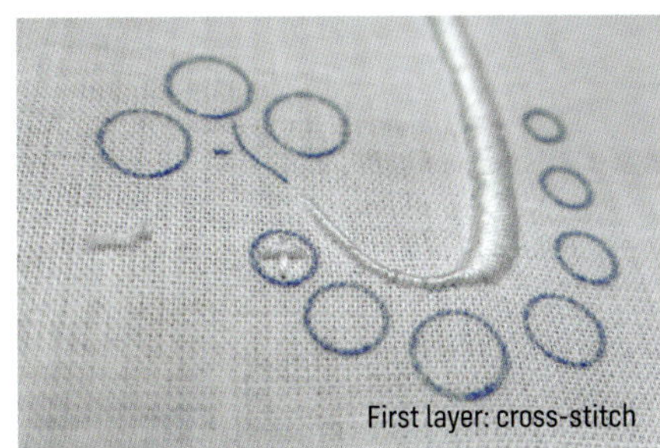
First layer: cross-stitch

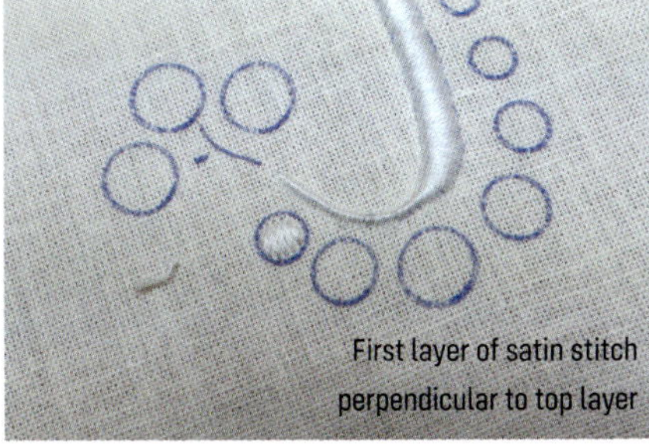
First layer of satin stitch perpendicular to top layer

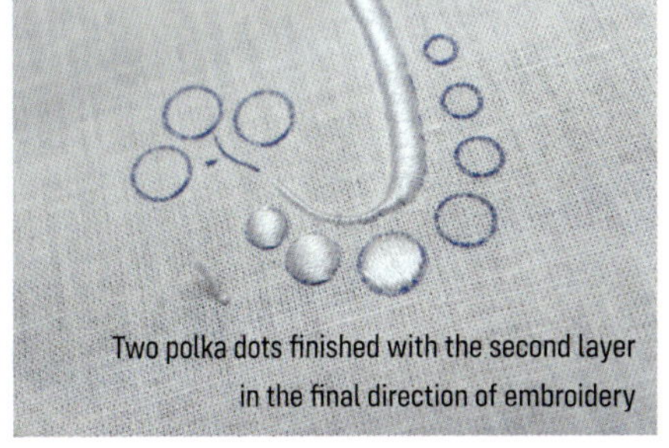
Two polka dots finished with the second layer in the final direction of embroidery

Third dot being embroidered

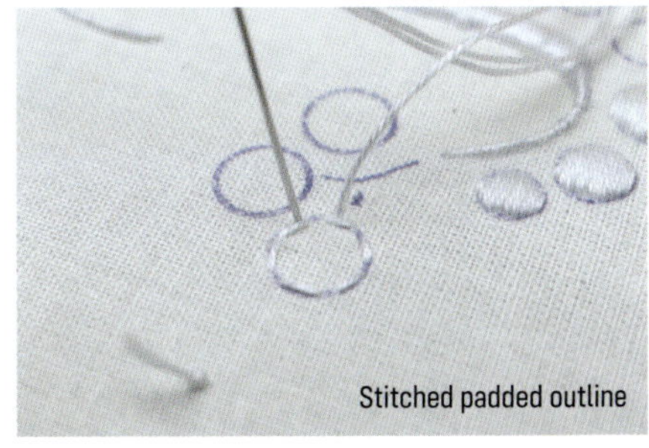
Stitched padded outline

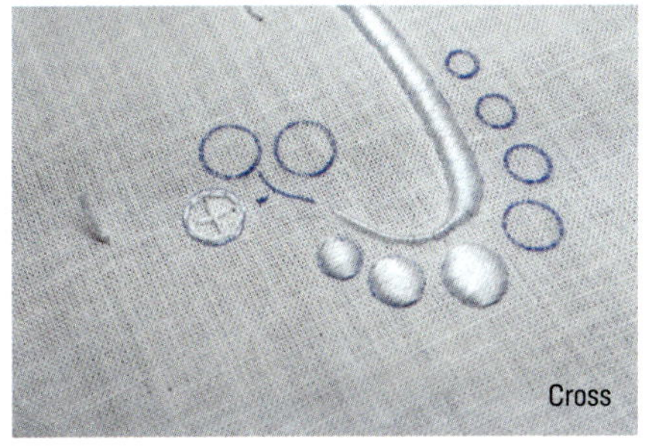
Cross

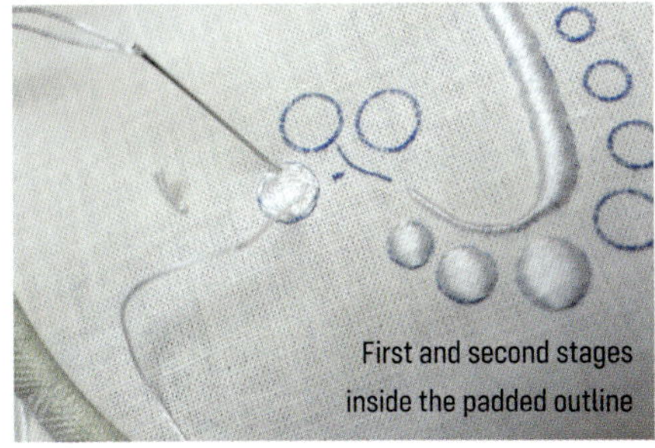
First and second stages inside the padded outline

Final stitching stretches over the padding

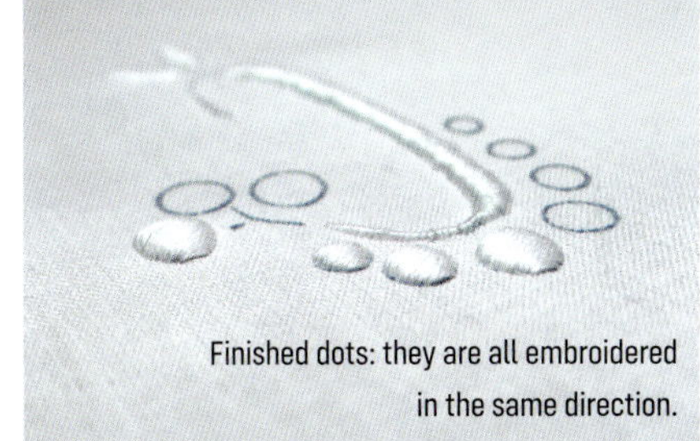
Finished dots: they are all embroidered in the same direction.

GOING THE EXTRA MILE

Threads	
Coton à Broder no. 25 DMC	◯ White
Coton à Broder no. 35 DMC	◯ White
Pattern	Personal creation

1 Embroider with satin stitch the entire motif with thread no. 35.

2 Backstitch the congress cloth with no. 25 thread.

Stitch padded outline on petals

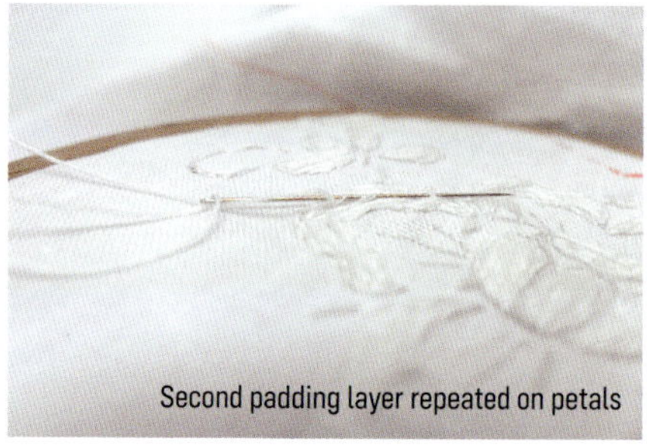
Second padding layer repeated on petals

Finished padding

Satin stitch on the first petal

Reverse side

Satin stitch on the last petal: tuck the needle out at an angle under the padding. Don't forget the guides.

The stem splits into a Y shape: prepare and place a second guide to align with the design.

Embroider the fork of the Y until it breaks into the two sides.

Embroider the first, then the second stem.

Template size 100%

DRAWN THREAD BORDERS

Pages 228 to 240

DISCOVER

Thread	
Coton à Broder no. 30 DMC	◯ White
Fabric	Fine linen canvas, color White (Stragier, ref. 0000 2589)
Supplies	Round-tipped needle
Pattern	Personal creation

1 Cut the front in linen along the straight grain.

2 Starting from the center front, remove a weft thread 7 cm from the neckline.

3 Create a drawn-thread border 2 mm in height from that thread 7 cm below neckline, according to the following pattern:

> Remove nine threads (for a total of ten with the first thread pulled) and leave eight threads.

> Remove ten threads and leave eight threads.

> Remove ten threads.

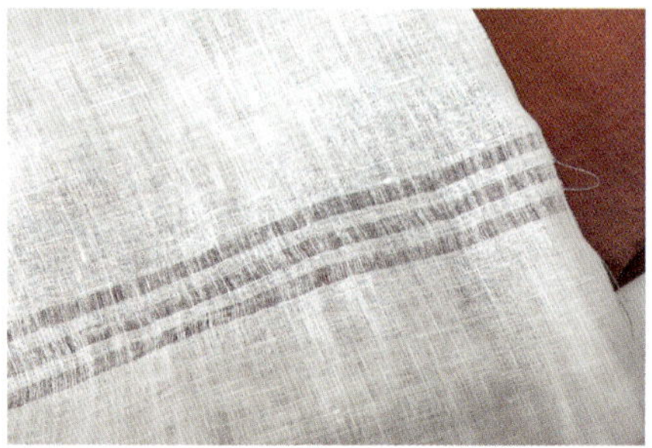

4 Remove the appropriate threads the full width of the front panel.

5 Embroider a ladder hemstitch on the middle band.

6 Embroider a diagonal hemstitch on the top and bottom bands.

7 Finish the armholes with a bound hem to hide the drawn-thread border edge.

GOING THE EXTRA MILE

Thread	
Coton à Broder no. 30 DMC	◯ White
Fabric	Fine linen evenweave, color White (Stragier, ref. 0000 2589)
Supplies	Round-tipped needle
Pattern	Alex Mum blouse by Ikatee

1 Cut the sleeves from the linen, along the straight grain.

> **Attention**
>
> **Do not cut the cuff slit until you have completed the embroidery.**

2 11 cm from the cuff edge of the sleeve, remove a weft thread shown as A.

3 Prepare the 2cm drawn-thread band as follows:

> Leave six threads in B.

> Remove eight threads in C and leave six threads in D.

> Remove three threads through E and leave.

> Leave eight threads in F.

> Remove one thread at G and leave eight threads at H.

> Remove three threads in I and leave 16 threads in J.

> Remove three threads through I' and leave eight threads through H'.

> Remove one thread at G' and leave eight at F'.

> Remove three threads through E' and leave six threads through D'.

> Remove eight threads at C' and leave six threads at B'.

> Remove a thread.

4 Continue to remove the threads from side to side to mark the entire width of the sleeve.

5 Embroider with a stitch height of four vertical threads.

> **Tips for Good Embroidery**
>
> **Make sure you always work on the same threads.**

> Square eyelet border on band J.

> Basic hemstitch in G and overcast in H.

> Basic hemstitch in E and overcast in D.

> Basic hemstitch in C and overcast in D.

> Between A and C, waves stitch on double border with single wrap around the bundles in A.

6 Do the same opposite work on the bands for G', H', E', D', C', A'.

7 Repeat steps 2 to 5 on the other sleeve.

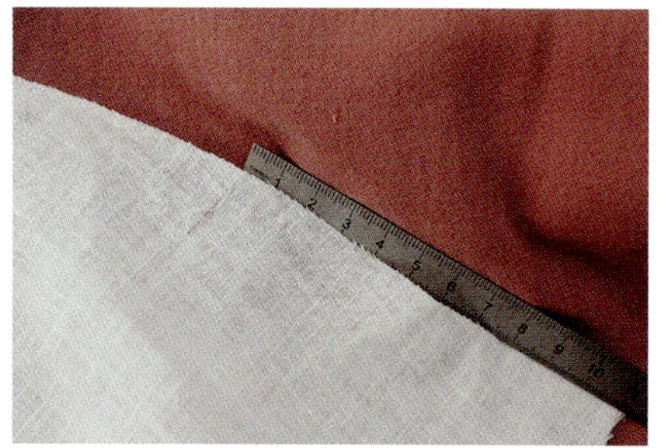

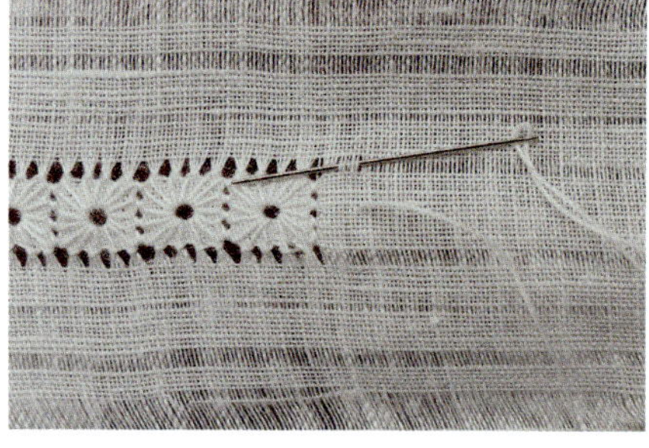

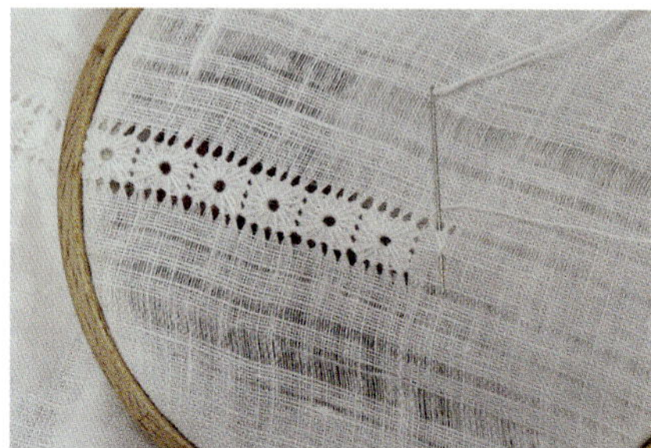

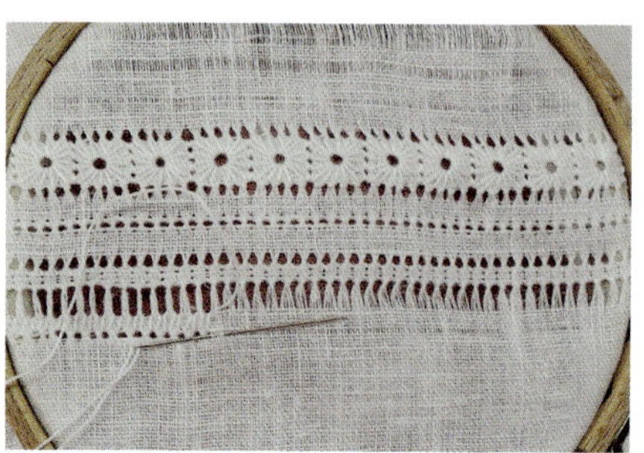

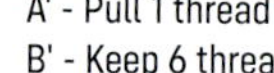

A' - Pull 1 thread
B' - Keep 6 threads
C' - Pull 8 threads
D' - Keep 6 threads
E' - Pull 3 threads
F' - Keep 8 threads
G' - Pull 1 thread
H' - Keep 8 threads
I' - Pull 3 threads
J - Keep 16 threads
I - Pull 3 threads
H - Keep 8 threads
G - Pull 1 thread
F - Keep 8 threads
E - Pull 3 threads
D - Keep 6 threads
C - Pull 8 threads
B - Keep 6 threads
A - Pull 1 thread

BORDERS AND LINES WITH PULLED THREADS

Pages 241 to 244

DISCOVER

Threads	
Coton à Broder no. 25 DMC	815
Coton à Broder no. 30 DMC	White
Cotton Retors embroidery DMC	2815
Fabric	Fine linen canvas, color White (Stragier, ref. 0001 4807)
Supplies	Long needle no. 10 Hoop Ø 15 cm (for presentation)

1 Make a ladder stitch without added relief on the letter B: embroider a ladder stitch with couched relief on both sides on the vertical bar (solid) and a ladder stitch with relief on one side on the curving portion of the B. Embroider the hemstitch with the white thread straddling the Retors cotton.

2 Embroider the rest of the word in backstitch (two rows in the thinner parts and three rows in the thicker parts) with color 815.

3 Embroider the center using the padded or flat satin stitch technique with color 815.

Template size 50%

Reverse side
Bisou
doux

GOING THE EXTRA MILE

Threads	
Coton à Broder no. 25 DMC	◯ White
Coton à Broder no. 30 DMC	◯ White
Quilt Machine Thread 100% cotton DMC	◯ White
Fabric	Fine linen evenweave, color White (Stragier, ref. 0001 4807)
Supplies	Embroidery needle no. 9 Embroidery needle no. 10 Ordinary sewing thread in contrasting colors
Pattern	Personal creation

1 Transfer the pattern to the front along the straight grain. If necessary, adapt the design to the neckline of your garment.

2 Prepare the work. To do this, use ordinary sewing thread to thread-trace the embroidery design lines; this will make it easier to locate the threads on which to work. Allow a width of 5 mm per column along the straight grain.

3 Embroider a three-sided stitch between these spaces. Work the stitch over a height of 10 threads.

Tips for Good Embroidery

Do not stitch into the basting threads, but right next to them, inside the column.

4 Remove thread-tracing threads.

5 Finish the neckline by hiding the neckline edge with a bound hem. Stitch the binding to the wrong side of the neckline, fold over to the right side and baste. Sew right sides together, using hemstitch.

6 Hem the sleeves and the bottom of the blouse in hemstitch, making two 5mm turns for the hem.

What You Need to Know

These lines of three-sided stitch have been worked along the straight grain of the fabric but can also be worked on a curved pattern.

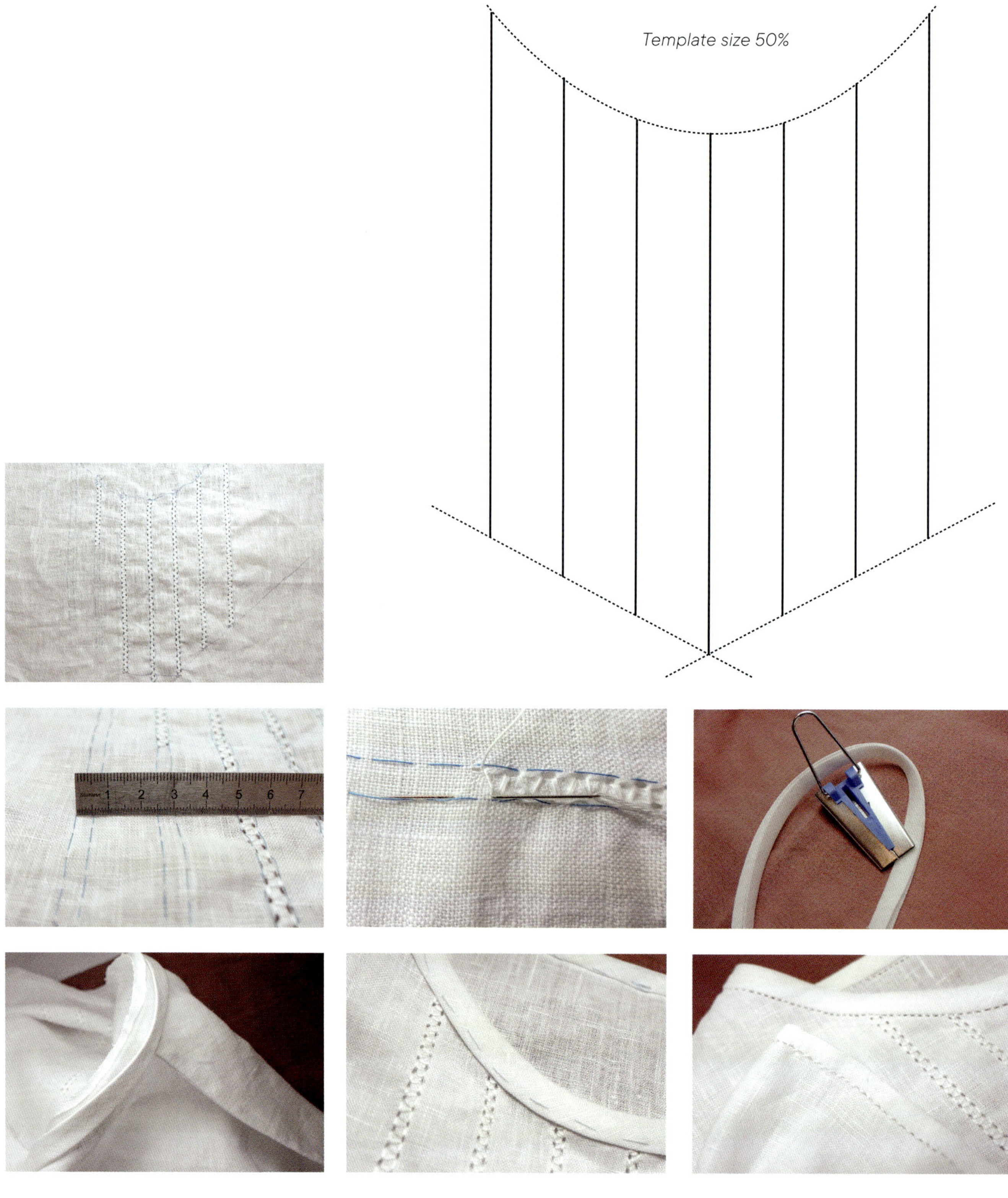
Template size 50%

OPENWORK GROUNDS

Pages 245 to 257

DISCOVER

Threads	
Coton à Broder no. 16 DMC	◯ White
Coton à Broder no. 25 DMC	◯ White
Quilt Machine Thread 100% cotton DMC	◯ White
Fabric	Fine linen evenweave, color Ivoire (Stragier, ref. 0000 2588)
Supplies	Embroidery needle no. 7
	Embroidery needle no. 9 (for openwork grounds)
	Embroidery needle no. 10

1 Embroider the perimeter of the rhombus in coral stitch with Coton à Broder no. 16 thread.

2 Embroider scallops in buttonhole stitch with Coton à Broder no. 25 thread.

3 On the reverse side of the work, thin the ground fabric by removing horizontal threads in the following pattern: remove one thread and leave three. Start with the center of the rhombus for the first thread, continue by preparing the following ones, then remove all the threads up to the coral stitch outline and cut flush.

4 Embroider on the right side in double wave stitch with Coton à Broder thread no. 25, starting at the center line. Work on six vertical threads, starting from the horizontal line in the middle of the design. Embroider the bottom half of motif then the top half of motif up to the top line.

What You Need to Know

If you wish, embroider all the hems and binding seams of the garment in hemstitch, using machine-quilting sewing thread.

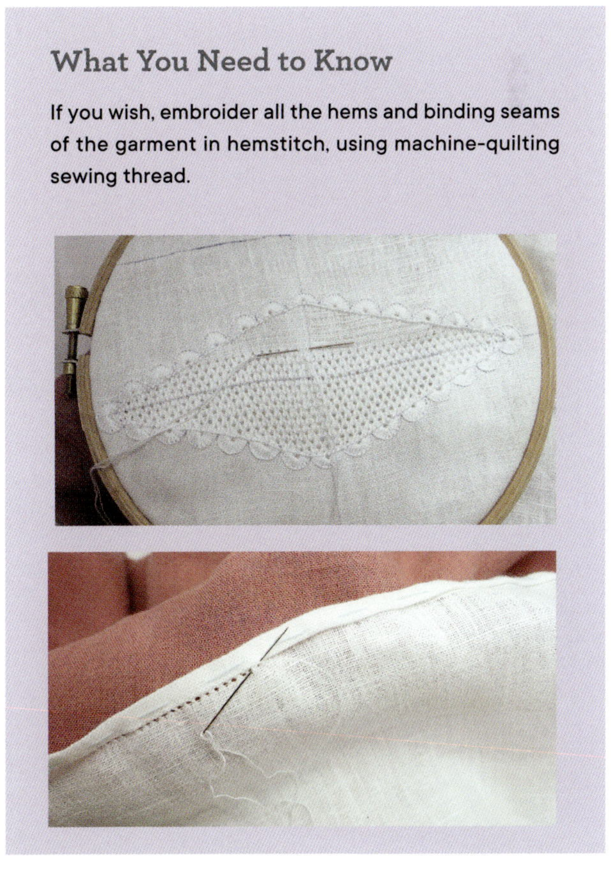

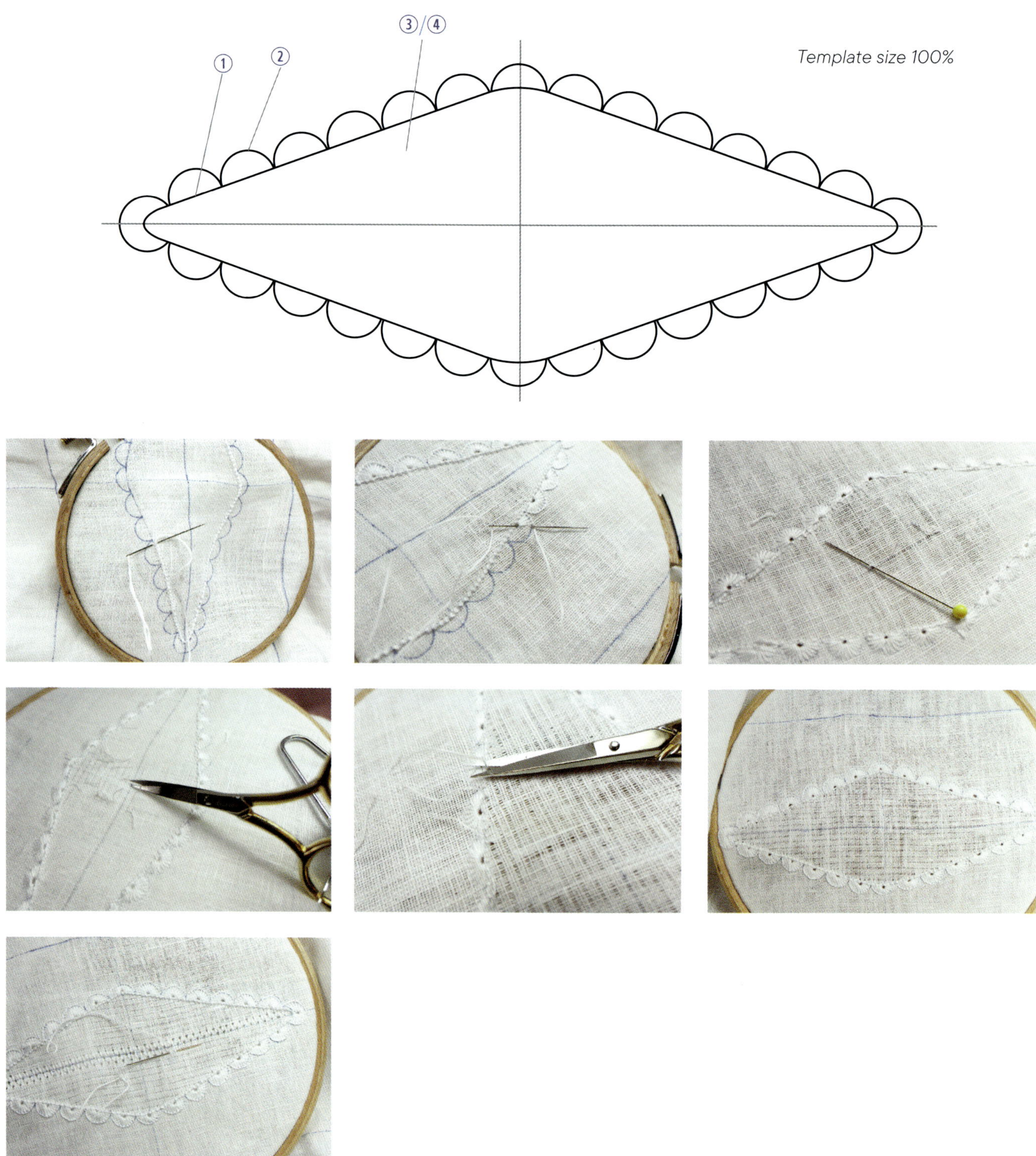
③/④
①
②
Template size 100%

GOING THE EXTRA MILE

Threads	
Coton à Broder no. 16 DMC	3713 ◯ White
Coton à Broder no. 25 DMC	Écru
Coton à Broder no. 30 DMC	◯ White
Machine Quilting Thread 100% cotton DMC	◯ White
Fabric	Fine linen evenweave, color Ivoire (Stragier, ref. 0000 2588)
Supplies	Embroidery needle no. 9 (for openwork grounds) Embroidery needle no. 9 (for outline) Embroidery needle no. 10
Pattern	Personal creation

1. Embroider the edges of the flower's center and petals in stitched padded outline, using Coton à Broder no. 25 thread: make two lines of stitch padding side by side, then tightly satin-stitch over them together.
2. Thin the area of the center of the flower on the reverse: remove a thread and leave three threads in both directions.
3. Embroider on the right side in four-sided stitch with Coton à Broder no. 30 thread.
4. Thin the ground fabric of the petal area on the reverse: remove a thread and leave three threads in both directions. Remove the same threads as for the center of the flower.
5. Embroider on the right side in Greek cross filling with Coton à Broder no. 16 thread.

Tips for Good Embroidery

Start all the petals at the same time to make it easier to spot the right diagonals: all the petals are embroidered in the same direction.

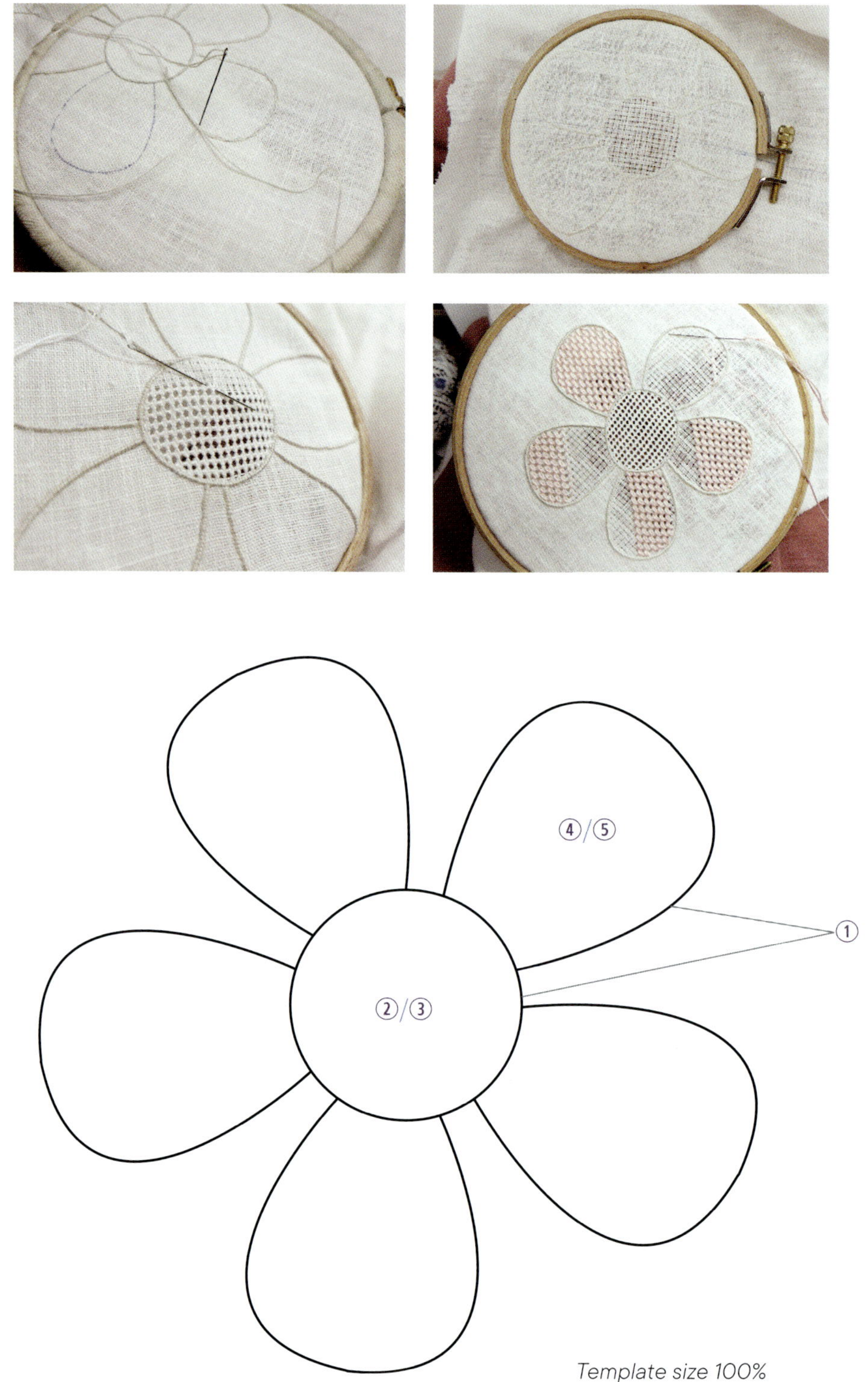

Template size 100%

RICHELIEU AND RENAISSANCE EMBROIDERY

Pages 258 to 263

DISCOVER

Threads	
Embroidery Special no.30 DMC	◯ White
Machine Quilting Thread 100% cotton DMC	◯ White
Fabric	Linen Percale, color Optique White (Stragier, ref. 0000 2666)
Supplies	HB mechanical pencil
Pattern	Madrid jumpsuit by Ikatee

① Renaissance embroidery.

② Satin stitch.

Template size 100%

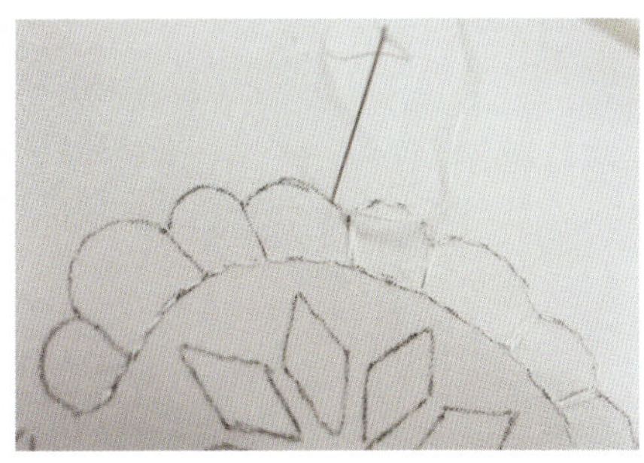

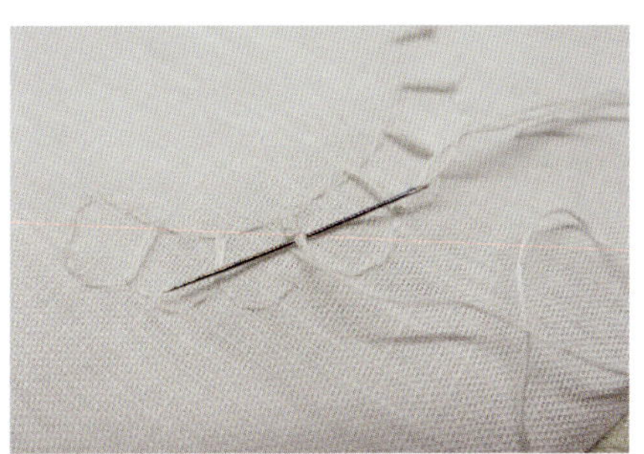

GOING THE EXTRA MILE

Threads	
Embroidery Special no. 30 DMC	◯ White
Machine Quilting Thread 100% cotton DMC	◯ White
Fabric	Linen Percale, color Optique White (Stragier, ref. 0000 2666)
Supplies	HB mechanical pencil
Pattern	Personal creation

Template size 80%

① Renaissance embroidery.

② Stem stitch.

③ Satin stitch around the edges and seeding inside the leaf.

④ Stem stitch outline and center vein, and darning stitch in the leaf.

⑤ Double seeding stitch.

BOUTIS

Pages 264 to 271

What You Need to Know

See pages 264 to 266 for boutis supplies.

FRIEZE

Fabrics	Batiste de Lawn, color White (Stragier, ref. 0001 6573) Pure combed cotton poplin, color White (Stragier, ref. 0000 2390)
Pattern	Roma dress by Ikatee

1 Starting from the center front of the waistband, transfer the frieze design to the poplin as many times as necessary to make the waistband of the dress. Leave 2 cm without embroidery at each end.

2 Embroider the boutis.

> Running stitch.

> Padding inside the heart.

> Padding outline of the heart.

> Padding the circles.

> Pad the large stripes.

3 Remove the dissolvable pen with an iron, then wash in hot, soapy water before drying flat.

4 Cut the waistband, leaving a 1cm seam allowance, and assemble the dress according to the pattern—the waistband is set into the garment.

What You Need to Know

The two fabric pieces should be 15 cm larger in width and length than the final dimensions of the waistband. Don't forget to allow for the shrinkage of the boutis: the 16cm frieze on the paper will shrink to 15 cm once the boutis has been washed.

Template size 50%

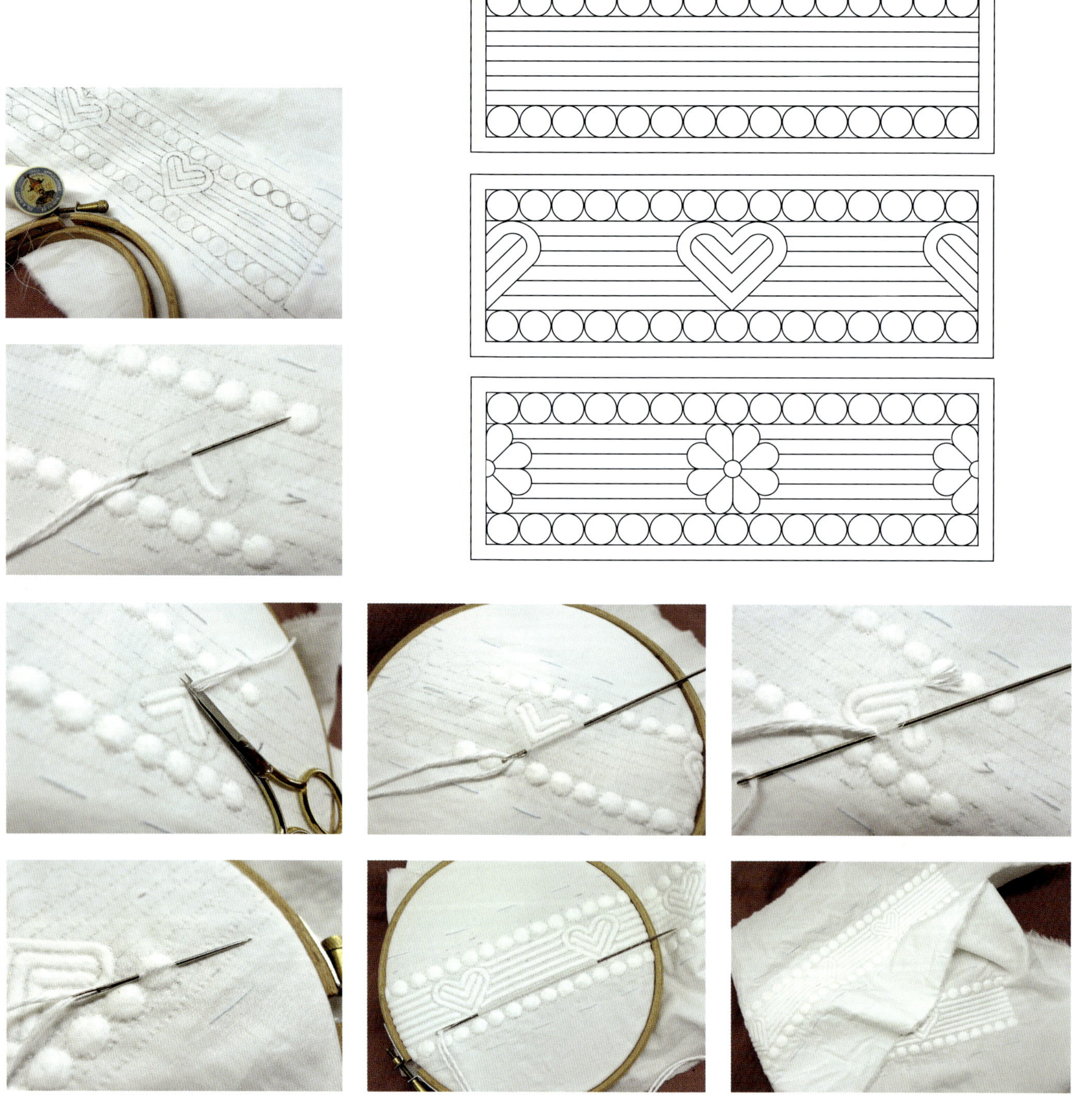

DISCOVER

Fabrics	Batiste de Lawn, color White (Stragier, ref. 0001 6573): 20 × 20 cm Pure combed cotton poplin, color White (Stragier, ref. 0000 2390): 20 × 20 cm
Supplies	Wooden beads White cotton twill ribbon

1 Embroider the boutis.
 > Trace on the poplin.
 > Running stitch.
 > Padding.
2 Baste the edges by turning them in twice to create a hem.
3 Hand-stitch the hem, using a small invisible stitch.
4 Remove the dissolvable pen with the iron, then wash the piece in hot, soapy water before drying flat.

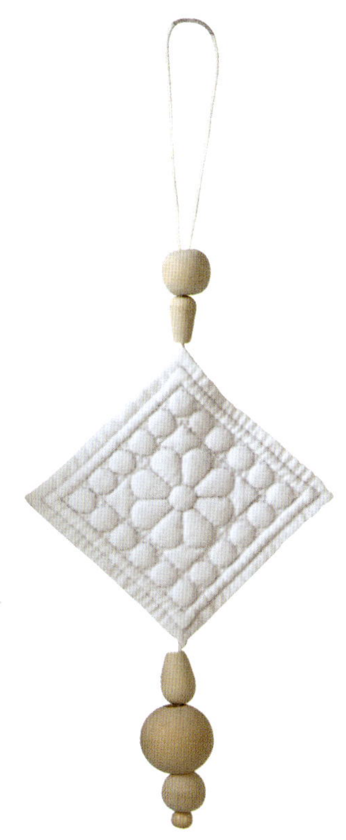

5 Hang the beads on the tassel with the twill ribbon.

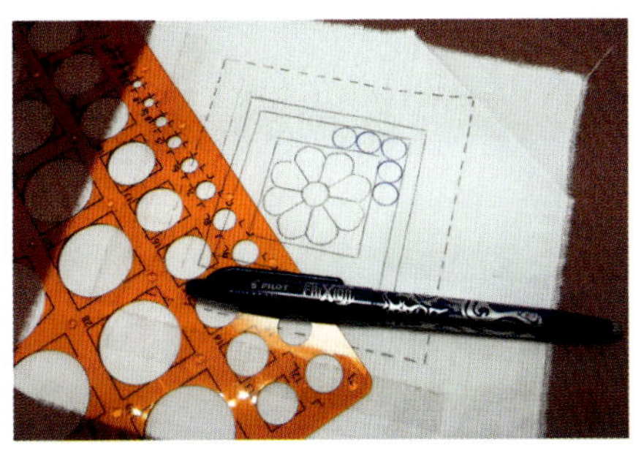

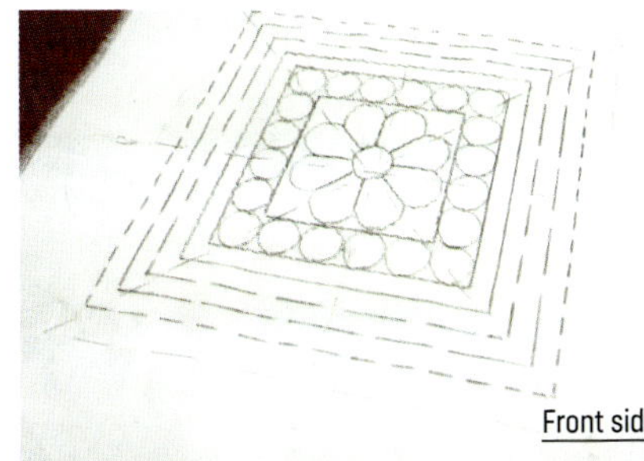

Front side

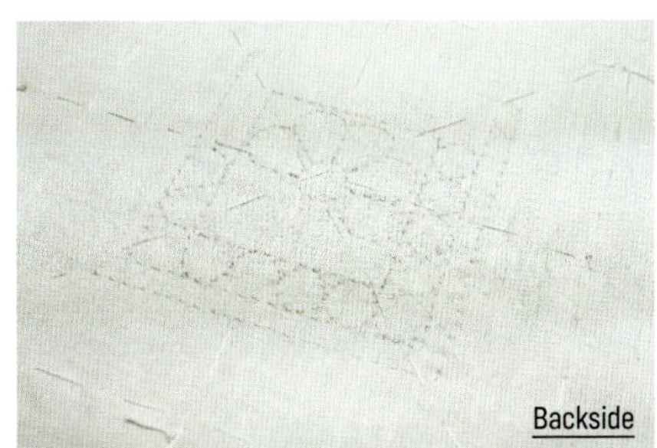

Backside

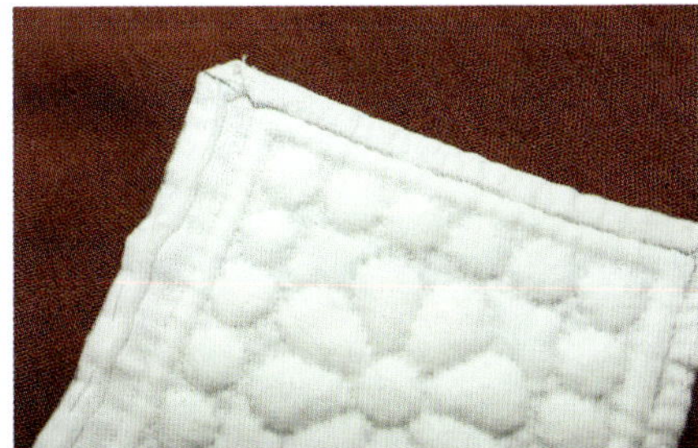

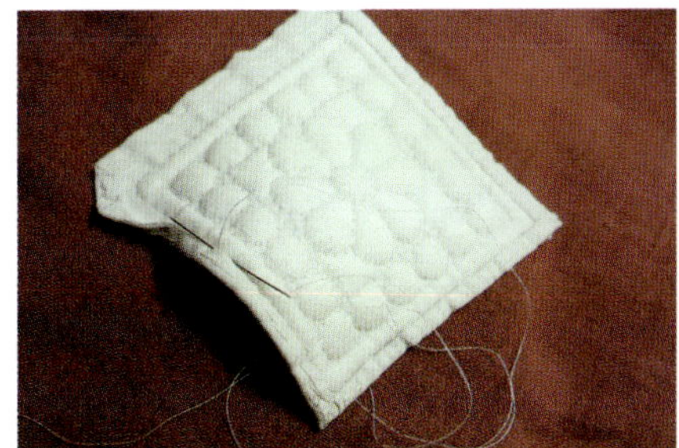

Template size 100%

VARIATION

Template size 50%

APPENDIXES

Reference Books

Bayle-Mouillard, É.-F. *Nouveau Manuel complet de la broderie par Mme Celnart. Roret*, 1840.

Bouet, P., and F. Neveux. *La Tapisserie de Bayeux.* Ouest-France, 2015.

Broderie: Leçons pratiques par Cousine Claire. La Bibliothèque des Métiers, 2015 (originally published in 1920).

Clech, J., and M. Fouriscot. *Les Jours brodés: 70 modèles traditionnels.* Éditions Didier Carpentier, 2005.

Conilleau, R. *La Broderie de Plombières-les-Bains.* Musée de Plombières-les-Bains, 1991.

De Dillmont, T. *Encyclopédie des ouvrages de dames.* T. de Dillmont Éditeur, 1886.

Denizot-Marquant, G. *L'Art de la broderie: Le passé empiétant.* Espaces Loisirs, 2007.

Di van Niekerk. *A Perfect World in Ribbon Embroidery & Stumpwork.* Search Press, 2018.

Dobler, A. *Savoir-broder.* Femmes d'aujourd'hui, 1965.

Dobler-Sauget, K. *Passion Smocks.* Mango, 2016.

Fouriscot, M., S. Château, and M.-H. César. *La Broderie or de Rochefort.* Éditions Didier Carpentier, 2003.

Latard-Gayraud, M. *Apprendre le boutis et transmettre.* France Boutis, 2020.

Le Goaziou, M., and N. Bresson. *La France au fil de l'aiguille.* Ouest-France, 2002.

Livolsi, E., et al. *École Lesage chez vous.* Tana, 2006.

Michaud, S. *Jours oubliés: Fonds ajourés sur fils tirés.* La Caneterie, 2020.

Michaud, S. *Les Jours d'Angles, cahier technique.* La Caneterie, 2019.

Nicolle, F., and J.-L. Aubert. *Boutis des villes, boutis des champs.* Edisud, 2000.

Siegler-Lathrop, D. *Les Secrets de la tapisserie à l'aiguille.* Le Temps Apprivoisé, 1997.

Sinton, K. *Essential Stitch Guides: Stumpwork.* Royal School of Needlework, 2011.

Thomas, M. *L'Encyclopédie de la broderie.* Fleurus, 1991.

Van de Velde-Malbranche, Y., and C. Rosenthal. *Cours de broderie à la main.* Armand Colin, 1995.

Vannier, C. *De fil en aiguille: La broderie dans l'art contemporain.* Pyramyd, 2021.

Author's Partners

ARTESANE

Platform for online video courses in the arts (embroidery, sewing, wool art, graphic arts). Here's a list of embroidery courses offered:

- traditional embroidery course
- heritage embroidery course
- traditional embroidery: basic embroidery stitches (beginner, intermediate, and expert courses)
- white embroidery (pulled-thread days, Renaissance, boutis)
- gold embroidery
- ribbon embroidery
- raffia embroidery

www.artesane.com I *Instagram: @artesane_france*

ATELIER 196.COM

Dealer for Au Ver à Soie threads and Once Upon Une Fois embroidery kits. It's also a haberdashery where you can buy embroidery supplies and embroidery threads. You'll also find my embroidery designs and the corresponding thread packs.
www.atelier196.com I *Instagram: @onceuponunefois*

AU VER À SOIE

Silk thread manufacturer. This living heritage company develops all circuits around its silk thread, from fishing to embroidery, haute couture, lace, couture, boutis, bookbinding, tapestry, and restoration. All these fields highlight the know-how of a job well done. Find Au Ver à Soie embroidery threads at Atelier 196.com.
www.auverasoie.com I *Instagram: @auverasoie*

BOHIN

Manufacturer of needles and pins and haberdashery supplies.
www.bohin.com I *Instagram: @bohin_france*

DMC

Manufacturer of embroidery thread who also sells haberdashery for embroidery, embroidery canvas, and kits.
www.dmc.com I *Instagram: @dmc_france*

IKATEE

Designer of sewing patterns for women and children.
www.ikatee.fr I *Instagram: @ikateecouture*

KAREN DOBLER-SAUGET

Specialist in Liberty fabrics (London) and smocked embroideries.
Instagram: @liberty_smocks_addict

MAISON SAJOU

Manufacturer of haberdashery and embroidery items, also selling embroidery haberdashery, embroidery canvas, Au Chinois thread, and Saint-Pierre wool.
www.sajou.fr I *Instagram: @maisonsajouofficiel*

NEELAM

Reseller of smooth purls and jaserons for gold embroidery.
www.neelam.fr I *Instagram: @neelam.textile*

PERLES PAILLETTES ET BRODERIE

Reseller of pearls, sequins, and embroidery supplies (Au Ver à Soie threads, Aubusson wool).
www.perlespaillettesetbroderie.com

RÉPUBLIQUE DU CHIFFON

Designer of sewing patterns for women and children.
www.republiqueduchiffon.com
Instagram: @republiqueduchiffon

STRAGIER

Reseller of the finest fabrics.
www.stragier.com I *Instagram: @s.t.r.a.g.i.e.r*

Other Resources

In addition to my partners previously mentioned, here are a few other suppliers you might want to check out.

FOR HABERDASHERY AND THREAD

Bohin
www.bohin.com
Instagram: @bohin_france

DMC
www.dmc.com
Instagram: @dmc_france

Rascol Mercerie
www.rascol.com

FOR GOLD EMBROIDERY

Le Bégonia d'or
www.broderieor.com
Instagram: @x.latelierdubegoniador

Golden Hinde
www.golden-hinde.co.uk

FOR BEADS AND SEQUINS

Paillettes & Broderie
www.paillettesetbroderie.com

Perles & Co
www.perlesandco.com

FOR TAPESTRIES

Tapisseries de la Bûcherie
www.bucherie.com
Instagram: @tapisseries_la_bucherie

FOR THE EMBROIDERY OF DAYS

Stéphanie Michaud MOF (jours d'angles)
www.stephaniemichaud.fr
Instagram: @joursdefil

Sylvie Lezziero MOF (broderie de Touraine)
www.lsbroderie.com
Instagram: @sylvie_lezziero_mof

FOR BOUTIS

France Boutis
www.franceboutis.com

La maison du Boutis
www.la-maison-du-boutis.fr

Acknowledgments

First of all, I'd like to thank the teams at Editions Eyrolles, without whom this adventure would not have been possible. Their constant support throughout the long process of producing this book was invaluable. This was without taking into account the pandemic's passage from 2020 to 2022. Despite the many pitfalls, this book is finally here! Special thanks to Anne-Lise for her unfailing patience and to Armelle for her careful proofreading. Thanks to all those who contributed to this project. First on my list: Eloïse and Isaure, my granddaughters; Maëna, my daughter; and Manon, my daughter-in-law, who kindly agreed to pose for the photos in this book. Manon (@manonpontillo and @studio_novembre on Instagram) also drew the zodiac signs for the chapter "Satin Stitches," as well as the patterns for the chapters "Embroidering Text, Letters, and Numbers" and "Cross Stitch." Thanks to my husband, who has been a great support during times of doubt, and there have been many! Thanks to Quentin, my son, who inspires the patterns I create for little boys (although he's not one anymore); the Big Five are dedicated to him! Thanks to Karen Dobler-Sauget, who embroidered all the designs in the smocking chapter and proofread it several times. Thanks to Ariane Andraud and Guilaine Millour, who embroidered some of the works in the chapters "Satin Stitches" and "Bead and Sequin Embroidery." Last but not least, thanks to my partners (in alphabetical order): Artesane, Atelier 196 (Once Upon Une Fois), Au Ver à Soie, Bohin, DMC, Ikatee, Maison Sajou, Neelam, Perles Paillettes et Broderie, République du Chiffon, and Stragier.

About the Author

Born into a family of dressmakers and blouses, I spent my childhood surrounded by threads and fabrics. My maternal grandmother and my mother passed on to me their know-how in embroidery, sewing, knitting and crochet. I was sewing and knitting my own clothes from the age of 14! After training in industrial design and international trade, I worked for a dozen years as an engineer in sectors as varied as the automotive industry and water treatment. The search for technical solutions for the customer and the commercial relationship are what interested me most in these experiences. In 1998, married with two young children, an expatriation opportunity in Africa completely changed my life. I finally had the time to get back into needlework and to enrich my knowledge in this field through my encounters with French women who were also passionate about embroidery. At the same time, I began teaching technology at the Lycée français Jean-Mermoz in Dakar. It was at this time that I developed my taste for teaching. In the first few years of the 2000s, in Johannesburg, with the help of the White Fathers and a few friends, I taught embroidery in workshops for women suffering from AIDS. The South African press took an interest in my work, and I produced several designs for a hobby magazine. At the same time, I trained at leading embroidery schools in France and abroad. After more than six years abroad, when I returned to France, it was only natural for me to continue in this direction. Designing for *Marie Claire Idées* magazine, writing four books, taking embroidery classes.. I haven't stopped! In 2016, I began my first embroidery video courses for Artesane, an online course platform. In 2019, Éditions Eyrolles asked me to produce a book for them. I had reached a stage in my life where I felt the need to put on paper all the needlepoint knowledge I had acquired over five decades. After all these years, this is a real achievement. This book, which is close to my heart, enables me to pass on all my embroidery knowledge.

Index of Embroidery Stitches

L

P

R

S

T

V

W

Photographic Credits

p. 46: MET/Purchase, Mrs. Jackson Burke Gift, 1979; **p. 53:** MET/Purchase, Friends of European Sculpture and Decorative Arts Gifts and Rogers Fund, 2006; **p. 67**: DMC/Archives DMC; **p. 85:** MET/From the Collection of Mrs. Lathrop Colgate Harper, Bequest of Mabel Herbert Harper, 1957; **p. 87:** COOPER HEWITT/Bequest of Gertrude M. Oppenheimer; **p. 90**: DMC/Archives DMC; **p. 122:** Wikipédia/LadyofHat; **p. 123:** COOPER HEWITT/Museum purchase through gift of George A. Hearn; **p. 127** top: COOPER HEWITT/Gift of Mrs. Edward C. Post; **p. 127** bottom: COOPER HEWITT/Bequest of Richard Cranch Greenleaf in memory of his mother, Adeline Emma Greenleaf; **p. 128:** COOPER HEWITT/Museum purchase from Au Panier Fleuri Fund; **p. 130** top: COOPER HEWITT/Museum purchase from Au Panier Fleuri Fund; **p. 132**: COOPER HEWITT/Museum purchase from Pauline Riggs Noyes Fund; **p. 157:** Gift of Cora Ginsburg in memory of Jean Mailey; **p. 167** left: COOPER HEWITT/Gift of Myra and William H. Mathers; **p. 168** left: COOPER HEWITT/Gift of Mrs. Hollis French; **p. 175:** The Metropolitan Museum of Art, Dist. RMN-Grand Palais/image of the MMA; **p. 188** left: MET/Fletcher Fund, 1936; **p. 188** right: MET/Gift of Lois and Anthony Blumka, in memory of Victoria Blumka, 1990; **p. 189** top: Gift of Ida-Gro Dahlerup; **p. 189** bottom: Gift of Ida-Gro Dahlerup; **p. 205** left: COOPER HEWITT/Gift of Marian Hague; **p. 205** right: MET/Purchase, Mrs. Thomas J. Watson Gift, 1939; **p. 211** left: LACMA/Gift in honor of Sara Marie Habib (M.86.133); **p. 221** top left: COOPER HEWITT/Gift of Robert B. Noyes; **p. 221** bottom left: Broderie Sylvie Lezziero (Mof broderie blanche 2004); **p. 245** left and right: Association Sauvegarde et Rayonnement des Jours d'Angles/Angles-sur-l'Anglin; **p. 259** top: DMC/Archives DMC; **p. 259** bottom: TRC Leiden; **p. 265**, except for the last photo at the bottom right: collection privée de la Maison du Boutis, Musée de Calvisson/Gard.

All other photos are by **Pierre Nicou,** except those on pages 86, 211 (right-hand column); 275 (mosaic), 277 (mosaic), 302 (left column), 303 (right column), 316, 317 (mosaic), 318 (left column and right column, bottom), 325, 328, 332 (right column), 333 (left column), 349, 351, 352, 355, 357, 359, 360, 362 (left column), 363, 364 (mosaic), 366, 367 (mosaic), 368, 370, 371, 372 (mosaic), 374, 376, 377 (mosaic), 380, 384, 385, 386 (mosaic), 388 (mosaic), 390, 392, 394, 395 (framed), 396, 398, 399 (mosaic), 402, 403 (mosaic). The latter were made by **Martine Biessy.**

Despite our best efforts, mistakes may have crept in and we apologize for them. If a reproduction in the book is not correctly identified, we invite you to contact Éditions Eyrolles.